The Edinburgh Companion to the Short Story in English

Edinburgh Companions to Literature

Published

The Edinburgh Companion to Virginia Woolf and the Arts
Edited by Maggie Humm

The Edinburgh Companion to Twentieth-Century Literatures in English
Edited by Brian McHale and Randall Stevenson

A Historical Companion to Postcolonial Literatures in English
Edited by David Johnson and Prem Poddar

A Historical Companion to Postcolonial Literatures - Continental Europe and its Empires
Edited by Prem Poddar, Rajeev Patke and Lars Jensen

The Edinburgh Companion to Twentieth-Century British and American War Literature
Edited by Adam Piette and Mark Rowlinson

The Edinburgh Companion to Shakespeare and the Arts
Edited by Mark Thornton Burnett, Adrian Streete and Ramona Wray

The Edinburgh Companion to Samuel Beckett and the Arts
Edited by S. E. Gontarski

The Edinburgh Companion to the Bible and the Arts
Edited by Stephen Prickett

The Edinburgh Companion to Modern Jewish Fiction
Edited by David Brauner and Axel Stähler

The Edinburgh Companion to Critical Theory
Edited by Stuart Sim

The Edinburgh Companion to the Critical Medical Humanities
Edited by Anne Whitehead, Angela Woods, Sarah Atkinson, Jane Macnaughton and Jennifer Richards

The Edinburgh Companion to Nineteenth-Century American Letters and Letter-Writing
Edited by Celeste-Marie Bernier, Judie Newman and Matthew Pethers

The Edinburgh Companion to T. S. Eliot and the Arts
Edited by Frances Dickey and John D. Morgenstern

The Edinburgh Companion to Children's Literature
Edited by Clémentine Beauvais and Maria Nikolajeva

The Edinburgh Companion to Atlantic Literary Studies
Edited by Leslie Eckel and Clare Elliott

The Edinburgh Companion to the First World War and the Arts
Edited by Ann-Marie Einhaus and Katherine Isobel Baxter

The Edinburgh Companion to Fin de Siècle Literature, Culture and the Arts
Edited by Josephine M. Guy

The Edinburgh Companion to Animal Studies
Edited by Lynn Turner, Undine Sellbach and Ron Broglio

The Edinburgh Companion to Contemporary Narrative Theories
Edited by Zara Dinnen and Robyn Warhol

The Edinburgh Companion to Anthony Trollope
Edited by Frederik Van Dam, David Skilton and Ortwin Graef

The Edinburgh Companion to the Short Story in English
Edited by Paul Delaney and Adrian Hunter

Forthcoming

The Edinburgh Companion to the Postcolonial Middle East
Edited by Anna Ball and Karim Matar

The Edinburgh Companion to Literature and Music
Edited by Delia da Sousa Correa

The Edinburgh Companion to Elizabeth Bishop
Edited by Jonathan Ellis

The Edinburgh Companion to Charles Dickens and the Arts
Edited by Juliet John and Claire Wood

The Edinburgh Companion to Gothic and the Arts
Edited by David Punter

The Edinburgh Companion to Ezra Pound and the Arts
Edited by Roxana Preda

The Edinburgh Companion to Virginia Woolf and Contemporary Global Literature
Edited by Jeanne Dubino & Paulina Pajak

The Edinburgh History of Reading, Volume 1: Early and Modern Readers
Edited by Mary Hammond and Jonathan Rose

The Edinburgh History of Reading, Volume 2: Common and Subversive Readers
Edited by Mary Hammond and Jonathan Rose

The Edinburgh Companion to the Short Story in English

Edited by Paul Delaney and Adrian Hunter

EDINBURGH
University Press

Edinburgh University Press is one of the leading university presses in the UK. We publish academic books and journals in our selected subject areas across the humanities and social sciences, combining cutting-edge scholarship with high editorial and production values to produce academic works of lasting importance. For more information visit our website: edinburghuniversitypress.com

© editorial matter and organisation Paul Delaney and Adrian Hunter, 2019, 2024
© the chapters their several authors, 2019

Edinburgh University Press Ltd
13 Infirmary Street,
Edinburgh, EH1 1LT

Typeset in 10/12 Adobe Sabon by
IDSUK (DataConnection) Ltd

A CIP record for this book is available from the British Library

ISBN 978 1 4744 0065 7 (hardback)
ISBN 978 1 3995 4677 5 (paperback)
ISBN 978 1 4744 0066 4 (webready PDF)
ISBN 978 1 4744 4223 7 (epub)

The right of Paul Delaney and Adrian Hunter to be identified as the editors of this work has been asserted in accordance with the Copyright, Designs and Patents Act 1988, and the Copyright and Related Rights Regulations 2003 (SI No. 2498).

Contents

Acknowledgements	vii
Notes on Contributors	viii
Introduction *Paul Delaney and Adrian Hunter*	1

Part I: Historicising the Short Story

1	Transnationalism and the Transatlantic Short Story *Michael J. Collins*	9
2	The Short Story and the Professionalisation of English Studies *Adrian Hunter*	24
3	Impressionism and the Short Story *Paul March-Russell*	40
4	Writers on the Short Story: 1950–present *Ailsa Cox*	56

Part II: Publishing the Short Story

5	The Short Story and the 'Little Magazine' *Beryl Pong*	75
6	Collections, Cycles and Sequences *Jennifer J. Smith*	93
7	The Short Story Anthology *Elke D'hoker*	108
8	The Short Story and Digital Media *Laura Dietz*	125

Part III: Forms of the Short Story

9 Short-Short Fiction — Michael Basseler — 147

10 The Weird Tale — Timothy Jones — 160

11 The Horror Story — Darryl Jones — 175

12 Experimental Short Stories — Jeremy Scott — 193

13 The War Story — Adam Piette — 211

Part IV: Placing the Short Story

14 Regionalism and the Short Story — Lucy Evans — 227

15 The Short Story and the City — Philip Coleman — 242

16 The Short Story in Suburbia — Joanna Price — 256

17 The Short Story and the Environment — Deborah Lilley and Samuel Solnick — 272

Part V: Identity and the Short Story

18 Gender and Genre in the Short Story — Ruth Robbins — 293

19 Diaspora and the Short Story — Sam Naidu — 313

20 The Queer Short Story — Brett Josef Grubisic — 328

21 Disability and the Short Story — Alice Hall — 346

Index of Short Story Titles — 363
General Index — 369

Acknowledgements

A book of this sort incurs many debts in the making.

Our warmest thanks go to the contributors – friends and colleagues around the world who have written so wonderfully about the short story, and who have shown great patience in the closing stages of the project.

Staff in the libraries of Trinity College Dublin and the University of Stirling have been unfailingly helpful at moments of greatest need.

Special thanks to Jackie Jones for commissioning this *Companion* and for championing the project from its infancy; and to Ersev Ersoy and Edinburgh University Press for advice and assistance.

Finally, heartfelt thanks to Finola and Mairi, Katie Rose, Molly-Rose, and Joe, for your unwavering support and patience. Families among us, us among you: this book is dedicated with love and gratitude.

Notes on Contributors

Michael Basseler is Academic Manager at the International Graduate Centre for the Study of Culture (GCSC) at the University of Giessen, Germany. His research focuses mainly on twentieth- and twenty-first-century American literature. His second book (post-doctoral thesis) on the North American Short Story as a genre of 'life knowledge' was published in 2018.

Philip Coleman is Associate Professor in the School of English, Trinity College Dublin, where he is also a Fellow. He has published widely on US American poetry and short fiction: recent books include *John Berryman's Public Vision* (2014) and *George Saunders: Critical Essays* (with Steve Gronert, Ellerhoff, 2017).

Michael Collins is a Senior Lecturer in American Literature at the University of Kent. His first monograph, *The Drama of the American Short Story, 1800–1865* was published in 2016 by University of Michigan Press. He is currently working on two book projects, a study of the relationship between class consciousness and the development of the anthropological culture concept in the USA between 1880 and 1945, entitled *After Haymarket*, and a cultural history of intelligence testing and the Anglo-American novel from 1880 to 1930 as part of the AHRC funded *Literary Culture, Meritocracy, and the Assessment of Intelligence* project.

Ailsa Cox is Professor of Short Fiction at Edge Hill University. Her books include *Alice Munro* (Northcote House), *Writing Short Stories* (Routledge) and *The Real Louise and Other Stories* (Headland Press). She is also the editor of the peer-reviewed journal *Short Fiction in Theory and Practice* (Intellect Press).

Paul Delaney is Associate Professor in the School of English, Trinity College Dublin. He is the author of *Seán O'Faoláin: Literature, Inheritance and the 1930s* (Irish Academic Press, 2014), and editor of *Reading Colm Tóibín* (Liffey Press, 2008) and *William Trevor: Revaluations*, with Michael Parker (Manchester University Press, 2013).

Laura Dietz is Senior Lecturer in Writing and Publishing at Anglia Ruskin University. Her first novel is *In the Tenth House* (Crown, Penguin Random House) and her recent scholarly publications include chapters and journal articles on digital novels, electronic literary magazines, cognitive approaches to literature, and literary careers in the digital era.

Lucy Evans is Lecturer in Postcolonial Literature at the University of Leicester, UK. Her monograph *Communities in Contemporary Anglophone Caribbean Short Stories* appeared in 2014, and she also co-edited *The Caribbean Short Story: Critical Perspectives* (Peepal Tree, 2011). She is currently leading two research networking projects: 'Crime and its Representation in the Anglophone Caribbean, 1834–2018', funded by the British Academy, and 'Dons, Yardies and Posses: Representations of Jamaican Organised Crime', funded by the UK Arts and Humanities Research Council.

Elke D'hoker is Senior Lecturer of English literature at the University of Leuven, Belgium. She is the author of *Irish Women Writers and the Modern Short Story* (Palgrave, 2016) and editor of *Mary Lavin* (Irish Academic Press, 2013) and *The Irish Short Story* (Peter Lang, 2015). Her research interests include British and Irish short fiction, the short story cycle and the composite novel.

Brett Josef Grubisic lectures on Canada's west coast, specialising in queer, Canadian and contemporary literature. A fiction writer as well, his novels include *The Age of Cities* and *Oldness; or, the Last-Ditch Efforts of Marcus O.*

Alice Hall is a Lecturer in Contemporary and Global Literature in the Department of English and Related Literature at the University of York. She is the author of *Literature and Disability: Contemporary Critical Thought* (2015) and *Disability and Modern Fiction: Faulkner, Morrison, Coetzee and the Nobel Prize for Literature* (2012). Alice has research and teaching interests in modern literature and the body, disability studies, and medical humanities.

Adrian Hunter is Senior Lecturer in English Studies at the University of Stirling. He is author of *The Cambridge Introduction to the Short Story in English*, and of several articles and chapters on British and North American short fiction. He is currently editing a volume of James Hogg's contributions to international periodicals for the definitive Stirling/South Carolina Research Edition of Hogg's work, also published by Edinburgh University Press.

Darryl Jones is Professor of English at Trinity College Dublin, where he teaches nineteenth-century literature and popular literature. He is the author or editor of twelve books, including the Oxford editions of the *Collected Ghost Stories* of M. R. James, the *Gothic Tales* of Arthur Conan Doyle and *Horror Stories: Classic Tales from Hoffmann to Hodgson*. His latest book, *Sleeping with the Lights On: The Unsettling Story of Horror* will be published by Oxford University Press in 2018.

Timothy Jones teaches the Gothic Imagination at the University of Stirling. He is the author of *The Gothic and the Carnivalesque in American Culture*, which co-won the Allan Lloyd Smith prize.

Deborah Lilley specialises in contemporary literature, critical theory and the environment, especially through the lens of the pastoral. She has published several journal articles and book chapters on these topics, and her monograph, *The New Pastoral in Contemporary British Writing*, is forthcoming. She has taught English at Royal Holloway, University of London, and the University of San Francisco.

Paul March-Russell teaches Comparative Literature at the University of Kent. He is a member of the European Research Network for Short Fiction, and an editorial advisor for both *Journal of the Short Story in English* and *Short Fiction in Theory and Practice*. His most recent publications include articles on Zoe Lambert and Lucy Wood, and a chapter on feminist fairy tales after Angela Carter, as part of the Women's Tales project based at the University of Santiago de Compostela. When not working on the short story, he edits the SF journal, *Foundation*, and is commissioning editor for SF Storyworlds (Gylphi Press).

Sam Naidu is Associate Professor in the Department of English, Rhodes University, South Africa. Her main research and teaching interests are transnational literature, crime and detective fiction, and the oral-written interface in the colonial Eastern Cape. Recent publications include *Sherlock Holmes in Context* (Palgrave Macmillan, 2017) and *A Survey of South African Crime Fiction: Critical Analysis and Publishing History* (2017). She has also guest edited a special issue of *Current Writing* on South African crime fiction (2013) and of *The Journal of Commonwealth and Postcolonial Studies* (2017) on postcolonial and transnational crime fiction.

Adam Piette is a Professor of Modern Literature at the University of Sheffield. He is the author of *Remembering and the Sound of Words: Mallarmé, Proust, Joyce, Beckett* (Oxford University Press, 1996), *Imagination at War: British Fiction and Poetry, 1939–1945* (Macmillan, 1995), and *The Literary Cold War, 1945 to Vietnam* (Edinburgh University Press, 2009). He co-edited *The Edinburgh Companion to Twentieth-century British and American War Literature* (Edinburgh University Press, 2012) and is co-editor of the poetry journal *Blackbox Manifold*.

Beryl Pong is currently a Vice-Chancellor's Fellow at the University of Sheffield. As well as short fiction, she specialises in modernism, British and global anglophone literature, war studies, narrative and film. She is completing a literary-cultural history of time surrounding the Blitz on London, *For the Duration: British Literature and Culture in Blitz-Time*, and has begun a study of semicolonial modern short fiction.

Joanna Price teaches English and American literature at Liverpool John Moores University. She is currently writing a book about how affect and memory shape the experience of place and its representation in literature and art. This project builds on her previous publications on trauma, memory and mourning in American literature since the 1980s.

Ruth Robbins is Professor of English and Director of Research for Cultural Studies at Leeds Beckett University. She is the author of *Literary Feminisms* (2000), *Pater to Forster* (2003), *Subjectivity* (2005) and *Oscar Wilde* (2011). With Andrew Maunder and Emma Liggins she is also the author of *The British Short Story* (2010).

Jeremy Scott works on the border between language and literary studies. His current research interests are in fictional technique, literary representations of dialect, the relationship between narratives and identity, stylistics-based approaches to creative writing, and portrayals of Englishness in fiction. He has published on style and narrative technique in contemporary British and Irish writing, and has also published his own fiction.

Jennifer J. Smith is an Assistant Professor of English at Franklin College. Her recent book, *The American Short Story Cycle* (Edinburgh University Press) gives a name and theory to the genre that has fostered the aesthetics of fragmentation, as well as recurrence, that characterise fiction today.

Samuel Solnick is a Lecturer in English at the University of Liverpool where he is co-director of the Literature and Science Hub. He writes primarily on contemporary literature and the environmental humanities. His first monograph, *Poetry and the Anthropocene,* was published by Routledge in 2017.

INTRODUCTION

Paul Delaney and Adrian Hunter

In her treatise on the condition of contemporary literary criticism, *The Limits of Critique*, Rita Felski notes how, following 'a long period of historically orientated scholarship, scholars of literature and art are returning to aesthetics, beauty, and form'.[1] On the one hand, Felski says, this is to be welcomed, kicking as it does against contextual and sociological approaches that would treat writing as a 'symptom, mirror, index, or antithesis of some larger social structure'.[2] On the other hand, proponents of the New Aestheticism and New Formalism risk repeating errors of old, reverencing the text as timeless, transcendent and self-enclosed in ways that merely bracket the 'problem of temporality' without resolving it.[3]

The dilemma Felski outlines here will be familiar to any scholar of the short story. Since its inception in the late nineteenth century, academic criticism has been marked by precisely the kind of 'zigzagging between dichotomies of text versus context, word versus world'[4] Felski describes – between the attempt to construct an abstract, transhistorical definition of the form that would distinguish it categorically from the novel, and a countervailing desire to account for the short story's cultural-historical specificity, by aligning it with the development of a particular national literature, say, or with a specific conception of authorship. That the trend in recent years has been strongly in the latter direction is evident from a survey of recent titles: *The Postcolonial Short Story*, *Irish Women Writers and the Modern Short Story*, *British Women Short Story Writers*, *The Short Story and the First World War*, and *Art and Commerce in the British Short Story* – studies whose stress on history, materialism and identity is rooted, more or less explicitly, in a rejection of the kind of formalist and cognitivist approaches favoured by proponents of the so-called 'new short story studies' of the 1980s and 1990s: Susan Lohafer, John Gerlach, Charles E. May and others. Where for these earlier critics questions of formal and generic definition were central, today it is the cultural, historical and ideological functions of the short story that predominate.

Of course, such oscillations are ubiquitous across the field of literary studies, as Felski and other surveyors of the 'postcritical' future point out.[5] The curious thing about short story criticism, however, is not so much that these shifts have been very pronounced – which they have been – but that they have occurred out of sync with broader institutional and disciplinary trends. Only very recently, for example, have gender and feminist theories begun to make their presence felt, as the appearance of volumes such as Emma Young and James Bailey's *British Women Short Story Writers: The New Woman to Now* (2015) attests. Prior to that, attention was sporadic at best with Mary Eagleton's 1989 essay 'Gender and Genre'[6] and Janet Beer's 1997 study of

Kate Chopin, Edith Wharton and Charlotte Perkins Gilman[7] among the few studies to engage in theoretical terms with the question of why women writers have gravitated toward the short form. Similarly, the short story had to wait until 2013 for the first extended treatment of its postcolonial formations, despite the obvious centrality of the form over many decades to diasporic and global anglophone literatures.[8] Short story criticism has also been oddly prone to attacks from within its own ranks – attacks that go as far as to question the foundational principles on which discussion of the form rests. Mary Louise Pratt's widely cited account of the short story as 'the smaller and lesser' genre, necessarily 'dependent' both in conception and in practice on the novel, is perhaps the best known of these.[9] More recently, Timothy Clark has taken issue with formalist as well as contextual approaches, arguing that where the former are constructed around a highly questionable 'metaphorics of sight' and a 'visual bias . . . so strong that it raises the question of how much it may be a form of denial', the latter too often settle for 'rather cosy models of cultural determinism'.[10]

To a great extent, the instability in short fiction's critical discourse reflects the uncertain status of the form itself, which, as Pratt points out, is named and defined relativistically (shortness not being in itself an intrinsic quality of anything). The sense of the short story's identity as equivocal or unfixed – bracketed somewhere between the prose poem and the novella – is compounded by other factors: by a literary culture overwhelmingly geared to recognising and rewarding the longer form; by the relegation of the short story to low-capital venues such as the magazine and anthology, whose multi-author, thematised modes of publication can conspire to diffuse and degrade the text's singularity; and, particularly in recent decades, by institutionalised reproduction and programmatisation through the Creative Writing industry.[11] At the same time, academic criticism has been skewed by the recurrence of certain procedural biases (Timothy Clark's point) and by a patchy account of the historical development of the form. We see this most obviously in the persistence of two key ideational frameworks: modernism and nationalism. While it is certainly true that modernist writers such as Woolf and Joyce transformed the theory and practice of the short story, raising it to the status of a prestigious art form,[12] subsequent scholarship has tended to reproduce unwittingly or uncritically modernism's aesthetic and cultural values, with the result that 'literariness' has become aligned with a specific repertoire of formal characteristics. To that extent, Dominic Head's often-quoted characterisation of the short story as the 'distilled essence'[13] of modernist narrative becomes as much a reflection of a dominant critical perspective on the form as it is a statement of literary-historical reality. At the same time, more or less politicised cultural-nationalist agendas have been played out with particular intensity around the short story. The referencing of Poe and his ideas about unity and totality – a feature of short story criticism since its inception in the American academy – is part of this narrative, as is Frank O'Connor's famous assertion that a definably 'national attitude toward society'[14] accounted for the pre-eminence of the short story in Ireland and America, a claim partly intended to underscore O'Connor's argument that a lack of such collective self-identification could explain the telling *in*sufficiency of English (British) achievement in the form. While modern criticism has moved well beyond O'Connor's brand of chauvinism, the idea that national preponderance in the short story – particularly true of the United States, for example – has an identitarian significance continues to circulate, most obviously through country-specific anthologies.[15]

Yet it is also undoubtedly true that such instability and disciplinary 'zigzagging' has proven uniquely productive for scholars willing to tread the dialectical fault lines between critical regimes. As Ann-Marie Einhaus points out, among the most significant studies to emerge from the structuralist and post-structuralist heyday of the 1980s and 1990s was Clare Hanson's *Short Stories and Short Fiction, 1880–1980* (1985),[16] a book that, as its title suggests, sought to weave history into narratology and vice versa. Head, likewise, in his landmark book from 1992, pursued the ideological functions of the modernist short story through an innovative (and still widely admired) analysis of its key formal feature, the epiphany; while in the United States Andrew Levy examined the impact of magazine publishing and the development of institutional literary criticism on the creation of a literary aesthetic of the form.[17] Further back in the century, writer-critics working in the afterglow of high modernism, such as Elizabeth Bowen, Seán O'Faoláin, Frank O'Connor, A. E. Coppard and H. E. Bates, brought an equally rich pancultural awareness to their often dazzling accounts of the aesthetics of the post-Chekhovian short story. Coppard and Bowen, for example, saw deep affinities between the short story and cinema, which they regarded as new art forms uniquely capable of rendering 'the disorientated romanticism of the age'.[18] For Bates, meanwhile, defining the modern short story meant taking into account the processes of social and cultural change responsible for the 'evolution of the general reader'.[19]

In other words, it is possible both to overstate the importance of short story criticism's disorderly history, and to understate the extent to which that disorderliness has been a spur to innovation, the hiding place of its power. Governing *The Edinburgh Companion to the Short Story in English* has been a desire to reflect some of that variety and, in the best sense, inconsistency. The chapters have not been written to prescription but, rather, guided by the authors' sense of their subject. Privileging neither text over context, nor form over function, but, rather, their interanimation, the book traverses many critical, conceptual and circumstantial fault lines. Its central aim is to provide a wide-ranging portrait of the historical, cultural, material and critical contexts that have shaped the production, dissemination and reception of short fiction across the English-speaking world through a detailed study of the formal and aesthetic particularities of individual texts and story collections. The structure and organisation of the volume is thus designed to facilitate an international and comparative perspective. For example, instead of corralling stories and writers by country of origin ('the Scottish short story', 'the Irish short story', 'the Caribbean short story'), the role of the short story in relation to place and identity is explored. Instead of 'modernist short stories', modernism features as a material and ideational construct that permeates institutional and historical definitions of the form and the structures of commercial publishing alike. Instead of 'Victorian short stories', the nineteenth century recurs across numerous chapters as an extensible phenomenon of transnational transmission and cultural exchange, the implications of which resonate through time and place, from Melvillean New York to modern-day Mumbai.

The chapters that follow are accordingly grouped into five sections. Part I, 'Historicising the Short Story', establishes a temporal starting point for the volume, in the late eighteenth century. However, its larger purpose is to explore the *historicity* of the form by examining how the tale of its origins and development has been, and continues to be, narrated. That is a journey that takes us from what Michael Collins, in Chapter 1, terms 'the experience of Atlantic intercultures', in which short fiction took many and various guises and exercised a 'seemingly endless play with identities', through the conceptual narrowings of institutional literary criticism and modernist-impressionist rationalisations of the 'short story proper',[20] to increasingly metaphorised renderings of the form favoured by writers since the Second World War.

Part II, 'Publishing the Short Story', takes up with recent work in the field of Book History to address the variety of forms and venues in which the short story is published, and the relationships between those forms and venues. There is a particular emphasis here on how the periodical differs as a venue of publication from the book, and the role of the anthology in, for example, defining 'national' story types. The section concludes with an exploration of the impact of digital media on the future of short story publishing, and in particular on the status of short fiction in what Ellen McCracken calls 'transitional literature', that is, 'electronic texts that mimic the format and appearance of print'.[21]

The chapters in Part III, 'Forms of the Short Story', focus on some of the major generic modes inhabited by the short story in English. Extending from short-short stories, through horror, supernaturalism and the weird, to postmodernist experimentalism and war writing, the chapters address both 'literary' and popular incarnations of the short story, and, building on Part II, consider the role that modes and venues of publication have played in conditioning the textual forms and contextual functions of short fiction since the nineteenth century.

'Placing the Short Story', Part IV, engages with the subject of 'place' in an expansive way, eschewing conventional, location-specific studies in favour of models which are comparative, transnational and theoretically informed. The opening chapter explores the short story as a phenomenon of regionalist writing, before attention turns to the evolving spaces of suburbia and the city, in which the short story has long predominated. In the final chapter, which brings the fruits of ecocriticism to bear on the short story, geographical place is 'hitched', as Deborah Lilley and Sam Solnick put it, across time and space to The Environment writ-large, and to 'tradition' understood not as a linear or historical process but as 'cultural environment'.

The volume concludes with 'Identity and the Short Story'. As noted earlier, perhaps the clearest indication of the short story's haphazard theorisation is the shortage of critical studies taking up questions of gender, sexuality, ethnicity, disability and other identity formations. This is all the more remarkable when one considers that the short story, since the late nineteenth century, has been found to be peculiarly amenable to the expression of 'minority', eccentric, and counter-normative identities and ideological positions. This section addresses matters that have for too long been neglected, such as: why, and in what ways, women writers have excelled in the short form in particular historical periods; how short fiction has been used to enact critiques of heteronormative values; what the role of the short story has been in the development of literatures of intercultural and multicultural exchange; and why we still have so much to discover about the short story's excursions into what Alice Hall terms the '"undiscovered country" of illness and invalidity in literary writing'.

Notes

1. Rita Felski, *The Limits of Critique* (Chicago and London: University of Chicago Press, 2015), p. 154.
2. Ibid. p. 11.

3. Ibid. p. 154.
4. Ibid. p. 153.
5. See, for example, Valentine Cunningham, *Reading After Theory* (Oxford: Blackwell, 2002); Derek Attridge, *The Singularity of Literature* (Abingdon and New York: Routledge, 2004); and Timothy Bewes, 'Reading with the Grain: A New World in Literary Criticism', *differences*, 21.3 (2010): 1–33.
6. Mary Eagleton, 'Gender and Genre', in Clare Hanson (ed.), *Rereading the Short Story* (Basingstoke: Macmillan, 1989), pp. 55–68.
7. Janet Beer, *Kate Chopin, Edith Wharton and Charlotte Perkins Gilman: Studies in Short Fiction* (London: Macmillan, 1997).
8. See Maggie Awadalla and Paul March-Russell (eds), *The Postcolonial Short Story* (Basingstoke: Palgrave Macmillan, 2013).
9. Mary Louise Pratt, 'The Short Story: The Long and the Short of It', in Charles E. May (ed.), *The New Short Story Theories* (Athens: Ohio University Press, 1994), pp. 91–113.
10. Timothy Clark, 'Not Seeing the Short Story: A Blind Phenomenology of Reading', *Oxford Literary Review*, 26.1 (2012): 10–11; 7.
11. On the central role of the short story in the development of university Creative Writing see Andrew Levy, *The Culture and Commerce of the American Short Story* (Cambridge: Cambridge University Press, 1993), pp. 102–32. See also Mark McGurl, *The Program Era: Postwar Fiction and the Rise of Creative Writing* (Cambridge, MA: Harvard University Press, 2011).
12. See Adrian Hunter, 'The "Custom" of Fiction: Virginia Woolf, the Hogarth Press, and the Modernist Short Story', *English* 56 (2007): 147–69.
13. Dominic Head, *The Modernist Short Story: A Study in Theory and Practice* (Cambridge: Cambridge University Press, 1992), p. 6.
14. Frank O'Connor, *The Lonely Voice: A Study of the Short Story* (London: Macmillan, 1963), pp. 20–1.
15. Richard Ford provides a searching account of post-war American writers' attraction to the form in the introduction to his *Granta Book of the American Short Story* (London: Granta, 1992).
16. Ann-Marie Einhaus (ed.), *The Cambridge Companion to the English Short Story* (Cambridge: Cambridge University Press, 2016), p. 1.
17. See Head's, *Modernist Short Story* and Levy's *Cultural and Commerce of the American Short Story*.
18. Elizabeth Bowen, 'The Faber Book of Modern Short Stories', in *After-Thought: Pieces About Writing* (London: Longmans, 1962), p. 38.
19. H. E. Bates, *The Modern Short Story: A Critical Survey* (London: Thomas Nelson, 1943), p. 23.
20. Ibid. p. 13
21. Ellen McCracken, 'Expanding Genette's Epitext/Paritext model for transitional electronic literature: Centrifugal and centripedal vectors on Kindles and iPads', *Narrative*, 21.1 (2013): 104.

Bibliography

Attridge, Derek, *The Singularity of Literature* (Abingdon and New York: Routledge, 2004).
Awadalla, Maggie and Paul March-Russell (eds), *The Postcolonial Short Story* (Basingstoke: Palgrave Macmillan, 2013).
Baldwin, Dean, *Art and Commerce in the British Short Story* (London: Routledge, 2013).
Bates, H. E., *The Modern Short Story: A Critical Survey* (London: Thomas Nelson, 1943).
Beer, Janet, *Kate Chopin, Edith Wharton and Charlotte Perkins Gilman: Studies in Short Fiction* (London: Macmillan, 1997).

Bewes, Timothy, 'Reading with the Grain: A New World in Literary Criticism', *differences*, 21.3 (2010): 1–33.
Bowen, Elizabeth, 'The Faber Book of Modern Short Stories', in *After-Thought: Pieces About Writing* (London: Longmans, 1962).
Clark, Timothy, 'Not Seeing the Short Story: A Blind Phenomenology of Reading', *Oxford Literary Review*, 26.1 (2012): 10–11; 5–30.
Cunningham, Valentine, *Reading After Theory* (Oxford: Blackwell, 2002).
D'hoker, Elke, *Irish Women Writers and the Modern Short Story* (Basingstoke and London: Palgrave Macmillan, 2016).
Eagleton, Mary, 'Gender and Genre', in Clare Hanson (ed.), *Rereading the Short Story* (Basingstoke: Macmillan, 1989), pp. 55–68.
Einhaus, Ann-Marie, *The Short Story and the First World War* (Cambridge: Cambridge University Press, 2013).
— (ed.), *The Cambridge Companion to the English Short Story* (Cambridge: Cambridge University Press, 2016).
Felski, Rita, *The Limits of Critique* (Chicago and London: University of Chicago Press, 2015).
Ford, Richard (ed.), *The Granta Book of the American Short Story* (London: Granta, 1992).
Head, Dominic, *The Modernist Short Story: A Study in Theory and Practice* (Cambridge: Cambridge University Press, 1992).
Hunter, Adrian, 'The "Custom" of Fiction: Virginia Woolf, the Hogarth Press, and the Modernist Short Story', *English*, 56 (2007): 147–69.
Levy, Andrew, *The Culture and Commerce of the American Short Story* (Cambridge: Cambridge University Press, 1993).
McCracken, Ellen, 'Expanding Genette's Epitext/Paritext model for transitional electronic literature: Centrifugal and centripedal vectors on Kindles and iPads', *Narrative*, 21.1(2013): 105–24.
McGurl, Mark, *The Program Era: Postwar Fiction and the Rise of Creative Writing* (Cambridge, MA: Harvard University Press, 2011).
O'Connor, Frank, *The Lonely Voice: A Study of the Short Story* (London: Macmillan, 1963).
Pratt, Mary Louise, 'The Short Story: The Long and the Short of It', in Charles E. May (ed.), *The New Short Story Theories* (Athens: Ohio University Press, 1994), pp. 91–113.
Young, Emma and James Bailey (eds), *British Women Short Story Writers: The New Woman to Now* (Edinburgh: Edinburgh University Press, 2015).

Part I
Historicising the Short Story

1

Transnationalism and the Transatlantic Short Story

Michael J. Collins

Conventional narratives concerning the origins of the short story in English have been challenged recently by new scholarly approaches that engage with important questions of nationalism, cosmopolitanism, literary transmission and print culture. Before the so-called 'transnational turn' in the twenty-first century, critics of the short story were prone to afford an especial place in the development of the genre to a certain restricted canon of nineteenth-century practitioners, normally including Washington Irving, Edgar Allan Poe, Nathaniel Hawthorne, Herman Melville and Sir Walter Scott, all of whose aesthetic achievements were tracked to prevalent conceptions of national traditions and 'origins' that have now been revealed as problematic.[1]

Nationalism has often reared its head in discussions of the short story. Galvanised, yet certainly not inaugurated, in the twentieth century by influential critical works such as Frank O'Connor's *The Lonely Voice* (1963), which argued that an alienation from the hegemonic imperial metropole of London afforded a particular richness to the work of Scottish, Irish and American writers in the genre (who could be seen as exemplars of subaltern 'cultures'), critics have often sidestepped the material facts of publication history so as to pin short stories to specific national traditions. Even when some account of publication is made, formalist critical approaches that try to locate distinctive, recurrent features of the short story are marked by a persistent, though often subtle, nationalist undertone. This nationalism reflects older concepts of canonicity: an artificial understanding of a work's literary value, rooted in a subjective assessment of its ability to capture national 'traits', that can be traced back to Matthew Arnold.[2] However, it also reflects the so-called origins of the 'short story' in late eighteenth- and early nineteenth-century German philology and folklore data collection by such figures as Johan Gottfried Herder, Wilhelm Von Humboldt and the Brothers Grimm.[3] It is generally acknowledged that the collections of folk tales and legends assembled by these figures had significant circulations in the Atlantic world and contributed to an emerging Romantic project of celebrating the 'primitive', 'indigenous' and professedly 'anti-modern' as potential wellsprings of national renewal in the wake of exhaustion with late eighteenth-century revolutionary modernising projects associated with a French conception of progressive civilisation.[4] These texts, particularly those of the Grimms (whose first collection of *Kinder- und Hausmärchen* was published in 1812), were widely read in German, which operated effectively as a second national language in America. However, it was with the translations of Edgar Taylor into English in 1823 that the tradition of the German folk tale really took off in Britain and the US. Matti Bunzl has remarked of the institutional logic of these German philological projects that

> [t]he comparison of any given nation or age with the Enlightenment or any other external standard was . . . unacceptable: each human group could be understood as a product of its particular history. Embodying a unique genius, or *Geist*, each *Volk* formed an organic whole, the values, beliefs, traditions, and language of which could only be understood from within by entering into the viewpoint of the members.[5]

For these important German pioneers of anthropology, short folk stories could be understood to contain the essence of a national, or local, culture/*Kultur* within the vehicle of their form. The 'short story', then, was sutured to a conception of nationalism rooted, at least at first, in German Romantic theories of '*der volk*' – a focus on localised specificity that contributed to the counter-revolutionary project of challenging the universalism of the French Enlightenment.

Returning to the American short story, Charles May's influential work has cleaved doggedly to nationalist tropes through repeated claims that 'short fiction's combination of the romantic and the realistic begins most vigorously in the United States . . .'[6] and that the nation gave specific force to American authors' aesthetic practices. For May, as indeed for other influential critics such as Susan Lohafer, the short story is notable for combining a descriptive realism with Romantic lyric effects (epiphanies, reversals, slippages between worlds) that push the narrative into the realm of the fantastical. The balance struck between these two modes by writers such as Hawthorne or Poe has come to constitute many of the defining features of the genre. The argument follows that the modern short story's remarkable combination of realism and romance suited authors working either on the so-called fringes of the British Empire or in postcolonial nations with historical attachments to England, because their tangential relationship to dominant, metropolitan mythologies of Enlightenment empiricism (embodied in the realistic imperative to describe events without recourse to Platonic other worlds that came to define the nineteenth-century realist novel) *and* unequal economic/literary relationships, forced authors to experiment in alternative and hybrid narrative forms.[7] For critics in the middle decades of the twentieth century, the formal lyrical epiphanies of key works such as Hawthorne's 'Young Goodman Brown' and 'My Kinsman, Major Molineux' or Melville's 'Bartleby, The Scrivener' were used to argue for the evolution of a national consciousness – a revolutionary rupture that was aesthetic *and* political. Key works in this mode include Frederick Crews's *Sins of the Fathers* (1966), Leo Marx's *The Machine in the Garden* (1964) and Daniel Hoffman's *Form and Fable in American Fiction* (1965). The institutionalisation of formalist approaches to the short story in the 1950s coincided with the rise of American Studies (with its associated critical tradition of 'myth and symbol') and the transatlantic movement of New Criticism, both of which adopted a selective approach to the canon based on traditions of close reading in universities. In this landscape the search for authentically 'American' (or 'Scottish', 'English', 'Irish', etc.) cultural forms led to a renewed interest in the achievements of key exponents of the nineteenth-century short story. This was because an inheritance from German *Kultur* scholarship of seeing the genre as culturally authoritative and 'authentic' dovetailed neatly with pedagogical practices in the university that venerated close textual analysis.⁸ The formal hermeticism of the short story – its brevity and seeming 'completeness' – served this national project beautifully, since it seemed to embody synecdochally nationalist scholarship's claims about the autonomy and inviolate nature of cultures.

Such nationalist-formalist readings actually belie the complex position of literature in the transatlantic world of the nineteenth century. Rather than short fiction issuing from clear and definable sites of origin (playing into Romantic narratives of the indigeneity and national provenance of literature), the Atlantic and imperial world of the eighteenth and early nineteenth centuries was one marked by what Oliver Scheiding has called a 'vast field of global textual traffic'⁹ in which 'alleged metropolitan textual hegemonies and national trajectories [were] frequently out of sync with the actual local literatures'.¹⁰ This is to say, the relationships of centre to periphery were far more vexed than O'Connor, May and others imagined. The 'textual traffic' between the metropolis and the provinces, or Britain and America, was generated and sustained by practices of reprinting, anonymous authorship, hoaxing and plagiarism that conferred less a state of fixity to national character (registered by some twentieth-century critics as a comparable stability in the generic traits of short fiction) than an opportunity for a seemingly endless play with identities: masquerades, burlesques, and, significantly, formal discontinuity.¹¹ Indeed, pinning aesthetics to the nation-state, or to a Herderian concept of 'culture' is, in fact, an anti-historical exercise, since the national traits that nineteenth-century philologists tried to find in the short story (and twentieth-century critics saw revealed in it) were far from established in the period. Without the systematic protections of copyright, which was not officially mandated in the Atlantic world until the Berne Convention for the Protection of Literary And Artistic Works in 1886 (or the Chace Act of 1891 in the USA), short stories could appear nearly simultaneously in transatlantic periodicals without clearly identifiable sites of origin, or indeed, 'authors'.¹² That scholars have often interpreted this fact as a travesty that arrested the development of literary culture in the Atlantic world reflects an inherent nationalism within academic approaches to literary form. It is better to think of it as one of the shaping forces of the short story tradition that was utilised by authors to produce literary effects in the form.

This overemphasis on Romantic nationalism in understandings of the origins of the short story has had other consequences. Not only does it effectively exclude all forms of short fiction other than the folk tale, 'romantic fragment' or 'short story proper' (whatever that may be taken to mean), it also relegates achievements during practically the whole eighteenth century to the position of prophesying the eventual arrival of figures like Hawthorne, Poe and Scott. This is, of course, a profoundly anti-historicist exercise that makes common eighteenth-century periodical forms such as the 'sketch', 'Socratic dialogues', 'reveries', 'didactic tales', 'epistolary fictions' and the like, with their own particular audiences and identities, seem not only inferior to the so-called 'short story proper' but invalidates them even in their own time through an anachronistic conception of aesthetic value.¹³ As Tim Killick has written, 'The notion of a clear-cut and homogenous Romantic tradition of the short story does not exist . . . there is often little sense of a collective ideology, even amongst those writers whose works are connected thematically, stylistically, or geographically.'¹⁴ It is worth saying that much of what is understood to be the 'short story proper', as Charles May and others have defined it, was the provenance of authors working for bourgeois audiences. A fuller account of the short story's 'origins' would include the work of writers operating in alternative traditions such as the enormously influential *Cheap Repository Tracts* of Hannah More or the innumerable broadsides and pamphlets that circulated in the Atlantic world of the eighteenth and nineteenth centuries. For all the insufficiencies of form and content, for the modern reader what the didactic tales of More and others indicate is an alternative historical trajectory for short prose fiction. For More the tale was not a romantic exercise in subjectivity but largely a disciplinary one with deep roots in the eighteenth century and only a few wild tendrils to be seen stretching into the nineteenth. From an American perspective this eighteenth-century market culture, the world of Franklin more than Shelley, was central to the meaning of the short story. The same might be said of Scott or Hogg, where the Scottish Enlightenment's centralisation of commerce and exchange looms at least as large in their literary imaginations as the fairy tales of a pre- or anti-modern peasantry that were held in such regard by Romanticists. For the moment, though, it is perhaps enough to say that there is more than simply one form of the short story – just as there is not one form of cosmopolitanism. Many different classes and cultures shaped, and were shaped by, the vast movements of people and resources across and around the Atlantic world. Significantly, all of these groups of people became 'cultures' in the anthropological sense because, not in spite, of this movement. The same can be said of the short story, which became what it was through exchange and diffusion.

Many of the texts that have been used by critics to establish a definable nationalist lineage and a recognisable form of the 'short story' operated by means of their 'remote performances' as much as, if not more than, their national ones. Texts often served utterly different purposes in Massachusetts than in Edinburgh or London. Furthermore, many texts drew on the position of uncertain provenance, or the mutual exchanges of the Atlantic world, as crucial sources of creativity. Kasia Boddy has argued a similar point in relation to paratext in a later era of publishing, claiming, 'where we read the story shapes the expectations we bring to our reading of it, and thus the effect it has on us'.[15] National identities and genres, such as they are, are contingent phenomena that because of the nature of publishing and writing in the age of print always perform themselves at a geographical remove from their source by means of an intersubjective and dialectical exchange with the matter around them. This is one of the crucial effects of publication; as true when the Grimms printed their collected folk stories in 1812 as when Kate Chopin published her local color tales of Creole life as *Bayou Folk* in 1894. In fact, in the case of culture and folklore in the modern age, diffusion and transmission beyond the hermetic boundaries of the 'interior' of the culture itself is how meaning is generated. James Clifford has described this process in relation to his own field of ethnography:

> [e]thnographic writings can properly be called fictions in the sense of 'something made or fashioned,' the principal burden of the word's Latin root, *fingere* . . . [b]ut it is important to preserve the meaning not merely of making, but also of making up, of inventing things not actually real.[16]

The history of the short story from the Brothers Grimm onwards has been defined by how stories were marketed or fashioned as the specific products of intrinsic and innate cultures, understood as bulwarks against the myriad threats imposed by encroaching modernity; yet at the same time they were created by and through processes of collection and writing that were themselves performances of a distinctly 'modern' nature.

Modernity's philological, academic projects and literary marketplaces created cultures that then performed themselves as autochthonic – the product of some early-Romantic logic of place. In the transatlantic world of the nineteenth century, short stories became 'marked and marketed as something like cultural things'[17] that affected a relationship to some imagined homeland but were actually created for the purpose of movement. Laura Doyle puts this quite beautifully in 'Toward a Philosophy of Transnationalism':

> [T]here certainly are nations – they are still with us clearly – but there is no a *priori*, Herderian spirit, or purely indigenous and liberatory 'inside' of the nation: rather there are radically coformed nations, arising from material and ideological forces that continuously transform the existence of both or all national sides.[18]

In other words, the underlying logic of the transnational literary project is that the experience of Atlantic intercultures should not be taken to be an extension of the reach of traditional literary study beyond a nation understood as always already fully formed (a literary version of an imperial 'mission'), but the *genius loci* of national and cultural formation in the modern age of empires and print. This is important for the short story since much of what have been reified as generic traits have been so bound up in Romantic-nationalist traditions of reading that have taken as truth the existence of a definitive American, Scottish, Irish or English national culture from which writers drew.

The short story in English has a distinctive set of generic forms and concerns only in so far as the genre in the eighteenth and nineteenth centuries was peculiarly suited to diffusion. Its brevity, and the fact that an editor did not need to commit to numerous 'episodes' month to month (as in the case of the serial novel), permitted its rapid and easy transmission within an Atlantic world where the financial success of a journal or publishing venture was often tenuous. Indeed, as Meredith McGill has argued in relation to Hawthorne and Poe, the push for many authors to collect their disparate short fictions within the more stable and locatable form of the book, or short story cycle, occurred precisely because of the fact of these transnational flows; the Atlantic shaping the national once again.[19] The short story collection, which brought the unstable genre of the short story under the auspices of the evolving form of the modern novel through means of framing devices, identifiable narrators (singular and plural) and thematic consistency, served to relocate texts within the national, or identifiably local, frameworks that frequently eluded short fiction. Crucial examples of this include James Hogg's *Winter Evening Tales* (1820), Washington Irving's *Sketchbook of Geoffrey Crayon, Gent* (1819–20), Mary Russell Mitford's *Our Village* (1824), Walter Scott's *Chronicles of the Canongate* (1827) and Nathaniel Hawthorne's *Twice-Told Tales* (1837), which were all the products of struggles by the authors to find a nationalist voice in a transatlantic literary space wholly resistant to the logic of nationalism. After the passage of the 1814 Copyright Act in Britain, writers were afforded copyrights to their works for a period of twenty-five years. However, these protections were based upon a policy of library deposit that relied upon the technology of 'the book'. This did not apply to the short story in the form it most often began its life, as magazine or newspaper fiction. As such, the short story was seldom as easily registered for purposes of copyright and so existed in parallel to the emerging nationalist formations undergirded by the juro-political protections of copyright and the nation state.[20]

At times the recent move towards transnational methodologies seems inclined to do away with close reading altogether, seeing such interest in focused formal attention as complicit with the outmoded nationalist reading practices. Recent work by figures such as Franco Moretti on 'world systems theory' and 'distant reading' that approach literature from the point of view of big data has moved analysis well beyond the nation, but also runs the risk of missing out on local and contingent features that play an important part in building a historicist picture of the meaning of a literary text.[21] The study of the short story, it happens, thrives on such specific details. What frequently falls under the radar of 'distant reading' is the fact that short fictions typically appeared in parallel marketplaces – gift books, anonymous reprinted texts, ephemeral media forms – and so did not always register with legitimating sources of authority.

The nationalist-formalist tradition can be misleading for scholars as it often fails to register how the short story developed out of transatlantic, transnational or global networks that signified differently according to local particularities. Importantly, this must not take the form of a new claim to nationalist exceptionalism. Rather, it should ask us to look at a text's 'performance' of national or local particularity: not what it is, but what it does. For this reason, the most important counterpart for short fiction in the period was not the novel, or poetry, but theatre; specifically, a kind of touring show that adapted its meaning to localised needs and audiences.[22] Connecting short fiction to performance culture is a surprisingly revealing enterprise, since the transatlantic drama of the Romantic era attests materially to the very complex and tangled nature of nationalism at the time. Matthew Pethers has noted:

> Perhaps the most striking indication of the cultural heterogeneity of the post-Augustan theatre ... is the plethora of regional and ethnic types which filled its stages. On both sides of the Atlantic, Scotsmen, Irishmen, Frenchmen, Jews, Africans and Arabs were regularly played off against each other as well as against the English; and into this theatrical melting pot we can also throw ... the Yankee.[23]

Along with Heather Nathans, Jeffrey H. Richards and others, Pethers has demonstrated how performances of the 'Scot' in America or the 'Yankee' in England created meaning out of their localised context rather than out of some generic conception of universalised national traits. This is much the same for short fiction in the period, especially since there was a very distinctly 'theatrical' and carnivalesque quality to the magazine form.[24] The connection of short fiction to performance is both a new and an old way of reading. It is a development of a long-standing theory of the short story that attests to its relationship to orality and older technologies of the folk tale. However, whereas that work was often part of a Romantic synthesis that tried to claim a work's originary relationship to the land, or to a pre-modern culture, it is more accurate to see this 'performativity' as a product of Atlantic modernity and one of its major traits.

Performances of nationalism functioned most effectively in sites quite geographically distant from their presumed points of origin. Indeed, they positively relied on distance for the simple reason that there is no innate 'truth' to nationalism at the location of its supposed formation. Close analysis will therefore always reveal the mythological nature of so-called 'national traits' and the reality, instead, of diversity and multiplicity. Consequently, any contemporary assessment of the early short story must account for the following: the local context in which a work appears in print, how it 'performs' its meaning or identity at that location, and how that local publication history relates to the migrancy of texts in eighteenth- and nineteenth-century transatlantic space. Two texts seldom included in official lineages and taxonomies of the short story can serve to illustrate these claims: Benjamin Franklin's 'The Speech of Miss Polly Baker' and James Hogg's 'The Story of Two Highlanders'.

By the late 1740s Franklin had already made a name for himself as a humourist and fabricator of hoaxes. Shortly after purchasing the paper that became *The Pennsylvania Gazette* in 1729 he began to use it as a vehicle for a distinctive mixture of satire, reportage and advice that utilised numerous aliases to cover his near single-handed authorship of the paper.[25] Franklin was known for relying on female pseudonyms such as 'Celia Single' and 'Alice Addertongue' in his work for the *Gazette*, building on his earlier success with the character of 'Silence Dogood' in the *New-England Courant*. Franklin's gendered ventriloquism revealed not only the important role played by women in the pre-revolutionary American public sphere, but also the interrelationship of regional and international news. As much as being an important colonial news source, the *Gazette* was a site of burlesque theatre that allowed Franklin to demonstrate how concerns in Europe were received in his local Philadelphian context. Yet it was with 'The Speech of Miss Polly Baker' in 1747 that Franklin was able to most fully probe the relationship of the local and regional to the international through the performative use of a female narrator.

'Polly Baker' is the fictional report of a speech given before a 'Court of Judicature, At Connecticut'[26] by a young woman on trial for her fifth 'offense' of having brought, out of wedlock, 'Five fine Children into the World, at the Risque of my Life'. Polly's speech draws attention to the hypocrisy of the penal code of New England, which prosecuted women for having illegitimate children but not men for fathering them. Polly remarks that the nature of the punishment was severe:

> [i]f mine, then, is a religious Offence, leave it to religious Punishments. You have already excluded me from the Comforts of your Church-Communion. Is not that sufficient? You believe I have offended Heaven, and must suffer eternal Fire: Will not that be sufficient? What Need is there, then, of your additional Fines and Whipping?

It is noted that Polly's plea is so eloquent and impassioned that it 'induced one of her Judges to marry her the next Day'. This marriage serves to effectively return the children to a condition of paternal legitimacy that is itself complicit with colonialism. Since the judge represents not only masculine authority but also colonial law itself, the speech constitutes at once a challenge to the authority of the Crown, through Polly's questioning of its civil and religious laws, and the possibility of a union between a 'wayward' colonial subject and the sovereignty of the British Empire. As a performance of an individuated speaking subject, the story oscillates between autonomy (understood in liberal terms as the right of the subject to speak) and dependence. Indeed, this is the very nature of a plea, which functions through the recognition of individual particularity in relation to a collective. Franklin alludes to this in having Polly describe herself as a 'Subject in particular Circumstances', evoking simultaneously the condition of being a generic, loyal 'Subject' of the Crown, a person in a challenging position in relation to it and, of course, a pun on maternity itself.

The story constitutes an early instance of an evolving 'American' consciousness that was not autochthonic but operated by exploiting crucial legal and social ties to the homeland. Polly's argument contains within it a veiled threat to colonial authority when she calls out a magistrate as the father of one of her illegitimate children. Polly's claim is that the 'great and growing Number of Batchelors in the Country', who were transatlantically mobile and required by the empire for the maintenance of law, order and trade, was entailing a backsliding in morality and the possibility of numerous illegitimate children that would be a tax burden and a threat to civil order. Consequently, Polly pleas for changes to the Crown's laws, a challenge to its authority over American women, in order to produce a greater surveillance of men by the Crown and protection of Britain's interests in the colonies. The condition of illegitimacy is further problematised by Polly's claim that she is doing her duty by the Crown, because what she has really achieved is 'to add to the Number of the King's Subjects, in a new Country that really wants People'. Yet the possibility that those people may result in 'burthening the Township' demonstrates an irony in misogynistic British imperialism that without the full and unequivocal rights of women over their own bodies, the colonial economy will be stretched to breaking point. The safety of the empire then relies on challenging male privilege. Polly's speech creates a complex ambiguity as it becomes questionable whether the decision of the judge to marry her (as described by the unnamed reporter at the beginning of the text) is a means of protecting patriarchal colonial law against the threat of female speech (an act of silencing), a desire to avoid a tax burden on the colony of Connecticut, or a genuine act of compassion.

As Elizabeth Barnes has noted, early 'American' literature often 'work[ed] out socio-political questions and conflicts through a gendered body – the woman's'.[27] For this reason, Franklin's performance as Polly is an act of what Joseph Roach calls 'surrogacy' in transatlantic space, albeit performed in expectation of a future condition of liberty. In Franklin's story, a woman in crisis becomes synecdochal of the ironies of empire facing all colonial American subjects in the years before the Stamp Act crisis and the outbreak of the War of Independence. 'The Speech of Miss Polly Baker' is a key text in the development of the short story in the transatlantic world because it utilises a condition of subalterneity in a transnational space as a means to perform an evolving 'national' consciousness. It 'stands in', as Roach would have it, for the nation that is not established institutionally but that existed as an affective condition in relation to the 'Faults and Miscarriages' (Baker) of the colonial juro-political order.

Franklin published the story anonymously, but chose not to use his own American ventures or connections to do so. Instead, the first appearance of the 'Speech' was in London's *The General Advertiser* on 15 April 1715, before then being reprinted in *The Gentleman's Magazine*, *The British Magazine* and *The Scot's Magazine* later in the month. It was not until 20 July 1720 that the piece appeared in the American publications *The Boston Weekly Post-Boy*, *The New York Gazette* and *The New York Weekly Journal*. The 'Speech' was soon translated into French 'where several writers, among them Voltaire, Diderot, and Morellet – found its contents helpful and made use of it in their fight for a more enlightened society'.[28] The condition of anonymity allowed the text to operate differently in different locations, aided by its form and non-authorial attribution. In America, the 'Speech' would have functioned as another example of a common genre in the newspaper press – the hoax – which Franklin had himself been influential in establishing. Certainly, local audiences would have picked up on the relationship between the story and some of the more famous instances in Puritan New England history, specifically the trials of Mary Dyer and Anne Hutchinson, whose conversions to Quakerism and challenge to the Elders during the Antinomian Controversy respectively constituted major local precedents for stories about the destabilising power of female speech in the colonies.[29] However, the story works most effectively as a remote performance in England, where it operates as an early instance of the significant tradition of 'American humour', playing off stereotypes of the American colonists as unruly and presenting a form of 'American' identity that resonates by specifically burlesquing its complex relationship to the homeland. Undoubtedly, though, English readers would have recognised in the speech a playful burlesque of their own commitment to the colonial rule of law. The delay in appearing in America also allowed the text to draw on the prestige associated with publication in Europe, demonstrating how authentication of short fiction often happened within an expanded geographical space that is not captured by the Romantic-nationalist critical tradition.

The character of Polly's challenge to colonial power does not take the form of wholesale rejection of the values of England or the British Empire. In fact, Polly appears to believe that she stands to save it from itself. The story expresses the voice of its time in its complex modal shifts between dependence and independence. A formalist analysis has little space for the emotional complexities of a work like 'The Speech', because the tendency would be to reject eighteenth-century precedents of the short story proper either on grounds of imitation or for their inability to articulate a fully coherent national consciousness. 'The Speech' is shaped by the influence of the transatlantic republic of letters that allowed it to diffuse so widely. Specifically, it is firm in its challenge, but polite, and its humour is gently satiric about national differences. Nationalist-formalist reading practices would reject 'The Speech' on the ground that it builds to no epiphany or lyric moment. Instead of a coming to consciousness or a falling away of the veil of reality that formalist critics have seen as central to the form, 'The Speech' turns on something more like a punchline: 'I have hazarded the Loss of the Publick Esteem, and have frequently endured Publick Disgrace and Punishment; and therefore ought, in my humble Opinion, instead of a Whipping, to have a Statue erected to my Memory'. According to the logic of Charles May's approach, the lyrical epiphany is crucial to the American short story because it is the aesthetic version of revolutionary rejection, a new understanding of the individual's relationship to the collective that has come to serve as an exemplary moment of nationalist formation. By thinking beyond the lyric in the short story it is possible to conceptualise a transnational cultural tradition for the form. The bathetic humour of Polly Baker's performance raises British-American dispute only to then undercut it, creating a shared sense of meaning for transatlantic readers.

'The Speech' is more than just an anonymous media joke. Its themes of anonymity and illegitimacy serve as a reflection upon the nature of the 'short story' in a world of transatlantic reprinting. By choosing not to attach his name to the piece, Franklin was fully expecting the work to be reprinted widely and liberally without his consent. Indeed, the decision to send a text to be anonymously printed in London, rather than holding some position of copyright that would come from a text being locally published in a paper under his control, constitutes an implicit disavowal of his engendering author function; the 'Speech' is an unattributed, unclaimed gift to the Atlantic world. By not acknowledging his authorship, Franklin becomes the father of an illegitimate child that he then refuses to claim. There is a clear self-parody in the fact that Franklin is one of the libidinous transatlantic bachelors Polly attacks in her speech, having his fun at the expense of an impelled and precarious woman that results in an unclaimed bastard. The physical movement of the text-object in transatlantic space dramatises its themes. Its anonymous authorship mobilises important questions of ownership that reflect the story's engagement with ideas of illegitimacy and the transatlantic movement of peoples in the eighteenth century. In being 'taken in' by the magistrate, Polly's children find a surrogate father who is not their own, but who performs as if he were, much as the transatlantic reprinter of a short story claims the story as theirs and performs as if it were, even though it is clearly not his authorial or legal property.

This process also worked in reverse. A European author might make use of American themes to dramatise their own local concerns in the short story. Hogg's 'Story of Two Highlanders' (1810), which uses American references to make claims about Scottish identity, is a good example. Hogg's tale engages with the real historical diaspora of Hudson River Scots to make claims about the interpenetration of national cultures in the Atlantic world. The appeal of Hogg's story is twofold. First, it clearly thinks about transnationalism in terms of imperialism and considers the implications of such a move for claims to a distinctive 'Scottish' national or cultural identity. Second, it seems formally more like a fragment, or what would become known as a 'short-short story', than like a 'short story proper', as May would have it. Hogg's story allows us to situate short fiction in a landscape less saturated with the concerns of Romanticism and more comprehensively shaped by an eighteenth-century discourse of circulation and mobility. The tale is not structured around an epiphany or moments of lyrical clarity. Instead, like Franklin's, it works through burlesque humour and anecdote.

'Two Highlanders' begins with an aphoristic statement that deliberately cuts in two directions, evoking universalism but also a logic of human difference. Hogg writes: 'There is perhaps no quality of mind, in which mankind differ more than in a prompt readiness either to act or answer to a point, in the most imminent and sudden dangers and difficulties.'[30] In this way Hogg attempts to balance two competing traditions, the German Romantic sensibilities of *'der volk'* (in Scotland the tradition of bardic nationalism) *and* an Enlightenment universalism that attributes common traits to all of mankind. This generalisation serves to evoke bathos, undercutting the authority of the writer to make pronouncements on universal human character. The 'perhaps' here performs uncertainty, even as the statement itself resembles similar claims in the Anglo-American literary tradition – among them Jane Austen's famed 'It is a truth universally acknowledged' or Thomas Jefferson's 'We hold these truths to be self-evident that all men are created equal.' Indeed, the Enlightenment nationalism of the Declaration of Independence seems to be specifically evoked in Hogg's next paragraph, only to be similarly burlesqued. Following this uncertain claim to universalism Hogg then reduces his scope to a very specific locale and cultural frame: 'the banks of the Albany River, which falls into Hudson's Bay . . . a small colony settled . . .[by] emigrants from the Highlands of Scotland'.[31] For Scottish readers this setting simultaneously performs distance and proximity, and when read in relation to the opening phrase of the story it establishes a thematic connection between universalism and particularity in a transatlantic frame.

What follows is a tale reminiscent of others in Hogg's *oeuvre*, featuring Scottish dialect and madcap humour. It is the story of Mack and Donald, who come across a den of baby boar while in the woods. Mack decides to climb into the den to 'commence [. . .] the work of death'[32] against the piglets. In the meantime, Donald is confronted outside the cave by the boar's mother, who charges him, before returning to the entrance to protect her piglets from Mack. Donald's struggle with the boar, thereby protecting his own life and that of his oblivious partner, constitutes the plot.

The plot, though, is not as significant as the specific evocation of place to the tale. The story generates meaning very distinctly out of the ambiguities of its transnational performance. It is either a tale about Scottish 'national character' (playing off stereotypes of canniness, wit and camaraderie) that fits within the Romantic project of describing distinctive features of '*der volk*' through short fiction, which utilises a geographically distant diaspora that transforms the territorialised logic of '*volk*' into a set of racial characteristics that transcend place, or it is a work of American frontier humour that makes its claims out of a performance of identity that is both specifically Scottish and specifically 'American'. In effect, the story triangulates identities between Scotland, the USA and Britain. Rather than operating in a bardic nationalist mode, Hogg is specifically using the short story to demonstrate the interrelation of cultural particularity and Atlantic modernity.

It is important to note that the tale is not just about camaraderie and sociality. Donald's decision to return to assist Mack is partly motivated by self-interest: Hogg repeatedly refers to the 'fine half-grown pigs' as a 'prize',[33] implying a kind of treasure and prospect of personal gain. It is for this reason that the mythology of American bounty and trade is so significant to the tale. Indeed, the tale reads a little like an American treasure-hunting story. Hogg is drawing on Scottish Enlightenment theories of the benevolent effects of personal enrichment that contributed to the expansionist vision of the British and American Empires.[34] On one level 'Two Highlanders' is base humour, but on another it is brutal and genocidal. Mack and Donald do not need to murder the baby pigs: more 'common game' is apparently plentiful. Indeed, Hogg artfully notes that there were 'few wild swine remaining,'[35] having been hunted to near extinction by the British settlers. What we see in the two Highlanders' actions is the cruel logic of imperialism. Scottish emigration to the Hudson Valley was partly established in the late eighteenth century to populate regions lately taken from the nearly exterminated Mohican and Mohawk people. The pigs (and their defence of their babies) serve, therefore, as a metaphorical stand-in for a human genocide committed, at least in part, by Scottish and Scots-Irish people in upstate New York.

Consequently, 'The Story of Two Highlanders' does not set up Scottish identity in contradistinction to the expansionist and imperialist projects of Enlightenment modernity (as works like Grimm's tales performed German ethnic identity against the claims of revolutionary French Enlightenment modernity to universality), but conducts its performance of national traits against the backdrop of those decisive 'modern' and transatlantic histories. Hogg's choice of the Hudson River Valley is not accidental. Historically, it was a site of large Scottish migration. However, Hogg's choice is also specifically literary. In the early nineteenth century the Hudson River (adjoining the Catskill Mountains and, eventually, the Appalachians), was known as a site for the production of 'tall tales' – fictional accounts emerging from a famous trope of Atlantic literary culture, the Backwoods Roarer, which circulated widely. Washington Irving's *History of New York* and Salmagundi pieces would draw on this figure. Frequently from Scottish or Ulster-Scottish ethnic stock, the Backwoods Roarer was a major figure in antebellum stage and print comedy. The excessiveness, daring and thinly-masked imperialism of 'The Story of Two Highlanders' fits perfectly within this so-called 'American' literary tradition, defined by James E. Caron as personifying 'the bestial potential of people, especially the untutored common man and woman ... an uncouth lubber at best and a ruffian at worst, capable of eye-gouging in a rough-and-tumble fight'.[36] When read in Britain, Hogg's tale performed both backwoods 'Americanness' and tropes associated with 'Scottishness' simultaneously, generating its complex humour out of circumatlantic intercultural connections and literary histories. The reason for the performance of ethnicity in the short story is modernity itself, which shaped the experience and understanding of 'cultures' and national traits. The ambiguities of the opening are reflective of the tangled nature of the story as a whole. For this reason, the tale's appearance in US periodicals (*The Emerald* and *Baltimore Literary Gazette*), two rival New York-based editions of *Winter Evening Tales*, and in British magazines and publications, dramatises in physical space the cosmopolitan and imperial thematics of the tale. Its transmission around the Atlantic is made possible by its form, which, in turn, assists in the expression of its literary and thematic concerns. It does not operate around a lyrical epiphany or formal continuity, but by its rapidly shifting surfaces and implications – a subtlety that relies on the Atlantic world.

Both Franklin and Hogg reveal how circumatlantic intercultures affected literary production and reception in the eighteenth and nineteenth centuries through their deployment of self-reflexive techniques that called attention to the vexed position of the very idea of culture that has been a shaping discourse in short story theory. However, this is not the only characteristic that links these two authors, both of whom have been featured inadequately in genealogies of the short story. Hogg and Franklin also conducted their discussions of transnationalism in a way that revealed the presence of empire. Postmodern readings of short fiction have often drawn attention to humour and formal play as a means to reject the essentialisms of the past, yet for scholars it is important to repeatedly return to how the short story in English produced its forms of cultural diffusion against the backdrop of an imperial mercantile project whose unequal distributions of wealth and influence can be seen in works like those by Hogg and Franklin. Donald and Mack are emigrant Scots seeking their fortunes in a New World through the genocide of native peoples and wildlife, reflecting the nested histories of British imperialism and American expansionism simultaneously. The story turns that genocide into a cruel humour that circulates as a product around the English-speaking Atlantic world. Polly Baker's claim that population growth will place a burden on the colonies is directed both to the homeland and against the imperial expansion and settler colonialism of the north-eastern US colonies. Yet, for all its seeming progressivism the story makes its joke quite specifically from within an Atlantic imperial culture. The counter-revolutionary project that motivated the German Romantic *volk*, and to which subsequent short story theory has owed such a debt, made claims to 'culture' as the alternative to imperial, Enlightenment modernity and so rendered the short story as an oppositional literary mode that operated through the enclosures of form. What is shown here is how ironic such a claim truly is. The short story was a product of modernity and issued its challenges from within it, making the genre an exercise in alterity and complicity and inviting us to consider all that lies outside of the form itself. Ultimately, the short story is a genre that doth protest too much its coherence and formal stability. Challenging that coherence by paying attention to local reception and meaning should be a major task of our criticism in the coming years.

Notes

1. As John Plotz notes, this conventional list periodically also includes James Hogg, although this is far more rare. For Plotz, the reason for this lies in Hogg's deviation from Poe's commitment to unity of effect and formal coherence, which have become critical commonplaces in formalist analyses of the genre, and has placed him beyond the critical purview of many critics. See John Plotz, 'James Hogg and the Short Story', in Ian Duncan and Douglas Mack (eds), *The Edinburgh Companion to James Hogg* (Edinburgh: Edinburgh University Press, 2012), pp. 113–21, and R. J. Lyell 'Intimations of Orality: Scotland, America and the Early Development of the Short Story in English', *Studies in Short Fiction*, 36 (1999): 311–25.
2. See Arnold, *Culture and Anarchy* (Oxford and London: Oxford University Press, [1869] 2006).
3. For more on canonicity and Atlantic literatures see Julia Straub, 'Early American Literature: Canon Theory in a Transatlantic Context', *Comparative American Studies*, 9.2 (2012): 106–18.
4. Maria Tatar at Harvard has been influential in making this argument.
5. Matti Bunzl, 'Franz Boas and the Humboldtian Tradition', in George W. Stocking Jr (ed.), *Volkgeist as Method and Ethic: Essays on Boasian Ethnography and the German Anthropological Tradition* (Madison: The University of Wisconsin Press, 1996), p. 20.
6. Charles E. May, *The Short Story: The Reality of Artifice* (New York: Routledge, 2002), p. 24.
7. See Douglas Tallack, *The Nineteenth-Century American Short-Story: Language, Form and Ideology* (London: Routledge, 1993) for a good survey of the significance of theories of 'lyric epiphany' to short fiction.
8. See Daniel Hoffman, *Form and Fable in American Fiction* (New York: Oxford University Press, 1965).
9. Oliver Scheiding, 'Migrant Fictions: The Early Story in North American Magazines', in Berensmeyer, Ehland and Grabes (eds), *Mobility in Literature and Culture, 1500–1900* (Tübingen: Narr Verlag, 2012), p. 197.
10. Scheiding, 'Migrant Fictions', p. 198.
11. See Meredith L. McGill, *American Literature and the Culture of Reprinting, 1834–1853* (Philadelphia: University of Pennsylvania Press, 2003).
12. For more on the concept of the 'author' and copyright see Martha Woodmandsee and Peter Jaszi (eds), *The Construction of Authorship. The Construction of Authorship: Textual Appropriation in Law and Literature* (Durham, NC and New York: Duke University Press, 1994).
13. See Jared Gardner, *The Rise and Fall of Early American Magazine Culture* (Urbana, Chicago and Springfield: University of Illinois Press, 2012).
14. Tim Killick, *British Short Fiction in the Early Nineteenth Century: The Rise of the Tale* (Burlington, VT: Ashgate, 2008), p. 8.
15. Kasia Boddy, *The American Short Story since 1950* (Edinburgh: Edinburgh University Press, 2010), p. 17.
16. James Clifford, 'Introduction: Partial Truths', in James Clifford and George E. Marcus (eds), *Writing Culture: The Poetics and Politics of Ethnography* (Berkeley: University of California Press, 1986), p. 6.
17. Brad Evans, *Before Cultures: The Ethnographic Imagination in American Literature, 1865 to 1920* (Chicago: University of Chicago Press, 2005), p. 7.

18. Doyle, Laura, 'Toward a Philosophy of Transnationalism', *Journal of Transnational American Studies*, 1.1 (2009).
19. See McGill, *American Literature and the Culture of Reprinting*.
20. Jennie Batchelor's Leverhulme-Trust-funded *Ladies' Magazine Project* at the University of Kent captures brilliantly some of the complexities of assigning short fiction to authors in romantic magazines. The series of blog posts hunting down authors testify to the strange transatlantic landscape the genre found itself negotiating. Available at <https://blogs.kent.ac.uk/ladys-magazine/> (last accessed 15 April 2018).
21. See Franco Moretti, *Distant Reading* (London: Verso, 2013).
22. See Michael J. Collins, *The Drama of the American Short Story, 1800–1865* (Ann Arbor: University of Michigan Press, 2016).
23. Pethers in Daniel Maudlin and Robin Peel (eds), *The Materials of Exchange Between Britain and North East America, 1750–1900* (Farnham, Surrey and Burlington, VT: Ashgate, 2013), p. 85.
24. Isabelle Lehuu, *Carnival on the Page: Popular Print Culture in Antebellum America* (Chapel Hill: University of North Carolina Press, 2000).
25. Alfred Owen Aldridge, 'Benjamin Franklin and the *Pennsylvania Gazette*', *Proceedings of the American Philosophical Society*, 106.1 (1962): 77–81.
26. All quotations of text from 'The Speech of Miss Polly Baker'. Available at <http://franklinpapers.org> (last accessed 15 April 2018).
27. Elizabeth Barnes, *States of Sympathy: Seduction and Democracy in the American Novel* (New York: Columbia University Press, 1997), p. 8.
28. Marcello Maestro, 'Benjamin Franklin and the Penal Laws', *Journal of the History of Ideas*, 36.3 (1975): 552.
29. See Amy Schrager Lang, *Anne Hutchinson and the Problem of Dissent in the Literature of New England* (Berkeley: University of California Press, 1987).
30. James Hogg, *Winter Evening Tales*, ed. Ian Duncan (Edinburgh: Edinburgh University Press, 2004), p. 148.
31. Ibid.
32. Ibid.
33. Ibid.
34. See Susan Manning, *Fragments of Union: Making Connections in Scottish and American Writing* (New York: Palgrave, 2002).
35. Hogg, *Winter Evening Tales*, p. 148.
36. James E. Caron, *Mark Twain: Unsanctified Newspaper Reporter* (Columbia and London: University of Missouri Press, 2008), p. 8.

Bibliography

Aldridge, Alfred Owen, 'Benjamin Franklin and the *Pennsylvania Gazette*', *Proceedings of the American Philosophical Society*, 106.1 (1962): 77–81.
Arnold, Matthew, *Culture and Anarchy* (Oxford and London: Oxford University Press, [1869] 2006).
Barnes, Elizabeth, *States of Sympathy: Seduction and Democracy in the American Novel* (New York: Columbia University Press, 1997).
Boddy, Kasia, *The American Short Story since 1950* (Edinburgh: Edinburgh University Press, 2010).
Caron, James E., *Mark Twain: Unsanctified Newspaper Reporter* (Columbia and London: University of Missouri Press, 2008).
Clifford, James and George E. Marcus (eds), *Writing Culture: The Poetics and Politics of Ethnography* (Berkeley: University of California Press, 1986).

Collins, Michael J., *The Drama of the American Short Story, 1800–1865* (Ann Arbor: University of Michigan Press, 2016).
Doyle, Laura, 'Toward a Philosophy of Transnationalism', *Journal of Transnational American Studies*, 1.1 (2009).
Duncan, Ian and Douglas Mack (eds), *The Edinburgh Companion to James Hogg* (Edinburgh: Edinburgh University Press, 2012).
Evans, Brad, *Before Cultures: The Ethnographic Imagination in American Literature, 1865 to 1920* (Chicago: University of Chicago Press, 2005).
Gardner, Jared, *The Rise and Fall of Early American Magazine Culture* (Urbana, Chicago and Springfield: University of Illinois Press, 2012).
Hoffman, Daniel, *Form and Fable in American Fiction* (New York: Oxford University Press, 1965).
Hogg, James, *Winter Evening Tales*, ed. Ian Duncan (Edinburgh: Edinburgh University Press, 2004).
Killick, Tim, *British Short Fiction in the Early Nineteenth Century: The Rise of the Tale* (Burlington, VT: Ashgate, 2008).
Lang, Amy Schrager, *Prophetic Woman: Anne Hutchinson and the Problem of Dissent in the Literature of New England* (Berkeley: University of California Press, 1987).
Lehuu, Isabelle, *Carnival on the Page: Popular Print Culture in Antebellum America* (Chapel Hill: University of North Carolina Press, 2000).
Lohafer, Susan and Jo Ellyn Clarey (eds), *Short Story Theory at a Crossroads* (Baton Rouge: Louisiana State University Press, 1989).
Lyell, R. J., 'Intimations of Orality: Scotland, America and the Early Development of the Short Story in English', *Studies in Short Fiction*, 36 (1999): 311–25.
McGill, Meredith L., *American Literature and the Culture of Reprinting, 1834–1853* (Philadelphia: University of Pennsylvania Press, 2003).
Maestro, Marcello, 'Benjamin Franklin and the Penal Laws', *Journal of the History of Ideas*, 36.3 (1975): 551–62.
Manning, Susan, *Fragments of Union: Making Connections in Scottish and American Writing* (New York: Palgrave, 2002).
Maudlin, Daniel and Robin Peel (eds), *The Materials of Exchange Between Britain and North East America, 1750–1900* (Farnham, Surrey and Burlington, VT: Ashgate, 2013).
May, Charles E., *The Short Story: The Reality of Artifice* (New York: Routledge, 2002).
Moretti, Franco, *Distant Reading* (London: Verso, 2013).
O'Connor, Frank, *The Lonely Voice: A Study of the Short Story* (London: Macmillan, 1963).
Roach, Joseph, *Cities of the Dead: Circum-Atlantic Performance* (New York: Columbia University Press, 1996).
Scheiding, Oliver, 'Migrant Fictions: The Early Story in North American Magazines', in Berensmeyer, Ehland and Grabes (eds), *Mobility in Literature and Culture, 1500–1900* (Tübingen: Narr Verlag, 2012).
Stocking, George W. Jr (ed.), *Volkgeist as Method and Ethic: Essays on Boasian Ethnography and the German Anthropological Tradition* (Madison: The University of Wisconsin Press, 1996).
Straub, Julia, 'Early American Literature: Canon Theory in a Transatlantic Context', *Comparative American Studies*, 9.2 (2012): 106–18.
Tallack, Douglas, *The Nineteenth-Century American Short-Story: Language, Form and Ideology* (London: Routledge, 1993).
Woodmandsee, Martha and Peter Jaszi (eds), *The Construction of Authorship: Textual Appropriation in Law and Literature* (Durham, NC and New York: Duke University Press, 1994).

2

The Short Story and the Professionalisation of English Studies

Adrian Hunter

In his landmark study of Romantic short fiction, Tim Killick notes a tendency among scholars to read 'backwards' from Hawthorne and Poe, treating the decades prior to the 1840s as, at best, preparatory to the emergence of the short story as a modern literary form. The result, Killick argues, is a historical and geographical bias that neglects the polygenetic array of 'innovative modes and sub-genres' of shorter fiction flourishing on both sides of the Atlantic during the preceding half century.[1] Much subsequent scholarship has taken Killick's cue, prising open the hitherto neglected history of Romantic-period short fiction. From Ian Duncan's account of short-form 'nonnovelistic experimentation' in the British miscellany,[2] to Amanpal Garcha's exploration of the 1830s sketch as a radical form calibrated to the 'newness, disconnection, and detachment' of urban life,[3] our understanding of the short story's beginnings has shifted backward in time, and outward in kind to embrace all manner of brief fictional texts.

Alongside this new historicist work has run a corresponding effort to overturn what Michael Collins identifies as the dominant nationalist-formalist paradigm in short story criticism.[4] The persistence of that paradigm – which owes much to the writings of Charles E. May, Susan Lohafer and the so-called 'new' short story criticism of the 1980s and 1990s – has had the effect not only of distorting the historical record but of perpetuating a fundamentally Americentric view of the form. Collins's own solution is to reconfigure the early nineteenth-century short story as a phenomenon of transatlantic and transnational literary exchange. Timothy Clark goes further still, arguing for the abandonment of reading practices that inherently privilege 'specific characteristics' and 'inherent properties'[5] conventionally associated with founding American practitioners of the short story. Clark singles out in this connection a critical over-reliance on visual analogies, 'countervailing metaphors of sight, of the striving to "see" a text whole, the flash of revelation, etc'[6] – a conceptual apparatus that has its roots in Poe's 'unity of impression' and the notion of the short story as a 'totality' readily visualisable in the way the novel is not ('a picture is at length painted which leaves in the mind of him who contemplates it with a kindred art, a sense of the fullest satisfaction', as Poe would have it).[7] Thus do 'accounts of the short story *per se*' proceed on the assumption, Clark says, that the form is 'fundamentally "American" in some sense'.[8] His conclusion is that short story criticism, if it is interested in revitalisation, must begin by 'divorcing' itself from an 'institutional Americanism that is perhaps more deeply ingrained in this field than in any part of literary culture'.[9]

As several recent publications attest,[10] that work of revitalisation, if not quite divorce, is well underway. Yet such revisionary moments bring dangers of their own, not least in their potential to unduly simplify or even misrepresent earlier critical regimes. Something of this sort has occurred in recent scholarship, which, for all its concern with redrawing the ideational map of the nineteenth century and challenging the nationalist-formalist consensus, has shown little interest in understanding where that map and that consensus came from in the first place. Why was it, indeed, that a particular constellation of conceptual, temporal and geographical convictions about short stories, centring on the origin point of the American 1840s, achieved the status and influence it did? It is now almost thirty years since Andrew Levy suggested that the myth of origination surrounding Hawthorne and Poe was largely an invention of the 1890s,[11] yet that key period of historicist reconstruction has rarely been considered in detail since, despite the fact that many of the claims and concepts that revisionist criticism now seeks to overturn originate with it.

What follows is an attempt to reorientate our understanding of this formative period in the critical conceptualisation of the short story, 1890–1920, by situating it within a wider *professional* history of institutional literary criticism. Where for Levy short story theory instantiated the triumph of analytical methods over older approaches to literary culture,[12] this chapter contends that the reverse was in fact the case – that the field was dominated by so-called 'generalist' scholars, as opposed to 'researchers', whose desire to identify the short story with the 'literary' as a transcendent and transhistorical value was part of a broader ideological struggle within the academy between rival conceptions of literary-critical labour. Recognising this casts a somewhat different light not only on these critics' reclamation of the 1840s – which was as much about locating an origin point for a particular aesthetic of the short story as it was about the nationalist effort to grant American literature a 'usable past' – but on the subsequent development of criticism and theory toward a modernist-impressionist rationalisation of the form.

According to Gerald Graff's history of literary studies in the American academy, the modern English department arose out of a struggle for disciplinary supremacy between older forms of literary-cultural historicism, and new quasi-scientific approaches rooted in Germanic philology. As representatives of the former, Graff names, among others, Brander Matthews, Bliss Perry, Henry Van Dyke, Henry Siedel Canby, Edward Everett Hale and Fred Lewis Pattee – 'generalists' united by a distrust of the 'research establishment' and its incorporated professional body, the Modern Language Association of America (MLA), which they regarded as facilitating the 'assimilation of higher education by the values of the industrial marketplace'.[13] Although it is somewhat beyond the purview of Graff's study to note this, what these individuals also had in common was a deep and abiding fascination with the short story, which they effectively brought into being as a subject for university study.

Andrew Levy is correct to attribute the 'Americanisation' of the form to these pioneering critics, whose cultural-nationalist leanings are apparent enough, and who promoted the short story as embodying a new 'egalitarian and efficient literature' uniquely adapted to expressing 'the rich heterogeneity of American life'.[14] However, Levy's further assertion that their interest in form and genre aligned with new 'scientific, or pseudo-scientific'[15] methodologies rooted in philology unduly simplifies the contested disciplinary history of which they were part. In reality, the careers of these scholars were shaped largely in opposition to the philological approaches Levy outlines, and in explicit rejection of claims that the study of literature could or should be approached 'with the same rigor and discipline as chemistry or mathematics'.[16] Short story theory in its early incarnation, that is to say, was a phenomenon of literary-critical 'generalism', and developed against rather than within the dominant disciplinary culture. While the researchers may ultimately have prevailed in the larger institutional struggle to define English studies, it was the generalists who lastingly shaped our understanding of the short story, setting the critical terms of debate on the form for a generation and more.

Nowhere is this more apparent than in the case of Brander Matthews. For a critic variously dismissed as a genteel amateur, an 'old ass', and 'as naive as Jackie Coogan',[17] Matthews has cast an extraordinary influence over the study of the short story. His presence can be traced throughout twentieth-century scholarship, from landmark works such as Frank O'Connor's *The Lonely Voice* (1963) and Mary Rohrherger's *Hawthorne and the Modern Short Story* (1966),[18] to Charles E. May's *The New Short Story Theories* (1994). The inclusion by May of extracts from Matthews's *The Philosophy of the Short-story* (1901) served to confirm his reputation as the form's founding critic in the Anglo-American tradition, while marking him out as largely responsible for the 'extension and formalization' of Poe's scattered statements into a working definition of the modern short story.[19] For many critics today, Matthews remains significant as a 'populariser' and 'disciple'[20] of Poe (a judgement curiously at odds with the uses Matthews in fact makes of his predecessor in *The Philosophy of the Short-story* and elsewhere, as we shall see). For others, he is the originator, if not the principal exponent, of the formalist-nationalist mythology of American exceptionalism in the form. Levy, again, has had an important role to play here, arguing that behind Matthews's 'genre-fication of the short story' was a polemical urge to stage an 'informal declaration of independence from ... European literature'.[21] It is a claim readily evidenced in Matthews's activities as anthologiser and pedagogue, through which he campaigned for the short story's inclusion in the American canon,[22] and by his tendency to make broad, transhistorical claims about the form based on a highly selective reading of (mostly) American authors.

If anything, however, the canonisation and nationalisation of Matthews has served to impede a properly historicised and contextualised reading of his work, which was very much the product of his status and standing as an academic during a period of tumultuous institutional change. In his long career as Professor of Dramatic Literature at Columbia University, Matthews was at the forefront of the struggle between research and generalism, and of the increasingly polarised and policitised debate over what it meant to be a literary professional. As one who had risen to the rank of professor without any formal qualification beyond a broad schooling in the classics and humanities, Matthews was always susceptible to accusations of amateurism, genteelism and belletrism. Such accusations had acquired an incorporated power with the establishment of the MLA, whose early proceedings were littered with attacks on men who, like Matthews, presumed to profess the subject on the basis of little more than 'a general society knowledge of literature'.[23] As the 1899 MLA presidential address declared, 'without the spirit of research, teaching becomes formal and learning fragmentary'.[24] The MLA spoke to, and on behalf of, a constituency of scholars intent on refashioning English studies into a 'knowledge subject'[25] of equal disciplinary standing to the modern sciences, a transformation that required 'serious workers'[26] – accredited professionals with specialised interests, capable of rendering literary-critical labour into forms of meaningful work appropriate to the needs of a modern technocratic democracy. In common with many of his social class and intellectual background, Matthews, by contrast, continued to nurture a professional persona rooted in an essentially Arnoldian apprehension of the critic as 'man of letters'. His academic identity, that is to say, operated as an extension of his private existence as a book reviewer, society 'clubber' and elite networker.[27]

It is this institutional context that fundamentally conditioned the work of Matthews and his fellow generalists on the short story. Two contemporary responses to *The Philosophy of the Short-story* serve to illustrate how that context impinged on Matthews, while highlighting the stake generalism had in the disciplinary controversies of the day. The first is an excoriating notice published in *The Academy* in March 1901. While the review notes Matthews's evident American bias, it is the book's theoretical pretensions that earn the greater rebuke, in particular its proposal to differentiate between the 'Short-story', so-called, and other forms of short fiction. 'How can a Short-story be "something other than" a short story?' the reviewer rails. 'The answer is that it cannot':

> It is an ancient game to fit facts to a theory by arbitrarily limiting the significance of everyday words, but a very tiresome game; and no one will follow the Professor in his attempt to lay down a rule that short stories are not short stories unless they happen to be short stories of a particular sort. There is no difference whatever of *kind* between a Novel and a Short-story. The latter relates an episode, the former a succession of episodes: each is self-complete . . . The truth is that the Professor has excogitated this part of his theory from the well-known paradoxical essay in which Poe tries to demonstrate that there can be no such thing as a long poem, and that every so-called long poem is, in fact, a succession of short ones.[28]

The problem with Matthews's study is that it is impressionistic where it ought to be scholastic. Any 'philosophy' worth the name must be able to 'lay down a rule' that can be shown to be both internally consistent and generally true. If Matthews fails the latter test by dint of his 'careless and absurd'[29] choice of representative stories, he fails the former owing to his fundamental shortcomings as a scholar – his 'vague' understanding of the workings of literary form and his signal failure to convert Poe's strictures on 'unity of impression' from poetry to prose fiction.[30] If *The Philosophy of the Short-story* proves anything, the reviewer suggests, it is that Matthews's reputation as an 'amiable *flaneur* of letters'[31] is justified, for he is no literary critic.

Similarly concerned with Matthews's professional shortcomings is C. Alphonso Smith, in his study *The American Short Story* (1912). Smith, whose presidential remarks to the MLA are quoted above, sets out to test the central propositions of Matthews's treatise against current research on genre emanating from critics who (like Smith himself) had undergone philological training.[32] The key distinction Matthews presents between the novel and the short story has, Smith argues, already been established with much greater clarity and precision in the work of German philologists and literary theorists such as Anton E. Schönbach and Friedrich Spielhagen.[33] Key again is Poe, whose various statements on the short story Smith regards as essential to any study of the genre. Matthews fundamentally misunderstands Poe, Smith suggests, when he approaches 'unity' and 'totality' from the point of view of the reading experience. Rather, these concepts are to be understood as elements in a clearly developed theory of textual *production*. That being so, the critic's task is to examine the means by which the writer institutes 'structure' and 'predetermined effect' in his narrative, and from such analysis to discern the 'criterion by which the short story is distinguished from the novel'.[34] Unsurprisingly, Smith regards Poe's own stories as the superlative examples of the form, controlled as they are by the artful construction of 'one dominating impression' to which 'every incident, every explanation, every sentence, every word contributes directly and cumulatively'.[35] Of Hawthorne, by contrast, he is scathing, finding him too often 'blunder[ing]' against formal considerations in an effort to appeal to the reader's 'conscience'[36] – a judgement clearly directed at Matthews who, in *The Philosophy of the Short-story* and elsewhere, champions the 'moral' complexity and 'ethical beauty' of Hawthorne over the 'physical', ratiocinative strategies of Poe.[37]

In stressing Matthews's misapplication of Poe and his ignorance of the Germanic philological tradition, these readers recycle the terms of the wider philological assault on the generalists. The striking thing, however, is how little traction such criticisms would ultimately gain among the scholarly community then thronging to the short story. On the contrary, as the field expanded rapidly over the following two decades, Matthews would see his ideas widely, if not always uncritically, reproduced, while philological approaches to the form were largely disregarded. Two explanations for this suggest themselves. The first is that Matthews's book struck a nationalist chord. As Gerald Graff has pointed out, generalist approaches to literature continued to flourish long after the institutional tide had begun to turn against them in part by tapping into the cult of 'Anglo-Saxon mystique'[38] promoted in the writings of Hippolyte Taine. Thus did the nationalist case for the study of American literature come to be carried not by the 'research scholars', Graff says, but by their 'belletristic detractors'.[39] While it is certainly true that Matthews was an important figure in the wider cultural-nationalist project – his *Introduction to American Literature* (1896) sold more than a quarter of a million copies during his lifetime – it was not his Americanism that subsequent short story criticism would primarily reproduce. Rather, it was the ready alignment of his approach to the form with wider generalist convictions about the function and values of literary scholarship that ensured the extension of his ideas into the modernist period and beyond.

Key here is Matthews's positioning of himself both as a critic and as a professional. In his memoir *These Many Years* (1917), Matthews describes his own practice as that of writing 'literary history', a pursuit quite distinct from literary *criticism*, to which it is 'not a brother . . . only a first cousin'.[40] Insofar as Matthews is interested in questions of literary form, or 'technic' as he terms it, it is in order to bring history 'alive'. This was, of course, a task of no small importance to the nationalist project, given Matthews's belief that American literature provided 'the most significant record of the changing temper and the modifying moods of the American people'.[41] However, more searchingly, the distinction Matthews makes between literary criticism and literary history expresses his rejection of the role of 'critic' where that is taken to imply subordination of questions of identity and aesthetic value to the technical study of writing. As a pedagogue and scholar, Matthews was never in the position to disregard the demands of literary-critical professionalism *tout court*; rather, he aimed to reinvisage and repurpose them, carving out a hybrid identity for himself as what Susanna Ashton terms a 'Professional Man of Letters'.[42] By speaking across the new academicism from within its own precincts, he aimed to preserve a broadly Arnoldian vision of culture and criticism in an arena of increasing specialisation and marketisation. Far from capitulating to the new institutional reality, Matthews, in common with other generalists, staged a subtle counter-reaction to it by forging his own distinctive form of professional labour centred on the defence of the literary as a transcendent, self-sufficient and, most importantly, self-interpreting category. To that extent, philological critiques of *The Philosophy of the Short-story* mistook Matthews's methodology, which was not to execute a definitional study in 'technic' and genre but to locate the sources of the form's affective and aesthetic power, and establish its literary bona fides.

The distinction becomes clearer when we examine the book's treatment of Poe. Given how much emphasis commentators continue to place on Matthews's indebtedness to Poe, it can come as a surprise to find that very little of his work actually features in Matthews's argument. Of the major essays, only 'The Philosophy of Composition', Poe's study in techniques of poetic assembly, is remarked in the main body of the text. Extracts from the 1842 review of Hawthorne's *Twice-told Tales* are included as an appendix, but these are prefaced by the disclaimer that while Poe may have 'felt' the distinctiveness of the short story, he did not recognise that it was 'in reality a *genre*, a separate kind, a genus by itself'.[43] Where Matthews does take up directly with Poe's ideas, it is to repurpose them for his own moral and historicist approach to the form. In this respect at least, Alphonso Smith was right to suggest that Matthews misrepresents Poe's ideas about 'unity of impression' and 'totality' by considering them aspects of reception rather than production: Matthews is indeed primarily concerned with the singular ways in which the short story 'impresses the reader'.[44] Throughout his study, we find him de-emphasising formalist considerations in this way in order to concentrate instead on what he terms 'moral effects'.[45] 'Important as are form and style', he argues, 'the subject of the short story is of more importance yet. What you have to tell is of greater interest than how you tell it.'[46] Thus is a limit quickly reached beyond which discussion of generic classification and formalistic prescriptiveness becomes otiose:

> Perhaps the difference between a Short-story and a Sketch can best be indicated by saying that, while a Sketch may be still-life, in a Short-story something always happens. A Sketch may be an outline of character, or even a picture of a mood of mind, but in a Short-story there must be something done, there must be an action. Yet the distinction, like that between the Novel and the Romance, is no longer of vital importance ... The fact is, that the Short-story and the Sketch, the Novel and the Romance, melt and merge into one another, and no man may mete the boundaries of each, though their extremes lie far apart. With the more complete understanding of the principle of development and evolution in literary art, as in physical nature, we see the futility of a strict and rigid classification into precisely defined genera and species.[47]

Matthews's conception of 'literary art' as an evolving organism bound to exceed the categories devised to contain it in part betrays his interest in Lamarckian and Spencerian ideas about evolutionary development;[48] but it also serves to establish his identity as a critic operating somewhere between 'pure science and pure impressionism',[49] as Graff says of the generalist mindset. To that extent, the *Academy* reviewer's complaint that in 'the matter of form the Professor is somewhat vague',[50] was both true and beside the point. Matthews's desire to square professional reading with a moralist-humanist defence of literature meant resisting precisely the kind of critical dissection that would render writing's mystical treasures into forms of workable, quantifiable 'knowledge'. His approach to the short story was thus consciously anti-formalist – a descriptive rather than prescriptive account intended to preserve the genre's insusceptibility to a particular sort of analytical capture.

This in turn helps to account for Matthews's preference for the elusiveness and moral suggestiveness of Hawthorne's stories over the deterministic machinations of Poe's, an aspect of *The Philosophy of the Short-story* that Alphonso Smith in particular found baffling. While Matthews acknowledges Poe's mastery in the arts of 'imaginative ratiocination' and in conjuring scenarios of 'intellectual desolation',[51] he also notes their susceptibility to mechanistic, formulaic reproduction. There is in Poe, he suggests, a troubling preponderance of the 'flimsiest and most tawdry tales' that 'too often sink to the grade of the ordinary "Tale from *Blackwood*"'.[52] Where Poe derives a calculated intrigue from the application of 'cold logic . . . and mathematical analysis', Hawthorne, by contrast, dwells in the deeper waters of 'introspective conscience . . . the subtile and the invisible':

> There is a propriety in Hawthorne's fantasy to which Poe could not attain. Hawthorne's effects are moral, where Poe's are merely physical. The situation and its logical development, and the effects to be got out of it, are all Poe thinks of. In Hawthorne the situation, however strange and weird, is only the outward and visible sign of an inward and spiritual struggle. Ethical consequences are always worrying Hawthorne's soul: but Poe did not know there were any ethics.[53]

By way of example, Matthews singles out Hawthorne's 'The Ambitious Guest', a story rich in 'ethical beauty' that in Poe's hands would have remained 'a mere feat of verbal legerdemain'.[54] Hawthorne's blackly ironic, wilfully ambivalent story tells of a family and their 'ambitious' young guest who, when alerted by the noise of an approaching avalanche, leave the safety of their cabin only to run into the path of destruction. The cabin is spared, and the fate of the young man who dreamt of fame and renown remains obscure: 'His name and person utterly unknown; his history, his view of life, his plans, a mystery never to be solved, his death and his existence equally a doubt!'[55] In his book on the American short story, Alphonso Smith highlights the technical deficiencies of 'The Ambitious Guest', arguing that Hawthorne's failure to allow the main theme to indirectly 'suggest itself' burdens the tale with the aspect of a 'formal sermon'.[56] For Matthews, its superiority lies precisely in the fact that the 'moral' *is* the 'technic', the 'sustaining skeleton of his narrative'.[57] The result, he argues, is a story in which, *contra* Poe, the operations of circumstance and plot dissolve into an ethical and affective concern with character and theme: 'The art of the narrator is perfect . . .

his adjustment of his characters to his theme is so complete, that we do not always perceive the adroitness of the craftsman . . . Hawthorne wanted us to be interested in the characters rather than in the scene.'[58]

For a reader of Smith's professional orientation, Matthews's preference for Hawthorne over Poe was symptomatic of the wider deficiencies in his study when judged as a coherent theory of genre or as an exercise in applied literary criticism. To a great extent, modern scholarship has persisted in viewing Matthews on these terms, at least insofar as it regards him as an epigone of Poe whose intention was to establish definitional maxims for the short story. Yet that was not at all how the *The Philosophy of the Short-story* was received by those critics who, immediately following Matthews, sought to establish short story studies as a legitimate field of critical enquiry. In the work of Bliss Perry, H. S. Canby, Edward Everett Hale, Fred Lewis Pattee and others, it is Matthews's interest in developing an impressionist and affective aesthetic of the form, rather than any concern with systematising Poe's ideas, that is taken up, and that serves to stake out the territory on which short story criticism should proceed. That all these critics were generalists like Matthews bears out the important point that short story criticism, in its inception and early formulation, was never a phenomenon of research. Rather, its procedures are closer to the 'higher method' set out by Theodore Hunt in his hugely influential *Studies in Literature and Style* (1890). Noting how often '[r]ecognised authorities' in science and philology turned out to be 'signally devoid of literary taste',[59] Hunt advocates a mode of critical reading that is 'suggestive, comprehensive and logical, as distinct from being technical, narrow and superficial', and that addresses form not on its own account but with 'primary reference to the thought that is in it'.[60] Matthews and his successors were both professional and professorial enough to recognise the importance of coherence and terminological consistency and the need to transcend the limitations of subjective, purely 'judicial'[61] forms of criticism, as Hunt cautioned they should be; but they were equally clear that the insights into 'technic' generated by 'scientific' critical methods were ultimately inadequate to the task of representing the short story's distinctive modes of meaning.

In such key works as Perry's *A Study in Prose Fiction* (1902; revised 1920), Canby's *The Short Story* (1902), *The Short Story in English* (1909) and *A Study of the Short Story* (1913), Hale's *The Elements of the Short Story* (1915) and Pattee's *The Development of the American Short Story* (1923) we find reproduced, above all, the conjunction Matthews establishes between moral complexity and impressionistic openness – a conjunction that in turn serves to exemplify the generalist rejection of philological and taxonomic critical models. This, according to Perry, is the 'critical trail blazed'[62] by Matthews, clearing the way for Perry's own attempts to make the short story's obliquity not only the basis of its difference from the novel, but the explanation for how uniquely it seems able to probe moral issues in a culture otherwise grown 'suspicious of its preachers'.[63] Central for Perry is the short story's freedom to 'pose questions without answering them',[64] a freedom born, paradoxically, of constraint. As he explains, from 'the laws of brevity and unity of effect'[65] arise techniques of expressive indirection by which the writer is able 'to make use of the vaguest suggestion, a delicate symbolism, a poetic impressionism, fancies too tenuous to hold in the stout texture of the novel'.[66] The 'large liberty'[67] afforded to both reader and writer by such indirection thus aligns the short story with the lyric poem rather than with the novel,

Perry suggests. What is more, the development of these techniques by exemplary modern practitioners has succeeded in elevating the short story to the front rank of literary culture, making it possible now to speak of Maupassant in the same breath as Ibsen.[68] At the same time, the form makes peculiar demands on the critic, who is forced to reckon with a mode of writing that deals 'not with wholes, but with fragments', and which makes an aesthetic virtue of its own failure to be 'consistent' or to 'think things through'.[69] Again echoing Matthews, Perry uses this generic multifariousness as an opportunity to expose the limits of 'scientific' criticism and by implication the continuing value of more 'judicial' forms of reading. That each critic 'can easily find the sort of facts he is looking for', Perry suggests, reflects the deeper truth 'that literary criticism has no apparatus delicate enough to measure the currents, the depths and the tideways, the reactions and interactions of literary forms'.[70] In so saying, Perry deploys the short story to instantiate the bigger anti-philological argument of his book, which is that professional criticism, while remaining alert to the pitfalls of subjectivism, has nonetheless a responsibility to ensure that 'knowledge and feeling' are 'kept in their due relations'. As he puts it, 'To know is good. To feel is better, when it is a question of appropriating the form and meaning of a work of art. Analysis must be subordinated to synthesis; the details must be forgotten in the cumulative impression given by the work as a whole.'[71]

Formulating a critical practice around the notion of the text's resistance to interpretative capture is a central concern, too, of H. S. Canby, Yale Professor and the author of several studies of the short story. More explicitly even than Matthews and Perry, Canby rejects the claims of academic 'research', which he considers at best preparatory to the real work of 'synthesis' and 'prophecy'[72] entailed in the pursuit of a 'fundamental, creative criticism'.[73] Criticism properly understood is, for Canby, an art of 'Defining the Indefinable', as the title of one of his chapters puts it, with 'definition' signifying not 'formal . . . rigid formulas' or any attempt to 'classify' but rather a species of criticism calibrated to the ineffable, transcendent 'literary':

> For definition, in the sense in which I am using it, like literature, has much of the indefinable. It is a tool merely, or better still, because broader, a device by which the things we enjoy and that profit us may be placed in perspective, ranged, compared, sorted, and distinguished. It is what Arnold meant by seeing steadily and seeing whole. It is the scientist's microscope that defines relationship, and equally the painter's brush that by a touch reveals the hidden shapes of nature and the blend of colors. It is, like these instruments, a *means* and not an *end*. May pedants, scholiasters, formalists, and dilettantes take to heart this final description of literary definition![74]

Canby's approach to the short story embodies this nuanced position. His first book on the subject, *The Short Story* (1902), opens with the claim that definition is best conceived of as a kind of short code or 'literary algebra', there to provide 'a word or a phrase for a development or a tendency' and in so doing to 'facilitate thinking and writing'.[75] Concepts like 'sentimentalism', 'preraphelite' and, especially, 'impressionism' are useful precisely because 'almost defying exact definition'.[76] What attracts Canby to the short story is its capacity to operate within that kind of inexactitude;

hence his predominant interest in what he terms 'impressionist' and 'psychological' stories. Although his historical range is broad – *A Study of the Short Story* (1913) begins in the Middle Ages – Canby takes from Matthews the idea that the short story fully distinguishes itself from other prose forms only in the nineteenth century, and that it does so by making a virtue of brevity and indirection. Here, for example, is his reading of Hawthorne's 'The White Old Maid':

> This, too, is a story, in the sense that something happens; and yet the real story, by which I mean the narrative which would logically connect and develop these events, is just hinted at, and is not very important. It is subordinated, indeed, to a new aim. 'The White Old Maid' is narrative for a purpose, and this purpose is to suggest an impression, and to leave us with a vivid sensation rather than a number of remembered facts. In short, it is contrived, not to leave a record of such and such an old woman who did this or that, but rather to stamp upon our minds the impression of a mystery-haunted house, mysterious figures entering, strange words, and a terrible sorrow behind all ... It is this, which, for want of a less abused word, may be called impressionism, that is characteristic to some extent of all typical Short Stories, and serves as the most fundamental distinction between them and the earlier tales.[77]

For Canby, the difference between Hawthorne's story and Irving's 'The Legend of Sleepy Hollow', with which he compares it, is to be understood at the intuitive level: it is a difference not readily quantified but intimately 'felt' by the qualified reader. Canby thus elevates the 'judicial' appreciation of the short story to the status of a quasi-theory of form, making the stimulation of subjective feeling and the mobilisation of the reader's co-productive capacities, rather than any formal or generic properties, its defining characteristic. Favouring 'impressionist' and 'psychological' stories, in which 'character exposition' is approached 'through an impression' in order to make the reader first 'feel' the character's 'mental make-up and personality',[78] Canby extends Matthews's preference for stories that tend toward moral complexity and open-endedness, and which typically de-emphasise plot.

Furthermore, in separating out the story of 'serious situation'[79] from more populist strains, both Canby and Perry mirror Matthews's concern with establishing the form's literary credentials – a concern that, again, underscores the alignment of short story theory with an anti-scientific, 'judicial' critical praxis. 'Distinction' (in the Bourdieusian sense) displaces 'definition' as the function of criticism. Edward Everett Hale and Fredrick T. Dawson's *The Elements of the Short Story* (1915), for example, argues against any kind of formalist prescriptiveness, aiming instead to 'train the mind to look at a short story so as to perceive instinctively certain things'.[80] Hale and Dawson's mission is to develop suitably qualified readers for short fiction, an aim they pursue through guided study of selected stories (all of them American and of recent vintage) and with a strong emphasis on the 'moral' complexities that compressed narratives invariably give rise to. Fred Lewis Pattee, meanwhile, in *The Development of the American Short Story* (1923), looks to defend what he calls 'short-story art', on the one hand against scholars who would 'exploit' it 'as if it were an exact science', enchaining it in 'laws as elaborate as those governing the sonnet', and on the other against promulgators of popular 'how-to' handbooks with their 'ten commandments' for the writing of mass-reproducible magazine tales.[81] As an antidote to such mechanisers and popularisers (among whom is mentioned Alphonso Smith), Pattee directs readers to the tentative, exploratory work of Perry, Canby and, of course, Matthews, whom he credits with having originated a 'startlingly new'[82] understanding of the form.

In the work of all these critics, impressionism is privileged over rationalism, literariness over populism, the aesthetic over the instrumental, interpretative openness over scholastic prescription. Such are the terms on which generalism co-opts the short story for its wider campaign of resistance to the research-led rationalisation of English studies. That such resistance would prove futile is a guiding assumption of Gerald Graff's history of the subject, according to which generalism was ultimately undone by its inability to reproduce (via the PhD system) and its lack of an effective counter-argument to the disciplinary systematisations of research. As Graff puts it, 'Generalist manifestos were frequently no more than vapid attacks on the analytical approach ... incanting words like "literature" in talismanic fashion, as if the power of literature were in and of itself sufficient to overcome an institutional problem.'[83] Yet it may be that the short story was an exception – not because its generalist advocates were any less obsolescent in institutional terms, but because of the ways in which their ideas about the form readily aligned with the aesthetic and cultural priorities of an emergent literary modernism. From William Carlos Williams's imagistic adventures in 'lacunae of sense, loups ... amputations'[84] to Virginia Woolf's sensitive explorations of Chekhovian modes of expressive indigence, in which 'half the conclusions of fiction fade into thin air',[85] high modernism was similarly drawn to the creative possibilities of writing 'short', whether as a means of exceeding what Ezra Pound called the 'conventional form of a "story"',[86] or of resisting the encroachments of a vulgar materialism on the imaginative life. For Woolf in particular the short story offered a space in which the 'indefinable', in Canby's terms, could be preserved – in which, as Matthews supposed, an 'effect of spirituality' could be produced, and the 'note of interrogation' sounded.[87]

Notes

1. Tim Killick, *British Short Fiction in the Early Nineteenth Century* (Aldershot: Ashgate, 2007), p. 7.
2. Ian Duncan, 'Altered States: Galt, Serial Fiction, and the Romantic Miscellany', in Regina Hewitt (ed.), *John Galt: Observations and Conjectures on Literature, History, and Society* (Lewisburg: Bucknell University Press, 2012), p. 47.
3. Amanpal Garcha, *From Sketch to Novel: The Development of Victorian Fiction* (Cambridge: Cambridge University Press, 2009), p. 25. See also Anthony Jarrells, 'Provincializing Enlightenment: Edinburgh Historicism and the Blackwoodian Regional Tale', *Studies in Romanticism*, 48.2 (2009): 257–77; and David Stewart, 'Romantic Short Fiction', in Ann-Marie Einhaus (ed.), *The Cambridge Companion to the English Short Story* (Cambridge: Cambridge University Press, 2016), pp. 73–86.
4. See the preceding chapter, 'Transnationalism and the Transatlantic Short Story'.
5. Timothy Clark, 'Not Seeing the Short Story: A Blind Phenomenology of Reading', *Oxford Literary Review*, 26.1 (2012): 9.
6. Ibid.

7. Edgar Allan Poe, 'Review of *Twice-Told Tales* by Nathaniel Hawthorne', *Graham's Monthly Magazine*, 20 (May 1842): 299.
8. Clark, 'Not Seeing the Short Story': 6.
9. Ibid. 7.
10. See, for example, Maggie Awadalla and Paul March-Russell (eds), *The Postcolonial Short Story* (Basingstoke: Palgrave Macmillan, 2013). In her introduction to *The Cambridge Companion to the English Short Story* (Cambridge: Cambridge University Press, 2016), Ann-Marie Einhaus notes ways in which the 'strong American slant in English-language short story criticism' is now being challenged (p. 2). See also Dominic Head's introduction to *The Cambridge History of the English Short Story* (Cambridge: Cambridge University Press, 2016), and chapters in that volume by Donald J. Newman and Abigail Ward.
11. Andrew Levy, *The Culture and Commerce of the American Short Story* (Cambridge: Cambridge University Press, 1993), pp. 27–57.
12. Levy, *Culture and Commerce*, p. 82.
13. Gerald Graff, *Professing Literature: An Institutional History* (Chicago: University of Chicago Press, 1987), p. 82.
14. Levy, *Culture and Commerce*, p. 30, p. 43.
15. Ibid. p. 82.
16. Ibid.
17. These judgements, by H. L. Mencken and an anonymous essayist in *The Bookman* of 1923, are recorded in Susanna Ashton, 'Authorial Affiliations, or, The Clubbing and Collaborating of Brander Matthews', *symploke*, 7, 1–2 (1999): 171; 184.
18. Viorca Patea, 'The Short Story: An Overview of the History and Development of a Genre', in Viorica Patea (ed.), *Short Story Theories: A Twenty-First-Century Perspective* (Amsterdam: Rodopi, 2012), p. 4.
19. Charles E. May (ed.), *The New Short Story Theories* (Athens: Ohio University Press, 1994), p. xvi.
20. See Paul March-Russell, *The Short Story: An Introduction* (Edinburgh: Edinburgh University Press, 2009), pp. 34–6. See also Erik Van Achter, 'Revising Theory: Poe's Legacy in Short Story Criticism', in Patea (ed.), *Short Story Theories*, pp. 84–5.
21. Levy, *Culture and Commerce*, p. 34.
22. See Levy, *Culture and Commerce*, pp. 34–5 and pp. 82–5. Matthews's influential anthology *The Short-story: Specimens Illustrating Its Development* appeared in 1907.
23. Theodore Hunt, 'The Place of English in the College Curriculum', *Transactions of the Modern Language Association of America*, 1 (1884): 118–39, as quoted in Warner, 'Professionalization and the Rewards of Literature': 5.
24. C. Alphonso Smith, 'The Work of the Modern Language Association of America', *PMLA*, 14.2 (1899): 243.
25. Elizabeth Renker, *The Origins of American Literature Studies: An Institutional History* (Cambridge: Cambridge University Press, 2007), p. 14.
26. Michael Warner, 'Professionalization and the Rewards of Literature: 1875–1900', *Criticism*, 27.1 (1985): 5.
27. See Ashton, 'Authorial Affiliations', *passim*.
28. Anonymous, 'The Philosophy of the Short Story', *The Academy* (30 March 1901): 288.
29. Ibid. 287.
30. Ibid.
31. Ibid.
32. Smith, who had gained his PhD from Johns Hopkins, established the journal *Studies in Philology* while at the University of North Carolina. See Graff, *Professing Literature*, p. 76.

33. C. Alphonso Smith, *The American Short Story* (Boston and London: Ginn and Company, 1912), pp. 5–9.
34. Smith, *American Short Story*, p. 11.
35. Ibid. p. 16.
36. Ibid. p. 20.
37. Matthews, *Philosophy of the Short-story*, p. 41, p. 39, p. 43. On Matthews's choice of Hawthorne's 'The Ambitious Guest' for his anthology of exemplary short stories, see below.
38. Graff, *Professing Literature*, p. 70.
39. Graff, *Professing Literature*, p. 72. On Matthews's enthusiasm for Taine see Lawrence J. Oliver, *Brander Matthews, Theodore Roosevelt, and the Politics of American Literature, 1880–1920* (Knoxville: University of Tennessee Press, 1992), pp. 9–12.
40. Matthews, *These Many Years: Recollections of a New Yorker* (New York: Charles Scribner's Sons, 1917), p. 403.
41. Ibid. p. 408, p. 403.
42. Ashton, 'Authorial Affiliations': 184.
43. Matthews, *Philosophy of the Short Story*, p. 77.
44. Ibid. p. 17.
45. Ibid. p. 39.
46. Ibid. pp. 33–4.
47. Ibid. pp. 35–7.
48. On Matthews's views about race, see Oliver, *Brander Matthews*, pp. 35–65. For the wider intellectual context surrounding race, academia and progressivism see Louis Menand, *The Metaphysical Club* (London: Harper Collins, 2001), pp. 382–408. See also Graff, *Professing Literature*, pp. 70–2.
49. Graff, *Professing Literature*, p. 126.
50. Anonymous, 'Philosophy of the Short Story': 287.
51. Matthews, *Philosophy of the Short Story*, pp. 44–5.
52. Ibid. p. 46.
53. Ibid. pp. 39–40.
54. Ibid. p. 43.
55. Nathaniel Hawthorne, 'The Ambitious Guest', in Brander Matthews (ed.), *The Short Story: Specimens Illustrating Its Development* (New York: American Book Company, 1907), p. 221.
56. Smith, *American Short Story*, p. 18.
57. Matthews, *The Short Story: Specimens*, p. 210.
58. Ibid. p. 222.
59. Theodore W. Hunt, *Studies in Literature and Style* (New York: A. C. Armstrong, 1890), p. 15.
60. Ibid. p. 19.
61. The distinction between 'judicial' and 'scientific' critical methods originates with Richard G. Moulton's *Shakespeare as a Dramatic Artist: A Popular Illustration of the Principles of Scientific Criticism* (Oxford: Clarendon, 1885). See the introduction, 'Plea for an Inductive Science of Literary Criticism', pp. 1–40.
62. Bliss Perry, *A Study of Prose Fiction*, rev. edn (Boston and New York: Houghton Mifflin, 1920), p. 302.
63. Perry, *Study of Prose Fiction*, p. 318.
64. Ibid.
65. Ibid. p. 320.
66. Ibid. p. 322.
67. Ibid.
68. Ibid. p. 318.

69. Ibid. pp. 328–9.
70. Ibid. pp. 331–2.
71. Ibid. p. 11.
72. Ibid.
73. H. S. Canby, *Definitions: Essays in Contemporary Criticism* (New York: Harcourt Brace, 1922), pp. 294–5.
74. Canby, *Definitions*, p. 303 (emphases in the original).
75. H. S. Canby, *The Short Story* (New York: Henry Holt, 1902), p. 5.
76. Ibid.
77. Ibid. pp. 11–12.
78. Ibid. p. 18.
79. H. S. Canby, *The Short Story in English* (New York: Henry Holt, 1909), p. 307.
80. Edward Everett Hale and Fredrick T. Dawson *The Elements of the Short Story* (New York: Henry Holt, 1915), p. 78.
81. Fred Lewis Pattee, *The Development of the American Short Story* (New York and London: Harper, 1923), pp. 364–5.
82. Ibid. p. 294.
83. Graff, *Professing Literature*, p. 88.
84. William Carlos Williams, 'Notes in Diary Form', in *Selected Essays of William Carlos Williams* (New York: New Directions, 1969), p. 71.
85. Woolf, Virginia, 'The Russian Point of View', in Andrew McNeillie (ed.), *The Essays of Virginia Woolf, Volume 4: 1925–1928* (London: Hogarth Press, 1994), p. 185.
86. Ezra Pound, 'Dubliners and Mr James Joyce', in T. S. Eliot (ed.), *Literary Essays of Ezra Pound* (London: Faber, 1960), p. 401.
87. Virginia Woolf, *The Essays of Virginia Woolf, Volume 2: 1912–1918* (London: Hogarth Press, 1988), p. 245, p. 342. See also Adrian Hunter, 'The "Custom" of Fiction: Virginia Woolf, the Hogarth Press, and the Modernist Short Story', *English*, 56 (2007): 147–69.

Bibliography

Achter, Erik Van, 'Revising Theory: Poe's Legacy in Short Story Criticism', in Viorica Patea (ed.), *Short Story Theories: A Twenty-First-Century Perspective* (Amsterdam: Rodopi, 2012), pp. 75–88.
Anonymous, 'The Philosophy of the Short Story', *The Academy* (30 March 1901): 287–8.
Ashton, Susanna, 'Authorial Affiliations, or, The Clubbing and Collaborating of Brander Matthews', *symploke*, 7.1–2 (1999): 165–87.
Awadalla, Maggie and Paul March-Russell (eds), *The Postcolonial Short Story* (Basingstoke: Palgrave Macmillan, 2013).
Canby, H. S., *The Short Story* (New York: Henry Holt, 1902).
— *The Short Story in English* (New York: Henry Holt, 1909).
— *A Study of the Short Story* (New York: Henry Holt, 1913).
— *Definitions: Essays in Contemporary Criticism* (New York: Harcourt Brace, 1922), pp. 294–5.
Clark, Timothy, 'Not Seeing the Short Story: A Blind Phenomenology of Reading', *Oxford Literary Review*, 26.1 (2012): 5–30.
Duncan, Ian, 'Altered States: Galt, Serial Fiction, and the Romantic Miscellany', in Regina Hewitt (ed.), *John Galt: Observations and Conjectures on Literature, History, and Society* (Lewisburg, PA: Bucknell University Press, 2012), pp. 46–60.
Einhause, Ann-Marie (ed.) *The Cambridge Companion to the English Short Story* (Cambridge: Cambridge University Press, 2016).

Garcha, Amanpal, *From Sketch to Novel: The Development of Victorian Fiction* (Cambridge: Cambridge University Press, 2009).

Graff, Gerald. *Professing Literature: An Institutional History* (Chicago: University of Chicago Press, 1987).

Hale, Edward Everett and Frederick T. Dawson, *The Elements of the Short Story* (New York: Henry Holt, 1915).

Head, Dominic (ed.), *The Cambridge History of the English Short Story* (Cambridge: Cambridge University Press, 2016).

Hunt, Theodore W., 'The Place of English in the College Curriculum', *Transactions of the Modern Language Association of America*, 1 (1884): 118–39.

— *Studies in Literature and Style* (New York: A. C. Armstrong, 1890), p. 15.

Hunter, Adrian, 'The "Custom" of Fiction: Virginia Woolf, the Hogarth Press, and the Modernist Short Story', *English*, 56 (2007): 147–69.

Jarrells, Anthony, 'Provincializing Enlightenment: Edinburgh Historicism and the Blackwoodian Regional Tale', *Studies in Romanticism*, 48.2 (2009): 257–77.

Killick, Tim, *British Short Fiction in the Early Nineteenth Century* (Aldershot: Ashgate, 2007).

Levy, Andrew, *The Culture and Commerce of the American Short Story* (Cambridge: Cambridge University Press, 1993).

March-Russell, Paul, *The Short Story: An Introduction* (Edinburgh: Edinburgh University Press, 2009), pp. 34–6.

Matthews, Brander, *An Introduction to American Literature* (New York: American Book Company, 1896).

— *The Philosophy of the Short-story* (New York: Longmans, Green and Co., 1901).

— *The Short-story: Specimens Illustrating Its Development* (New York: American Book Company, 1907).

— *These Many Years: Recollections of a New Yorker* (New York: Charles Scribner's Sons, 1917).

May, Charles E. (ed.), *The New Short Story Theories* (Athens : Ohio University Press, 1994), p. xvi.

Menand, Louis, *The Metaphysical Club* (London: Harper Collins, 2001), pp. 382–408.

Moulton, Richard G., *Shakespeare as a Dramatic Artist: A Popular Illustration of the Principles of Scientific Criticism* (Oxford: Clarendon, 1885).

Oliver, Lawrence J., *Brander Matthews, Theodore Roosevelt, and the Politics of American Literature, 1880–1920* (Knoxville: University of Tennessee Press, 1992), pp. 9–12.

Patea, Viorica, 'The Short Story: An Overview of the History and Evolution of a Genre', in Viorica Patea (ed.), *Short Story Theories: A Twenty-First-Century Perspective* (Amsterdam: Rodopi, 2012), pp. 1–24.

Pattee, Fred Lewis, *The Development of the American Short Story* (New York and London: Harper, 1923).

Perry, Bliss, *A Study of Prose Fiction*, rev. edn (Boston and New York: Houghton Mifflin, 1920).

Poe, Edgar Allan, 'Review of *Twice-Told Tales* by Nathaniel Hawthorne', *Graham's Monthly Magazine*, 20 (May 1842): 298–300.

Pound, Ezra, 'Dubliners and Mr James Joyce', in T. S. Eliot (ed.), *Literary Essays of Ezra Pound* (London: Faber, 1960), pp. 339–402.

Renker, Elizabeth, *The Origins of American Literature Studies: An Institutional History* (Cambridge: Cambridge University Press, 2007).

Smith, C. Alphonso, 'The Work of the Modern Language Association of America', *PMLA*, 14.2 (1899): 240–56.

— *The American Short Story* (Boston and London: Ginn and Company, 1912).

Stewart, David, 'Romantic Short Fiction', in Ann-Marie Einhaus (ed.), *The Cambridge Companion to the English Short Story* (Cambridge: Cambridge University Press, 2016), pp. 73–86.

Warner, Michael, 'Professionalization and the Rewards of Literature: 1875–1900', *Criticism*, 27.1 (1985): 1–28.

Williams, William Carlos, 'Notes in Diary Form', in *Selected Essays of William Carlos William* (New York: New Directions, 1969), pp. 62–74.

Woolf, Virginia, *The Essays of Virginia Woolf, Volume 2: 1912–1918* (London: Hogarth Press, 1988).

— 'The Russian Point of View', in Andrew McNeillie (ed.), *The Essays of Virginia Woolf, Volume 4: 1925–1928* (London: Hogarth Press, 1994), pp. 181–9.

3

IMPRESSIONISM AND THE SHORT STORY

Paul March-Russell

SPEAKING IN 2006, the Scottish writer A. L. Kennedy observed:

> If you have a generally correct appreciation . . . of the point of view of the characters, then you have everything. You have the world, the colour of description, you have the density of description – you have this sense of genuinely being within someone else's skin or this genuine understanding of someone else. The short story is the form where you most need to have a grip of point of view or it just doesn't work.[1]

Kennedy's observation indicates not only the extent to which one of the key organisational principles of literary Impressionism – the focus and selectivity of perspective – has become ingrained in contemporary practice but also how far it is associated with the short story form. Indeed, Edgar Allan Poe had long ago argued, with reference to Nathaniel Hawthorne's *Twice-Told Tales* (1842), that 'in almost all classes of composition, the unity of effect or impression is a point of the greatest importance'.[2] Although Poe's emphases upon concision, precision and foreshadowing prefigure key tenets of literary Impressionism, his usage echoes David Hume's association of the impression with the realm of the body, the senses and the passions. As Jesse Matz has argued, Hume's distinction forms part of a more complex negotiation between what is most memorable and most ephemeral about the impression, between profundity and banality, which destabilises the alleged philosophic roots to literary Impressionism.[3] In charting the recent historiography of the concept, its origins, rise and fall, and subsequent dissemination into modernist techniques such as the epiphany and stream of consciousness, this chapter will argue that not only are critical attempts to define the short story in terms of Impressionism sundered by its very instability but also its range of potential meaning is complemented by the diversity of the short story form.

As several critics have emphasised, the high watermark for both Impressionist literature and its criticism was in the period from the end of the nineteenth century to the start of the 1920s. First eclipsed by the more combative and non-representational avant-garde movements such as Cubism, Futurism and Vorticism,[4] literary Impressionism was subsequently overshadowed by the consolidation of the modernist canon during the 1940s and 50s by academics such as F. R. Leavis and the New Critics, working on either side of the Atlantic. The question mark as to whether writers such as Joseph Conrad, Stephen Crane, Ford Madox Ford and Henry James should be viewed either as the tail end of the nineteenth century or precursors to modernism not only obscured their role but put them at odds with the more recognisably modernist aesthetics of Imagism, Symbolism and the Bloomsbury Group as practised variously by T. S. Eliot, Ezra Pound, Virginia Woolf and W. B. Yeats. In the mid-1970s, however, critical interest in literary Impressionism was renewed, perhaps symptomatic of the extent to which the formalist orthodoxy of Leavis and the New Critics was then under attack from the rise of critical theory and, with it, their conception of the modernist canon.

Prefigured by a symposium on literary Impressionism in the *Yearbook of Comparative Literature* in 1968 and by Elizabeth Maria Kronegger's book-length study in 1973, monographs by James Nagel, Peter Stowell and Ian Watt on, respectively, Stephen Crane, Henry James and Anton Chekhov, and Joseph Conrad not only re-evaluated the role that Impressionism had played in each of these authors' works but reassessed the similarities between Impressionism in literature and the visual arts, as well as its overall contribution to the making of a modernist aesthetic.[5] In addition to Watt's influential notion of delayed decoding, between them these authors developed a useful checklist of tropes that could (at the very least) delineate the outline of what literary Impressionism was. Andrzej Gasiorek has summarised them as follows: 'impersonality; suppression of the author; refusal of moral didacticism; presentation versus description (with the goal of making the reader see); linguistic economy; *progression d'effet*; the time-shift; illusionism (no breaking of the fictional frame); attention to style and form'.[6] The effect of these techniques was to concentrate the point of view, whether in the first or third person or an intermingling of the two through the use of free indirect discourse, such that 'beginning with impressionism, unknowability rather than knowability became a major concern in literature'.[7] While, on the one hand, the focus upon the selective and mediated role of perception associated literary Impressionism with an emergent psychological realism, on the other hand, the representation of character tended to be opaque, elusive or contradictory, dependent upon the shifts between multiple and partial points of view. For Stowell, this apparent inconsistency could be resolved by reference to 'the modern world of science and technology' which, as it 'became more chaotically threatening, so too did society and its individual members': 'Impressionism's goal was to render effects, understanding that causes and motives were too often unknowable.'[8] For Nagel, if life is, as Conrad and Ford averred, 'a series of disjointed sensory experiences' then fiction too must concentrate on 'the minds and actions of the characters rather than on the interpretative analysis of the narrator'.[9] As a further consequence, while sticking fixedly to the objective realism of the description, literary Impressionism tended towards the spatialisation of the narrative: incidents are described out of chronological sequence but effects accumulated so as to offer a whole picture of the events rather than a resolution of the plot; thus suggesting further affinities with the visual arts.

Within what might appear to be a series of constraints upon artistic freedom, Nagel suggests a number of modalities. 'In the subjective mode', he writes, 'the images derive their significance ... from what they suggest about the mind of the character' and so, somewhat paradoxically, the effects become more expressionist in quality.[10] The more objective the details are described, Nagel proposes, the more they resemble an imagistic quality: the direct presentation, in Ezra Pound's words, of 'an intellectual and emotional complex in an instant of time'.[11] Consequently, whilst literary Impressionism can be described in terms of its tropes, their precise handling and combination can produce a variety of effects and linguistic and visual registers. And while this complexity can be understood in terms of Stowell's emphasis upon the chaos of modern experience – what appears to be chaotic in the text is actually the discreet manipulation of a finite set of techniques; the realisation of which restores (at the very least) a tentative order to otherwise apparent randomness and chance – it also indicates the variance in the midst of perception. Stowell, in particular, associates literary Impressionism with the emergence of a phenomenological turn across physics, psychology and philosophy during the early years of the twentieth century, encompassing such thinkers as Henri Bergson, Albert Einstein, Edmund Husserl and William James.[12]

Although more recent critics have sought to substantiate the associations between modernism and phenomenology in the period in and around the First World War, through a generalised sense of crisis, rupture or breakdown in social relations,[13] the terms in which Stowell presents their resemblance tend towards analogy, recapitulating the ways in which the relationship between visual and literary Impressionism has often been described. More substantively, Watt draws upon the recorded reflections of Conrad and Ford for the basis of his delayed decoding, but Crane left few insights behind him, whilst both Nagel and Stowell tend to paraphrase the observations of Chekhov, Conrad, Ford and James rather than critique them. On this account, the critical reclamation of literary Impressionism in the late 1970s was instrumental in constructing a more unified and consistent version of the method than was necessarily the case.

The effect of this critique can be seen when the short story was applied to this revival of interest in literary Impressionism (Nagel, Stowell and Watt having largely concentrated upon the novel form). In 1982, Suzanne Ferguson attempted to define the short story in terms of Impressionism by first asserting that 'there is no single characteristic or cluster of characteristics that the critics agree absolutely distinguishes the short story from other fictions'.[14] Ferguson adopts a structuralist approach, derived from such critics as Roland Barthes, Seymour Chatman, A. J. Greimas and Vladimir Propp, to argue that 'all stories can be reduced to minimal statements of the required elements or expanded by the inclusion of optional developments in the narrative chain, as long as they maintain a discoverable coherence in their interrelationships'. Whereas maximalist novels such as James Joyce's *Ulysses* (1922) or Laurence Sterne's *Tristram Shandy* (1759–67) suggest almost limitless expansion, 'the "best" short stories give us a sense of the inevitability of each sentence and persuade us that they are as complete as possible',[15] precisely because of their brevity and compactness. Ferguson argues then that, although the modern short story developed along similar lines to the early modernist novel from the late nineteenth century onwards, 'it has fewer "optional" narrative elements in its structural "slots"', and so 'manifests its formal allegiances to impressionism even more obviously than does the novel'.[16] Ferguson adopts Flaubert as the starting point for literary Impressionism, which she defines in terms of the following characteristics, most of which had already been enumerated by Nagel, Stowell and Watt: selective points of view, inner states of mind, non-causality, the figurative uses of metaphor and metonymy, non-linearity, concision, and an emphasis upon style over plot. Like Stowell, Ferguson makes the further claim by equating the rise of modernist fiction, of which the short story is exemplary, with an intellectual move 'away from positivism and toward phenomenology': 'the representation of experience *as experienced by individuals*' with a concomitant emphasis upon the unresolved understanding of subjective truth.[17]

In her analysis, then, Ferguson rejects a generic approach to the short story but re-casts a critical terminology derived from Poe in the context of a proto-modernist vocabulary inherited from Gustave Flaubert. Although this reading allows Ferguson to consider the rise of the modern short story in relation to other developments within the poetics of modernism, she does not define Impressionism in itself but instead all too readily assumes the terms laid out by the modernists themselves. Her analysis considers neither the market conditions in which modernist fiction emerged, nor the ambiguous relationship between different kinds of modernist practice from the wide spectrum of small presses, little magazines and dominant, commercial production. In other words, although Ferguson does expand the discussion on what constitutes a short story via her focus on Impressionist techniques, she ultimately concentrates upon a narrow cross section of short stories, texts that Eileen Baldeshwiler would term 'lyrical': 'internal changes, moods, and feelings, utilizing a variety of structural patterns depending on the shape of the emotion itself, [relying] for the most part on the open ending . . . expressed in the condensed, evocative, often figured language of the poem'.[18] The close similarities between the list of characteristics associated with Impressionism and lyricism means that Ferguson, like Baldeshwiler, implicitly contrasts the Impressionist short story with the majority of short fictions that Baldeshwiler dismisses as 'epical': 'realistic, conventional' narratives that constitute 'the mainstream'.[19] It is worth noting, however, that this usage of the word 'mainstream' dates from the mid-1950s, when it was first used within jazz and science-fiction fandoms, subcultures anxious to preserve their own precarious and non-canonical identities. The binary approach that underwrites the analyses of Baldeshwiler and Ferguson describes a similar anxious relationship between the short story and its more culturally dominant counterpart, the novel.

In the wake of Ferguson's essay, other critics sought to substantiate the short story's affinities with visual Impressionism. Valerie Shaw, for example, wrote that 'the impact of many modern short stories resemble the effect of looking at an Impressionist canvas because it leaves a sense of something complete yet unfinished'.[20] In 1985, Clare Hanson took Walter Pater's conclusion to *The Renaissance* (1873) as her starting point for a generalised 'movement towards subjective impressionism in literature and the visual arts and a hedonistic emphasis on the value of the passing moment',[21] impulses that she sees as influencing the rise of the prose poem and the psychological sketch in such journals as *The Yellow Book* (1894–7). By contrast, Dominic Head takes such comparisons to task by arguing that the visual analogy 'risks obscuring the basic distinction between the metaphorical story "picture" and the literal spatial image on a painter's canvas': in the short story, 'spatial pattern is grasped by accumulation, or with hindsight, and, as such, is a kind of illusion generated progressively as the text is produced through reading. In short, the perception of story unity, in a spatial sense, is at odds with the inherent temporality of reading and writing.'[22] Head's critique, although not dismissive of literary Impressionism in itself, indicates the categorical errors that can accrue when seeking ready analogies between media.

In any event, the critical debate on literary Impressionism had already moved on, which threatened to render anachronistic such later studies as Julia van Gunsteren's

1990 analysis of Katherine Mansfield that primarily takes a hermeneutic approach to the topic of Mansfield's possible debt to Impressionism.[23] The transformation of the debate was largely due to Paul Armstrong's analysis of Conrad, Ford and James, *The Challenge of Bewilderment* (1987). Instead of regarding the trio as working from an agreed definition of Impressionism, Armstrong sees each of them as developing their own individual impressionistic method, a divergence that arises from the same dilemma in their fictions: the question of epistemology, or the representation of understanding. In this regard, Armstrong sees them motivated by a mutual sense of bewilderment not as 'a negative but a positive value' which calls 'into question our confidence in the "roads" that make up "reality"'.[24] Instead of the tendency towards artistic unity (however subjective), as suggested in the evaluations of literary Impressionism by Nagel, Stowell and Watt, and then in their application to short story criticism by critics such as Ferguson, Armstrong suggests that their impressionistic narratives disperse into further fragments that ask 'whether reality is a unified whole or a collection of conflicting interpretations that may not be ultimately reconcilable'.[25] Although, like Stowell, Armstrong turns to phenomenology as a philosophic method for illustrating his argument, he does so not to reacquaint writing with the world of the senses but, following Husserl's notion of reduction, to dwell on 'the processes of consciousness' which constitute the world of objects: to question 'our assurances about what we are most familiar with'.[26] In other words, whilst short story criticism of the 1980s was adapting the recent revival of interest in literary Impressionism to a pre-existing and over-determined model of formal unity (consonant also with other developments in short story criticism toward narratology and neuroscience, for example, in the work of John Gerlach and Susan Lohafer), the wider debate was moving in the opposite direction: towards the dispersal and fragmentation of perspective, consciousness and cognition.

Such contradictions were present from the initial naming of the movement in art. As has been emphasised, the term was originally coined by the French art critic, Louis Leroy, as a sign of derision.[27] Taking Claude Monet's painting, *Impression: Soleil Levant* (1872), as his inspiration, Leroy sought to dismiss Monet and his immediate contemporaries such as Edgar Degas, Camille Pissarro and Jean Renoir as light and insubstantial. Instead, the term caught on both as a means of grouping not only these artists but also painters such as Paul Cézanne, Paul Gauguin and Georges Seurat, who exhibited alongside them and sought to expand upon Impressionism, and also as an indication of the basic style and content: the quick outline of something seen – and as it is seen from the painter's perspective – within a restricted period of time. By 1882, the term had entered the lexicon of British periodicals such as the *Athenaeum* although, as Max Saunders argues following the contemporary art critic Richard Brettell, the concept subdivided further into artists, such as Monet, concerned primarily with visual experience – the authentic albeit subjective representation of light, colour, shadow and shape – and artists, such as Renoir, preoccupied with psychological realism: the relationship between subjects and objects in a social setting.[28] As Matz argues, however, once the term crosses over into literature, the writer is confronted with the same dilemma postulated by Leroy: can something as ephemeral as an impression be recuperated into an ideology (an 'ism') that offers a cogent understanding of time, space, memory and perception?[29] Matz's solution is to define the concept in terms of its diversity although this plurality also suggests the inherent inconsistency of any ideology. Seen in this light, when the idea of Impressionism confronted the real-world conditions of production, distribution and consumption, its internal contradictions were exposed.

This instability can be observed in the first anglophone critic to apply the term to literature, the aesthetic writer and critic Vernon Lee. Writing in the *Academy* in December 1883, she acknowledged her appropriation of what was, up to then, an artistic concept introduced into English criticism by Lee's then confidante, Henry James, in his *Parisian Sketches* (1876). A year later however, and in her volume of critical dialogues, *Baldwin* (1884), Lee's use of the word 'impression' indicates less her indebtedness to the visual arts than to the aestheticism of her intellectual mentor, Pater: 'our aesthetic life consists really in the fluctuations, the movements, of these, if I may call them so, living molecules of aesthetic feeling; it consists of the action and reactions produced within us by any new impression that we receive'.[30] The selection and handling of these impressions, and even more so their residue, 'the living dust of broken impressions' that 'live on within us',[31] is what for Lee constitutes the beautiful in fiction. She is mindful, however, to consider the role of the reader, 'the idealist thinks also of the mind for whose benefit the impression from without is to be elicited',[32] and the effect that it is to have. Lee, then, as the earliest proponent of what would subsequently be termed literary Impressionism makes three important distinctions: firstly, she suggests an affinity between Impressionism in art and in literature that goes beyond realism by connecting with the realm of the senses; secondly, she acknowledges the debt to Pater's 'stream' of impressions, 'that continual vanishing away, that strange perpetual weaving and unweaving of ourselves';[33] and thirdly, she stresses the importance of reception – the impression that the author seeks to make upon the reader so that they experience all the more clearly. From the outset, then, the idea of Impressionism in literature seeks to achieve more than one effect, to move between varying conditions of experience (the visual, the sensual, the cognitive), to draw upon more than one intellectual or artistic discipline, and to work between the subjective and inter-subjective relations of the observer, the observed and the communicant.

Following Leroy's lead, the idea of literary Impressionism was first developed in 1879 in an ambivalent essay by Ferdinand Brunetière on the work of Alphonse Daudet. Van Gunsteren argues that by the end of the 1890s the concept had developed from a purely stylistic consideration of writers as diverse as Honoré de Balzac, Gustave Flaubert and Émile Zola to a more specific and appreciative understanding of Impressionism as a method of representing the intensity and subjectivity of modern experience. These ideas were then disseminated into German literary culture by influential critics, such as Hermann Bahr, working on French literature.[34] Whether or not Lee would have been aware of these developments, especially in France, is unclear although her multilingualism and strong ties to continental Europe suggest that she might. What is clear though, on both sides of the English Channel, is that there was an emerging sense that literary Impressionism was not only a formal or stylistic technique, with affinities to the visual arts, but that it was also a means for portraying what appears to be a characteristically modern sense of experience. G. K. Chesterton expressed it thus:

> Our modern attraction to short stories is not an accident of form; it is a sign of a real sense of fleetingness and fragility; it means that existence is only an impression, and, perhaps, only an illusion. . . . The moderns, in a word, describe life in short stories because they are possessed with the sentiment that life itself is an uncommonly short story, and perhaps not a true one.[35]

Although Chesterton offers an unmediated, reflectionist account of literature's relationship to modernity, in which he sees both Impressionism and the short story as a falling-away from the permanence of great art, he draws upon the terms of the critical debate that surrounded Impressionism at the turn of the century. As Adrian Hunter has argued, this discussion was also informed by wider debates surrounding the purpose, content, composition and consumption of fiction following the Education Act of 1870, the growth of the periodical market, the collapse of the three-volume novel in the mid-1890s, the increasing professionalisation of the publishing industry and the fragmentation of the literary marketplace into separate genres and niche audiences.[36] The short story had already featured as an appendage to the so-called 'art of fiction' debate in 1884 between Walter Besant, Henry James and Robert Louis Stevenson, thanks to Brander Matthews's little-read *Saturday Review* article that became better known on its republication in 1901 as *The Philosophy of the Short-story*. The occasional commentaries on this newly coined genre that appeared during the *fin de siècle* complemented other, more celebrated debates on art for art's sake, moral censorship and candour in literature. In short, these dialogues – including those on Impressionism and the short story – were indivisible from one another, and from their place within wider cultural, socio-economic and demographic changes.

Ford Madox Ford has been characterised by Andrzej Gasiorek as discriminating 'between traditions in order to situate his writing and that of authors he admires within a precisely defined literary current'.[37] Ford's advocacy for Impressionism is viewed by Gasiorek as a further instance in this process: 'impressionism's refusal of easy answers to social problems, of moral generalisations about complex realities, indeed of didacticism of any kind . . . marks out its modernism',[38] an aesthetic whose origins Ford associates with French authors such as Flaubert, Théophile Gautier and Guy de Maupassant so as to displace the lineage of mid-Victorian novelists such as Charles Dickens and George Eliot. If the rise of literary Impressionism, as advocated by Ford, necessitated a reorientation of literary traditions so as to appeal to the senses of an expanding and newly enfranchised reading public, then Impressionism's possible affinities with the short story, rather than the traditional novel, must also be taken into account.

As Michael Levenson has argued, Ford's doctrine on Impressionism was formulated between 1912 and 1914.[39] At the heart of this mantra is a concern with mimesis: an artfully produced 'illusion of reality'.[40] Authorial intrusion would not only disturb this illusion but also call attention to it: the Impressionist aims for objective detachment. Yet, at the same time, Ford also believed that 'all art must be the expression of an ego' and 'that Impressionism is a frank expression of personality'.[41] While this apparent contradiction could be resolved either by Nagel's emphasis upon the modalities in Impressionist technique or by recalling the inherent inconsistencies between theory and practice, it also invokes the earlier tensions within visual Impressionism: objectivity on the one hand, amounting almost to abstraction, and subjective, psychological realism on the other hand. Ford resolves this seeming paradox by arguing 'that the Impressionist gives you, as a rule, the fruits of his own observations and the fruits of his own observations alone'.[42] In other words, the mimetic representation of reality – unmediated by the authorial voice – collapses into the subjective ego of the narrator: it is objective from his or her point of view. Such a get-out, complementing the first rule of Pound's so-called Imagist manifesto, 'Direct treatment of the "thing", whether subjective or objective',[43] may help to explain why Wyndham Lewis incorporated the first chapter of Ford's *The Good Soldier* (1915), entitled 'The Saddest Story', in the first issue of *Blast* in 1914 alongside Rebecca West's non-Impressionistic short story, 'Indissoluble Matrimony'.

However, although Ford later explained how his Impressionist ethos was worked out in collaboration with Joseph Conrad, two contrasting statements from Conrad help to undermine the apparent security of the doctrine. One is an extract from his famous preface to *The Nigger of the 'Narcissus'* (1897):

> Art itself may be defined as a single-minded attempt to render the highest kind of justice to the visible universe, by bringing to light the truth, manifold and one, underlying its every aspect. ... My task which I am trying to achieve is, by the power of the written word, to make you hear, to make you feel – it is, before all, to make you *see*.[44]

Conrad's emphasis on vision is not exclusively Impressionist in ethos; the moral force that lies behind it echoes nineteenth-century commentators such as John Ruskin: 'Hundreds of people can talk for one who can think, but thousands can think for one who can see. To see clearly is poetry, prophecy, and religion – all in one.'[45] Yet, as Saunders suggests, 'while Conrad's art renders the visible universe as a way of revealing the secrets that lie beneath it, what it finds is precisely that they *are* secrets; enigmas, mysteries'.[46] A second extract, a letter to Edward Garnett in 1899, helps to develop this point:

> All is illusion – the words written, the mind at which they are aimed, the truth they are intended to express, the hands that will hold the paper, the eyes that will glance along the lines. Every image floats in a sea of doubt – and the doubt itself is lost in an unexplored universe of incertitudes.[47]

This letter, meant for private consumption unlike the preface, suggests that Ford's 'illusion of reality' is indeed just that, an illusion, and that Conrad's visual metaphor does not so much comprehend the truth as illuminate it: 'seeing as physical vision and seeing as seeing through ... of seeing the darkness in terms of the light.'[48]

This distinction, indicated by Conrad more than a decade before Ford's consolidation of Impressionism into a doctrine, sunders it since it implies that 'Ford's Impressionism ... is a subjectivity in which the subject has disappeared.'[49] Ford himself suggested as much when he wrote, 'Impressionism is a thing altogether momentary',[50] while this crisis of subjectivity also dogged Pound (even as he rejected Impressionism in favour of Imagism): 'One says "I am" this, that, or the other, and with the words scarcely uttered one ceases to be that thing.'[51] The reader is suddenly in the same dilemma as Virginia Woolf:

> Examine for a moment an ordinary mind on an ordinary day. The mind receives a myriad impressions . . . From all sides they come, an incessant shower of innumerable atoms; and as they fall, as they shape themselves into the life of Monday or Tuesday, the accent falls differently from of old . . . Life is not a series of gig lamps symmetrically arranged; life is a luminous halo, a semi-transparent envelope surrounding us from the beginning of consciousness to the end.[52]

In other words, at the very height of its critical ascent at the outbreak of the First World War, Ford's Impressionism disintegrated but, ironically, its ruins would not only provide 'one very influential basis of Modernism' but also 'its most productive, voluble, self-conscious and lucrative stage'.[53]

It is a curious feature of the critical accounts upon literary Impressionism that, with the exception of Crane, they largely concentrate upon the novel – although cryptic short stories such as James's 'The Beast in the Jungle' (1903) and Conrad's 'Il Conde' (1908) and 'The Tale' (1917), with their enigmatic uses of point of view and multiple narrators, surely contributed to its formal development. Instead, the heyday of literary Impressionism in the short story occurred just as Ford's doctrinal use imploded and the form scattered into other devices. This dissemination, although marking the limits of literary Impressionism (we can, quite literally, talk about a post-Impressionism that emerged 'in or about December 1910'),[54] also marked its afterlife in the work of writers such as Mansfield and Woolf.

To say, however, that these authors are post-Impressionist and modernist is not simply a chronological statement: they are also reflecting upon what it means to be modern. As Woolf's narrator comments in 'The Mark on the Wall' (1917), speculating upon a time *after* the lessons of modernism have been learnt:

> As we face each other in omnibuses and underground railways we are looking into the mirror; that accounts for the vagueness, the gleam of glassiness, in our eyes. And the novelists in future will realise more and more the importance of these reflections, for of course there is not one reflection but an almost infinite number; those are the depths they will explore . . . leaving the description of reality more and more out of their stories.[55]

Unlike the tales of Conrad and James, written alongside their major novels, Woolf's experiments in short fiction prefigure her key phase as a novelist; they are instrumental in her development as a writer. Yet, Woolf's self-reflection also echoes one of the seminal documents of proto-modernism, Charles Baudelaire's 'The Painter of Modern Life' (1863), in particular, his description of what he terms 'mnemonic art':

> Thus two elements are to be discerned in Monsieur G.'s execution: the first, an intense effort of memory that evokes and calls back to life . . . the second, a fire, an intoxication of the pencil or the brush, amounting almost to a frenzy. It is the fear of not going fast enough, of letting the phantom escape before the synthesis has been extracted and pinned down.[56]

And, of course, embedded in Baudelaire's essay is a reading of Poe's 'The Man of the Crowd' (1840): the *flâneur* as the prototypical Impressionist. By these divergent pathways – a serendipity consonant with the messy history of Impressionism outlined here – Woolf's experimentalism is nonetheless rooted in the originary documents of both pictorial Impressionism and short story criticism.

The stream of consciousness techniques developed by Woolf – the term was popularised by May Sinclair in her 1918 review of Dorothy Richardson's multi-volume sequence *Pilgrimage* – were a direct offshoot from the crisis of subjectivity that undermined Ford's Impressionist credo. Sandra Kemp, paraphrasing a quotation from Woolf's novel, *The Waves* (1931), regards the effects achieved by the stories of Richardson, Sinclair and Woolf as stemming from the description of 'a world seen without a self',[57] in which, as for the child-protagonist of Richardson's 'The Garden' (1924), the boundaries between self and other, subject and object, have collapsed or not yet formed:

> There was no one there. The sound of feet and no one there. The gravel stopped making its noise when she stood still. When the last foot came down all the flowers stood still.[58]

Kemp, significantly, omits from her analysis Mansfield who, despite being reclaimed for Impressionism by van Gunsteren, was hostile in her criticism of Richardson and Sinclair. She accused the former of having 'no memory': 'Things just "happen" one after another with incredible rapidity and at break-neck speed'; 'bits, fragments, flashing glimpses, half scenes and whole scenes, all of them quite distinct and separate, and all of them of equal importance'.[59] The latter – and in terms not unlike Wyndham Lewis – Mansfield describes as pandering to a new cult of childishness: 'At two (poor infant staggerer!) the vast barn of impressions opens upon her . . . At forty-seven . . . she is still turning them over and over, still wondering whether any of them did happen to have in one of their ignoble pockets the happiness she has missed in life.'[60] Although Mansfield did find room to acknowledge Richardson's novels 'as a nest of short stories',[61] she only praises an actual short story, Woolf's 'Kew Gardens' (1919), and then maybe because it was perhaps written at her suggestion.[62] For sure, Mansfield does use post-Impressionist techniques – Kezia viewing the world through differently coloured panes of glass, for example, in 'Prelude' (1918) – but only once did she write an exclusively impressionistic story, 'The Wind Blows' (1915), and then as a divergence. Instead, Mansfield implies that there is something prematurely utopian in the work of her near-contemporaries, in which not only are the boundaries between self and other dissolved but also the social relations through which the self is constituted. Mansfield does not so much hold on to a controlling centre of consciousness for stylistic purposes, as in James, as to refuse to let go of a self, however tentative and provisional. Instead, one could argue that her stories oscillate between Impressionism, and a kind of fleeting mimetic realism, and Symbolism, the escape (or should that be flight?) into poetry and metaphor. Likewise, her characters are pulled between their internal desires and external pressures – the temporary respite of female community in 'At the Bay' (1922) is a fine illustration of that – but in which the self operates as the battle-ground where these competing forces are played out. Mansfield's fiction is arguably darker than the work of her near-contemporaries but this darkness can also be understood, as with Conrad, in terms of an Impressionism that does not so much offer insight as illumination.

Mansfield's scepticism dovetails with the short fiction of James Joyce. Like stream of consciousness, Joyce's early doctrine of the epiphany was a further offshoot from literary Impressionism. In *Stephen Hero* (1906), Joyce's alter ego, Stephen Dedalus, considers compiling 'a book of epiphanies' by which he means 'a sudden spiritual manifestation, whether in the vulgarity of speech or of gesture or in a memorable phase of the mind'.[63] In conversation with his friend, Cranly, Stephen describes the three-way process of epiphany:

> First we recognise that the object is one integral thing, then we recognise that it is an organised composite structure, a *thing* in fact: finally, when the relation of the parts is exquisite, when the parts are adjusted to the special point, we recognise that it is *that* thing which it is. Its soul, its whatness, leaps to us from the vestment of its appearance.[64]

However, even in this early formulation, the credo is not to be fully trusted. Stephen's reflection 'that it was for the man of letters to record these epiphanies with extreme care, seeing that they themselves are the most delicate and evanescent of moments' not only suggests his adolescent egotism but also plays ironically upon what was already a standard critical discourse on Impressionism in British literary periodicals.[65]

By the time that *Dubliners* finally appeared in 1914, Joyce had not only consolidated the epiphany as an organisational principle but had also – as in the Impressionist commentary upon perception itself – made it into an object of ironic scrutiny. A celebrated epiphanic moment from 'The Dead' captures this double-aspect to Joyce's methodology:

> He asked himself what is a woman standing on the stairs in the shadow, listening to distant music, a symbol of. If he were a painter he would paint her in that attitude. Her blue felt hat would show off the bronze of her hair against the darkness and the dark panels of her skirt would show off the light ones. *Distant Music* he would call the picture if he were a painter.[66]

While, on the one hand, this scene in which Gabriel Conroy sees his wife, Gretta, listening distractedly to a far-off tune calls attention to the affinities between literary and visual Impressionism, on the other hand, this analogy is undercut by the repeated use of the conditional. Gabriel is no artist but he wants to render this spiritual illumination, and by extension how he perceives Gretta, as an aesthetic experience. The epiphanic moment is undermined by it being no more than a projection of Gabriel's egotism. Yet, Joyce also provides a double bluff. Gabriel's subsequent realisation of the truth that lies behind the tune, seemingly suggesting that – as in Stephen's description of epiphany as a process of revelation – a false insight veils a true one, may be no more revelatory than Gabriel's earlier perception of Gretta; the snow, signifier of the whitening-out of meaning, 'faintly falling, like the descent of their last end, upon all the living and the dead'.[67] Although the use of epiphany, often in an impressionistic context, has become a byword in short story criticism and a standard technique amongst such contemporary practitioners as Raymond Carver and William Trevor, it is notable how two architects of the modernist short story, Joyce and Mansfield (in numerous stories such as 'Bliss', 'The Garden Party', 'Miss Brill' and 'The Stranger'), undermine the epiphany; drawing the story back into the materiality of its content and what James termed the 'abyss of ambiguities'.[68]

Opacity, then, rather than transparency underlines literary Impressionism: a form of blindness or, in musical terms, silence that the modernist, post-Impressionist techniques of writers such as Joyce, Mansfield and Woolf draw out. By the same token, a critical blindness underlines short story criticism even as it turns to the tenets of literary Impressionism to define the form. For Timothy Clark, reversing the terms of a debate in which visual metaphors have been over-privileged, 'blankness, remoteness and not-knowing are themselves an essential part of the realm called up in literary narrative';[69] a sense of what he terms 'enclosure', 'of having reached a limit or a border but without being able to formulate what might be beyond it'.[70] Although Clark ranges over a wide array of examples, from Kate Chopin to Alice Munro, his observations upon communicability could equally apply to what might be termed popular short fictions, from the unlikely lightning strike that might or might not have incinerated the lovers in Rudyard Kipling's 'Mrs Bathurst' (1904) to the dreamworld of Elizabeth Bowen's supernatural tale, 'Mysterious Kôr' (1944), and the titular 'new rays' of M. John Harrison's 1982 weird fiction that provokes grotesque transformations of self and other. As Harrison comments in terms that are strikingly post-Impressionist:

> A book – its meaning – is not what the light discovers. What is interesting in any book, or picture, or film, is the light itself. . . . This light, though experiential, serves paradoxically to familiarise the object it falls on. The moment in which it falls is the moment of being.[71]

In this regard, the impressionistic transgression of the boundaries between subject and object not only endures within contemporary short fiction but also questions how we define the short story in terms of its 'literariness'.

Notes

1. A. L. Kennedy, 'Small in a Way That a Bullet is Small', in Ailsa Cox (ed.), *The Short Story* (Newcastle upon Tyne: Cambridge Scholars Publishing, 2008), p. 4.
2. Edgar Allan Poe, 'Review of *Twice-Told Tales*', in Charles E. May (ed.), *The New Short Story Theories* (Athens: Ohio University Press, 1994), p. 60.
3. Jesse Matz, *Literary Impressionism and Modernist Aesthetics* (Cambridge: Cambridge University Press, 2001), pp. 20–5.
4. Wyndham Lewis's petulant response to Ford, 'What is the sense of you and Conrad and Impressionism?', quoted in Ford Madox Ford, *Return to Yesterday*, ed. Bill Hutchings (Manchester: Carcanet, 1999), p. 311, is emblematic of this eclipsing of early modernism.
5. See respectively James Nagel, *Stephen Crane and Literary Impressionism* (University Park: Pennsylvania State University Press, 1980); H. Peter Stowell, *Literary Impressionism, James and Chekhov* (Athens: University of Georgia Press, 1980); and Ian Watt, *Conrad in the Nineteenth Century* (Berkeley: University of California Press, 1979).
6. Andrzej Gasiorek, 'Ford Madox Ford's Modernism and the Question of Tradition', *English Literature in Transition*, 44.1 (2001): 13.
7. Stowell, *Literary Impressionism*, p. 23.
8. Ibid.
9. Nagel, *Stephen Crane*, p. 24.
10. Ibid. p. 29.

11. Ezra Pound, *Gaudier-Brzeska: A Memoir* (New York: New Directions, 1970), p. 86.
12. Stowell, *Literary Impressionism*, pp. 16–19.
13. See, for example, Ariane Mildenberg, 'Openings: *Epoché* as Aesthetic Tool in Modernist Texts', in Carol Bourne-Taylor and Ariane Mildenberg (eds), *Phenomenology, Modernism and Beyond* (Bern: Peter Lang, 2010), esp. pp. 41–9.
14. Suzanne C. Ferguson, 'Defining the Short Story: Impressionism and Form', in May (ed.), *New Short Story Theories*, p. 218.
15. Ibid. p. 219.
16. Ibid. pp. 219–20.
17. Ibid. p. 220.
18. Eileen Baldeshwiler, 'The Lyric Short Story: The Sketch of a History' (1969), in May (ed.), *New Short Story Theories*, p. 231.
19. Ibid. p. 241.
20. Valerie Shaw, *The Short Story: A Critical Introduction* (Harlow: Longman, 1983), p. 13.
21. Clare Hanson, *Short Stories and Short Fictions, 1880–1980* (London: Macmillan, 1985), p. 13.
22. Dominic Head, *The Modernist Short Story: A Study in Theory and Practice* (Cambridge: Cambridge University Press, 1992), pp. 9–10.
23. See Julia van Gunsteren, *Katherine Mansfield and Literary Impressionism* (Amsterdam: Rodopi, 1990).
24. Paul B. Armstrong, *The Challenge of Bewilderment: Understanding and Representation in James, Conrad, and Ford* (Ithaca, NY: Cornell University Press, 1987), p. 3.
25. Ibid.
26. Ibid. p. 4.
27. See, for example, Matz, *Literary Impressionism*, p. 12; and Max Saunders, 'Literary Impressionism', in David Bradshaw and Kevin J. H. Dettmar (eds), *A Companion to Modernist Literature and Culture* (Malden, MA and Oxford: Blackwell Publishing, 2006), p. 204.
28. Saunders, 'Literary Impressionism', p. 205.
29. Matz, *Literary Impressionism*, p. 17.
30. Vernon Lee, *Baldwin: Being Dialogues on Views and Aspirations* (London: T. Fisher Unwin, 1886), p. 276.
31. Ibid. p. 275.
32. Ibid. p. 301.
33. Walter Pater, 'Conclusion to *The Renaissance*', in *Essays on Literature and Art*, ed. Jennifer Uglow (London: Dent, 1973), p. 45.
34. Van Gunsteren, *Katherine Mansfield*, pp. 38–40.
35. G. K. Chesterton, *Charles Dickens* (London: Methuen, 1906), p. 69.
36. Adrian Hunter, *The Cambridge Introduction to the Short Story in English* (Cambridge: Cambridge University Press, 2007), pp. 6–9.
37. Gasiorek, 'Ford Madox Ford's Modernism', p. 4.
38. Ibid. p. 13.
39. Michael H. Levenson, *A Genealogy of Modernism: A Study of English Literary Doctrine 1908–1922* (Cambridge: Cambridge University Press, 1984), p. 107.
40. Ford, 'On Impressionism' (1914), in *Critical Writings of Ford Madox Ford*, ed. Frank MacShane (Lincoln: University of Nebraska Press, 1964), p. 43.
41. Ibid. p. 34 and p. 36.
42. Ibid. p. 37.
43. Pound, *Gaudier-Brzeska*, p. 83.
44. Joseph Conrad, preface to *The Nigger of the 'Narcissus'*, ed. Cedric Watts (London: Penguin, 1988), p. xlvii and p. xlix.

45. John Ruskin, *Modern Painters*, ed. David Barrie (London: André Deutsch, 1987), p. 404.
46. Saunders, 'Literary Impressionism', p. 208.
47. Conrad, letter to Edward Garnett (16 September 1899), in *The Collected Letters of Joseph Conrad, vol. 2*, ed. Frederick R. Karl and Laurence Davies (Cambridge: Cambridge University Press, 1986), p. 198.
48. J. Hillis Miller, '*Heart of Darkness* Revisited', in Ross C. Murfin (ed.), *Conrad Revisited: Essays for the Eighties* (Tuscaloosa: University of Alabama Press, 1985), p. 37.
49. Levenson, *Genealogy of Modernism*, p. 119.
50. Ford, 'On Impressionism', p. 40.
51. Pound, *Gaudier-Brzeska*, p. 85.
52. Virginia Woolf, 'Modern Fiction' (1919), in *The Crowded Dance of Modern Life*, ed. Rachel Bowlby (London: Penguin, 1993), p. 8.
53. Matz, *Literary Impressionism*, p. 173; and Paul Mann, *The Theory Death of the Avant-Garde* (Bloomington: Indiana University Press, 1991), p. 3.
54. Woolf, 'Mr Bennett and Mrs Brown' (1924), in *A Writer's Essays*, ed. Rachel Bowlby (London: Penguin, 1992), p. 70.
55. Woolf, *A Haunted House: The Complete Shorter Fiction*, ed. Susan Dick (London: Vintage, 2003), pp. 79–80.
56. Charles Baudelaire, *The Painter of Modern Life and Other Essays*, trans. and ed. Jonathan Mayne, 2nd edn (London: Phaidon Press, 1995), p. 17.
57. Sandra Kemp, 'But how describe a world seen without a self?': Feminism, Fiction and Modernism', *Critical Quarterly*, 32.1: 99–118.
58. Dorothy Richardson, *Journey to Paradise*, ed. Trudi Tate (London: Virago, 1989), p. 21.
59. Katherine Mansfield, 'Three Women Novelists' (1919), in *The Poetry and Critical Writings of Katherine Mansfield*, ed. Gerri Kimber and Angela Smith (Edinburgh: Edinburgh University Press, 2014), p. 446.
60. Mansfield, 'The New Infancy' (1919), in *Poetry and Critical Writings*, p. 479.
61. Mansfield, 'Dragonflies' (1920), in *Poetry and Critical Writings*, p. 558.
62. Mansfield, 'A Short Story' (1919), in *Poetry and Critical Writings*, pp. 473–5.
63. James Joyce, *Stephen Hero*, ed. Theodore Spencer et al. (London: Paladin, 1991), p. 216.
64. Ibid. p. 218.
65. Ibid. p. 216.
66. Joyce, *Dubliners* (London: Grafton, 1977), p. 240.
67. Ibid. p. 256.
68. Henry James, preface to *The Princess Casamassima* (1908), in *The Critical Muse: Selected Literary Criticism*, ed. Roger Gard (London: Penguin, 1987), p. 500.
69. Timothy Clark, 'Not Seeing the Short Story: A Blind Phenomenology of Reading', *Oxford Literary Review*, 26 (2004): 9.
70. Ibid. p. 18.
71. M. John Harrison, 'The Profession of Science Fiction' (1989), in *Critical Writings by and on M. John Harrison*, ed. Mark Bould and Michelle Reid (London: SF Foundation, 2005), p. 147.

Bibliography

Armstrong, Paul B., *The Challenge of Bewilderment: Understanding and Representation in James, Conrad, and Ford* (Ithaca, NY: Cornell University Press, 1987).

Baudelaire, Charles, *The Painter of Modern Life and Other Essays*, trans. and ed. Jonathan Mayne, 2nd edn (London: Phaidon Press, 1995).

Bourne-Taylor, Carol and Ariane Mildenberg (eds), *Phenomenology, Modernism and Beyond* (Bern: Peter Lang, 2010).

Chesterton, G. K., *Charles Dickens* (London: Methuen, 1906).
Clark, Timothy, 'Not Seeing the Short Story: A Blind Phenomenology of Reading', *Oxford Literary Review*, 26 (2004): 5–30.
Conrad, Joseph, *The Collected Letters of Joseph Conrad, vol. 2*, ed. Frederick R. Karl and Laurence Davies (Cambridge: Cambridge University Press, 1986).
— *The Nigger of the 'Narcissus'*, ed. Cedric Watts (London: Penguin, 1988).
Ford, Ford Madox, *Critical Writings of Ford Madox Ford*, ed. Frank MacShane (Lincoln: University of Nebraska Press, 1964).
— *Return to Yesterday*, ed. Bill Hutchings (Manchester: Carcanet, 1999).
Gasiorek, Andrzej, 'Ford Madox Ford's Modernism and the Question of Tradition', *English Literature in Transition*, 44.1 (2001): 3–27.
Gunsteren, Julia Van, *Katherine Mansfield and Literary Impressionism* (Amsterdam: Rodopi, 1990).
Hanson, Clare, *Short Stories and Short Fictions, 1880–1980* (London: Macmillan, 1985).
Harrison, M. John, *Critical Writings by and on M. John Harrison*, ed. Mark Bould and Michelle Reid (London: SF Foundation, 2005).
Head, Dominic, *The Modernist Short Story: A Study in Theory and Practice* (Cambridge: Cambridge University Press, 1992).
Hunter, Adrian, *The Cambridge Introduction to the Short Story in English* (Cambridge: Cambridge University Press, 2007).
James, Henry, *The Critical Muse: Selected Literary Criticism*, ed. Roger Gard (London: Penguin, 1987).
Joyce, James, *Dubliners* (London: Grafton, 1977).
— *Stephen Hero*, ed. Theodore Spencer, John J. Slocum and Herbert Cahoon (London: Paladin, 1991).
Kemp, Sandra, '"But how describe a world seen without a self?": Feminism, Fiction and Modernism', *Critical Quarterly*, 32.1: 99–118.
Kennedy, A. L., 'Small in a Way That a Bullet is Small', in Ailsa Cox (ed.), *The Short Story* (Newcastle upon Tyne: Cambridge Scholars Publishing, 2008), pp. 1–11.
Lee, Vernon, *Baldwin: Being Dialogues on Views and Aspirations* (London: T. Fisher Unwin, 1886).
Levenson, Michael H., *A Genealogy of Modernism: A Study of English Literary Doctrine 1908–1922* (Cambridge: Cambridge University Press, 1984).
Mann, Paul, *The Theory Death of the Avant-Garde* (Bloomington: Indiana University Press, 1991).
Mansfield, Katherine, *The Poetry and Critical Writings of Katherine Mansfield*, ed. Gerri Kimber and Angela Smith (Edinburgh: Edinburgh University Press, 2014).
Matz, Jesse, *Literary Impressionism and Modernist Aesthetics* (Cambridge: Cambridge University Press, 2001).
May, Charles E. (ed.), *The New Short Story Theories* (Athens: Ohio University Press, 2004).
Miller, J. Hillis, 'Heart of Darkness Revisited', in Ross C. Murfin (ed.), *Conrad Revisited: Essays for the Eighties* (Tuscaloosa: University of Alabama Press, 1985), pp. 31–50.
Nagel, James, *Stephen Crane and Literary Impressionism* (University Park: Pennsylvania State University Press, 1980).
Pater, Walter, 'Conclusion to *The Renaissance*', in *Essays on Literature and Art*, ed. Jennifer Uglow (London: Dent, 1973).
Pound, Ezra, *Gaudier-Brzeska: A Memoir* (New York: New Directions, 1970).
Richardson, Dorothy, *Journey to Paradise*, ed. Trudi Tate (London: Virago, 1989).
Ruskin, John, *Modern Painters*, ed. David Barrie (London: André Deutsch, 1987).
Saunders, Max 'Literary Impressionism', in David Bradshaw and Kevin J. H. Dettmar (eds), *A Companion to Modernist Literature and Culture* (Malden, MA and Oxford: Blackwell Publishing, 2006), pp. 204–11.

Shaw, Valerie, *The Short Story: A Critical Introduction* (Harlow: Longman, 1983).
Stowell, H. Peter, *Literary Impressionism, James and Chekhov* (Athens: University of Georgia Press, 1980).
Watt, Ian, *Conrad in the Nineteenth Century* (Berkeley: University of California Press, 1979).
Woolf, Virginia, *A Haunted House: The Complete Shorter Fiction*, ed. Susan Dick (London: Vintage, 2003).
— *The Crowded Dance of Modern Life*, ed. Rachel Bowlby (London: Penguin, 1993).
— *A Writer's Essays*, ed. Rachel Bowlby (London: Penguin, 1992).

4

Writers on the Short Story: 1950–present

Ailsa Cox

Looking back nostalgically on his early career, John Updike recalled a time when 'a young family that by 1960 included four children under six' could support a modest existence on the basis of short stories accepted by *The New Yorker*.[1] *The New Yorker* still pays handsomely, but it is one of the last remnants of the magazine culture that, as so many commentators have observed, sustained the careers of short story writers in the first half of the twentieth century. Such figures included V. S. Pritchett, who, in later life, proclaimed the short story 'one of the inextinguishable lost causes':[2]

> The periodicals on which the writer can rely have almost all vanished, driven out by expensive printing, by television and the hundred and one new diversions of an extravert and leisured society. Yet the annual number of volumes published is said to have increased and if the public is painfully small, it is also addicted.[3]

Pritchett's article, 'The Short Story', published in the small-circulation *London Magazine*, encapsulates the enduring relationship between economic vulnerability and status anxiety exhibited by short story writers in their comments on the form. From the post-war period to the present day, pronouncements about the death of the novel, the undermining of literary culture, or its atrophy, are not uncommon. The threat posed by television, in Pritchett's article, multiplies, and is finally dwarfed by the ubiquity of social media. But short story writing is conditioned by its marginality to a far greater degree than other literary genres. As Paul March-Russell notes, a dependence on magazine publication also generates a sense of the text's ephemerality, no matter how healthy the circulation figures.[4]

Pritchett's 'inextinguishable lost cause' suggests a quixotic attachment to failure which, in some writers, becomes an aesthetic strategy, as they appropriate the notion of the incomplete or the inexpressible. A self-consciousness about the choice of form perpetuates a constant re-examination of its attributes, usually in contrast with the novel, and a need to identify a canonical tradition as a context for the writer's own practice. These tendencies are all evident in Pritchett's 1966 article, and recur in the critical writings of his successors, published sometimes in essays and newspaper articles, and often in the introductions to anthologies. Pritchett and his contemporary, Frank O'Connor begin a conversation that continues up until this day, as practitioners negotiate a role for the short story in contemporary culture.

Pritchett's saviour, like Updike's, was *The New Yorker*, where he had secured a yearly payment in return for first refusal of his work in addition to the sums paid for each of the stories accepted. The contrast he draws between the short story's neglect in the UK and its comparative health in the US is another recurring theme, reiterated most recently in Philip Hensher's Introduction to *The Penguin Book of the British Short Story* (2015). Yet, even in the US, the perception of the short story as a threatened species is deeply entrenched. Writing in 2007, Richard Ford complains about the pressures on young writers to switch to the novel, and recalls the editor of *Esquire* magazine telling him he wouldn't bother with short stories at all, if he could find something cheaper to fill the space between advertisements.[5]

Pritchett's argument is that this endangered species is not only worthy of interest but is an elite form, uniquely challenging for its practitioner and rewarding for the reader:

> The great novels are, almost all, imperfect; indeed the 'perfect' ones become tedious; the very shortness of the short story is a protection here, but the real advantages are its varying mixture of the poetic, the reported and what is, essentially, the wit of the closed form; also its closeness (in some writers) to the perpetual, unconscious story-telling of people in real life.[6]

Because the short story is so highly condensed, any small weakness in the writing is disastrous, fatally undermining the entire text.

Pritchett ends his article with some faint optimism, his hope for some kind of synergy between television drama and the short story inspired by Granada Television's D. H. Lawrence adaptations. This series of sixteen short stories, broadcast between 1966 and 1967, seemed to suggest an appetite for the storyteller's art that might cross over into the new medium. Pritchett's belief that 'the short story is perfectly fitted to the glancing, allusive, nervously decisive and summary moods of contemporary life'[7] echoes both Edgar Allan Poe and Elizabeth Bowen in its alignment of the short story with a modern, fragmented sensibility. Referring, once again, to the more hospitable climate for short story writers in the US, he paraphrases Frank O'Connor: 'the form is more natural to anarchic societies, not to closely-knit ones like our own'.[8] His source is O'Connor's full-length study, *The Lonely Voice* (first published in New York in 1962, and in London in 1963), a systematic attempt to establish the generic specificity of the short story.

The Lonely Voice has retained its influence largely through the concept of the 'submerged population group',[9] marginalised characters who are the protagonists of the short story, a role they could never fulfil within the fixed social structures necessary for the novel. O'Connor is a provocative and a polemical writer, given to absolute statements based on his writerly instincts rather than any kind of scholastic apparatus. As his 1957 interview with *The Paris Review* reveals, his views on the novel are as definitive as those on short fiction.[10] Modernist novels such as *Ulysses* which take place in a single day are not novels at all, but long short stories; for O'Connor, a novel must unfold through an extended period of time, following standard conventions.

According to *The Lonely Voice*, both the novel and short fiction trace their origins to oral storytelling. But the emergence of a distinctive short story tradition is marked by Gogol's 'The Overcoat' (1842). What draws O'Connor's attention to this particular story is 'the first appearance in fiction of the Little Man . . . Everything about Akakey Akaeivitch, from his absurd name to his absurd job, is on the same level of mediocrity, and yet his absurdity is somehow transfigured by Gogol.'[11] There may be examples of 'the Little Man' in novels, as O'Connor himself admits; but his argument is based not only on the introduction of a new type of anti-hero, but also on the reader's ambivalent response.

The religious connotations of 'transfigured' are developed in O'Connor's close reading of a key passage in the story. Describing the routine bullying suffered by the clerk, Gogol suggests moments of self-reproach in one of his tormentors by evoking the phrase 'I am your brother'.[12] O'Connor consequently maps the discourse of the New Testament onto Gogol's text:

> What Gogol has done so boldly and brilliantly is to take the mock-heroic character, the absurd little copying clerk, and impose his image over that of the crucified Jesus, so that even while we laugh we are filled with horror at the resemblance.[13]

O'Connor is categorical in his insistence that 'this is something that the novel cannot do',[14] because a novel depends on the reader's ability to identify with its protagonist. The short story, on the other hand, is typically filled by a 'submerged population . . . outlawed figures wandering about the fringes of society, superimposed sometimes on symbolic figures whom they caricature and echo – Christ, Socrates, Moses'.[15]

O'Connor discusses the short story's historical prominence in the literatures of countries such as Russia, the US and Ireland, where cultures are contested. This aspect of O'Connor's thinking is easily transferred to the postcolonial context. O'Connor looks to South East Asia and the Caribbean for the future of the genre; and as Michael O'Sullivan points out, 'recent criticism would presumably rephrase this feature in terms of such notions as alterity and the subaltern'.[16] But the 'loneliness' that gives the book its title is primarily an existential solitude, as O'Connor's spiritual references imply – 'an intense awareness of human loneliness'.[17] The epigraph from Pascal in the paratext, quoted in French, 'the eternal silence of those infinite spaces terrifies me', refers to the essential horror of the human condition, the brevity of the individual lifespan in relation to the endless universe.

This existential loneliness informs tone and subject matter; it also shapes the short story's formal attributes. The author is 'lonely', in the sense that he or she stands outside formal tradition and is forced to constantly re-invent the genre, in the absence of the settled conventions O'Connor associates with the traditional novel:

> For the short-story writer there is no such thing as essential form. Because his frame of reference can never be the totality of a human life, he must be forever selecting the point at which he can approach it, and each selection he makes contains the possibility of a complete fiasco.[18]

Like many others seeking to distance the short story from the novel, O'Connor affirms a generic alignment with poetry, illustrating this argument with reference to Robert Browning's 'My Last Duchess' (1842): 'since a whole lifetime must be crowded into a few minutes, those minutes must be carefully chosen indeed and lit by an unearthly glow, one that enables us to distinguish present, past, and future as though they were all contemporaneous'.[19] In his view, the short story presents time as a continuum; it is for this reason that he is compelled to re-categorise modernist novels that engage with Bergsonian duration as essentially short stories in disguise. The difference between short stories and novels has nothing to do with length; 'it is a difference between pure and applied storytelling'.[20]

The Lonely Voice consists of a series of avowedly personal responses to the author's peers and predecessors. O'Connor's prejudices often make him seem dated, particularly his attitude to gender and sexuality. Almost all of the overviews of individual writers that make up the bulk of the volume are ambivalent, exposing deficiencies that may be as much spiritual as technical. The superficial certainties expressed by his theories are tempered by the suggestion that these ideas are provisional, subjective and playful.

The Lonely Voice lays the groundwork for almost all subsequent analyses of the short story conducted by practitioners. Some re-examine the book's central thesis. Others repeat the emphasis on the riskiness and artistry of short story writing. O'Connor's self-image as a freewheeling intellectual maverick, keeping a distance from the academic establishment, is also shared by many of his successors in a period when short story writing is increasingly embedded in the university. O'Connor's epilogue, reflecting on his experiences teaching Creative Writing, is a sign of what is to come. The rapid expansion of Creative Writing programmes in the late twentieth and early twenty-first century has changed the relationship between short story writing, publishing and reading. It has also increased short story writers' self-consciousness about their choice of form to an even great extent than in the time when O'Connor was writing his seminal study.

Mark McGurl's *The Program Era: Postwar Fiction and the Rise of Creative Writing* (2009, reprinted 2011) examines the synergy that has developed between the individual writer, universities and literary culture in the US since the emergence of the discipline in the mid-twentieth century. In the US, and in the anglophone world generally, there are now very few universities that do not offer an MA or MFA in Creative Writing, most also offering opportunities to study at undergraduate and PhD level. As McGurl himself observes, the effects on short fiction are especially pronounced. The short story adapts itself to the workshop method more readily than full-length fiction for the obvious reason that a student is able to complete an entire first draft, present it for discussion, polish the text, and submit for assessment within the tightly organised academic cycle.

For some emerging writers, the short story serves as a showcase for talents that, in the long term, are invested in the novel. Short stories provide an initial route to publication, perhaps through one of the many literary journals linked to universities, especially in the US. But others remain committed to short fiction throughout their careers, attracted by its potential for experiment and technical innovation. For these individuals, university teaching will subsidise the habit. Even those who seem to reject 'the cold, suffocating hands of the American writing-program industry'[21] cannot help but feed that industry, writing for a readership largely generated by its activities. Creative Writing, as a discipline, encourages writers to be self-reflexive; the critical writings of practitioners in McGurl's 'program era' reveal their individual process and poetics to a greater extent than their predecessors.

If, as Andrew Levy suggests, Edgar Allan Poe is 'the patron saint and the neighborhood bully of the American short story',[22] then Raymond Carver is the patron saint of the short fiction workshop, and a 'bully' in the sense that his influence pervades the classroom. His thinking can be placed in a direct line of succession to O'Connor and Pritchett, particularly in their reverence for Chekhov as the pre-eminent figure in the short story canon. All three are cited as major creative influences in the foreword to *Where I'm Calling From*, the volume of his selected stories, published in the year of his death. Here Carver writes:

> I love the swift leap of a good story, the excitement that often commences in the first sentence, the sense of beauty and mystery found in the best of them: and the fact – so crucially important to me at the beginning and even now a consideration – that the story can be written and read in one sitting.[23]

But according to his essay, 'Fires', first published earlier in the 1980s, literary influences, including those of his teacher, John Gardner, and his editor, Gordon Lish, are outweighed by 'the greatest single influence on my life, and on my writing, directly and indirectly', the fact of parenthood.[24] The practical advantages of condensed forms of writing, alluded to in the foreword, drive his choice of genre, and ultimately generate a poetics of short fiction, developed in dialogue with his peers and predecessors.

In 'Fires', Carver recalls a hand-to-mouth existence in his early years, and, in particular, an epiphanic moment, waiting for a dryer at the laundromat:

> At that moment I felt – I knew – that the life I was in was vastly different to the lives of the writers I most admired. I understood writers to be people who didn't spend their Saturdays at the laundromat and every waking hour subject to the needs and caprices of their children.[25]

These constraints restrict Carver to abbreviated forms such as poetry and short fiction, a choice that becomes an aesthetic preference when those conditions no longer apply. The reference to a single sitting in the foreword is, however, slightly misleading. Carver's oft-quoted mantra, 'Get in, get out. Don't linger. Go on',[26] belies the slow precision of the compositional process. A first draft is dashed out in short bursts, but a lengthier period of revision has to follow before the story is finally completed:

> I had great patience with a piece of work after I'd done the initial writing. I'd keep something around the house for what seemed like a very long time, fooling with it, changing this, adding that, cutting out something else.[27]

When Carver says that 'to write a novel, it seems to me, a writer should be living in a world that makes sense, a world that the writer can believe in, draw a bead on, and then write about accurately',[28] he is remembering the instability of his own lifestyle. But his comments also suggest a wider affinity between the short story and postmodern fragmentation. Carver's belief that a novelist needs to reflect 'the essential correctness' of a settled universe[29] echoes O'Connor's contrast between the secure world of the novel and the marginal territory that belongs to short fiction. The dedication to stylistic precision recalls both O'Connor's and Pritchett's comments on the unforgiving nature of the form.

Carver explains his stylistic preferences more fully in the essay 'On Writing', remarking that 'the words can be so precise that they may even sound flat, but they can still carry, if used right, they can hit all the notes'.[30] In this essay he refers again to Pritchett, quoting his definition of a short story as 'something glimpsed from the corner of the eye, in passing'.[31] By engaging with the half-concealed or fractured, Carver is not merely coping with the 'position of unrelieved responsibility and permanent distraction' that he blames on parenthood, but incorporating his existential predicament into an aesthetic that continues long after his practical personal circumstances have improved.

As Joyce Carol Oates points out, the term 'minimalism', now generally applied to writers such as Carver, Richard Ford and Bobbie Ann Mason, who specialise in pared down prose and are sparing in descriptive detail, is problematic; 'even to classify them as "realists" is reductive and misleading'.[32] The aversion Carver expresses towards experimental writing derives from a feeling that it is emotionally disengaging. In the foreword to *Where I'm Calling From*, he says that in his own fiction his aim has always been to:

> line up the right words, the precise images, as well as the correct and exact punctuation so that the reader got pulled in and involved in the story and wouldn't be able to turn his eyes from the text unless the house caught fire.[33]

He even suggests that completing the story induces physiological changes in both writer and reader: 'then breathing evenly and steadily once more, we'll collect ourselves, writers and readers alike, get up, "created of warm blood and nerves", as a Chekhov character puts it, and go on to the next thing: Life. Always Life'.[34]

Like other literary labels, 'minimalism' is not a term that many writers feel comfortable with, but it has become a shorthand term for many who might be situated more accurately within the Chekhovian tradition. Amongst them is Alice Munro, rarely classified as a minimalist and sometimes contrasted with Carver. Munro's reflections on her own practice are less extensive than his, tending to be contained in the fiction itself, or in interviews, but she also places the concrete and observable at the core of her writing: 'This ordinary place is sufficient, everything here touchable and mysterious.'[35] She also exploits the elliptical properties of the form – as Carver puts it, 'the things that are left out, that are implied, the landscape just under the smooth (but sometimes broken and unsettled) surface of things'.[36] Both Carver and Munro acknowledge an insufficiency in language, a tension between the scrupulous transmission of experience and that project's ultimate failure.

Amongst US writers, Richard Ford perpetuates the line of influence from Chekhov, O'Connor, Pritchett and Carver, but also interrogates that heritage and acknowledges parallel developments in American fiction. Ford begins his introduction to *The Granta Book of the American Short Story* (1993) by fondly lampooning *The Lonely Voice*, and especially O'Connor's view 'that stories are natively romantic, individualistic and intransigent; and that America is a brutal place full of dislocated people who sometimes fool you and act nice, thereby making the US a natural place for short stories to flourish'.[37] Ford argues that O'Connor's concept of the short story, limited by his faith in the 'mimetic-realist unites', was outdated within a few years of his study. A new generation of postmodern short story writers challenged that concept, regarding texts as 'narrative *objets* with arbitrary, sometimes ironically-assigned references, palpable shapes, audible sounds, rhythms – all of whose intricacies and ironies produced aesthetic as well as ordinary cognitive pleasure'.[38]

Ford refers to the 1971 volume *Anti-Story: An Anthology of Experimental Fiction*, which juxtaposes texts by US writers, including Robert Coover and Donald Barthelme with metafictions from Jorge Luis Borges, Nathalie Sarraute, Julio Cortazar and others. The introduction by Philip Stevick contrasts the innovations of the modernist short story with the atrophied 'self-imitative' fiction currently produced in the US,[39] claiming that it is the long form that now represents innovation. The purpose of his anthology is an attempt to reclaim the short form for the avant-garde.

In the 1993 introduction, Ford seeks to reconcile the polarities represented by *The Lonely Voice* and *Anti-Story*, blaming this schism on a tendency amongst Creative Writing teachers to regard their preferences as the model for their disciples, at the expense of the form's inherent fluidity. The legacy of these battles is, in his view, 'a feeling of unsettlement among writers as well as a preoccupation with invigorating the story's form as a way of creating effects in stories which would transcend form altogether'.[40]

Fifteen years later, the introduction to *The New Granta Book of the American Short Story* is equally disparaging towards Creative Writing programmes, but is less defensive, and less tentative in its observations on the form. Short stories are 'the high-wire act of literature, the man keeping all those pretty plates up and spinning on skinny sticks'.[41] In both introductions, Ford repeats the claim made by O'Connor and Pritchett that the stakes are higher in short story writing than in any other type of fiction:

> A novel with a defective structure, a wrong opening movement, a dead end, or a fractured end part can still be novel and may – on balance – be good (think of *Tender is the Night, The Sound and the Fury, The Sheltering Sky*). But if a short story suffers these aesthetic flaws, it risks being nothing at all. A minor aesthetic nullity.[42]

Ford stresses the high degree of artifice and stylisation called for in short story writing. He implies that, like the circus performance, this 'high-wire act' deceives the eye: because brevity forces omission, short stories 'succeed by willfully falsifying many of the observable qualities of the lived life they draw upon'.[43]

In this introduction, 'post 9/11, post-Katrina, mid-George-Bush-11, mid-Gulf war 11, mid-oil crisis, early-eco disaster', 'all imaginative writing feels experimental'.[44] The literary battles of the 1960s and 1970s become irrelevant in an age when the readership for literary fiction is dwindling, and '"the news" in all its compromised forms and conveyances threatens to become our modern novel, and when our high-speed sensation of event occurs faster than we can transact it imaginatively'.[45]

Ford resists applying abstract or totalising theories to the fluid and pragmatic practice of writing. But in this introduction, he concentrates on the generic characteristics of short fiction to a greater degree than in 1993, exploring a delicate balance between authorial design and happenstance. He introduces the term 'election' to describe the precise linguistic choices a writer must make in the exercise of authority over the reader:

This power drawn from good election is part of the story's potent capacity to command our attention and assure us that while there's blessedly, dismayingly, more to life than we can ever say ... it is specifically by these choices that something crucial within life is illumined as nowhere else and put on radiant, consequential display.[46]

Although Ford is more open to formal experimentation than Carver, they share a very similar aesthetic, particularly in the emphasis on stylistic precision. Ford's phrase 'radiant, consequential display' recalls the imagery of illumination in Carver's critical work (and, indeed, in the fiction), with its evocation of the epiphanic and its appeal to an elusive and boundless reality called 'life'. The sometimes contentious dialogue between the so-called 'minimalists', their predecessors, their opponents and their peers continues to this day.

Nadine Gordimer's essay, 'The Flash of Fireflies', based on a lecture she gave at an American short story symposium in 1968, celebrates the survival of the short story at a time when the novel is increasingly supplanted by film and television. In her view, novelists struggle to represent heterogeneity; 'each of us has a thousand lives and the novelist gives a character only one'.[47] But 'short story writers see by the light of the flash; theirs is the art of the only thing one can be sure of – the present moment'.[48] By isolating a discrete moment, the short story is able to engage with a complex contemporary reality. Gordimer's remarks suggest the modernist affinity with transient moods and epiphanic insights, but she also refers to a postmodern breakdown of certainties:

The short story as a form and as a kind of creative vision must be better equipped to attempt the capture of ultimate reality at a time when ... we are drawing nearer to the mystery of life or are losing ourselves in a bellowing wilderness of mirrors, as the nature of that reality becomes more fully understood or more bewilderingly concealed by the discoveries of science and the proliferation of communication media outside the printed word.[49]

Undistracted by the ongoing campus squabbles between the minimalist and postmodern tendencies, Gordimer's essay places all varieties of contemporary short fiction within a continuum. She does, however, place special emphasis on the fantastic. The fantastic, she argues, is more easily accommodated within the short form than the novel because of an inherent self-sufficiency; there is no need to sustain or develop the world it contains. While she sees no existing art forms are entirely adequate – 'our age is threshing about desperately for a way out of human isolation'[50] – she is much more positive in her assessment of the short story's cultural and economic standing than Pritchett. Gordimer points out, for instance, that short stories can be republished several times, a good investment for writers who are frequently anthologised.

Raymond Carver's exact contemporary, Joyce Carol Oates addresses generic specificity more directly in her essay 'Beginnings: "The Origins and Art of the Short Story"': 'Formal definitions of the short story are commonplace, yet there is none quite democratic enough to accommodate an art that includes so much variety and lends itself so readily to experimentation and idiosyncratic voices.'[51] She concludes that the simplest, least prescriptive definition is: 'that it represents a concentration of the imagination, and not an expansion; it is no more than 10,000 words; and, no matter its mysteries of experimental properties, it achieves closure – meaning that, when it ends, the attentive reader understands why'.[52]

Oates was herself included in Stevick's 1971 *Anti-Story* anthology (in fact she was the only female contributor from the US), but in her later writing she reveals no ideological bias towards one style over another. Other writers take a less sanguine approach, especially when focusing on contemporary writing in the US, attacking a predominantly 'minimalist' orthodoxy promulgated by Creative Writing programmes. In an article written for the *New York Times Book Review* in 1988, the Indian-born writer Bharati Mukherjee argues that 'Minimalism is nativist, it speaks in whispers to the initiated. As a newcomer, I can feel its chill, as though it were designed to keep out anyone with too much story to tell.'[53]

An immigrant to the US, Mukherjee has resisted being categorised as an Indian writer, expressing much disdain towards postcolonial concepts of subalternity that are often applied to her fiction. A product of the Iowa Writers' Workshop, Mukherjee insists on her identity as 'an American writer, in the American mainstream, trying to extend it'.[54] In her essay 'A Four-Hundred-Year-Old Woman', she takes Moghul miniature painting as her aesthetic model, 'with its crazy foreshortening of vanishing point, its insistence that everything happens simultaneously, bound only by shape and color'.[55] In contrast to the starkness and temporal unity that is the minimalist ideal, this type of writing would embrace excess, juxtaposing personal experience with oral tradition.

Mark McGurl's critical study of the 'Program Era' provides an invaluable analysis of minimalist tendencies and its opponents, including Mukherjee. He relates this aesthetic to a growth in mass higher education, coining the term 'lower-middle-class modernism' to describe literature produced 'in and around the scene of creative writing instruction in the postwar period, which formalises and textualises the modern "life story" in and as the production of self-reflexive fictions'.[56] He links the discourse of painstaking stylistic precision to nostalgia for artisanal labour, made extinct in a post-industrial society:

> the prideful attention to 'craft' associated with literary minimalism can also be understood as the utopian return of unalienated labor in an economic order characterised by a large increase in jobs that are 'white collar' in standard social definition but no less 'alienated' – and often worse paid and less secure – than the unionised blue-collar jobs of the past.[57]

The discourse of 'craft' evokes white male values that may be seen as narrow and exclusive to those who choose not to identify with that tradition. In her introduction to the *The Best American Short Stories 1999*, the Chinese-American Amy Tan evokes a sense of alienation from the short stories she was encouraged to read as a beginner writer: 'The stories concerned ordinary people doing ordinary things with just a bit of inner unease, and an omniscient narrator who provided the precise details that proved their lives were moving at glacial speed.'[58] Unlike Mukherjee, she does not relate her sense of ennui to ethnicity, but she does seem to be trying to break away from a cramped, claustrophobic aesthetic in favour of a more expansive style with 'a distinctive voice that tells a story only that voice can tell'.[59]

Writing in *The New Yorker* in 2014, Junot Diaz is more confrontational than either Tan or Mukherjee in his assertion that the Creative Writing MFA (in his case at Cornell in the 1990s) perpetuates white cultural values:

> The plurality of students and faculty had been educated exclusively in the tradition of writers like William Gaddis, Francine Prose, or Alice Munro – and not at all in the traditions of Toni Morrison, Cherrie Moraga, Maxine Hong-Kingston, Arundhati Roy, Edwidge Danticat, Alice Walker, or Jamaica Kincaid.[60]

Many anthologies articulate or interrogate national tradition. The selections in *The Penguin Book of Caribbean Short Stories* (1996), edited by E. A. Markham, are divided into two sections, one dedicated to re-workings of folk tales, and the other, much larger in proportion, consisting of wholly original stories. Markham's introduction promotes the global significance of short story writing from the Caribbean, a lineage overlooked because so many of its practitioners, from Jean Rhys to Olive Senior and Jamaica Kincaid, have been expatriates. He advocates a more inclusive and more female canon, one which can accommodate the fantastic, whether as traditional tale or postmodern experiment, observing that: 'the anthology, itself, is an artefact, a modernist text with its great theme, large structure, its chaotic-seeming detail and (perhaps) an underlying sense of portentousness'.[61]

Several other writers also use the anthology to challenge current assumptions. Anne Enright's introduction to *The Granta Book of the Irish Short Story* (2011) is a playful interrogation of the need for unitary theories, whether they concern generic or national identity: 'The short story is, for me, a natural form, as difficult and as easy to talk about as, say, walking. Do we need a theory about going for a walk? About one foot in front of the other? Probably, yes.'[62] Quoting Carver and Flannery O'Connor, Enright privileges intuition over self-analysis. Like Richard Ford, she challenges the sweeping assertions made in *The Lonely Voice*:

> Are all short stories, Russian, French, American, Irish, in fact about loneliness? I am not sure. This may be part of writers' nonsense about themselves, or O'Connor's nonsense about being Irish, or it may just be the general nonsense of being alive.[63]

Nonetheless she is not altogether dismissive of O'Connor, especially in the Irish context. His theories 'place the short story as the genre of the cusp between tradition and modernity',[64] as a predominantly oral culture collides with literary modernism. She also makes the intriguing suggestion that 'much of what is written about the short story form is actually anxiety about the unknowability of the novel' just as 'much of what is written about Irish writing is, in fact, anxiety about England. Sometimes, indeed, the terms "England" and "the novel" seem almost interchangeable'.[65]

National and generic characteristics are also intertwined in Philip Hensher's two-volume *The Penguin Book of the British Short Story* (2015). Hensher's introduction makes it clear from the beginning that 'Britishness is slippery and debatable, as indeed the British short story often is.'[66] Most introductions to anthologies work their way through the contents, commenting on the individual stories and making connections or contrasts. Hensher is unusual in the amount of attention he pays to writers whose work is not included, whether for reasons of space or as a deliberate policy. The introduction makes a strong case for a uniquely British strand in short story writing, but it also demonstrates the impossibility of the fixed canon, and of taxonomical classifications, whether applied to national or generic characteristics. He includes, for instance, the Irish-born Elizabeth Bowen (who is also in Enright's anthology) but excludes the New Zealander Katherine Mansfield.

Hensher challenges theories derived from Poe's concepts of artistic unity. Many of the anthology's earliest selections, from Fielding, Swift and Poe, would not normally be regarded as short stories at all, but Hensher would argue that these sketches and essays are essential precursors of contemporary short fiction. According to Hensher, the British short story is marked by the playful, the comic and the macabre, forming a tradition which, thanks to a post-imperial fear of jingoism, has been seriously undervalued. Like Pritchett, he yokes the fortunes of the short story in the UK to the disappearance of the magazines, and paltry rates of pay, which are compared to the more generous American market. There are other implications in the decline of the magazine market, besides the financial. Hensher regrets the absence of topicality in contemporary writing, a journalistic capacity to respond quickly to current events. Instead the British market is dominated by competitions which reward 'present tense solitary reflections, often with characters lying on their beds affectlessly pondering; major historical events were considered gravely; social media . . . dutifully brought in to indicate an eye on the contemporary without disturbing the safely solitary nature of the character'.[67]

Writing on the short story continues to be haunted by a never-ending quest for generic definition in contradistinction to the novel. Frank O'Connor and Nadine Gordimer liken short fiction to poetry, a comparison made by many other writers, including Amy Tan, Sarah Hall, A. L. Kennedy and William Boyd. In an article written for *The Guardian* newspaper, Boyd proposes seven categories of story – the event-plot story, the Chekhovian story, the modernist story, the cryptic-ludic story, the mini-novel story, the poetic/mythic story and the biographical story – but even as he explains this taxonomy, they overlap, and their purpose is obscure. Boyd does, however, challenge the assumption, made by many promoting the short story, that abbreviated forms are naturally suited to an attenuated mass culture, catering to short attention spans:

> The well-written short story is not suited to the soundbite culture: it's too dense, its effects are too complex for easy digestion. If the zeitgeist is influencing this taste then it may be a sign that we are coming to prefer our art in highly concentrated form. Like a multivitamin pill, a good short story can provide a compressed blast of discerning, intellectual pleasure, one no less intense than that delivered by a novel, despite the shorter duration of its consumption.[68]

Boyd is unapologetic about the demands short story reading makes on the reader. Sarah Hall's article, published nine years later in the same newspaper, goes still further, by acknowledging that the 'strong meat' of the short story will inevitably be a minority taste:

> Often the experience is exquisitely unsettling; one might feel like a voyeur suddenly looming at the window of an intimate scene. At first glance normal-seeming events are taking place, but mundanity gives way to the peculiar, the perilous, the

capricious. Short stories are manifestations, their own literary phenomena. Mostly there is no explanatory narrative ramp or roof, there are no stabilisers giving support over scary subject matter – sex and death, classically – and there are no solvent, tonic or consoling endings. The reader is left to decide what everything might mean, and in this way the form is inordinately respectful. Some might want such a reading experience infrequently, some every day, many never.[69]

In writing about the short story, its practitioners frequently resort to metaphor: Boyd's 'multivitamin pill', Hall's 'strong meat' and 'stabilisers' (the latter evoking not only architectural analogies, but a child learning to ride a bicycle). Alarmingly, Boyd also likens the short story to a 'daisycutter bomb';[70] in another military analogy, A. L. Kennedy says the short story is 'small in a way that a bullet is small'.[71] The image is repeated in a later blog posting; in the same entry she compares the short story to 'holding your empty hand until it's satisfactorily and strangely filled with your granny's cameo and the powder-sweet scent of her long-gone lipstick'.[72] In 'The Craft of the Short Story', Clark Blaise gives us a 'canary in a mineshaft', then uses the double metaphor of 'a transparent membrane ... like a jellyfish, like an IMac',[73] before concluding his essay with one implosive metaphor: 'Stories are like smashed atoms, and the tracing in nanoseconds of an evidence that something was there, but it disappeared in the very act of discovering or describing it. Schrödinger's Cat; Heisenberg's Uncertainty.'[74]

These self-parodying metaphorical definitions reach their apogee in Ali Smith's metafictions. Her 'True Short Story' challenges remarks made at the launch of a National Short Story Prize in the UK, comparing the 'capacious old whore' of the novel with the 'nimble goddess' that is the short story.[75] Smith changes 'goddess' to 'nymph', paraphrasing a number of writers and critics, including Elizabeth Bowen, Nadine Gordimer, Ernest Hemingway and Alice Munro, in the search for definition. However, the text's polyphonic structure and its own hybridity, fusing autobiography, fiction and the essay, problematise the very notion of a fixed definition. Alluding to the myth of Echo and Narcissus, Smith's closing lines suggest an infinity of voices at play: 'So when is a short story like a nymph? When the echo of it answers back.'[76] 'True Short Story' ends with a riddle; Smith's foreword to *British Women Short Story Writers: The New Woman to Now* (2015) starts with a joke: 'A short story walked into a bar.'[77] The conceit expands into a parodic fable:

> The barmaid looked apologetic.
>   Ah. I'm sorry, she said. We don't serve stories here.
>   What about them, then? the short story said and nodded towards a group of inebriated-looking novels, some thick, some thin, carousing round a table covered in emptied glasses, the sides of the glasses laced with the realist foam of the beer they'd been drinking.[78]

As in 'True Short Story', Smith aligns short fiction with that which is perceived as feminine and marginal, and therefore subversive, evading the logocentric drive to classify and contain. Her fable ends with the barmaid joining the short story outside the pub, where children are playing football on the grass despite the signs ordering 'NO BALL GAMES. NO DOGS'.[79] Her closing lines, evoking the moon, the scent of jasmine and the glow of streetlamps, is almost a pastiche of Katherine Mansfield, a figure she returns to in her essay collection, *Artful* (2013). Prefacing her comments with a brief quotation from Mansfield's 'At the Bay' (1922), Smith argues that the short story's distinguishing characteristic is brevity as temporal experience, rather than simple word length: 'Because of this, the short story can do anything it likes with notions of time; it moves and works spatially regardless of whether it adheres to chronology or conventional plot. It is an elastic form; it can be as imagistic and achronological as it likes and it will still hold its form.'[80]

Smith's comments liberate the short story from the constrictions of generic definitions that, however well-intentioned, ultimately suggest its limitations. Her understanding of the short story's engagement with temporality owes something to the modernist inheritance but also accommodates the plot-driven tale. Above all, she reclaims the short story for women writers, whose contribution to its development has often been overshadowed by male progenitors. Frank O'Connor's *The Lonely Voice* is notoriously dismissive towards Mansfield, despite his admiration for some of her New Zealand-based stories. But for Smith, Mansfield encapsulates the short story's engagement with brevity, in the textual strategies she used in her fiction and the sensibility that informed them.

While the search for generic definition continues, there are signs that it is losing its relevance to contemporary culture. In her introduction to *The Best American Short Stories 2014*, Jennifer Egan proclaims: 'I don't care very much about genre, either as a reader or as a writer. To me, fiction writing at any length, in any form, is a feat of radical compression.'[81] While this compression might be more pronounced in short fiction than the novel, any further distinctions are irrelevant. Egan is much more interested in the historical ability of all forms of fiction to engage with technological change. The precedents she gives here include eighteenth-century epistolary novels alongside James Joyce's interest in the cinema. More recently, literary transmission itself has been affected by technological innovation; she notes that even the term 'printed' feels anachronistic in the age of the smartphone.[82]

Yet Egan focuses on the psychic effects of the new media, rather than any formal repercussions of these new means of transmission: 'the commingling of online with actual experience; the disappearance of a certain kind of solitude; the illusion of safety that goes along with being in touch; surveillance as a fact of everyday life; the gulf between those who are technologically connected and those still isolated'.[83] Egan's 'disappearance of a certain kind of solitude' raises interesting questions for students of *The Lonely Voice*. Short story writers will no doubt continue in O'Connor's footsteps, searching for essential definitions that can only be expressed in metaphor. But for many, including Smith, Kennedy and Egan, the pleasure of writing short fiction lies in the creative freedom to roam beyond generic boundaries.

Notes

1. John Updike, 'Foreword', *The Early Short Stories, 1953–1975* (London: Hamish Hamilton, 2004), p. x.
2. V. S. Pritchett, 'The Short Story', *London Magazine*, 6.6 (1966): 6.
3. Ibid.
4. Paul March-Russell, *The Short Story: An Introduction* (Edinburgh: Edinburgh University Press, 2009), p. 43.

5. Richard Ford, 'Introduction', in Richard Ford (ed.), *The New Granta Book of the American Short Story* (London: Granta Books, 2007), pp. viii–ix.
6. Pritchett, 'The Short Story', p. 7.
7. Ibid.
8. Ibid. p. 8.
9. Frank O'Connor, *The Lonely Voice: A Study of the Short Story* (London: Macmillan, 1963), p. 18.
10. Anthony Whittier, 'Frank O'Connor, The Art of Fiction No. 19'. Available at <http://www.theparisreview.org/interviews/4847/the-art-of-fiction-no-19-frank-oconnor> (last accessed 15 April 2018).
11. O'Connor, *The Lonely Voice*, p. 15.
12. Ibid. p. 16.
13. Ibid.
14. Ibid.
15. Ibid. p. 19.
16. Michael O'Sullivan, 'Loneliness and the Submerged Population: Frank O'Connor's *The Lonely Voice* and Joyce's "The Dead"', in Elke D'hoker and Stephanie Eggermont (eds), *The Irish Short Story: Tradition and Trends* (Bern: Peter Lang, 2015), p. 105.
17. O'Connor, *The Lonely Voice*, p. 19.
18. Ibid. p. 21.
19. Ibid. p. 22.
20. Ibid. p. 27.
21. Ford, 'Introduction' (2007), p. xxi.
22. Andrew Levy, *The Culture and Commerce of the American Short Story* (Cambridge: Cambridge University Press, 1993), p. 10.
23. Raymond Carver, 'Author's Foreword', in *Where I'm Calling from: The Selected Stories* (London: Harvill, 1998), p. xi.
24. Raymond Carver, *Fires* (London: Harvill, 1994), p. 31.
25. Ibid. p. 33.
26. Ibid. p. 22.
27. Ibid. p. 36.
28. Ibid. p. 35.
29. Ibid.
30. Ibid. p. 27.
31. Ibid. p. 26.
32. Joyce Carol Oates, 'Introduction', in Joyce Carol Oates (ed.), *The Oxford Book of American Short Stories* (Oxford: Oxford University Press, 1992), p. 6.
33. Carver, 'Author's Foreword', p. xii.
34. Ibid. p. xiv.
35. Alice Munro, 'Everything Here is Touchable and Mysterious', *Weekend Magazine, Toronto Star*, 11 May 1974, p. 33.
36. Carver, *Fires*, p. 26.
37. Richard Ford, 'Introduction', in Richard Ford (ed.), *The Granta Book of the American Short Story* (London: Granta Books, 1993), pp. viii–ix.
38. Ibid. p. viii.
39. Philip Stevick, 'Introduction', in Philip Stevick (ed.), *Anti-Story: An Anthology of Experimental Fiction* (New York: The Free Press, 1971), p. xii.
40. Ford, 'Introduction' (1993), p. xi.
41. Ford, 'Introduction' (2007), p. vii.
42. Ibid. p. viii.
43. Ibid. p. vii.

44. Ibid. p. xxiii.
45. Ibid.
46. Ford, 'Introduction' (2007), p. xviii.
47. Nadine Gordimer, 'The Flash of Fireflies', in Charles E. May (ed.), *The New Short Story Theories* (Athens: Ohio University Press, 1994), p. 264.
48. Ibid.
49. Ibid.
50. Gordimer, 'Flash of Fireflies', p. 266.
51. Joyce Carol Oates, 'Beginnings: "The Origins and Art of the Short Story"', in Barbara Lounsberry, Susan Lohafer, Mary Rohrberger, Stephen Pett and R. C. Feddersen (eds), *The Tales We Tell: Perspectives on the Short Story* (Westport, CT: Greenwood Press, 1998), p. 47.
52. Ibid.
53. Bharati Mukherjee, 'Immigrant Writing: Give Us Your Maximalists!', *New York Times Book Review*, 28 August 1988, p. 28.
54. Bharati Mukherjee, 'A Four-Hundred-Year-Old Woman', in Janet Sternburg (ed.), *The Writer on Her Work* (London: Virago, 1992), p. 53.
55. Ibid. p. 56.
56. Mark McGurl, *The Program Era: Postwar Fiction and the Rise of Creative Writing* (Cambridge, MA: Harvard University Press, 2011), p. 286.
57. Ibid. pp. 296–7.
58. Amy Tan, 'Introduction', in Amy Tan with Katrina Kenison (eds), *The Best American Short Stories 1999* (New York: Houghton Mifflin, 1999), pp. xxi–xxii.
59. Ibid. p. xxvii.
60. Junot Diaz, 'MFA vs. POC', *The New Yorker*, 30 April 2014. Available at <http://www.newyorker.com/books/page-turner/mfa-vs-poc> (last accessed 15 April 2018).
61. E. A. Markham, 'Introduction', in E. A. Markham (ed.), *The Penguin Book of Caribbean Short Stories* (London: Penguin, 1996), p. xxxii.
62. Anne Enright, 'Introduction', in Anne Enright (ed.), *The Granta Book of the Irish Short Story* (London: Granta Books, 2011), p. ix.
63. Ibid. p. xv.
64. Ibid. p. xii.
65. Ibid. p. xiii.
66. Philip Hensher, 'General Introduction', in Philip Hensher (ed.), *The Penguin Book of the British Short Story*, Vol. 1 (London: Penguin, 2015), p. xi.
67. Ibid. p. xxv.
68. William Boyd, 'Brief Encounters', *The Guardian*, 2 October 2004. Available at <http://www.theguardian.com/books/2004/oct/02/featuresreviews.guardianreview38> (last accessed 15 April 2018).
69. Sarah Hall, 'Sarah Hall on Why we Should have a Short Story Laureate', *The Guardian*, 11 October 2013. Available at <http://www.theguardian.com/books/2013/oct/11/sarah-hall-short-story-laureate> (last accessed 15 April 2018).
70. Boyd, 'Brief Encounters'.
71. A. L. Kennedy, 'Small in a Way that a Bullet is Small', in Ailsa Cox (ed.), *The Short Story* (Newcastle upon Tyne: Cambridge Scholars Publishing, 2008), p. 3.
72. A. L. Kennedy, *On Writing* (London: Vintage Books, 2014), p. 62.
73. Clark Blaise, 'The Craft of the Short Story', in John Metcalf and J. R. (Tim) Struthers (eds), *Selected Essays* (Windsor, ON: Biblioasis, 2008), p. 189.
74. Ibid. p. 190
75. Michelle Pauli, 'Short Story Scores with New Prize and Amazon Project', *The Guardian*, 23 August 2005. Available at <http://www.theguardian.com/books/2005/aug/23/news.michellepauli> (last accessed 15 April 2018).

76. Ali Smith, 'True Short Story', in *The First Person and Other Stories* (London: Penguin, 2009), p. 17.
77. Ali Smith, 'Foreword', in Emma Young and James Bailey (eds), *British Women Short Story Writers: The New Woman to Now* (Edinburgh: Edinburgh University Press, 2015), p. viii.
78. Ibid.
79. Smith, 'Foreword', p. x.
80. Ali Smith, *Artful* (London: Penguin, 2013), p. 29.
81. Jennifer Egan, 'Introduction', in Jennifer Egan with Heidi Pitlor (eds), *The Best American Short Stories 2014* (Boston, MA: Houghton Mifflin, 2014), p. xiv.
82. Egan, 'Introduction', p. xix.
83. Ibid.

Bibliography

Blaise, Clark 'The Craft of the Short Story', in John Metcalf and J. R. (Tim) Struthers (eds.), *Selected Essays* (Windsor, ON: Biblioasis, 2008), pp. 181–90.

Boyd, William, 'Brief Encounters', *The Guardian*, 2 October 2004, <http://www.theguardian.com/books/2004/oct/02/featuresreviews.guardianreview38> (last accessed 15 April 2018).

Carver, Raymond, *Fires* (London: Harvill, 1994).

— 'Author's Foreword', in *Where I'm Calling from: The Selected Stories* (London: Harvill, 1998), pp. xi–xiv.

Diaz, Junot, 'MFA vs. POC', *The New Yorker*, 30 April 2014, <http://www.newyorker.com/books/page-turner/mfa-vs-poc> (last accessed 15 April 2018).

Egan, Jennifer, 'Introduction', in Jennifer Egan with Heidi Pitlor (eds), *The Best American Short Stories 2014* (Boston, MA: Houghton Mifflin, 2014), pp. xii–xix.

Enright, Anne, 'Introduction', in Anne Enright (ed.), *The Granta Book of the Irish Short Story* (London: Granta Books, 2011), pp. ix–xviii.

Ford, Richard, 'Introduction', in Richard Ford (ed.), *The Granta Book of the American Short Story* (London: Granta Books, 1993), pp. vii–xxii.

— 'Introduction', in Richard Ford (ed.), *The New Granta Book of the American Short Story* (London: Granta Books, 2007), pp. vii–xxvi.

Gordimer, Nadine, 'The Flash of Fireflies', in Charles E. May (ed.), *The New Short Story Theories* (Athens: Ohio University Press, 1994), pp. 263–7.

Hall, Sarah, 'Sarah Hall on Why we Should have a Short Story Laureate', *The Guardian*, 11 October 2013, <http://www.theguardian.com/books/2013/oct/11/sarah-hall-short-story-laureate> (last accessed 15 April 2018).

Hensher, Philip, 'General Introduction', in Philip Hensher (ed.), *The Penguin Book of the British Short Story*, Vol. 1 (London: Penguin, 2015), pp. xi–xxxvi.

Kennedy, A. L. *On Writing* (London: Vintage Books, 2014).

— 'Small in a Way that a Bullet is Small', in Ailsa Cox (ed.) *The Short Story* (Newcastle upon Tyne: Cambridge Scholars Publishing, 2008), pp. 1–11.

Levy, Andrew, *The Culture and Commerce of the American Short Story* (Cambridge: Cambridge University Press, 1993).

McGurl, Mark, *The Program Era: Postwar Fiction and the Rise of Creative Writing* (Cambridge, MA: Harvard University Press, 2011).

March-Russell, Paul, *The Short Story: An Introduction* (Edinburgh: Edinburgh University Press, 2009).

Markham, E. A. (ed.), 'Introduction', *The Penguin Book of Caribbean Short Stories* (London: Penguin, 1996), pp. xi–xlv.

Mukherjee, Bharati, 'A Four-Hundred-Year-Old Woman', in Janet Sternburg (ed.), *The Writer on Her Work* (London: Virago, 1992), pp. 52–6.
— 'Immigrant Writing: Give Us Your Maximalists!', *New York Times Book Review*, 28 August 1988, pp. 28–9.
Munro, Alice, 'Everything Here is Touchable and Mysterious', *Weekend Magazine, Toronto Star*, 11 May 1974, p. 33.
Oates, Joyce Carol (ed.), 'Introduction', *The Oxford Book of American Short Stories* (Oxford: Oxford University Press, 1992), pp. 3–16.
— 'Beginnings: "The Origins and Art of the Short Story"', in Barbara Lounsberry, Susan Lohafer, Mary Rohrberger, Stephen Pett and R. C. Feddersen (eds), *The Tales We Tell: Perspectives on the Short Story* (Westport, CT: Greenwood Press, 1998), pp. 47–52.
O'Connor, Frank, *The Lonely Voice: A Study of the Short Story* (London: Macmillan, 1963).
O'Sullivan, Michael 'Loneliness and the Submerged Population: Frank O'Connor's *The Lonely Voice* and Joyce's "The Dead"', in Elke D'hoker and Stephanie Eggermont (eds), *The Irish Short Story: Tradition and Trends* (Bern: Peter Lang, 2015), pp. 105–19.
Pauli, Michelle, 'Short Story Scores with New Prize and Amazon Project', *The Guardian*, 23 August 2005, <http://www.theguardian.com/books/2005/aug/23/news.michellepauli> (last accessed 15 April 2018).
Pritchett, V. S., 'The Short Story', *London Magazine*, 6.6 (1966): 6–9.
Smith, Ali, 'True Short Story', in *The First Person and Other Stories* (London: Penguin, 2009), pp. 1–18.
— *Artful* (London: Penguin, 2013).
— 'Foreword', in Emma Young and James Bailey (eds), *British Women Short Story Writers: The New Woman to Now* (Edinburgh: Edinburgh University Press, 2015), pp. viii–x.
Stevick, Philip, 'Introduction', in Philip Stevick (ed.), *Anti-Story: An Anthology of Experimental Fiction* (New York: The Free Press, 1971), pp. ix–xxiii.
Tan, Amy, 'Introduction', in Amy Tan with Katrina Kenison (eds), *The Best American Short Stories 1999* (New York: Houghton Mifflin, 1999), pp. xii–xxviii.
Updike, John, 'Foreword', *The Early Short Stories, 1953–1975* (London: Hamish Hamilton, 2004), pp. ix–xv.
Whittier, Anthony, 'Frank O'Connor, The Art of Fiction No. 19', <http://www.theparisreview.org/interviews/4847/the-art-of-fiction-no-19-frank-oconnor> (last accessed 15 April 2018).

Part II

Publishing the Short Story

5

THE SHORT STORY AND THE 'LITTLE MAGAZINE'

Beryl Pong

IN HER ESSAY 'MODERNISM, Geopolitics, Globalization', Melba Cuddy-Keane notes that the end of the nineteenth and the early twentieth centuries saw the beginnings of modern globalisation. Phenomena such as technological advances in global communications, the development of transnational ideologies and discourses like liberalism and Marxism, the increased engagement of ideas at an international level – involving high-profile events like the Olympics and the awarding of Nobel Prizes, for example – all point to globalisation, not as a late twentieth-century phenomenon, but as a long historical process of burgeoning international consciousness.[1] Linking this context to writing and literature, Cuddy-Keane asks: '[D]id increasing encounters with cultural others help to *produce* the multipersonal novel? Did an expanding awareness of *inter*-cultural connectivity inform the new *intra*-cultural discourse that was beginning, at that time, to emerge?'[2] Many have indeed focused on the novel in relation to such ideas; the history of short fiction, in contrast, has itself received short shrift. Despite the fact that literary histories of the modern short story tend to pin its origins and development to roughly the same period as that discussed by Cuddy-Keane, it is the novel – whether the nineteenth-century realist text, or the twentieth-century multipersonal panorama – that dominates.

Short fiction's place within the context of internationalism was itself an issue raised by writers in the early twentieth century. In her introduction to *The Faber Book of Modern Stories* (1937), Elizabeth Bowen made two arguments concerning the short story in English: one related to aesthetic form, the other to literary history. First, she argued that the short story 'was once the condensed novel; it needed a complex subject and depended for merit on the skill with which condensation had been effected'.[3] Second, discussing Thomas Hardy and Henry James, she claims that 'the English short story had to get from abroad. Rumour, the translation and easier circulation of foreign books, also a widening curiosity, brought Tchehov and Maupassant into the English view.'[4] James himself had, on more than one occasion, acknowledged Maupassant and Turgenev as masters of the form to whom he looked for instruction, so Bowen's latter observation is not unfounded.[5] But he and Hardy are used to support a larger point: that, influenced by modern travel and technology, and by globalisation, the English short story is a heterogeneous and international form, a product of cross-cultural importation and development.

What Bowen suggests of the English short story, we should consider of anglophone short fiction more generally. Adapting Cuddy-Keane's hypotheses, we might ask: Did encounters with cultural others influence the development of certain types of short fiction? How did an expanding awareness of intercultural connectivity impact the aesthetics, as well as the production and reception, of short stories? How do short stories 'get from abroad'? And, combining this with Bowen's arguments: How – and why – did a 'condensed' form gain momentum during the 'widening curiosity' of globalism in the late nineteenth and early twentieth centuries?

The response is necessarily manifold, concerning a variety of literary, political and socio-economic conditions which not only contextualise but shape short fiction production and dissemination. As Raymond Williams writes:

> the problem of form is a problem of the relations between social (collective) modes and individual projects . . . For a social and historical theory based on the materiality of language and the related materiality of cultural production, it is a problem of the description of (these) variable relations within specifiable material practices. Thus a social theory can show that form is inevitably a relationship.[6]

For Williams, writing is as much an individual as it is a socially informed event. Language is tied to the pragmatics of the way it is produced, communicated and transmitted, and the form that storytelling takes is dynamically related to variable material circumstances.

A key element of a 'social and historical theory' of the short story is print culture. For the inter-animating conjunction between the materiality of language and the related materiality of cultural production is hardly more evident here, given the short story's intertwined history with the medium of the periodical, and its maturation within the culture of increasing consumerism in the late nineteenth and early twentieth centuries. The 'little magazine', especially, in both Anglo-American and mid-century (post)colonial contexts, is a site of specifiable material practices that circulated experimental short fiction all the while impacting the texts' aesthetics and reception in significant ways. What the 'little magazine' ultimately makes visible is a history of the short story genre beyond frameworks of regional or national exceptionalism. Although short fiction criticism has tended, and continues, to revolve around particular national traditions – American, Canadian, Irish, South African and Australian short fiction, among others, have all been described as a 'national art form', with the genre viewed as uniquely representative of those geographies and identities[7] – as Bowen noted, national forms developed through international influence. The status of being both national and international, culturally specific yet cosmopolitan, define many short stories and coterie publications in and of themselves, as well as their feedback and imbricated developments in a progressively networked world.

Historically, major arguments in short fiction genre theory have centred on matters of form while material conditions have been of implicit concern. The emphasis on form dates back to at least Edgar Allan Poe's review of Nathaniel Hawthorne's *Twice-Told Tales* (1837), where Poe famously stated that a 'single' and 'preconceived effect' defines short fiction, and that the genre has a 'unity of effect' and a 'one pre-established design'.[8] The dictum was enormously influential and came to underpin the work of early critics like Brander Matthews, who described the short story as a 'complete and self-contained' work of art.[9] Arguably, what Dominic Head calls the 'unity aesthetic' has also influenced later critics like Susan Lohafer and John Gerlach, whose 'closure' theories emphasise the short story as an 'end-oriented totality' – for Lohafer, even on the level of individual sentences.[10] But Poe's original criticism is predicated on the short story within a historical-material context: Hawthorne's *Twice-Told Tales* is, after all, a text whose stories were themselves printed separately in magazine form and 'read at one sitting', Poe claims, before they appeared together as a collection (hence 'twice-told'). The short story is thus part and parcel of 'the whole energetic, busy spirit of the age [that] tended wholly to the Magazine literature, to the curt, the terse, the well-timed, and the readily diffused'.[11]

As numerous critics have established, a myriad of social, economic and legal factors helped to spur a 'magazine revolution'[12] in the eighteenth and nineteenth centuries that significantly impacted the form and popularity of the short story. From the repeal of advertising duties to the cheaper costs of printing due to machine-made paper, from the increased competition in the literary marketplace to the professionalisation of authors and literary agents: circumstances favoured short fiction for its comparatively brief length and corresponding ease of production.[13] The short story's 'symbolic economy', in Winnie Chan's cogent phrase, 'could seldom extricate itself from the pecuniary one'.[14] According to Peter Keating, the short story may not have even developed very much at all 'if the market had not been so desperate to fill periodical columns with fiction'.[15]

Many of the innovations now associated with the genre took place within and through the 'little magazine': a type of publication whose definition remains open to debate, though most agree on traits of investment in artistic innovation, often at the expense of financial gain, and of alternative, unconventional or radical politics.[16] In Paul March-Russell's summation, 'little magazines' are 'characterised first by their fugitive quality, and second by their passionate (if irreverent) commitment to a way of conceptualising art and society. They are driven less by commercial desires (though commercial relations ultimately determine their continued existence) than by an overarching belief.'[17] Varying widely in size, duration of publication and editorial ethos, 'little magazines' are literary-artistic journals driven by an 'overarching belief' in art, and, to borrow from Adam McKible and Suzanne Churchill's working definition, as 'non-commercial enterprises founded by individuals and groups for publishing untried, unpopular, or under-represented writers'.[18]

A prototypical 'little magazine' from the British *fin de siècle* with an indelible influence on the shape of modern short fiction is *The Yellow Book*. Established by John Lane, *The Yellow Book* emphasised the aesthetic and decadent creed of art for art's sake, publishing works that challenged 'accepted hierarchies in art, literature, and life'.[19] The magazine was founded to capitalise on the controversies surrounding figures like Oscar Wilde, though he never actually appeared in it. It gained a 'notoriety [which] was due less to its Decadent associations . . . than to Lane's acumen for publicity'.[20] Handsomely produced in hardback, and expensive, it targeted a wide readership, likely 'a middle-class reader who is mildly daring', while suggesting admission into an elite group.[21] Its broad appeal is both reflected and created by the diversity of its short stories: throughout the magazine's thirteen issues, it published over a hundred titles by writers as varied as Henry James, Vernon Lee and Ernest Dowson, as well as 'New Women' writers like George Egerton and Charlotte Mew.

Where earlier magazines in Britain prescribed word lengths for their contributors, engaged in serial publishing and often used pictures to illustrate their texts' plots, *The*

Yellow Book eschewed these conventions and led the short story down a different path. Freedom from word count enabled James to publish longer short stories, for example, but the magazine's rejection of serialisation also led to short, impressionistic sketches evoking psychological or emotional states. In Simon James's observation, this helped to develop the short story into a 'quintessential Decadent art form': one whose brevity is not only predisposed to magazine publication, but to focusing on brief moments, thus chiming with Walter Pater's appeal to 'value a moment's experience for that experience's own sake'.[22] Such aesthetics would become significant precursors to those of the modernist short story, and in its cosmopolitanism, too, *The Yellow Book* anticipated the transatlantic production and reach of modernist 'little magazines'. Although known as a British periodical and London-based, *The Yellow Book* was published, marketed and reviewed in the United States as well as in Britain; its contributors and readers hailed from around the world, including France, Denmark, the Netherlands and Serbia.[23] Literary editor Henry Harland was himself an American expat, and the origin of the magazine 'was seeded in an artists' community in Dieppe'.[24] *The Yellow Book* is an important bridge between the illustrated periodicals of the nineteenth century and the modernist coterie magazines to come, and it evidences early ways in which the generic form of the short story became imbricated with periodical publication.

By the time that Anglo-American modernist 'little magazines' were established, the link between experimental writing and fugitive, avant-garde periodicals reached new heights. These magazines remain the most well-known examples of coterie magazines, due in large part to their publishing of canonical texts like Ezra Pound's 'In a Station of the Metro' (1913) (in *Poetry*) and T. S. Eliot's *The Waste Land* (1922) (in *The Dial* and *The Criterion*). The cosmopolitanism of these magazines played a crucial role in contributing to modernism's status as 'a uniquely international and polyglot body of arts' known for mobility, restlessness and migration.[25] As Michael Levenson notes, 'little magazines' enabled the formation of 'a micro-sociology of modernist innovation, within which small groups of artists were able to sustain their resolve ... to create small flourishing communities'.[26] Such 'small' communities typically involved sprawling networks. *Broom*, for instance, featured transnational literary and visual modernists from North America and Europe, and it shifted offices from Rome to Berlin to New York, always in search of cheaper printing to allay production costs. Cosmopolitan peripateticism similarly characterises Ford Madox Ford's *the transatlantic review*, an English journal edited in Paris, and Kenneth Macpherson's *Close Up*, which was edited in Switzerland and printed in France and England, and which dealt with the cinema of Moscow, Berlin, London, New York and Paris.

Arguably, the representative modernist 'little magazine' is *The Little Review*, which was little in readership, large in cultural capital. Operating first from Chicago and briefly San Francisco, it migrated to New York and then Paris, where advantageous exchange rates between America and Europe meant cheaper and easier publication. The magazine was also notoriously cliquish: during Pound's tenure as its foreign editor, the only poetry Eliot published between 1917 and 1919 appeared in *The Little Review*, and Wyndham Lewis contributed fifteen pieces to Pound without even going through the magazine's other editors.[27] The magazine's epigraph, 'Making No Compromise with the Public Taste', captures this insular relationship, though constant financial hardship meant that *The Little Review* was very much engaged with the consumerist market; advertisements featured frequently for other literary journals in addition to popular fiction, and for commercial products like typewriters and Goodyear Tyres.[28] The international nature of the magazine's production and circulation is underpinned by its self-consciously cosmopolitan ambitions. 'The Little Review was the first magazine to reassure Europe as to America, and the first to give America the tang of Europe', editor Margaret Anderson wrote in an advertisement for the September–December 1920 issue.[29] Counterbalancing cosmopolitanism with nationalism, the magazine remained committed to American culture; indeed, it worked to construct an American canon by producing 'American Number' special issues throughout. National interests did not necessarily pivot on American geography or history; instead, the magazine's 'nationalism was not based on the country's past and its traditions', but on its prioritisation of experimentalism, 'on a sense of the limitless possibilities inherent in its very newness'.[30]

In this, Ernest Hemingway's short story cycle *In Our Time* (1925) certainly fit the bill as an innovative exploration of nationalism and internationalism. Composed of interlocking yet disjointed 'chapters' and vignettes, and covering a wide geography encompassing America, Europe and Asia Minor, *In Our Time* was a groundbreaking portrait of the modern age rendered through the interplay between the contemporary and the immemorial. Hemingway's desolate subject matter – revolving around themes and scenes of unwanted pregnancy, death, crime and bullfighting (all recurring preoccupations in his *oeuvre*) – is exacerbated by the author's austere writing style, where short, declarative statements coldly render moments that would otherwise provoke emotion and anxiety. The work is thus widely considered to be the first instance of the writer's theory of omission or 'Iceberg Theory'.[31]

It is easy to forget the importance of 'little magazines' to the development of this work because it is typically studied as one of three book versions, which are, in increasing degrees of availability, the 1924 collection *in our time*, published by Three Mountains Press in Paris; the 1925 collection *In Our Time*, published by Boni and Liveright in New York; and the 1938 Scribner's version, also called *In Our Time*. But while the evolution from one book to the next is anything but straightforward, with various parts being altered or cannibalised into others, the text undeniably developed through *The Little Review*. Six of the vignettes which comprise the first half of the 1924 *in our time* first appeared in the Spring 1923 'Exiles' issue, under the title 'In Our Time'. The magazine subsequently published another section, what Hemingway later called a 'chapter', in October 1924. Other parts appeared in other 'little magazines': two sections were published in *the transatlantic review* in December 1924 and January 1925, and another in *This Quarter* in May 1925.[32] In Michael Reynolds's assessment, 'the form had not dictated content; rather, the sketches created the form. If there was a [unifying] principle involved, it came from the title, *in our time*, which itself had not appeared until the first six vignettes were finished.'[33] While *In Our Time* criss-crossed between publishing houses and editors, the text's entangled bibliography includes the confusing but integral role played by 'little magazines' in its reception as well as conception. To put it another way, Hemingway's aesthetics developed alongside and through its print contexts, and *In Our Time* is a text that reveals its own process as a product of periodical and book publication – in its time, over time.

The work's extended spatial and temporal diffusion across multiple print venues have also influenced the work's final shape as a short story cycle. Typical conventions of this genre involve a set of stories linked by plot, character, setting, motif or thematic pattern, such that the composite illuminates both the individual episodes and the total cycle or sequence as a whole. Hemingway's work is a textbook example of such strategies of juxtaposition and collage: Nick Adams makes a recurring appearance, obviously, but the text is also held together by various themes and motifs, and attending to the missing and unstated emotion of one episode (such as the matador's feelings during the bullfight) reveals the way it might be repressed in another (Mon's shooting of enemy Germans in the Great War). For this reason, the work's individual 'chapters' and stories have inspired as much criticism and interest as the larger cycle. As Susan Garland Mann has noted, the short story cycle's play between the fragment and the whole, between heterogeneity and unity, relates to the way they appeared over different spaces and times in 'little magazines'. Among other modernist cycles, Sherwood Anderson's *Winesburg, Ohio* (1919) also appeared disparately across journals like *The Little Review*, *The Masses* and *Seven Arts* before being brought together as a 'final' book, again testifying to how contingencies of publication and dissemination can become essential to textual pattern and design.[34]

But one needs to stress that beyond being, in part, a by-product of 'little magazines', Hemingway's work and its aesthetics of fragmentation and collage are essential to his overall concern with international violence. This is important to keep in mind because the short story cycle is often studied as a quintessentially American form: in one critic's words, the feedback between individual stories and the cycle as a whole creates a 'networked logic of interplay' that 'works in a variety of ways to rethink national space' by representing the pull between coherent national identity and American individualism.[35] However, Hemingway's case is also clearly about how to think and understand globally. While roundly praised for being an American masterpiece, the work is both about, and enabled by, the tightening of international networks in the early twentieth century. Yoking together different geographies, and depicting domestic violence alongside large-scale geopolitical conflicts like the First World War and the Greco-Turkish War, Hemingway's paratactic style is central to his conception of 'our time' as international rather than national, as a fragmented age of untimely violence. Among its many other concerns, the work addresses the difficulties and ethics of apprehending war both distant and near in a world where global communications – which Hemingway as an international journalist and correspondent knew too well – has enabled the 'experiencing' of violence on other shores without being physically there.

In Our Time and its interplay between the fragment and whole presents a heuristic for theorising how to read texts within periodicals more generally. When do we read a text in and of itself, and when do we read it alongside the magazine as a whole? What role should literary criticism ascribe to a magazine's 'periodical codes' – its advertisements and illustrations, its layout and size, its networks of distribution and sales?[36] How does our reading of 'In Our Time' (and *In Our Time*) change, knowing that the vignettes were immediately followed by the writings of Gertrude Stein in the 'Exiles' issue, for example, or the fact that Hemingway's poem 'They All Made Peace – What is Peace?' appeared several pages after that? Such matters surrounding the methodology of reading within periodicals are captured by Ann Ardis's concept of 'magazine dialogism'. On one hand, periodicals have *'external dialogics'* which involve 'discursive exchanges with other print media; the mapping of geographical (and temporal) space that they perform as they claim the territories that they report on, distribute copies to, take advertisements from'.[37] On the other hand, they have *'internal dialogics'*.[38] In collaborating with different editors, writers and readers; in presenting a mixture of text, image and paratext, like advertisements and readers' letters; in maintaining a generally consistent editorial approach and design, yet circulating new content in every issue: the magazine is an inherently heterogeneous form, across its run but also within a single issue.

Because magazine dialogism describes a periodical's relationships to the world beyond as well as within its pages, it is an important component in understanding how marginalised writers, particularly colonial modernists, were featured and figured within or alongside dominant metropolitan culture in the early twentieth century. Colonial modernists, Elleke Boehmer writes, 'shaped their modernist techniques within the crucible of their outsider colonial experience, or from their perspective as colonial others who felt themselves to be players within, yet to some degree alienated from, the metropolitan city'.[39] In addition to writers like Claude MacKay, William Plomer and Mulk Raj Anand, colonial modernists include women like Katherine Mansfield, a figure without whom the history of the short story and the 'little magazine' – and the history of modernist short fiction more generally – would be incomplete. Born to a settler-colonial family in Wellington, New Zealand, Mansfield relocated at a young age to metropolitan Europe, where she established her writing career. She published almost exclusively in the short story form and had a long relationship with both mass-market periodicals and coterie magazines throughout her short life.[40] She was thus dubbed disparagingly as the 'New Zealand mag.-story writer', and 'dismissed as cheap, ambitious, brittle, déraciné'.[41] While it is difficult to confirm whether Mansfield's preference for shorter forms is related to her creative development through magazine culture, one cannot ignore the correlation.

Mansfield's early short stories were published in the British periodical *The New Age* under the editorship of A. R. Orage, who belittled her colonial background even as he mentored her.[42] Drawing from her travels in Germany, these texts are not colonial in content, but their preoccupations with the perspective of the outsider, and with cultural miscommunication and stereotyping, resonate with the sense of bilocation that she often wrote about in her diaries. It was not until her involvement with John Middleton Murry's 'little magazine' *Rhythm*, however, of which she eventually became a co-editor, that she published short fiction with an explicitly colonial bent. Like *The Little Review*, cosmopolitan and national interests were mutually reflexive for *Rhythm*. Considered by some to be 'the first English little magazine', it was born out of a time when the Continental 'little magazine' was still held as the ideal and 'the textual negative of English philistinism'.[43] 'The understanding that 'little magazines such as *Rhythm*, like the artist and writers who appeared in them, were struggling to establish themselves upon unremittingly stony ground', Faith Binckes writes, 'placed the issue of national literary culture firmly on the agenda'.[44] *Rhythm*'s national-cosmopolitanism manifested in a strong attraction to experimental, international art movements such as Fauvism, primitivism and neo-impressionism.

There was no better magazine for the publication of Mansfield's colonial-modernist short fiction, which also negotiates between nationalism and cosmopolitanism, between Antipodean filiation and European affiliation. But while *Rhythm* raised her profile as a 'European' writer, the magazine's broader interests in aesthetic primitivism also created paratextual fissures with her stories. 'The Woman at the Store', for instance, published in *Rhythm*'s Spring 1912 issue, was presented in such a way that challenges, and conflicts with, the text's themes. Depicting the encounter between a group of travellers and an indigenous woman and her child, Mansfield's text reworks an Australian colonial short story, Henry Lawson's 'The Drover's Wife' (1892), to de-romanticise colonial narratives. Where the Drover's Wife is the local variant of the 'New Woman', known for handling her harsh environment with independence and resilience, Mansfield's character is a victim of domestic abuse and outback isolation in New Zealand. These political themes are undercut by the magazine's illustrations, especially by Albert Marquet's and Lionel Halpert's primitivist drawings – of a dog and a naked woman, respectively – which splice through the story, seeming to emphasise stereotypes of indigenous animalism and to further sexualise the eponymous character. For Kate Krueger, the periodical even problematically overwrites and aestheticises Mansfield's anti-colonial and anti-masculinist message.[45]

Despite this contradiction between text and paratext, the story and its circumstances of publication are also representative of Mansfield herself, who was by turns dismissive of and nostalgic about New Zealand. Furthermore, while the choice of an avant-garde publication like *Rhythm* can be seen to mitigate the association between the story and the 'outback school' whose tropes are being referenced, according to Binckes, 'it is also clear that Murry expressly sought to advance *Rhythm*'s avant-garde status by virtue of those very qualities'.[46] The story projects 'the image of a country still possessed of its rough edges', and its position 'in a magazine that promoted so many international connections prevented the backwoods from seeming too much of a backwater': it makes New Zealand itself into an avant-garde setting.[47] However we reconcile the way the story draws upon, even while rejecting, colonial literary form and stereotypes, this much is sure: given that much of the text takes place in the store's 'large room, the walls plastered with old pages of English periodicals' – where 'Queen Victoria's Jubilee appeared to be the most recent number' – Mansfield is undoubtedly drawing attention to the power of print culture, and to the way empire can make itself felt through its circuitry.[48] The sharpness of this resonance, and of the way *Rhythm* simultaneously exploits and ironises this fact, is lost if we do not examine the story within the venue of its original publication.

Another female colonial modernist who first published in twentieth-century modernist 'little magazines' is Jean Rhys, who was of Welsh heritage but with a West Indian upbringing. Rhys's status as a Left Bank artist was vastly different to other writers who made Paris home, like Hemingway, since she was more colonial migrant than cosmopolitan expatriate. When Ford Madox Ford published her first story 'Vienne' (1924) in *the transatlantic review*, he placed her within the cultural space of international modernism and within the same textual space as Hemingway, Stein and Tristan Tzara. Remarkably, though, Ford attributes Rhys's uniqueness and quality of writing to her colonial background, to her 'coming from the Antilles, with a terrifying insight and a terrific – an almost lurid! – passion for stating the case of the underdog'.[49] While not necessarily the only reason for Rhys's aesthetic, Ford's observation is given weight in stories like 'Again the Antilles' (1927). Depicting the sparring between an Englishman and a brown-skinned 'Mulatto' editor from Dominica over a late nineteenth-century newspaper, the text echoes Mansfield's awareness of the relationship between colonial politics and print culture.[50] When the Englishman condescendingly criticises the editor for misquoting Chaucer (whom the Englishman himself slightly misquotes too), Rhys highlights the way that the English language and literature, through international print culture, can perpetuate prejudice and inequality – a theme she would famously feature in her later prequel of *Jane Eyre*, *Wide Sargasso Sea* (1966).[51] As Peter Kalliney points out, Rhys is a significant compass for 'the changing demands and interests of readers and scholars', since critical interest in her modernist-bohemian days followed only after the success of *Wide Sargasso Sea* and her later re-positioning as a postcolonial writer.[52] She is thus evidence of how the emergence of postcolonial writing and the post-war history of modernism are related developments.

During the time that Rhys made her name abroad, a number of 'little magazines' were founded in her native West Indies during the mid-century and beyond, including Trinidad's *The Beacon*, Guyana's *Kyk-Over-Al*, Jamaica's *Focus* and Barbados's *Bim*. These magazines serve as a reminder that coterie publications flourished outside of Anglo-European contexts, and they offered a forum for writings that might not have fit the narrower readerships of European journals, as Rhys's did. These magazines therefore sustained the 'national linguistic expression', as one anonymous reviewer in *Bim* put it.[53] By encouraging emergent West Indian writing, *Bim* became vital to developing both cultural and national self-awareness in Barbados, as well as a sense of historical recovery within postcolonial West Indian communities at large. Such magazines would have a significant impact on the popularity and development of the anglophone West Indian short story, though the aesthetics of their 'local' and archipelagic writing, too, involved trans-oceanic influences.

Begun with Barbadian literature in mind, Frank Collymore's *Bim* quickly took on a pan-Caribbean remit and became a major outlet for creative writers, publishing works by Derek Walcott, George Lamming, V. S. Naipaul and others. It also published the early short stories of Sam Selvon, who had been working as a journalist and who had an acute awareness of the economics of print culture.[54] Selvon is now known for his linguistic achievements in rendering a Trinidadian dialect: as Hyacinth Simpson puts it, he 'set the standard for what was later to become a normative practice among West Indian writers of drawing on the linguistic spectrum of West Indian English to shape and provide their stories' perspective and set the rhythm and tone of their narratives'.[55] But while *The Lonely Londoners* (1956) is his defining work, his experiments with modes of West Indian orality and dialect began in *Bim* several years prior. The short story 'Calypsonian', for instance, published in *Bim* in 1952, describes the quick descent of calypso composer Razor Blade into a life of 'tiefing' and swindling through the language registers of Trinidadian speech.[56] Written from the character's perspective, and concerned with the composition of a calypso, the narrative style takes on the calypso's rhythms and insists on orality and dialect as literary. The style of the calypso itself, of course, has national as well as international origins, as it incorporates local carnival music in addition to European musical traditions and West African slave song. Representing 'part compromise and part defiance', John McLeod explains, it 'embodied the principle of creolisation in its combination of Anglophone and Francophone traditions with African influences'.[57]

This mixed status as 'internationally national' characterises Selvon's writing, which is representative of Trinidad but which is also nevertheless cosmopolitan. For Selvon had already emigrated to London by this point and was writing as both a Caribbean and a post-war British writer; as Nick Bentley argues, he represents 'an engagement with dominant literary practice in the West rather than simply an alternative that comes from the periphery', increasingly 'dramatiz[ing] and articulat[ing] many of the anxieties and concerns of both mainstream society and culture', as well as those of 'marginalized black subcultures in 1950s Britain'.[58] In fact, 'Calypsonian' was rewritten and revised many times, and a later 1957 version, titled 'Calypso in London', transposed the setting from the original Port of Spain to London's East End. Like Selvon's own migration, the short story came to address not only the West Indian, but the West Indian immigrant, experience. Moreover, 'Calypsonian' was intended for both domestic and international consumption. *Bim* not only had a strong readership in the West Indies as well as abroad, it had a long-standing collaboration with the BBC radio programme *Caribbean Voices*, which broadcast short fiction that had appeared in West Indian 'little magazines', as well as featured original, spoken short stories that were then reprinted in those journals. In and of themselves, the 'little magazine' and the radio are media already favourable to short fiction due to the brevity of material that both require. But the relationship between *Bim* and the BBC actively promoted West Indian orality as a literary language, and Selvon is one of several writers who capitalised on *Bim*'s international circulation and its relationship to oral media. Another writer, Daniel Samaroo Joseph, whose story 'Taxi, Mister!' (1949) appeared in *Bim*, similarly utilises the conventions of the dramatic monologue to bring his character and setting to life. He too was much lauded for having 'written a spoken language' accurately, as one English critic put it, and the story aired on *Caribbean Voices* in 1949.[59]

Bim not only gave West Indian writing wider recognition across the region and internationally, it influenced the way stories were conceived and received, forwarding 'an oral aesthetic wherein the speaking voice became as central to the stories' construction as it was to their on-air delivery and dissemination'.[60] Tellingly, *Caribbean Voices* typically hired West Indians as readers, so that West Indians heard their own voices being relayed back across the ocean through airwaves (and Selvon often read his own stories on air).[61] This intertwining of national and international reception – a textual and oral ricochet from Britain back to the West Indies – meant that literary aesthetics like orality were local and international phenomena simultaneously. Ironically, it also meant that *Bim* and West Indian short fiction benefited from the global associations linked to colonialism, since many of the stories garnered attention because of the BBC's authority among colonial territories and in Britain, which legitimated their 'quality'. Metropolitan and colonial literary institutions involved reciprocal exchanges, but cultural capital and power relations, especially during the period surrounding decolonisation, were not necessarily equal.

Whether in terms of generic innovations such as the short story cycle; of influencing textual interpretation through paratexts and illustrations; or of impacting aesthetic style through relationships to international audiences and other media: literary form and material form are mutually informing, and considerations of the short story genre in relation to the 'little magazine' demonstrate substantial transatlantic and international contexts to 'national' short fiction. And as literary and cultural criticism continues to expand the temporal and geographical reach of the 'little magazine', its importance to colonial and postcolonial literatures, beyond those of the Caribbean, becomes increasingly evident. Adrian Hunter points out that the short story has 'always ... been disproportionately represented' in colonial and postcolonial societies, in part because socio-economic circumstances encouraged coterie publication: 'In cultures with small or non-existent publishing infrastructures, the low-capital, low-circulation literary magazine tends to be the main outlet for new writing.'[62] Linking this to Gilles Deleuze and Félix Guattari's concept of 'minor literature' – 'that which a minority constructs within a major language' – Hunter also suggests that the short story's prominence in (post)colonial cultures is related to the form's inherently elusive and fragmentary features, which can counter the more totalising 'power and law' of 'major' cultures and literatures.[63] Here again, formal, material and social-historical theories are inextricable.

'The little magazine flourished for about forty years, from 1895 to 1935.'[64] Such outdated critical statements, clearly only about avant-garde modernist 'little magazines', no longer apply. And moving forward from the mid-century, another region requiring further examination regarding the conjunction between the 'minor' form of the short story and the 'minor' medium of the 'little magazine' is Africa. As decolonisation gathered steam in the 1950s and 1960s, Western publishers took advantage of a relatively new anglophone African literary market, and many African novelists in turn produced novels intended for Western readerships; most notably, Amos Tutuola's *Palm-Wine Drinkard* (1952) was endorsed by Eliot and published by Faber and Faber. But while foreign publishers focused on the novel, local publishers focused on the 'little magazine' and its attendant contents, which catered especially to poetry and short fiction. Examples of these magazines include Nairobi's *Zuka*, Ghana's *Okyeame* and Nigeria's *Okike*, the latter of which was founded by Chinua Achebe after the Nigerian civil war to uphold Igbo culture, though it quickly took on a broader African scope. Another Nigeria-based magazine, Ulli Beier's *Black Orpheus*, was inspired by *Présence Africaine* and Jean-Paul Sartre, and it provided opportunities for African writers to publish their work in dialogue with each other, and with writers around Europe, the United States and the West Indies. Meanwhile, Rajat Neogy's Ugandan-based *Transition* magazine was founded as a clear nod to Eugene Jolas's modernist 'little magazine' *transition*, taking from the former its ethos of aesthetic autonomy and extending it to concerns about political autonomy for colonial countries.[65] *Transition* intended to register the changes and readjustments impacting East Africa at a crucial sociopolitical juncture, when imperial powers were withdrawing and when nations were re-establishing themselves, even as local traditions were rapidly fading. Significant short stories by Grace Ogot and Nadine Gordimer appeared in its pages. While cultivating local literatures and cultures, such postcolonial 'little magazines' were also outward-looking and internationally oriented. They 'fostered the kinds of literary and critical affiliations that would end up reinforcing their status as both national *and* cosmopolitan', Eric Bulson writes, because they strove to assert themselves within a changing world system as British imperialism came to an end.[66] As Neogy declared after being forced to relocate *Transition* to Ghana: '*Transition*'s home is also all Africa. And it was at home in the world outside.'[67] The interactions between nationalism and cosmopolitanism that defined modernist writers took on different, politically urgent iterations for postcolonial writers who promoted an art and a nationalism within the sociocultural reconfigurations of empire's aftermath.

In his essay on 'world literature', Franco Moretti has argued that, because the novel has been translated and transposed around the world, it created a 'compromise' between 'foreign form, local material – and local form'.[68] 'But are there other "material texts" that are worldly, in Moretti's sense, that is, textual forms that cross boundaries and borders and dwell primarily in the *world* of literature, rather than within individual national cultures?' Andrew Thacker asks.[69] Drawing upon modernist magazines that borrowed, copied and collaborated with one another, Thacker suggests that the 'little magazine' itself is a world medium, and Bulson's recent work has expanded on this by considering the 'little magazine' as a world form in areas like the global South and the East beyond the early twentieth century. By bringing material form back to its implications for literary form, and by considering how 'worldliness' in the former can penetrate the latter, a 'social and historical theory' shows how short fiction, too, is a 'world form'. Short fiction criticism and historiography must therefore examine not just the genre's symbolic or pecuniary economy, but its political economy as well. Doing so reveals that the short story is key to expanding our understanding of the varieties of literary transnationalism.

Notes

1. Melba Cuddy-Keane, 'Modernism, Geopolitics, Globalization', *Modernism/Modernity*, 10.3 (2003): 539–40.
2. Cuddy-Keane, 'Modernism, Geopolitics, Globalization', p. 540 (her emphases).
3. Elizabeth Bowen, 'Introduction to *The Faber Book of Modern Short Stories*', in Charles E. May (ed.), *The New Short Story Theories* (Athens: Ohio University Press, 1994), p. 257. Published in 1937, the anthology is called *The Faber Book of Modern Stories*, though May, and Bowen's prose collection *Collected Impressions* (1950), have used the title *The Faber Book of Modern Short Stories*, dating its publication to 1936.
4. Ibid.
5. James mentions the writers in his book of literary criticism, *Partial Portraits* (1888), and he recalls discussing their work with Hippolyte Taine in his notebooks. See Alfred R. Ferguson, 'The Triple Quest of James: Fame, Art, and Fortune (1956)', in Edwin H. Cody and Louis J. Budd (eds), *On Henry James: The Best from 'American Literature'* (Durham, NC: Duke University Press, 1990), p. 69.
6. Raymond Williams, *Marxism and Literature* (Oxford: Oxford University Press, 1977), p. 187.
7. On the short story as a 'national art form' in the United States, see Frank O'Connor's *The Lonely Voice: A Study of the Short Story* (London: Macmillan, 1963) and Andrew Levy, *The Culture and Commerce of the American Short Story* (Cambridge: Cambridge University Press, 2008). In relation to Ireland, see Heather Ingman, *A History of the Irish Short Story* (Cambridge: Cambridge University Press, 2011). As the 'flagship genre of Canadian literature', see Reingard M. Nischik (ed.), *The Canadian Short Story: Interpretations* (Rochester: Camden House, 2007), p. 1. As the genre in which 'South African literature has most consistently excelled', see Gareth Cornwell, Dirk Klopper and Craig Mackenzie, *The Columbia Guide to South African Literature in English since 1945* (New York: Columbia University Press, 2010), p. 176. In relation to Australia, see Bruce Bennett, *Australian Short Fiction: A History* (St Lucia: University of Queensland Press, 2002).
8. Edgar Allan Poe, 'Poe on Short Fiction', in May (ed.), *New Short Story Theories*, p. 61.
9. Brander Matthews, 'The Philosophy of the Short-story', in May (ed.), *New Short Story Theories*, p. 73.
10. Dominic Head, *The Modernist Short Story: A Study in Theory and Practice* (Cambridge: Cambridge University Press, 2009), pp. 13–14. See Susan Lohafer, *Coming to Terms with the Short Story* (Baton Rouge: Louisiana State University Press, 1983) and John Gerlach, *Toward the End: Closure and Structure in the American Short Story* (Tuscaloosa: University of Alabama Press, 1985).

11. Edgar Allan Poe, *The Letters of Edgar Allan Poe*, Vol. 2 (Cambridge, MA: Harvard University Press, 1948), p. 271.
12. Richard Ohmann, *Selling Culture* (London: Verso, 1996), p. 234.
13. Dean Baldwin, *Art and Commerce in the British Short Story, 1880–1950* (London: Chatto & Windus, 2013).
14. Winnie Chan, *The Economy of the Short Story in British Periodicals of the 1890s* (London: Routledge, 2007), p. xi.
15. Peter Keating, *The Haunted Study: A Social History of the English Novel 1875–1914* (London: Secker, 1989), p. 40.
16. For definitions of the 'little magazine', see Ezra Pound, 'Small Magazines', *English Journal*, 19 (1930): 689–704; Frederick J. Hoffman, Charles Allen and Carolyn F. Ulrich (eds), *The Little Magazine: A History and a Bibliography* (Princeton: Princeton University Press, 1947); Lionel Trilling, 'The Function of the Little Magazine', in *The Liberal Imagination: Essays on Literature and Society* (New York: Harcourt, 1979), pp. 89–99; and Paul Bixler, 'Little Magazine, What Now?', *The Antioch Review*, 50 (1992): 75–99.
17. Paul March-Russell, *The Short Story: An Introduction* (Edinburgh: Edinburgh University Press, 2009), p. 68.
18. Adam McKible and Suzanne Churchill, 'Little Magazines and Modernism: An Introduction', *American Periodicals: A Journal of History, Criticism and Bibliography*, 15.1 (2005): 3.
19. Lorraine Janzen Kooistra, 'The Yellow Book (1894–1897): An Overview', in Dennis Denisoff and Lorraine Janzen Kooistra (eds), *The Yellow Nineties Online* (Toronto: Ryerson University, 2010). Available at <www.1890s.ca> (last accessed 15 April 2018).
20. March-Russell, *The Short Story*, p. 69.
21. Edward Bishop, 'Re:Covering Modernism—Format and Function in the Little Magazines', in Ian Willison, Warwick Gould and Warren Chernaik (eds), *Modernist Writers and the Marketplace* (Basingstoke: Macmillan, 1996), p. 291.
22. Simon J. James, 'Foreword', in Kostas Boyiopoulos, Yoonjoung Choi and Matthew Brinton Tildesley (eds), *The Decadent Short Story: An Annotated Anthology* (Edinburgh: Edinburgh University Press, 2014), p. xi.
23. Kooistra, 'The Yellow Book', n. p.
24. Ibid.
25. Malcolm Bradbury and James McFarlane (eds), 'Preface', in *Modernism: A Guide to European Literature 1890–1930* (Harmondsworth: Penguin, 1991), p. 13.
26. Michael Levenson (ed.), 'Introduction', *The Cambridge Companion to Modernism* (Cambridge: Cambridge University Press, 1999), p. 6.
27. Alan C. Golding, 'The Little Review (1914–1929)', in Peter Brooker and Andrew Thacker (eds), *The Oxford Critical and Cultural History of Modernist Magazines, Vol. 2. North America 1894–1960* (Oxford: Oxford University Press, 2012), pp. 61–84.
28. Golding, 'The Little Review', p. 69.
29. Quoted in Mark Morrisson, 'Nationalism and the modern American canon', in Walter Kalaidjian (ed.), *The Cambridge Companion to American Modernism* (Cambridge: Cambridge University Press, 2005), p. 24.
30. Morrisson, 'Nationalism and the modern American canon', p. 21.
31. See James Gifford, 'Introduction', '*"In Our Time" & "They All Made Peace – What is Peace?": The 1923 Text*' (Victoria: Modernist Journals Project, 2015), pp. i–ix. Available at <http://web.uvic.ca/~mvp1922/wp-content/uploads/2015/07/Hemingway-In-Our-Time-1923.pdf> (last accessed 15 April 2018).
32. For the publishing history of *In Our Time*, see Michael Reynolds, 'Hemingway's *In Our Time*: The Biography of the Book', in J. Gerald Kennedy (ed.), *Modern American Short Story Sequences: Composite Fictions and Fictive Communities* (Cambridge: Cambridge University Press, 1995), pp. 48–9.

33. Reynolds, 'Hemingway's *In Our Time*', p. 39.
34. Susan Garland Mann, *The Short Story Cycle: A Genre Companion and Reference Guide* (Westport, CT: Greenwood Press, 1988), p. 8.
35. Wesley Beal, *Networks of Modernism: Reorganizing American Narrative* (Iowa City: University of Iowa Press, 2015), pp. 18–19.
36. Peter Brooker and Andrew Thacker (eds), 'General Introduction', *The Oxford Critical and Cultural History of Modernist Magazines, Vol. 1. Britain and Ireland 1880–1955* (Oxford: Oxford University Press, 2009), pp. 1–26 (p. 5).
37. Ann Ardis, 'Staging the Public Sphere: Magazine Dialogism and the Prosthetics of Authorship at the Turn of the Twentieth Century', in Ann Ardis and Patrick Collier (eds), *Transatlantic Print Culture, 1880–1914: Emerging Media, Emerging Modernisms* (Basingstoke: Palgrave Macmillan, 2008), p. 38 (her emphases).
38. Ibid.
39. Elleke Boehmer, 'Mansfield as Colonial Modernist: Difference Within', in Gerri Kimber and Janet Wilson (eds), *Celebrating Katherine Mansfield: A Centenary Volume of Essays* (Basingstoke: Palgrave Macmillan, 2011), p. 58.
40. Jenny McDonnell shows that Mansfield was a 'shrewd author at work in the literary marketplace' in *Katherine Mansfield and the Modernist Marketplace: At the Mercy of the Public* (Basingstoke: Palgrave Macmillan, 2010), p. 173.
41. Faith Binckes, *Modernism, Magazines, and the British Avant-Garde: Reading 'Rhythm' (1911–1914)* (Oxford: Oxford University Press, 2010), p. 100. 'New Zealand mag.-story writer' is from Wyndham Lewis. Quoted in Antony Alpers, *The Life of Katherine Mansfield* (London: Jonathan Cape, 1980), p. 372.
42. Carey Snyder, 'Katherine Mansfield and *The New Age* School of Satire', *Journal of Modern Periodical Studies*, 1.2 (2010): 147.
43. Binckes, *Modernism, Magazines, and the British Avant-Garde*, p. 1, p. 71.
44. Ibid. p. 73.
45. Kate Krueger, *British Women Writers and the Short Story, 1850–1930: Reclaiming Social Space* (Basingstoke: Palgrave Macmillan, 2014), pp. 142–3.
46. Binckes, *Modernism, Magazines, and the British Avant-Garde*, p. 125.
47. Ibid. p. 81.
48. Katherine Mansfield, 'The Woman at the Store', *Rhythm*, 1.4 (Spring 1912): 12. Retrieved online at *The Modernist Journals Project* (Brown and Tulsa Universities, ongoing). Available at <www.modjourn.org> (last accessed 15 April 2018).
49. Ford Madox Ford, 'Preface to a Selection of Stories from *The Left Bank*', in Jean Rhys, *Tigers Are Better-Looking, With a Selection from the Left Bank* (Harmondsworth: Penguin, 1972), p. 138.
50. Dominica, Rhys's island of birth, was the first and only British Caribbean colony to have a mixed-race elite controlling the House of Assembly, known as the 'Mulatto Ascendancy'.
51. Rhys, *Tigers Are Better-Looking*, pp. 166–8.
52. Peter Kalliney, 'Jean Rhys: Left Bank Modernist as Postcolonial Intellectual', in Mark Wollaeger and Matt Eatough (eds), *The Oxford Handbook of Global Modernisms* (Oxford: Oxford University Press, 2012), p. 417.
53. Quoted in Eric Bulson, 'Little Magazine, World Form', in Wollaeger and Eatough (eds), *The Oxford Handbook of Global Modernisms*, p. 274.
54. Selvon worked for the *Trinidad Guardian* and as literary editor for the *Sunday Guardian Weekly*, contributing his own poems, stories and articles when deadlines loomed and material was short.
55. Hyacinth M. Simpson, 'The BBC's *Caribbean Voices* and the Making of an Oral Aesthetic in the West Indian Short Story', *Journal of the Short Story in English*, 57 (Autumn 2011): n. p. Available at <http://jsse.revues.org/1184?lang=en> (last accessed 15 April 2018). On

56. West Indian literary orality, see Kenneth Ramchand, 'West Indian Literary History: Literariness, Orality and Periodization', *Callaloo*, 34 (Winter 1988): 91–110.
56. The story is reprinted in Sam Selvon's *Foreday Morning: Selected Prose 1946–1986* (London: Longman, 1989).
57. John McLeod, *Rewriting the Metropolis* (London: Routledge, 2004), p. 31. The phrase 'part compromise and part defiance' is cited from John Cowley, *Carnival, Canboulay and Calypso: Traditions in the Making* (Cambridge: Cambridge University Press, 1996).
58. Nick Bentley, 'Form and Language in Sam Selvon's *The Lonely Londoners*', *ARIEL: A Review of International English Literature*, 36.3–4 (2005): 68. See also See Mark Looker, *Atlantic Passages: History, Fiction and Language in the Fiction of Sam Selvon* (New York: Peter Lang, 1996).
59. The story appeared in *Bim*, 3.11 (1949): 216–18. Repr. in Barbara Howes (ed.), *From the Green Antilles: Writings of the Caribbean* (London: Souvenir Press, 1967). See also Simpson's discussion of Samaroo Joseph in 'The BBC's *Caribbean Voices*'.
60. Simpson, 'The BBC's *Caribbean Voices*', n. p.
61. Ibid.
62. Adrian Hunter, *The Cambridge Introduction to the Short Story in English* (Cambridge: Cambridge University Press, 2007), p. 138.
63. Hunter, *The Cambridge Introduction to the Short Story in English*, p. 138, p. 140.
64. Bishop, 'Re:Covering Modernism', p. 287.
65. Peter Kalliney, *Modernism in a Global Context* (London: Bloomsbury, 2016), p. 101.
66. Bulson, 'Little Magazine, World Form', pp. 273–4 (his emphasis).
67. Rajat Neogy, 'Letter to the Editor', *Transition*, 38 (1971): 6.
68. Franco Moretti, 'Conjectures on World Literature,' *New Left Review*, 1 (2000): 65.
69. Andrew Thacker, 'Crossing Borders with Modernist Magazines', *Variants*, 9 (2011): 200.

Bibliography

Alpers, Antony, *The Life of Katherine Mansfield* (London: Jonathan Cape, 1980).
Ardis, Ann, 'Staging the Public Sphere: Magazine Dialogism and the Prosthetics of Authorship at the Turn of the Twentieth Century', in Ann Ardis and Patrick Collier (eds), *Transatlantic Print Culture, 1880–1914: Emerging Media, Emerging Modernisms* (Basingstoke: Palgrave Macmillan, 2008), pp. 30–47.
Baldwin, Dean, *Art and Commerce in the British Short Story, 1880–1950* (London: Chatto & Windus, 2013).
Beal, Wesley, *Networks of Modernism: Reorganizing American Narrative* (Iowa City: University of Iowa Press, 2015).
Bennett, Bruce, *Australian Short Fiction: A History* (St Lucia: University of Queensland Press, 2002).
Bentley, Nick, 'Form and Language in Sam Selvon's *The Lonely Londoners*', *ARIEL: A Review of International English Literature*, 36.3–4 (2005): 67–84.
Binckes, Faith, *Modernism, Magazines, and the British Avant-Garde: Reading 'Rhythm' (1911–1914)* (Oxford: Oxford University Press, 2010).
Bishop, Edward, 'Re:Covering Modernism – Format and Function in the Little Magazines', in Ian Willison, Warwick Gould and Warren Chernaik (eds), *Modernist Writers and the Marketplace* (Basingstoke: Macmillan, 1996), pp. 287–319.
Bixler, Paul, 'Little Magazine, What Now?', *The Antioch Review*, 50 (1992): 75–99.
Boehmer, Elleke, 'Mansfield as Colonial Modernist: Difference Within', in Gerri Kimber and Janet Wilson (eds), *Celebrating Katherine Mansfield: A Centenary Volume of Essays* (Basingstoke: Palgrave Macmillan, 2011), pp. 57–71.

Bowen, Elizabeth, 'Introduction to *The Faber Book of Modern Short Stories*', in Charles E. May (ed.), *The New Short Story Theories* (Athens: Ohio University Press, 1994), pp. 256–62.

Bradbury, Malcolm and James McFarlane (eds), 'Preface', *Modernism: A Guide to European Literature 1890–1930* (Harmondsworth: Penguin, 1991), pp. 11–16.

Brooker, Peter and Andrew Thacker (eds), 'General Introduction', *The Oxford Critical and Cultural History of Modernist Magazines, Vol. 1. Britain and Ireland 1880–1955* (Oxford: Oxford University Press, 2009), pp. 1–26.

Bulson, Eric, 'Little Magazine, World Form', in Mark Wollaeger and Matt Eatough (eds), *The Oxford Handbook of Global Modernisms* (Oxford: Oxford University Press, 2012), pp. 267–87.

Chan, Winnie, *The Economy of the Short Story in British Periodicals of the 1890s* (London; Routledge, 2007).

Cornwell, Gareth, Dirk Klopper and Craig Mackenzie, *The Columbia Guide to South African Literature in English since 1945* (New York: Columbia University Press, 2010).

Cowley, John, *Carnival, Canboulay and Calypso: Traditions in the Making* (Cambridge: Cambridge University Press, 1996).

Cuddy-Keane, Melba, 'Modernism, Geopolitics, Globalization', *Modernism/Modernity*, 10.3 (2003): 539–58.

Ferguson, Alfred R., 'The Triple Quest of James: Fame, Art, and Fortune (1956)', in Edwin H. Cody and Louis J. Budd (eds), *On Henry James: The Best from 'American Literature'* (Durham, NC: Duke University Press, 1990), pp. 53–76.

Ford, Ford Madox, 'Preface to a Selection of Stories from *The Left Bank*', in Jean Rhys, *Tigers Are Better-Looking, With a Selection from the Left Bank* (Harmondsworth: Penguin, 1972), pp. 137–40.

Gerlach, John, *Toward the End: Closure and Structure in the American Short Story* (Tuscaloosa: University of Alabama Press, 1985).

Gifford, James, 'Introduction', '*"In Our Time" & "They All Made Peace—What is Peace?"*: *The 1923 Text*' (Victoria: Modernist Journals Project, 2015), pp. i–ix. Available at <http://web.uvic.ca/~mvp1922/wp-content/uploads/2015/07/Hemingway-In-Our-Time-1923.pdf> (last accessed 15 April 2018).

Golding, Alan C., 'The Little Review (1914–1929)', in Peter Brooker and Andrew Thacker (eds), *The Oxford Critical and Cultural History of Modernist Magazines, Vol. 2. North America 1894–1960* (Oxford: Oxford University Press, 2012), pp. 61–84.

Head, Dominic, *The Modernist Short Story: A Study in Theory and Practice* (Cambridge: Cambridge University Press, 2009).

Hoffman, Frederick J., Charles Allen and Carolyn F. Ulrich (eds), *The Little Magazine: A History and a Bibliography* (Princeton: Princeton University Press, 1947).

Howes, Barbara (ed.), *From the Green Antilles: Writings of the Caribbean* (London: Souvenir Press, 1967).

Hunter, Adrian, *The Cambridge Introduction to the Short Story in English* (Cambridge: Cambridge University Press, 2007).

Ingman, Heather, *A History of the Irish Short Story* (Cambridge: Cambridge University Press, 2011).

James, Simon J., 'Foreword', in Kostas Boyiopoulos, Yoonjoung Choi and Matthew Brinton Tildesley (eds), *The Decadent Short Story: An Annotated Anthology* (Edinburgh: Edinburgh University Press, 2014), pp. xi–xii.

Kalliney, Peter, 'Jean Rhys: Left Bank Modernist as Postcolonial Intellectual', in Wollaeger and Eatough (eds), *The Oxford Handbook of Global Modernisms* (Oxford: Oxford University Press, 2012), pp. 413–32.

— *Modernism in a Global Context* (London: Bloomsbury, 2016).

Keating, Peter, *The Haunted Study: A Social History of the English Novel 1875–1914* (London: Secker, 1989).
Kooistra, Lorraine Janzen, 'The Yellow Book (1894–1897): An Overview', in Dennis Denisoff and Lorraine Janzen Kooistra (eds), *The Yellow Nineties Online* (Toronto: Ryerson University, 2010). Available at <www.1890s.ca> (last accessed 15 April 2018).
Krueger, Kate, *British Women Writers and the Short Story, 1850–1930: Reclaiming Social Space* (Basingstoke: Palgrave Macmillan, 2014).
Levenson, Michael (ed.), 'Introduction', *The Cambridge Companion to Modernism* (Cambridge: Cambridge University Press, 1999), pp. 1–8.
Levy, Andrew, *The Culture and Commerce of the American Short Story* (Cambridge: Cambridge University Press, 2008).
Lohafer, Susan, *Coming to Terms with the Short Story* (Baton Rouge: Louisiana State University Press, 1983).
Looker, Mark, *Atlantic Passages: History, Fiction and Language in the Fiction of Sam Selvon* (New York: Peter Lang, 1996).
McDonnell, Jenny, *Katherine Mansfield and the Modernist Marketplace: At the Mercy of the Public* (Basingstoke: Palgrave Macmillan, 2010).
McKible, Adam and Suzanne Churchill, 'Little Magazines and Modernism: An Introduction', *American Periodicals: A Journal of History, Criticism and Bibliography*, 15:1 (2005): 1–5.
McLeod, John, *Rewriting the Metropolis* (London: Routledge, 2004).
Mann, Susan Garland, *The Short Story Cycle: A Genre Companion and Reference Guide* (Westport, CT: Greenwood Press, 1988).
Mansfield, Katherine, 'The Woman at the Store', *Rhythm*, 1.4 (Spring 1912): 7–21.
March-Russell, Paul, *The Short Story: An Introduction* (Edinburgh: Edinburgh University Press, 2009).
Matthews, Brander, 'The Philosophy of the Short-story', in May (ed.), *New Short Story Theories*, pp. 73–80.
May, Charles E. (ed.), *The New Short story Theories* (Athens: Ohio University Press, 1994).
Moretti, Franco, 'Conjectures on World Literature', *New Left Review*, 1 (2000): 54–68.
Morrisson, Mark, 'Nationalism and the modern American canon', in Walter Kalaidjian (ed.), *The Cambridge Companion to American Modernism* (Cambridge: Cambridge University Press, 2005), pp. 12–35.
Neogy, Rajat, 'Letter to the Editor', *Transition*, 38 (1971): 6.
Nischik, Reingard M. (ed.), *The Canadian Short Story: Interpretations* (Rochester, NY: Camden House, 2007).
O'Connor, Frank, *The Lonely Voice: A Study of the Short Story* (London: Macmillan, 1963).
Ohmann, Richard, *Selling Culture* (London: Verso, 1996).
Poe, Edgar Allan, *The Letters of Edgar Allan Poe, Vol. 2* (Cambridge, MA: Harvard University Press, 1948).
— 'Poe on Short Fiction', in May (ed.), *New Short Story Theories*, pp. 59–72.
Pound, Ezra, 'Small Magazines', *English Journal*, 19 (1930): 689–704.
Ramchand, Kenneth, 'West Indian Literary History: Literariness, Orality and Periodization', *Callaloo*, 34 (Winter 1988): 91–110.
Reynolds, Michael, 'Hemingway's *In Our Time*: The Biography of the Book', in J. Gerald Kennedy (ed.), *Modern American Short Story Sequences: Composite Fictions and Fictive Communities* (Cambridge: Cambridge University Press, 1995), pp. 35–51.
Rhys, Jean, *Tigers Are Better-Looking, With a Selection from the Left Bank* (Harmondsworth: Penguin, 1972).
Selvon, Sam, *Foreday Morning: Selected Prose 1946–1986* (London: Longman, 1989).

Simpson, Hyacinth M., 'The BBC's *Caribbean Voices* and the Making of an Oral Aesthetic in the West Indian Short Story', *Journal of the Short Story in English* 57 (Autumn 2011): n. p. Available at <http://jsse.revues.org/1184?lang=en> (last accessed 15 April 2018).

Snyder, Carey, 'Katherine Mansfield and *The New Age* School of Satire', *Journal of Modern Periodical Studies*, 1.2 (2010): 125–58.

Thacker, Andrew, 'Crossing Borders with Modernist Magazines', *Variants*, 9 (2011): 199–208.

Trilling, Lionel, 'The Function of the Little Magazine', in *The Liberal Imagination: Essays on Literature and Society* (New York: Harcourt, 1979), pp. 89–99.

Williams, Raymond, *Marxism and Literature* (Oxford: Oxford University Press, 1977).

Wollaeger, Mark and Matt Eatough (eds), *The Oxford Handbook of Global Modernisms* (Oxford: Oxford University Press, 2012).

6

Collections, Cycles and Sequences

Jennifer J. Smith

In 'Art Work', at the centre of *The Matisse Stories* (1993), A. S. Byatt translates Henri-Émile-Benoît Matisse's aesthetics into fiction. She renders a domestic scene in dynamic sentences that alternate between long and languid and short and layered, resonant with Matisse's experimentations with colour and brushstroke. The story itself concerns a full-time, yet unproductive painter supported by his wife, once a sculptor and now a graphic designer in the magazine business. Their lives are held together by Mrs Brown, who is their maid, nanny and emotional lifesaver. Unbeknownst to them, Mrs Brown turns out to be a wildly talented curator of junk, which earns her the art exhibition and respect the husband so desperately craves. Byatt turns medium into message in this beautiful, humane story; as the wife, Debbie, takes stock of her husband's neorealist productions, which are 'just this side of kitsch', she realises that his work is really 'a serious attempt at a serious and terrible problem, an attempt to answer the question every artist must ask him or herself, at some time, why bother, why make representations of anything at all?'[1] That is the question that connects the three seemingly disparate stories that make up *The Matisse Stories*. What is the point of art? Or storytelling? What do we gain by putting pieces of art, junk or stories together?

When Mrs Brown exhibits the mass of stuff she has collected, the public and critics alike love it, because each person leaves impressed with some element. By weaving ostensibly different pieces into a tapestry, she creates something much more meaningful than the singularity of the husband's neorealist representations. In this meta-artistic story, Byatt celebrates the possibilities of the short story collection, sequence or cycle; like the newly lauded Mrs Brown, Byatt knows that stories gain meaning and resonance with accretion and addition. This story's treatment of Matisse's aesthetic, the role of art in everyday life, the buried lives of our intimates, the frustrated ambitions of middle age all recur – in somewhat different forms – in the stories that precede and follow 'Art Work'. Byatt, working in the late twentieth century, is a particularly emblematic case of a writer who straddles a commitment to realism in plot and characterisation with an experimentalist's fascination with the production and reception of art. Byatt's sequence, then, is one example of a much bigger trend in short fiction.

Short story collections, cycles and sequences are the ideal forms for resolving two major strands of literary expression in general. The first is a turn to realism, often articulated in third-person narrative tales grounded in place. These collections tend to be concerned with articulating regional, national and ethnic identities. The second is a seeming rejection of realism in favour of avant-garde experimentation with narrative voice, non-linear temporalities and placelessness. These cycles also interrogate issues of identity but typically focus on the individual and the artist. Cycles, collections and sequences show that these strands co-exist – often within the same book. Byatt's stories suggest that realist and avant-garde stories are connected by their fascination with what cannot be expressed in language. The cycle and sequence, because of their pronounced experimentations with cohesion and fragmentation, attempt to work out in form the problem of expression itself. For this reason, these genres repeatedly turn to intertextuality and metanarrative; they allude to literature, music and visual art to reveal how meaning flourishes in fragments.

The distinctions between a short story collection, cycle or sequence are ambiguous at best. Criticism on these genres debates these labels. In 1971, Forrest L. Ingram introduced the genre as the short story cycle; since then J. Gerald Kennedy proposes short story sequence, Maggie Dunn and Ann Morris prefer composite novel, and Rolf Lundén suggests short story composite. Debates about these terms reveal the generic diversity of short stories and short story monographs. However, in taxonomic debates we lose the larger sense of what such stories contribute to the larger field of fiction. I propose that we think about what the short story as a genre does when we read a story as part of a book.[2] In this chapter, I will survey several books of short stories, focusing on modernist and contemporary sequences and cycles, to trace how short stories balance realism and avant-garde experimentation through metafiction and intertextuality.

Although the tale is ancient and the modern short story enjoys a complex history in the nineteenth century, perhaps the best place to start is Gertrude Stein's *Three Lives* (1909).[3] Each story is set in Bridgepoint, a fictionalised Baltimore; however, the stories do not otherwise share characters or connecting elements. Each examines the idiosyncrasies and psychological motivations of its central female character. Stein began the stories when her brother, Leo, encouraged her to translate Gustave Flaubert's 'Un Coeur Simple' from *Trois Contes* (1877). Departing from the original text, she wrote the opening story, 'The Good Anna', by marrying Flaubert's realism in characterisation to a modernist experimentation with syntax and form. Like the heroine of Flaubert's story, Stein depicts humble characters, focusing on migrant women and African American women.

Stein's use of portraiture as a model takes realism's commitment to characterisation to its end point. Informed by her work with William James and her interest in cognition, Stein's prose suggests a belief that people are static and dominated by singular traits. The first such portrait transforms Flaubert's original source material into a psychological study of Anna, who is of 'solid lower middle-class south german [sic] stock'.[4] Anna seeks to control everything and everyone around her. Rather than repressing that drive, her role as a servant liberates her to extend and exploit it by managing dogs, the under-servants, storekeepers and even her mistress. Stein's stories are realist in their opposition to idealism. Stein offers Anna no transcendence or growth; her static commitment to power is itself the source of conflict in the story, as she repeatedly becomes close to and then falls out with friends, family, fellow servants, dogs and employers.

Told in three parts, 'The Good Anna' exceeds the length of a conventional story, bending toward a novella. These experimentations with length signal the ongoing debates about form among avant-garde writers. Stein embraces a modernist turn towards fragmentation to disrupt the realist elements of plot and characterisation; this fracturing happens in the division of the story, the syntactical complexity of her prose, and the very form of the book. Anna's story is distinct from but resonates with the other stories in the volume, as each woman embraces compulsions that determine the course of their lives. Stein varies the nature of these compulsions but each story examines the origin, manifestation and effects of singular aims.

Like Byatt, Stein takes Matisse and other impressionist and post-impressionist painters as inspiration for the style and subject of her trio. Paul Cézanne's work, especially his *Portrait of Madame Cézanne* (c. 1881), prompted a new theory of composition for Stein, as she explained to Robert Haas in 'A Transatlantic Interview, 1946':

> Cézanne conceived the idea that in composition one thing was as important as another thing. Each part is as important as the whole, and that impressed me enormously, and it impressed me so much that I began to write Three Lives [*sic*] under this influence and this idea of composition and I was more interested in composition at that moment, this background of word-system, which had come to me from this reading that I had done. I was obsessed by this idea of composition.[5]

This sense that each part is as important as the whole applies to her portraits of these women: Anna's treatment of bad dogs is just as important as her ill-treatment of her brother's wife. At the level of the sentence, this theory is even more apparent in 'Melanctha'.

Stein famously reworked a conventional autobiographical fiction, *Q.E.D.*, into her classic story 'Melanctha' transferring her experiences onto those of Dr Jeff Campbell. The story retains realism's commitment to deep characterisation of everyday figures but evinces modernism's obsession with 'personae, metamorphoses, doubles, and mythic parallels'.[6] In the opening description, Stein describes Melanctha as 'patient, submissive, soothing, and untiring' in her assistance to Rose, whom she terms 'sullen, childish, cowardly, black'.[7] Stein uses adjectives the way Cézanne uses brushstroke; the terms deposit and accumulate, their accretion defining Melanctha as a character. She repeats these adjectives, but their connotations shift as she arranges them differently and at different points in the story. Ann Charters explains that in *Three Lives* Stein 'tried to replace conventional linear narrative with incremental blocks of description . . . including repetition in her descriptions and dialogue as a conscious literary device'.[8] Most significantly for scholars has been Stein's repetition of words such as 'real', 'really', 'certainly' and 'very', which reflect how people use hyperbole to express scepticism. By seeing the same words repeated over and over, Stein constructs a fragmentary experience where all sayings and expressions simultaneously express truth yet induce doubt. The instability of what is knowable about a person, word, or idea is a driving force of the avant-garde throughout the century.

And yet, Stein's use of dialogue, which departs from more prevalent versions of dialect at the end of the nineteenth century, has been championed as the height of realism. Readers and writers alike have often found Stein's depiction of black language and experience to be exact. Richard Wright adored Stein's prose, explaining that, 'As I read it my ears were open for the first time to the magic of the spoken word. I began to hear the speech of my grandmother, who spoke a deep, pure Negro dialect . . . Miss Stein's struggling words made the speech of the people around me so vivid.'[9] In a letter to Stein, Nella Larsen said of 'Melanctha': 'I never cease to wonder how you came to write it and why you and not some one of us should so accurately have caught the spirit of this race of mine.'[10] Her publishers even sent someone to investigate whether Stein was black because they found her prose so authentic.[11] Yet, the dialogue is also extraordinarily stylised in that her characters speak in repetitious phrases that operate according to context and sequence. In one scene, for instance, Melanctha calls out Dr Jeff Campbell for not meaning what he says. Dr Campbell has been visiting Jane Harden, a woman with a reputation for trouble, to which Melanctha replies,

> [it] seems to me Dr. Campbell you find her to have something in her, and you go there very often, and you talk to her much more than you do to the nice girls that stay at home with their people, the kind you say you are really wanting. It don't seem to me Dr. Campbell, that what you say and what you do seem to have much to do with each other. And about your being so good ... You don't care about going to church much yourself, and yet you always are saying you believe so much in things like that, for people ... it certainly does seem to me you don't know very well yourself, what you mean, when you are talking.[12]

For Wright and Larsen, such passages render the spoken words of black Americans with verisimilitude. Her repetitious use of the second person, 'do,' and 'really' create a language thick with double meanings. For instance, when she wishes to say she knows he is hypocritical, she chooses the word 'seems'. Melanctha uses elliptical language to accuse Dr Campbell of being unclear. Melanctha's diction appears to be at odds with her meaning, but the repetition of 'seems' reflects her certainty about the disjunction between what Dr Campbell says and what he does. This experimentation is possible because Stein 'create[s] a dialect in which conventions of verbal verisimilitude are played against themselves so that the speech seems simultaneously concrete and highly artificial'.[13]

Michael North argues that 'the step away from conventional verisimilitude into abstractions is accomplished by a figurative change of race'.[14] That is, Stein achieves something more real by embracing an abstraction made possible by depicting black experiences. While she was writing 'Melanctha', she sat for Picasso's famous portrait. She sat as many as ninety-two times as he reworked the likeness before finding Stein's reality in a stylised depiction of her face modelled on an African mask. African masks appealed to Picasso, Stein and others for their ability to balance abstraction and naturalism. Her cultivation of avant-garde painters shaped her prose: Cézanne compelled her to explore beyond linear narrative; Matisse upheld the possibility of complex, psychological portraits; and Picasso's practice and friendship encouraged her to experiment with 'obsessive syntactical repetitions' akin to Cubism.[15]

Shortly before and during the time Stein was composing *Three Lives*, James Joyce was at work on *Dubliners* (1914), another story cycle that leans on portraits and intertextuality to balance the demands of realism and experimentation. Grounded in the city, Joyce's stories embrace realism's attention to space and identity. In a letter to Constantine Curan in 1904, Joyce explains that the aim of the volume is to 'betray the soul of that hemiplegia or paralysis which many consider a city'.[16] Like Stein, Joyce's stories illuminate the origins, manifestations and effects of stasis. Although each story is distinct, taken together they construct a vision of the city and the paralysis that plagues its citizens: three of childhood, four of adolescence, four of maturity and three of public life. The final story, 'The Dead,' brings these elements together to illustrate how the private bleeds into the public and the events of adolescence linger into maturity. Joyce wrote to his brother, Stanislaus, 'When you remember that Dublin has been a capital for thousands of years, that it is the "second" city of the British Empire, that it is nearly three times as big as Venice it seems strange that no artist has given it to the world', and to render Dublin to the world is an intention of the cycle.[17]

Scarlett Baron argues that Joyce's lifelong study of Flaubert's works and letters were absolutely formative to his fiction. She cites Flaubert's *Trois Contes* as shaping Joyce's sense that the purpose of fiction is to be 'absolutely, uncompromisingly true to his vision of Dublin and its problems'.[18] According to Baron, Joyce signals Flaubert's influence through shared use of the linked short story, multivalent irony, symbolic language drawn from geometry, impersonality in characterisation, 'cinematographic modes,' a balance of realism and symbolism, and the 'frozen permanence' of epiphanic endings.[19] Robert Scholes goes so far as to argue that 'Joyce's larger aim . . . was to follow Flaubert in making every detail of description and dialogue part of both a "mood" and a highly developed symbolic pattern.'[20] Beyond mere allusion, Joyce draws on Flaubert's fictive practices in subject and style; in *Dubliners*, this manifests itself in short stories that explore the stasis of characterisation and place that unite their works.

Ezra Pound too noted this likeness in his review of *Dubliners*: 'The followers of Flaubert deal in exact presentation . . . They are perhaps the most clarifying and they have been perhaps the most beneficial force in modern writing.'[21] Pound contrasts Joyce and Flaubert to a mass of (unnamed) writers who lean towards Monet's impressionism, immersed by descriptions of soft colours but missing their subjects' difficult realities. For Pound, Joyce's impressionism is more centrally aligned with realism in that:

> He presents his people swiftly and vividly, he does not sentimentalise over them, he does not weave convolutions [sic] He is a realist. He does not believe 'life' would be all right if we stopped vivisection or if we instituted a new sort of 'economics.' He gives the thing as it is.[22]

Joyce's short fiction evinces Pound's sense that realism and the experimentation of impressionism are intrinsically linked. Further, Pound described Joyce's writing as 'prose free from sloppiness'.[23]

Like Stein, Joyce's portraits focus on solitary, marginalised figures. Following Joyce, characters in short fiction tend to be 'alienated, solipsistic, socially dysfunctional, and largely uncomprehending of their own predicaments'.[24] They initiated the widespread turn away from plot twists toward moments-of-truth, what Joyce called epiphanies. Joyce uses epiphanies to communicate but not cure the paralysis from which his characters suffer. The effect of reading one epiphany after another in the cycle is to create a world in which growth or resolution is impossible. Some paralyses have greater consequences than others – for instance, the alcoholism and abuse of Farrington in 'Counterparts' is much more destructive than the vanity of the boy's romantic quest in 'Araby'. However, the source in both is a frustration with how reality and expectation do not line up for the protagonists and the effect is that neither can produce something good with their lives and efforts. The fragmented form thwarts progression or resolution, even as it shows how connected each situation is. To illustrate the point, Sean Latham traces the number of times characters appear to be looking out of a window, initially in 'The Sisters', then in 'Araby' and 'Eveline', and ultimately in 'The Dead' so that

> some boys skipping a day at school, a young man having a drink with a successful friend, and a cynical political campaign all become linked, both to one another and to a larger visions of modernity oscillating in the gap between ellipsis and epiphany.[25]

Joyce uses portrait-like stories to chronicle the city's denizens in a realist mode; the spare prose and fragmentation of the cycle bespeak an avant-garde concern with the medium of art itself. Later writers draw from Joyce's sense of modernity's spiritual, economic and artistic paralysis and have taken up this theme as a primary concern for their short fiction – from V. S. Naipaul to Raymond Carver to Junot Díaz.

The intertextual link between Flaubert's realism and the avant-garde reaches yet another articulation in Samuel Beckett's *More Pricks than Kicks* (1934), which signals also a heightened attention to metafiction. Beckett merged fragments of an earlier novel, *Dream of Fair to Middling Women*, with separate short stories to create the sequence. The ten stories centre on a single character, Belacqua Shuah, and Beckett announces the sequence's intertextuality in the opening story when Belacqua, whose name alludes to a minor character in *Purgatorio* who epitomises laziness, is depicted reading Dante. The stories trace Belacqua's life and stunted development, focusing on moments of estrangement and the idiosyncrasies of an everyday person. Narrating his life from youth through middle age to his death, Beckett's stories are 'self-consciously experimental, self-referential, and often mannered'.[26]

Often studied for its place in Beckett's canon of anti-heroes, the short stories also provide an important bridge between literary movements, as they embrace realism and modernism and anticipate postmodernism. The sequence's fissured form makes this possible, with Beckett bouncing between highly experimental stories, such as 'The Smeraldina's Billet Doux' – an epistolary story narrated in a German's misspelled and idiosyncratic English – and more realist stories like 'Yellow', which depicts Belacqua's last night as he awaits surgery in the morning. The former is all interiority, placeless and stream-of-consciousness, while the latter is a third-person linear narrative deeply invested in details of place and context. When the former enters the sequence, the reader has no idea who Smeraldina is and why she is so in love with Belacqua. The latter explains that they met following his second wife's death, when Smeraldina fairly crushed him with her adoration and love, which makes sense in light of her effusive, tortured love letter. Andrew Fox makes the case that *More Pricks* represents a critical point in Beckett's career where he turned away from naturalism toward the experimentation of his later works; in this sequence, though, he holds the two strands in tension.[27]

What Stein and Joyce do in individual stories, Beckett extends to the entire sequence: he creates a portrait of a person driven by singular compulsions to lead a thwarted life. The opening story, 'Dante and the Lobster', establishes the sequence's commitment to portraiture and static characterisation in the realist tradition. As Belacqua goes about the quotidian tasks of preparing lunch, buying a lobster and going to an Italian lesson, the protagonist's fastidious nature is immediately apparent and threatens to overturn his day every day:

> If his lunch was to be enjoyable, and it could be very enjoyable indeed, he must be left in absolute tranquillity to prepare it. But if he were disturbed now, if some brisk tattler were to come bouncing in now big with a big idea or a petition, he might just as well not eat at all, for the food would turn to bitterness on his palate, or worse again, taste of nothing.[28]

His attitude towards the preparation of his lunch foreshadows his responses to complexities and disruptions in love and friendships; Belacqua's preparation of lunch reveals his abiding need to script out his life. Subsequent stories prove that when life veers from the script, Belacqua retreats. This failure to adapt and learn from context initiates the irony at the end of the story when Belacqua is shocked to learn that lobsters are cooked alive. His aunt attempts to reassure him that 'They feel nothing', but the tragedy of the lobster's survival from the 'depths of the sea', 'the Frenchwoman's cat', and 'his witless clutch' only to be boiled alive for his dinner is too much revision to the narrative he has created of the lobster. He consoles himself, 'Well, thought Belacqua, it's a quick death, God help us all', to which the narrative voice intercedes simply 'It is not.'[29] The ending of the story disrupts the preceding realism of Beckett's portrait with a conclusion replete with self-awareness and dramatic irony.

As the sequence progresses, the portraits get increasingly metafictional. Stories have a Cézanne-like effect in that 'Each part is as important as the whole.'[30] In 'Love and Lethe', about halfway through the sequence, Belacqua plans (and fails) to script a quick murder-suicide for a dying woman. The narrator comments:

> we feel confident that even the most captious reader must acknowledge, not merely the extreme wretchedness of Ruby's situation, but the verisimilitude of what we hope to relate in the not too distant future. For we assume the irresponsibility of Belacqua, his faculty for acting with insufficient motivation, to have been so far evinced in previous misadventures as to be no longer a matter of surprise.[31]

The narrator uses the first-person plural to create a consensus about Belacqua as a person, whom the narrator later calls 'a cretinous Tom Jones'.[32] In this story, as with the lobster, Belacqua fails to register the meaning and nature of death. In intratextual irony, his own accidental death in the penultimate story is swift and largely unnarrated.

The stories are replete with intertextual experimentation as Beckett places his antihero against the entire Western canon, as the opening story intimates. Mark Nixon argues that early in his career the protagonists of Beckett's writing 'are unable to avoid giving voice to their past learning by way of allusion or quotation' so much so that 'Beckett's early works in particular is [sic] heavily reliant on other texts, pursuing an intertextual strategy that creates a web of erudite references, and which surely owes something to the model of Joyce.' Drawing as it does from the form of *Dubliners*, the whole sequence is in conversation with Joyce. For Nixon, 'Beckett's work from the early 1930s would simply not exist without the material he took from his reading. . . . the text at times approaching the status of pastiche with its extensive use of quotations and allusions.'[33] The Tom Jones allusion above highlights the life-story elements of the sequence as well as its satiric elements; unlike Henry Fielding, Beckett denounces his protagonist as a cretin better suited to a 'mental home'[34] incapable of redemption through love; if anything, romantic love triggers his worst tendencies. Beckett alludes to Thomas Hardy at the beginning of 'Yellow', with his depiction of a night spent in the hospital before surgery. He meditates on a line from *Tess of the D'Urbervilles* (1891) which has been with him since childhood: '*When grief ceases to be speculative, sleep sees her opportunity.*'[35] The treatment of Hardy is an interesting one, as Hardy is often deemed the last great British realist but also a harbinger of the alienation and sexual exploration that marks modernism. Tess is an ironic choice as she is a woman destroyed by romantic whims, just as Belacqua has destroyed the women in his life (his wives are especially short-lived). At his funeral, the subject of the final story, his best friend, Hairy, takes up with his third wife, Smeraldina, much like the ending of *Tess*. Hairy, 'gaz[es] straight before him through the anti-dazzle windscreen, whose effect by the way on the mountains was to make them look not unlike the picture by Paul Henry'.[36] Here, Hairy envisions Belacqua's funeral plot as akin to the Irish post-impressionist Paul Henry, whose stark landscapes of the west of Ireland give a final referent to Beckett's meditations on landscape throughout the stories.

Stein, Joyce, Beckett and other modernists such as Anderson, Faulkner, Hemingway and Jean Toomer, established the cycle and sequence as the pre-eminent genres for resolving the tensions between realism and experimentation, which would remain the case through the early twentieth century. Modernism and avant-garde experimentation are associated with the examination of interiority, often rendered in disorienting prose. Such writing has a conscious desire to break with tradition, opposing the scientific and social mandates of realism and naturalism, even while often borrowing their emphasis on the actual. According to Paul March-Russell:

> Following in the wake of precise stylists such as Gustave Flaubert and Anton Chekhov, modernists such as James Joyce and Ernest Hemingway sought methods of capturing the many points of view that constitute an objective reality without either dissolving the text altogether or subsuming these multiple perspectives within the homogenising tendency of the realist novel. Instead, they found a solution in the use of interlinked short stories.[37]

In the mid-century a number of books continued this tradition, even leaning toward full-blown postmodernist expression, most notably John Barth's *Lost in the Funhouse* (1968). Barth credits the ancient story cycle tradition for the form of his book and continues in the intertextual and metafictional play. But it is not until the 1980s and 1990s that the genre makes a major resurgence on par with its modernist heyday. The reasons for this include a rise in writing by authors for whom the interlinked collection offers commonalities with indigenous traditions; the rise of MFA programs; and the general decline in short story outlets and sales so that linked stories hold more commercial appeal.[38] The reach of the cycle and sequence extends far beyond Britain and the United States. From Naipaul to Jamaica Kincaid to Junot Díaz to Edwidge Danticat, the cycle and sequence are especially robust forms in Caribbean literatures, among writers of dramatically various styles and subjects.[39]

In British short fiction, the cycle and sequence remain especially dominant for balancing the tensions between realism and experimentation through intertextuality. For instance, in Byatt's trio of stories, the first story concerns a casual observer of art, the second story depicts the lives of artists, and the third turns to scholars of art. Each has an explicit treatment of Matisse's work, and Byatt's experiments in texture and sound mirror the painter's techniques and subject. In 'Art Work', the story that opened this chapter, Robin, the husband, paints portraits of common objects against a grey or beige background. An art curator interprets his work as being about the 'littleness of our life'; although he cannot express it in words, he disagrees and maintains that his work is about 'the infinite terror of the brilliance of colour'.[40] His view is certainly in keeping with Matisse's aesthetic, which so powerfully renders colour, in both its singularity and in combination. What the husband does not understand about Matisse's work is how it celebrates connection – bodies dancing together, colours bursting next to each other, the subject staring at the artist or viewer. Robin's work isolates the object but misses the importance of seeing the object in relation to other objects, which is why the exhibition and art of Mrs Brown, the maid, are so much more powerful and inspiring (after all, both the wife and the husband renew their art in response to the show). Of her art, she says, 'it all just comes to me in a coloured rush, I just like putting things together, there's so much in this world, isn't there, and making things is a natural enough way of showing your excitement'.[41] Mrs Brown answers the question that began this chapter: Why do we make things? She is excited to do so. Why do we put objects and stories together? She does so to replicate how she experiences the world in a coloured rush of objects and people. Collections, cycles and sequences render that rush in their very form. Matisse, then, is the perfect artist for Byatt to articulate the necessity of seeing these stories in relation to each other: the first depicts people who see Matisse in their everyday lives almost as background; the second portrays artists' attempt to create art; and the third focuses on the lives of academics who have made a life and career from interpreting Matisse. These stories isolate the characters' distinct lives and become a full picture of the way art moves people.

Byatt includes black and white sketches by Matisse on the title page of each story: *La chevelure* (1931–2), *L'artiste et le modéle reflétés dans le mirior* (1937) and *Nymphe et faune* (1931–2). In several editions, three other reproductions, alluded to in the stories, appear on the front and back covers: *Silence habite des maisons* (1947), *Le Nu rose* (1935) and *La Porte noire* (1942). With these paratextual materials, Byatt constructs a threshold across which the stories are placed in conversation with the visual art. They announce that 'the figure of the artist and the practice of artistic creation' loom large in the stories.[42] Byatt also borrows two of Matisse's objectives: 'to flesh out a fictional location or landscape and second, to shed light on the workings of the creative process in which their often troubled protagonists are engaged'.[43] Byatt constructs settings with the sensory details that saturate Matisse's work. In the final story, 'The Chinese Lobster', she describes the Cantonese Musak that plays and the overgrown plants that give a Chinese restaurant its particular sense of comfort to the protagonist, Professor Himmelblau, who has been going there for seven years.

As she enters on the day of the story, Professor Himmelblau observes the fish in their tank while mediating the conflict between a student and another professor. The lobster – so reminiscent of Belacqua's lobster – moves 'slowly in this unbreathable element, moves her long feelers and can be seen to move her little claws on the end of her legs, which cannot go forward or back' (96). The student, Peggi Nollet, has accused Professor Perry Diss of sexual harassment and blocking her ability to complete a degree. Nollet is painting original productions that revise Matisse and writing an academic thesis arguing that Matisse can only see women as objects of lust. Professor Diss wholeheartedly disagrees and argues that Matisse seeks primarily to understand pleasure. Professor Himmelblau tries to argue Peggi's side until they are fighting about the meaning of Matisse's vision. Underlying this debate is a difference of opinion about the artist's relationship to inspiration: 'Professor Diss endorses a mode of artistic practice underpinned by the principles of respectful imitation and disciplined emulation. Nollett, on the other hand, views art as a medium for reworking and challenging artistic conventions and ideological positions.'[44] Byatt's stories enact this duality as they are both an imitation of and an ideological challenge to Matisse. Byatt embraces Matisse's use of sensory details but rejects his objectification of women by making complex female interiority central to each story. The stories are inside his subjects' minds looking out at the world, rather than adoring their physicality and aloofness as his paintings would have us do. The characters in this final story recognise that, like the lobster, they are stuck. All they can really do is give Peggi another advisor, one more sympathetic to her work. Byatt seems to be saying that the conversation a person has with a painter or with a story matters immensely and not at all. This theme recurs in all three stories; in 'Art Work', the artists' sense of what their work means is vitally important to its production but so often irrelevant to its reception, as the debate in the final story shows.

A metafictional angst about the ways form matters across artistic mediums is at the very centre of Gabriel Josipovici's *Goldberg: Variations* (2002). Monika Fludernik cites Josipovici's sense of himself as 'resolutely modern' and in the tradition of Picasso, Duchamp and Beckett as the basis for his blend of experimentation and realism.[45] Josipovici takes his formal structure not predominantly from visual art or literature but music. Werner Wolf argues that Josipovici seeks to capture 'the condition of music' – that is, its essence, form and effects.[46] The volume fictionalises a famous – and likely apocryphal – tale of how J. S. Bach came to compose his *Goldberg Variations* (*Klavier-übung* 1741). According to Johann Nikolaus Forkel, one of his earliest biographers, Count Kaiserling, a patron, suffered from insomnia so he asked Bach to create music that a talented musician, Johann Gottlieb Goldberg, could play for him at night to induce sleep. Bach's *Goldberg Variations* include an aria and thirty variations; Josipovici's volume contains thirty numbered and titled stories. In the stories, a wealthy gentleman, Westfield, asks a writer named Goldberg to tell him stories to fall asleep after a musician failed to have a soporific effect. What follows then are interweaving tales, relating to Goldberg, Westfield and an authorial figure, Gerald, akin to Josipovici, who narrates the struggle of writing this book. In its framed structure and nightly interludes, another, unnamed intertext for the volume is *One Thousand and One Nights*. Although Goldberg's life is not literally at stake, he relies on his storytelling powers to appease a notoriously demanding auditor who needs a story to amuse, engage and relax, all at once. Thus, the volume meditates on the function and form of stories. Jopsipovici's variations contemplate art in all its form, obsess over the production and effects of art, and analyse intimacy in all of its forms especially in terms of romance and friendship. Josipovici is in conversation with Bach but is not mirroring him directly.[47]

Josipovici sets the tales in eighteenth-century England, announcing an experimentation with realism and narrative voice in the opening tales. In the opening passage, Goldberg describes his arrival:

> We arrived at nightfall. Mr Hammond set me down at the manor and drove on to see his son. Mr Westfield was expecting me. His manservant showed me to my room. It is larger than our living-room and freshly painted. The windows are large and look directly down on to the kitchen garden, but the big oak and elm trees of the park are visible beyond. It is all together very pleasant and peaceful, and I am sure I will be able to do very good work here.[48]

The depth of detail and the description of emotion all mirror early realist novels, yet Goldberg's exhaustive thought and tendency toward effusion also satirises these conventions. The parodic treatment of narrative voice in eighteenth- and nineteenth-century novels pays homage to the playfulness and digressions of writers like Laurence Sterne, suggesting that experimentation is not new to realism but central to it. Bach, too, is an important eighteenth-century figure as he stands at the crossroads of Romanticism and the Enlightenment, which resonates with the characters' debates about the value of reason and feeling. Even in this opening passage, Goldberg embraces the studied empiricism of the Enlightenment while inferring menace and delight from the near-Gothic setting.

The story sequence allows Josipovici to embrace the proto-realism of the eighteenth century and the experimentation of the contemporary avant-garde simultaneously. For instance, he includes a plotless story describing the content of shelves, a story in which only one of the speakers' dialogue is present, and a number of epistolary stories that embrace a variety of voices and styles. The main plot of the book follows the author Goldberg telling Westfield stories to help him fall asleep. But his stories must incite irritation as Goldberg articulates points of view, such as his wives' and his sons', which Westfield seems to misunderstand. There is also a diversion into a three-part (but not contiguous) story of the carriage ride that Goldberg took to the house. Halfway through, Josipovici introduces another thread: that of the present-day author reaching a crisis in the writing of his Goldberg book as his marriage falls apart. All three plots question the nature and purpose of storytelling itself.

The intertextuality with eighteenth-century novels, with music and interweaving storylines illuminate Josipovici's central question: why write? Westfield longs for a story because:

> A new story, a story which is really new and really a story, will give the person who reads or hears it the sense that the world had become alive again for him. I would put it like this: the world will start to breath for him where before it had seemed as made of ice or rock.[49]

Westfield's optimism about the restorative power of storytelling is immediately undercut by Goldberg's uncertainty about composing such a story. For the authorial figure, Paul Klee's *Wander-Artist (ein Plakat)* (1940) seems to inspire the completion of his book. Near the end of the volume, Josipovici writes a story voiced from the perspective of Klee's figure, but he is just as much an enigma to himself. His story is largely a series of questions about his origins and purpose. He, at least, is at peace with the meaninglessness of his words. But Gerald's attempts to unite his book with the same principles as the painting fail. In the final story, he contemplates, 'I am racked by doubts about whether there is any point in expressing anything?'[50] Following this moment and elsewhere, he pokes holes in his Goldberg tales by pointing out their historical ignorance and errors.[51] In a letter to his wife, Goldberg confesses, '[Art] purports to speak of man and all his doings, but in effect it speaks only of those things most amenable to speech.'[52] He realises that so much exceeds language's ability, and that all we can do is capture the surface of dialogue, expression, and art, hoping that this intimates what lies beneath.

The writer finds Klee's image of the waving man compelling for his ambiguity:

> Like so many of the paintings Klee did in his last year it exuded a sense of desperate urgency yet remained curiously aloof, inhabiting its own still world. Is he waving airily to us as he passes by or is he raising his hand in warning? Is it melancholy or indifference that is to be read into his expression? . . . Klee knew better than anyone how to give and withhold at the same time, and the *Wander-Artist* is the supreme example of his art.[53]

To give and withhold – this is the central task that animates both realism and avant-garde experimentation. In contemporary and modernist story cycles and sequences, authors resolve this paradox through intertextuality and metafiction. The multiplicity of the stories allows such books to straddle the divide between what is said and what remains unspoken. The gaps between stories in such collections are thus the ideal formal articulation of a problem of fiction since modernism: how does the artist capture the ineffable?

Notes

1. A. S. Byatt, *The Matisse Stories* (London: Chatto & Windus, 1993), p. 52.
2. For an excellent overview of the scholarly debates on the genre and the diversity of global story collections and cycles, see Elke D'hoker, 'The short story cycle: broadening the perspective', *Short Fiction in Theory and Practice*, 3.2 (2013): 151–9.
3. On the origins of the short story cycle in ancient story cycles, see Forrest L. Ingram, *Representative Short Story Cycles of the Twentieth Century: Studies in a Literary Genre* (The Hague: Mouton, 1971); Rolf Lundén, *The United Stories of America: Studies in the Short Story Composite* (Amsterdam: Rodopi, 1999); James Nagel, *The Contemporary American Short-Story Cycle: The Ethnic Resonance of Genre* (Baton Rouge: Louisiana University Press, 2001); Michelle Pacht, *The Subversive Storyteller: The Short Story Cycle and the Politics of Identity in America* (Newcastle upon Tyne: Cambridge Scholars, 2009); and Sue Marais, '"Queer small town people": Fixations and fictions of fellowship in the modern short story cycle', *Current Writing: Text and Reception in Southern Africa*, 17.1 (June 2011): 14–36.
4. Gertrude Stein, *Three Lives*, ed. Ann Charters (New York: Penguin, 1990), p. 13.
5. Quoted in Philip Heldrich, 'Connecting Surfaces: Gertrude Stein's *Three Lives*, Cubism, and the Metonymy of the Short Story Cycle', *Studies in Short Fiction*, 34.4 (1997): 427.
6. Michael North, *The Dialect of Modernism: Race, Language, and Twentieth-Century Literature* (Oxford: Oxford University Press, 1998), p. 67.
7. Stein, *Three Lives*, p. 59.
8. Ann Charters, 'Introduction', in Ann Charters (ed.), *Three Lives* (New York: Penguin, 1990), p. ix.
9. Gertrude Stein, *The Collected Writings of Gertrude Stein*, ed. Carl Van Vechten (New York: Vintage, 1990), p. 338.

10. Donald Gallup, *Flowers of Friendship: Letters Written to Gertrude Stein* (London: Octagon, 1979), p. 216.
11. North, *Dialect of Modernism*, pp. 72–3.
12. Stein, *Three Lives*, p. 82.
13. North, *Dialect of Modernism*, p. 73.
14. Ibid. p. 61.
15. Charters, 'Introduction', p. x.
16. James Joyce, *Dubliners*, ed. Robert Scholes and A. Walton Litz (New York: Penguin, 1996), p. 253.
17. Ibid. p. 256.
18. Scarlett Baron, *Strandentwining Cable: Joyce, Flaubert, and Intertextuality* (Oxford: Oxford University Press, 2012), p. 59.
19. Ibid. p. 70.
20. Robert Scholes and A. Walton Litz, 'Editors' Introduction to Criticism Section', in James Joyce, *Dubliners,* ed. Robert Scholes and A. Walton Litz (New York: Penguin, 1996), pp. 290–1.
21. Ezra Pound, '"Dubliners" and Mr. James Joyce', *The Egoist*, 1.14 (15 July 1914): 267.
22. Ibid.
23. Ibid.
24. Marais, '"Queer small town people"': 17.
25. Sean Latham (ed.), 'Introduction', in James Joyce, *Dubliners* (New York: Longman, 2010), p. xv.
26. S. E. Gontarski (ed.), 'Introduction,' in *Samuel Beckett: The Complete Short Prose, 1929–1989* (New York: Grove, 1996), p. xii.
27. Andrew Fox, 'Samuel Beckett: The Last Naturalist', in Catriona Ryan (ed.), *Writing from the Margins: The Aesthetics of Disruption in the Irish Short Story* (Newcastle upon Tyne: Cambridge Scholars), pp. 23–6.
28. Samuel Beckett, *More Pricks than Kicks* (New York: Grover, 1970), p. 10.
29. Ibid. p. 22.
30. Quoted in Heldrich, *Connecting Surfaces*, p. 427.
31. Beckett, *More Pricks*, p. 89.
32. Ibid. p. 103.
33. Mark Nixon, '"Guess where": From Reading to Writing in Beckett', *Genetic Joyce Studies*, 6 (Spring 2006). Available at <http://www.antwerpjamesjoycecenter.com/articles/GJS6/GJS6Nixon> (last accessed 15 April 2018), n.p.
34. Beckett, *More Pricks*, p. 89.
35. Ibid. p. 158.
36. Ibid. p. 190.
37. Paul March-Russell, *The Short Story: An Introduction* (Edinburgh: Edinburgh University Press, 2009), p. 103.
38. For more on why the short story flourishes in such contexts, see Nagel, *Contemporary American Short-Story Cycle*; Rocío G. Davis, *Transcultural Reinventions: Asian American and Asian Canadian Short-story Cycles* (Toronto: TSAR Publications, 2002); and Mark McGurl, *The Program Era: Postwar Fiction and the Rise of Creative Writing* (Cambridge, MA: Harvard University Press, 2009).
39. For more on Caribbean volumes, see Julie Barak, '"Turning and Turning in the Widening Gyre": A Second Coming into Language in Julia Alvarez's *How the García Girls Lost Their Accents*', *MELUS*, 23.1 (1998): 159–76; and Benjamin Forkner, 'Short Story Cycles of the Americas, A Transitional Post-Colonial Form: A Study of V. S. Naipaul's *Miguel Street*, Ernest Gaines's *Bloodline*, and Gabriel Garcia Marquez's *Los Funerales De Mama Grande*.' Dissertation (Baton Rouge: Louisiana State University, 2012).

40. Byatt, *Matisse Stories*, p. 72.
41. Ibid. p. 85.
42. Sarah Fishwick, 'Encounters with Matisse: Space, Art, And Intertextuality in A. S. Byatt's *The Matisse Stories* and Marie Redonnet's *Villa Rosa*', *Modern Language Review*, 99.1 (2004): 53.
43. Ibid. 54.
44. Byatt, *Matisse Stories*, p. 60.
45. Fludernik, Monika. 'Introduction'. Available at <www.gabrieljosipovici.org> (last accessed 15 April 2018), n.p.
46. Werner Wolf, 'The Role of Music in Gabriel Josipovici's *Goldberg: Variations*', *Style*, 37.3 (2003): 294.
47. Theodore Ziolkowski, 'Literary Variations on Bach's *Goldberg*', *Modern Language Review*, 105.3 (July 2010): 637.
48. Gabriel Josipovici, *Goldberg: Variations* (Manchester: Carcanet, 2002), p. 1.
49. Ibid. p. 3.
50. Ibid. p. 171.
51. Ibid. p. 175.
52. Ibid. p. 166.
53. Ibid. pp. 97–8.

Bibliography

Barak, Julie, '"Turning and Turning in the Widening Gyre": A Second Coming into Language', in Julia Alvarez's *How the García Girls Lost Their Accents*,' *MELUS*, 23.1 (1998): 159–76.

Baron, Scarlett, *Strandentwining Cable: Joyce, Flaubert, and Intertextuality* (Oxford: Oxford University Press, 2012).

Barth, John, *Lost in the Funhouse* (New York: Anchor, 1988).

Beckett, Samuel, *More Pricks than Kicks* (New York: Grover, 1970).

Byatt, A. S., *The Matisse Stories* (London: Chatto & Windus, 1993).

Charters, Ann, 'Introduction', in Ann Charters (ed.), *Three Lives* (New York: Penguin, 1990), pp. vii–xx.

Davis, Rocío G., *Transcultural Reinventions: Asian American and Asian Canadian Short-story Cycles* (Toronto: TSAR Publications, 2002).

D'hoker, Elke, 'The short story cycle: broadening the perspective', *Short Fiction in Theory and Practice*, 3.2 (2013): 151–9.

Dunn, Maggie and Ann Morris, *The Composite Novel, the Short Story Cycle in Transition* (New York: Twayne; Toronto: Maxwell Macmillan Canada, 1995).

Fishwick, Sarah, 'Encounters with Matisse: Space, Art, And Intertextuality in A. S. Byatt's *The Matisse Stories* and Marie Redonnet's *Villa Rosa*', *Modern Language Review*, 99.1 (2004): 52–64.

Fludernik, Monika, 'Introduction', <www.gabrieljosipovici.org> (last accessed 15 April 2018).

Forkner, Benjamin, 'Short Story Cycles of the Americas, A Transitional Post-Colonial Form: A Study of V. S. Naipaul's *Miguel Street*, Ernest Gaines's *Bloodline*, and Gabriel Garcia Marquez's *Los Funerales De Mama Grande*'. Dissertation (Baton Rouge: Louisiana State University, 2012).

Fox, Andrew, 'Samuel Beckett: The Last Naturalist', in Catriona Ryan (ed.), *Writing from the Margins: The Aesthetics of Disruption in the Irish Short Story* (Newcastle upon Tyne: Cambridge Scholars), pp. 23–36.

Gallup, Donald, *Flowers of Friendship: Letters Written to Gertrude Stein* (London: Octagon, 1979).

Gontarski, S. E. (ed.), 'Introduction', in *Samuel Beckett: The Complete Short Prose, 1929–1989* (New York: Grove, 1996), pp. xi–xxix.

Heldrich, Philip, 'Connecting Surfaces: Gertrude Stein's *Three Lives*, Cubism, and the Metonymy of the Short Story Cycle', *Studies in Short Fiction*, 34.4 (1997): 427–40.

Ingram, Forrest L., *Representative Short Story Cycles of the Twentieth Century: Studies in a Literary Genre* (The Hague: Mouton, 1971).

Josipovici, Gabriel, *Goldberg: Variations* (Manchester: Carcanet, 2002).

Joyce, James, *Dubliners*, ed. Robert Scholes and A. Walton Litz (New York: Penguin, 1996).

Kennedy, J. Gerald, *Modern American Short Story Sequences: Composite Fictions and Fictive Communities* (Cambridge: Cambridge University Press, 1995).

Latham, Sean (ed.), 'Introduction', in James Joyce, *Dubliners* (New York: Longman, 2010), pp. xiii–xvii.

Lundén, Rolf, *The United Stories of America: Studies in the Short Story Composite* (Amsterdam: Rodopi, 1999).

McGurl, Mark, *The Program Era: Postwar Fiction and the Rise of Creative Writing* (Cambridge, MA: Harvard University Press, 2009).

Marais, Sue, '"Queer small town people": Fixations and fictions of fellowship in the modern short story cycle', *Current Writing: Text and Reception in Southern Africa*, 17.1 (2011): 14–36.

March-Russell, Paul, *The Short Story: An Introduction* (Edinburgh: Edinburgh University Press, 2009).

Nagel, James, *The Contemporary American Short-Story Cycle: The Ethnic Resonance of Genre* (Baton Rouge: Louisiana University Press, 2001).

Nixon, Mark, '"Guess where": From Reading to Writing in Beckett', *Genetic Joyce Studies*, 6 (Spring 2006): n.p. <http://www.antwerpjamesjoycecenter.com/articles/GJS6/GJS6Nixon> (last accessed 15 April 2018).

North, Michael, *The Dialect of Modernism: Race, Language, and Twentieth-Century Literature* (Oxford: Oxford University Press, 1998).

Pacht, Michelle, *The Subversive Storyteller: The Short Story Cycle and the Politics of Identity in America* (Newcastle upon Tyne: Cambridge Scholars, 2009).

Pound, Ezra. '"Dubliners" and Mr. James Joyce', *The Egoist*, 1.14 (15 July 1914): 267.

Scholes, Robert and A. Walton Litz (eds), James Joyce, *Dubliners* (New York: Penguin, 1996).

Stein, Gertrude, *The Collected Writings of Gertrude Stein*, ed. Carl Van Vechten (New York: Vintage, 1990).

— *Three Lives*, ed. Ann Charters (New York: Penguin, 1990).

Wolf, Werner, 'The Role of Music in Gabriel Josipovici's *Goldberg: Variations*', *Style*, 37.3 (2003): 294–317.

Ziolkowski, Theodore, 'Literary Variations on Bach's *Goldberg*', *Modern Language Review*, 105.3 (2010): 625–40.

7

The Short Story Anthology

Elke D'hoker

In his 1901 essay 'Some Anomalies of the Short Story', W. D. Howells tackled the vexing question why short story collections don't sell:

> What is the solution as to the form of publication for short stories, since people do not object to them singly but collectively, and not in variety, but in identity of authorship? Are they to be printed only in the magazines, or are they to be collected in volumes combining a variety of authorship?[1]

Finding both solutions inadequate, magazines being too ephemeral and anthologies too uneven and distracting, he 'wish[ed]' instead that 'it might be found feasible to purvey them in some pretty shape where each would appeal singly to the reader'.[2] If publishers have often repeated the mantra that story collections don't sell, critics have often echoed Howells's frustration with the anthology as an all too fragmented and disparate format for publishing short fiction. 'The role of the anthology is fraught with problems', Paul March-Russell writes: apart from the problem of selection, 'there is also an aesthetic concern . . . reading several short stories together violates Poe's contention that a short story is to be read as a single and self-sufficient unit'.[3] Leah Price concurs, commenting that 'the anthology violates modern readers' sense that the material unit (the book) should coincide with the verbal unit (the text)'.[4]

Yet, it is precisely this non-coincidence of the material unit of publication and the verbal unit of the story that characterises the short story as a genre. A short story is by necessity published together with other texts: in a magazine, a newspaper, a collection, online or, indeed, in an anthology. If this context proves distracting or problematic to some critics, it can also be viewed in a more positive light: as a polyphonic echo chamber that creates meanings and resonances beyond those of the single text. Especially in the miscellaneous context of an anthology, a story's 'juxtaposition with other stories, either through the reader's choice or because of the editor's ordering of the selection, can have unexpected (and possibly creative) outcomes'.[5] Taken out of their original publication context, stories in an anthology can forge new and unexpected connections with other texts. Far more than in the case of the novel, where material and verbal units coincide, the publication context of a short story has an influence on the reader's understanding of that story. Reading a short story in a magazine, next to reportage or advertisements, is a very different experience from reading a story in a single-authored collection or in a thematically organised anthology. Different co-texts evoke different meanings, so that the understanding of the short story is altered, however slightly.

In short, whether one approves or disapproves of anthologies, it is clear that they have a certain power. Not only do anthologies affect individual readings by placing existing stories in a new textual environment, they also play a part in canon formation, by promoting some authors and relegating others. Moreover, anthologies shape expectations of literary form, thus helping to mould and define genres. Price makes a convincing case in this respect for the role of the prose anthology in the rise of the novel in the nineteenth century. Bestselling gift books, annuals and anthologies, which sampled favourite extracts from novels, she argues, were crucial in forming readers' tastes, reading strategies and expectations. In this way, they 'shaped the production of new novels even more than the re-production of the literary past'.[6] This genre-shaping potential also characterised the short fiction anthologies which started to appear around the middle of the nineteenth century. Such books 'were central to establishing the generic credentials of short fiction', Tim Killick argues, 'defining the form as both literarily distinct and relevant'.[7] Two centuries later, anthologies remain popular, and the form retains importance in shaping readerly expectations about what constitutes the short story. In order to better understand the short story, therefore, the anthology needs to be studied as a literary form with a literary, cultural, and ideological power of its own.

Derived from the Greek word *anthologein*, to collect flowers, anthologies of epigrams already existed in Ancient Greece.[8] The practice of collecting quotations from literary and philosophical texts, mainly for educational purposes, was continued in subsequent centuries. In the Middle Ages, anthologies, or *florilegia* as they were more often called, presented extracts from the classical and/or Christian tradition around a given theme. While the terms *anthologia* and *florilegium* seem to have been used interchangeably in medieval literature,[9] in the Renaissance, the term miscellany was often used to denote anthologies of poetry in the vernacular. *Tottel's Miscellany* (1557) was the first of many such collections, but miscellanies could incorporate prose or drama extracts as well as verse. From the end of the eighteenth century, excerpts from novels were also extracted and anthologised.[10] In short, the practice of selecting, extracting and editing previously published work was already well-established by the beginning of the nineteenth century, when the first short story anthologies started to appear.

In *The English Novel, 1830–1836*, Peter Garside mentions as one of the 'manifestations of a transformational fiction market', 'compilations of shorter fiction, usually presented as edited by one person, such as Andrew Picken's *The Club-Book*'.[11] Miscellanies of tales also appeared around this time, mostly in the form of translations from German or French: *German Stories* (1826), *Specimens of German Romance* (1826) and *Popular Tales and Romances of the Northern Nations* (1823).[12] Two other antecedents to the short story anthology are the collections of, mostly anonymous, folk and fairy tales and the gift books or annuals that were bestsellers in the first half of the nineteenth century.[13] These beautifully illustrated books contained short fiction, as well as verse and prose fragments. As a rule, publishers of gift books commissioned, and paid handsomely for, new work from established authors. Some early short fiction anthologies, such as *The Encyclopedia of Romance* (1833) and *The Continental Annual and Romantic Cabinet* (1832), seem to have been modelled on these gift books in terms of illustration and marketing.[14] What makes them short story anthologies is that they reprinted previously published work from different authors. Indeed, unlike the gift books and other multi-authored books, the anthology typically selects and presents literary texts that have already been published elsewhere.[15]

It should come as no surprise, therefore, that the short fiction anthology only really took off when the publication of short stories or tales in magazines became more common. Killick notes how an early anthology, *The Story-Teller* (1830), 'drew together stories from *Blackwood's Edinburgh Magazine,* the *New Monthly Magazine,* the *Ladies' Museum,* and *Arliss's Pocket Magazine*, as well as translations from the French and German'.[16] As Wendell Harris has argued, in Britain *Blackwood's* was particularly important for the development of short fiction throughout the century. Its popularity was attested to by the publication of a series of story anthologies, *Tales from Blackwood*, which went through several reprints and helped to determine generic conventions: 'The form and content of these tales ... provided a constant model of what respectable short fiction was expected to be.'[17] It is interesting to observe how already in the first half of the nineteenth century, short fiction anthologies were organised in ways that are still current today. Stories could be gathered on the basis of origin (the German or Northern tales), genre (romance stories or Gothic tales), or their link to a particular magazine. Moreover, editors, who were often also authors, prided themselves on 'cherry-picking the best examples' from the ever-increasing body of short fiction that was being published.[18] With the boom of short fiction in the later decades of the nineteenth century, the number of anthologies increased. And even as the short story's popularity waned in the second half of the twentieth century, and the amount of short fiction published in periodicals dwindled considerably, the anthology seems to have remained a popular format for short fiction.[19] Every year, major publishers as well as independent presses in the anglophone world bring out new short story anthologies, catering to different tastes, needs and audiences. In order to bring some clarity to this varied and ever-expanding domain, some distinctions can be introduced to classify anthologies according to type, structure, scope and aim.

A distinction is sometimes drawn by critics between 'commercial' and 'literary' anthologies, the first 'published for the purpose of entertainment', the second composed with aesthetic rather than commercial ambitions.[20] For March-Russell, the very success of the commercial anthology constitutes a threat to the literary anthology: 'Due to the invisibility of literary anthologies, commercial collections not only dominate the marketplace but also make it potentially difficult for readers to access literary short fiction.'[21] His remarks echo Laura Riding's and Robert Graves' attack on 'the all too numerous trade anthologies that turn poetry into an industrial packet-commodity'. As they argued in their 1928 *A Pamphlet against Anthologies*, the 'salad-mixing of a popular anthology' corrupts readers by making them read too superficially and blinding them to individual style and talent.[22] To the 'trade anthology', they oppose the 'true anthology', even though they would prefer to do away with anthologies altogether. As these two quotations suggest, the distinction between literary and commercial anthologies is highly judgemental and subject to debate. Even such obviously commercial projects as anthologies devoted to different sports or animals typically contain stories by canonical literary authors,[23] for instance, while anthologies edited by respected authors or critics, and issued by publishers of literary fiction, remain commercial ventures. To give one example: in 2009, Ali Smith, Kasia Boddy and Sarah Wood edited the anthology *Let's Call the Whole Thing Off: Love Quarrels from Anton Chekhov to ZZ Packer*, with stories by a variety of celebrated authors. The topic of the collection, however, its handsome binding, and its launch just before Valentine's Day, clearly marked the book as a commercial product. Moreover, contrary to March-Russell's complaint, this 'literary' anthology was given extensive coverage in the press. The same holds true for two recent anthologies of Irish women writers, edited by Sinéad Gleeson, which received a lot of attention in Ireland and were awarded the Best Irish Published Book Award in 2015 and 2016, respectively. Since sales figures tend to be jealously guarded by publishers, it is difficult to find exact information about the commercial success of short story anthologies. Nonetheless, as Dean Baldwin has demonstrated, anthologies are 'often very profitable for their publishers and appear to have involved little risk', even though authors 'could expect little more than pin money and a bit of prestige from appearing in an anthology of any kind'.[24]

A better way of classifying anthologies than the problematic distinction between commercial and literary is to look at the criteria governing selection. First, anthologies may be organised around a specific theme or topic. These can range from the frivolous to the serious: from the anonymously edited *The Dover Anthology of Cat Stories* (2015) to Diane Secker Tesdell's *Stories of Motherhood* and *Stories of Fatherhood* (2012, 2014 respectively) to Trudi Tate's *Women, Men, and the Great War: An Anthology of Stories*, published by Manchester University Press (1996). Popular themes include love, death and war, as well as sports, regions or animals, and childhood, adolescence and family relations. Typically, these themed anthologies advertise canonical or bestselling authors on their covers, even though the entire selection usually consists of a mixture of major and minor writers. Many of these themed anthologies are also marketed as gift books, recalling the nineteenth-century annuals which invited new stories from established authors.

A second, equally popular group, consists of anthologies devoted to specific sub-genres of the short story. Anthologies of horror and terror, of romance stories, ghost stories and Gothic stories were already popular in the early nineteenth century and continue to sell. In *The Supernatural Index: A Listing of Fantasy, Supernatural, Occult, Weird, Horror Anthologies* (1995), Michael Ashley and William D. Contento list over 2,100 anthologies published over the course of two centuries. The twentieth century also saw the rise of other genre anthologies, such as detective stories, science fiction stories, comic stories, erotic stories and fantasy stories.[25] Arguably, anthologies of genre short fiction became even more important in the second half of the twentieth century, as the market for specialised periodicals shrank dramatically, in Britain and in the US. More recent additions to this group of anthologies defined by genre include flash fiction anthologies, such as Robert Shapard's series of *Sudden Fiction*, the annual anthologies issued by the National Flash-Fiction Day, or the recent *Flash Fiction International: Very Short Stories from Around the World* (2015).[26] Especially in the case of new – or newly fashionable – genres such as flash fiction, the prefaces to these anthologies are important in shaping genre consciousness among readers. For instance, in their preface to *Jawbreakers* (2012), the first anthology of the (British) National Flash-Fiction Day, the editors address the question 'what *exactly* . . . are these things called flash-fictions?', and argue that 'these are tiny, concise tales that condense, like our titular jawbreakers, an enormity of flavour and energy into a very dense space'.[27] Given the relative obscurity of flash fiction in Britain, their anthology proposes 'to celebrate this form of story and to bring it to the attention of the wider public'.

As a series of anthologies linked with a literary event, *Jawbreakers* and the three volumes of *Scraps* that followed, can also be said to belong to a third group of anthologies, those connected to literary institutions of different kinds. The first to emerge in this group were the anthologies linked to literary magazines: successive series of *Tales from Blackwood*, *Atlantic Tales* and *Choice Stories from Dickens' Household Words* were followed in the early twentieth century by anthologies such as *The Time and Tide Album* (1932), *The English Review Book of Short Stories* (1933–4)[28] and, in 1940, the first of many collections associated with *The New Yorker*.[29] As the publication of short fiction in literary magazines decreased in the second half of the twentieth century, even more so in Britain than in the US, so did the number of anthologies to come out of magazines. Nevertheless, some recent examples include Dave Eggers's *The Best of McSweeney's* (2013), published to celebrate the fifteenth anniversary of *McSweeney's Quarterly*, and Lorin and Sadie Stern's *Object Lessons: The Paris Review Presents the Art of the Short Story* (2012). In general, though, the role of magazine anthologies has been overtaken by anthologies linked to literary prizes. The most famous of these is the annual anthology of the O. Henry Prize, which has run in different formats since 1918 and selects the twenty 'best' stories published in American and Canadian magazines in a given year. In 2005, the BBC National Short Story Award was established on this very model and its shortlisted stories have also been published in annual anthologies.

The *O. Henry Prize Stories* anthologies are also closely related to the ever-expanding group of 'best of' anthologies, which have been popular since the late nineteenth century. A canonical series in this respect is the long-running *Best American Short Stories*, launched in 1915 by Edward J. O'Brien, who edited the series until his death in 1941. Next to the 'best' stories of any given year, O'Brien's anthologies also contained his own views on the form, a classification of all stories following grades of 'distinctiveness', a bibliographical list of articles or books on the short story form, and an exhaustive list of all the magazine stories, story collections and anthologies published in that year.[30] O'Brien made a lasting mark on the development of the short story as a literary genre, and many important authors found recognition and support in his collections.[31] After O'Brien's death, the American series was continued by Martha Foley for thirty years; since 1978, authors have been invited to act as guest editors for individual volumes. The British equivalent, *Best British Short Stories*, which O'Brien edited between 1922 and 1940, was not continued.[32] Faber and Faber have partially filled that gap with their practice of publishing a variety of 'best of' anthologies, from a series of *My Best Story* in the 1920s and 30s,[33] to the *Faber Book of Best New Irish Stories* series which has appeared almost annually since 2005. Other 'best of' anthologies are more ambitious in their reach, simply presenting 'the' best stories of the world. Well-known examples which have gone through many reprints are Milton Crane's *50 Great Stories* (1952), *Short Story Masterpieces*, edited by Robert Penn Warren and Albert Erskine (1954), *Randall Jarrell's Book of Stories* (1958) and V. S. Pritchett's *The Oxford Book of Short Stories* (1981). Recently, Andrew Miller selected '100 of the finest stories ever written', for his anthology *That Glimpse of Truth* (2014).

Even though the titles or subtitles of these anthologies suggest a global reach, most have a strong anglophone bias. Pritchett, Warren and Erskine limit themselves to short stories originally written in English. Three of Crane's 'greatest' stories are translated works and so are sixteen of Miller's hundred 'finest' stories. Only *Randall Jarrell's Book of Stories* is perhaps a truly global anthology, with thirteen stories from anglophone writers and seventeen originally written in other languages. While the English language bias is not commented on in any of the prefaces or subtitles of these anthologies, other subjective preferences involved in the selection tend to be highlighted, whether implicitly, through the foregrounding of the editor's name in the title or on the cover of the book, or explicitly, by means of the preface. 'Any anthology is a weird, wonky wonder', Andrew Miller writes in his introduction to *That Glimpse of Truth*, 'Are all the short stories selected here *really* the "finest"? *Who* says – and *why*, let alone *how*?'[34] The preface thus becomes the place to explain and to justify one's aesthetic criteria and the processes of selection.

If the 'best of' anthologies claim to make their selection on the basis of aesthetic excellence and generic norms, anthologies premised on a region, country or continent usually add representativeness to the selection criteria: a story will be selected if it is understood to speak for the region, country or continent as a whole. Anthologies of Irish and Scottish short fiction have been popular in Britain since the beginning of the nineteenth century. Samuel Lover, for instance, edited *Popular Tales and Legends of the Irish Peasantry* in 1834, while Andrew Picken's *The Club-Book* (1836) included tales by Scottish authors such as James Hogg, John Galt, William Jerdan, Alan Cunningham and Picken himself.[35] Later, these anthologies were added to by other collections claiming to offer the best or most representative of stories from a particular country, whether in English or in translation. For the early twentieth century, Baldwin mentions as new developments such titles as *Australian Short Stories* (1929/30), *Stories of Africa* (1931/2) and *Tales by New Zealanders* (1938/9),[36] while the second half of the twentieth century saw major publishers on both sides of the Atlantic promoting anthologies of short fiction from France and Russia to the Caribbean and Japan. While such anthologies are mostly drawn from countries and regions peripheral to the centre in which they are published, recent years have also seen the publication of two volumes of *The Granta Book of the American Short Story*, edited by Richard Ford and the two-volume *Penguin Book of the British Short Story*, edited by Philip Hensher. As these titles also show, it is common practice for publishers to explicitly lend their name to such regional or national anthologies and to invite well-known authors to select and introduce the stories. Hensher's introduction to *The Penguin Book of the British Short Story* offers a good illustration of the mixture of aesthetic criteria, genre expectations and concerns for representativeness and comprehensiveness that can motivate an editor's selection. 'Britishness' is here an inclusive, if slippery, notion: while Elizabeth Bowen, Jean Rhys and Sam Selvon are included, Henry James and Katherine Mansfield are not. At the same time, Hensher has taken care to represent different regions and population groups within Britain. Comprehensiveness also informs his temporal reach – stories from Defoe to the present – as well as his wish 'to go beyond the *oeuvres* of celebrated and once-celebrated authors' by including short stories from a larger variety of writers who published in periodicals.[37] Finally, Hensher draws on aesthetic and generic norms to justify his selection: stories he 'admired' but which also serve to illustrate the 'distinctive qualities' of the British short story: playfulness, performance, surprise and topicality.[38]

Like many 'national' anthologies, *The Penguin Book of the British Short Story* also celebrates the merits of the tradition that is represented. 'The British short story is probably the richest, most varied and most historically extensive tradition anywhere in the world', Hensher claims, even as he acknowledges certain hesitations about who does, or does not, belong to that tradition.[39] Interesting exceptions to this assertion of national pride include such explicitly non-national anthologies as Ova Adagha and Molara Woods's *One World: A Global Anthology of Short Stories* (2009) and Linda Prescott's *A World of Difference: An Anthology of Short Stories from Five Continents* (2008). As with the 'best ever' short story anthologies, however, these publications have an implicit anglophone bias and only include stories originally written in English.

In the titles of the latter two texts (*One World* and *A World of Difference*), one can also trace the influence of recent critical and cultural movements on the organisation and marketing of anthologies in recent years. The canon wars of the 1970s and 1980s have made editors more conscious of the legacy effect of anthologies, and collections have since been used as powerful tools in the recovery of forgotten writers and the promotion of new voices. These anthologies are mostly construed around the identity of authors, determined by such markers as gender, sexuality, race, ethnicity or class. Women writers were among the first to benefit from this recovery project, through such anthologies as *The Secret Self: Short Stories by Women*, edited by Hermione Lee (1985), *The Penguin Book of Modern Women's Short Stories*, edited, in several versions, by Susan Hill (1991), *The Unforgetting Heart: An Anthology of Short Stories by African-American Women*, edited by Asha Kanwar (1993), *Nineteenth-Century Short Stories by Women: A Routledge Anthology*, edited by Harriet Devine Jump (2003), and the monumental *The Story: Love, Loss and the Lives of Women*, edited by Victoria Hislop (2013). In the prefaces to these anthologies, the editors emphasise the necessity to foreground women's short fiction because of its omission from earlier anthologies; they also engage with the potential problem of linking gender and genre in this way. Hermione Lee writes, for instance, 'It doesn't seem profitable . . . to pursue a separatist aesthetic of the twentieth century woman's short story', yet this does not stop her from locating the difference of the female perspective in the specific 'conflicts' women short stories seek to express, 'between secret visions and unwelcome realities, between personal desires and family restrictions, between consolatory dreams and hostile circumstances'.[40]

Other anthologies which have followed in the wake of new developments in literary and cultural studies are anthologies of gay and lesbian stories, such as *The New Penguin Book of Gay Short Stories* (2004), edited by David Leavitt and Mark Mitchell, and *The Mammoth Book of Lesbian Short Stores* (1999), edited by Emma Donoghue. The increased attention to issues of race and ethnicity in literature has also left its imprint on short story anthologies. A ground-breaking example is Langston Hughes's *The Best Stories by Black Writers: 1899–1967* (1967), which was brought up to date by Gloria Naylor with *Children of the Night: The Best Stories by Black Writers, 1967 to the present* (1995). A more recent example is *Closure: Contemporary Black British Short Stories* (2015), edited by Jacob Ross. The changing discourse of identity politics is also reflected in the preface to each of these anthologies. Langston Hughes offered his stories as testimony to the increasing literary prominence of black writers: 'In fiction as in life Negroes get around. They have been covering various grounds for a considerable time via the written word.'[41] Gloria Naylor, on the other hand, remarked that the stories 'are examples of affirmation', an affirmation of survival and identity alike.[42] Jacob Ross, finally, has a more pragmatic view of the shared ethnic identity on which his anthology is based: '"Black Britishness" is what it is, a lived reality that is like air or breath or blood: important, but hardly at the forefront of one's consciousness.'[43] Yet, like Hughes and Naylor, he is at the same time eager to endorse this group of writers as 'capable of bringing a distinctive and striking fluency to the form', and expresses the hope that his anthology will bring these writers more attention and recognition.[44]

Promoting new writers, delineating a tradition, or affirming an identity: these are only some of the many different functions anthologies have served over the centuries. At its simplest, the anthology offers a solution to the problem of how best to publish a short story which, precisely because of its limited length, is difficult to bring out as a separate text. This question of publication also underscores the commercial function of short story anthologies as a means not just of publishing stories, but also of selling them, and making them sell. Throughout the 1930s and 1940s, Dean Baldwin has calculated, short story anthologies were more profitable to publishers than to authors or editors. Since many anthologies still advertise the name of the publisher in their title, the same may hold true today. Yet, authors and editors may have other reasons for collaborating with anthologies. For authors, obviously, anthologies offer promotion and publicity. Editors, on the other hand, may be drawn by the opportunity to foreground a certain group of possibly neglected writers, or to advance a certain idea about the short story form. This ties in with the canon-shaping function of the short story anthology. As Karen Kilcup puts it, 'composing an anthology creates a miniature canon, no matter how resistant the editor is to the vexed notions of goodness and importance'.[45] If in poetry criticism, the role of anthologies in canon formation has been the subject of intense controversy and debate,[46] short story anthologies have not yet received similar scrutiny. Nevertheless, the role of anthologies in shaping particular conceptualisations of a national tradition, promoting certain writers and marginalising others, cannot be overstated. Apart from influencing the general reader, who may wish to sample the 'highlights' of a certain period, region or group, anthologies are also widely used in educational contexts, which further strengthens the role they play in shaping a canon and promoting a certain idea of excellence. It is therefore important to remain aware of the often highly subjective criteria that inform the selection of stories for an anthology: general criteria of aesthetic value as well as more specific ones of generic propriety. To these are added equally problematic notions of national, regional or ethnic identity, and concerns about representativeness, readability and literary status.

A brief comparison of four anthologies of Irish short fiction illustrates the extent to which editorial convictions influence the selection of stories. The anthologies are Vivian Mercier's *Great Irish Short Stories* (1964), Frank O'Connor's *Modern Irish Short Stories* (1957), William Trevor's *The Oxford Book of Irish Short Stories* (1989) and Benedict Kiely's *The Penguin Book of Irish Short Stories* (1981). While each of these anthologies claims to reflect the tradition of the Irish short story, they are all instrumental in shaping that tradition. Their influence in this respect may be gauged by the fact that they have all gone through several editions and only Mercier's collection is currently out of print. A first difference between these anthologies concerns the starting point they envisage for the Irish short story tradition. Mercier starts his chronological selection with a story extracted from Muirchú's life of Saint Patrick, published in Latin around 700, arguing 'All books about Irish literature should begin with St. Patrick ... for it was he, or other Christian missionaries like him, who brought the Roman alphabet to Ireland, and thus made Gaelic literature possible.'[47] Mercier also includes several medieval stories, translated from Middle Irish, before moving to nineteenth-century transcriptions of oral folkloric or mythic tales, and then, finally, to the first 'original' short story written by William Carleton in 1834.

In his anthology, Trevor starts with a selection of oral folk tales, since 'it is against this background of a pervasive, deeply rooted oral tradition that the modern short story in Ireland must inevitably be considered'.[48] His first story proper is Oliver Goldsmith's 'Adventures of a Strolling Player', which was published in *The British Magazine* in 1765. O'Connor, to the contrary, has the Irish short story tradition start at the turn of the twentieth century with George Moore, as he claims that 'the short story as an art form [is] distinct from the tale'.[49] Kiely takes yet another starting point: Lady Gregory's 'The Daughter of King Under-Wave', taken from her cycle of Gaelic myths, *Gods and Fighting Men* (1904). Clearly, each of these selections depends on the editor's notion of what constitutes a short story: any story that is short and that can even be extracted from a longer text, in the case of Mercier; a stand-alone tale, written or oral, according to Trevor and Kiely; or a specific modern literary genre, as O'Connor suggests. The selections also betray the editors' contrasting views on the origins of the genre: did it develop from the folk tale tradition or from the novel, or did it emerge as a new literary form as a consequence of colonial conquest and foreign influence?

A second point of divergence concerns the question of nationality: what makes a short story an Irish short story? Mercier, with his very inclusive definition of short fiction, has the most exclusive idea of an 'Irish' short story: 'I have deliberately confined myself not merely to authors of Irish birth but to stories with an Irish background and/or characters.'[50] Hence, stories by Goldsmith, Oscar Wilde or Elizabeth Bowen find no place in his anthology, even though W. B. Yeats and Samuel Beckett do. These writers are excluded by Trevor, 'because they conveyed their ideas more skilfully in another medium'.[51] Yet Trevor includes Wilde's 'The Sphinx Without a Secret', a story with no overt link to Ireland, and several of the stories chosen by Kiely are not set in Ireland and do not have a distinctively 'Irish' subject matter. Thirdly, the anthologies differ in their stance towards Irish-language short stories: Trevor and Mercier include one or two such stories in translation, Kiely and O'Connor omit the Irish-language tradition altogether. Finally, in each case, the Irish short story is a predominantly male affair: the proportion of stories by women writers in all of the anthologies is unrepresentative. As Sinéad Gleeson notes in her preface to *The Long Gaze Back: An Anthology of Irish Women Writers* (2015), in 'any anthology of Irish short stories published between 1950 and 1990', 'a reader would usually find there were rarely more than five stories by women. Many anthologies had none, others had just two female writers, and it was always the ubiquitous names, the female stalwarts of the form.'[52] Gleeson's all-female anthologies seek to redress this imbalance. Still, in terms of canon formation, Anne Enright's *The Granta Book of the Irish Short Story* (2010) is probably more effective: she includes ten stories by women writers next to twenty-one by men.

In all of these anthologies, the normative effect of the selection is further underscored by the introductions or prefaces, in which editors explicitly voice their opinions about the genre of the short story, its tradition, and – in the case of Vivian Mercier – its aesthetic 'greatness'. Mercier's anthology also explicitly advertises its educational function, as it introduces every story with information about the author and offers a preliminary interpretation of the story. This practice also characterises Ann Charters's *The Story and its Writer*, which has been updated in nine editions since 1983 and has shaped the ideas about the short story of many generations of American students. Nevertheless, in her introduction, Charters says nothing about the criteria or ideals governing her selection and only briefly touches upon the short story's distinct characteristics of 'unity' and 'concentration', by means of which it allows the reader 'to catch a glimpse of what life is like'.[53]

More explicit in voicing ideas about aesthetic excellence and generic norms are anthologies that seek to introduce and promote a new generation of writers. Such anthologies have a clear programmatic function and provide a way for emerging writers to generate critical and public attention. A well-known example of such an anthology is *Anti-Story: An Anthology of Experimental Fiction* (1971), which brought the postmodern and metafictional short story to wide attention. The anthology, which is still in print, contains stories by John Barth, Donald Barthelme and Robert Coover, as well as translated works by European and South American writers. In his introduction, Philip Stevick was keen to launch a new art form, criticising the 'narrow range' of early-twentieth-century short fiction, ridiculing its reliance on epiphany, praising the 'daring and imagination' of the new writers, and drawing attention to their shared concerns. 'Anti-stories', he argued, are marked by a strong degree of 'contrariness' and reject all the trappings of the 'classic story'; in different ways, the writers are 'against mimesis', 'against "reality"', 'against meaning', 'against subject' and 'against event'.[54] In 2003, *The Burned Children of America* similarly launched a new generation of writers, with stories by writers such as George Saunders, David Foster Wallace and A. M. Homes. While both of these anthologies were explicitly aimed at a renewal of the short story form, other programmatic anthologies have used stories as a convenient form through which to advance new ideas about writing more generally.

A case in point is *All Hail the New Puritans* (2000), edited by Nicolas Blincoe and Matt Thorne, who invited a new generation of British writers, all born around 1970 to write short stories that followed the ten aesthetic rules outlined in their preface, 'The New Puritan Manifesto'. While the editors were vocal in their advertisement of these rules, their minimalist credo was less about the short story, specifically, than about writing in general. Blincoe and Thorne even admitted to 'worries about using short stories as our medium rather than novels', and most of the authors included would identify themselves as novelists rather than as short story writers.[55] Moreover, although the collection was marketed and received as an anthology, it hovers on the margins of the form, since the anthology is traditionally defined as a form that selects and reprints previously published material. A programmatic intention can also be found in some anthologies devoted to specific sub-genres, such as the flash fiction anthologies mentioned earlier which seek to delineate and promote the form of the very short short story.

Programmatic anthologies, which are devoted to specific sub-genres, or which are intent on promoting a new generation of writers, are explicitly concerned with defining genres and creating a sense of tradition. However, as the Irish examples suggest, a normative dimension is embedded within most national or 'best of' anthologies as well. In this respect, the prefaces to these anthologies are often as important as the stories they present. For the editor, indeed, the preface is the place to outline ideas about the short story form, to make explicit certain principles of selection, and to assess the current or past development of the genre. For the reader, these prefaces can shape the reading experience, influence the interpretation of individual stories, and contribute to a more general sense of genre. For instance, readers of *The Penguin Book of the British Short Story* will probably look for signs of the comedy, playfulness and surprise which the editor, Philip Henscher, singles out as the distinctive characteristics of British short fiction. Similarly, readers of Hermione Lee's *The Secret Self* should be guided by the quotation from Katherine Mansfield which provides the anthology's title and thematic focus: 'One tries to go deep – to speak to the secret self we all have – to acknowledge that.'[56] More generally, prefaces to anthologies often contain statements by editors which illustrate their understanding of the most typical characteristics of the short story form. Given the time-honoured practice of inviting writers to edit anthologies, these prefaces have often been mined by critics for authorial statements about the form.

A famous example is Elizabeth Bowen's preface to *The Faber Book of Modern Stories* (1937), which has often been reprinted as a separate essay. In this preface, Bowen traced the development of the modern short story in Britain and Ireland, criticising the 'cult of Tchehov' which has led to too much 'lax, unconvincing or arty work', and called for a dose of Maupassant's 'vitality', 'astringency and iron relevance' to rectify the present imbalance.[57] In a long passage, marked by a series of compulsive verbs, Bowen dictated what she considered norms for the short story:

> The short story . . . must spring from an impression or perception pressing enough, acute enough, to have made the writer write . . . [it] should have the valid central emotion and inner spontaneity of the lyric; it should magnetize the imagination and give pleasure – of however disturbing, painful or complex a kind. The short story should be as composed, in the plastic sense, and as visual as a picture; it must have tautness and clearness; it must contain no passage not aesthetically relevant to the whole. . . . The subject must have implicit dignity . . . The plot . . . ought to raise some issue, so that it may continue in the mind.[58]

While some of these prescriptions echo the thoughts of earlier writers, such as Poe's insistence on unity or the modernist emphasis on 'impression or perception', others express Bowen's personal conviction that the best short stories strike a balance between the popular, plotted story which entertains and 'give[s] pleasure' and the modernist, plotless story, governed by 'emotion' or the desire to 'raise some issue'. For Bowen, the future of the short story lay in this middle ground, hence her warning: 'if the short story is to keep a living divinity, it is not to be side-tracked into preciousness, popular impatience on the one hand and minority fervour on the other will have to be kept in check'.[59] The short stories Bowen selected for *The Faber Book of Modern Stories* reflect this aesthetic credo. They include stories by Frank O'Connor, Seán O'Faoláin, A. E. Coppard, Stephen Spender, Osbert Sitwell and Bowen herself.

Few editors have been as detailed or as prescriptive as Bowen. Nonetheless, most prefaces include a definition of form. In her preface to *The Oxford Book of American Short Stories* (1992), for instance, Joyce Carol Oates writes:

> My personal definition of the form is that it represents a concentration of imagination, and not an expansion; it is no more than 10,000 words; and, no matter its mysteries or experimental properties, it achieves closure – meaning that, when it ends, the attentive reader understands why.[60]

For Pritchett in *The Oxford Book of Short Stories*, 'The short story springs from a spontaneously poetic as distinct from a prosaic impulse . . . A short story is always a disclosure, often an evocation . . . frequently the celebration of a character at bursting-point:

it approaches the mythical.'[61] Referring back to Pritchett's preface in his introduction to the *The New Granta Book of the American Short Story* (2007), Richard Ford finds the story's 'basic self' to be linked to 'its brevity and to its bravura quality, its daring and (again) its audacity, to how it makes much of little, and to how it wields its authority as – to borrow from Auden – a "verbal artefact"'.[62] Contemporary editors, perhaps, have become more wary of normative or universal definitions, and have chosen to instead advance an anecdote, an evocation or a metaphor. According to Anne Enright in *The Granta Book of the Irish Short Story*, '[short stories] are the cats of literary form; beautiful, but a little too self-contained for readers' tastes',[63] while in his introduction to *New American Stories* (2015), Ben Marcus describes at length his experience of reading – and the daunting task of selecting – short stories before claiming 'the idea was to put together a book that shows just what the short story can do . . . Each story here is a different weapon, built to custom specifications. Let's get bloodied and killed in thirty-two different ways.'[64]

If the best anthologies demonstrate 'that a short story can do pretty much anything', as Miller puts it in his preface to *That Glimpse of Truth*,[65] the purpose of this chapter has been to show just what an anthology can do. Far more than a mere solution to the problem of publishing short fiction, the anthology is a literary form which plays a major part in the production, promotion, reception, evaluation and understanding of the short story. Although the production and marketing of anthologies is itself influenced by the developments of the genre, by critical movements, and by broader national, cultural or social concerns, the anthology does not merely reflect these factors and concerns. It also reinforces and consolidates them. Throughout the history of the short story, anthologies have been instrumental in raising the profile and shaping the general understanding of this literary form. As instruments in education and canon formation, anthologies have also been used to establish a specific tradition, to promote new writers or to recover forgotten ones. Further research is necessary to probe deeper into the forms and functions of the anthology: the nineteenth-century roots of the short story anthology and its contribution to the development of the genre; the influence of its multi-textual format on the reading experience; the role of anthologies in the creation of specific national canons; and the generic norms and aesthetic criteria that shape – and are shaped by – its processes of selection. In addition, further research would be needed to provide more facts and figures about the publication of anthologies: titles, editions, sales figures and profits. Still, the anthologies discussed are representative of larger trends and, taken together, offer an overview of the many functions and forms of this often underestimated literary form.

Notes

1. W. D. Howells, 'Some Anomalies of the Short Story', *The North American Review*, 173.538 (1901): 424.
2. Ibid.
3. Paul March-Russell, *The Short Story: An Introduction* (Edinburgh: Edinburgh University Press, 2009), p. 53.
4. Leah Price, *The Anthology and the Rise of the Novel: From Richardson to George Eliot* (Cambridge: Cambridge University Press, 2000), p. 3.
5. Emma Liggins et al., *The British Short Story* (Basingstoke: Palgrave Macmillan, 2011), pp. 16–17.

6. Price, *The Anthology and the Rise of the Novel*, p. 99.
7. Tim Killick, *British Short Fiction in the Early Nineteenth Century: The Rise of the Tale* (Aldershot: Ashgate, 2008), p. 162.
8. J. A. Cuddon, *The Penguin Dictionary of Literary Terms and Literary Theory* (London: Penguin, 1999), p. 41.
9. Some critics distinguish these terms on the basis of either their content (religious vs. secular) or the length of the extracts, but there is no critical consensus about this. See Anthony Grafton et al., *The Classical Tradition* (Cambridge, MA: Harvard University Press, 2010), pp. 47–8; see also Simon Hornblower et al. (eds), *The Oxford Classical Dictionary* (Oxford: Oxford University Press, 2012), pp. 98–9.
10. Price, *The Anthology and the Rise of the Novel*, p. 2 ff.
11. Anthony Mandal and Peter Garside (eds), *The English Novel, 1830–1836: A Bibliographical Survey of Prose Fiction Published in the British Isles* (Cardiff: Centre for Editorial and Intertextual Research, 2003).
12. Hilary Brown, 'German Women Writers in English Short Story Anthologies of the 1820s', *The Modern Language Review*, 97.3 (July 2002): 621–2.
13. Wendell V. Harris, *British Short Fiction in the Nineteenth Century: A Literary and Bibliographic Guide* (Detroit: Wayne State University Press, 1979), pp. 24–5.
14. Killick, *British Short Fiction*, p. 160.
15. While this is indeed what defines the anthology as a literary form, it must be noted that short story anthologies may occasionally contain a mixture of previously published stories and newly commissioned work. Recent examples are the two anthologies of Irish women's short fiction edited by Sinéad Gleeson.
16. Killick, *British Short Fiction*, p. 160.
17. Three series of selections appeared: twelve volumes between 1858 and 1861, another twelve between 1878 and 1880, and a third series of six volumes in 1889–90. Other nineteenth-century anthologies connected to a magazine were *Tales from Bentley* (1859–60), *Stories from Black and White* (1893), *Pic Nics: From the Dublin Penny Journal* (1836) and *Choice Stories from Dickens' Household Words* (1854). Harris, *British Short Fiction*, pp. 28–9, pp. 166–7.
18. Killick, *British Short Fiction*, p. 161.
19. See Dean Baldwin, *Art and Commerce in the British Short Story: 1880–1950* (London: Pickering and Chatto, 2013), pp. 35–50. In 2004, *The Short Story in the UK report* revealed that while the publishing of short story collections was declining, a rise could be noted in the publication of anthologies since 2000. Jenny Brown Associates, *The Short Story in the UK Report*. Available at <http://www.theshortstory.org.uk/aboutus/The_Short_Story_in_the_UK_Report.pdf> (last accessed 15 April 2018), p. 6.
20. March-Russell, *The Short Story*, p. 55. David Hopkins pursues a roughly similar classification of 'academic' as opposed to 'trade' anthologies; David Hopkins, 'On Anthologies', *The Cambridge Quarterly*, 37.3 (2008): 290.
21. March-Russell, *The Short Story*, p. 55.
22. Laura Riding and Robert Graves, *A Pamphlet Against Anthologies* (London: Jonathan Cape, 1928), p. 185, p. 140.
23. To give just one example: *The Dover Anthology of Cat Stories* contains stories by Saki, Mark Twain, Guy de Maupassant, Rudyard Kipling and H. P. Lovecraft, next to other, lesser-known, names.
24. Baldwin, *Art and Commerce*, p. 115.
25. See Baldwin, *Art and Commerce*, p. 114 for a list of representative British titles from the first half of the twentieth century.
26. Robert Shapard has edited several *Sudden Fiction* anthologies devoted to American 'short short stories' since 1986. The British-based *Scraps* series of anthologies comes out of the *National Flash-Fiction Day*; four volumes have been published since 2012.

27. Calum Kerr and Valerie O'Riordan (eds), 'Foreword' to *Jawbreakers: 2012 National Flash-Fiction Day Anthology* (Southampton: National Flash-Fiction Day, 2012), p. 9.
28. Baldwin, *Art and Commerce*, p. 113.
29. The first anthology, *Stories from the New Yorker*, was published by Simon and Schuster in 1940, and would be followed by many similar titles: e.g. *55 Stories from the New Yorker* (1949), *Short Stories from the New Yorker 1950–1960* (1960), and *20 under 40: Stories from the New Yorker* (2010, ed. Deborah Treisman).
30. Andrew Levy, *The Culture and Commerce of the American Short Story* (Cambridge: Cambridge University Press, 1993), p. 36.
31. In a tribute to O'Brien in the preface to her own anthology, *The Best American Short Stories of the Century*, Katrina Kenison relates how O'Brien singlehandedly launched Hemingway's literary career in his 1923 anthology. Breaking his own rule of only selecting already published stories, he was the first to print one of Hemingway's stories, 'My Old Man', which had been rejected by several other editors. John Updike and Katrina Kenison, 'Introduction', in *The Best American Short Stories of the Century* (New York: Houghton Mifflin, 1999), p. viii.
32. For a discussion of the status of Irish short stories within these 'British' anthologies, See Wei H. Kao, *The Formation of an Irish Literary Canon in the Mid-Twentieth Century* (Stuttgart: Ibidem, 2007), pp. 153–5.
33. Baldwin, *Art and Commerce*, p. 114.
34. Andrew Miller, 'Introduction', in *That Glimpse of Truth: 100 of the Finest Stories Ever Written* (London: Head of Zeus, 2014), p. viii.
35. Killick, *British Short Fiction*, p. 119.
36. Baldwin, *Art and Commerce*, p. 114.
37. Philip Hensher, 'General Introduction', in *The Penguin Book of the British Short Story*, Volume 1 (London: Penguin, 2015), p. xviii.
38. Ibid. pp. xxx–xxxiv.
39. Ibid. p. xi.
40. Hermione Lee, 'Introduction', in *The Secret Self: A Century of Short Stories by Women* (London: Dent, 1985), pp. ix–x.
41. Langston Hughes, 'Introduction', in *The Best Stories by Black Writers: 1899 to 1967* (Boston, MA: Little, Brown, 1967), p. xiii.
42. Gloria Naylor, 'Introduction', in *Children of the Night: The Best Stories by Black Writers, 1967 to the present* (Boston, MA: Little, Brown, 1995), p. xx.
43. Jacob Ross, 'Introduction', in *Closure: Contemporary Black British Short Stories* (Leeds: Peepal Tree, 2015), p. 11.
44. Ibid.
45. Karen L. Kilcup, 'Anthologizing Matters: The Poetry and Prose of Anthology Work', *symploke*, 8.1/2 (2000): 37.
46. See Hopkins, 'On Anthologies'; see also Marjorie Perloff, 'Whose New American Poetry? Anthologizing in the Nineties', *Diacritics*, 26.3/4 (1996): 104–23.
47. Vivian Mercier, 'Introduction', in *Great Irish Short Stories* (New York: Dell, 1964), p. 19.
48. William Trevor, 'Introduction', in *The Oxford Book of Irish Short Stories* (Oxford: Oxford University Press 1989), p. xiv.
49. Ibid. p. xv
50. Mercier, *Great Irish Short Stories*, p. 15
51. Trevor, *Oxford Book of Irish Short Stories*, p. xvi.
52. Sinéad Gleeson, 'Introduction', in *The Long Gaze Back: An Anthology of Irish Women Writers* (Dublin: New Island, 2015), p. 1.
53. Ann Charters, 'Introduction', in *The Story and Its Writer: An Introduction to Short Fiction*, 9th edn (Bedford: St Martin's Press, 2014), pp. 1–2.

54. Philip Stevick, *Anti-Story: An Anthology of Experimental Fiction* (New York: Free Press, 1971), pp. xiv–xxxiii.
55. Nicholas Blincoe and Matt Thorne, 'The New Puritan Manifesto', in *All Hail the New Puritans* (London: Fourth Estate, 2000), p. xvii.
56. Lee, 'Introduction', p. xv.
57. Elizabeth Bowen, 'The Faber Book of Modern Short Stories', *Collected Impressions* (London: Longmans, 1950), pp. 39–40.
58. Ibid. pp. 42–3.
59. Ibid. p. 45.
60. Joyce Carol Oates, 'Introduction', in *The Oxford Book of American Short Stories* (Oxford: Oxford University Press, 1992), p. 7.
61. V. S. Pritchett, *The Oxford Book of Short Stories* (Oxford: Oxford University Press, 1981) p. xiv.
62. Richard Ford, 'Introduction', in *The New Granta Books of the American Short Story* (London: Granta, 2007), p. viii.
63. Enright, 'Introduction', p. x.
64. Ben Marcus, 'Introduction', in *New American Stories* (New York: Vintage, 2015), p. xx.
65. Miller, 'Introduction', n.p.

Bibliography

Adagha, Ovo and Molara Wood (eds and introd.), *One World: A Global Anthology of Short Stories* (Oxford: New Internationalist Publications, 2009).
Anon., *The Dover Anthology of Cat Stories* (New York: Dover Publishing, 2015).
Ashley, Michael and William D. Contento (eds), *The Supernatural Index: A Listing of Fantasy, Supernatural, Occult, Weird, Horror Anthologies* (Westport, CT: Greenwood, 1995).
Baldwin, Dean, *Art and Commerce in the British Short Story: 1880–1950* (London: Pickering and Chatto, 2013).
Blincoe, Nicholas and Matt Thorne (eds and introd.), *All Hail the New Puritans* (London: Fourth Estate, 2000).
Bowen, Elizabeth, 'The Faber Book of Modern Short Stories', *Collected Impressions* (London: Longmans, 1950), pp. 38–52.
Brown, Hilary, 'German Women Writers in English Short Story Anthologies of the 1820s', *The Modern Language Review*, 97.3 (July 2002): 620–31.
Charters, Ann (ed. and introd.), *The Story and Its Writer: An Introduction to Short Fiction*, 9th edn (Boston and New York: Bedford/St. Martin's, 2014).
Crane, Milton (ed. and introd.), *50 Great Short Stories* (New York: Bantam, 1952).
Cuddon, J. A., *The Penguin Dictionary of Literary Terms and Literary Theory* (London: Penguin, 1999).
Donoghue, Emma (ed. and introd.), *The Mammoth Book of Lesbian Short Stories* (New York: Caroll & Graff, 1999).
Eggers, Dave (ed. and introd.), *The Best of McSweeney's* (San Francisco: McSweeney's, 2013).
Enright, Anne (ed. and introd.), *The Granta Book of the Irish Short Story* (London: Granta, 2010).
Ford, Richard (ed. and introd.), *The Granta Book of the American Short Story* (London: Granta, 1992).
— (ed. and introd.), *The New Granta Book of the American Short Story* (London: Granta, 2007).
Gleeson, Sinéad (ed. and introd.), *The Long Gaze Back: An Anthology of Irish Women Writers* (Dublin: New Island, 2015).

— (ed. and introd.), *The Glass Shore: Short Stories by Women from the North of Ireland* (Dublin: New Island, 2016).

Grafton, Anthony, Glenn W. Most and Salvatore Settis, *The Classical Tradition* (Cambridge, MA: Harvard University Press, 2010).

Harris, Wendell V., *British Short Fiction in the Nineteenth Century: A Literary and Bibliographic Guide* (Detroit: Wayne State University Press, 1979).

Hensher, Philip (ed. and introd.), *The Penguin Book of the British Short Story*, Vols. 1 and 2 (London: Penguin, 2015).

Hill, Susan (ed. and introd.), *The Penguin Book of Modern Women's Short Stories* (London: Penguin, 1991).

Hislop, Victoria (ed. and introd.), *The Story: Love, Loss and the Lives of Women* (London: Head of Zeus, 2013).

Hopkins, David, 'On Anthologies', *The Cambridge Quarterly*, 37.3 (2008): 285–304.

Hornblower, Simon, Antony Spawforth and Esther Eidinow (eds), *The Oxford Classical Dictionary* (Oxford: Oxford University Press, 2012).

Howells, W. D., 'Some Anomalies of the Short Story', *The North American Review*, 173.538 (1901): 422–32.

Hughes, Langston (ed. and introd.), *The Best Stories by Black Writers: 1899 to 1967* (Boston, MA: Little, Brown, 1967).

Jarrell, Randall (ed. and introd.), *Randall Jarrell's Book of Stories* (New York: Doubleday, 1958).

Jenny Brown Associates, *The Short Story in the UK Report*, 2004. Online. <http://www.theshortstory.org.uk/aboutus/The_Short_Story_in_the_UK_Report.pdf> (last accessed 15 April 2018).

Jump, Harriet Devine (ed. and introd.), *Nineteenth-Century Short Stories by Women: A Routledge Anthology* (London: Routledge, 2003).

Kanwar, Asha (ed. and introd.), *The Unforgetting Heart: An Anthology of Short Stories by African-American Women* (San Francisco: Aunt Lute Books, 1993).

Kao, Wei H., *The Formation of an Irish Literary Canon in the Mid-Twentieth Century* (Stuttgart: Ibidem, 2007).

Kerr, Calum and Valerie O'Riordan (eds), *Jawbreakers: 2012 National Flash-Fiction Day Anthology* (Southampton: National Flash-Fiction Day), 2012).

Kiely, Benedict (ed. and introd.), *The Penguin Book of Irish Short Stories* (London: Penguin, 1981).

Kilcup, Karen L., 'Anthologizing Matters: The Poetry and Prose of Anthology Work', *symplokē*, 8.1/2 (2000): 36–56.

Killick, Tim, *British Short Fiction in the Early Nineteenth Century: The Rise of the Tale* (Aldershot: Ashgate, 2008).

Leavitt, David and Mark Mitchell (eds and introd.), *The New Penguin Book of Gay Short Stories* (London: Penguin, 2004).

Lee, Hermione (ed. and introd.), *The Secret Self: A Century of Short Stories by Women* (London: Dent, 1985).

Levy, Andrew. *The Culture and Commerce of the American Short Story* (Cambridge: Cambridge University Press, 1993).

Liggins, Emma, Andrew Maunder and Ruth Robbins, *The British Short Story* (Basingstoke: Palgrave Macmillan, 2011).

Lover, Samuel (ed.), *Popular Tales and Legends of the Irish Peasantry* (Dublin: Wakeman, 1834).

Mandal, Anthony and Peter Garside (eds), *The English Novel, 1830–1836: A Bibliographical Survey of Prose Fiction Published in the British Isles* (Cardiff: Centre for Editorial and Intertextual Research, 2003).

March-Russell, Paul, *The Short Story: An Introduction* (Edinburgh: Edinburgh University Press, 2009).

Marcus, Ben (ed. and introd.), *New American Stories* (New York: Vintage, 2015).

Mercier, Vivian (ed. and introd.), *Great Irish Short Stories* (Boston, MA: Little, Brown, 1964).

Miller, Andrew (ed. and introd.), *That Glimpse of Truth: 100 of the Finest Stories Ever Written* (London: Head of Zeus, 2014).

Naylor, Gloria (ed. and introd.), *Children of the Night: The Best Stories by Black Writers, 1967 to the present* (Boston, MA: Little, Brown, 1995).

Oates, Joyce Carol (ed. and introd.), *The Oxford Book of American Short Stories* (Oxford: Oxford University Press, 1992).

O'Connor, Frank (ed. and introd.), *Classic Irish Short Stories* (Oxford: Oxford University Press [1957], 1985).

Perloff, Marjorie, 'Whose New American Poetry? Anthologizing in the Nineties', *Diacritics*, 26.3/4 (1996): 104–23.

Picken, Andrew (ed.), *The Club-Book: Being Original Tales, &c. by Various Authors* (London: Cochrane & Pickersgill, 1836).

Prescott, Linda (ed. and introd.), *A World of Difference: An Anthology of Short Stories from Five Continents* (Basingstoke: Palgrave, 2008).

Price, Leah, *The Anthology and the Rise of the Novel: From Richardson to George Eliot* (Cambridge: Cambridge University Press, 2000).

Pritchett, V. S. (ed. and introd.), *The Oxford Book of Short Stories* (Oxford: Oxford University Press, 1981).

Riding, Laura and Robert Graves, *A Pamphlet Against Anthologies* (London: Jonathan Cape, 1928).

Ross, Jacob (ed. and introd.), *Closure: Contemporary Black British Short Stories* (Leeds: Peepal Tree, 2015).

Shapard, Robert and James Thomas (eds and introd.), *Sudden Fiction: American Short Stories* (Layton, UT: Gibbes M. Smith, 1986).

Smith, Ali, Kasia Boddy and Sarah Wood (eds and introd.), *Let's Call the Whole Thing Off: Love Quarrels from Anton Chekhov to ZZ Packer* (London: Penguin, 2009).

Stein, Lorin and Sadie Stein (eds and introd.), *Object Lessons: The Paris Review Presents the Art of the Short Story* (London: Heinemann, 2012).

Stevick, Philip, *Anti-Story: An Anthology of Experimental Fiction* (New York: Free Press, 1971).

Tate, Trudi (ed. and introd.), *Women, Men, and the Great War: An Anthology of Stories* (Manchester: Manchester University Press, 1996).

Tesdell, Diane Secker (ed.), *Stories of Motherhood* (Everyman's Pocket Classics) (New York: Knopf, 2012).

— (ed.), *Stories of Fatherhood* (Everyman's Pocket Classics) (New York: Knopf, 2014).

Thomas, James, Robert Shapard and Christopher Merrill (eds and introd.), *Flash Fiction International: Very Short Stories from Around the World* (New York: Norton, 2015).

Trevor, William (ed. and introd.), *The Oxford Book of Irish Short Stories* (Oxford: Oxford University Press, 1989).

Updike, John and Katrina Kenison (eds and introd.), *The Best American Short Stories of the Century* (New York: Houghton Mifflin, 1999).

Warren, Robert Penn and Albert Erskine (eds and introd.), *Short Story Masterpieces* (New York: Dell, 1954).

8

THE SHORT STORY AND DIGITAL MEDIA

Laura Dietz

E-READING, AS JOHN THOMPSON has pointed out, is only the most public and visible aspect of a digital revolution that has transformed nearly every aspect of publishing.[1] Evolving modes of distribution change what it means to write a short story for publication. If 'publishing' means making a short story available, the Internet makes this technically trivial. If 'publishing' is to make that story 'real', to make it legitimate and potentially influential, to earn for its author rewards – money, prestige, audience, credibility, and so on – then electronic publishing presents new opportunities without resolving old conflicts between pursuit of those rewards, most notably between wide readership and high status.

The digital age has not (at least not yet) ushered in a dramatic resurgence for the popularity of the short story form. The on-screen short story contends with an electronic publishing arena only beginning to pull away from print-based norms. It does have one advantage over the short story in print: it can appear in company, but does not have to. After a century and more of the dominance of the periodical and the bound collection (single-author and anthology), with only the rarest examples of stand-alone print publication, the digital short story can go out into the world on its own, unfettered as a pamphlet or ballad sheet, or allied to a greater range of non-textual material. For a short story to have its own distinct paratext is potentially revolutionary. But such an unfettered short story is forced, for the moment, to make its way in digital spaces occupied primarily by, and in many cases designed for, book-length works of prose. The accommodations required to reach readers – in pricing, in distribution and in paratextual packaging – mean that the solo story is often allied to larger series, books and brands. This lingering on the sidelines, however, has not proved a calamity: innovation is possible, as the component of the short story's identity most relevant to its digital future appears to be not brevity or non-commercial distribution or modernist values, but portability.

This chapter does not aspire to offer a comprehensive survey of a large and rapidly changing field, or even a list of key players. It considers enhanced stories but devotes most attention to traditional forms, what Ellen McCracken calls 'transitional literature':[2] 'electronic texts that mimic the format and appearance of print', adding few or no features that take advantage of the affordances of screen reading, and consequently keeping open the possibility of moving, or returning, to print without significant alterations. As exciting as it is to consider the aesthetic and commercial possibilities of digital fiction – what the Digital Fiction Network defines as fiction written for the screen that 'pursues its verbal, discursive and/or conceptual complexity through the digital medium and would lose something of its aesthetic and semiotic function if it were removed from the medium'[3] – to focus on it would be to ignore the vast bulk of the art created and shared. The passage of traditional stories (those that work in older traditions or that innovate in ways unrelated to digital delivery) through the new digital landscape is just as interesting. Considering the digital short story in terms of publishing contexts 'opens the way', as Adrian Hunter puts it, 'for us to think of innovation in literary form less in terms of superlative gestures of non-conformist genius, and more as the result of interactions between the creative imagination and the material, ideological, and technological conditions prevailing at a particular historical moment.'[4]

For an industry famous for its pessimism, talk of the new era of the short story is striking in its optimism, almost shocking compared to the general e-gloom and digital despair. Over the course of the twentieth century the short story became in many senses a genre with its back against the wall: squeezed out by the popularity of the novel, relegated to an arid artistic tradition more often seen in the classroom than on the news-stand, threatened by a vicious circle of contracting outlet options and declining readership. Though writers – at least, writers interested in a certain aesthetic, or trained in story-friendly university programmes – never abandoned the form, they increasingly pursued it like poets, with the understanding that their work would rarely pay and would likely appear, when it was published at all, in 'little magazines' and in other volumes from small or subsidised presses. But as the twenty-first century neared, the digital era was spoken of as a second chance: a new world where the downward spiral would be reversed. Publishing textbooks confidently predicted that the new environment would positively favour the form.[5] In one sense the assumption was emotional: short stories, like poetry, deserved better, and if revolutions have winners as well as losers, unjustly neglected genres would be deserving beneficiaries of upheaval. But commercially speaking, the dire sales of short story collections and little magazines meant that there was little revenue to lose, and in terms of readership nowhere to go but up. As the short story has been widely described as a quintessentially American form,[6] the American-born[7] Internet, bestridden by American colossi like Apple and Facebook and Amazon, might seem a perfect home. Artistically, the argument that short stories are a '"modern art" attuned to "modern conditions – to printing, science, and individual religion"',[8] singles out the form as specially selected for, even burdened with, reflection and depiction of an era of rapid technological change. And as the Victorian boom in periodical publishing saw what Henry James called 'a huge open mouth which has to be fed – a vessel of immense capacity which has to be filled'[9] – it is plausible to look at the new vessel, all the bright screens awaiting content, and to anticipate at least some opportunity for every literary form. But two factors presumed to favour the form have not played out as expected.

The first supposed competitive advantage of the short story was in the name. The future, it was promised, would be for the brief. The earliest digitised texts favoured short forms because of the brutal economics of disk storage: one MB, roughly the space required for a 300-page book in Plain Vanilla ASCII, was scarce and expensive in 1971.[10] (It is easy to forget how recently storage space and file transfer speeds were a major consideration. In the dial-up era, the time and expense of downloading large files mitigated against books with illustrations, but also long, unbroken blocks of text; a download in segments, like short stories, was more likely to survive the experience. Early e-readers like the Rocket Book could hold, in 2000, about ten books at a time.) The computer scientists tapping John Donne on to mainframes through DOS command windows were rightly confident that storage would soon drop rapidly in cost, putting Trollope, Eliot and even Stephen King tantalisingly within reach. But interface designers had additional reasons to 'go short'. 'Usability experts', sometimes computer scientists and ergonomists with long experience of user interface design, sometimes self-appointed experts reporting back on their own experiences with varying levels of rigour, made swift pronouncements. Subjects were sat down in testing suites before vast, beige desktop PCs, their eye movements tracked as they navigated through America Online portal content on Mosaic browsers. One consistent finding was that users skimmed: on screen, people read approximately 50 per cent of the text, so the prescription was to make the text 50 per cent shorter.[11] Brevity became, like F-shaped web page navigation and avoidance of red and green, 90s' design dogma. Few usability experts were looking at the fringe content category of e-books. Even when they were, apart from Gutenberg classics, early digital texts leaned heavily towards reference, technical and educational titles.[12] Extrapolating from observations on the usage of non-fiction, particularly reference materials, meant that patterns of information-seeking[13] were applied to fiction and other immersive forms of reading.[14] Every form of reading, fiction and non-fiction, was examined to consider how shortness, now often discussed as an absolute requirement, would be realised. In the future, it was rumoured (and, by authors of scholarly monographs, feared), content previously presented in the form of a book would be 'chunked' because readers would no longer tolerate the screen-staring required to wade through a book-length resource to get to the information they desired. If encyclopaedias were to be replaced by Wikipedia-style discrete entries, newspapers reduced to a flurry of individual articles, and monographs salami-sliced into the smallest possible coherent chapters, it stood to reason that 'chunkable' short story collections would outcompete tiresome, exhausting long-form fiction.

At the same time that 'short is good' was making itself comfortable as received wisdom, millions of readers in Japan, primarily but not exclusively young, were consuming *keitai shosetsu*, cell phone novels,[15] through glowing green Nokia screens the size of a passport photo. Fiction appearing on blogs and fan fiction archives came in many sizes, with novel-length works regularly posted and consumed in vast scroll-down web pages or RTF files. This was not an embrace of screen reading, but a different idea of how to respond to the problems of screen reading. Early focus groups on the Kindle found that while an e-ink display was consistently rated as superior to reading on a backlit screen, any e-reader was still rated as awkward and unsatisfying compared to reading on the page.[16] What made the irritating medium tolerable was not brevity but immersion: story, particularly long and involving story, could overcome the interface barrier between reader and text, a barrier only thickened, not created, when narrative moved from paper to screen. When we read a short story, however, 'there is no time . . . to forget it is only "literature" and not "life"', which is why, says Tzvetan Todorov, 'the public prefer novels to tales, long books to short texts'.[17] As Kasia Boddy points out, the short story has for generations been hailed as the 'solution' to uniquely (always uniquely) fractured modern attention spans,[18] offering 'literature for those who had more pressing concerns than literature'.[19]

The second supposed competitive advantage of the short story was price. Many early observers predicted that music would be the closest model, and that the breakdown of the album presaged the breakdown of the book. Consumers buying 99-cent singles would, they reasoned, be just as interested in 99-cent stories; that one tenth of a short story collection would sell better than the full collection because price-sensitive buyers would take a chance if the cost barrier was low. These observers were correct in their prediction that readers are price-sensitive: Amazon e-book rankings demonstrate that a small change in cost, for any text, can have dramatic effects on sales. What observers did not predict was the chaotic e-reading market to come: a vast array of prices for similar products, wild fluctuations resulting from dynamic pricing, battles between publishers and retailers for control of that pricing, and perhaps most significantly the deluge of free or near-free literature, some of it excellent in quality, and much of it tremendously popular. Inexpensive literature has appeal, but there is so much available, and prices for even book-length works have fallen so far, that the idea of a short story representing particular *value*, in terms of price per word, does not stand up as a unique selling point. $2.48 for a 44-page Jack Reacher e-short story does not represent a bargain when it is sold next to a 494-page Jack Reacher novel, in paperback, for $4.61.[20] And if the aim is to try out a new author, Amazon's 'send a free sample' and 'look inside' features mean that while one might have to pay to get a complete novel, many window-shoppers can have one complete short story from a given collection or anthology for free. Even if these two assumed advantages, brevity and value, are not proving to be reliable assets, however, the short story is carving a space in digital media, through the comparatively slow evolution of existing forms and the creative application of new ones.

The short story's faltering as a commercial genre now looks more like an opportunity than a handicap. The two great difficulties of electronic publishing are establishing legitimacy and getting anyone to pay for content.[21] Digital publishing and self-publishing remain stigmas, but separate stigmas, and a piece of writing can suffer from either or both. At time of press, readers retain a tremendous degree of respect for print and for the gatekeeping functions of traditional publishing, and a 'book' that appears graced by neither is assumed, witheringly, to have been 'rejected by every publishing house in Britain'.[22] A short story, however, has an excuse. As a commercially neglected form, it can make the case that its 'failure' to appear in print, or to find a traditional publisher, is for reasons that have nothing to do with quality or value, especially if the author or publisher (or author/publisher) can provide evidence of gatekeeping and/or investment in some other way. As a publisher or editor, if one has effectively given up on making money, a non-commercial form is as attractive as any other – more so, in fact, if it means having scant competition from commercially minded publishers for the best work. And for authors, resigned to earning little and facing enormous barriers to getting their writing seen at all, creative control or higher digital royalties are proving reason enough to step away from the considerable advantages of print.

Fiction is staggeringly popular on screen. In the US and UK, e-books account for only a quarter of the ISBN book market (i.e. books from traditional publishers and from self-published authors who have paid for ISBN numbers) but half of the fiction market.[23] No reliable statistics exist for the non-ISBN e-books, much less digital reading that does not fit easily into the category of 'book', but most experts agree that the non-ISBN market is even more tilted towards fiction, particularly fantasy, science fiction, romance and fanfic. Digital appears to have hurt print sales of fiction but it has helped fiction sales overall.[24] Short story collections do not do badly as e-books – Nielsen statistics find them to be a slightly bigger slice of the market in digital than in print – but they have not exploded in the way that the digital novel has. What is notable about the digital short story collection is not how digital versions of print-original collections perform commercially (broadly, similar to the way they perform in print), but how digital-original publishing provides an outlet for collections that have no print prospects at all.

Single-author short story collections are pushed to the margins of the print book market. With modest sales compared to novels and a reputation as a hard sell to bookstores and to readers, many collections are blocked before they have a chance to go into print, and often even before they are composed, as agents and editors urge authors to devote their energies to long-form fiction with a better chance of publication. While there are small and specialist presses that make short story collections part of their mission, often with arts or institutional funding (like Salt or Comma Press, both having been supported at times by Arts Council England), there is nothing like the variety of non-commercial publishers for collections as there are 'little magazines' for individual stories. The coherent collection, with its opportunities to arrange stories into a cycle, cluster or other pattern that adds a further level of resonance, is not just a neglected form, it is almost a suppressed form. Digital editions can offer a lower-cost way of releasing any kind of book for which a print run covering projected sales would be uneconomically small, though it is a myth that digital is invariably cheaper. Collections need not be digital-only, or even digital-first. Finding a traditional publisher to perform the gatekeeping function is not necessarily easy, but the short story's unique position as a respected but unprofitable form makes it acceptable as something on which to experiment.

Major publishers began largely with genre material: Penguin Random House's digital-only Hydra, Alibi, Loveswept and Flirt imprints offer novels as example titles, but do not exclude short story collections in their submission guidelines, while Bloomsbury Spark, aimed at Young Adult and New Adult readers, explicitly welcomes 'interconnected short stories'.[25] Digital-only literary imprints are rare, but Amazon's Little A does release some short story collections, sometimes with a Print on Demand option for physical copies. Some Little A collections come from authors like David Gordon, who also publish literary novels via Amazon, but others from authors with a mixed digital and print portfolio. For these hybrid authors, who release different books or different categories of books in parallel with traditional publishers and self-publishing platforms, short fiction is a common category of work to put into the second column. A self-published book does not make a self-published author. It is proving possible for writers who have been traditionally published to stretch that endorsement beyond individual works and to validate an entire career – at least when the 'outlaw' portion of that career is in a form like the short story, where the mainstream industry is acknowledged to be generally inactive, and/or sufficiently distanced from one's other work. (A 'literary' writer self-publishing crime fiction, or a novelist self-publishing short stories, is one thing, but a literary novelist self-publishing a literary novel might be asked why his or her mainstream publisher was not interested.)²⁶ An established writer with a self-published story collection might use one of the dedicated (and often transitory) digital-first publishers like Byliner (purchased by Vook, then rebranded with a new business model as Pronoun, finally out of business in early 2018). The writer might draw on existing professional connections and release work via semi-supported self-publishing services linked to their agents or to managers like David Mamet self-publishing with ICM. Or, he or she might truly go it alone, like John Edgar Wideman self-publishing his collection of 'microstories' through Lulu. Out-of-print collections can be resurrected by digital-only or print-and-digital imprints (like Faber Finds), or by the author him or herself, taking advantage of revision of rights. Out-of-print anthologies could be similarly resurrected if authors pulled together to resolve complicated rights questions, but it is another form of multi-author volume that is at present making a greater impact on screen.

The currency of the 'little magazine' – the capital with which it rewards or perhaps recompenses its authors – is prestige.²⁷ The question is how 'little magazines' adapt to continue minting prestige in the digital environment, when selectivity, investment and gatekeeping are not always obvious to the reader. The exchange between author and publisher, as previously noted, is not so much non-commercial as anti-commercial: an outgrowth of more than a century of the fostering of 'literary' short stories in periodicals where exclusivity is the point. As Hunter points out, to certain strata of the modernist movement insignificant sales were not a tolerated consequence of 'challenging' material, but a celebrated consequence, evidence that the writing was literally repellent: actively driving away the populist, the middlebrow, the conservative, the artistically compromised.²⁸ The appearance of selectivity presents particular problems for digital publications. The classic printed magazine at least looks as though selectivity is in play, simply because of the cost of paper. An online magazine runs the risk of appearing fatally inclusive: of infinite length and able to expand to include anyone and everyone.²⁹

In the pre-web era, awareness of the existence of journals and their place in the literary ecosystem, let alone awareness of the customs surrounding submission of one's own work, was an example of implicit knowledge handed between initiated members of a select group. As Mark McGurl has demonstrated, this implicit knowledge once typically circulated via personal networks – friends in the know – increasingly came to be circulated via university-based writing programmes.³⁰ Students paying tuition could stop by the university library or bookstore to view a copy and jot down the submissions address, if not hand-delivering stories to the offices of a prestigious magazine based at and supported by their institution. Then, having honed and perfected their stories in workshops led by writers in tune with the aesthetic, they might note the name of their mentor and their institution in the cover letter as a handshake of introduction. A copy of *The Writers' and Artists' Yearbook* is a poor second to the personal touch. Now, online visibility – even with a 'business card' website that offers no content – leads to inclusion in web search results and, more significantly, writer services, including online databases like Duotrope. Submission-management software linked to listings further accelerates quick, cheap mass mailings, with which magazines must cope. For a writer, inclusion after such fierce competition confers its own kind of bragging rights: one has triumphed over greater odds. But this distinction of achievement displaces another form: the distinction of belonging to a peer group, of having been in the know.

For magazines, the loss of sales to would-be contributors, who can now easily submit without having bought a copy, plus the burden of reading so many submissions, has added expense to going digital. Even in a low-capital (or rather, low financial capital) publishing environment like that of a little magazine, investment counts. Digital-only or digital-first publications face the same exacting standards for editing and design,[31] and have arguably more demanding standards for remaining current. Being up to date in terms of look is hard enough, but remaining up to date in terms of functionality (e.g. usability on the latest platforms and operating systems) is an additional burden. A publication, or individual work, that aims to make an impression with its look as well as its prose soon faces the reality that their intended audience does read widely and can recognise inexpensive off-the-shelf packages for what they are. The most conspicuous investment on screen may be customisation. Stories published to the web on a free Wordpress blog template represent one end of the technical investment continuum. Stories presented as a stand-alone app, or as a conspicuously enhanced e-book, represent the other. The future value of 'heritage digital' is unknowable; a digital artefact could conceivably develop its own sort of aura, or it could disappear with its platform, becoming inaccessible to all but media archaeologists. With no way to put many digital short stories on a shelf, constant updating and renewal is frequently necessary not just to appear fashionable, but to continue to exist.

Academic environments see creative writing through the lens of peer review. Sales and anything that can count as 'impact' are not irrelevant, but what matters most is the esteem of one's peers, and that esteem had best be expressed in recorded and quantifiable form. Publication in even the most celebrated 'little magazine' is by these lights problematic: selection by an editorial board of experts would be inferior to blind, anonymous review (more like being chosen to take part in a conference or be published in an edited collection than to find one's way into an issue of *Nature* or *The Journal of Neuroscience*). Citation indexes are utterly unsuited to capturing the status or influence on other writers of a 'little magazine' story, although these are often apt for the open publishing platforms discussed below. This tension has led to the emergence of peer-reviewed creative writing journals, featuring a mix of articles and fiction, with major academic publishers, such as *New Writing* from Taylor & Francis. The open access movement adds another layer of complication. Under pressure to make research carried out in universities, with direct or indirect state support in the form of grants, freely available online, many institutions, such as University College London, are adopting a policy of ensuring that all research is free by default. The next major national university research evaluation exercise in the UK (REF 2021) will only evaluate open access material. Short stories can find themselves lumped in with academic papers, with the most stringent standards for access, where novels might be classed alongside scholarly monographs, which at times cross over into commercial publishing and may make a claim to be excused from open access demands. Short story writers who have granted first publication rights to any trade publisher, even a supposedly non-commercial 'little magazine', may face a painful negotiation as they try to make their work, already visible in a way credible to their writing community, similarly prominent to their academic community. Similarly, writers who have made their work visible in public (and, ironically, 'impactful') ways via the web or apps sold directly through iTunes or other retailers may struggle to define their stories as 'published'. A well-meaning faculty mentor might advise against spending time on 'little magazine' stories, the way a well-meaning agent might discourage a writer from spending time on a collection.

It is characteristic of the short story to appear in more than one venue: perhaps published first in a magazine, then in a 'best of' anthology, and later as part of a single-author collection, possibly revised along the way. Adding the possibility of appearing unfettered merely expands the portfolio of options; the choice is not a binary one, and digital-first in no way blocks later or even simultaneous appearance in a periodical, anthology, collection, or game or app. Appearing solo does not so much cut a story off from its traditional forms of context as foreground other, less physical contexts for its sale and interpretation.

It is not unprecedented for short stories to appear alone; a vibrant form with a long history of formal experimentation will have turned most turnable stones. *One Story* is an example of the rare but important series model: its 'one story per month' booklets, bound and shipped (or sent electronically to their Kindles) to subscribers one by one, invite discrete reading and consideration even as the prominent series title and common cover design underscore links. Separated by time but not aesthetic or brand, the stories represent an intriguing semi-independence, a different way to be part of a whole. Digital delivery's innovation is to make this commonplace and, in at least some instances, financially viable. Any author or publisher can post a story in the form of a web page, as 4th Estate does for complete stories selected from collections currently in print.[32] But now, any author or publisher with a download of Calibre or an iBooks iAuthor app can release that story as a digital reading file: .epub, .azw, etc.

The e-story (a story presented for download as a single file) may be released by a traditional publisher or sold directly by the author. A number of established literary magazines and small presses have begun to sell e-stories via their websites, often echoing *One Story* by presenting them as a series with 'issues'. *Ploughshares Solos*, meant for 'longer stories and essays', have widely varying covers linked only by a small logo, but appear with series numbers appended to their titles (*Solo 3.9, Solo 4.5*, etc.).[33] *Galley Beggar Singles*[34] share a common cover design, a common price and the offer of a subscription. All of these traditional presses, small presses, little-magazines-turned-small-presses and individual authors can also sell e-stories via retailers, like Amazon or iBooks. But the framework provided by the leading retailer makes selling an e-story more difficult, in many ways, than selling an e-book.

Amazon, the leading retailer of ISBN digital fiction, has wide criteria for what it will accept via Kindle Direct Publishing. It hews (as plagiarised authors have found to their cost) to a policy of inclusion, questioning content, when it does question content, often only after a challenge from a rights holder or unsatisfied customer. It will at least consider selling a 300-word microshort or a 1,000,000 word mega-anthology. It even has a Short Reads category allowing buyers to browse texts organised by 'reading time' (15 minutes, 45 minutes, etc.),[35] which intriguingly mingles short fiction with celebrity mini-biographies and urban foraging guides. But Amazon began as an online retailer of physical books. It extended its reach to e-book by promoting 'vanilla' e-books, direct analogues of mainstream published bestsellers, at heavily discounted prices.[36] It was born selling 'volumes' and remains optimised for the sale of book-length, book-shaped products, with commercial terms that do not favour e-stories. Its current terms (keeping in mind that Amazon changes these terms frequently and without warning) mean that works must be of a certain file size and sit in a narrow price band (in the US currently $2.99 to $9.99) to qualify for full 70 per cent royalties.[37] (A shorter or cheaper story languishes at 35 per cent royalty.) Amazon's few CreateSpace requirements (e.g. no copyright infringement, nothing 'poorly translated', etc.) bar 'disappointing content', which includes 'content that is too short' (as well as 'content that does not provide an enjoyable reading experience', a statement so vague that eligibility can only be described as 'what Amazon says it is, today').[38] But how short is too short? Amazon leaves it to its own discretion to decide, but makes clear that e-stories must meet undefined and evolving expectations in terms of length, for a retailer and an audience trained to think in terms of books. These rules do not apply to Kindle Singles.

Kindle Singles are Amazon's 'curated' stable of fiction and non-fiction work, 'compelling ideas expressed at their natural length – writing that doesn't easily fit into the conventional space limitations of magazines or print books'.[39] 'Typically' between 5,000 and 30,000 words in length, the works are submitted by traditional publishers, including Amazon's own imprints, like Thomas & Mercer and Mortlake Romance, or by authors directly. Amazon's description could serve as a mission statement for 'long-shorts', short stories shy of novella status, as much as for long essays and capsule memoirs. This genre-free term, 'ideas', and minimal Single-specific branding (pages list 'Kindle Single' after the title, and most give a page count for users willing to scroll down far enough, but otherwise the page is as that of any other text for sale), make for an ambiguous, even evasive paratext – not so much creating a revolutionary new length-agnostic space as dropping 'writing that doesn't easily fit' into a book space to fend for itself.

The result is that publishers and authors are free to treat the ambiguous space as a flexible one. An informal survey of the top twenty-five Kindle Singles on a given day and hour (10.30 a.m. on 29 March 2016), saw fiction Singles presented variously as 'short story', 'novella' or (curiously) 'short novel'. There appears to be little pattern in terms of length; some 'short stories' are longer than 'novellas'. The choice of how to label the work is down to what the publisher, author or author/publisher feels will represent the content but will also sell.

Some e-stories are presented as parts of a whole and others as stand-alone works. That 'whole' could be a collection (as with Hilary Mantel's *The Assassination of Margaret Thatcher*, from which 4th Estate sells individual stories), but, in the case of Kindle Singles, the 'whole' is likely to be a book series. Amazon does not offer statistics on the performance of author-submitted vs. publisher-submitted works, nor about the odds of a given author-submitted work being selected from the slush pile. But Kindle Singles top sellers (which are, as Michael Bhaskar reminds us, a brutally self-reinforcing group, where sales lead to visibility which leads to further sales)[40] are overwhelmingly linked to a small cohort of bestselling crime, romance, horror or thriller authors. Titles are frequently released by the same publishers as their novels, and presented with covers sharing design elements with recent editions of the main novel series. Some are connected to the author, as with Jennifer Weiner or Dean Koontz. Others are connected with the author and also with a specific character and series; for crime and thrillers, often to the detective (e.g. 'a Jack Reacher story', 'a Paul Madriani novella'). When produced by major publishers and selected by Amazon, these tie-in e-stories can make money, but they also serve as a means to market novels. Publishers promoting a popular series are concerned with keeping the public interested between novel instalments, and authors report pressure to produce not only a new novel every year, but a shorter piece in between novels.[41] For marketing purposes these short stories really are 'short novels': substitutes that publishers release not because they think that shorter works are the best way to expand readership or maximise profit, or find them artistically interesting, but because they are the closest authors can get to the desired two novels a year. The 'short novel' does not describe every series tie-in Kindle Single, and 'unaffiliated' Kindle Singles do sometimes find success (though 'success' may be defined, as for Robin Sloan's *Mr. Penumbra's 24 Hour Bookstore*, as 'graduating' to extension into a full novel). It is notable how many e-story breakout authors, in common with many e-novel breakout authors, are like Robin Sloan expert publicists and/or social media professionals.

'All writers lead a double life' where they are evaluated in terms of sales and in terms of recognition.[42] Recognition, once conferred solely by insiders like prize judges and broadsheet and journal reviewers, now sits alongside the wisdom of crowds. Free-to-read short fiction collectives cater to readers who are not customers but community members, and generate the clicks, 'likes', ratings and tags that are the local currency. Networks of mutually supporting writer/readers on platforms like Wattpad offer an intriguing glimpse of an alternative hierarchy, where hits, numbers of ratings and length and persuasiveness of reviews are the mechanism by which the cream is meant to rise to the top. This model, where there is no money and little cultural capital in play, leaves as the only currencies time and a screen-based form of social capital.

Self-publishing platforms are proliferating; in part, as companies like Pronoun (previously Vook) abandon struggling 'reader-pays' business models in favour of 'writer-pays', or simply advertising-based revenue models.[43] Some of the current platforms, such as Amazon CreateSpace or Wattpad, are unapologetically for-profit, finding value in advertising, writer services (e.g. editing, cover design, promotion, etc.) and simply the data provided by large numbers of readers. Others, including Comma Press's MacGuffin, are at least partially supported by arts funding.[44]

MacGuffin has been described as a 'jukebox for stories', offering audio as well as text for every story on the site (while evoking, intriguingly, the fun of a diner novelty rather than the gravity of more typical library imagery).[45] But the jukebox analogy is not a very good one: on such a machine, the records stay separate. On a platform, the more the stories are read the less stand-alone they become. Comments, recommendations and tags, combined with platform algorithms, become a crowd-sourced paratext, a categorisation that groups the story with what readers consider to be comparable texts (or, in the case of automatically generated 'if you liked that, you'll like this' results, at least texts that have attracted the attention of the same readers). Even a story with no tags, no comments, no comparisons, is still grouped by rank: how many stars, how many readers, how many lists. Wattpad emphasises serialisation as a means of 'hooking' readers, both with the suspense of awaiting the next instalment and the immediacy and excitement of feeling involved with the story and author in the white heat of creation.[46] This emphasis favours novels even if the stated publication criteria claim to be length-agnostic. On these platforms, an unaffiliated story is a failed story. In the face of such a loss of control, an author might be even more likely to embrace a digital merger on his or her own terms, via links to non-textual forms.

A further form of affiliation is to other digital media: video, audio, interaction and games. Some fiction projects set traditional short stories within an interactive frame, like jewels in a digital crown: Comma Press's Litnav (much like its predecessor Gimbal) presents stories alongside maps of their settings,[47] while other app-based 'ambient literature' projects, currently in use for poetry[48] and other forms of literature but adaptable to short stories, use mapping to select texts based on the reader's geographic location. Other projects weave interaction and enhanced content in to the point that it becomes 'digital literature' as per Bell and Ensslin's definition, where the story cannot be removed from the screen without stripping the text of meaning. In Kate Pullinger's *Inanimate Alice*,[49] readers switch back and forth between feeds of information as Alice, the young protagonist, draws on both physical and digital-within-digital environments as she confronts her father's disappearance. Five Dials's *The Role of Music in Your Life*[50] reworks the familiar conceit of a story in the form of a questionnaire. Readers cannot simply skim or skip ahead, nor hover above the action as a blameless observer. They must input answers if they are to proceed to the next question and advance the narrative, in this case one of a child and parent whose squabbles over music lessons poorly conceal darker conflict beneath. The reader is complicit, forced to select from a menu of unsatisfactory options and become a guilty participant. Branching and multiple pathways are not the only ways to emphasise reader involvement. Both examples, one emphasising sharing a protagonist's agency and the other an employee's excruciating lack of agency, are actively ergodic, where a 'nontrivial effort is required to allow the reader to traverse the text',[51] and if the reader declines to engage, the story freezes in place, inert and unable to unfold. Game developers like Simogo approach the game/story border from the other direction, producing products/artworks like *Device 6* that rely so heavily on typography as well as text that the line between playing and reading is blurred.[52] The Random House *Black Crown* experiment ambitiously combined original texts with custom-developed gameplay, created to work together rather than to see one designed to accommodate the other. (The expense of the model contributed to Random House's decision to discontinue.)[53] Gamification is often discussed as a means to an end, a way to feed words into reluctant readers or for literature to compete with digital entertainment, but for authors like Naomi Alderman games simply offer the best tools and territory to tell certain stories, and are for good reason many writers' method of choice.[54]

Short stories are no less suited to gamification, interaction and digital enhancement than other types of prose. But they are no more suited, and perhaps de-emphasise their identity as 'short stories' when presented as part of an integrated multimedia whole. Intuitively, it might seem that combined forms, like 90s-era web content, favour the short: that digital elements would crowd out long-form prose and require a sort of length compromise, a 50–50 split. In practice, modern games and interactive forms are receptive to long works, even requiring them when the piece involves reader/player agency: a choice between text paths requires a minimum of two text paths, each complete and satisfying in itself. Jules Verne's *Around the World in Eighty Days* was roughly 60,000 words long, while Meg Jayanth's script for the highly acclaimed game *80 Days*, which adapted some aspects of its plot into a new interactive narrative, required over 500,000 words of prose.[55] For commercial reasons, games and interactive works with narrative elements often market themselves as 'novels', whatever the style and whatever the length of the text component.[56] 'Story' and 'short story' have specific and generally understood meanings in academic and literary circles; this is not the case in other contexts – a fact underscored by the diversity of labels attached to short-form fiction on Amazon. 'Novel', on the other hand, has a more broadly understood identity – if anything, the concept is more coherent and generally accepted outside specialist circles than within them. It is something with weight and cultural significance, which a game or comic or interactive text piece (or indeed, a walk-through life-size narrative art installation)[57] can access by sharing the name. The novel is something with which even the most occasional readers have an experience,[58] and crucially, for anyone trying to sell, the novel is something people are accustomed to paying for.

Even on a purely artistic level, digital is not such an obvious fit for the short story. The interconnectedness and opportunities for reader agency can support dilation and plotlessness,[59] as in an app like McSweeney's *The Silent History* that allows readers to explore at will and encounter facets of the story in a different order or not at all.[60] But this releasing of the reins, allowing readers time and licence to poke around, can be harsh to the equally central 'implication, ambiguity' and 'suggestion' that make short stories in some traditions both more challenging and less overtly novelistic.[61] Can readers be given freedom to explore without that freedom including the right to interrogate, to press for answers where no answers were meant to be? Digital incarnations thrive on linkage and search, the promise that someone, somewhere, shares one's curiosity, and that the right query will forge the connection one needs to learn more. That promise is the antithesis of reticence, of acceptance of or respect for limits. It may be a cliché that short stories are like still photographs or Kennedy's 'bullet', compressed and contained, but that cliché, shared in innumerable workshops and how-to books, is a part of the form's reputation and identity. The 'pliable', 'mongrel'[62] novel has enjoyed vast success in the zone of search and linkage, but the short story does not share its tradition of promiscuous expansion. Online, the author can't so easily cut off the conversation, leave words unsaid, close the door.

It is customary at the end of any piece on digital publishing, academic or journalistic, to completely evade conclusions, ending coyly with some version of 'no one knows, time will tell'. Predictions are impossible: the market changes too fast and shifts are at the whim of larger currents in legislation, technology and digital culture. (Invariably, the company one cites as interesting will be the one out of business or sold to Google within six months.) But it is possible to highlight pressures that are likely to persist, and remain factors in short story publishing in the near future. Digital delivery opens up opportunities for stand-alone short fiction, but publishing frameworks mean that today's e-story is rarely truly stand-alone, and is more often presented as part of a different whole, be it a series like *Ploughshares Solos*, a brand author like Lee Childs's book series, or a tag or ranking on a free access platform like MacGuffin. Digital-only editions, from mainstream publishers and digital self-publishing, have expanded the release options for single-author short story collections, particularly 'hybrid authors' who use digital-only and self-publishing for some but not all of their work and still rely on mainstream publishing to establish career legitimacy. Digital has enabled a burgeoning exchange in free, community-based material, from which commercially viable works (but mainly novels) can spring. Digital has left many aspects of the 'little magazine' world unchanged, where the currency is prestige and legitimacy comes not from sales figures but from recognition by 'people who matter'; it has not, however, necessarily reduced costs, and changes to the way university-based writers are evaluated make 'little magazine' publications potentially less attractive from a career point of view. Digital fiction, a niche once heavily dependent on arts funding, now has the possibility of commercial viability, but such narratives have powerful incentives to ally themselves with the novel, not the short story, and some traditional characteristics of the short story, like ambiguity and suggestion, can clash with a web ethos of openness and interconnection.

After decades of concern over a short story monoculture, as cultivated by university creative writing programmes[63] or the dominant aesthetics of a single important magazine like *The New Yorker*,[64] an uncertain future does at least foster experimentation – experimentation out of desperation, perhaps, but unquestionably a flowering of publication and paratextual options. Which of these flourish is of immense concern to individual publishers who have climbed out on various artistic and commercial limbs. But for the writer, one fallen branch is not the end. Their lifeline is portability. Writers can afford to experiment with new forms of publication with their short stories because no one publication is definitive: a story is defined by its publishing context, but redefined by the next one. There is little conflict between following a 'little magazine' tradition or *New Yorker* aesthetic while also forging a path in self-published stand-alone e-stories or narrative apps. It is required only that something calling itself a short story survive: that writers now, as writers have in the past, 'consistently [find] in the short story a form well adapted to their most fundamental preoccupations'.[65]

Notes

1. John B. Thompson, *Merchants of Culture: The Publishing Business in the Twenty-First Century* (Cambridge: Polity, 2012), p. 326.
2. Ellen McCracken, 'Expanding Genette's Epitext/Paritext model for transitional electronic literature: Centrifugal and centripedal vectors on Kindles and iPads', *Narrative*, 21.1 (2013): 104.
3. Bell et al. 2010, quoted in Alice Bell, Astrid Ensslin and Hans Rustad, 'From Theorising to Analysing Digital Fiction', in Alice Bell, Astrid Ensslin, and Hans Rustad (eds), *Analysing Digital Fiction* (New York: Routledge, 2014), p. 3.
4. Adrian Hunter, *The Cambridge Introduction to the Short Story in English* (Cambridge: Cambridge University Press, 2007), p. 46.
5. See Kelvin Smith, *The Publishing Business: From P-books to E-books* (Lausanne: AVA Publishing SA, 2012).
6. See 'Introduction', p. 1–18, in Kasia Boddy, *The American Short Story Since 1950* (Edinburgh: Edinburgh University Press, 2010).
7. Passing over the fact that the Web on which all of these stories actually sit owes its existence to an Englishman working in Switzerland.

8. Frank O'Connor, quoted in Hunter, *The Cambridge Introduction to the Short Story in English*, p. 3
9. Hunter, *The Cambridge Introduction to the Short Story in English*, p. 7.
10. See Marie Lebert, 'History of Project Gutenberg'. Available at <http://www.gutenbergnews.org/about/history-of-project-gutenberg/> (last accessed 15 April 2018), and Michael Hart, 'The history and philosophy of Project Gutenberg by Michael Hart'. Available at <https://www.gutenberg.org/wiki/Gutenberg:The_History_and_Philosophy_of_Project_Gutenberg_by_Michael_Hart> (last accessed 15 April 2018).
11. See Jakob Nielsen and John Morkes, 'Concise, SCANNABLE, and objective: How to write for the web'. Available at <https://www.nngroup.com/articles/concise-scannable-and-objective-how-to-write-for-the-web/> (last accessed 15 April 2018).
12. Doris Small Helfer, 'E-Books in Libraries: Some Early Experiences and Reactions', *Searcher: The Magazine for Database Professionals*, 8.9 (2000): 63–5.
13. Ann Blandford and Simon Attfield, *Interacting with information* (San Rafael, CA: Morgan & Claypool, 2010).
14. 'Features of books and e-books', INKE Project website. Available at <http://inke.ca/projects/features-of-books-and-e-books/> (last accessed 15 April 2018).
15. Dana Goodyear, 'I love novels' *The New Yorker*, 22 December. Available at <http://www.newyorker.com/magazine/2008/12/22/i-%E2%99%A5-novels> (last accessed 15 April 2018).
16. Karen Coyle, quoted in D. T. Clark, 'A qualitative assessment of the kindle e-book reader: Results from initial focus groups', *Performance Measurement and Metrics*, 9.2 (2008): 118–29.
17. Quoted in Boddy, *The American Short Story Since 1950*, p. 63.
18. Ibid. pp. 77–8.
19. Ibid. p. 3.
20. See Amazon.com, Lee Child author page. Available at <https://www.amazon.com/Lee%20Child/e/B000APO0PQ/ref=la_B000APO0PQ_pg_2?rh=n%3A283155%2Cp_82%3AB000APO0PQ&page=2&sort=author-pages-popularity-rank&ie=UTF8&qid=1491558286> (last accessed 15 April 2018).
21. Angus Phillips, *Turning the Page: The Evolution of the Book* (Abingdon: Routledge, 2014).
22. Laura Dietz, Claire Warwick and Samantha Rayner, 'Auditioning for permanence: reputation and legitimacy of electronically distributed novels', *Logos*, 26.4 (2015): 26.
23. See Steve Bohme, 'Books & consumers in 2016', presentation at Quantum Conference, London Book Fair, 13 March. Available at <http://quantum.londonbookfair.co.uk/RXUK/RXUK_PDMC/responsive/images/2017/Steve%20Bohme%20-%20The%202016%20Book%20Market%20Highlights%20from%20the%20Books%20and%20Consumers%202016%20Survey.pdf?v=636257834636180655> (last accessed 15 April 2018), and Jonathan Nowell, quoted in Jane Tappuni, 'What Nielsen Bookscan tells us about ebook sales cycles and the ebook plateau', *Publishing Technology*. Available at <http://www.publishingtechnology.com/2015/01/what-nielsen-bookscan-data-tells-us-about-ebook-sales-cycles-the-ebook-plateau/> (last accessed 15 April 2018).
24. Jonathan Nowell, quoted in Jane Tappuni, 'What Nielsen Bookscan tells us about ebook sales cycles and the ebook plateau', *Publishing Technology*. Available at <http://www.publishingtechnology.com/2015/01/what-nielsen-bookscan-data-tells-us-about-ebook-sales-cycles-the-ebook-plateau/> (last accessed 15 April 2018).
25. See the submission guidelines for Penguin Random House digital imprints (such as Hydra). Available at <http://www.randomhousebooks.com/hydra/> (last accessed 15 April 2018) and Bloomsbury Spark. Available at <http://www.bloomsbury.com/uk/bloomsbury-spark/faqs/> (last accessed 15 April 2018).

26. See Laura Dietz, 'Who are You Calling an Author? Changing Definitions of Career Legitimacy for Novelists in the Digital Era', in Guy Davidson and Nicola Evans (eds), *Literary Careers in the Modern Era* (Basingstoke, Hampshire: Palgrave Macmillan, 2015).
27. See James English, *The Economy of Prestige: Prizes, Awards, and the Circulation of Cultural Value* (Cambridge, MA: Harvard University Press, 2005).
28. Hunter, *The Cambridge Introduction to the Short Story in English*, p. 47.
29. See Laura Dietz, 'Online vs. print reputation of literary fiction magazines', *The Short Story in Theory and Practice*, 4.1 (2014): 7–21.
30. See Mark McGurl, *The Program Era: Postwar Fiction and the Rise of Creative Writing* (Cambridge, MA: Harvard University Press, 2011).
31. See Dietz, 'Online vs. print reputation of literary fiction magazines'.
32. See the 'Shorts' section of the 4th Estate website. Available at <http://www.4thestate.co.uk/shorts/> (last accessed 15 April 2018).
33. See the 'Ploughshares Solos' section of the *Ploughshares* website. Available at <https://www.pshares.org/solos> (last accessed 15 April 2018).
34. See the 'Galley Beggar Singles' section of the *Galley Beggar Press* website. Available at <https://galleybeggar.co.uk/store/books/type/singles> (last accessed 15 April 2018).
35. See the 'Short Reads' section of the Amazon.com website. Available at <https://www.amazon.com/Kindle-Short-Reads/b/ref=kbhp_bb_SRd_c?ie=UTF8&node=8584457011&pd_rd_r=W766E2NRSCQDZAHJ5B7T&pd_rd_w=Q0Ryr&pd_rd_wg=mMZzA&pf_rd_m=ATVPDKIKX0DER&pf_rd_s=merchandised-search-leftnav&pf_rd_r=W766E2NRSCQDZAHJ5B7T&pf_rd_r=W766E2NRSCQDZAHJ5B7T&pf_rd_t=101&pf_rd_p=9522fca1-50db-421c-ad32-6dd558151a05&pf_rd_p=9522fca1-50db-421c-ad32-6dd558151a05&pf_rd_i=154606011> (last accessed 15 April 2018).
36. Phillips, *Turning the Page*.
37. See the 'Publishing process: Getting started' section of the Kindle Direct Publishing website. Available at <https://kdp.amazon.com/help/topic/A37Z49E2DDQPP3?ref_=gs> (last accessed 15 April 2018).
38. Ibid.
39. See the 'Kindle Singles' section of the Amazon.com website. Available at <https://www.amazon.com/Kindle-Singles/b/ref=amb_link_7?ie=UTF8&node=2486013011&pd_rd_r=NWYV5QK1EVMQQRJJC3P5&pd_rd_w=iGyHr&pd_rd_wg=9qBPu&pf_rd_m=ATVPDKIKX0DER&pf_rd_s=merchandised-search-leftnav&pf_rd_r=NWYV5QK1EVMQQRJJC3P5&pf_rd_r=NWYV5QK1EVMQQRJJC3P5&pf_rd_t=101&pf_rd_p=f9b7c7f1-8fce-4041-83d3-b03e754547f9&pf_rd_p=f9b7c7f1-8fce-4041-83d3-b03e754547f9&pf_rd_i=8584457011> (last accessed 15 April 2018).
40. Michael Bhaskar, *Curation: The power of selection in a world of excess* (London: Piatkus, 2016).
41. Julie Bosman, 'Writer's cramp: in the E-reader era, a book a year is slacking', *The New York Times*, 12 May. Available at <http://www.nytimes.com/2012/05/13/business/in-e-reader-age-of-writers-cramp-a-book-a-year-is-slacking.html> (last accessed 15 April 2018).
42. Gunter Leypoldt, 'All Writers Lead a Double Life,' *Books in the Making* symposium, Cambridge University, 15 March 2016.
43. Ravi Somaiya, 'Byliner, an online publisher of long-form writing, seeks partners', *The New York Times*, 3 June. Available at <http://www.nytimes.com/2014/06/04/business/media/byliner-an-online-publisher-of-long-form-writing-seeks-partners.html> (last accessed 15 April 2018).
44. Comma Press, 'Macguffin'. Available at <http://commapress.co.uk/digital/macguffin/> (last accessed 15 April 2018).
45. Ibid.

46. David Streitfeld, 'Web fiction, serialised and social', *The New York Times*, 23 March. Available at <http://www.nytimes.com/2014/03/24/technology/web-fiction-serialized-and-social.html> (last accessed 15 April 2018).
47. Comma Press, *Litnav*. Available at <http://www.litnav.com/#about> (last accessed 15 April 2018).
48. Sarah Cole, *Poetic places*. Available at <http://www.poeticplaces.uk/> (last accessed 15 April 2018).
49. Kate Pullinger, *Inanimate Alice*. Available at <http://www.inanimatealice.com/> (last accessed 15 April 2018).
50. Anon., *The role of music in your life*. Available at <http://fivedials.com/experiments/#cover> (last accessed 15 April 2018).
51. Bell et al., 'From Theorising to Analysing Digital Fiction', p. 1.
52. Simogo, *Device 6*. Available at <http://simogo.com/work/device-6/> (last accessed 15 April 2018).
53. Philip Jones, 'Arcadia's vision for a new way of reading', *The Bookseller*, 30 June. Available at <http://www.thebookseller.com/futurebook/arcadias-vision-new-way-reading-305033> (last accessed 15 April 2018).
54. Naomi Alderman, 'The first great works of digital literature are already being written', *The Guardian*, 13 October. Available at <https://www.theguardian.com/technology/2015/oct/13/video-games-digital-storytelling-naomi-alderman> (last accessed 15 April 2018).
55. Simon Parkin, 'Meg Jayanth: The 80 days writer on the interactive power of game play', *The Guardian*, 10 January. Available at <https://www.theguardian.com/technology/2016/jan/10/video-game-makers-meg-jayanth-80-days> (last accessed 15 April 2018).
56. Simogo, *Device 6*, 2013.
57. See the website of the Meow Wolf art collective, describing their work *The House of Eternal Return*. Available at <https://meowwolf.com/> (last accessed 15 April 2018).
58. Andrew Perrin, *Book Reading 2016* (Washington, DC: Pew Research Center, 2016).
59. See Hunter, *The Cambridge Introduction to the Short Story in English*.
60. Amy Hungerford, *Making Literature Now* (Stanford: Stanford University Press, 2016), p. 108–10.
61. Hunter, *The Cambridge Introduction to the Short Story in English*, p. 7.
62. Virginia Woolf, quoted in Terry Eagleton, *The English Novel: An Introduction* (Malden, MA: Blackwell, 2004), and Eagleton, p. 1.
63. See McGurl, *The Program Era*.
64. Boddy, *The American Short Story Since 1950*, pp. 37–54.
65. Ibid. p. 1.

Bibliography

Alderman, Naomi, 'The first great works of digital literature are already being written', *The Guardian*, 13 October, <https://www.theguardian.com/technology/2015/oct/13/video-games-digital-storytelling-naomi-alderman> (accessed 15 April 2018).

Amazon.com, 'Kindle Singles' <https://www.amazon.com/Kindle-Singles/b/ref=amb_link_7?ie=UTF8&node=2486013011&pd_rd_r=NWYV5QK1EVMQQRJJC3P5&pd_rd_w=iGyHr&pd_rd_wg=9qBPu&pf_rd_m=ATVPDKIKX0DER&pf_rd_s=merchandised-search-leftnav&pf_rd_r=NWYV5QK1EVMQQRJJC3P5&pf_rd_r=NWYV5QK1EVMQQRJJC3P5&pf_rd_t=101&pf_rd_p=f9b7c7f1-8fce-4041-83d3-b03e754547f9&pf_rd_p=f9b7c7f1-8fce-4041-83d3-b03e754547f9&pf_rd_i=8584457011> (last accessed 15 April 2018).

Amazon.com, Lee Child author page <https://www.amazon.com/Lee%20Child/e/B000APO0PQ/ref=la_B000APO0PQ_pg_2?rh=n%3A283155%2Cp_82%3AB000APO0PQ&page=2&sort=author-pages-popularity-rank&ie=UTF8&qid=1491558286> (last accessed 15 April 2018).

Amazon.com, 'Short Reads' <https://www.amazon.com/Kindle-Short-Reads/b/ref=kbhp_bb_SRd_c?ie=UTF8&node=8584457011&pd_rd_r=W766E2NRSCQDZAHJ5B7T&pd_rd_w=Q0Ryr&pd_rd_wg=mMZzA&pf_rd_m=ATVPDKIKX0DER&pf_rd_s=merchandised-search-leftnav&pf_rd_r=W766E2NRSCQDZAHJ5B7T&pf_rd_r=W766E2NRSCQDZAHJ5B7T&pf_rd_t=101&pf_rd_p=9522fca1-50db-421c-ad32-6dd558151a05&pf_rd_p=9522fca1-50db-421c-ad32-6dd558151a05&pf_rd_i=154606011> (last accessed 15 April 2018).

Anon., *The role of music in your life* http://fivedials.com/experiments/#cover (last accessed 15 April 2018).

Bell, Alice, Astrid Ensslin and Hans Rustad, 'From Theorising to Analysing Digital Fiction', in Alice Bell, Astrid Ensslin, and Hans Rustad (eds), *Analysing Digital Fiction* (New York: Routledge, 2014).

Bhaskar, Michael, *Curation: The power of selection in a world of excess* (London: Piatkus, 2016).

Blandford, Ann and Simon Attfield, *Interacting with information* (San Rafael, CA: Morgan & Claypool, 2010).

Bloomsbury, 'Bloomsbury Spark Frequently Asked Questions' <http://www.bloomsbury.com/uk/bloomsbury-spark/faqs/> (last accessed 15 April 2018).

Boddy, Kasia, *The American Short Story Since 1950* (Edinburgh: Edinburgh University Press, 2010).

Bohme, Steve, 'Books & consumers in 2016', presentation at Quantum Conference, London Book Fair, 13 March, <http://quantum.londonbookfair.co.uk/RXUK/RXUK_PDMC/responsive/images/2017/Steve%20Bohme%20-%20The%202016%20Book%20Market%20Highlights%20from%20the%20Books%20and%20Consumers%202016%20Survey.pdf?v=636257834636180655> (last accessed 15 April 2018).

Bosman, Julie, 'Writer's cramp: in the E-reader era, a book a year is slacking', *The New York Times*, 12 May, <http://www.nytimes.com/2012/05/13/business/in-e-reader-age-of-writers-cramp-a-book-a-year-is-slacking.html> (last accessed 15 April 2018).

Clark, D. T., 'A qualitative assessment of the kindle e-book reader: Results from initial focus groups', *Performance Measurement and Metrics*, 9.2 (2008): 118–29.

Cole, Sarah, *Poetic places* <http://www.poeticplaces.uk/> (last accessed 15 April 2018).

Comma Press, *Litnav* <http://www.litnav.com/#about> (last accessed 15 April 2018).

Comma Press, 'Macguffin' <http://commapress.co.uk/digital/macguffin/> (last accessed 15 April 2018).

Dietz, Laura, 'Online vs. print reputation of literary fiction magazines', *The Short Story in Theory and Practice*, 4.1 (2014): 7–21.

— 'Who are You Calling an Author? Changing Definitions of Career Legitimacy for Novelists in the Digital Era', in Guy Davidson and Nicola Evans (eds), *Literary Careers in the Modern Era* (Basingstoke, Hampshire: Palgrave Macmillan, 2015).

Dietz, Laura, Claire Warwick and Samantha Rayner, 'Auditioning for permanence: reputation and legitimacy of electronically distributed novels', *Logos*, 26.4 (2015): 22–36.

Eagleton, Terry, *The English Novel: An Introduction* (Malden, MA: Blackwell, 2004).

English, James, *The Economy of Prestige: Prizes, Awards, and the Circulation of Cultural Value* (Cambridge, MA: Harvard University Press, 2005).

4th Estate, 'Shorts' <http://www.4thestate.co.uk/shorts/> (last accessed 15 April 2018).

Galley Beggar Press, 'Galley Beggar Singles' <https://galleybeggar.co.uk/store/books/type/singles> (last accessed 15 April 2018).

Goodyear, Dana, 'I love novels', *The New Yorker*, 22 December, http://www.newyorker.com/magazine/2008/12/22/i-%E2%99%A5-novels (last accessed 15 April 2018).

Hart, Michael, 'The history and philosophy of Project Gutenberg by Michael Hart' <https://www.gutenberg.org/wiki/Gutenberg:The_History_and_Philosophy_of_Project_Gutenberg_by_Michael_Hart> (last accessed 15 April 2018).

Helfer, Doris Small, 'E-Books in Libraries: Some Early Experiences and Reactions', *Searcher: The Magazine for Database Professionals*, 8.9 (2000): 63–5.

Hungerford, Amy, *Making Literature Now* (Stanford: Stanford University Press, 2016).

Hunter, Adrian, *The Cambridge Introduction to the Short Story in English* (Cambridge: Cambridge University Press, 2007).

INKE Project, 'Features of books and e-books', INKE Project website <http://inke.ca/projects/features-of-books-and-e-books/> (last accessed 15 April 2018).

Jones, Philip, 'Arcadia's vision for a new way of reading', *The Bookseller*, 30 June, <http://www.thebookseller.com/futurebook/arcadias-vision-new-way-reading-305033> (last accessed 15 April 2018).

Kindle Direct Publishing, 'Publishing process: Getting started' <https://kdp.amazon.com/help/topic/A37Z49E2DDQPP3?ref_=gs> (last accessed 15 April 2018).

Lebert, Marie, 'History of Project Gutenberg' <http://www.gutenbergnews.org/about/history-of-project-gutenberg/> (last accessed 15 April 2018).

Leypoldt, Gunter, 'All Writers Lead a Double Life', *Books in the Making* symposium, Cambridge University, 15 March 2016.

McCracken, Ellen, 'Expanding Genette's Epitext/Paritext model for transitional electronic literature: Centrifugal and centripedal vectors on Kindles and iPads', *Narrative*, 21.1 (2013): 105–24.

McGurl, Mark, *The Program Era: Postwar Fiction and the Rise of Creative Writing* (Cambridge, MA: Harvard University Press, 2011).

Meow Wolf, <https://meowwolf.com/> (last accessed 15 April 2018).

Nielsen, Jakob and John Morkes, 'Concise, SCANNABLE, and objective: How to write for the web' <https://www.nngroup.com/articles/concise-scannable-and-objective-how-to-write-for-the-web/> (last accessed 15 April 2018).

Parkin, Simon, 'Meg Jayanth: The 80 days writer on the interactive power of game play', *The Guardian*, 10 January, <https://www.theguardian.com/technology/2016/jan/10/video-game-makers-meg-jayanth-80-days> (last accessed 15 April 2018).

Perrin, Andrew, *Book Reading 2016* (Washington, DC: Pew Research Center, 2016).

Penguin Random House, 'Hydra' <http://www.randomhousebooks.com/hydra/> (last accessed 15 April 2018).

Phillips, Angus, *Turning the Page: The Evolution of the Book* (Abingdon: Routledge, 2014).

Ploughshares, 'Ploughshares Solos' <https://www.pshares.org/solos> (last accessed 15 April 2018).

Pullinger, Kate, *Inanimate Alice* <http://www.inanimatealice.com/> (last accessed 15 April 2018).

Simogo, *Device 6* <http://simogo.com/work/device-6/> (last accessed 15 April 2018).

Smith, Kelvin, *The Publishing Business: From P-books to E-books* (Lausanne: AVA Publishing SA, 2012).

Somaiya, Ravi, 'Byliner, an online publisher of long-form writing, seeks partners', *The New York Times*, 3 June, <http://www.nytimes.com/2014/06/04/business/media/byliner-an-online-publisher-of-long-form-writing-seeks-partners.html> (last accessed 15 April 2018).

Streitfeld, David, 'Web fiction, serialised and social', *The New York Times*, 23 March, <http://www.nytimes.com/2014/03/24/technology/web-fiction-serialized-and-social.html> (last accessed 15 April 2018).

Tappuni, Jane, 'What Nielsen Bookscan tells us about ebook sales cycles and the ebook plateau', *Publishing Technology* <http://www.publishingtechnology.com/2015/01/what-nielsen-bookscan-data-tells-us-about-ebook-sales-cycles-the-ebook-plateau/> (last accessed 15 April 2018).

Thompson, John B., *Merchants of Culture: The Publishing Business in the Twenty-First Century* (Cambridge: Polity, 2012).

Part III

Forms of the Short Story

9

Short-Short Fiction

Michael Basseler

THE QUESTION OF LENGTH – what makes a short story short – has never been far from view in critical discussions of the form. As early as the nineteenth century, the matter of upper and lower limits was debated, and quickly became entwined with questions about the short story's aesthetics and its particularities in relation to other literary genres. Edgar Allan Poe famously established brevity as the key generic marker of the short story by emphasising 'unity of effect', a quality that for Poe depended on the possibility that short stories could and should be read 'at one sitting', that is, without any interruptions or distractions. Brevity, for Poe, entailed a complex interaction between three elements: theme, structure and temporal length.[1] While Poe's poetics valorised brevity mainly by patrolling the short story's upper limit, he also warned that there was a lower limit at which 'extreme brevity will degenerate into epigrammatism'.[2] Ever since, shortness, however defined, has been part and parcel of almost every discussion of the genre, and has often been treated as if it were an absolute rather than a relative category.

In recent decades, there has been a surge in popularity of very short narrative forms of various kinds, and this has brought with it renewed attention to questions of length. Broadly speaking, critical discussion has concentrated on two main issues: the formal properties and characteristics of these often radically truncated texts, and the sociocultural significance of their proliferation. On the latter, interest has fallen on the extent to which short-short fiction can be regarded as a peculiarly contemporary phenomenon, a response to the social and cultural realities of our historical moment. Some accounts have stressed that these forms are especially well equipped to capture an incoherent (post)modern world that can, if at all, only be adequately represented in fragments and vignettes. Short-shorts, so this argument goes, address the pluralisation and acceleration of a culture in which *grand récits* have been rendered obsolete and ideologically, but also aesthetically, questionable. A version of this thesis can be found in David Shields's much-noted *Reality Hunger* (2010), which reasons that short-shorts 'gain access to contemporary feeling states more effectively than the conventional story does',[3] and goes on to compare such texts with other cultural forms of abbreviated expression, from movie trailers to fast food to bumper stickers.[4] Ashley Chantler likewise sees the short-short boom as 'a sign of the times', suggesting that 'the internet buzzes with numerous e-zines, websites, forums and blogs containing short-shorts, no doubt because they are perfect for the emailing, texting, abbreviating ADD generation'.[5]

Short-short fiction in such accounts is largely conceived as a response to, or consequence of, a changing cultural and media landscape. Under the influence of, first, radio and then television, and, later, the Internet, social media and smart phone apps, the ways in which we process information and perceive reality have changed dramatically. These changes have, in turn, contributed to an aesthetic and epistemological valorisation of the literary fragment. It seems beyond question that social media platforms and phenomena like twitterature, though still in their infancy, have begun altering and shaping how we tell and read stories in our 'one-byte-and-go-culture';[6] and it seems highly likely that this 'new economy' of miniature narrative forms will continue to proliferate as writers and artists learn to make ever more creative use of the technical features and quantitative restrictions of electronic mass communication. At the same time, however, it is worth recalling that such correlations between short narrative forms and 'modernity' broadly conceived have been made before, particularly in the modernist period, and that claims to the effect that short fiction presents a challenge to dominant modes of realism promulgated by the novel and other forms of popular discourse have been advanced throughout the twentieth century.[7] Moreover, extreme brevity is only *one* characteristic of our contemporary cultural economy, which is equally saturated with popular epic forms: one only has to think about the persistence of the serial novel and the success of extensive, multi-episodic narratives across different media, such as Harry Potter, *Game of Thrones*, *Breaking Bad* or *House of Cards*.

If sociocultural accounts of short-short fiction's rise to prominence are prone to broad statement and even speculation, formalist readings show a contrasting tendency towards restrictive definition. One can see this most obviously in the roster of terms that has developed since the 1980s to address the form: along with short-short stories, or just short-shorts, we find flash fiction, minute stories, microfiction, sudden fiction, hint fiction and quick fiction; beyond anglophone traditions, meanwhile, we encounter *microrrelato*, *microcuento*, *Kürzestgeschichte* and *micronouvelle*. The surge in nomenclature is symptomatic of the thorny questions about limits and definitions with which short fiction criticism in general tends to be preoccupied: how short can a story be before it degenerates into something else? How do the forms of short-short fiction probe or enlarge our definitions of narrative? To what extent does short-short fiction dissolve or subvert generic boundaries between, say, narrative and poetry? Where should one draw the line between a short story and even shorter narrative forms? And what further taxonomic classifications are justified to differentiate, for example, a two-page story and a fifty-word 'flash'?

In attempting to answer such questions – attempting, that is, to define the outer limits of short-short fiction – many critics inevitably end up making assertions about what they take to be essential and distinguishing properties of the form. Anthologies like Howe and Howe's *Short Shorts* (1982), Shapard and Thomas's *Sudden Fiction* (1983) and Thomas et al. *Flash Fiction* (1992), for example, proceed on the conviction that the stories they present are categorically different from what one might understand by the traditional short story. As Robert Shapard and James Thomas say in the foreword to *Sudden Fiction*, almost all of the writers who contributed to the volume 'accepted the short-short as a form of its own';[8] that is, as a form distinct from what would commonly be regarded as the short story. The physical extent of the text is prerequisite in such definitions. Flash fiction, when the term was coined by James Thomas in 1992, was reserved for prose narratives of up to 750 words. Other generic terms like 'new sudden fiction'[9] and 'microfiction'[10] similarly rely on quantitative restrictions, sometimes on a mere counting of words, and sometimes on putative reading time, as in 'four-minute fiction'.[11] In truth, the range of what counts as a short-short story seems to run anywhere from as little as fifty (or even less) to two thousand words.[12]

Matters get considerably more complicated when claims are made, *pace* Poe, about the relative merits or qualities of different lengths of text. In the most systematic contribution to date, William Nelles argues for an appreciation of the qualitative differences between stories of up to 700 words and stories above that length; as he puts it, 'microfiction seems to me not just shorter than the short story, but different: if it's not a different genre, then at least it's a different species'.[13] According to Nelles, a 'different set of narrative principles does seem to kick in as stories shrink down to a couple of pages or less'.[14] However, if one takes a closer look at this 'different set of narrative principles' – extreme action, reduced character, indistinct setting, linear temporality and short duration of related events, intertextual referentiality, and closure – it becomes highly doubtful whether they can really be said to be unique to microfiction, and whether, indeed, they constitute a generic quality at all. Among other things, Nelles claims that the action in microfictions tends to be 'more palpable and extreme'.[15] While this might be true for the case studies he uses – the 240-word, stream of consciousness-like miniatures that constitute Robert Olen Butler's *Severance* (2006), all of which are told by narrators in the last conscious moment after their beheading – it simply does not apply to a vast number of other microfictions. The pieces in Lydia Davis's *Can't and Won't* (2014), for instance, are arguably among the best work produced in this genre, yet almost none of them contain any kind of extreme action, but are often self-reflexive meditations on very mundane happenings, or simply narrativised observations of the seemingly trivial. As the writer Charles Johnson, a professed phenomenologist, puts it, 'Only a fool would rigidly define the short-short because, above all else, it must be an innovative, attention-grabbing exploration of that perennial mystery that is the origin and end of expression itself: language.'[16]

Such attempts at theorising the short-short story, conditioned as they are by structuralist and formalist approaches, run the risk of continuing the unduly taxonomic approach that has dominated short story theory for decades, and which has tended to produce unyielding enquiries into essential generic differences between the form and neighbouring genres such as the novel, novella or (at the other end of the scale) prose poem.[17] While many scholars, particularly in the 1980s and 1990s, set out to identify textual, formal and content-based elements that could be said to be unique to the short story, more often than not they emerged from this endeavour with the realisation that no such essential differences, at least at the textual level, could be said to exist. Even the most systematic, empirically saturated works of this sort, such as Helmut Bonheim's *The Narrative Modes: Techniques of the Short Story* (1982), eventually succumb to the sober recognition that there 'is no single ingredient of the many short story definitions other than its form of publication that cannot be claimed for countless novels as well'.[18] As deconstruction many years ago established, the 'law of genre' is one of impurity rather than purity;[19] and despite the individuating names we give them, genres are not 'taxonomic classes of equal solidity but fields at once emerging and ephemeral, defined over and over again by new entries that are still being produced'.[20] Nor has the concentration on length by itself been any less problematic. As Graham Good points out in an essay surveying the relationship of the short story to the novella form, 'Categories based purely on length are bound to be arbitrary; there is no magic number of words which constitutes the minimum for a novel or the maximum for a short story, and there are always borderline cases.'[21]

An alternative approach to short-short fiction sets aside vexatious questions of definition and taxonomy in favour of a focus on the ways in which individual texts produce meaning and handle knowledge. This is expressly *not* to say that we should abandon the attempt to address the form *tout court*, or that we must surrender the effort to explain our evident contemporary preference for it; rather, it is to substitute the question of what a short-short story *is*, definitionally speaking, for an emphasis on what it *does*, that is, on the cognitive and cultural work it performs. The issue of genre remains central in such an approach, but not as the definitional frame or ideational purpose of the discussion. Instead, genre arises as something that radically condensed narratives invariably problematise – this might go some way to explain why the form has proven so elusive. Such an approach owes something to Charles E. May, who in his work on the relationship between brevity and particular forms or modes of knowing argues that short fiction can seem 'closer to the nature of reality as we experience it in those moments when we are made aware of the inauthenticity of everyday life'.[22] Where for May the distinctiveness of the genre is a matter of its being more adequately reflective of reality ('closer to the nature of reality') than other fictional modes, however, it is less an a priori reality that is the source for short fiction's 'mode of knowing'. Rather, such a mode of knowing is grounded in, and only produced by, particular generic structures. In other words, short forms of fiction do not simply 'contain' or 'embody' a certain form or mode of knowing, they construe and prefigure it in the first place. It is in this sense that this chapter follows Rita Felski's argument that 'genre and knowledge are inescapably intertwined'.[23]

The status of knowledge in short-short fiction – what is known, disclosed or withheld – is intimately bound up with the brevity of the form. As Irving Howe puts it, the reader is required to 'supply the contexts . . . since if the contexts were there, they'd no longer be short shorts'.[24] The critical literature affords many accounts of this particular aspect of radically condensed or abbreviated narration. Umberto Eco, for example, calls such texts 'open works' that to an unusual degree require the 'theoretical, mental collaboration of the consumer'.[25] John Gerlach, meanwhile, reflects on how such stories present 'an invitation to construct explanations, explanations about causality, connections, motives. When we feel we are constructing them significantly . . . we sense story. . . . Story proper is more accurately defined by speculations it encourages on the part of the reader than by what actually occurs in the reported event.'[26] More recently, Renate Brosch has described how the reader must engage in 'projective reading': the text 'does not aim at a comprehensive depiction of its material, but wants to leave an irritation that calls for completion'.[27]

Dave Eggers's 'A Circle Like Some Circles', published in his collection *Short Short Stories* (2005), provides a good example of both the extent and the limits of this 'projective' openness as it operates in short-short fiction. In the story, a character called Ron visits his friend Mina, who years before had been severely injured in a train accident and is now living with her grandmother because 'her brain doesn't work quite the way it did before the accident'.[28] The story is told by a heterodiegetic narrator, with Ron serving as the focalising centre. As the trio sits by an artificial, gas-powered fireplace, the reader is afforded insights into Ron's thoughts and feelings: 'He is looking at Mina, smiling at her; in many ways she seems precisely the same as when she was when they were young together, years before, when they flirted and drove over the hills too fast.'[29] We learn that Ron used to date Mina and thought they would marry, but now he visits her only once a year, since she 'lives six hours away from Ron and he is lazy'.[30] Oscillating between memories of his love affair with Mina and his recognition of the morbidity of the present situation, Ron's lugubrious reflections turn, in the closing sentences, to the future: 'He sits near the fire, very warm and shuddering, close to Mina's scar and her grandmother's pacemaker, and he thinks the inevitable thoughts: that there is no God, that there had better not be any kind of God, because he doesn't want someone to blame for all this bullshit.'[31]

'A Circle Like Some Circles' stages a scenario one comes across repeatedly in contemporary short-short stories, in which characters of whose lives we are afforded only a glimpse are brought together in a brief, inconclusive encounter. The story is both highly compressed – repeatedly gesturing toward an unelaborated prehistory, for example – and semiotically open, with details like the artificial fireplace and the grandmother's pacemaker charged with metonymic suggestiveness. Compared with many short-short stories, Eggers's narrative is thematically quite elaborate, staging a collision between present and past and condensing a large span of years into an ephemeral moment. That moment functions as an epiphany for Ron, signalling the disparity between life as it is and life as it could have been. Any sense of heightened realisation is undermined by the closing statements, however, as the reader is told that Ron thinks 'inevitable' thoughts, which amount to his reiterating an untestable philosophical platitude ('there is no God') before lapsing into inarticulacy ('all this bullshit'). It is a bathetic ending, but it serves a greater purpose as a moment of textual self-reflexiveness, in which Eggers, having briefly liberated Ron from the meaninglessness of contemporary existence, resubmerges him in its dominant, Godless metanarrative.

The rather conventional, epiphanic element to 'A Circle Like Some Circles' has the effect of cancelling out the exceptionalism of Ron and Mina's story, swamping their particular narrative in a sea of equivalent narratives that have the same meaning (as the title also suggests). As the story loses its singularity and becomes generic, it displays how meaning-making is closely entwined with generic structures, conventions and reader expectations. A more overt form of self-referentiality is evident in the work of David Foster Wallace. His 'A Radically Condensed History of Postindustrial Life', the opening piece in the collection *Brief Interviews With Hideous Men* (1999), consists of a mere eighty-five words, including the title. As with Eggers's work, the text ends up referring back to its own procedures in order to blur generic boundaries and invite projective reading:

> When they were introduced, he made a witticism, hoping to be liked. She laughed extremely hard, hoping to be liked. Then each drove home alone, staring straight ahead, with the same twist to their faces.
>
> The man who'd introduced them didn't much like either of them, though he acted as if he did, anxious as he was to preserve good relations at all times. One never knew, after all, now did one now did one now did one.[32]

There are a number of inferential levels on which the reader works to navigate a text like this. But crucially, the text is not equally 'open' on every level. In respect of the situational framing of the scene, disclosure is minimal: we may be at a party or a similar social event, with the man who introduces the other characters perhaps being the host; but the setting could easily be otherwise. The point is that the reader is free to make whatever inference he or she pleases within the loosely marked parameters of the story. On an affective level, the text is more directive. All three characters perform specific cultural rituals and follow social protocols, pretending to like each other and 'hoping to be liked' in return. The perspectival shift in the second paragraph, toward the host and his social anxiety, reinforces the dominant affect of the encounter, while the repetitive rhetorical questioning ('now did one now did one now did one') universalises it, closing the story in a kind of social *perpetuum mobile*.

This paradigmatic expansion of the characters' anxieties to imply something about the wider psycho-social infrastructure of post-industrial life is reinforced by a number of devices in the text, such as the repetition in the first two sentences of the phrase 'hoping to be liked', which signals a contradictory desire for the simultaneous recognition of difference and sameness. The title likewise functions metonymically to suggest that the story stands for the history of post-industrial life *pars pro toto*. In this 'radically condensed history', knowledge of a historically general kind is attained not by means of comprehension, but by means of omission, exemplification and compression: what is to be known about the history of post-industrial life, Wallace suggests, can be said in less than a hundred words, through a private encounter between anonymous interchangeable subjects. In this way, the text's brevity begins to impinge on the question of generic identity. Lacking the conventional markers of 'storyness', and alluding to the idea of a history of post-industrial best told as a *petite histoire*, Wallace's text, precisely because of its brevity, transcends its own generic status as narrative fiction.

The transgression of generic boundaries is a hallmark, too, of the work of Lydia Davis, perhaps the most celebrated exponent of short-short fiction in America today, and a writer whose career has been almost entirely based on an exploration of the possibilities inherent in short forms. 'My Childhood Friend', from her recent collection *Can't and Won't* (2014), is typical of her writing in the strategies of omission and condensation it employs. Here it is entire:

> Who is this old man walking along looking a little grim with a wool cap on his head?
>
> But when I call out to him and he turns around, he doesn't know me at first, either – this old woman smiling foolishly at him in her winter coat.[33]

Davis's work is so abstemious that in order to conceptualise it as a story at all we have to rely on a radically simplified definition of what constitutes narrative act. Something like Monika Fludernik's definition of narrativity as 'the quasi-mimetic evocation of real-life experience'[34] is as much as Davis's story seems willing to assert. Yet even at this level of brevity, the text is highly active and surprisingly richly patterned. It imposes cognitive parameters that are temporally framed: this is what it feels like to meet an old friend after so many years. It has a metaphorical dimension: the season is winter, which is also, we infer, the season of the characters' lives. Typical of an 'open work', as Eco describes, all that is omitted – everything that has happened between this meeting between the characters and their last – persists in the form of questions the reader is encouraged to pursue. What kind of friendship did they share, and for how long? What, in fact, do we mean if we call someone a 'childhood friend'? Why does he look 'a little grim'? What does it mean that she smiles at him 'foolishly'? And as with Wallace's 'A Radically Condensed History of Postindustrial Life', Davis causes us to contemplate the effects of this brevity and openness on generic designation. Davis's use of an autodiegetic narrator, and her stressing of the I-narrator's subjectivity ('*my* childhood friend'), prevents the development of that narrator as a fictional character but also gives the text the quality of autobiographical disclosure. Where Wallace blurs the boundaries between fiction and history, however, Davis switches between narrating and narrated selves, between autobiography and fiction, with the text dissolving at a moment of perspectival shift in which the narrator suddenly sees herself in the third person ('this old woman . . .'). The effect is akin to what Roland Barthes, contemplating the haiku form, calls an 'acute dialectic of time', a 'brief, searing contradiction, like a kind of logical flash',[35] in which the momentariness and fleetingness of an instant in time is captured in memory only to be immediately consumed.[36] Davis's text can be understood as trying to evade the grasp of generic containment in this way. As Claudia Öhlschläger, summarising Barthes, puts it: 'Small forms . . . provide the formal framework for the immediacy of the instant, while in the act of recording they already archive its disappearance.'[37]

Short-short fiction can be characterised (rather than defined) by the ways in which it interacts with established genres and, as a result of its extreme brevity, problematises the boundaries between genre and expectation. As John Frow has remarked, 'far from being merely "stylistic" devices, genres create effects of reality and truth, authority and plausibility, which are central to the different ways the world is understood'. Texts, Frow goes on to say, do not so much 'belong' to a single genre as enter into relation with 'a field or economy of genres'; what complexity a text can be said to possess 'derives largely from the complexity of that relation'.[38] This point can be illustrated with reference to Jamaica Kincaid's 'Girl' (1978), one of the most anthologised pieces of short-short fiction in English. Originally published in *The New Yorker*, this 650-word piece consists entirely of dialogue or, more precisely, of a series of exhortations, presented in paratactic, often repetitive sentences:

> Wash the white clothes on Monday and put them on the stone heap; wash the color clothes on Tuesday and put them on the clothesline to dry; don't walk bare-head in the hot sun; cook pumpkin fritters in very hot sweet oil; soak your little cloths right after you take them off; when buying cotton to make yourself a nice blouse, be sure that it doesn't have gum in it, because that way it won't hold up well after a wash; soak salt fish overnight before you cook it; is it true that you sing benna in Sunday school?; always eat your food in such a way that it won't turn someone else's stomach; on Sundays try to walk like a lady and not like the slut you are so bent on becoming; don't sing benna in Sunday school; you mustn't speak to wharf-rat boys, not even to give directions; don't eat fruits on the street – flies will follow you; *but I don't sing benna on Sundays at all and never in Sunday school;* this is how to sew on a button; this is how to make a buttonhole for the button you have just sewed on; this is how to hem a dress when you see the hem coming down and so to prevent yourself from looking like the slut I know you are so bent on becoming; this is how you iron your father's khaki shirt so that it doesn't have a crease; this is

how you iron your father's khaki pants so that they don't have a crease; this is how you grow okra – far from the house, because okra tree harbors red ants; when you are growing dasheen, make sure it gets plenty of water or else it makes your throat itch when you are eating it; this is how you sweep a corner; this is how you sweep a whole house; this is how you sweep a yard; this is how you smile to someone you don't like too much; this is how you smile to someone you don't like at all; this is how you smile to someone you like completely; this is how you set a table for tea; this is how you set a table for dinner; this is how you set a table for dinner with an important guest; this is how you set a table for lunch; this is how you set a table for breakfast; this is how to behave in the presence of men who don't know you very well, and this way they won't recognize immediately the slut I have warned you against becoming; be sure to wash every day, even if it is with your own spit; don't squat down to play marbles – you are not a boy, you know; don't pick people's flowers – you might catch something; don't throw stones at blackbirds, because it might not be a blackbird at all; this is how to make a bread pudding; this is how to make doukona; this is how to make pepper pot; this is how to make a good medicine for a cold; this is how to make a good medicine to throw away a child before it even becomes a child; this is how to catch a fish; this is how to throw back a fish you don't like, and that way something bad won't fall on you; this is how to bully a man; this is how a man bullies you; this is how to love a man, and if this doesn't work there are other ways, and if they don't work don't feel too bad about giving up; this is how to spit up in the air if you feel like it, and this is how to move quick so that it doesn't fall on you; this is how to make ends meet; always squeeze bread to make sure it's fresh; *but what if the baker won't let me feel the bread?*; you mean to say that after all you are really going to be the kind of woman who the baker won't let near the bread?[39]

Reviewing the collection in which 'Girl' was later reprinted, the novelist Anne Tyler criticised Kincaid's writing for being 'insultingly obscure', and for 'fail[ing] to pull us forward with any semblance of plot. . . . Not once do we feel that the writer is leaning forward and taking our hands and telling us a story.'[40] Echoing Poe's warning against epigrammatism at the lower limits of narrative, Tyler protested that Kincaid's work was too often closer to poetry than to the short story. Yet one could equally argue that the text is replete with story, each of the mother's advices constituting a mini-narrative in itself. Her warning that her daughter 'mustn't speak to wharf-rat boys, not even give directions', for instance, activates a subplot about the implications of inappropriate sexual contact that extends throughout the text, from the advice on how to fix a torn dress, to the singing of benna (a vernacular call-and-response musical form characterised by licentious gossip and scandal-mongering), to the question with which the story ends: 'you mean to say that after all you are really going to be the kind of woman who the baker won't let near the bread?' Taken together, these instructions-as-micro-stories constitute a condensed initiation narrative. But where in the classical initiation story the young (male) protagonist advances from a state of innocence toward a self-actualising 'change of knowledge about the world or himself',[41] 'Girl' projects a future for its female protagonist that is entirely conditioned by prohibition and moral exhortation: 'this is how to behave in the presence of men who don't know you very well'; 'don't eat fruits on the street'; 'always squeeze bread to make sure it's fresh'.

'Girl''s truth-effect – its powerful evocation of a girl's life in Antigua and her initiation into the adult world – is less the result of its attunement to certain kinds of reality or experience (Charles May's argument) than of the complex interaction within it of literary and non-literary genres. Reading the story, we encounter a subtle fusing of everyday-life genres of 'advice' or 'instruction' rooted in a specific cultural experience, with conventions marked as 'literary', such as poetic language (repetition, parallelism, metaphor) and the initiation theme. As Frow suggests, the 'decoding' of such generically encoded knowledge presupposes our familiarity with generic conventions and structures; but at the same time Kincaid's text challenges the idea that those genres are readily distinguishable from one another. Perhaps this fluidity in its relations to a 'field or economy of genres', as Frow puts it, explains the difficulty taxonomic criticism has faced in accounting for short-short fiction. It might also help to explain something of the continuing fascination readers evidently have with very short narrative forms.

Literature, as Stathis Gourgouris claims, 'challenges our usual definitions of knowledge in strict conceptual terms' and 'demands that we account for the implicit, the nonpalpable, the ineffable, the perfectly contingent'.[42] As condensed literary forms that operate on the principle of economy to convey the implicit and inexpressible, the genres of short narrative fiction create effects of reality and truth that are at once exemplary of literary discourse at large *and* generically specific. The task for future approaches to very short fiction is therefore to develop what Ottmar Ette has called 'nanophilology',[43] that is an approach to short narrative texts that overcomes the formalist and structuralist legacy by providing explanatory frameworks for the ways in which these forms experimentally deploy knowledge in the microcosmos they zero in on, and how they always signal the macrocosmos of the wider cultural processes of the production and exchange of meaning. The forms of short fiction – from short-short fiction to the novella – are not only closely interrelated in an economy of genres, but are also interesting case studies for what one might call the 'knowledge of literature',[44] or 'literature as knowledge for living'.[45] Rather than erecting or solidifying generic boundaries and categories, a central question for research in short fiction should be how short narrative forms constitute a system of cultural and narrative exchange in which meanings and knowledge are produced in the generically conditioned interaction between authors, texts, publishers and readers.[46]

Notes

1. Kirk Curnutt, *Wise Economies: Brevity and Storytelling in American Short Stories* (Moscow: University of Idaho Press, 1997), p. 4.
2. Edgar Allan Poe, *Essays and Reviews*, ed. Gary Richard Thompson (New York: Library of America, 1984), p. 572.
3. David Shields, *Reality Hunger* (London: Penguin, 2010), p. 126.
4. See the introduction to David Shields and Elizabeth Cooperman (eds), *Life is Short – Art is Shorter: In Praise of Brevity* (Portland: Hawthorne Books, 2015).
5. Ashley Chantler, 'Notes Towards the Definition of the Short-Short Story', in Ailsa Cox (ed.), *The Short Story* (Newcastle upon Tyne: Cambridge Scholars, 2008), p. 49.
6. Laila Al-Sharqi and Irum S. Abbasi, 'Flash Fiction: A Unique Writer-Reader Partnership', *Studies in Literature and Language*, 11:1 (2015): 52.

7. Christopher Gair, '"Perhaps the Words Remember Me": Richard Brautigan's Very Short Stories', *Western American Literature*, 47.1 (2012): 8.
8. Robert Shapard and James Thomas (eds), *New Sudden Fiction. Short-Short Stories from America and Beyond* (New York and London: W. W. Norton, 2007), p. xiv.
9. Shapard and Thomas, *New Sudden Fiction,* p. 15.
10. William Nelles, 'Microfiction: What Makes a Very Short Story Very Short?', *Narrative*, 20: 1 (2012): 89.
11. See Robley Wilson Jr (ed.), *Four-Minute Fictions: 50 Short-Short Stories from the North American Review* (Flagstaff: Word Beat Press, 1987).
12. Al-Sharqi and Abbasi, 'Flash Fiction': 52.
13. Nelles, 'Microfiction': 97.
14. Ibid. 91.
15. Ibid.
16. Charles Johnson, 'Afterword', in Robert Shapard and James Thomas (eds), *Sudden Fiction* (Layton, UT: Peregrine Smith, 1986), p. 233.
17. See, for instance, John Gerlach, 'The Margins of Narrative: The Very Short Story, the Prose Poem, and the Lyric', in Susan Lohafer and Jo Ellyn Clarey (eds), *Short Story Theory at a Crossroads* (Baton Rouge: Louisiana State University Press, 1989), pp. 74–84; Graham Good, 'Notes on the Novella', in Charles E. May (ed.), *The New Short Story Theories* (Athens: Ohio University Press, 1994), pp. 147–64; Ted Morrissey, 'Great Works of Literature Betwixt Short Story and Novella', *Eureka Studies in Teaching Short Fiction*, 2: 2 (2002): 9–12; and Mary Louise Pratt, 'The Short Story: The Long and the Short of It', in May (ed.), *The New Short Story Theories*, pp. 91–113.
18. Helmut Bonheim, *The Narrative Modes. Techniques of the Short Story* (Cambridge: Brewer, 1982), p. 166.
19. See Jacques Derrida, 'The Law of Genre', in David Duff (ed.), *Modern Genre Theory* (Harlow: Pearson, 2000), pp. 219–31.
20. Wai Chee Dimock, 'Introduction: Genres as Fields of Knowledge', *PMLA*, 122:5 (2007): 1379.
21. Good, 'Notes on the Novella', p. 149.
22. Charles E. May, 'The Nature of Knowledge in Short Fiction', in May (ed.), *The New Short Story Theories*, p. 137.
23. Rita Felski, *Uses of Literature* (Malden, MA: Blackwell, 2008), p. 83.
24. Irving Howe, 'Introduction', in Irving Howe and I. W. Howe (eds), *Short Shorts. An Anthology of the Shortest Stories* (Boston and London: David R. Godine, 1982), p. xv.
25. Umberto Eco, *The Open Work*, trans. Anna Cancogni (Cambridge, MA: Harvard University Press, 1989), p. 12.
26. Gerlach, 'The Margins of Narrative', pp. 79–80.
27. Renate Brosch, *Short Story. Textsorte und Leseerfahrung* (Trier: Wissenschaftlicher Verlag Trier, 2007), p. 83 [my translation].
28. Dave Eggers, 'A Circle Like Some Circles', in Dave Eggers, *Short Short Stories* (London: Penguin, 2005), p. 16.
29. Ibid. p. 16.
30. Ibid.
31. Ibid. p. 17.
32. David Foster Wallace, 'A Radically Condensed History of Postindustrial Life', in *Brief Interviews with Hideous Men* (New York: Little, Brown, 1999), n.p.
33. Lydia Davis, 'My Childhood Friend', in Lydia Davis, *Can't and Won't* (London: Penguin, 2014), p. 235.
34. Monika Fludernik, *Towards A 'Natural' Narratology* (London: Routledge, 1996), p. 12.

35. Roland Barthes, *The Preparation of the Novel: Lecture Courses and Seminars at the Collège de France, 1978–1979 and 1979–1980*, trans. N. Léger (New York: Columbia University Press, 2011), p. 48.
36. Ibid. p. 49.
37. Claudia Öhlschläger, '"Feindialektik Der Zeit." Aspekte einer Epistemologie der Kleinen Form in Transnationaler Perspektive', in Sabine Autsch et al. (eds), *Kulturen des Kleinen. Mikroformate in Literatur, Kunst Und Medien* (Paderborn: Wilhelm Fink, 2014), p. 60 [my translation].
38. John Frow, *Genre* (London: Routledge, 2010), p. 2.
39. Jamaica Kincaid, 'Girl', *The New Yorker*, 26 June 1978. Available at <http://www.newyorker.com/magazine/1978/06/26/girl> (last accessed 15 April 2018).
40. Anne Tyler, 'Mothers and Mysteries', *The New Republic*, 189 (1983): 33.
41. Mordecai Marcus, 'What Is an Initiation Story?', *The Journal of Aesthetics and Art Criticism*, 19.2 (1960): 222.
42. Stathis Gourgouris, *Does Literature Think? Literature as Theory for an Antimythical Era* (Stanford: Stanford University Press, 2003), p. 18.
43. Ottmar Ette, 'Zur Einführung – Nanophilologie und Mikrotextualität', in Ottmar Ette (ed.), *Nanophilologie: Literarische Kurz- Und Kürzestformen in der Romania* (Tübingen: Niemeyer, 2008), p. 1.
44. See Angela Locatelli (ed.), *La conoscenza della letteratura/The Knowledge of Literature*, 9 vols (Bergamo: Bergamo University Press, 2002–10).
45. Ottmar Ette, 'Literature as Knowledge for Living, Literary Studies as Science for Living', *PMLA*, 125.4 (2010): 983.
46. See Curnutt, *Wise Economies*, p. 2.

Bibliography

Al-Sharqi, Laila and Irum S. Abbasi, 'Flash Fiction: A Unique Writer-Reader Partnership', *Studies in Literature and Language*, 11:1 (2015): 52–6.
Barthes, Roland, *The Preparation of the Novel: Lecture Courses and Seminars at the Collège de France, 1978–1979 and 1979–1980*, trans. N. Léger (New York: Columbia University Press, 2011).
Bonheim, Helmut, *The Narrative Modes. Techniques of the Short Story* (Cambridge: Brewer, 1982).
Brosch, Renate, *Short Story. Textsorte und Leseerfahrung* (Trier: Wissenschaftlicher Verlag Trier, 2007).
Butler, Robert Olen, *Severance* (San Francisco: Chronicle Books, 2006).
Chantler, Ashley, 'Notes Towards the Definition of the Short-Short Story', in Ailsa Cox (ed.), *The Short Story* (Newcastle upon Tyne: Cambridge Scholars, 2008), pp. 32–58.
Curnutt, Kirk, *Wise Economies: Brevity and Storytelling in American Short Stories* (Moscow: University of Idaho Press, 1997).
Davis, Lydia, 'My Childhood Friend', in Lydia Davis, *Can't and Won't* (London: Penguin, 2014), p. 235.
Derrida, Jacques, 'The Law of Genre', in David Duff (ed.), *Modern Genre Theory* (Harlow: Pearson, 2000), pp. 219–231.
Dimock, Wai Chee, 'Introduction: Genres as Fields of Knowledge', *PMLA*, 122:5 (2007): 1377–88.
Eco, Umberto, *The Open Work*, trans. Anna Cancogni (Cambridge: Harvard University Press, 1989).

Eggers, Dave, 'A Circle Like Some Circles', in Dave Eggers, *Short Short Stories* (London: Penguin, 2005), pp. 16–17.
Ette, Ottmar, 'Zur Einführung – Nanophilologie und Mikrotextualität', in Ottmar Ette (ed.), *Nanophilologie: Literarische Kurz- Und Kürzestformen in der Romania* (Tübingen: Niemeyer, 2008), pp. 1–5.
— 'Literature as Knowledge for Living, Literary Studies as Science for Living', *PMLA*, 125.4 (2010): 977–93.
Felski, Rita, *Uses of Literature* (Malden, MA: Blackwell, 2008).
Fludernik, Monika, *Towards A 'Natural' Narratology* (London: Routledge, 1996).
Frow, John, *Genre* (London: Routledge, 2010).
Gair, Christopher, '"Perhaps the Words Remember Me": Richard Brautigan's Very Short Stories', *Western American Literature*, 47.1 (2012): 4–21.
Gerlach, John, 'The Margins of Narrative: The Very Short Story, the Prose Poem, and the Lyric', in Susan Lohafer and Jo Ellyn Clarey (eds), *Short Story Theory at a Crossroads* (Baton Rouge: Louisiana State University Press, 1989), pp. 74–84.
Good, Graham, 'Notes on the Novella', in Charles E. May (ed.), *The New Short Story Theories* (Athens: Ohio University Press, 1994), pp. 147–64.
Gourgouris, Stathis, *Does Literature Think? Literature as Theory for an Antimythical Era* (Stanford: Stanford University Press, 2003).
Howe, Irving, 'Introduction', in Irving Howe and I. W. Howe (eds), *Short Shorts. An Anthology of the Shortest Stories* (Boston and London: David R. Godine, 1982), pp. ix–xvii.
Johnson, Charles, 'Afterword', in Robert Shapard and James Thomas (eds), *Sudden Fiction* (Layton, UT: Peregrine Smith, 1986), pp. 232–3.
Kincaid, Jamaica, 'Girl', *The New Yorker*, 26 June 1978, <http://www.newyorker.com/magazine/1978/06/26/girl> (last accessed 15 April 2018).
Locatelli, Angela (ed.), *La conoscenza della letteratura/The Knowledge of Literature*, 9 vols (Bergamo: Bergamo University Press, 2002–10).
Marcus, Mordecai, 'What Is an Initiation Story?', *The Journal of Aesthetics and Art Criticism*, 19.2 (1960): 221–8.
May, Charles E., 'The Nature of Knowledge in Short Fiction', in Charles E. May (ed.), *The New Short Story Theories* (Athens: Ohio University Press, 1994), pp. 131–46.
— (ed.), *The New Short Story Theories* (Athens: Ohio University Press, 1994).
Morrissey, Ted, 'Great Works of Literature Betwixt Short Story and Novella', *Eureka Studies in Teaching Short Fiction*, 2: 2 (2002): 9–12.
Nelles, William, 'Microfiction: What Makes a Very Short Story Very Short?', *Narrative*, 20: 1 (2012): 87–104.
Öhlschläger, Claudia, '"Feindialektik Der Zeit." Aspekte einer Epistemologie der Kleinen Form in Transnationaler Perspektive', in Sabine Autsch, Claudia Öhlschläger and Leonie Süwolto (eds), *Kulturen des Kleinen. Mikroformate in Literatur, Kunst Und Medien* (Paderborn: Wilhelm Fink, 2014), pp. 57–68.
Poe, Edgar Allan, *Essays and Reviews*, ed. Gary Richard Thompson (New York: Library of America, 1984).
Pratt, Mary Louise, 'The Short Story: The Long and the Short of It', in Charles E. May (ed.), *The New Short Story Theories* (Athens: Ohio University Press, 1994), pp. 91–113.
Shapard, Robert and James Thomas (eds), *New Sudden Fiction. Short-Short Stories from America and Beyond* (New York and London: W. W. Norton, 2007).
Shields, David, *Reality Hunger* (London: Penguin, 2010).
Shields, David and Elizabeth Cooperman (eds), *Life is Short – Art is Shorter: In Praise of Brevity* (Portland: Hawthorne Books, 2015).

Thomas, James, Robert Shapard and Christopher Merrill (eds), *Flash Fiction International* (New York: W. W. Norton, 2015).

Thomas, James, Denise Thomas and Tom Hazuka (eds), *Flash Fiction: 72 Very Short Stories* (New York: W. W. Norton, 1992).

Tyler, Anne, 'Mothers and Mysteries', *The New Republic*, 189 (1983): 32–3.

Wallace, David Foster, 'A Radically Condensed History of Postindustrial Life', in *Brief Interviews with Hideous Men* (New York: Little, Brown, 1999).

Wilson Jr, Robley (ed.), *Four-Minute Fictions: 50 Short-Short Stories from the North American Review* (Flagstaff: Word Beat Press, 1987).

10

THE WEIRD TALE

Timothy Jones

To offer a history or even a definition of the weird tale risks unweirding it, potentially placing an unearthly and sometimes wide-eyed literature too squarely in the world. The weird, perhaps more than most categories, exists between periods, nations and movements, while regularly narrating events that break with the particular circumstances of history. The weird tale begins somewhere in the world, but often departs, or glimpses a departure, from it. That departure is also visible in the ongoing reception of the weird. Shaped by the practices of magazine publication and anthologisation, readers have been encouraged to take the weird tale *out* of historical context. Readers who have no interest in American literature in the twenties and thirties more generally will nevertheless happily devour the works of H. P. Lovecraft without needing to connect them to the historical moment they emerged from. This unworldly placelessness is one of the distinguishing features of the weird. Mark Fisher suggests the 'weird' and the 'eerie' (a term Fisher associates with, and distinguishes from, the weird) are preoccupied 'with the ... strange – not the horrific. The allure that the weird and the eerie possess is not captured by the idea that we "enjoy what scares us". It has, rather, to do with a fascination for the outside, for that which lies beyond standard perception, cognition and experience.'[1] Perception, cognition and experience exist within history; the weird potentially offers a glimpse of something outside. In doing this, it often becomes preoccupied with mysterious or unauthorised forms of knowing and knowledge. Intuition becomes at least as important as ratiocination, and occult tomes hold the weight of accepted philosophies. The weird can be difficult to make sense of, suggesting both a recognisable human feeling and a literature of illegible and inhuman circumstance.

Although the weird nods to various genres, critics often suggest it is not really a genre in itself.[2] In some ways, the history of the weird tale is really a history of the conversation about what constitutes the weird. The most stable elements in this discussion are the work of H. P. Lovecraft, noted for his creation of a misanthropic fiction of unclassifiable beings, distant times and planes, and tentacle-headed gods; and the publication of the American pulp magazine *Weird Tales*, 'The Unique Magazine' (1923–54), which is generally noted for having championed Lovecraft and his circle. The magazine was the first to specialise in publishing fantasy, horror and 'scienti-fiction' tales, alongside then-modish subgenres such as the oriental tale. The advent of the magazine signals the development of a specialised audience for the weird,[3] and this doubtless contributed to an ongoing sense that weird and genre writing constitutes a special class of fiction, distinct from what would later be described as the literary 'mainstream'.

Lovecraft remains as fine a critic as he was an author of the weird. For him, the weird is 'a persistent and permanent type of expression, as old as literature itself'.[4] For S. T. Joshi, however, the form effloresced between 1880 and 1940,[5] with more recent efforts too involved in representing humanity to grasp the cosmic stance of the weird.[6] China Miéville, on the other hand, sees the weird as an historical more than a cosmic phenomenon, suggesting that the 'great Weird Fiction writers are responding to capitalist modernity entering, in the late nineteenth and early twentieth centuries, a period of crisis in which its cruder nostrums of progressive bourgeois rationality are shattered'.[7] Yet the term is increasingly regarded as unconfined to any particular historical moment. Jeff VanderMeer postulates the emergence of a 'new weird' around the turn of the millenium,[8] and together with Ann VanderMeer, has edited a capaciously inclusive collection of weird tales,[9] whose contents describe the phenomenon as international in scope, as originating in the twentieth century, and as shifting into the twenty-first. Whatever the weird is, the canon is growing and the term is gathering a degree of critical interest.

Ann and Jeff VanderMeer attempt to describe the weird tale with precision when they write that it is 'a story that has a supernatural element but does not fall into the category of traditional ghost story or Gothic tale ... it represents the pursuit of some indefinable and perhaps maddeningly unreachable understanding of the world beyond the mundane'.[10] Miéville similarly looks to define the weird tale as a 'breathless and generically slippery macabre fiction, a dark fantastic ("horror" plus "fantasy") often featuring nontraditional alien monsters (thus plus "science fiction")',[11] becoming somewhat breathless himself when he suggests that 'Weird Fiction writers are in a lineage with those religious visionaries and ecstatics who perceive an unmediated relationship with numinosity – Godhead itself.'[12] In these accounts, the weird becomes a progressive form that shrugs off stultifying tradition, offering both critique and, perhaps, a form of faux-religious encounter acceptable to secular readers. Chloe Buckley is not entirely credulous when she notes the critical consensus that the weird is a '*radical* form of literature, one that *exceeds* what has come before ... that sits on the *margins*, in opposition to mainstream modes of thought'.[13]

Perhaps the weird tale can be these things, but it can also be a little preposterous. Lovecraft's 'The Dunwich Horror' (1929) asks us to agree with the narrator that it 'was no joke tracking down something as big as a house that one could not see, but that had all the vicious malevolence of a daemon'.[14] Robert E. Howard's 'The Hoofed Thing' (posthumously published 1970) opens with Marjory, the love interest, weeping over the loss of 'Bozo, her fat Maltese', who, it emerges, has fallen prey to a pet-gobbling demon locked up somewhere in the suburb.[15] Ray Bradbury's 'Usher II' (1950) features a sadistic recreation of Poe's horrors in a Martian house of Usher. Its architect checks that his client is satisfied: '"Is the color right? Is it *desolate* and *terrible*?"'[16] he asks. The weird can also be funny, and slight, and camp. It can exhaust its interest in the unreachable, become unweird. As reader Arthur E. Walker wrote into *Weird Tales* to complain,

> I have had enough of the forbidden books ... I am also getting fed up with the 'old ones' who are continually wriggling into the third dimension through forbidden nooks and crannies. Some of your yarns are too complex; they sound

more like half-baked lectures on higher mathematics than ghost stories. I lose interest in the story, trying to figure out the significance of triangles, trapezoids and pentagons.[17]

Walker sees the very things that critics remark upon as characterising the weird – the pursuit of the unreachable, the non-traditional monsters, the signs used to suggest the ineffable – as already banal and overbaked. These are tropes particularly associated with Lovecraft, who has been so often critically celebrated as the pre-eminent example of the weird[18] that the word is at risk of becoming a synonym for 'Lovecraftian'.

Weird Tales offered a wider range of writing than that authored by Lovecraft and writers who closely followed him. In fact, Lovecraft is an unusual *Weird Tales* writer, escaping the inherent disposability of the pulp medium to achieve something like cultural permanence. He is distinguished from writers who were important to the magazine's audience, whose work has had little influence on the development of the literature or criticism of the weird. Seabury Quinn's psychic detective, Jules de Grandin, was enormously popular in the *Weird Tales* letters pages, easily rivalling Lovecraft; yet Quinn receives almost no attention in weird scholarship. It should also be noted how many female writers were published regularly in the magazine, whose names – Greye La Spina and Mary Elizabeth Counselman – are now unfamiliar. If we look towards these other writers, or even to Lovecraft's associate, Howard, then quite un-Lovecraftian shades of adventure and even romance begin to colour the weird.

The weird could be understood as an assemblage.[19] It incorporates elements which emerge from lived experience – we perceive something odd, judge something to be wrong, feel a little strange. But at the same time, the weird collects and connects texts and textual habits (an emphasis on the short tale, twist endings, pulp cultural textures), that, without necessarily simply expressing the experience of the weird, nevertheless relate to it. An assemblage is not a permanent arrangement, gaining and losing territory over time. If the weird once seemed like a wholly marginal category, certain texts and elements of the weird now command critical attention; but it shifts internally too, so that any number of elements in the weird – like Quinn's tales – have receded from view in the constellation. The assemblage suggests connection but does not guarantee coherency.

If Lovecraft has been viewed as central to this arrangement, eclipsing his peers, this obscures not just the work of other pulp writers, but also the connection that canonical literary figures might have with the weird. Doubtless driven by economy as much as anything, *Weird Tales* particularly in the twenties, but also into the thirties, republished prose and poetry by various canonical writers, an editorial policy that had the effect of reading a weird canon back into older literature. Some of these were inclusions from authors associated with horror and the Gothic – Shelley, Stoker, Hawthorne. Continental writers were included in translation (Flaubert, Schiller, de Maupassant, and, with some regularity, Baudelaire), and there were careful selections from Keats, Shakespeare and even Whitman. The writer far and away most often republished was Edgar Allan Poe. He appeared in *Weird Tales* before Lovecraft, and eventually his likeness was to feature on the cover.[20] Poe is as much a part of the magazine's figuring of the weird as the names more often linked with it.

Poe's work suggests the range of the weird. He wrote across a number of associated genres – the horror story, science fiction, the tale of detection. Poe also authored less well-defined short narratives – the story of the city streets, the gaming story of codes, the hoax, pieces which sit somewhere between tale and essay. Even Poe's interest in the comic short with a cruel twist has gone forward into the weird in the work of writers like Shirley Jackson, Ray Bradbury and Roald Dahl. This diversity, along with a preference for short rather than long prose forms, began to distinguish the weird from the earlier Gothic. (Of course, this sense of Poe's polygeneric ability is an illusion, as these are generic distinctions not made in the period in which he wrote. Locating Poe as a forefather of any genre is a retrospective gesture – just as it is to describe him as central to the weird).

While Lovecraft returns to disorienting gulfs of time and space and the things that dwell within them, Poe's tales frequent the cities, but describe them as potentially alien places. Walter Benjamin's famous reading of 'The Man of the Crowd' (1840) understands Poe as capturing the quality of modernity through his depiction of the city's masses. Poe's narrator observes the people of London, noting their workaday lives, their 'business-like demeanor', the '*deskism*' of the clerks, and the depredations of hard labour and prostitution.[21] For Benjamin, Poe's 'pedestrians act as if they had adapted themselves to the machines and could express themselves only automatically. Their behaviour is a reaction to shocks';[22] they are barbaric and inspire horror.[23] *Flânerie* is recast as the appalled observation of modernity. The narrator becomes fixated by the sinister man of the crowd, who belongs in this shocked urban space, but remains distinct from it. The narrator cannot help but follow the eccentric figure who has 'a countenance which at once arrested and absorbed my whole attention, on account of the absolute idiosyncracy of its expression'.[24] Having pursued the man through the night, the narrator recognises that some things (a book, a human heart) resist being read, a recognition which provides the story's epigraph.

'The Man of the Crowd' describes concerns and themes of the weird tale that complement the beyondness and excess often read in Lovecraft's tales. Poe notes the strange texture of modern urban life before his protagonist becomes involved in something that exists outside of that texture – this departure is experienced as a feeling of shifting from a surface to a depth. Just as outsideness remains distant, so too does the outsider. Everything begins to seem remote and unstable in the weird. Reading is a vexed issue – whether this is of people or occult tomes – and the weird tale is interested in knowledge that cannot be authenticated; how can Poe's narrator know that the man is the 'genius of deep crime'?[25] The teeming city is an important site. In Lovecraft or Clark Ashton Smith, some other dimension would be described; for Poe, London can seem strange enough. The weird can play out at a human scale. Crowds are lonely places, potentially sinister, populated with the wrong sorts of people – although, contrarily, spaces are sometimes oddly emptied. People do not seem to be in control of their actions or destiny. There is a pervasive sense of wrongness, an ill-defined something that has gone amiss. Poe's weird does not always demand the hyperbolic distances other writers have preferred as an element of estrangement. Joshi has claimed that the weird tale emerges as '*the consequence of a world view*' possessed by its author.[26] This claim emerges out of Joshi's investment in antique critical modes that hope to discover authorly intentions; nevertheless, there is value in the observation that the weird emerges from a certain perception of, or feeling about, the world.

Lovecraft remarked that 'all . . . a wonder story can ever be is *a vivid picture of a certain type of human mood*'.[27] Certainly, nothing much *happens* in 'The Man of the Crowd' beyond an attempt to read a man, an attempt that finally must be abandoned. Elsewhere, Lovecraft wrote that the 'one test of the really weird is simply this – whether or not there be excited in the reader a profound sense of dread, and of contact with unknown spheres and powers; a subtle attitude of awed listening, as if for the beating of black wings or the scratching of outside shapes'.[28] Sensation, anticipation, vexed attempts to perceive are important in these tales. The weird is informed as much by a shocked response to modernity, by mood and enquiry, as it is by the Lovecraftian beyond or a canon of texts. That Poe's concern for human feeling and the urban sinister are in some ways quite different to Lovecraft's interests signals the breadth of the weird.

In April 1932, *Weird Tales* published a letter from regular contributor Clark Ashton Smith, where Smith evaluates a recent number before offering a prescription for an ideal issue. He praises 'The Tree-men of M'Bwa' as 'truly weird', while other contributions are described as an 'admirable weird-scientific story' and as '*contes cruels*'. For Smith, a good issue needs no more than 'one or two scientific tales', accompanied by 'one or two tales dealing with physical as opposed to supernatural horror' and 'at least one fantasy of poetic and atmospheric type'. The rest of the stories should be 'tales of sheer weirdness and pure terror' that feature 'the supernatural and the supermundane'.[29] The letter suggests that distinct sorts of stories all contribute to a satisfactorily weird issue. In this understanding, there is no epitome of the weird; it is something that could only ever be assembled from a variety of diverse sources. As Fisher notes, the form 'most appropriate to the weird is the montage – the conjoining of *two or more things which do not belong together*'.[30] (So many of Lovecraft's monsters are collages, whole but seemingly cobbled together out of bits of various other creatures.) The way in which the weird is assembled is its principle of organisation, and helps explain why the weird has favoured the short form. We read *a* novel, but we read tales *in serial*. Stories appear together in magazines and in themed anthologies. Because we read tales in serial, this facilitates the collaging, the comparison and contrast that signals the assembly of a weird constellation. Indeed, the anthology format of *Weird Tales* spilled over into other media through the middle parts of the twentieth century – anthology shows such as *The Twilight Zone* (1959–64) and *Thriller* (1960–2), and anthology horror comics, such as EC Comics' *Tales from the Crypt* (1950–5) and the later Warren magazines *Creepy* (1964–83) and *Eerie* (1966–83), presented a diverse range of strange tales. As the weird tale moved beyond the magazines, it retained connections with short narrative and the anthology.

Poe's depiction of the city as a terrible but fascinating spectacle is a theme the weird tale returns to throughout the twentieth century. Caitlín R Kiernan's 'The Long Hall on the Top Floor' (1999), is an example in this line. Story is incidental to Kiernan's piece, in the same way that it is to 'The Man of the Crowd'. Sadie leads Deacon into an abandoned building; Deacon has some claim to having psychic powers, but this is almost beside the point. Once within, in the long hall of the title, he perceives something at the end of the corridor which gives off 'indifference . . . the freezing temperature of an apathy, so absolute, so perfect'[31] that he is sick. A vision of a collaged form is glimpsed through a broken window: it is a stain, the shadow of wings, movement in a distant ocean. It is unclear if the thing glimpsed is a place or a being or a time; all three categories are inferred. Like Poe's story, 'The Long Hall on the Top Floor' is less interested in peril than it is in fixation, the spell the weird casts. After they've left the building, Sadie insists that 'the whole world's getting a little shittier, a little more hollow every goddamn day. And then something like *that* comes along . . . Something that means *something*, you know?'[32] The desultory urban environment the story sketches out, where Deacon works in a laundromat and drinks too much, functions as a counterpoint to Sadie's secret. What the phenomenon at the end of the corridor might 'mean' is scarcely elaborated upon, but hermeneutics are beside the point; that something should be meaningful at all has a weight, whatever the exact meaning. Sadie says she wanted Deacon the psychic to witness the thing because she thought he would be able to tell her if it was 'real'[33] – it lies outside her ability to be sure of her perceptions, a concern that emphasises its unprecedentedness, but also affirms that the thing is genuinely outside, not a product of any individual psyche. Readers are assumed to sympathise with Sadie's need to witness the outside and to have it validated. Kiernan's characters are listening, like the audience Lovecraft imagines, for the beating of black wings.[34]

Sadie's complaint about the shittiness of the world is as important as the thing in the hallway. City life is often repulsive in the weird. Clive Barker's 'Midnight Meat Train' (1984) describes Leon Kaufman's disappointment with New York, which he has recently moved to. Having once seen it as a 'promised land', Leon now feels that 'New York was just a city'.[35] He falls asleep on the subway after working late, only to wake and discover that he shares the train with a killer, Mahogany, who has strung up several carefully butchered victims in one of the carriages. The splatterpunk butchery in the subway seems to be an extension of the urban malaise. Leon unexpectedly bests the killer as they fight. Mahogany is a descendent of the man of the crowd, but where Poe's narrator abandons his pursuit of the criminal, Leon physically confronts him.

The surface of the city gives way to the depths beneath. Leon rides the train to its destination and is welcomed by a tribe of subterranean cannibals who introduce themselves as the city's Fathers and consume the prepared bodies while insisting Leon take up the role of the butcher he has slain. He meets an ancient thing whose form is as uncertain and multiple as Kiernan's thing in the hallway, and is, apparently, 'the original American'.[36] Leon's tongue is torn out, and he assumes the mantle of the butcher. Summarised thus, 'Midnight Meat Train' teeters on the edge of incoherence, although this is this is not the experience of reading it. Lovecraft noted that 'Atmosphere, not action, is the great desideratum of weird fiction.'[37] If the weird tale suggests the right feeling, it is excused some of the demands of becauseness. The curious point here is that Leon's assumption of the butcher's role is described in terms that are disinterested in a genuine psychological account of his resolution. Instead, his decision is understood in terms of initiatory rebirth, of religion and fate: the cleaver is 'the Butcher's symbol of office' and we are told that every 'day of his life had been leading to this day, every moment quickening to this incalculable moment of holy terror'.[38] This claim departs from the habits of psychologising realism. Moreover, that Leon more or less becomes Mahogany so swiftly and uncomplicatedly suggests there is nothing inwardly essential in either of them. Character is formed by whatever demands an exterior force – here, the Fathers – impose on the individual body. As the story keeps insisting, whatever else we are, we are meat.

At the story's close, Leon's feeling for New York has returned, but the city he loves has been revealed as different to the city initially described. New York is presented in familiar terms, as a dirty and deathly place where, as the papers keep reporting, a serial killer pointlessly went about his murders on the subway; but the city is revised by Leon's adventure, and newspaper accounts of the murderer are now inadequate. Instead, the city operates through a cult of sacrifice to subterranean forces that control its various networks of power. The received version of New York has been revealed as shallow, inauthentic, basically staged. Leon is invigorated rather than troubled by this, preferring the strange new arrangement, in much the same way Sadie prefers the weird to the everyday.

A secret community hidden in the interstices of the city is an idea that recurs in the weird. John Collier's 'Evening Primrose' (1941) offers shadowy comedy rather than horror. Collier's story is recorded in a diary – allegedly found on a 25¢ pad bought from Bracey's department store – which opens with the diarist's intention to 'turn my back for good and all upon the *bourgeois* world that hates a poet'.[39] The diarist conceives of himself as a writer, and retreats from that world to live within Bracey's, only to discover that the store is already inhabited by a 'midnight clan' who, like him, have fled from the everyday and now live hidden lives amidst the products and displays. These people are governed by 'intricate laws of silence and camouflage'[40] and are entirely bourgeois. The diarist may have found an underground, but it is only an extension of the poet-hating world he sought to flee – although he seems not to recognise this circumstance. The story offers an analogue for life in the city, presenting both artists and the well-to-do middle classes as near-phantasmal creatures trapped within snobberies and commerce – here, quite literally living in and between shops.

The poet falls for another shop dweller, pretty but socially marginal Ella, attempting to woo her by arranging a lakeside beach in the shop, using the displays and various goods for sale – a piece of fern from the florist's is put in the hand of a mannequin to simulate a 'young, spring tree'.[41] Under these inauthentic conditions, the gestures of romantic love are false and feeling can't quite be mustered. In any case, Ella prefers the store's night watchman, although her attachment to him is forbidden by the midnight people. The Dark Men, a group of living spectres resident in a nearby undertaker's shop are summoned to transform Ella into a shop mannequin using their embalming arts. Amidst the pleasant socialising of the ghostly department-store bourgeoisie, a young woman possessed of genuine feeling is converted into a senseless object, and put on display. 'Smoke them out! Obliterate them! Avenge us!' are the poet's last frantic jottings[42] – the story is the document that proves he too has met this end. As with 'Midnight Meat Train', the hidden powers of the city determine the fates of its citizens, but Collier makes it seem as if the powers of the urban bourgeois are wholly inescapable. The secret beyond offers no consolation.

Ray Bradbury's 'The Crowd' (1943) describes another clandestine sect. Spallner discovers – and is apparently pursued by – a group that appears at the scenes of serious motoring accidents. 'Vultures, hyenas, saints, I don't know which they are', says Spallner.[43] He assembles a dossier of evidence that shows the crowd is always composed of the same individuals, but we rely on Spallner's surmise to understand the purpose of the gathering: 'To make certain the right ones live and the right ones die.'[44] The story provides no sense of what the terms of this rightness or wrongness might be. Why are some apparently killed by the crowd, and why are others allowed to live? The accidents are refigured as unaccidental; they are no longer a result of bad luck, timing or carelessness, but rather have an obscure purpose. Once again, conventional (humanist, secular, modern) views of the working of the city are cast into doubt.

At the same time, the story seems to predict some of the observations made in Guy Debord's *The Society of the Spectacle*. For Debord, in a society where 'modern conditions of production prevail, life is presented as an immense accumulation of *spectacles*. Everything that was directly lived has receded into a representation.'[45] Spallner's involvement in the crashes that open and close the story seem to enact this claim. His potential death becomes a spectacle for the gathered crowd who 'form a circle, to peer down, to probe, to gawk, to question, to point, to disturb the privacy of a man's agony by their frank curiosity'.[46] The value of Spallner's bodily pain is apparently subsidiary to his value as a spectacle – a spectacle affirmed and enacted by the spectral crowd. After the first crash, the watchers appal Spallner; but as he dies in the second, he understands he will be 'joining up with' them,[47] so that he too will be a gawker. In Debord's terms, 'the spectacle is an *affirmation* of appearances . . . But a critique that grasps the spectacle's essential character reveals it to be a visible *negation* of life.'[48] Spallner's death suggests the negation of life the spectacle engenders, but also transmutes him from an embodied subject to a figure amid the watching crowd, themselves no more than an image, tied together only by their need to watch. The story's ending is not far removed from 'Evening Primrose', where the spectacle is reified and hero and heroine have become mannequins that will be used for commercial display.

The cannibals and their god run New York, the spectral bourgeoisie destroy both artists and lovers, the watchers transmute the watched into one of their number. The deathly spectacle carries on; the stories read like conspiracy theories. Individual agency evaporates, and the terms of the real are determined by hidden cliques and outré forces. If the weird tale has not been celebrated for its ability to render character, this is because it is less interested in human interiors and more interested in outside forces that act upon the individual.

Despite the weird tale's association with throwaway pulp culture, it has assembled something approximating a tradition. Kiernan, Barker, Collier and Bradbury are all authors whose work has been received as belonging to the lineage of *Weird Tales*. Nevertheless, there are a diverse range of 'literary' writers who would not recognise themselves as working in this pulp tradition, who are beginning to be seen – or legitimately could be seen – as connected to the weird assemblage. These connections recall the unique magazine's practice of reprinting 'classic' work, expanding the weird's purview while claiming legitimacy for it. Jorge Luis Borges, Isak Dinesen, Janet Frame and Shirley Jackson are all writers who, taken together, suggest the international dimension of this expansion.

Borges's 'The Lottery in Babylon' (1941) is an account of a complex system of gaming that shapes a city. The lives of the Babylonians are determined by drawings that reward, punish and otherwise determine their fates. The 'Lottery is a major element of reality' but the narrator has 'thought as little about it as about the conduct of the indecipherable gods or of my heart'.[49] Hearts, gods and the lottery are all apparently unreadable. The narrator does not understand the 'mighty purposes'[50] of the lottery, although he is completely in its power. A similar world is described in 'The Library of Babel' (1941), which imagines the titular city as an infinite library in which its inhabitants wander. The city becomes a lottery or a library, although there is little to distinguish the two arrangements. Both stories describe environments where the agency of individuals is compromised and it is impossible to tell how order and power function. The players in the lottery postulate a world ordered by a shadowy Corporation that oversees the determination of their fate, while the library seems a chaotically disordered space governed by chance discoveries. The librarians worry because the 'certainty that everything has already been written annuls us, or renders us phantasmal'.[51] If Borges's cities seem remote and bizarre, they still seem to carry the dissatisfactions that Kiernan's Sadie describes, and hold the threat described by Bradbury's crowd. Their ability to function as a metaphor for Western modernity is emphasised when the lottery is said to perhaps operate 'imperfectly or secretly'[52] elsewhere. The lottery (Jackson's 'The Lottery', discussed below) and the library (Lovecraft's 'The Shadow Out of Time') are sites the weird tale returns to. They are structures that signal what Fisher notes as the weird 'agency of the immaterial and the inanimate . . . the way "we" "ourselves" are caught up in the rhythms of pulsions and patternings of non-human forces'.[53]

The weird looks anxiously at powers that lie beyond the self. These exterior forces – whether figured as monsters or systems – often seem the weirdest things in the stories. However, if 'the weird is *that which does not belong*',[54] then the very fact that these forces do not belong suggests that, counter-intuitively, the weird tale amounts to a defence of the self. Readers are asked to recognise the wrongness of the powers without. In most weird tales, the self is presented as possessing essential qualities and an agency that ought to be preserved.

Isak Dinesen's exquisitely sad 'The Dreaming Child' (1942), however, considers weird influences in terms that are human in scale. Jens, an orphan raised by a washerwoman, is told untrue stories of his affluent heritage. When he is adopted by Jakob and Emilie Vandamm, a wealthy, childless couple, he immediately accepts them as his true parents and their house as his own. The little outsider then recognises the house and recalls parts of the family's life, as if he genuinely were a Vandamm. The child's dream of his lost bourgeois home seems to reshape the texture of the house itself, and Emilie is unable to scold him for lying. Instead, Jens's claims are charismatic fancies that begin to be accepted as truthful. Both the Vandamms and their household 'were made to see themselves with the eyes of the dreamer, and were impelled to live up to an ideal, and that for this their higher existence, they became dependent upon him'.[55] The story closes in the wake of Jens's death. Emilie, rather than allowing the dreamt house to die with him, tells Jakob that Jens was indeed her son by birth, the product of an imaginary dalliance. Dinesen's tale suggests the real is no more than a set of stories we tell ourselves, which might radically change under the pressure of a different story. Personal histories and even households are not stable or factual and might be revised by nothing more than a dream. Jens's power is not, in Fisher's terms, a 'non-human force', but neither is it 'human' or 'realist' in any familiar sense.

Janet Frame's work, likewise, traces lines between wholly outside powers and social or cultural forces. Her story 'The Terrible Screaming' (1963) dramatises an uncomfortable encounter between individuality and exteriority. The sound of screaming fills an unnamed city, but its citizens are worried they will be labelled 'insane'[56] if they admit to having heard it. The screaming is clearly worrying, but it is socially impossible to register or discuss it. 'Work and play, love and death, continued as usual. Yet the screaming persisted.'[57] While the weird tale tends to imagine strange phenomena as perceived only by a few, the screaming is perceived by all. The authority of any individual's take on reality is undermined by a shared refusal to acknowledge shared perception. In Frame, the space between individual experience and social agreement has something in common with the cosmic distances invoked in Lovecraft; each is an unnavigable reach.

Frame is better known for short fiction in a closer-to-realist mode, but even then, shades of the weird appear in her writing. 'The Reservoir' (1963) follows a group of children as they sneak away to a forbidden lake. The children are being kept home from school due to a polio outbreak, but the lessons sent to them by post seem 'makeshift and false', and the 'world was full of alarm'.[58] Once again, the immediate real is inauthentic and troubled, but the reservoir is remote and special, 'the end of the world; beyond it were paddocks of thorns ... strange farms, legendary people whom we would never know or recognize'.[59] The children believe the reservoir is connected with the occult powers of the town officials, and with death. Once the reservoir is finally reached, it has 'an appearance of neatness which concealed a disarray too frightening to be acknowledged except ... in moments of deep sleep and dreaming'.[60] The reservoir holds the ill-defined stuff of the adult world; there is nothing supernatural in the encounter, but as is often the case in Frame's writing, the adult sphere is distant and strange to her young narrators. The children return home possessing an ill-defined knowledge – the story can scarcely articulate what – which must be kept hidden from their parents. Worldly knowledge, from the child's perspective, is as eldritch as anything in Lovecraft.

Shirley Jackson is another writer who locates the weird within the flow of domestic life. In her most famous story, 'The Lottery' (1948), Mrs Hutchinson is sure to finish her dishes before unexpectedly being killed in the town square.[61] Jackson is often read in terms of the Gothic and the uncanny, but the lottery represents no atavistic passion or repressed urge. It is bureaucratic rather than violent in spirit. Mrs Hutchinson is killed without malice and for no reason. The lottery, although a social rather than a cosmic phenomenon, is so much a part of the town that it might as well be an external force, as it is in Borges; and as with Bradbury's 'The Crowd', the death of an individual is presented as spectacular.

Death is not the only way that Jackson's heroines lose themselves. 'The Tooth' relates how Clara Spencer, troubled by a toothache which she is managing with a combination of codeine, whisky and sleeping pills, takes a bus to the city to seek dental attention. The journey offers an escape from the hum-drum routine of her days, emphasised in the list of intricate instructions she gives to her husband for the running of house and family in her absence. Once she reaches the dentist's office she worries that 'her tooth, which had brought her here unerringly, seemed now the only part of her to have any identity ... it was the important creature which must be examined and recorded and gratified; she was only its unwilling vehicle'.[62] Addled, Clara begins to perceive what she regards as her self as separate and subsidiary to a part of her body. After anaesthetic, Clara is confused and finds herself in a washroom. She stands before a mirror with a group of others and finds she is unable to identify her own face. All she sees is 'a group of strangers, all staring at her or around her; no one was familiar in the group, no one smiled at her or looked at her with recognition; you'd think my own face would know me, she thought'.[63] She discards her hair-slide, which has her name on it, and takes stock of her possessions as if they are unfamiliar. Earlier, Clara complained that she felt 'as if I were all tooth. Nothing else.'[64] What remains of Clara once the tooth is gone is uncertain. The story seems to describe an interiority so unsteady it can be discarded like an accessory, or perhaps simply removed from the body. In Jackson, the self threatens to dissolve more or less completely.

Many of these stories can be read in terms that emphasise their psychological elements. 'The Dreaming Child' might recount Emilie's fantasies, 'The Reservoir' becomes a simple coming-of-age story, 'The Tooth' a mental collapse. Yet such readings would be symptomatic of what Fisher has called 'a secular retreat from the outside' where criticism that focuses on psychology and particularly on Freud's notion of the uncanny is 'commensurate with a compulsion towards a certain kind of critique, which operates by always processing the outside through the gaps and impasses of the inside'.[65] The tales tend to disregard the impressionistic psychological realism that short stories contemporary with them often favoured. Instead, they direct readers' interest outward, to things and effects that lie beyond the self.

Lovecraft suggested the weird appeals to those:

> who feel a burning curiosity about unknown outer space, and a burning desire to escape from the prison-house of the known and the real into those enchanted lands of incredible adventure and infinite possibilities which dreams open up to us, and which things like deep woods, fantastic urban towers, and flaming sunsets momentarily suggest.[66]

Lovecraft, like Kiernan's Sadie, conceives of known experience as a confinement. The weird tale scrutinises why this should be so, but tends to look without rather than within. Although he described the weird most often in a rhetoric of cosmic malignity ('the assaults of chaos and the daemons of unplumbed space'),[67] here Lovecraft notes the power of worldly things to 'open up' the distances of the weird. We cannot penetrate the woods, climb to the top of the looming tower, or meet the colours of the sunset. Rather, these things suggest there is something beyond but imminent. For Poe and many of the writers discussed here, this beyondness can play out on a human or social scale rather than a cosmic one.

In February 1929, Tom Cain, of Baltimore wrote into *Weird Tales* to say the magazine:

> fills a crying need in these days of steadily increasing materialism. To get away from hard facts for a while, to soar into realms of bizarrerie where one may meet witches and warlocks, shake hands with the celebrities of distant planets, be called a species of asparagus by [Seabury Quinn's character] Dr. de Grandin, or walk right through an old-fashioned spook – such release gives one time to catch one's breath, mentally speaking, or possibly to get a new slant on the world we live in.[68]

From the yarns published in the magazine, Cain appears to assemble a platform that allows both a critique of secular modernity, of materialism and 'facts', while looking towards the 'infinite possibilities' that Lovecraft suggests. The experience described isn't quite evoked in the whimsy of a word like 'escapism'. For Lovecraft the encounter with distance is motivated by a 'burning desire', while for Cain, it is a 'crying need'. If the weird tale unsettles, it has also acquired an audience who look to it for reassurance, to provide an imaginative break with the apparent tyranny of the everyday.

Notes

1. Mark Fisher, *The Weird and the Eerie* (London: Repeater, 2016), p. 8.
2. Fisher, *The Weird and the Eerie*, p. 9; S. T. Joshi, *The Weird Tale* (Holicong, PA: Wildside Press, [1990] 2003), p. 1.
3. S. T. Joshi, *The Modern Weird Tale* (Jefferson, NC: McFarland, 2001), pp. 3–4.
4. H. P. Lovecraft, 'Notes on Writing Weird Fiction'. Available at <http://www.hplovecraft.com/writings/texts/essays/nwwf.aspx> (last accessed 25 June 2017).
5. Joshi, *The Weird Tale*, p. 1.
6. Ibid. pp. 8–9.
7. China Miéville, 'Weird Fiction', in Mark Bould et al. (eds), *The Routledge Companion to Science Fiction* (Oxford: Routledge, 2009), p. 513.
8. Jeff VanderMeer, 'The New Weird: "It's Alive?"', in Ann and Jeff VanderMeer (eds), *The New Weird* (San Francisco: Tachyon Publications, 2008), pp. ix–xviii.
9. Ann VanderMeer and Jeff VanderMeer (eds), *The Weird* (New York: Tor, 2012).
10. Ann VanderMeer and Jeff VanderMeer, 'Introduction' to *The Weird* (New York: Tor, 2012), p. xv.
11. Miéville, 'Weird Fiction', p. 510.
12. Ibid. p. 511.
13. Chloe Buckley, '"Do Panic. They're Coming": Remaking the Weird in Contemporary Children's Fiction', in Anna Jackson (ed.), *New Directions in Children's Gothic: Debatable Lands* (New York: Routledge, 2017), p. 18 (emphases in the original).
14. H. P. Lovecraft, 'The Dunwich Horror', in *The H.P. Lovecraft Omnibus 3: The Haunter of the Dark* [1951] (London: HarperCollins, 1994), p. 146.
15. Robert E. Howard, 'The Hoofed Thing', in Rusty Burke (ed.), *The Horror Stories of Robert E. Howard* (New York: Del Ray, 2008), pp. 289.
16. Ray Bradbury, 'Usher II', in *The Silver Locusts (The Martian Chronicles)* [1951] (London: Corgi, 1963), p. 104.
17. Arthur E. Walker, 'Bouquets and Brickbats', *Weird Tales*, 30.1 (1937): 127.
18. See Joshi, *The Weird Tale*; Miéville, 'Weird Fiction', pp. 510, 512; Ann VanderMeer and Jeff VanderMeer, 'Introduction' to *The Weird*.
19. I borrow the term, loosely, from Gilles Deleuze and Felix Guattari, *A Thousand Plateaus: Capitalism and Schizophrenia* (Minneapolis: University of Minnesota Press, 1987), p. 88.
20. *Weird Tales*, 34.3 (1939).
21. Edgar Allan Poe, 'The Man of the Crowd' in Patrick F. Quinn (ed.), *Edgar Allan Poe: Poetry and Tales* (New York: Library of America, 1984), pp. 389–91.
22. Walter Benjamin, 'On Some Motifs in Baudelaire', in Hannah Arendt (ed.) and Harry Zohn (trans.), *Illuminations* [1970] (London: Pimlico, 1999) p. 172.
23. Ibid. p. 170.
24. Poe, 'The Man of the Crowd', p. 392.
25. Ibid. p. 396.
26. Joshi, *The Weird Tale*, p. 1 (emphases in the original).

27. Lovecraft, 'Notes on Writing Weird Fiction' (emphases in the original).
28. H. P. Lovecraft, 'Supernatural Horror in Literature', in *H.P. Lovecraft Omnibus 2: Dagon and Other Macabre Tales* [1967] (London: Grafton Books, 1985), p. 427.
29. Clark Ashton Smith, quoted in 'The Eyrie', *Weird Tales*, 19.3 (1932): 574.
30. Fisher, *The Weird and the Eerie*, p. 11.
31. Caitlín R. Kiernan, 'The Long Hall on the Top Floor', in *Tales of Pain and Wonder* (Decatur: Meisha Merlin, 2000), p. 310.
32. Ibid. p. 312.
33. Ibid.
34. Lovecraft, 'Supernatural Horror in Literature', p. 427.
35. Clive Barker, 'Midnight Meat Train' [1984], in *Books of Blood: Volume One* (London: Penguin, 1985), p. 12.
36. Ibid. p. 33.
37. Lovecraft, 'Notes on Writing Weird Fiction'.
38. Barker, 'Midnight Meat Train', p. 34
39. John Collier, 'Evening Primrose', in *Fancies and Goodnights* [1951] (New York: New York Review, 2003), p. 16.
40. Ibid. p. 20.
41. Ibid. p. 23.
42. Ibid. p. 27.
43. Ray Bradbury, 'The Crowd' in *The October Country* [1955] (Earthlight: London, 1998), p. 169.
44. Ibid. p. 172.
45. Guy Debord, *The Society of the Spectacle*, trans. Ken Knabb [1967] (Berkeley: Bureau of Public Secrets, 2014), p. 2.
46. Bradbury, 'The Crowd', p. 162.
47. Ibid. p. 172.
48. Debord, *Society of the Spectacle*, p. 4.
49. Jorge Luis Borges, 'The Lottery in Babylon', in Andrew Hurley (trans.), *Collected Fictions* (New York: Penguin, 1999), p. 101.
50. Ibid. p. 101.
51. Jorge Luis Borges, 'The Library of Babel', in *Collected Fictions*, p. 118.
52. Borges, 'The Lottery in Babylon', p. 101.
53. Fisher, *The Weird and the Eerie*, p. 11.
54. Ibid. p. 10 (emphases in the original).
55. Isak Dinesen, 'The Dreaming Child' in *Winter's Tales* [1942] (London: Penguin, 1983), pp. 94–5.
56. Janet Frame, 'The Terrible Screaming' [1963], in *Snowman, Snowman: Fables and Fantasies* (New York: George Braziller, 1993), p. 119.
57. Ibid. p. 120.
58. Janet Frame, 'The Reservoir' [1963] in *The Reservoir and Other Stories* (Christchurch: Pegasus, 1966), pp. 78, 79.
59. Ibid. p. 74.
60. Ibid. p. 87.
61. Shirley Jackson, 'The Lottery' [1949], in *The Lottery and Other Stories* (London: Penguin, 2009), p. 295.
62. Shirley Jackson, 'The Tooth' [1949], in *The Lottery and Other Stories*, p. 276.
63. Ibid. p. 283.
64. Ibid. p. 266.
65. Fisher, *The Weird and the Eerie*, p. 10.

66. H. P. Lovecraft, 'Notes on Writing Weird Fiction'.
67. Lovecraft, 'Supernatural Horror in Literature', p. 426.
68. Tom Cain, quoted in 'The Eyrie', *Weird Tales*, 13.2 (1929): 275.

Bibliography

Barker, Clive, 'Midnight Meat Train' [1984], in *Books of Blood: Volume One* (London: Penguin, 1985), pp. 12–37.
Benjamin, Walter, 'On Some Motifs in Baudelaire' [1970], in *Illuminations*, ed. Hannah Arendt and trans. Harry Zohn (London: Pimlico, 1999), pp. 152–96.
Borges, Jorge Luis, 'The Library of Babel', in *Collected Fictions*, trans. Andrew Hurley (New York: Penguin, 1999), pp. 112–18.
— 'The Lottery in Babylon', in *Collected Fictions*, trans. Andrew Hurley (New York: Penguin, 1999), pp. 101–6.
Bradbury, Ray, 'Usher II' [1951], in *The Silver Locusts (The Martian Chronicles)* (London: Corgi, 1963), pp. 103–18.
— 'The Crowd' [1955], in *The October Country* (Earthlight: London, 1998), pp. 161–72.
Buckley, Chloe, '"Do Panic. They're Coming": Remaking the Weird in Contemporary Children's Fiction', in *New Directions in Children's Gothic: Debatable Lands*, ed. Anna Jackson (New York: Routledge, 2017), pp. 16–31.
Collier, John, 'Evening Primrose' [1951], in *Fancies and Goodnights* (New York: New York Review, 2003), pp. 16–27.
Debord, Guy, *The Society of the Spectacle*, trans. Ken Knabb [1967] (Berkeley: Bureau of Public Secrets, 2014).
Deleuze, Gilles and Felix Guattari, *A Thousand Plateaus: Capitalism and Schizophrenia*, trans. Brian Massumi (Minneapolis: University of Minnesota Press, 1987).
Dinesen, Isak, 'The Dreaming Child' [1942], in *Winter's Tales* (London: Penguin, 1983), pp. 82–105.
'The Eyrie', *Weird Tales*, 13.2 (1929): 275–8.
'The Eyrie', *Weird Tales*, 19.3 (1932): 436–8, 574.
Fisher, Mark, *The Weird and the Eerie* (London: Repeater, 2016).
Frame, Janet, 'The Reservoir' [1963], in *The Reservoir and Other Stories* (Christchurch: Pegasus, 1966), pp. 73–89.
— 'The Terrible Screaming' [1963], in *Snowman, Snowman: Fables and Fantasies* (New York: George Braziller, 1993), pp. 119–22.
Howard, Robert E., 'The Hoofed Thing', in *The Horror Stories of Robert E. Howard*, ed. Rusty Burke (New York: Del Ray, 2008), pp. 289–303.
Jackson, Shirley, 'The Lottery' [1948], in *The Lottery and Other Stories* [1949] (London: Penguin, 2009), pp. 291–302.
— 'The Tooth' [1949], in *The Lottery and Other Stories* [1949] (London: Penguin, 2009), pp. 265–86.
Joshi, S. T., *The Modern Weird Tale* (Jefferson, NC: McFarland, 2001).
— *The Weird Tale* (Holicong, PA: Wildside Press, [1990] 2003).
Kiernan, Caitlín R., 'The Long Hall on the Top Floor', in *Tales of Pain and Wonder* (Decatur, GA: Meisha Merlin, 2000), pp. 301–13.
Lovecraft, H. P., 'Supernatural Horror in Literature' [1967], in *H. P. Lovecraft Omnibus 2: Dagon and Other Macabre Tales* (London: Grafton Books, 1985), pp. 423–512.
— 'The Dunwich Horror' [1951], in *The H. P. Lovecraft Omnibus 3: The Haunter of the Dark* (London: HarperCollins, 1994), pp. 99–153.

— 'Notes on Writing Weird Fiction'. Available at <http://www.hplovecraft.com/writings/texts/essays/nwwf.aspx> (last accessed 25 June 2017).

Miéville, China, 'Weird Fiction', in *The Routledge Companion to Science Fiction*, ed. Mark Bould, Andrew M. Butler, Adam Roberts and Sherryl Vint (Oxford: Routledge, 2009), pp. 510–15.

Poe, Edgar Allan, 'The Man of the Crowd', in *Edgar Allan Poe: Poetry and Tales*, ed. Patrick F. Quinn (New York: Library of America, 1984), pp. 388–96.

VanderMeer, Ann and Jeff VanderMeer (eds), *The Weird* (New York: Tor, 2012).

— Introduction to *The Weird* by Ann and Jeff VanderMeer (New York: Tor, 2012), pp. xv–xx.

VanderMeer, Jeff, 'The New Weird: "It's Alive?"', in *The New Weird*, ed. Ann and Jeff VanderMeer (San Francisco: Tachyon Publications, 2008), pp. ix–xviii.

Walker, Arthur E., 'Bouquets and Brickbats', *Weird Tales*, 30.1 (1937): 127.

Weird Tales, 34.3 (1939).

11

The Horror Story

Darryl Jones

The horror story is one of the enduring genres of short fiction. With its characteristic reliance on the unity of time and effect, and on the creation of an unsettling mood or atmosphere leading to a shocking denouement, horror has proved particularly amenable to the short form, deliberately designed to be consumed in one sitting for maximum impact. A number of the greatest horror writers – Edgar Allan Poe, Ambrose Bierce, M. R. James, H. P. Lovecraft, Robert Aickman – worked almost exclusively in the short story form, while others – Nathaniel Hawthorne, Sheridan Le Fanu, Arthur Conan Doyle, Shirley Jackson, Stephen King, Clive Barker – made important contributions in long and short fiction. It is also a genre of important anthologies, which have collected the enduring moments of otherwise minor or neglected writers: William Maginn, Amelia B. Edwards, Fitz-James O'Brien, Rhoda Broughton, W. W. Jacobs, Oscar Cook and numerous others have made unforgettable appearances in a variety of anthologies of horror and the supernatural.

In his fiction and his poetry, Poe built a whole aesthetic around this intensity of effect:

> Nothing is more clear than that every plot, worth the name, must be elaborated to its *dénouement* before anything be attempted with the pen. It is only with the *dénouement* constantly in view that we can give the plot its indispensable air of consequence, or causation, by making the incidents, and especially the tone at all points, tend to the development of the intention ... If any literary work is too long to be read in some sitting, we must be content to dispense with the immensely important effect derivable from unity of impression – for, if two sittings be required, the affairs of the world interfere, and everything like totality is at once destroyed.[1]

In Poe's work, at least, literary theory anticipates and governs the practice of writing, always and at all points subordinated to a priori aesthetic concerns. Horror was for Poe the most suitable mode for achieving his aesthetic goals. Poe's position is a typically extreme one, yet many of his aims and concerns have been shared by other writers of horror fiction. This has led to the creation of a very particular type of fiction, rigorously excluding anything which does not tend towards this shocking, unsettling or appalling denouement, with the result that the horror short story can often seem a very demanding formal exercise before it is anything else.

M. R. James was obsessed by particulars, and consequently highly resistant to theorising of any kind, but his occasional pronouncements on his chosen literary form reveal similar concerns to Poe's:

Often have I been asked to formulate my views about ghost stories and tales of the marvellous, the mysterious, the supernatural. Never have I been able to find out whether I had any views that could be formulated. The truth is, I suspect, that the *genre* is too small to bear the imposition of far-reaching principles. Widen the question, and ask what governs the construction of short stories in general and a great deal might be said, and has been said . . . The ghost story is, at its best, only a particular sort of short story, and is subject to the same broad rules as the whole mass of them. These rules, I imagine, no writer ever consciously follows. In fact, it is absurd to talk of them as rules; they are qualities which have been observed to accompany success . . . Well then: two ingredients most valuable in the concocting of a ghost story are, to me, the atmosphere and the nicely-managed crescendo.[2]

The power of 'the atmosphere and the nicely-managed crescendo' is manifest in many of the most influential and widely anthologised horror stories. In W. W. Jacobs's 'The Monkey's Paw', the story builds to its celebrated denouement – a knock on the door – as the titular magical talisman brought back from India by a colonial soldier allows grieving parents seemingly to reanimate the corpse of their dead son, mangled in industrial machinery:

'For God's sake don't let it in,' cried the old man, trembling.
   'You're afraid of your own son,' she cried, struggling. 'Let me go. I'm coming, Herbert; I'm coming.'[3]

Similarly, Shirley Jackson's 'The Lottery' is very strictly constructed on aesthetic grounds originating in Poe, as an idyllic American small town is revealed as conducting an annual ritual sacrifice, the victim chosen in a ceremonial lottery and then stoned to death to ensure the fertility of the crops: 'Used to be a saying about "Lottery in June, corn be heavy soon." . . . There's *always* been a lottery.'[4]

But *pace* Poe's theorising, horror stories are not only purely formal exercises. Like all significant forms of cultural expression, horror's appeal cannot be reduced to any one thing. As a popular cultural mode, horror often has a contextual immediacy, a tendency to finger, often in ways which are inchoate or inconsistent, contemporary concerns and anxieties. The development of colonial horror, to give just one example, is exactly contemporaneous with the major period of British imperial expansion in the second half of the nineteenth century, and often articulates what might be thought of as the uneasy unconscious of writers who were publicly highly committed to the Empire, most notably Rudyard Kipling and Arthur Conan Doyle. Viewed in this way, a story such as Kipling's 'The Mark of the Beast' is highly revealing. It is the tale of a colonial administrator who violates a Hindu altar, and is cursed with a form of lycanthropy. The story has as its epigraph a 'Native Proverb', 'Your Gods and my Gods – do you or I know which are the stronger?', and opens with a revealingly relativistic theological statement:

East of Suez, some hold, the direct control of Providence ceases; Man being there handed over to the power of the Gods and Devils of Asia, and the Church of England Providence only exercising an occasional and modified supervision in the case of Englishmen.[5]

The vengeful 'power of the Gods and Devils of Asia', or of Africa, a discourse of uneasy Orientalism, pervades much British imperial fiction. Conan Doyle specialised in tales of 'monstrous beasts giving nightmares to the aristocracy of deep England',[6] to use Christopher Frayling's phrase – from the English folklore of *The Hound of the Baskervilles* or 'The Terror of Blue John Gap' to the imperial monsters of *The Lost World*, 'The Brazilian Cat', 'The Adventure of the Speckled Band' and many others. The horror of 'The Monkey's Paw' is in effect the Empire knocking on the door of a suburban villa, bringing its terrors home. A generation later, colonial horror specialist Oscar Cook spent the 1910s as a civil servant in Borneo, an experience he used as the basis of a memorably ghoulish *oeuvre* of stories showcasing cannibalism, sacrificial rites, incest and a variety of imaginative forms of sexual revenge.

The genesis and development of the modern horror story across the course of the nineteenth century is inseparable from the history of the great nineteenth-century periodicals whose publication provided a vehicle for much genre fiction. The second half of the nineteenth century, most particularly, was, as Philip Waller has observed, 'the first and the *only* mass literary age'.[7] Many of the great popular fiction genres of the twentieth century – detective and crime fiction, espionage thrillers, adventure stories, science fiction – have their modern origins in the Victorian periodical boom.[8] Mass literacy was, to use Waller's phrase, an 'unprecedented phenomenon',[9] and the variety of periodicals produced across the century, from *Blackwood's Edinburgh Magazine* in the 1810s to the *Strand Magazine* and its many imitators in the 1890s, need to be understood as the cultural manifestations of the interlinked socio-historical forces of capitalism, industrialisation and urbanisation, which may be the defining characteristics of modernity.

Mass literacy presupposes mass humanity, and in the nineteenth century this meant London, which was not only the centre of the largest empire in the history of the world, but with 6.58 million inhabitants by the end of the century was, in the words of the city's historian Jerry White, 'incomparably the largest city the world had ever seen'.[10] Furthermore, as Nick Barratt has shown, the history of the growth of London across the nineteenth century is, profoundly, a history of *suburbanisation*.[11]

'Our parish is a suburban one', and moreover 'a very populous one',[12] Charles Dickens wrote in his first published book, *Sketches by Boz* (1836). Dickens is the greatest of all London novelists, and not coincidentally also a writer whose own career and practice is intimately interwoven with nineteenth-century periodical culture. He was the editor and sole contributor of *Master Humphrey's Clock* (1840–1), in which *The Old Curiosity Shop* and *Barnaby Rudge* were first published. More ambitiously, he was editor and proprietor of two of the great mid-century periodicals, *Household Words* (1850–9) and *All the Year Round* (1859–95). The horror story, the tale of terror, the Gothic tale, the ghost story, and their many subgenres, were pioneered and developed in periodicals such as these. Dickens's first novel proper, *The Pickwick Papers* (1837), contains a number of interpolated supernatural tales and horror stories – notably 'The Stroller's Tale' (Chapter 3) and 'The Story of the Goblins who stole a Sexton' (Chapter 28) – as well as a series of grim and ghoulish episodes and anecdotes such as those involving the medical students Bob Sawyer and Benjamin Allen ('Nothing like dissecting, to give one an appetite'), or Sam Weller's tale of the owner of a 'Celebrated Sassage factory', who falls into his own grinder and is turned into sausages and eaten.[13]

Dickens, in the famous words of *Pickwick*'s Fat Boy, often 'wants to make your flesh creep'.[14] He is a major figure in the history of the supernatural tale. 'A Christmas Carol' (1843) is easily the most celebrated Christmas story in English, and the most famous ghost story. These two genres are intimately connected, and more than any other figure Dickens established the tradition of the Christmas Ghost Story, which continued though the work of M. R. James (many of whose ghost stories were composed specifically to be read to his colleagues and students on Christmas Eve) and beyond. 'A Christmas Carol' is also, profoundly, an urban narrative, its action largely taking place in Scrooge's office and rooms in the City, and the Cratchit home in Camden Town. Scrooge's encounter with Marley's ghost enables him to see the city for what it really is – a city simultaneously of the living and the dead: 'The air was filled with phantoms, wandering hither and thither in restless haste, and moaning as they went.'[15] At the beginning of the story, Scrooge rebuffs the charitable collectors who call soliciting donations for 'the Poor and destitute':

> Are there no prisons? . . . And the Union workhouses? . . . Are they still in operation? . . . The Treadmill and the Poor Law are in full vigour, then? . . . If they [the Poor] would rather die, . . . they had better do it, and decrease the surplus population.[16]

The Malthusian problem of the 'surplus population' of Victorian London's poor, crowded into its notorious slums and rookeries, is counterpointed in the story with the similarly Malthusian problem of what to do with London's dead. Victorian London was indeed, as 'A Christmas Carol' makes clear, a city of the dead as well as of the living, and its crowded churchyards were overflowing. Notoriously, in the Enon Chapel scandal of 1839, an overpowering stench and an infestation of rats led to the discovery of thousands of bodies piled into a small pit right under the floorboards of a chapel off the Strand.[17] London's great municipal cemeteries – from Kensal Green (1833) and Highgate (1839) though to Golders Green Crematorium (1902) – were the city's solution to its problem of the dead.

'A Christmas Carol' inaugurated a series of Dickensian Christmas stories, some of which were overtly supernatural – such as 'The Chimes' (1844), or 'The Haunted Man' (1848). The best of these, and one of the most celebrated and frequently anthologised of all English ghost stories, is 'The Signal-Man', which first appeared as part of *Mugby Junction*, an interconnected series of narratives by Dickens and others in the Christmas 1866 edition of *All the Year Round*. It is one of the great tales of precognition, in which a railway signalman is haunted by visions of the train crash which will eventually cost him his life. Precognition, the uncanny possibility of being haunted by the future, is one of the recurring tropes of Victorian and Edwardian horror, in 'A Christmas Carol's Ghost of Christmas Yet to Come', and in stories such as Edith Wharton's 'Afterward' (1910), W. F. Harvey's 'August Heat' (1910), or E. F. Benson's 'The Room in the Tower' (1912). Classically, the appearance of ghosts served a variety of functions, one of which was to bring back, from beyond the grave, prophecies or important information about the future. In the presence of ghosts, the linear arrow of time breaks down. As with Scrooge's Christmas visitations (which, an attentive reading will show, simultaneously occur on three separate nights and the same Christmas Eve), ghosts occupy past, present and future at the same time.

Dickens's use of the railway as the locus for horror is characteristic of the nineteenth century, and again powerfully reflective of the social conditions which produced periodical fiction.[18] The Fat Boy's pronouncement, 'I wants to make your flesh creep', is contained in a chapter entitled 'Strongly illustrative of the Position, that the course of true love is not a Railway'. *Dombey and Son* was first published in novel form in 1848, the year in which the newsagent W. H. Smith opened its first railway kiosk, on Euston Station – an event which Raymond Williams has read as formative for Victorian fiction.[19] *Dombey* records the destruction of traditional London communities by the building of the railway, and closes with its villain, Carker, killed by a train, which the novel represents as a monster, with 'red eyes, bleared and dim', which 'struck him limb from limb, and licked his stream of life up with its fiery heart, and cast his mutilated fragments in the air'.[20] At the turn of the nineteenth into the twentieth century, in his first large-scale work of futurology, *Anticipations*, H. G. Wells wrote: 'The nineteenth century, when it takes its place with the other centuries in the chronological charts of the future, will, if it needs a symbol, almost inevitably have as that symbol a steam engine running upon a railway.'[21] 'The Signal Man' inaugurates a significant tradition of railway horror, which would include M. R. James's 'The Malice of Inanimate Objects' ('By some means and for some reason Mr. Burton contrived to reserve a compartment for himself ... But these precautions avail little against the angry dead'),[22] Andrew Caldecott's 'Branch Line to Benceston', Robert Aickman's 'The Trains' and 'The Waiting Room', and Clive Barker's 'The Midnight Meat Train'.

The presence of W. H. Smith on Euston station testifies to the overwhelming appeal of nineteenth-century periodical fiction for commuters. Wells, himself a significant writer of periodical fiction in the 1890s, was completely aware of this:

> To make the railway train a perfect symbol of our times, it should be presented as uncomfortably full in the third class – a few passengers standing – and everybody reading the current number either of the *Daily Mail*, *Pearson's Weekly*, *Answers*, *Tit Bits*, or whatever Greatest Novel of the Century happened to be going.[23]

Even *Sketches by Boz*, though it just predates the coming of the railways, is prescient in its awareness of the suburban commuter, and contains a chapter dedicated to a new phenomenon, 'Omnibuses' (Chapter 16). Writing a generation after Wells, the literary critic Q. D. Leavis, in her semi-sociological study of mass literacy, *Fiction and the Reading Public* (1932), identified 'the exhausted city worker' as the archetypal consumer of popular genre fiction.[24] Reading in relatively short bursts, often in the face of mental lassitude, this mass reading public demanded a literature of sensation, thrill and shock. Horror fiction – and especially *short* horror fiction – was made for such readers.

Some of the most successful horror fiction trades on viscerality, on the embodied nature of its aesthetic affect. Early in the nineteenth century, the Gothic novelist Ann Radcliffe formulated a taxonomy of the different kinds of fear, *terror* and *horror*: 'Terror and horror are so far opposite, that the first expands the soul, and awakens the faculties to a high degree of life; the other contracts, freezes, and nearly annihilates them.'[25] This distinction between 'terror' (numinous, metaphysical anticipation and dread) and 'horror' (shocking, often disgusting revelation) has proved a lasting and influential one, accepted by many (but not all) writers and commentators.

Blackwood's Edinburgh Magazine, founded in 1817, was the first of the great nineteenth-century periodicals. Its appeal was based on an interrelated combination of scurrilous and often libellous political journalism and sensational, often shocking fiction. It was, in Radcliffe's terms, often more interested in offering its readers the experience of horror, rather than terror, though its long history (it finally closed in 1980) contained plenty of both. Although *Blackwood's* mellowed somewhat across the century, publishing, amongst others, Anthony Trollope, George Eliot and Joseph Conrad, initially it specialised in lurid fiction.[26] A perennial favourite theme of *Blackwood's* was the tale of claustrophobia, entrapment or imprisonment, such as Daniel Keyte Sandford's 'A Night in the Catacombs' (1818), John Galt's 'The Buried Alive' (1821), William Mudford's 'The Iron Shroud' (1830), or best of all William Maginn's 'The Man in the Bell' (1821), written by the most scurrilous of all *Blackwood's* journalists, in which the narrator finds himself trapped in a church tower under a giant, swinging bell. *Blackwood's* in general, and this strain of its fiction in particular, was to prove very influential upon the works of Edgar Allan Poe, many of whose stories ('The Fall of the House of Usher', 'The Cask of Amontillado', 'The Pit and the Pendulum', 'The Premature Burial') and poems ('The Bells') draw on the *Blackwood's* template. Indeed, Poe initially framed his stories within the narrative of 'The Folio Club', as ghoulish tales told by a variety of characters, including 'Mr. Blackwood Blackwood, who had written certain articles for foreign Magazines.'[27] In his story 'How to Write a Blackwood's Article', the protagonist seeks advice on writing horror stories from William Blackwood himself, and is told that 'The first thing requisite is to get yourself into such a scrape as no one ever got into before' – trapped in an 'oven or big bell . . . tumbl[ing] out of a balloon . . . swallowed up in an earthquake, or . . . stuck fast in a chimney.'[28]

Blackwood's other characteristic genre was the medical horror story, a subgenre which was to prove lastingly influential across the nineteenth century and beyond, as perhaps the major manifestation of the *embodied* nature of some nineteenth-century horror. Samuel Warren's ongoing collection of tales, *Pages from the Diary of a Late Physician*, a long-running serial published in *Blackwood's* from 1830 to 1837, was a particularly successful example of this, often dealing in the ghoulish specifics of medical cases ('Then follow the details of his disease, which are so shocking as to be unfit for any but professional eyes . . .').[29] Enduring public anxieties about the activities of doctors and medical students, and particularly their associations with Resurrection Men, or bodysnatchers, illegally stealing corpses (or in the notorious Burke and Hare case of 1828, murdering) to provide specimens for medical research, led to the Anatomy Act of 1832, which legalised the medical dissection of donated cadavers. The relationship between doctors and bodysnatchers, and the class tensions implicit in this relationship, were ripe for fictional exploitation. The Chartist and journalist G. W. M. Reynolds's sprawling and hugely popular serial fiction *The Mysteries of London* (published from 1844) has as its most sensational narrative strand the activities of the Resurrection Man Anthony Tidkins. Decades later, Robert Louis Stevenson was still drawing on the Burke and Hare case for 'The Body Snatcher' (1884), one of a series of horror stories he wrote examining divided identity, professional repute and public respectability, and class relations (others include 'Deacon Brodie', and most famously *The Strange Case of Dr. Jekyll and Mr. Hyde*).

If the implications of the Anatomy Act were ripe for exploitation in horror fiction, so too were Martin's Act of 1822 and the Cruelty to Animals Act of 1876, both of which sought to regulate the practices of vivisection and animal experimentation in the light of a developing discourse of medical ethics. These practices had accompanied the rise of experimental physiology as a recognised medical discipline in the nineteenth century: William Sharpey was appointed Chair of General Anatomy and Physiology at University College London in 1836; the Physiological Society was founded in 1876.[30] The nineteenth-century vivisection debates were public and intensely political, led by activist organisations such as the RSPCA (founded 1824), or Frances Power Cobbe's Victoria Street Society (1875, and later renamed the British Anti-Vivisection Society).[31] Mary Shelley's *Frankenstein* (1818) is the archetypal fiction of unethical medical research, literalising the metaphor of the Resurrection Man. Nathaniel Hawthorne's tales 'The Birth-Mark' (1843) and 'Rappaccini's Daughter' (1844) both deal with the subject of human experimentation. H. G. Wells's *The Island of Doctor Moreau* (1896) contains a portrait of the archetypal Victorian archvivisector, experimenting without anaesthetic on live animal subjects in an attempt to transform them into human beings. Moreau, like many of fiction's mad doctors, is a sadist who carries out his activities under the guise of supposedly disinterested scientific research, claiming that 'To this day I have never troubled about the ethics of the matter.'[32] One of H. P. Lovecraft's earliest tales, 'Herbert West – Reanimator' (1922) is perhaps best read as a late outlier to nineteenth-century medical horror:

> as I have said, it happened when we were in the medical school, where West had already made himself notorious through his wild theories on the nature of death and the possibility of overcoming it artificially ... In his experiments with various animating solutions he had killed and treated immense numbers of rabbits, guinea-pigs, cats, dogs, and monkeys, till he had become the prime nuisance of the college.[33]

Burke and Hare supplied corpses for Dr Robert Knox, who taught anatomy at Edinburgh University Medical School – in the nineteenth century the foremost medical school in Britain and Ireland. Robert Louis Stevenson himself studied Engineering at Edinburgh. His younger contemporary Arthur Conan Doyle trained as a doctor at Edinburgh University, initially specialising in syphilis, before settling into general practice. Of all *fin-de-siècle* writers, Doyle's career was perhaps the one most closely imbricated with periodical fiction, because of his long-running relationship with *The Strand Magazine*, which owed a large part of its success to the unparalleled popularity of the Sherlock Holmes stories. Doyle very clearly understood himself as one of life's all-rounders, a general practitioner of fiction, and made distinguished contributions not only to the detective story, but also to the adventure story, to historical fiction, to sporting fiction and to the horror story.[34] This was a genre which allowed Doyle to put his medical expertise to good use, in tales such as 'The Case of Lady Sannox' (in which a brilliant surgeon is tricked into operating on the face of the women he loves), 'The Third Generation' (a young gentleman discovers on the eve of his wedding that he has hereditary syphilis), 'The Retirement of Signor Lambert' (a jealous husband cuts the vocal chords of an opera singer who is having an affair with his wife), or 'The Brown Hand' (the ghost of an Afghan tribesman haunts the doctor who amputated his hand). Doyle also wrote two astonishingly ghoulish collections of vignettes, 'A Medical Document' and 'The Surgeon Talks', in which gatherings of medical men seek to outdo one another with ever more lurid anecdotes drawn from their professional practices. In 'A Medical Document', an alienist remarks that

> there is a side of life which is too medical for the general public and too romantic for the professional journals, but which contains some of the richest human materials that a man could study. It's not a pleasant side, I am afraid, but if it is good enough for Providence to create, it is good enough for us to try and understand.[35]

A surgeon immediately provides an example of this, and tells the history of 'a famous beauty in London Society' who comes to his consulting rooms:

> a rodent ulcer was eating its way upwards, coiling on in its serpiginous fashion until the end of it was flush with her collar. The red streak of its trail was lost below the line of her bust. Year by year it had ascended and she had heightened her dress to hide it, until now it was about to invade her face.[36]

Nineteenth-century medical horror provided the source for one continuing, and often highly controversial, strain of viscerally embodied horror, which placed a strong and often graphic emphasis on the corpo-reality of fear. This is horror at its most straightforwardly transgressive, single-mindedly setting out to shock. From the publication of Matthew Lewis's *The Monk* in 1796 to modern 'moral panics' arising from video nasties or violent computer games, it has often occasioned a very public discourse on the ethics of representation, what could or should be shown: does exposure to violent or transgressive images cause violent or transgressive behaviour? The urge to censor, purge and ban is a familiar accompaniment to some horror.[37]

Visceral horror could afford even writers who later settled into mainstream, canonical respectability the opportunity to probe the limits of the ethics of representation. In Poe's *Blackwood's* pastiche, 'A Predicament', Psyche Zenobia narrates her own decapitation by the hands of an Edinburgh cathedral clock. In his most visceral tale, 'The Facts in the Case of M. Valdemar', a mesmerised man is kept suspended at the point of death for seven months. Released from his trance, 'his whole frame at once – within the space of a single minute, or even less, shrunk – crumbled – absolutely *rotted* away beneath my hands. Upon the bed, before that whole company, there lay a nearly liquid mass of loathsome – of detestable putrescence.'[38]

The activities of the Spanish Inquisition had long fascinated Gothic novelists. This is perhaps the most sensational manifestation of the anti-monastic, anti-Catholic animus of much Romantic Gothic. Inquisitorial dungeons and torture chambers play significant roles, for example, in *The Monk*, or in Charles Maturin's *Melmoth the Wanderer* (1820). Torture and its implements, often represented with a cultured, connoisseurish sadism, make frequent appearances in a variety of tales of terror. Poe's 'The Pit and the Pendulum' applies his own formalist aesthetic to the psychology of torture, adapting the basic premise of Maginn's 'The Man in the Bell' to a tale of an inquisition victim tied down under a giant blade attached to a swinging pendulum. Conan Doyle's 'The Leather Funnel' tells of the psychic resonances of an artefact used in 'The torture of water – the "Extraordinary question"'[39] – that is, the enforced drinking of sixteen pints of water. In Bram Stoker's 'The Squaw', an American tourist visits a torture chamber and is trapped inside 'The Iron Virgin of Nurnberg':

And then the spikes did their work. Happily the end was quick, for when I wrenched open the door they had pierced so deep that they had locked in the bones of the skull though which they had crushed, and actually tore him – it – out of his iron prison till, bound as he was, he fell at full length with a sickly thud upon the floor, the face turning upward as he fell.[40]

These ghoulish tales of bodily dismemberment and dissolution proved unsurprisingly irresistible to twentieth-century pulp writers. There are innumerable instances of this. Following the success, in particular, of Sax Rohmer's Fu Manchu series, beginning with *The Mystery of Dr. Fu-Manchu* (1913), a strain of 'Yellow Peril' horror often articulated geopolitical anxieties about Asian political and demographic power by writing them on the body, as a series of 'diabolical' tortures.[41] In George Fielding Eliot's 'The Copper Bowl', for example, a Chinese mandarin attempts to gain information about the location of a French legionary outpost by means of a rat placed inside a heated copper bowl, whose only means of escape is by gnawing its way through the prisoner's abdomen:

When he raised his head the pulse had ceased to beat. Where it had been, blood was flowing sluggishly – dark venous blood, flowing in purple horror.
    And from the midst of it, out of the girl's side, the grey, pointed head of the rat was thrust, its muzzle dripping gore, its black eyes glittering beadily at the madman who gibbered and frothed above it.[42]

Radically figuring and refiguring the body as its locus of fear and fascination, 1980s 'body horror' is the most extreme manifestation of this tradition. Published in 1984–5, Clive Barker's short story collections *The Books of Blood* are certainly the most celebrated short-form examples of body horror, recognised on publication as revolutionary works. Volumes 1–3 came emblazoned with *two* laudatory cover blurbs from Stephen King: 'I have seen the future of horror . . . and his name is Clive Barker' (on the front cover), and 'What Barker does makes the rest of us look like we've been asleep for the last ten years' (on the back).[43] Barker's aesthetic radicalism is inextricable from his political radicalism. His stories take what were certainly in the 1980s highly progressive stances on gender and sexual politics, both militantly feminist and avowedly gay. 'Jacqueline Ess: Her Will and Testament', for example, updates the concerns of Betty Friedan's pioneering 1963 feminist classic *The Feminine Mystique* in its tale of a bored and frustrated Yorkshire housewife who discovers the ability to reshape human flesh by the power of thought. She tests her powers on her sexist, patronising doctor, wishing him to 'Be a woman':

She willed his manly chest into making breasts of itself and it began to swell most fetchingly, until the skin burst and his sternum flew apart. His pelvis, teased to breaking point, fractured at its centre . . . It was from between his legs all the noise was coming; the splashing of his blood; the thud of his bowel on the carpet.[44]

Barker is a highly articulate theorist of his chosen form, and has repeatedly defended the graphic nature of his work:

> There is a very strong lobby which says you can show too much. Wrong. Not for me. You can never show too much . . . There is also a school that says that suggestion is best, that understatement is best. And there are occasions, certainly, where that is true. But for me, as a viewer, a reader, I like it there – I mean, it's show me, show me. Paradoxically, I thank God for them [censors]. I think it's important that there should always be somebody around who says that this is forbidden territory. We are, after all, trading on taboo.[45]

In 1848, the same year that W. H. Smith opened its Euston kiosk, the novelist Catherine Crowe published what was to become, in its strange way, one of the most influential books of the nineteenth century. *The Night Side of Nature* is a compendium of supernatural tales, anecdotes and folklore, whose range of interests – trance visions, dreams and precognition; ghosts, poltergeists and haunted houses; doppelgängers – effectively cover the range of subjects that were to be developed in the supernatural tale.[46] Crowe's work was a significant contribution to the Victorian climate of enchantment that was to exist in an uneasy dialectic with the era's dominant secularising discourses of utilitarianism, industrialisation, scientific naturalism and the concomitant 'crisis of faith' that characterised the 1860s and 1870s.[47] As Jarlath Killeen writes in his history of nineteenth-century Gothic, 'No major Victorian thinker or writer, from the Brontës to the Brownings, from Dickens to Darwin, was unconcerned about the occult.'[48]

The growth of spiritualism as a series of practices and beliefs was a major intellectual phenomenon of the second half of the nineteenth century, albeit in ways that were complex and often internally inconsistent. Spiritualism posited the survival of the human personality after death, and the existence of an 'other world' – an astral or spirit realm – coexisting and interpenetrating with our own material world, and most readily accessible through the intercession of a medium. For many – perhaps most – of its adherents, spiritualism was entirely compatible with Christianity, even of the most orthodox Anglican variety. For others it led on to an intellectual path that took them to the further shores of belief – to esoteric Buddhism, theosophy, hermetic philosophy or occultism. Janet Oppenheim, spiritualism's most authoritative historian, has argued that the spiritualists' 'concerns and aspirations placed them – far from the lunatic fringe of society – squarely amidst the cultural, intellectual, and emotional moods of the era.'[49] The Society for Psychical Research (SPR) was founded in Trinity College Cambridge in 1891 as an attempt to provide an empirical basis for testing the claims of spiritualists and mediums, which it took very seriously. The SPR's early membership included many of the foremost cultural and intellectual figures of the age, such as Henry Sidgwick, A. J. Balfour, William James and Henri Bergson.

Yet part of the great power of spiritualism was also its appeal for the marginalised voices of Victorian society, amongst the working class and especially, as Alex Owen has shown, for women.[50] It was this intellectual climate that produced – and, to an extent, that was produced by – the development of the ghost story in English. In this, as in so much else, Dickens was a pioneering figure. But the ghost story, with its recurring concerns of domesticity and entrapment, in which the secure and comforting environment of the home becomes inverted, uncanny, haunted, proved to be a powerful medium through which to articulate the anxieties of women. In her critical study *Victorian Ghosts in the Noontide*, Vanessa D. Dickerson persuasively situated the Victorian ghost story within the context of the 'ambiguous, marginal, ghostly' position of Victorian women: 'The ghost corresponded more particularly to the Victorian woman's visibility and invisibility, her power and powerlessness.'[51] The list of English-language women writers who have made important contributions to the ghost story is a very long one (just as a random sample, it would include Elizabeth Gaskell, Charlotte Riddell, Rhoda Broughton, Vernon Lee, Mary E. Wilkins Freeman and Edith Wharton), and any representative anthology of ghost stories contains (or should contain) many women writers.[52]

Amelia B. Edwards's 'The Phantom Coach' (1864) provides a good example of the tensions arising out of the ghost story, simultaneously ontological and gendered. A lawyer gets lost in a blizzard while out grouse shooting on the Yorkshire moors, and finds shelter in the house of a scholarly recluse. The scholar is a white-maned magus whose walls are 'scrawled over with strange diagrams' and who discourses at length on the limitations of Victorian scientific naturalism, in a manner which recalls the table of contents of *The Night Side of Nature*:

> He spoke of the soul and its aspirations; of the spirit and its powers; of second sight; of prophecy; of those phenomena which, under the names of ghosts, spectres, and supernatural appearances, have been denied by the sceptics and attested by the credulous, of all ages.[53]

Ostensibly, this is a characteristically masculinist Victorian narrative, in which a young bourgeois professional has his narrow intellectual horizons expanded by an authoritative older man – precisely the same dynamic of class and authority which underlies the relationship between the young newly wedded lawyer Jonathan Harker and the paternal polymath Van Helsing in Bram Stoker's *Dracula*. The scholar is himself an ambiguous character, liminally supernatural, and this meeting precipitates the lawyer's later encounter with a ghostly mail-coach, which leaves him lying in a snowdrift 'in a state of raving delirium, with a broken arm and a compound fracture of the skull'.[54] This is, indeed, where the story seems to end, but it is not where it begins. The lawyer is recently married, 'very much in love, and of course, very happy'.[55] Yet his wife is occluded from his story, rendered silent, a spectral presence: the story actually closes not with the phantom coach, but with the lawyer's assertion that 'I never told my wife the fearful events which I have just related to you.'[56]

The Victorians did not, of course, invent ghosts. But the historian Owen Davies has argued that the Victorian ghost may represent a new development in thinking about the supernatural in its very *purposelessness*. In his 1894 study of psychical research, the folklorist Andrew Lang concluded that the modern ghost was 'a purposeless creature', appearing 'nobody knows why; he has no message to deliver, no secret crime to reveal, no appointment to keep, no treasure to disclose, no commissions to be executed, and, as an almost invariable rule, he does not speak, even if you speak to him'.[57] With a small few exceptions, this is certainly the case in the work of the most influential of all ghost-story writers, M. R. James.

James was a manuscript scholar of enormous distinction. His stories generally arise out of his academic research, to which they are perhaps best viewed as a kind of by-product or imaginative surplus. One of the most interesting things about James's stories is the way in which they are very self-consciously removed from the tenor of their times, and attempt to deny or refute any ideological or contextual reading. For much of his scholarly life, James was based in King's College Cambridge. At exactly the same time, and right next door, the SPR was founded in Trinity College. And yet the foremost English ghost-story writer had little interest in, and no enthusiasm for, the activities of the most high-profile group of academic ghost-hunters. 'The Mezzotint' (1904) dismisses the SPR as 'the Phasmatological Society',[58] an interfering bunch from whom the story's supernatural artwork must be kept a secret. (The 'Phasmatological Society' translates as the 'Ghost Society'; the SPR began life as the Cambridge Ghost Society.) James himself displayed little interest in the actual existence of the supernatural, maintaining that 'I am prepared to consider evidence and accept it if it satisfies me'[59] – an answer which, admittedly, would also have satisfied the SPR. However, James drew very clear lines of demarcation between the literary ghost story and psychical investigation: 'I have not sought to embody in them any well-considered scheme of "psychical" theory', he wrote of his stories; 'The story that claims to be "veridical" (in the language of the Society of Psychical Research) is a very different affair.'[60]

James's ghost stories are learned, austere, highly formalised intellectual exercises, set in a confined and instantly recognisable milieu of repressed bachelor scholars, academic and religious institutions, isolated country houses, and uncanny inns and hotels. Deeply immersed in the concerns of James's own scholarship – medieval manuscripts, clerical architecture, academic politics – the stories self-consciously set out to repel modernity. Fascinatingly, the stories' anxieties often emerge out of what they attempt to occlude. 'Oh, Whistle, and I'll Come to You, My Lad' is perhaps James's most celebrated and widely discussed tale, but what is often overlooked is that it is in fact a Christmas ghost story, not only (as was common for James) in the occasion of its composition or telling (it was first read in King's College at Christmas 1903), but also in its setting. The rational materialist Professor Parkin takes himself off on a solitary East Anglian holiday during the Christmas vacation, and unearths the supernatural whistle on 'the Feast of St. Thomas the Apostle'.[61] This is 21 December, the winter solstice, when the forces of darkness are at their strongest, and therefore the time of doubt (the saint's day of Doubting Thomas). In its very solitariness, 'Oh, Whistle' self-consciously rejects the familial ideology – hearth and home – which underpinned the Dickensian ghost story. When domesticity intrudes upon the story, it does so characteristically for James as a locus of terror: the whistle summons up a ghost which takes the form of a bedsheet which rises from the bed next to Parkins, with 'a horrible, an intensely horrible face *of crumpled linen*'.[62]

James was a keen reader of supernatural fiction right up to the end of his life. He understood himself as, in the words of one of his characters, 'a Victorian by birth and education',[63] and thus found himself profoundly out of sympathy with most manifestations of modernity. In his chosen fictional genre, he disapproved of the weird tale, largely on the grounds of class and taste. He was equivocal about Arthur Machen, who 'has a nasty after-taste. Rather a foul mind I think, but as clever as they make 'em.'[64] He was downright dismissive of the weird tale's foremost practitioner, complaining after having read 'a disquisition of nearly 40 pages of double columns on Supernatural Horror in Literature by one H. P. Lovecraft, whose style is of the most offensive. He uses the word cosmic about 24 times.'[65] He disliked Christine Campbell Thomson's pulpish *Not at Night* series, whose stories were largely anthologised from *Weird Tales* magazine, and whose methods ran directly counter to his own:

On the whole, then, I say, you must have horror and also malevolence. Not less necessary, however, is reticence. There is a series of books I have read, I think American in origin, called *Not at Night* (and with other like titles), which sin glaringly against this law.[66]

These contrasts, and James's responses, encapsulate the dynamic between terror and horror which has animated the genre since the Romantic Gothic novel. At times, this has been played out in a series of wrangles over nomenclature, as though writers did not want to own up to the straightforward vulgarity of 'horror'. Thus, a survey of the history of the genre gives us 'Tales of Terror' (*Blackwood's*), 'Tales of the Grotesque and Arabesque' (Poe), 'Tales of Unease' (Conan Doyle), *Weird Tales*, 'Strange Stories' (Robert Aickman) and 'Dark Fantasy' (or even, heaven help us, 'The Dark Fantastique'). Clive Barker refers to himself as a 'Dark Imaginer'.[67] Refreshingly, Herbert Van Thal's honest and influential series of *Pan Books of Horror Stories*, distinguished by their memorably lurid covers (skulls and severed heads a speciality), was one of the great successes of post-war British publishing, appearing annually from 1959 to 1989, and selling 5.6 million copies.[68] There are, of course, notable subgeneric distinctions between these kinds of horror, which continue to be the subjects of discussion and argument for writers and critics. For as long as this is the case, the horror story will continue to develop.

Notes

1. Edgar Allan Poe, 'The Philosophy of Composition', in *Selected Writings*, ed. G. R. Thompson (New York: W. W. Norton, 2004), p. 675, p. 677.
2. M. R. James, 'Introduction' to V. H. Collins (ed.), *Ghosts and Marvels*, in *Collected Ghost Stories*, ed. Darryl Jones (Oxford: Oxford University Press, 2011), p. 400.
3. W. W. Jacobs, 'The Monkey's Paw', in Darryl Jones (ed.), *Horror Stories: Classic Tales from Hoffmann to Hodgson* (Oxford: Oxford University Press, 2014), p. 336.
4. Shirley Jackson, 'The Lottery', in *Novels and Stories*, ed. Joyce Carol Oates (New York: Library of America, 2010), p. 232.
5. Rudyard Kipling, 'The Mark of the Beast', in Jones (ed.), *Horror Stories*, p. 208.
6. Frayling, 'Introduction' to Doyle, *The Hound of the Baskervilles*, edited with an introduction and notes by Christopher Frayling (London: Penguin, 2001), p. xxii.
7. Philip Waller, *Writers, Readers and Reputations: Literary Life in Britain 1780–1918* (Oxford: Oxford University Press, 2006), p. 3.
8. For the importance of periodical publication for fiction in the late nineteenth century, particularly with the demise of the 'triple-decker' realist novel, see Peter Keating, *The Haunted Study: A Social History of the English Novel 1875–1914* (London: Secker and Warburg, 1989), pp. 9–87.
9. Waller, *Writers, Readers and Reputations*, p. 3.
10. Jerry White, *London in the Nineteenth Century: 'A Human Awful Wonder of God'* (London: Jonathan Cape, 2007), p. 3.
11. Nick Barratt, *Greater London: The Story of the Suburbs* (London: Random House, 2012).
12. Charles Dickens, *Sketches by Boz*, ed. Dennis Walder (London: Penguin, 1995), p. 26, p, 55.
13. Dickens, *The Pickwick Papers*, ed. Mark Wormald (London: Penguin, 1999), p. 397, p. 407.
14. Ibid. p. 114.
15. Dickens, 'A Christmas Carol', in *Christmas Books*, ed. Ruth Glancy (Oxford: Oxford University Press, 1988), p. 23.

16. Dickens, 'A Christmas Carol', pp. 10–11.
17. See Catharine Arnold, *Necropolis: London and its Dead* (London: Pocket Books, 2007), pp. 104–7.
18. For accounts of the significance of the railway to Victorian culture, see Wolfgang Schivelbusch, *The Railway Journey: The Industrialization and Perception of Time and Space*, 2nd edn (Berkeley: University of California Press, 2014); Nicholas Daly, 'Sensation drama, the railway and modernity', in *Literature, Technology and Modernity, 1860–2000* (Cambridge: Cambridge University Press, 2004), pp. 10–33; Simon Bradley, *The Railways: Nation, Network and People* (London: Profile, 2015). For a specific account of Dickens in this context, see Jonathan Grossman, *Charles Dickens's Networks: Public Transport and the Novel* (Oxford: Oxford University Press, 2013).
19. See Raymond Williams, 'Forms of English Fiction in 1848', in *Writing in Society* (London: Verso, 1983), p. 150.
20. Charles Dickens, *Dombey and Son*, ed. Dennis Walder (Oxford: Oxford University Press, 2001), p. 823.
21. H. G. Wells, *Anticipations*, in *The Works of H.G. Wells*, Atlantic Edition (London: T. Fisher Unwin, 1924), p. iv, p. 5.
22. M. R. James, 'The Malice of Inanimate Objects', in *Collected Ghost Stories*, p. 400.
23. Wells, *Anticipations*, p. 15.
24. Q. D. Leavis, *Fiction and the Reading Public* (London: Chatto and Windus, 1965), p. 32.
25. Ann Radcliffe, 'On the Supernatural in Poetry', *New Monthly Magazine*, 16: 1 (January 1826): 145–52. Repr. in E. J. Clery and Robert Miles (eds), *Gothic Documents: A Sourcebook 1700–1820* (Manchester: Manchester University Press, 2000), p. 168.
26. For an account of the genesis of *Blackwood's* and its fiction, on which I draw here, see Robert Morrison and Chris Baldick (eds), 'Introduction' to *Tales of Terror from Blackwood's Magazine* (Oxford: Oxford University Press, 1995), pp. vii–xviii.
27. Poe, 'The Folio Club', *Selected Writings*, p. 596.
28. Poe, 'How to Write a Blackwood Article', *Selected Writings*, p. 177.
29. Samuel Warren, 'A "Man About Town"', in Morrison and Baldick (eds), *Tales of Terror from Blackwood's Magazine*, p. 203.
30. These details are from the Physiological Society's website. Available at <http://www.physoc.org/society-history> (last accessed 15 April 2018).
31. See Richard D. French, *Antivivisection and Medical Science in Victorian Society* (Princeton: Princeton University Press, 1975).
32. H. G. Wells, *The Island of Doctor Moreau*, ed. Darryl Jones (Oxford: Oxford University Press, 2017).
33. H. P. Lovecraft, 'Herbert West – Reanimator', in *Tales*, ed. Peter Straub (New York: Library of America, 2005), p. 24.
34. For studies of Doyle as a literary 'all-rounder', see, for example, Douglas Kerr, *Conan Doyle: Writing, Profession, and Practice* (Oxford: Oxford University Press, 2013).
35. Arthur Conan Doyle, 'A Medical Document', in *The Conan Doyle Stories* (London: John Murray, 1929), p. 1045.
36. Ibid. pp. 1045–6.
37. There is an enormous body of literature on this subject, but see, for example, André Parreaux, *The Publication of 'The Monk': A Literary Event 1796–1798* (Paris: Didier, 1960); Stanley Cohen, *Folk Devils and Moral Panics* (St Albans: Paladin, 1973); Martin Barker, *The Video Nasties: Freedom and Censorship in the Media* (London: Pluto, 1984); David Kerekes and David Slater, *See No Evil: Banned Films and Video Controversies* (Manchester: Headpress, 2000); Martin Barker and Julian Petley (eds), *Ill-Effects: The Media/Violence Debate* (London: Routledge, 2001).
38. Poe, 'The Facts in the Case of M. Valdemar', *Selected Writings*, p. 414.

39. Conan Doyle, 'The Leather Funnel', in *Gothic Tales*, ed. Darryl Jones (Oxford: Oxford University Press, 2016), p. 405.
40. Bram Stoker, 'The Squaw', in *Horror Stories*, ed. Jones, p. 262.
41. In its modern form, 'Yellow Peril' fiction dates from the 1890s, and particularly the publication of M. P. Shiel's *The Yellow Danger* in 1898. For studies of the 'Yellow Peril', see, for example, David Glover, 'Die Gelbe Gefahr, le peril jaune, yellow peril: the geopolitics of a fear', in Kate Hebblethwaite and Elizabeth McCarthy (eds), *Fear: Essays on the Meaning and Experience of Fear* (Dublin: Four Courts, 2007), pp. 47–59. Christopher Frayling, *The Yellow Peril: Dr. Fu Manchu and the Rise of Chinaphobia* (London: Thames and Hudson, 2014); John Kuo Wei Tchen and Dylan Yeats (eds), *Yellow Peril!: An Archive of Anti-Asian Fear* (London: Verso, 2013).
42. George Fielding Eliot, 'The Copper Bowl', in Herbert van Thal (ed.), *The Pan Book of Horror Stories* (London: Pan, 1959), p. 60.
43. Volumes 1–3 were published by Sphere in 1984, and volumes 4–6 in 1985. For this chapter, I am using the two-volume anthology editions: *Clive Barker's Books of Blood*, vols 1–3 (London: Warner, 1994); *Clive Barker's Books of Blood*, vols 4–6 (London: Warner, 1994).
44. Barker, *Books of Blood*, vol. 2, p. 60.
45. Clive Barker, interviewed in Douglas E. Winter, 'Give Me B-Movies or Give Me Death!', *Faces of Fear* (1985). Available online at <http://www.clivebarker.info/censorship.html> (last accessed 15 April 2018).
46. Catherine Crowe, *The Night Side of Nature; or, Ghosts and Ghost Seers*, 2 vols. (London: T. C. Newby, 1848).
47. For scientific materialism (or scientific naturalism), see, for example, Gowan Dawson and Bernard Lightman (eds), *Victorian Scientific Naturalism: Community, Identity, Continuity* (Chicago: University of Chicago Press, 2014). For the Victorian 'crisis of faith', see, for example, Elisabeth Jay, *Faith and Doubt in Victorian Britain* (London: Macmillan 1986); Richard J. Helmstadter and Bernard Lightman (eds), *Victorian Faith in Crisis: Essays on Continuity and Change in 19th-century Religious Belief* (Palo Alto: Stanford University Press, 1991).
48. Jarlath Killeen, *Gothic Literature, 1814–1925* (Cardiff: University of Wales Press, 2009), p. 124. See also Nicola Bown et al., eds, *The Victorian Supernatural* (Cambridge: Cambridge University Press, 2004).
49. Janet Oppenheim, *The Other World: Spiritualism and Psychical Research in England, 1850–1914* (Cambridge, 1985), p. 4.
50. Alex Owen, *The Darkened Room: Women, Power and Spiritualism in Late-Victorian England* (Chicago: University of Chicago Press, 1989).
51. Vanessa D. Dickerson, *Victorian Ghosts in the Noontide: Women Writers and the Supernatural* (Columbia and London: University of Missouri Press, 1996), p. 5. For a counter-argument to this influential thesis, see Jarlath Killeen, 'Victorian Women and the Challenge of the Phantom', in Helen Conrad O'Briain and Julie-Anne Stevens (eds), *The Ghost Story from the Middle Ages to the Twentieth Century: A Ghostly Genre* (Dublin: Four Courts, 2010), pp. 81–96. See also Dara Downey, *American Women's Ghost Stories in the Gilded Age* (London: Palgrave Macmillan, 2014).
52. For example, *The Oxford Book of English Ghost Stories*, ed. Michael Cox and R. A. Gilbert (Oxford: Oxford University Press, 1986) contains eight stories by women writers; *The Oxford Book of Victorian Ghost Stories*, ed. Michael Cox and R. A. Gilbert (Oxford: Oxford University Press, 1991) has eleven; *The Penguin Book of Ghost Stories from Elizabeth Gaskell to Ambrose Bierce*, ed. Michael Newton (London: Penguin, 2010) has eight. For an anthology specifically dedicated to women writers, see Richard Dalby (ed.), *The Virago Book of Ghost Stories* (London: Virago, 1987). For American writers in particular, see Alfred Bendixen (ed.), *Haunted Women: The Best Supernatural Tales by American*

Women (New York: Frederick Ungar, 1985); Catherine A. Lundie (ed.), *Restless Spirits: Ghost Stories by American Women 1872–1926* (Amherst: University of Massachusetts Press, 1996).

53. Amelia B. Edwards, 'The Phantom Coach', in Cox and Gilbert (eds), *The Oxford Book of English Ghost Stories*, p. 16, p. 18.
54. Ibid. p. 24.
55. Ibid. p. 14.
56. Ibid. p. 24.
57. Owen Davies, *The Haunted: A Social History of Ghosts* (London: Palgrave, 2007).
58. James, 'The Mezzotint', *Collected Ghost Stories*, p. 31.
59. James, 'Ghosts – Treat them Gently!', *Collected Ghost Stories*, p. 418.
60. James, 'Introduction to *Ghosts and Marvels*', *Collected Ghost Stories*, p. 407, and 'Ghosts – Treat them Gently!', *Collected Ghost Stories*, p. 416.
61. James, 'Oh, Whistle, and I'll Come to You, My Lad', *Collected Ghost Stories*, p. 88.
62. Ibid. p. 92.
63. James, 'A Neighbour's Landmark', *Collected Ghost Stories*, p. 315.
64. M. R. James, letter to Nico Llewelyn Davies, 12 January 1928, in *A Pleasing Terror: The Complete Supernatural Writings*, ed. Christopher Roden and Barbara Roden (Ashcroft, BC: Ash-Tree Press, 2001), p. 642.
65. Ibid. p. 641.
66. James, 'Ghosts – Treat them Gently!', p. 418.
67. See Sorcha Ní Fhlainn (ed.), *Clive Barker: Dark Imaginer* (Manchester: Manchester University Press, 2017).
68. For the sales figures for the *Pan Books of Horror Stories*, see Johnny Mains, *Lest You Should Suffer Nightmares: A Biography of Herbert Van Thal* (Bargoed: Screaming Dreams, 2011), p. 21.

Bibliography

Arnold, Catharine, *Necropolis: London and its Dead* (London: Pocket Books, 2007).
Barker, Clive, *Clive Barker's Books of Blood*, vols 1–3 (London: Warner, 1994).
— *Clive Barker's Books of Blood*, vols 4–6 (London: Warner, 1994).
Barker, Martin, *The Video Nasties: Freedom and Censorship in the Media* (London: Pluto, 1984).
Barker, Martin and Julian Petley (eds), *Ill-Effects: The Media/Violence Debate* (London: Routledge, 2001).
Barratt, Nick, *Greater London: The Story of the Suburbs* (London: Random House, 2012).
Bendixen, Alfred (ed.), *Haunted Women: The Best Supernatural Tales by American Women* (New York: Frederick Ungar, 1985).
Bown, Nicola, Carolyn Burdett and Pamela Thurschwell (eds), *The Victorian Supernatural* (Cambridge: Cambridge University Press, 2004).
Bradley, Simon, *The Railways: Nation, Network and People* (London: Profile, 2015).
Clery, E. J. and Robert Miles (eds), *Gothic Documents: A Sourcebook 1700–1820* (Manchester: Manchester University Press, 2000).
Cohen, Stanley, *Folk Devils and Moral Panics* (St Albans: Paladin, 1973).
Conrad O'Briain, Helen and Julie-Anne Stevens (eds), *The Ghost Story from the Middle Ages to the Twentieth Century: A Ghostly Genre* (Dublin: Four Courts, 2010).
Cox, Michael and R. A. Gilbert (eds), *The Oxford Book of English Ghost Stories* (Oxford: Oxford University Press, 1986).
— (eds), *The Oxford Book of Victorian Ghost Stories* (Oxford: Oxford University Press, 1991).

Crowe, Catherine, *The Night Side of Nature; or, Ghosts and Ghost Seers*, 2 vols (London: T. C. Newby, 1848).
Dalby, Richard (ed.), *The Virago Book of Ghost Stories* (London: Virago, 1987).
Daly, Nicholas, *Literature, Technology and Modernity, 1860–2000* (Cambridge: Cambridge University Press, 2004).
Davies, Owen, *The Haunted: A Social History of Ghosts* (London: Palgrave, 2007).
Dawson, Gowan and Bernard Lightman (eds), *Victorian Scientific Naturalism: Community, Identity, Continuity* (Chicago: University of Chicago Press, 2014).
Dickens, Charles, *Christmas Books*, ed. Ruth Glancy (Oxford: Oxford University Press, 1988).
— *Sketches by Boz*, ed. Dennis Walder (London: Penguin, 1995).
— *The Pickwick Papers*, ed. Mark Wormald (London: Penguin, 1999).
— *Dombey and Son*, ed. Dennis Walder (Oxford: Oxford University Press, 2001).
Dickerson, Vanessa D., *Victorian Ghosts in the Noontide: Women Writers and the Supernatural* (Columbia and London: University of Missouri Press, 1996).
Downey, Dara, *American Women's Ghost Stories in the Gilded Age* (London: Palgrave Macmillan, 2014).
Doyle, Arthur Conan, *The Conan Doyle Stories* (London: John Murray, 1929).
— *The Hound of the Baskervilles*, ed. Christopher Frayling (London: Penguin, 2001).
— *Gothic Tales*, ed. Darryl Jones (Oxford: Oxford University Press, 2016).
Frayling, Christopher, *The Yellow Peril: Dr. Fu Manchu and the Rise of Chinaphobia* (London: Thames and Hudson, 2014).
French, Richard D., *Antivivisection and Medical Science in Victorian Society* (Princeton: Princeton University Press, 1975).
Grossman, Jonathan, *Charles Dickens's Networks: Public Transport and the Novel* (Oxford: Oxford University Press, 2013).
Hebblethwaite, Kate and Elizabeth McCarthy (eds), *Fear: Essays on the Meaning and Experience of Fear* (Dublin: Four Courts, 2007).
Helmstadter, Richard J. and Bernard Lightman (eds), *Victorian Faith in Crisis: Essays on Continuity and Change in 19th-century Religious Belief* (Palo Alto: Stanford University Press, 1991).
Jackson, Shirley, *Novels and Stories*, ed. Joyce Carol Oates (New York: Library of America, 2010).
James, M. R., *A Pleasing Terror: The Complete Supernatural Writings*, ed. Christopher Roden and Barbara Roden (Ashcroft, BC: Ash-Tree Press, 2001).
— *Collected Ghost Stories*, ed. Darryl Jones (Oxford: Oxford University Press, 2011).
Jay, Elisabeth, *Faith and Doubt in Victorian Britain* (London: Macmillan 1986).
Jones, Darryl (ed.), *Horror Stories: Classic Tales from Hoffmann to Hodgson* (Oxford: Oxford University Press, 2014).
Keating, Peter, *The Haunted Study: A Social History of the English Novel 1875–1914* (London: Secker and Warburg, 1989).
Kerekes, David and David Slater, *See No Evil: Banned Films and Video Controversies* (Manchester: Headpress, 2000).
Kerr, Douglas, *Conan Doyle: Writing, Profession, and Practice* (Oxford: Oxford University Press, 2013).
Killeen, Jarlath, *Gothic Literature, 1814–1925* (Cardiff: University of Wales Press, 2009).
Leavis, Q. D., *Fiction and the Reading Public* (London: Chatto and Windus, 1965).
Lovecraft, H. P., *Tales*, ed. Peter Straub (New York: Library of America, 2005).
Lundie, Catherine A. (ed.), *Restless Spirits: Ghost Stories by American Women 1872–1926* (Amherst: University of Massachusetts Press, 1996).
Mains, Johnny, *Lest You Should Suffer Nightmares: A Biography of Herbert Van Thal* (Bargoed: Screaming Dreams, 2011).

Morrison, Robert and Chris Baldick (eds), *Tales of Terror from Blackwood's Magazine* (Oxford: Oxford University Press, 1995).
Newton, Michael (ed.), *The Penguin Book of Ghost Stories from Elizabeth Gaskell to Ambrose Bierce* (London: Penguin, 2010).
Ní Fhlainn, Sorcha (ed.), *Clive Barker: Dark Imaginer* (Manchester: Manchester University Press, 2017).
Oppenheim, Janet, *The Other World: Spiritualism and Psychical Research in England, 1850–1914* (Cambridge: Cambridge University Press, 1985).
Owen, Alex, *The Darkened Room: Women, Power and Spiritualism in Late-Victorian England* (Chicago: University of Chicago Press, 1989).
Parreaux, André, *The Publication of 'The Monk': A Literary Event 1796–1798* (Paris: Didier, 1960).
Poe, Edgar Allan, *Selected Writings*, ed. G. R. Thompson (New York: W. W. Norton, 2004).
Physiological Society, <http://www.physoc.org/society-history> (last accessed 15 April 2018).
Schivelbusch, Wolfgang, *The Railway Journey: The Industrialization and Perception of Time and Space*, 2nd edn (Berkeley: University of California Press, 2014).
Tchen, John Kuo Wei and Dylan Yeats (eds), *Yellow Peril!: An Archive of Anti-Asian Fear* (London: Verso, 2013).
Thal, Herbert Van (ed.), *The Pan Book of Horror Stories* (London: Pan, 1959).
Waller, Philip, *Writers, Readers and Reputations: Literary Life in Britain 1780–1918* (Oxford: Oxford University Press, 2006).
Wells, H. G., *Anticipations*, in *The Works of H. G. Wells*, Atlantic Edition (London: T. Fisher Unwin, 1924), vol. 4.
— *The Island of Doctor Moreau*, ed. Darryl Jones (Oxford: Oxford University Press, 2017).
White, Jerry, *London in the Nineteenth Century: 'A Human Awful Wonder of God'* (London: Jonathan Cape, 2007).
Williams, Raymond, *Writing in Society* (London: Verso, 1983).

12

Experimental Short Stories

Jeremy Scott

The experimental short story is particularly amenable to analytical approaches based on the concept of *deviation* (or foregrounding) in relation to perceived norms; this is because the term 'experimental' itself implies and entails working against a prevailing paradigm. These deviations can take many forms. They can be linguistic, and thus at the level of discourse (the linguistic building blocks of the text), or narratological (at the level of story structure: the ways in which the 'matter' of the story itself is mediated by the writer for the reader). According to this formulation, experimentation is manifested as a type of deviation against the background of what readers expect a short story to be – against what Paul Simpson has termed our expectations of 'wellformedness'.[1] To draw on terminology from literary stylistics: the reader brings a pre-defined *narrative schema*[2] to bear upon the reading experience. This schema is a set of expectations and preconceptions of what a short story should be, learned and embedded during a life's experience of reading. If a story fails to accord with this schema in some way – if it challenges and/or modifies it – the reader views that story as 'experimental'.

However, it could be argued that there is another, equally interesting way to think about experimental short fiction, and that is to focus on its 'content' as distinct from its discourse. In other words, the very matter of what the story is about – the imaginary world that it cues up in the mind of the reader – can also be in some way deviant, and thus key to its experimental nature. To draw a broad example from literary history: much early literature involved princely, courtly or deified characters and concerned the deeds of gods, queens, kings and heroes, rarely if ever ordinary people living quotidian lives. Thus, Chaucer's *Canterbury Tales* were 'experimental' in their context, not only through their rendering of the contemporary oral vernacular (Middle English) as text but also in the tales' depictions of the trials and tribulations of pardoners, squires and millers. Now that the palette from which story subject matter can be drawn is so much larger, if not infinite, what might be said to constitute 'experimental' subject matter? Science fiction? Magic? Surrealism?

Is experimental fiction, then, only ever about technique and craft, the *manner* in which the story is mediated (linguistically deviant), and never about *content*? Or could it be argued that experimentalism and its subsequent refreshment of narrative schema in fact arises in the relationship between the two?

The troublesome distinction between 'mediation' and 'content', if it is to be useful, should be defined as rigorously as possible. Narratology proposes that the narrative act requires a series of key ingredients: a narrator, characters, a represented situation, a situation of representation (the physical artefact of the short story text), a medium of representation (language) and a listener, audience or reader.[3] Here, the term *discourse* will be substituted for 'medium of representation' and *storyworld*[4] for 'represented situation', borrowing distinctions originally made by the Russian Formalists[5] and later refined and expanded.[6] By way of explication: in 'traditional' realist stories the events of the storyworld should be relatable to a person who has not read the story itself. A reader should be able to read such a story, and then summarise what happens in its plot to a third party without difficulty. Crucially, another reader asked to do the same would come up with, broadly, the same pieces of key information. Furthermore, key categorical statements about the storyworld should be falsifiable (i.e. based on linguistic evidence to be found in the text, and not from inference). Events either happen or do not happen. Characters either perform certain actions or they do not. Given the existence of narrative schema, then, it should be possible, when exploring experimental short stories, to analyse them in terms of their deviance from these norms – in relation to both discourse and storyworld, linguistically and conceptually. The discourse itself can be deviant; so can the events of the storyworld.

Linguistic deviation at the level of discourse has been systematised extensively by Mick Short,[7] and sub-categorised as follows: syntactical (grammatical), morphological (the building blocks of words), graphological (the 'look' on the page), lexical (vocabulary choices), semantic (e.g. paradoxes of meaning), phonological (sound patterning) and pragmatic (how meaning is generated in part by context). Some revealing examples of the expressive effect of overt linguistic deviation (in all of its various manifestations) can be found in the work of the short story writers Ronald Sukenick, Gabriel Josipovici and Donald Barthelme.

Sukenick in particular refused to accede to the kinds of conventions associated with mimetic fiction; the narrative schema of the reader is continually challenged by his work. To return to the dichotomy between discourse and storyworld: much of Sukenick's work foregrounds the former, continually confronting the reader with his work's fundamental status as text.[8] Further, these texts, arguably, take the notion of linguistic deviation as far as it can go before moving beyond the realms of coherence. They are non-referential and explicitly deviant.

The extract below is from 'Doggy Bag' (1994), described in its blurb as 'an outrageous avant-pop answer to T. S. Eliot's *The Waste Land*'. In a pastiche of Eliot's collage-like technique in that poem, the blurb also gives the following advice to writers and readers: 'Don't waste anything: recycle it, cut it up and snarf it down like a Naked Lunch':

> who are these people?]--->
>
> name of the dog]=================================>
>
> doggy bag}######################:::::::::::::::::::::------------>
>
> a mummy's curse}*******************++++++++++===--->
>
> 50,010,008}}}}}}}}}}}))))))>>>>>////////%%%%%%%::::==>
>
> the wondering jew and the black widow murders, or the
>   return of the planet of the apes}*******"""",,,,,,,,,,,,,,,>
>
> the burial of count orgasm} llllllllllll::::::::::::. .. ..
>
> death on the supply side}_____------------""""""""" 9

Virtually all of forms of linguistic deviation as defined by Short are present in this story. Semantic deviation (collocational incongruity) can be in seen in the phrase 'death on the supply side' which, without context, has no discernible referential meaning beyond itself. There is also discoursal deviation; the text has none of the typical textual features associated with prose fiction: a title, distinct paragraphs, complete sentences and, more arguably, a discernible point of view or stable narrator. The most obvious form of deviation here, however, is graphological:[10] the unconventional use of punctuation marks and symbols at the end of each line of text, and the lack of any capitalisation of proper nouns and names. The opening page of the text, then, is constructed from a series of fragments with few if any features of textual cohesion[11] apart from some loose semantic fields: dogs, science fiction and horror film titles.

The story moves on to become (at first glance) more conventional, with standard grammar and graphology and with a coherent narrative point of view. However, closer examination reveals significant semantic deviation:

> I'm standing in line waiting to get into the Uffizi, but this is an understatement. I'm heading for the Uffizi yesterday in a leisurely way, expecting to 'do' it, as Henry James might say, for the third time after a lapse of twenty-odd years, when as my 'companion', as Henry James might call her, and myself turn into the piazza in front of the entrance, I lower my eyes from the huge imposition of the Palazzo della Signoria, the calculated imbalance of the tower implying that matter can always crush us, and whose rough elegance never fails to bowl me over, and behold a swarm of people in front of the museum.[12]

The opening sentence is a non sequitur; the second clause does not manifest the contradiction or qualification of the previous clause that its use of the conjunction 'but' predicts. The second sentence contains a paradox brought about by the use of the present progressive tense ('I'm heading') and past time deixis, 'yesterday'. The verb phrases that open both the first and second sentences also contradict each other: 'I'm standing in line' versus 'I'm heading for . . .' Both statements cannot be deemed semantically true in the terms of a storyworld based on the physical laws of the actual world, and thus effectively negate one another. If readers expect short stories to invite identification and empathy with a dynamic storyworld, then this text seems intent on disrupting that process.

In the first extract, there is little to engage with in terms of mediated storyworld. A reader asked to describe 'what happened?' would have little by way of an answer. The second extract seems more recognisable as narrative fiction. The narrator is in Florence, Italy, queuing (or on his way to queue?) for the Uffizi museum. But closer examination of the semantics of the paragraph reveals contradiction, paradox and untruths which effectively unpick and undercut any fixed readerly representation of the mediated storyworld. It is, in effect, impossible to extract a coherent storyworld from the discourse; the text aspires to project an alternative to 'received' reality. This highly deviant style of writing was labelled 'surfiction' by the American experimental writer Raymond Federman in his collection of essays *Surfiction: Fiction Now and Tomorrow*,[13] which also included a contribution by Sukenick. A distinctly American phenomenon of the early 1970s and 1980s, writers associated with it (e.g. Steve Katz, Ursule Molinaro and Jonathan Baumbach amongst others) were key figures in the formulation of early critical definitions of postmodernist fiction.[14] Rather than attempting to mimetically mediate a pre-existent reality, surfiction repeatedly foregrounds its own status as text and fiction, and foregoes the requirement 'to be meaningful, truthful or realistic'.[15]

In similar vein, Gabriel Josipovici's short fiction also disrupts (and refreshes) narrative schema. A good example of his approach can be found in the stories collected in *Mobius the Stripper* (1974). The title story of this collection is an example of extreme discoursal deviation from the norms of mimetic fiction. It is constructed from two narratives which are meant to be read at the same time; the first fills the upper half of each page of the text while the second can be found on the lower half. The story of Mobius, an overweight club stripper, is told in the third person while the second story, told in the first person, narrates the life of an aspiring writer who is afflicted by writer's block and, accordingly, struggling in front of an empty page. The stories have several thematic overlaps, chiefly the protagonists' search for some kind of authentic ipseity or self-knowledge. However, the most interesting relationship between the two stories is revealed by the pun of the title, which evokes the mathematical and geometrical figures of the Möbius strip: a model of a three-dimensional surface with only one side. This pun points to the fact that the stories are to be read simultaneously – but the order in which one reads them affects the relationship between them, and hence the reader's conception of the storyworld(s). The relationship between the two can be represented diagrammatically, thus:

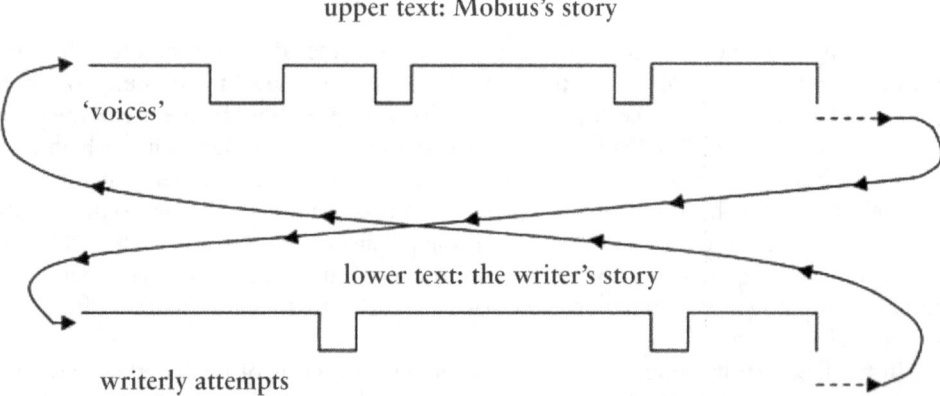

Mobius hears voices. If the reader reads about this first, then the second story becomes one of the voices that Mobius hears. If the reader begins with the story of the writer, then the story of Mobius might be the story that the writer eventually manages to write after he overcomes his writer's block. So, a device rooted in discoursal deviation becomes a neat dramatisation of Mobius's hopeless search for the truth during which he strips (literally and metaphorically) layer after layer of himself away, only to reveal an essential emptiness, faced with which he takes his own life. At the same time, the narrator agonises over his inability to write or say anything of note, until he arrives at the idea of the story of this dilemma as exemplified by Mobius. Just as in the work of Sukenick, the intersections and relationships between discourse and storyworlds and the nature of 'truth' and 'fiction' are intensely problematised. Is the writer a figment of Mobius's imagination? Who comes first? Who is creator, who is object? Which is 'author', which is 'text'? There are no falsifiable answers to these questions; like the world built by Sukenick's narrator, the competing discourses undercut one another.

The experimental short fiction of Donald Barthleme, in turn, seems to point to a similar impossibility of gaining true, falsifiable knowledge about the storyworlds of experimental short stories. In an essay entitled 'Not-Knowing',[16] he contends:

> Writing is a process of dealing with not-knowing, a forcing of what and how . . . The not-knowing is crucial to art, is what permits art to be made. Without the scanning process engendered by not-knowing, without the possibility of having the mind move in unanticipated directions, there would be no invention . . . The not-knowing is not simple, because it's hedged about with prohibitions, roads that may not be taken. The more serious the artist, the more problems he takes into account and the more considerations limit his possible initiatives.[17]

These remarks reinforce the approach of this chapter: in experimental short fiction, the assumption that the mediated storyworld is in some sense anterior to the discourse (that it has an independent existence and falsifiable knowledge about it can be gained separately from the linguistic code that builds it in the mind of the reader) is at least questioned, at most shown to be false. However, in the same essay, Barthleme contests the idea that experimental writing has 'turned its back on the world, is in some sense not about the world but about its own processes'.[18] He goes on to account for these criticisms of experimental writing as a misconception of its key aesthetic and philosophical aim which, he argues is a refreshment and reinvigoration of language itself:

> The problems that seem to me to define the writer's task at this moment . . . are not of a kind that make for ease of communication, for work that reissues toward the reader with out-flung arms – rather, they're the reverse. Let me cite three such difficulties that I take to be important, all having to do with language. First, there is art's project, since Mallarmé, of restoring freshness to a much-handled language. . . . Secondly, there is the political and social contamination of language by its use in manipulation of various kinds over time and the effort to find what might be called a 'clean' language. . . . Finally, there is the pressure on language from contemporary culture in the broadest sense – I mean our devouring commercial culture – which results in a double impoverishment: theft of complexity from the reader, theft of the reader from the writer.[19]

Accordingly, as with Sukenick, we find wide-ranging and characteristic linguistic deviation; e.g. literalising of figurative metaphor, blending of styles and registers, overt use of cliché and linguistic incongruity. The opening paragraph of 'For I'm the Boy' is graphologically deviant; it eschews punctuation distinguishing between direct speech and narrative voice:

> You weren't required Bloomsbury said explicitly, you were invited. Invited then Huber said, I don't see what we were invited for. As friends of the family Bloomsbury said.[20]

This technique of fragmentation continues in 'Me and Miss Mandible', which mediates its storyworld, the tale of a grown man returning to school, through a highly fragmented collage made up of diary excerpts. Something frightening, uncanny, seems to alienate the reader, impeding his or her schema-based ambition to understand the storyworld. In 'traditional' fiction, the ways in which the reader builds character are relatively straightforward: schema (top down information) are activated by the fictional entity in question as dictated by textual cues (bottom up information).[21] However, in the case of the narrator of 'Me and Miss Mandible', the reader will struggle to categorise or naturalise him. Is he eleven or thirty-five? He cannot be situated within the context of a coherent, concrete storyworld; the boundaries continually shift. The narrator constantly refers back to his own past in order to discover a sense of self, but it is ultimately undiscoverable. Like the reader, he has to be content with 'Not-Knowing'.

In 'Game', there is a similar disavowal of absolute knowledge, inexactness, negation and contradiction:

> Each of us wears a .45 and each of us is supposed to shoot the other if the other is behaving strangely. How strangely is strangely? I do not know. In addition to the .45 I have a .38 which Shotwell does not know about concealed in my attaché case, and Shotwell has a .25 calibre Beretta which I do not know about strapped to his right calf.[22]

'[S]upposed to shoot the other' implies outside direction or obligation, but from or to whom? The notion of any agreed truth is explicitly problematised. Of course, the narrator's knowledge of the existence of Shotwell's hidden Beretta could have come about with hindsight, but if that were the case, then surely the preferred form would be 'which I did not know about at the time'. It is hard to escape the conclusion that the discourse here is resolutely anti-mimetic. Eventually, accordingly, it dissolves into repeated negation:

> I am not well. I do not know our target. They do not tell us for which city the bird is targeted. I do not know. . . . I do not know for which city the bird is targeted. Shotwell is not himself. Sometimes I cannot sleep. Sometimes Shotwell cannot sleep.[23]

The opening of the story 'Alice' also embraces all of the forms of linguistic deviation defined previously:

> twirling around on my piano still my head beings to swim my head beings to swim twirling around on my piano stool twirling around on my piano stole dizzy spell eventuates twirling around on my piano stool I begin to feel dizzy twirling around on my piano stool.[24]

Reading Barthelme means accepting the essential unknowability and indeterminacy of storyworld. 'Fragments are the only forms I trust' remarks the narrator of 'See the Moon?'[25] and the reader searching for unity and textual cohesion will be frustrated. However, once narrative schema, linguistic norms and the need to establish the actuality of concrete storyworlds behind the array of discourses are discarded, then it is possible to engage with these stories and marvel at the breadth of their stylistic innovation, the freshness of their use of language and, indeed, to get a renewed sense of the genre's possibilities.

It should now be possible to advance a more detailed account of those elements that go to make up a general reader's narrative schema and to understand how experimental short stories disrupt and refresh it. First, an encounter with the discourse of narrative fiction (the act of reading itself) instigates processes of world-building in the mind of the reader. Second, these worlds correspond to a storyworld which the narrative discourse mediates; the reader, in Ron Carter and Walter Nash's phrase, is 'seeing through language'.[26] Third: against the background of these worlds, events take place according to archetypal narrative structures, and these events (as well as the characters who instigate and are affected by them) constitute points of interest and engagement for the reader.

What, then, is to be made of experimental writing such as that of Samuel Beckett that disrupts these norms at the level of storyworld? The following is from 'Malone Dies':

> I shall soon be quite dead at last in spite of all. Perhaps next month. Then it will be the month of April or of May. For the year is still young, a thousand little signs tell me so. Perhaps I am wrong, perhaps I shall survive Saint John the Baptist's Day and even the Fourteenth of July, festival of freedom. Indeed I would not put it past me to pant on to the Transfiguration, not to speak of the Assumption. But I do not think so, I do not think I am wrong in saying that these rejoicings will take place in my absence, this year.[27]

Beckett's writing has been characterised as 'anti-narrative', a term usually reserved for stories which violate the kinds of conventional narrative norms above.[28] However, this extract is linguistically standard. Although the deictic language and present tense ('soon', 'next month', 'this year', 'now', 'to-day') indicate a simultaneous narration in the here-and-now of the storyworld, it is hard for the reader to discern any storyworld beyond the discourse; in fact, there is little sense even of a concrete setting. Again: if a reader were asked to tell a third party 'what happened', there would be little to say. What does the reader know that could be falsified? Malone is an old man who lies naked in bed in an asylum or hospital. Most of his personal effects have been taken from him, though he has retained some: his exercise book, brimless hat and pencil. He writes both of his own situation and that of a boy, Sapo. When he reaches the point in the story where Sapo becomes a man, he changes Sapo's name to Macmann. Soon after, Malone admits to having killed six men, but seems to think this insignificant, particularly in the case of the last: a total stranger whom he cut across the neck with a razor. Macmann's story (such as it is) takes up the remainder of the text, as Malone fades from the reader's view – inasmuch as he was ever really visible:

> Lemuel is in charge, he raises his hatchet on which the blood will never dry, but *not* to hit anyone, he will not hit anyone, he will *not* hit *anyone any more*, he will *not* touch anyone any more, either with it or with it or with it or with or
>
> or with it or with his hammer or with his stick or with his fist or in thought in dream I mean *never* he will *never*

> or with his pencil or with his stick or
> or light light I mean
> ***never*** there he will ***never***
> ***never anything***
> there
> ***any more*** [my emphases]²⁹

The majority of the discourse, however, is observational in tone and deals with the minutiae of Malone's isolated existence, such as dropping his pencil or the dwindling amount of writing lead available to him, or with flights of fancy (such as riding down the stairs on his bed) and dark philosophical musings, tangential to the 'story' that Malone is intent on telling. Note also the repeated use of negation in the extract above (in bold), which is characteristic; indeed, the novella contains the famous line 'nothing is more real than nothing', encapsulating the narrative's refusal of the coherence, even existence, of storyworld – and reality.

This 'anti-narrativity' is even more pronounced in Beckett's later fiction. The following is from 'Lessness':

> Ruins true refuge long last towards which so many false time out of mind. All sides endlessness earth sky as one no sound no stir. Grey face two pale blue little body heart beating only up right. Blacked out fallen open four walls over backwards true refuge issueless.
>
> Scattered ruins same grey as the sand ash grey true refuge. Four square all light sheer white blank planes all gone from mind. Never was but grey air timeless no sound figment the passing light. No sound no stir ash grey sky mirrored earth mirrored sky. Never but this changelessness dream the passing hour.³⁰

This extract has similar linguistically deviant features to the Sukenick stories: grammatical, semantic and discoursal. Lexical deviation and parallelism (repeated patterns) are foregrounded; nouns are created from an adjectival or substantive root and the addition of the morpheme '-ness': 'endlessness', 'issueless', 'changelessness'. While 'issueless' is not deviant, its intended meaning here is ('without issue').

What if this text is analysed from the perspective of this chapter's central thesis on the relationship between discourse and storyworld? To explore this relationship further: Monica Fludernik attempts a re-conceptualising of 'natural narratology',³¹ which seeks to redefine narrativity not in terms of plot or story shape but within broadly *cognitive* parameters. These parameters are based on our subjective experience of the world, and on our sense of embodiment in it, as opposed to structuralist models of plot:

> [Embodiment] evokes all the parameters of a real-life schema of existence which always has to be situated in a specific time and space frame, and the motivational and experiential aspects of human actionality likewise relate to the knowledge about one's physical presence in the world.³²

Fludernik's use of the term 'experiential' here is crucial, and points to the fact that conventional narratives (e.g. oral storytelling) correlate in cognitive terms with perceptual parameters of human experience. Crucially, these parameters are still in place in so-called anti-narrative such as Beckett's.[33] Thus, narrative need not be defined in structuralist terms (e.g. plot), but can also arise from experientiality. There is a cognitively grounded inter-relationship between human experience and narrative fiction's human representations of experience, and any text that foregrounds these parameters can be treated as a narrative, regardless of whether it mediates an identifiable story. Thus, the inconsistencies of experimental texts cease to be problematic when they are no longer read as a series of events, but explained as the experience of the mediating consciousness or that of a reflective or 'registering' mind. A reader can make sense of and find meaning in what at first appears to be non-sense, and this happens because humans are conditioned to do so.

This model of the nature of narrativity allows the definition of a great number of 'plotless' narratives such as Beckett's to be viewed as fully satisfying the requirement of experientiality, since such texts operate by means of a projection of consciousness without necessarily needing any actantial, independent base structure (such as a storyworld). To summarise: although these texts have a discourse reference, what precisely (if anything) is their story (or plot) cannot be determined with any clarity. This textual non-specificity could be defined as *conceptual deviation*. Events, stories, interconnected happenings, drama, tension – these are no longer the focus of interest. Instead, the nature of experience itself takes centre stage.

To propose another norm against which to measure conceptual deviance, it could be posited that in classic realism, narrators and characters are foregrounded against the background of the storyworld in which they exist. They inhabit, move through and against, this background, and are the focus of the reader's attention. To generalise for a moment: fictional narratives are typically *anthropocentric*. However, writers influenced by the advent of *psychogeography* in the 1950s began to foreground the environment itself until it took on equal status as, almost, a character in its own right; the landscapes, often urban, that narrators and characters found themselves in and their effect on these entities became the centre of attention. It is in the peculiarly modern entanglement of mind and environment, what Will Self describes variously as 'the contemporary world warp[ing] the relationship between psyche and place' and as 'the personality of place itself',[34] that these stories find their inspiration.

One of the pioneers of psychogeography, Guy-Ernest Debord, defined it as 'the study of the precise laws and specific effects of the geographical environment . . . on the emotions and behaviour of individuals'.[35] As such, it could be viewed as a dehumanising way of thinking about literary characters – as harking back in some way to the nineteenth-century European naturalism of Zola, Balzac and Flaubert, which positions its characters as helpless in the face of the currents of history that swirl around them. However, it is more accurate to think of the psychogeographical project as concerned with characters' psychological responses to the environment they find themselves in. At the idea's beginnings in the Situationist movement in 1950s Paris, various points across the cityscape were observed to generate specific types of reaction, emotion and behaviour, either positive or negative. These key points were designated as *plaques tournantes* ('turning places'), and by mapping and tracking the distribution of these nodes, psychogeographers aimed to explain these reactions and connect them to wider sociocultural forces such as consumerism and capitalism.[36]

Thus, at its heart, psychogeography is inherently transgressive and subversive in an ideological sense. In a literary sense, it is subversive in its reversal of the classical relationship between psyche and place where the former exists to a large extent independently of the latter.

The short stories of Iain Sinclair swap Paris for London. Sinclair's London is a city of labyrinths, divisions, zones and disparities, and the style of the discourse, which is highly associative rather than narrative-driven, responding to the *plaque tournantes* of the city rather than events or interactions, reflects this. His work is full of cross-references, recurring and re-visited themes and topics, links between different texts and segments of texts; indeed, books which would normally be seen as entirely separate seem to blend and demand to be read holistically. Like all of the experimental writers discussed here, these texts can alienate the reader who arrives with a standard narrative schema. As with hyperlinks, the reader must learn to navigate between the many themes and preoccupations and tangential connections. Indeed, 'navigate' is an apposite description of the reading process, as Robert Macfarlane points out:

> It can take time to acquire a reading method for Sinclair's style: time to develop the necessary stamina and the requisite orientation devices. His style is forcibly intransitive: verbs are deprived of their objects, prepositions are suppressed, conjunctions vanish, full-stops proliferate. Passage through his prose is demanding, immersion is obligatory, and cognitive dissonance is high. . . . Sinclair is often described as 'digressive', but the term doesn't work, for it suggests a central path from which his divagations occur. A buzzword from the emergent critical vocabulary of 'ergodic'[37] literature may help: one doesn't read Sinclair so much as 'navigate' him.[38]

The collection of prose pieces that make up *Lud Heat* (1975) bears out Macfarlane's description of Sinclair's early style:

> These accusations go against the poet with equal force. If he is not truly 'here' the fevers will nail him. The continually drawn handkerchief is drenched with his melting ego. Discursive thoughts run out of his nose, the attention is concentrated in one place. He listens to the smell that is no longer there.
>
> Breakage, asthma priest, keeps his eye hidden in the cool socket of his viewfinder; concentrates all pain OUT into the captured image field.
>
> Which recalls the worst days of suffering – filming at Silbury Hill, or taking photographs of Avebury, the Ridgeway – punishment for defiling the mysteries. Thick midsummer drift of grass seed, midge helmet, surrounds these shrines, hovering over the aqua stats, spirals of protection and warning.[39]

The majority of the verbs in this excerpt exhibit material transitivity ('go', 'nail', 'drenched', 'run'), and some transitive verbs are used as other parts of speech ('drawn', 'drift'). The sentences of the first paragraph are short and terse, progressing relentlessly from subject to verb to object: 'accusations go', 'fevers nail', 'thoughts run'. Note, though, how the subjects of these sentences are abstract and inanimate emotions and thoughts, de-emphasising the role of the human subject and foregrounding the effect of the surroundings. It is the environment itself which is dynamic ('drift of grass seed ... surrounds'), not the humans within it, who struggle to externalise emotions ('concentrates all pain out') in the face of the landscape.

In *Suicide Bridge* (1979), the reader is faced with an equally 'ergodic' text in terms of its style and lack of coherence in narrative terms; however, this story is peopled with characters drawn from Blake's 'Jerusalem' and ancient English and Welsh folklore who take literal form and converge on London. The blend of mythic archetypes with contemporary setting is disorientating and unsettling, and the style, whilst materially transitive, much closer to the poetic than the prosaic. The City of London and its roads take on living form, enveloping and overarching the characters who move through it:

> Hutton the stiff one
> revolves through cement mixer
> conglomerate
> with flint & gravel, with sand dredged aggregate
> tipped
> born into the East Way Flyover ...
> a literal & continuing part of the city[40]

Again, in keeping with the premise of this chapter as a whole, Sinclair's work, through its foregrounding of setting and environment, redefines the relationship between discourse and storyword; to attempt a separation of the two is to misunderstand how these texts work. In another instance of Fludernik's natural narrative, psyche (experientiality) and place are intrinsically linked and co-existent. In support of this, Julian Wolfreys characterises Sinclair's deviant style as 'unreadable', but not in the standard sense of that term. He views the discourse's mediation of storyworld as an act of 'translation':

> I am tempted to argue that no reading of Sinclair is possible, if by reading the idea of a more or less coherent translation is implied. Put another way: Iain Sinclair's texts cannot be read, they are unreadable in a very real way, which has nothing to do with the language, the syntax, the grammar or any other formal element. They are unreadable inasmuch as *everything that is to be said already finds itself on the surface of the text.*[41]

In Sinclair's writing too, storyworld is anterior and subservient to discourse, and thus fits neatly into this chapter's broader definition of the experimental short story, radically refreshing the reader's narrative schema and eschewing narrative in favour of associative connections and the foregrounding of experientiality.

Narrative schema themselves were born, arguably, in the form of the folk tale, in which humankind first learned to tell stories, and first began to see the coherence of story as a stay against mutability, a way of capturing evanescent time and a method of teaching and passing on knowledge and wisdom. Vladimir Propp[42] systematised the familiar narrative elements and structures of folk tales into a set of detailed criteria, including what he termed 'functions': a significant action or event defined according to its place in the plot (such as 'family member absents himself from home' or 'an interdiction is addressed to the hero' and so on). Propp reckoned on there being a total of thirty-one functions available to the storyteller. In this sense, the structure of the folk tale becomes like a language with its own narrative syntax, similar in effect to the way individual lexical items (each with their own function) are assembled according to particular norms to construct a meaningful sentence. These structures offer universality and familiarity. However, they also have the potential for subversion: first, in the essential adaptability of their structures and the ways in which their conventions can be worked against and, second, in the fact that they appear to turn the experimental short story away from linguistic and conceptual deviation back towards the pre-eminence of *story*.

The short stories of A. S. Byatt collected in *The Djinn in the Nightingale's Eye* (1995) and *Elementals* (1998) are a contemporary renegotiation of schema as well as an acknowledgement of their power and indefatigability. 'I am in a pattern I know, and I suspect I have no power to break it', ponders the heroine of 'The Story of the Eldest Princess', paying tribute to the narratological self-reflexivity of Byatt's working of mythic structures. This is the story of a kingdom where the blue sky has vanished, replaced by a green one. Three princesses embark upon a quest to find a silver bird, which promises to return everything to normal. Propp's functions appear throughout (the quest, the acquisition of a magical item, the meeting with 'false heroes' and various adversaries or 'villains') – but the eldest princess rebels against her designated role. She then assumes that the others will continue the quest in her absence, that the plot will run on, relentless. However, the second princess also defeats the constraints of the narrative form, leaving the youngest 'without a story'. Each of the archetypal female figures rebels against what the machinery of the narrative expects and compels them to do. It turns out that they *do* have the power to break the pattern. When the eldest princess meets the Old Woman, the latter explains:

> There is always an old woman ahead of you on a journey, and there is always an old woman behind you too, and they are not always the same, and may be fearful or kindly, dangerous or delightful, as the road shifts and you speed along it. Certainly I was ahead of you, and behind you too, but not only I, and not only as I am now.[43]

Thus, the Old Woman becomes emblematic of a new narratological principle, pointing the way to the forging of new possibilities, new choices – and new stories.

Similarly, Byatt's story 'Cold' is in every respect a fairy tale, featuring many of the functions defined by Propp ('a member of a family lacks something or desires to have something', 'the hero leaves home'). It contains many familiar mythic tropes such as the magical cooling of the earth, palaces of ice and mysterious visitors. There are also cycles of events in threes: three bearers of gifts, three northmen, three envoys. However, once again the form is subverted in a way that has inescapable metafictional effects. Byatt has said of the story that it is 'a metaphor for the writer in myself', the story of an Ice Princess 'whose existence is predicated on not making contact'.[44] Princess Fiammarosa becomes encased within an icy second skin, a metaphor for her own self-imposed isolation:

> She had been so much loved, as a little child, and all that heaping of anxious love had simply made her feel ill and exhausted. There was more life in coldness. In solitude. Inside a crackling skin of protective ice that was also a sensuous delight.[45]

However, this isolation leads to bursts of creativity, expressed through 'tapestries, with silver threads and ice-blue threads . . . unlike anything seen before in that land'.[46] When Fiammarosa marries Prince Sasan, she does so because his glass clothing reminds her of frozen water; she moves to his hot desert kingdom, melts (literally and metaphorically), and he builds for her a glass palace on a snowy mountaintop in which her layer of ice re-forms. She begins studying and writing again, and thus the story ends with a moment of metaphorical flourish rather than a more traditional 'happily ever after'; it is through contact, not isolation, that creativity and well-being can thrive:

> She was resourceful and hopeful, and made a study of the vegetation off the Sassanian snow-line, and a further study of which plays could thrive in mountain air under glass windows, and corresponded – at long intervals – with authorities all over the world on these matters. Her greatest discovery was a sweet blueberry, that grew in the snow, but in the glass garden became twice the size, and almost as delicate in flavour.[47]

In Byatt's work, the expectations entailed by narrative schema are to a large extent met and satisfied; the reader will be able to relate details from the storyworld with certainty, and different readers will agree on their interpretations and understanding. The experimental nature of these stories, then, arises not through deviation from formal norms (although, as in metafiction,[48] characters do rebel against and usurp the dictates of story) but by a return to and manipulation of the kinds of mythic archetypes systemised and proved to be universal by Propp – an appeal to the essential narrativising instincts of humankind, and to its taste for the fantastic and magical. Thus, deviation is to be found within the context of contemporary fiction's resolute heterogeneity. Roger Caillois summarises the lure of ancient unities and coherence well:

> If a mystery can stir, if the unusual can grip, if poetry is possible, then perhaps this is because of the complex, confusing correspondences into which the unity of cosmos has disintegrated. Everything that reminds us of this unity calls forth within our feelings agreement and good will, an *ab initio* approving echo and longing for unanimity . . . Many philosophers have blithely defined the real and the rational. I am convinced that another, equally daring action, so long as it was based on and would inspire many very precise investigations, could discover the network of established analogy and hidden links that constitute the logic of the imaginative.[49]

Thus, for Caillois, experimental reworking of the mythic and fantastical is a continual reinvigoration of that which humanity has never really lost.

To summarise the argument developed throughout this chapter: as we read the narrative discourse of a short story, we envisage a storyworld beyond it. In much experimental writing, it is problematic to describe and discuss that storyworld or answer questions about it with certainty. The more problematic this process, the more overtly experimental the piece of writing. This argument can be augmented further by suggesting that the discourse and storyworld become progressively more difficult to disentangle because conception of the latter is based on an individualised reading experience, a subjective act of interpretation where appeals to the text for substantiation of positions and claims are less clear-cut. In the case of short stories that locate themselves within a conventional mimetic mode of realism, this process of disentanglement is more straightforward. This happened, then this happened. The protagonist's name was Maria, and she had a husband called Jon. They lived on the island of Svalbard. On a particular day, they had an accident involving a skidoo and a reindeer. And so on. In the case of experimental short stories, questions about the storyworld will be less easy to answer, will vary more widely from reader to reader, and responses will rely less on concrete linguistic evidence from the text itself. Cognitive poetics frameworks such as Text World Theory[50] would be very difficult to apply to a text like Beckett's 'Lessness'; the 'lessness' of the discourse itself, its paucity of conventional stylistic indicators of point of view, deixis, modality and focalisation means that processes of world-building are impeded.

So: the initial proposition of this chapter can now be modified slightly. It began by positing that perhaps storyworlds in and of themselves can be deviant, just like discourse. Instead, it should be said that it is in the level of *accessibility* of the storyworld and the corresponding emphasis upon the reader's subjective experience of the text that the deviance of experimental short stories lies. This in turn leads to an 'openness' or freeing of interpretation, characterised by Lyn Hejinian as a 'rejection of closure'.[51] The next step in providing firm evidence for this conclusion would be to analyse in a principled manner using robust psychological and linguistic frameworks the intuitions, inferences and assumptions that actual readers have during their experience of reading these kinds of texts.

Robert Coover's story 'The Magic Poker' (1969) begins with a useful illustration of the processes of world-building described from the perspective of the writer; the observation tower here is significant, a locus for the mediating imagination:

> I wander the island, inventing it. I make a sun for it, and trees – pines and birch and dogwood and first – and cause the water to lap the pebbles of its abandoned shored. This, and more: I deposit shadows and dampness, spin webs, and scatter ruins. Yes: ruins. A mansion and guest cabins and boat houses and docks. Terraces, too, and bath houses and even an observation tower. All gutted and window-busted and autographed and shat upon. I impose a hot midday silence, a profound and heavy stillness. But anything can happen.[52]

Experimental short fiction is about *vision*, about *experientiality*, about *ways of seeing* – and not just about what is seen. It seems that, not just from the point of the writer of experimental short fiction, but also, crucially, from its readers, anything can happen.

Notes

1. Jonathan Culpeper et al., *Exploring the Language of Drama: From Text to Context* (London: Routledge, 1998), p. 41.
2. For discussion of narrative schema, see Jessica Mason, 'Narrative', in *The Cambridge Handbook of Stylistics*, ed. Peter Stockwell and Sara Whiteley (Cambridge: Cambridge University Press, 2014).
3. For a detailed review of this taxonomy, see Jeremy Scott, *Creative Writing and Stylistics* (Basingstoke: Palgrave Macmillan, 2013), p. 22.
4. I am using the term 'storyworld' as a compound noun in order to distinguish its use from more general, less theoretical applications of the term. See James Phelan, *Living to Tell about It: A Rhetoric and Ethics of Character Narration* (Ithaca, NY: Cornell University Press, 2004), for example.
5. Vladimir Propp, *Morphology of the Folk Tale*, ed. Louis A. Wagner, trans. Laurence Scott (Austin: University of Texas Press, 1968).
6. See respectively Gerard Genette, *Narrative Discourse: An Essay in Method* (New York: Cornwell University Press, 1983); Wayne C. Booth, *The Rhetoric of Fiction* (Chicago: The University of Chicago Press, 1983); and Phelan, *Living to Tell About It*.
7. Mick Short, *Exploring the Language of Poetry, Plays and Prose* (Harlow: Longman Pearson, 1996).
8. Jerzy Kutnik, *The Novel as Performance: The Fiction of Ronald Sukenick and Raymond Federman* (Carbondale: Southern Illinois University Press, 1986).
9. Ronald Sukenick, *Doggy Bag* (Boulder: Northwestern University Press, 1994), p. 7.
10. Short, *Exploring the Language of Poetry, Plays and Prose*, p. 54.
11. Michael Toolan, *Language in Literature: An Introduction to Stylistics* (London: Arnold, 1998).
12. Sukenick, *Doggy Bag*, p. 9.
13. Raymond Federman, *Surfiction: Fiction Now and Tomorrow*, 2nd rev. edn (Athens: Ohio University Press, 1981).
14. See Brian McHale, *Postmodernist Fiction* (London: Routledge, 1987) for a review of this movement.
15. Federman (ed.), *Surfiction: Fiction Now and Tomorrow*, p. 142.
16. Donald Barthelme, 'Not-Knowing', in Donald Barthelme and John Barth, *Not-Knowing: The Essays and Interviews of Donald Barthelme*, ed. Kim Herzinger (New York: Random House, 1997).
17. Ibid. p. 12.
18. Ibid. p. 15.
19. Ibid.
20. Donald Barthelme, *Sixty Stories* (New York: Penguin Classics, 2005), p. 29.
21. For discussion of this approach to literary characterisation, see Jonathan Culpeper, *Language and Characterisation: People in Plays and Other Texts* (Harlow: Longman, 2001).
22. Barthelme, *Sixty Stories*, p. 57.
23. Ibid. p. 60.
24. Ibid.
25. Ibid. p. 90.
26. Ron Carter and Walter Nash, *Seeing Through Language: A Guide to Styles of English Writing* (Oxford: Blackwell, 1990).
27. Samuel Beckett, *Trilogy: 'Molloy', 'Malone Dies', 'Unnameable'* (London: Calder Publications, 1973), p. 179.
28. Marie-Laure Ryan, *Possible Worlds, Artificial Intelligence, and Narrative Theory* (Bloomington: Indiana University Press, 1992)

29. Beckett, *Trilogy*, p. 289.
30. Samuel Beckett, 'Lessness' (1970). Available at <http://www.samuel-beckett.net/lessness.html> (last accessed 15 April 2018).
31. Monica Fludernik, *Towards a 'Natural' Narratology* (London: Routledge, 1996); Jan Alber, "The 'Moreness' or 'Lessness' of 'Natural' Narratology: Samuel Beckett's 'Lessness' Reconsidered", *Style*, 36.1 (2002): 54–75.
32. Fludernik, *Towards a 'Natural' Narratology*, p. 30.
33. Alber, 'The "Moreness" or "Lessness"'.
34. Will Self, *Psychogeography* (New York: Bloomsbury, 2007), p. 11.
35. Guy-Ernest Debord, 'Introduction to a Critique of Urban Geography' (1995). Available at <http://library.nothingness.org/articles/SI/en/display/2> (last accessed 15 April 2018).
36. Ken Knabb (ed.), *Situationist International Anthology* (Berkeley: Bureau of Public Secrets, 2006), pp. 50–4.
37. 'Ergodic' is a term coined by Espen Aarseth (1997) to describe literary texts which are resistant to straightforward engagement on the part of the reader. In Aarseth's terms, 'non-trivial effort is required to traverse the text'.
38. Robert Macfarlane, 'Iain Sinclair's Struggles with the City of London', *The Guardian*, 15 July 2011. Available at <https://www.theguardian.com/books/2011/jul/15/ghost-milk-iain-sinclair-olympics> (last accessed 15 April 2018).
39. Iain Sinclair, *Lud Heat: A Book of the Dead Hamlets* (Cheltenham: Skylight Press, 2012), p. 68.
40. Iain Sinclair, *Suicide Bridge* (Cheltenham: Skylight Press, 2013).
41. Julian Wolfreys, *Writing London: Volume 2: Materiality, Memory, Spectrality* (New York: Springer, 2011), pp. 161–2 (emphasis added).
42. Propp, *Morphology of the Folk Tale*.
43. A. S. Byatt, *The Djinn in The Nightingale's Eye: Five Fairy Stories* (London: Vintage, 1995), pp. 71–2.
44. Quoted in Sarah Gooderson, 'Writing a Tale', *The Guardian*, 22 September 2005. Available at <https://www.theguardian.com/books/2005/sep/22/fiction.asbyatt> (last accessed 15 April 2018).
45. A. S. Byatt, *Elementals: Stories of Fire and Ice* (London: Chatto & Windus, 1998), p. 133.
46. Ibid. pp. 134–5.
47. Ibid. p. 182.
48. Patricia Waugh, *Metafiction: The Theory and Practice of Self-conscious Fiction* (London: Routledge, 1984).
49. Roger Caillois, *The Kraken: Experiments in the Logic of the Imaginative*, trans. Brigitte Weidmann (Munich: Carl Hanser, 1986).
50. Joanna Gavins, *Text World Theory: An Introduction* (Edinburgh: Edinburgh University Press, 2007).
51. Lyn Hejinian, 'The Rejection of Closure' (1985). Available at <https://www.poetryfoundation.org/resources/learning/essays/detail/69401> (last accessed 15 April 2018).
52. Robert Coover, *Pricksongs and Descants* (London: Penguin Modern Classics, 2011).

Bibliography

Aarseth, Espen, *Cybertext: Perspectives on Ergodic Literature* (Baltimore: Johns Hopkins University Press, 1997).
Alber, Jan, 'The "Moreness" or "Lessness" of "Natural" Narratology: Samuel Beckett's "Lessness" Reconsidered', *Style*, 36.1 (2002): 54–75.

Barthelme, Donald, *Sixty Stories* (New York: Penguin Classics, 2005).
Barthelme, Donald and John Barth, *Not-Knowing: The Essays and Interviews of Donald Barthelme* (New York: Random House, 1997).
Beckett, Samuel, 'Lessness' (1970), <http://www.samuel-beckett.net/lessness.html> (last accessed 15 April 2018).
— *Trilogy: 'Molloy', 'Malone Dies', 'The Unnameable'* (London: Calder Publications, 1973).
Booth, Wayne C., *The Rhetoric of Fiction* (Chicago: The University of Chicago Press, 1983).
Byatt, A. S., *The Djinn in The Nightingale's Eye: Five Fairy Stories* (London: Vintage, 1995).
— *Elementals: Stories of Fire and Ice* (London: Chatto & Windus, 1998).
Caillois, Roger, *The Kraken: Experiments in the Logic of the Imaginative*, trans. Brigitte Weidmann (Munich: Carl Hanser, 1986).
Carter, Ron and Walter Nash, *Seeing Through Language: A Guide to Styles of English Writing* (Oxford: Blackwell, 1990).
Coover, Robert, *Pricksongs and Descants* (London: Penguin Modern Classics, 2011).
Culpeper, Jonathan, *Language and Characterisation: People in Plays and Other Texts* (Harlow: Longman, 2001).
Culpeper, Jonathan, Mick Short and Peter Verdonk, *Exploring the Language of Drama: From Text to Context* (London: Routledge, 1998).
Debord, Guy-Ernest, 'Introduction to a Critique of Urban Georgraphy' (1995), <http://library.nothingness.org/articles/SI/en/display/2> (last accessed 15 April 2018).
Federman, Raymond (ed.), *Surfiction: Fiction Now and Tomorrow*, 2nd rev. edn (Athens: Ohio University Press, 1981).
Fludernik, Monika, *Towards a 'Natural' Narratology* (London: Routledge, 1996).
Gavins, Joanna, *Text World Theory: An Introduction* (Edinburgh: Edinburgh University Press, 2007).
Genette, Gérard, *Narrative Discourse: An Essay in Method* (New York: Cornell University Press, 1983).
Gooderson, Sarah, 'Writing a Tale', *The Guardian*, 22 September, <https://www.theguardian.com/books/2005/sep/22/fiction.asbyatt> (last accessed 15 April 2018).
Hejinian, Lyn, 'The Rejection of Closure' (1985), <https://www.poetryfoundation.org/resources/learning/essays/detail/69401> (last accessed 15 April 2018).
Josipovici, Gabriel, *Mobius the Stripper: Stories and Short Plays* (London: Victor Gollancz, 1974).
Knabb, Ken (ed.), *Situationist International Anthology* (Berkeley: Bureau of Public Secrets, 2006).
Kutnik, Jerzy, *The Novel as Performance: The Fiction of Ronald Sukenick and Raymond Federman* (Carbondale: Southern Illinois University Press, 1986).
Macfarlane, Robert, 'Iain Sinclair's Struggles with the City of London', *The Guardian*, 15 July, <https://www.theguardian.com/books/2011/jul/15/ghost-milk-iain-sinclair-olympics> (last accessed 15 April 2018).
McHale, Brian, *Postmodernist Fiction* (London: Routledge, 1987).
Phelan, James, *Living to Tell about It: A Rhetoric and Ethics of Character Narration* (Ithaca, NY: Cornell University Press, 2004).
Propp, Vladimir, *Morphology of the Folk Tale*, ed. Louis A. Wagner, trans. Laurence Scott (Austin: University of Texas Press, 1968).
Ryan, Marie-Laure, *Possible Worlds, Artificial Intelligence, and Narrative Theory* (Bloomington: Indiana University Press, 1992).
Scott, Jeremy, *Creative Writing and Stylistics: Creative and Critical Approaches* (Basingstoke: Palgrave Macmillan, 2013).
Self, Will, *Psychogeography* (New York: Bloomsbury Publishing, 2007).

Short, Mick, *Exploring the Language of Poetry, Plays and Prose* (Harlow: Longman Pearson, 1996).
Sinclair, Iain, *Lud Heat: A Book of the Dead Hamlets* (Cheltenham: Skylight Press, 2012).
— *Suicide Bridge* (Cheltenham: Skylight Press, 2013).
Stockwell, Peter and Sara Whiteley, *The Cambridge Handbook of Stylistics* (Cambridge: Cambridge University Press, 2014).
Sukenick, Ronald, *Doggy Bag* (New York: Northwestern University Press, 1994).
Toolan, Michael, *Language in Literature: An Introduction to Stylistics* (London: Arnold, 1998).
Waugh, Patricia, *Metafiction: The Theory and Practice of Self-conscious Fiction* (London: Routledge, 1984).
Wolfreys, Julian, *Writing London: Volume 2: Materiality, Memory, Spectrality* (New York: Springer, 2011).

13

The War Story

Adam Piette

The brevity of the short story lends itself to war narratives, one would have thought, because of the suddenness of war's violence and the traumatic singularity of the battlefield event. And yet, in literary terms, war found expression in large scale narratives, the saga text of mythology (*Cath Maige Tuired*), the epic poem (the *Illiad*, the *Aeneid*), the detailed history (Thucydides' *History of the Peloponnesian War*), the gigantic Romance (*Le Morte d'Arthur*), the endless ballad (*Chevy Chase*), the epic drama film (*Birth of a Nation*). However, looked at more closely, these texts break up into discrete episodes and tales, and each tale zeroes in on a scene so powerful or strange that it effectively splits off from the epic form it is nestled within, releasing its own vivid meanings as an isolated story event. One thinks of Achilles dragging the body of Hector round the walls of Troy; the brothers Balin and Balan killing each other unwittingly; Aeneas witnessing the death of Priam. These nodal events cohere as war stories, tellable, iconic, detached. The war story as short story might arguably issue from the epic as if broken from it as fragment; retaining the epic's scope as though it were secreted into the violent detail. This secret intensity need not have to do with representativeness, necessarily. Part of the mystery of war stories often lies in the ways they can block easy symbolism because of the uncanny horror of their core events. And yet the war story's central event does carry its significances at such a pitch that it will often summon up an alienating otherness of sorts from the dark edges of the short form that reads and feels as though epic were being assumed as environment. This chapter will look at the war story from a number of different major conflict zones to track the interrelation of short story form and war, in particular hoping to define the war story in terms of the variety of its sub-genres: the war story as yarn, traumatic dreamwork, metafictional enigma, historical and cultural document, witness record, epic-lyric fragment, propaganda text, dramatic newspaper story, wartime sketch or diary entry, soldier's tale, meditation on violence and death in the world. The chapter will draw on examples from such writers as Ambrose Bierce, Louisa May Alcott, Stephen Crane, Sapper, Elizabeth Bowen, Tim O'Brien, Shusaku Endo, Bao Ninh and others, and will consider how these writers have exploited the formal properties of the short story and the short story cycle in representing conflict and its social, cultural and ideological consequences.

The rise of the short story as a popular genre is linked to the rapid expansion of the periodical press in the late nineteenth century as paper taxes were repealed, middle-class readerships boomed, and the appetite for sensational genre fiction accompanied high art proto-modernist experiments in form. The genre received its most significant boost in the United States. As Kenneth Price and Susan Belasco Smith put it, 'by the 1870s, the inexpensive weekly magazines, an estimated 4,295 of them, had a combined circulation of 10.5 million', that is a third of the entire population of the United States.[1] The periodicals favoured a mix of 'popular and elite forms',[2] and genre and literary writing meet in the short story form, favoured, inevitably, since serialisation had the effect of experientially presenting novels as short story cycles. Short stories were shorter in the States than was commonly the case in the more condensed novel tradition in the UK.[3] This has to do with the closer relationship of periodical presses to newspaper journalistic conventions. As Gary Hoppenstand has argued, looking at Ambrose Bierce's influence on the popularity of Gothic fiction in San Francisco, 'in contrast to European models, the American Gothic tale became sparser and less ornate, influenced by the evolving journalistic vernacular in a print media pressured by publication deadlines, considerations of space, and the changing tastes of an expanded readership'.[4] And it was the dissemination of Civil War stories which provided the staple of many of the magazines when turning to violent history for sensationalist genre fare.

The Civil War as it was fought had been narrated to the nation in the form of colourful and dramatic dispatches by front line war correspondents. Washington was close to many of the major battles and became the fulcrum for a horde of war writers, including Henry Adams at the *Boston Daily Advertiser*.[5] Many of the 'letters' from the battle scenes mixed news with short bursts of impressions, as though hosting the nuggets of real story. The *New York Tribune* correspondent at Antietam, George Smalley, lapses into Tennysonian / border ballad lyric: 'Back across the corn-field, leaving dead and wounded behind them, over the fence, and across the road, and then back again into the dark woods which closed around them, went the retreating rebels.' And lapses, too, into guilty spectatorship as he walked his horse through the cornfield after the battle:

> The dead are strewn so thickly that as you ride over it you can not guide your horse's steps too carefully. Pale and bloody faces are every where upturned. They are sad and terrible, but there is nothing which makes one's heart beat so quickly as the imploring look of sorely wounded men who beckon wearily for help which you can not stay to give.[6]

His account, telegraphed from Frederick, Maryland, was sent first straight to Lincoln at the War Department, desperate for news, and it was only then forwarded to his paper. These letters more than matched the military dispatches in speed, were similarly compromised by rumour, propaganda, misinformation; but were laced through with witness affect, storytelling zeal, the kernel of war story. And, as telegraphed texts designed for the tight compass of the newspaper page, they had to be economical, concise, packed with telling detail. This strange combination, of journalist economy with eyewitness colour, rhetoric and feeling, had an intoxicating effect, as though each reader were a Lincoln at the end of a telegraph line: and arguably generated the ways and means of the war story genre. The dispatch was a hybrid style that forms the groundwork of the tales of Ambrose Bierce, who had fought in the war as a scout and topographer. He adapted the correspondent blend of newspaper economy of means (boosted by a rhetoric of suspense to simulate wartime 'telegraph' urgency) with rhetorical shows of sensational emotion that zero in, not on patriotic feeling, but on an eyewitness's shock, guilt, cynical war-weariness. He also enhanced the storytelling fictionalising of the dispatch by overt and stagy Gothic effects. The fictionality of these manoeuvres is deliberate: it is designed to make the war story recall the correspondent's allusive drawing on other genres, like Smalley lapsing into uncanny lyric. But in so doing it releases and reveals the allegorising power of the core violent event as witnessed by the imagination. Just as Smalley wading through the dead and dying on his horse at Antietam resembles Dante on his boat in hell, so does Bierce Gothicise in order to fathom the uncanny meanings of the war scene. To tell the tale of the horrors of Chickamauga, Bierce invents a runaway child who accidentally falls upon maimed and disfigured soldiers dragging themselves to a creek to drink. The child cannot understand what he sees, and plays at war as he is wont, riding the crawling men, leading them to the water as play general. The boy's unfeeling gaze on the horrifically destroyed bodies is eerie:

> He moved among them freely, going from one to another and peering into their faces with childish curiosity. All their faces were singularly white and many were streaked and gouged with red. Something in this – something, too, perhaps, in their grotesque attitudes and movements – reminded him of the painted clown whom he had seen last summer in the circus.[7]

The child takes on the affectlessness of the war-numbed combatant, but also the attitude of the war-story-reading public, animated by prurient though innocent curiosity, enjoying the suffering as odd, grotesque, a scary-comic entertainment, merely. Bierce also, just by recording with such vivid concision the ghastly scene, releases cartoon-like satirical meaning: the poor men destroyed by the Civil War were drawn to their deaths by generals playing at soldiers, ridden by cruel little boys with their heartless war games. The poised cruelty of Bierce's own stylishness is self-confessedly complicit in the game, also: as survivor remembering, he moves among the dead too freely, and profits from the shocking display of the dead men's wounds and 'grotesque attitudes'.

Bierce has a sophisticated sense, moreover, of the short story form as an ideal vehicle for war story: many of his tales focus, with a bold metafictionality, on wartime as traumatic experiencing of violence. That experiencing telescopes temporality into concentrated quanta: wartime at the battlefront, for Bierce, is time experienced at crazy intensity so that it slows, the mind registering a multiplexing of detail, a concentrate of feeling, fantasy and sensation that is pure war story, dispatches from the edge of reason where time consciousness itself is warped and traumatised. In 'An Occurrence at Owl Creek Bridge', a bridge-saboteur is about to be hung and imagines a full-scale miraculous escape in the seconds it takes before he dies. The reader is fooled into believing the escape is the real story, only to be rudely awakened to the harsh fact of death at the close.[8] The effect is both to bolster a sense of Bierce's miracle-working narrative powers, but also to demonstrate the confabulation of wartime; the compression of long *syuzhet* time into brief chronological *fabula*-temporality – the immense psychological pressure generated by the violence, in other words, has triggered tachypsychia (distortion of perceived time).[9] But Bierce is also feeding into his tale the very brevity of the short story form: or rather its brevity is being reflected upon as revelatory of the distinction between real temporal experiencing of time and narrative textual temporality: 'these thoughts, which have here to be set down in words, were flashed into the doomed man's brain rather than evolved from it'.[10]

In 'A Son of the Gods: A Study in the Present Tense', wartime coalesces round the extraordinary bravery of a single horse rider who offers to scout for the army on his own to save the lives of the skirmishers. The present tense of the style heightens the focus on the specific incident as temporal experience, with the uncanny attention fostered by war's strangeness (the story opens with Bierce noting how 'curiously we had regarded everything' owned by the invisible enemy).[11] The whole army watching the gallant cavalryman is riveted in what Bierce calls 'a new kind of "attention", each man in the attitude in which he was caught by the consciousness of what is going on'.[12] And the very distance from which the army observes, wrapt as they are in this new attention, slows what is seen to what one might call 'war story time', a temporality decelerated down to the aesthetic reading speed of a hungry detail-consuming, baitedly suspenseful and death-entranced readership. The army collectively watching the young man die is superimposed on Bierce's numberless collective readers consuming his war story time.

In 'One of the Missing', Bierce contrives a situation whereby a scout topographer like he had been during the war is trapped by a shellburst in a cabin, his gun cocked and aiming at his forehead. The 4,600-word story spends 2,700 of them in Jerome Searing's mind as he wrestles with the mental torment of his own fear facing the barrel of his own weapon: for the reader that stretch of time, though in short story form, seems to take up hours of imagined storytime. The tale ends with the discovery of the body and a noting of the time by the officer: 'Six o'clock and forty minutes' – earlier we have been told the shell that trapped Jerome had struck at 6.18: so in clockwork terms, those 2,700 words occupy a mere twenty-two minutes. Bierce plays with the paradox of the war story, its fusion of packed emotional detail and economy of scale, and seduces readers into the new kind of attention being generated both by the war and by the post-bellum war story. What the story discovers is an eerie parallel between the war story's time paradox (we relish these very short tales so *slowly*) and the uncanny tachypsychia of the fear-crazed combatant: 'Here in this confusion of timbers and boards is the sole universe. Here is immortality in time – each pain an everlasting life. The throbs tick off eternities.'[13]

Wartime as tachypsychic proximity to death is too easily associated with battlefield experiences. The Civil War stories of Louise May Alcott, who served as a nurse in the war, reveal how the delayed deaths of combatants in hospitals after battle can trigger the same 'slow storytime' temporal disturbance. Her moving and consciously melodramatic account of the protracted death of a Virginia blacksmith soldier, John, in 'A Night', takes the short story form as an opportunity to fuse periodical war story with sermon-length patriotic-religious homily. The fusion works because the blend of agonisingly extended deathbed experience with the brevity of the short story matches how sermons meditating on last things will dwell at length on the moment of death. The unnatural death in wartime sucks in energies and conventions from rival genres, adopting and adapting them to the uncanny narrative drive it generates amongst its witnesses. Alcott's sentimentality draws strength, also, from the opportunity the war story offers to link levels of storytelling, extra-diegetic and diegetic. Her story's power leans on her character's own need to tell stories about his own terminating life. After one particularly poignant memory about his mother, the narrator remarks: 'A short story and a simple one, but the man and the mother were portrayed better than pages of fine writing could have done it.'[14] The fusion of homily and war story works, Alcott is saying here, because writing the tragically short simple stories left behind by war-foreshortened lives simply matches the way nursing the dying is a loving reception of deathbed storytelling.

The Civil War in the United States inaugurated the modern war story with the new media technologies and expanded reading public, its writers at the same time successfully preserving older sub-genres such as the homiletic tale. Stephen Crane's war stories are indebted to French naturalism for their candour about the unconscious motivations in extreme situations that unleash 'primitive' unconscious forces in a collective. The stories he wrote about the 1898 Spanish-American war in Cuba, which he had witnessed as a war correspondent for the *World*, combine naturalist psychology with the Bierce style, a potent combination. We have the same exuberance, colour, wit; Crane developing the sheer craziness of warfare to settle on the absurdity of the mind under fire. In a tale like 'The Sergeant's Private Madhouse', a sergeant Peasley has to appease a sentry, Dryden, driven insane by terror at his outpost. The sentry will not leave or allow the sergeant to move since it will draw Spanish guerrilla fire. A Bierce-like tachypsychia is generated: '[Peasley] became aware of the slow wheeling of eternity, its majesty incomprehensibility of movement. Seconds, moments, were quaint little things, tangible as toys, and there were billions of them, all alike.'[15] This little episode is forgotten after he drags the mad sentry back to the camp; but Dryden's insanity seems to infect the way the whole war is being registered, especially the surreality of night-time combat:

> Sometimes guerrillas crept so close that the flame from their rifles seemed to scorch the faces of the marines, and the reports sounded as if within two or three inches of their very noses. If a pause came, one could hear the guerrillas gabbling to each other in a kind of delirium.[16]

Crane's prose keeps things as close to the reader's mind's eye as the marines to the guerrillas; and the extreme psychology of the war's events is registered semi-comically, with a cool impersonality that allows for that precious war story resource, zest in the telling. And a naturalist attention to weird psychology is there in the acknowledgement of Dryden's panic as core to the war.

Another war story, 'A Episode of War', was written before Cuba in 1897, a Civil War story narrated as though with Bierce's eyewitness control. The story ponders the strange suddenness and uncanny experiential feel of casualty, and discovers modernist fragmentariness in the shock of it. A lieutenant is shot whilst distributing coffee, and the men in his platoon enter into a strange ritual of alternating gazes, at the distant wood from where the shot had been fired and at the wounded officer – their gazing enacts the semi-sacral magic of violence ('they gazed statue-like and silent, astonished and awed by this catastrophe').[17] The officer is locked into a similar shock, all that is his become outlandishly other ('[his sword] had of a sudden become a strange thing to him') as he becomes as though blessed by the uncanny grace conferred by his wound ('the power of [the wound] sheds radiance upon a bloody form'). The story follows him as he walks back through the lines to the dressing station, each thing seen witnessed with the same revelatory intensity: 'As the wounded officer passed from the line of battle, he was enabled to see many things which as a participant in the fight were unknown to him.'[18] Those things are like little snapshots, a general receiving a message just 'like a historical painting', the sight of men trying to control their horses under artillery fire, a battery swerving toward the right. Everything is seen as with an artist's insight:

> The battery swept in curves that stirred the heart; it made halts as dramatic as the crash of a wave on the rocks, and when it fled onward, this aggregation of wheels, levers, motors, had a beautiful unity, as if it were a missile. The sound of it was a war-chorus that reached into the depths of man's emotion.[19]

The lieutenant is suffering from shell shock, as we see later when he refuses medical aid and loses his arm: but that same shock is giving him visions of things, a proto-futurist sense of the war machine, a war aesthetic that sings of arms and the man. Crane's ability to summon this aesthetic, even without any combat experience, impressed contemporaries, not least Bierce. His command over the representation of war psychology is fused extraordinarily with a modernist war story technique of violence-induced impressionism, war-machine aesthetics related in a shell-shocked style of delirious witness, fragmentariness and episodic tachypsychia; yet never quite abandoning the absurdist comic tone that registers, with an amusement masquerading as shocked impersonality, the powerful heart-stirring emotions of warfare.

Crane's imagination registered and exploited the resemblances between the post-Bierce war story's fidelity to what is seen and felt in wartime and the psychological extremes that French naturalism was recording. The 1895 story 'A Mystery of Heroism' dwells on the collective sensations of a regiment forced to witness the struggle of a battery on a hill above them, and is written with the 'eye of the infantry' as its focalised core.[20] That collective experiencing of an episode of the war takes its time to register the psychological predicament: the soldiers stare as the blades of grass of the meadow around them, kin to them under the assault of the war machine, are 'torn, burnt, obliterated'. The predicament seems to be Crane's but is fashioned as a collective envisioning of the episode. When a shell strikes the grey ruin of a nearby farmhouse, they hear the flapping of the shutters as if during a 'wild gale of winter'; and this draws the regiment into an other world of apocalyptic insanity and vision:

> Indeed, the infantry paused in the shelter of the bank appeared as men standing upon a shore contemplating a madness of the sea. The angel of calamity had under its glance the battery upon the hill.[21]

The infantry appeared *to themselves* as men witnessing a madness of the sea. To them in their fear, the war machine assumes the eye of divine power, that might so easily see them next after it has dealt with the battery on the hill. When Crane does zero in on one man's experience – the mind of a foolishly brave infantryman, Collins, who risks his life to fetch water – then it is to dwell more intimately on and with the collective superstition and comic absurdity generated by war's terrors: 'So, through this terrible field over which screamed practical angels of death, Collins ran in the manner of a farmer chased out of a dairy by a bull.'[22]

Kipling's war stories of the Boer War record a growing disillusionment with belligerent propaganda which he had sponsored as war correspondent. Malvern Van Wyk Smith has correlated this disillusionment with an increase in narrative indeterminacy in the tales, as if Kipling were both acknowledging the breakdown of racist imperial ideology, and concealing the consequences from himself through obliquity.[23] This gathering distance from patriotic writing exploits the puzzling plurality and complexity of the modernist short story as it emerged from Russian and French models: so that, in the post-Boer War 1904 story 'Mrs Bathurst', for instance, an intradiegetic narrator tells the story of an infatuation and affair between Vickery and Mrs Bathurst that is relayed second hand, and occluded by Vickery's obsession with a random film that captures her at Paddington, an obsession which drives him to desert. The story ends with the enigma of two tramps fried by lightening discovered in South Africa, one of whom might be Vickery. Nicholas Daly relates the tale to the Boer War and the ghostly correlation between the war's distant and invisible trauma and cinematic channelling of romance.[24] It becomes a war story because of our own suspicions about Kipling's guilt at the war dead, and the potential crazy sacrificial sexual economy that drives war's lusts. That supposition of war guilt is retrospective, to a certain extent: based on the story of Kipling's loss of his son in the trenches, and the turn against his own propaganda role in savage stories like 'Mary Postgate'. The tale tells the story of Mary's adoption of a young man, Wyn, as substitute son, and, when he dies and she discovers a wounded German airman in her garden, she takes her revenge by gloating over him as he dies. The tale relates to atrocity stories of the Great War in its theatrical portrayal of Mary's Home Front hatred of the enemy. But it equally has great subtlety in the mounting hysteria and obsessive mania the story reveals as underbelly to her barely contained bereavement. She takes sexual pleasure in the airman's death; and this fanaticism is related to a savage freedom gained by her own grim determination to burn Wyn's things in a garden 'destructor'. Something of the shock of the short story form, that it gives us so much life so quickly only to so quickly end it, is written in to the cold-bloodedness of her sadistic bacchanal of murder and memory-obliteration. The war story has taken on board other comparably condensed sub-genres, such as the propaganda atrocity tale in wartime news, the psychological case study, and fused them into an unholy mix that both reveals war ideology at work in the unconscious, but also invites us to take guilty relish in collective acts of sadistic sacrifice too. The tale draws into its orbit other contemporary war stories about militarised thinking that cross sex and death, such as D. H. Lawrence's account of the killing of an officer by his orderly, in the 1914 'The Prussian Officer': a grimly frank tale about homoerotic bullying, hinting at rape and sadistic sex, that leads to murder followed by the orderly's death; as with 'Mrs Bathurst', the two bodies are displayed together, revealing the deep dynamic of war hierarchies for Lawrence.

More traditional war stories were produced by writers like 'Sapper' (pseudonym of H. C. McNeile), who turned his experience in the Royal Engineers into popular stories for the *Daily Mail*. What he specialised in were war story cycles which stitched together impressionistic scenes or presented typical trench characters or telling episodes. 'A Fortnight in France' fictionalises Sapper's own experiences of Ypres, and takes the form of a slowly evolving set of anecdotes that show a lazy rich-kid nonentity being toughened by the war. 'The Education of Bunny Smith' does a similar job of displaying, clearly for propaganda purposes, the ways a rather useless bank clerk becomes minor hero by learning 'the lessons of true leadership and unselfishness' at the Front.[25] But it is the sequence 'Seven Stories' which does real writerly work, with its first tale 'Morphia' accompanying a soldier as he dies in hospital, desperately imagining his nurse is his loved one. This is followed by a tale of a waster, an Irishman O'Shea, who redeems himself with some excellent action with a bayonet. The third tale stages a 'company idiot' so useless yet also redeemed by the 'religion of esprit de corps'[26] so that he dies trying to fix cut telegraph wire; and the fourth recounts the tale of a futurist artist commissioned to create a camouflaged tree thankfully destroyed by a shell. And so on: the sequence works to spread the same set of recruiting values across its different zones and topics. Sapper's technique sentimentalises the war, turns harsh conditions into fluent anecdote, wry fireside yarn, and propaganda tale. McNeile's journalistic glibness and patriotic zeal led him to channel his own experiences as easy-going recruiter lore; and agreeably censored the darker side to war's motivations.

It was not only Freudian psychology that encouraged a darker vision of the sexual drives running the war story: naturalism had discovered similar core drives in its representations. But it is true that the First World War in its magnitude and machinic apocalyptic power obliterated patriotic sentiment – like Wyn's things being burnt in Mary Postgate's destructor. Irish writing of the 1919–21 Irish War of Independence and the 1922–3 Civil War that followed blends ancient storytelling traditions and ultra-modern conflict. In the short stories of Frank O'Connor and Sean O'Faolain, civil war splits in identity are figured in the trope of two men on the run in the countryside. In O'Connor's 'September Dawn', two republicans on the run from the British, Keown and Hickey, act out the division, and in O'Faolain's 'Fugue', there are two men again on the run, reduced to one when Rory is shot by the Black and Tans; but the split persists, between the solitary imagination hunted by enemy and the unreadable landscape of the nation at war with itself. The memory of this psychic 'civil war', turning the Irish landscape into a war zone, both hostile enemy's country and loving-patriotic refuge, draws on Gaelic legends of the renegade outlaw mad king Sweeney on the run in the moors and hills and fields; and the runaways' encounter with kindly inspirational women at isolated farmhouses summons Cathleen ni Houlihan or the Spéirbhean figure of the Aisling vision poem, Ireland personified. These stories and the ways they modernise semi-ironically the dreamy sentimentalities of the Irish Revival (especially their revival of the visionary Gaelic allegorical tale) feed in to Irish modernism obliquely, pitching Joyce against Yeats in contestation over the meaning of the Irish war story.

With the Second World War and Irish neutrality, the Irish war story, for Elizabeth Bowen, turned to interrogate its own form as modernist, Irish, as national-mythological tale. In her introduction to *The Faber Book of Modern Short Stories* in 1937, she had allied the modernist short story, which she saw as specialising in 'an affair of reflexes, of immediate susceptibility, of associations not examined by reason', with experience of war; which explains, for her, the dominance of Irish and American short story writers in English – for their cultures have known war and civil war. Both nations are places where 'either sexual or political passion makes society unsafe', leading to cultures of 'high nervous tension', attributable to experience of war: 'The younger Irish writers have almost all carried arms; American civilization keeps the Americans, nervously, armed men.'[27] The Second World War, for Bowen, especially in Blitzed London which she witnessed first-hand, was a war of the unconscious; as she remarked in her postscript to the US edition of her wartime collection, *The Demon Lover*: 'It seems to me that during the war the overcharged subconsciousnesses of everybody overflowed and merged.'[28]

'The Demon Lover' is consciously Jamesian, reprising psychological ghost stories like 'The Jolly Corner' or *The Turn of the Screw*, featuring uncanny returns to abandoned houses and hauntedness which is undecideably mental or supernatural. Kathleen Drover returns in August 1941 to her 'shut-up house', under the gaze of 'no human eye', meeting the '[d]ead air' as she opens the door.[29] She receives a mysterious letter that is delivered to her from the deep past, a lover of twenty-five years back arranging a rendezvous: it triggers a nervousness in her that drives her to the mirror to check on her identity in time. The story shifts then back to the past moment being summoned by the writing: August 1916 and the time she said farewell to her soldier fiancé – the moment in a transitional space at the end of the garden, her looking back to house and family, making a sinister troth with him that they will meet no matter what. In order to stave off the fear of the supernatural, she takes comfort in the mundane reality of ringing for a taxi to carry her and her parcels to the train station. The comforting sense of the taxi driver emboldens her, but this feeling alternates with being spooked by the certainty that someone is heard leaving the house. Outside, signs of 'the ordinary flow of life' and she takes a taxi that seems strangely to know where she is going. The taxi is stopped suddenly, and the driver turns to stare at his passenger, then drives off as 'Mrs Drover' screams and screams.

The taxi might be taken to signal the modernist war story: its lethal machine mobility, the brevity of its journeys, the sense of being controlled by something driving you, its combination of technology and transitional power. In the taxi, Bowen concentrates her hybrid sense of the war story as both tight realist prosaic space of encounter with death and supernaturally expansive forcefield for unconscious dreamwork. The struggle between a brutal modernity and female psychology under war compulsions creates an unmistakeable Bowen hybrid: 'After that she continued to scream freely and to beat with her gloved hands on the glass all round as the taxi, accelerating without mercy, made off with her into the hinterland of deserted streets.'[30]

After the Second World War, late modernism spawned metafictional doubt about its own literary procedures with regard to the war story, following on from manoeuvres with form readable in high modernist tales like 'The Demon Lover'. In the wars of late modernity, the media channelling war's violence also channelled metafictional reflection, and it was with Vietnam that this came most clearly to consciousness, technically and culturally. Michael Herr's *Dispatches*, written, ironically, years after the conflict, take the form of New Journalistic creative non-fictional pieces that read like a sequence of short stories, stories based on his work as war correspondent for *Esquire* and *Rolling Stone*, 1967–8. Each dispatch ponders its own status within the Bierce tradition of creative war correspondence, and takes the measure of Vietnam's transformation by television and the immediacies of a news-mediatised warscape. As Mark Heberle has argued, *Dispatches* is 'non-linear, particularly in the catalogue of violent and ironic epiphanies titled "Illumination Rounds"',[31] and deliberately unpicks the capacity of any history to account for the war's immensities and surrealities with straight chronologies and smoothly long-winded storytelling. What the episodic, media-deranged and treacherous structure of the book encourages is less metafictional reflection in the technical sense, than a hyperawareness of lethal fictions and their crazy networking of death-entranced minds in-country. Herr becomes addicted to the war story, like everybody else, like, even, the dead themselves: 'After a year I felt so plugged in to all the stories and the images and the fear that even the dead started telling me stories.'[32] The war story through the attrition of dispatch after dispatch, interview after interview, reduces itself to this: 'a story that was as simple as it had always been, men hunting men, a hideous war and all kinds of victims'.[33] As Ty Hawkins argues, the fact of violent death is not only the essence of the war for the war correspondent but has an addictive, viral effect, a story-generating and story-fissional effect, isolating the druggy hit of each death story.[34] A typical hit is a fragmentary narrative without link either to past or future, but only to the text of annihilation as such. A violence-addicted Lurp (marine in a long-range reconnaissance unit) tells him this typical core war story: '"Patrol went up the mountain. One man came back. He died before he could tell us what happened".'[35] Herr waits for the story to be developed: 'I waited for the rest, but it seemed not to be that kind of story; when I asked him what had happened he just looked like he felt sorry for me, fucked if he'd waste time telling stories to anyone dumb as I was.'[36] War turning into story becomes narrative without beginning or end, arbitrarily end-stopped, chartless, barely communicable, formlessly simple in its fixation on violent death as broken episode: and so, as its own lethal Ur-fragment, becomes war story.

The American War in Vietnam caused immeasurable suffering to the Vietnamese, civilians and Viet Cong alike, with the quite mind-numbing bombing campaigns contributing to a death toll that Robert McNamara himself judged to be around 3.5 million. Vietnamese short stories that came out of the conflict and its long aftermath, either by Vietnamese writers or from the Vietnamese-American community, do not display the same postmodern tricksiness and ultra-mediatised surface, necessarily, but engage with the conflict using forms that draw on other conventions. In 1995, Wayne Karlin worked with Vietnamese editors Le Minh Khue and Truong Vu to produce *The Other Side of Heaven*, an anthology of post-war fiction by both Vietnamese and American writers. Bao Ninh has a story in the book, 'Wandering Souls', which tracks the same spookiness encountered by Herr with its representation of a shell-shocked veteran surviving into the post-war yet wracked by hypnagogic lucid dreams of the war dead, in his room, singing on the air, sequencing terrible war memories before his very eyes. The PTSD focuses on the sheer scale of the bombing, and on the endless dead blasted into the other dreamworld by the US war machine; here, from a litany of terrible reminiscences:

> And a rain of arms and legs dropping before him onto the grass by the Sa Thay river during a night raid by B52s. Hamburger Hill, after three days of bloody fighting, looked like a dome roof built with corpses. A soldier stepping onto a mine and being blown to the top of a tree, as if he had wings. Kien's deaths had more shapes, colors and reality of atmosphere than anyone else's war stories. Kien's soldiers' stories came from beyond the grave and told of their lives beyond death.[37]

The war machine commands the weather (lethal rain), controls the environment like a master-builder (bodies as bricks); commands like a godlike trickster, a supernatural agent directing the dead to generate war stories for the dreamer. The war story becomes a textual space for the scening of the war machine's dreams, just as it is an arena for the lethal spectrality of the war in Vietnam; Vietnam where death had undone so many, the postmodern wasteland where the victims of the B52s (so many dead) still crowd.

Bao Ninh's sense of the terrible, endless, broken sequences of war memories that modern warfare blasts into spectral being, and their spooky relation to traumatic war story, chimes with the haunted violent unreality of Vietnam in Tim O'Brien's fictions. His 1990 short story cycle, *The Things They Carried*, takes that unreality and bases upon it a trauma model of metafictionality that is, O'Brien might be said to argue, made by Vietnam. The stories were published separately in *Esquire*, *Playboy* and elsewhere between 1976 and 1990, then revised as a story cycle with each story following the characters in, and events experienced by, one infantry company.[38] The genius of the move from isolated war story to cycle lies in the attention to genre as traumatised; the 'they' of the title are a mini-collective, an aggregate of characters comparable to the eccentrics and wasters focused on by Sapper, yet their experiences do not quite ring true, and generate severe contradiction and falsehood as tale superimposes on memory of tale. O'Brien is not just exercising a postmodern slipperiness of fact and fiction, though that is the effect; it is more that the war story itself has somehow slipped its moorings under the pressure of the war's collective trauma, its lethal unreality functioning as a generator of destructive fictions within the minds and texts of survivor combatants. O'Brien's stories stage a fictive O'Brien as member of 'A' company and the tales have the vivid nightmarish shock and awe of eyewitness accounts – tales return again and again to recycling the deaths of key comrades-in-arms, Lavender, Kiowa, Lemon. Curt Lemon's death is eerily identical to one of the deaths witnessed by Kien in the Bao Ninh story:

> he took a peculiar half step, moving from shade into bright sunlight, and booby-trapped 105 round blew him into a tree. The parts were just hanging there, so Dave Jensen and I were ordered to shinny up and peel him off.[39]

The fact of the coincidence is supplemented by suspicion when Jensen starts to sing 'Lemon Tree' 'as he threw down the parts', and by the narrator's confession of the unbelievability of the story at this point; for he follows through with 'You can tell a true war story by the questions you ask.'[40] What emerges from the tissue of fictions and mock truths is that any naïve desire for these war stories to be true (because based on O'Brien's real experiences as an ex-combatant writer) is not only itself dangerous, because so gullibly blind to the warping fictions and lies of the American mission in Vietnam, but also misses the whole point of any war story: 'A thing may happen and be a total lie; another thing might not happen and be truer to the truth',[41] is the way the narrator puts it.

This is slippery since the story cycle reveals the myriad ways special pleading, guilt-oblation, traumatic condensation, fantasy, displacement and wish fulfilment twist and turn the war story from any textworld intradiegetic sense of true. O'Brien's war stories attend to odd little fragments that stick to the memory; to the Fantasyland that is the whole war effort such that combatants cannot remember what the real *is*; to the ways war story mimes war's targeting killing attention (like the gaze of Crane's angel of calamity): it is story which makes the dead talk. O'Brien's war storytelling turns inwards and thinks about war story as war's story-making power, generated partly by the fog of war: 'war has the feel – the spiritual textures – of a great ghostly fog, thick and permanent. There is no clarity.'[42] Without clarity, the 'sense of truth' is lost, a Conradian point: 'the only certainty is overwhelming ambiguity'.[43] The texture of the tales as we move through the cycle is made more menacing, and more shocking, somehow, by the raw fictiveness of the procedure, and by the bold satirical anarchic energy released on realising just how treacherous the war storytellers are in the collection. For war stories exploit the ambiguity and fog of war to tell it as it never quite was: so we have several versions of key deaths, for instance, which accumulate new detail as contradictions. The tour de force story is the death of Kiowa who drowns in a shit field (the unit camps on a field used for centuries as a village's latrine, rendered liquid by a firefight). Not only is the story too good or bad to be true ('we're in deep shit' and its many variants being so common a tag about Vietnam); even its allegorical truth falls down as an unconscionable number of his comrades confess to and evade responsibility for not saving Kiowa's life. Kiowa becomes part of the general waste that is Vietnam: the waste of life and the waste that the dead become in the wasting away of lives in the conflict. But what wastes away most of all is the very language of war story: storytelling simplicities, confession's plain style, the accent of integrity are all wasted by the in-your-face fog and shite of lying fictions that were the war effort en masse, collectively and neocolonially. Nothing can redeem that, and O'Brien turns the war story's weapons of creative-realistic representation, cleaned and prepped and handed on down by generations of war correspondent witness-writers since Bierce, against the genre's own brains and pulls the trigger.

Notes

1. Kenneth Price and Susan Belasco Smith (eds), *Periodical Literature in Nineteenth-Century America* (Charlottesville: University of Virginia Press, 1995), p. 6.
2. Ibid.
3. See Winnie Chan, *The Economy of the Short Story in British Periodicals of the 1890s* (London: Routledge, 2007).
4. Gary Hoppenstand's argument as summarised in Price and Smith, *Periodical Literature*, p. 14. See also 'Ambrose Bierce' in the same book, pp. 220–38.
5. See Henry Adams, *Henry Adams in the Secession Crisis: Dispatches to the Boston Daily Advertiser, December 1860–March 1861*, ed. Mark Joseph Stegmaier (Baton Rouge: Louisiana University Press, 2012).
6. As extracted in *Harper's Weekly*, 4 October 1862. Available at the Illustrated Civil War website < http://www.lincolnandthecivilwar.com> (last accessed 18 April 2018). See also HistoryNet website on Smalley and the battle. Available at <http://www.historynet.com/george-smalley-battle-of-antietam.htm> (last accessed 18 April 2018).
7. Ambrose Bierce, 'Chickamagua', in *Civil War Stories* (New York: Dover Publications, 1994), p. 43.
8. Bierce, *Civil War Stories*, pp. 33–40.
9. See Eric Haanstadf, 'Violence and Temporal Subjectivity', *Anthropology and Humanism*, 34 (2009): 71–82.
10. Bierce, *Civil War Stories*, p. 35.
11. Ibid. p. 47.
12. Ibid. p. 49.
13. Ibid. p. 60.

14. Louisa May Alcott, *Short Stories* (New York: Dover, 1996), p. 18.
15. Stephen Crane, 'The Sergeant's Private Madhouse', in *Wounds in the Rain: War Stories* (North Hollywood: Aegypan, 2005), pp. 38–42.
16. Ibid. p. 41.
17. Stephen Crane, 'An Episode of War', *Great Short Works of Stephen Crane* (New York: Harper and Row, 1965), p. 268.
18. Crane, *Great Short* Works, p. 270.
19. Ibid.
20. Ibid. p. 259.
21. Ibid. p. 261.
22. Ibid. p. 266.
23. See Malvern Van Wyk Smith, 'Telling the Boer War: Narrative Indeterminacy in Kipling's Stories of the South African War', *South African Historical Journal*, 41.1 (1999): 349–69.
24. See Nicholas Daly, *Literature, Technology, and Modernity, 1860–2000* (Cambridge: Cambridge University Press, 2004), pp. 68–75.
25. H. C. (Sapper) McNeile, *Sapper's War Stories* (London: Hodder & Stoughton, 1930), p. 299.
26. Ibid. p. 426.
27. Elizabeth Bowen, 'The Short Story', introduction to *The Faber Book of Modern Short Stories* [1937] (Stockholm: A/B Ljus Förlag, 1944), p. 11.
28. Elizabeth Bowen, 'The Demon Lover' postscript [1945], *The Mulberry Tree: Writings of Elizabeth Bowen*, ed. Hermione Lee (London: Vintage, 1999), p. 95.
29. Elizabeth Bowen, 'The Demon Lover', in *The Collected Stories of Elizabeth Bowen* (London: Vintage, 1999), p. 743.
30. Ibid. p. 749.
31. Mark Heberle, 'Vietnam Fictions', in Adam Piette and Mark Rawlinson (eds), *The Edinburgh Companion to Twentieth-century British and American War Literature* (Edinburgh: Edinburgh University Press, 2012), p. 207.
32. Michael Herr, *Dispatches* (New York: Knopf, 1977), p. 31.
33. Ibid. p. 214.
34. See Ty Hawkins, 'Violent Death as Essential Truth in *Dispatches*: Re-Reading Michael Herr's "secret history" of the Vietnam War', *War, Literature and the Arts*, 21.1/2 (2009): 129–43.
35. Herr, *Dispatches*, p. 6.
36. Ibid.
37. Bao Ninh, 'Wandering Souls', in Wayne Karlin, Le Minh Khue and Truong Vu (eds), *The Other Side of Heaven: Postwar Fiction by Vietnamese and American Writers* (Willimantic, CT: Curbston Press, 1995), p. 17.
38. James Nagel analyses O'Brien's use of the cycle to unify the tales of the company usefully in Chapter 5 of his *The Contemporary American Short-Story Cycle: The Ethnic Resonance of Genre* (Baton Rouge: Louisiana State University Press, 2004).
39. Tim O'Brien, *The Things They Carried* (London: Flamingo, 1991), p. 78.
40. Ibid. p. 79.
41. Ibid.
42. Ibid. p. 78.
43. Ibid.

Bibliography

Adams, Henry, *Henry Adams in the Secession Crisis: Dispatches to the Boston Daily Advertiser, December 1860–March 1861*, ed. Mark Joseph Stegmaier (Baton Rouge: Louisiana University Press, 2012).

Alcott, Louisa May, *Short Stories* (New York: Dover, 1996).
Bierce, Ambrose, *Civil War Stories* (New York: Dover Publications, 1994).
Bowen, Elizabeth, 'The Short Story', introduction to *The Faber Book of Modern Short Stories* [1937] (Stockholm: A/B Ljus Förlag, 1944), pp. 7–19.
— *The Collected Stories of Elizabeth Bowen* (London: Vintage, 1999).
— *The Mulberry Tree: Writings of Elizabeth Bowen*, ed. Hermione Lee (London: Vintage, 1999).
Chan, Winnie, *The Economy of the Short Story in British Periodicals of the 1890s* (London: Routledge, 2007).
Crane, Stephen, *Great Short Works of Stephen Crane* (New York: Harper and Row, 1965).
— *Wounds in the Rain: War Stories* (North Hollywood: Aegypan, 2005).
Daly, Nicholas, *Literature, Technology, and Modernity, 1860–2000* (Cambridge: Cambridge University Press, 2004).
Haanstadf, Eric, 'Violence and Temporal Subjectivity', *Anthropology and Humanism*, 34 (2009): 71–82.
Hawkins, Ty, 'Violent Death as Essential Truth in *Dispatches*: Re-Reading Michael Herr's "secret history" of the Vietnam War', *War, Literature and the Arts*, 21.1/2 (2009): 129–43.
Heberle, Mark, 'Vietnam Fictions', in Adam Piette and Mark Rawlinson (eds), *The Edinburgh Companion to Twentieth-century British and American War Literature* (Edinburgh: Edinburgh University Press, 2012), pp. 205–13.
Herr, Michael, *Dispatches* (New York: Knopf, 1977).
Hoppenstand, Gary, 'Ambrose Bierce and the Transformation of the Gothic Tale in the Nineteenth-Century American Periodical', in Kenneth Price and Susan Belasco Smith (eds), *Periodical Literature in Nineteenth-Century America* (Charlottesville: University of Virginia Press, 1995), pp. 220–38.
Karlin, Wayne, Le Minh Khue and Truong Vu (eds), *The Other Side of Heaven: Postwar Fiction by Vietnamese and American Writers* (Willimantic, CT: Curbston Press, 1995).
Kipling, Rudyard, *War Stories and Poems*, ed. Andrew Rutherford (Oxford: Oxford University Press, 1999).
Lawrence, D. H., *The Prussian Officer and Other Stories*, ed. John Worthen (London: Penguin, 1995).
McNeile, H. C. (Sapper), *Sapper's War Stories* (London: Hodder & Stoughton, 1930).
Nagel, James, *The Contemporary American Short-Story Cycle: The Ethnic Resonance of Genre* (Baton Rouge: Louisiana State University Press, 2004).
O'Brien, Tim, *The Things They Carried* (London: Flamingo, 1991).
O'Connor, Frank, 'September Dawn', *The Best of Frank O'Connor* (New York: Alfred A. Knopf, 2009).
O'Faolain, Sean, *The Collected Stories of Sean O'Faolain*, vol. 1 (London: Constable, 1980).
Price, Kenneth, and Susan Belasco Smith (eds), *Periodical Literature in Nineteenth-Century America* (Charlottesville: University of Virginia Press, 1995).
Smith, Malvern Van Wyk 'Telling the Boer War: Narrative Indeterminacy in Kipling's Stories of the South African War', *South African Historical Journal*, 41.1 (1999): 349–69.

Part IV

Placing the Short Story

14

Regionalism and the Short Story

Lucy Evans

'The hurricane does not roar in pentameters', Kamau Brathwaite remarked in *History of the Voice* (1984). 'And that's the problem: how do you get a rhythm which approximates the natural experience, the environmental experience?'[1] Brathwaite's comments stress the need for a form of poetry which is appropriate to the social, cultural and natural environment of the Caribbean. However, the questions he raises are equally pertinent to anglophone Caribbean short fiction. The iambic pentameter, in Brathwaite's estimation, 'carries with it a certain kind of experience'[2] from outside the region; something similar can be said for the formal conventions of the modern European and American short story. Building on Brathwaite's claims, and with a focus on anglophone Caribbean short stories, this chapter asserts the value of reading literary forms – and particularly the form of the short story – in regional terms.

Short story theory has not, as yet, sufficiently engaged with the variety of cultural traditions which constitute the genre, although recent research has begun to broaden the range of reference. In formalist studies of the 1960s and 1970s, some of the characteristics of European and American short stories were regarded as distinguishing features of the form more broadly and were therefore presented as universally applicable.[3] Subsequent criticism has moved away from such taxonomies, and from attempts to define the 'short story proper',[4] and has instead positioned short stories within the contexts of specific modes or periods, such as modernism and modernity.[5] While many of these studies do not make essentialising claims about the nature or the function of the short story, they nevertheless often incorporate a falsely universalising rhetoric through their use of such labels as 'modernist short fiction' and 'the modern short story'. In doing so, they present a particular tradition of short story writing (invariably a tradition of European and American writers) as *the* tradition rather than as one of several traditions which have developed in different parts of the world. The centrality of Euro-American literary culture to discussions of the short story is also demonstrated by the significant influence of Edgar Allan Poe, who is often seen as the progenitor and first theorist of the 'modern short story'.[6]

In his 1842 review of Nathaniel Hawthorne's *Twice-Told Tales*, Poe claimed that the short story's most important feature was 'unity of effect or impression', and proposed that this unity or 'single effect' could not be achieved in works 'whose perusal cannot be completed at one sitting'.[7] The enduring currency of Poe's ideas in short story theory does not allow for the variety of forms of prose writing that have evolved in other contexts around the world. It is over thirty years since W. H. New critiqued critical and theoretical debates of the genre, observing that 'most commentary does not adequately apply to the practice of the short story outside America, England and continental Europe'.⁸ New's pioneering work on Canadian and New Zealand writing, which corresponded with the emergence of postcolonial studies in the 1980s, drew attention to the need for critics to consider regional variations in the narrative mode, structure and patterns of short fiction. Relatively few studies of the genre have responded in kind. However, some critics have focused on short story writing in particular regions outside Europe and America;⁹ and others have taken a broader comparative approach. Jacqueline Bardolph's edited collection *Telling Stories: Postcolonial Short Fiction in English* (2001), for instance, includes sections on 'Canada', 'The West Indies', 'Southern Africa', 'India, Sri Lanka and the Diaspora', 'New Zealand' and 'Australia', while Maggie Awadalla and Paul March-Russell's *The Postcolonial Short Story* (2012) is geographically and culturally wide-ranging, covering short fiction from across several continents.

This chapter extends New's work, highlighting the regionally specific elements of anglophone Caribbean short stories. However, whereas New warns against the tendency of cultural critics to identify the distinctive characteristics of a region's literature, since 'to limit by region is to accept a form of geo-historical determinism that excludes any account of influence and impact from outside',¹⁰ this chapter contends that a focus on the regional dimensions of Caribbean short fiction need not preclude consideration of external influences. On the contrary, in a Caribbean context, any engagement with the idea of a regional aesthetic necessarily involves a concern with oral and literary traditions from other parts of the world.

The question as to what constitutes Caribbean regional identity has long occupied writers, artists and philosophers. The process of theorising a pan-Caribbean identity is a challenging task, complicated as it is by the region's history, topography and demographics. The archipelago's geographical fragmentation, compounded by political differences and the linguistic divisions generated by Spanish, French, Dutch and British colonial rule, has led to entrenched divisions between Caribbean territories. These territories contain further differences, and the distinct yet overlapping histories of colonialism, slavery and indenture, have meant that Caribbean nations are composed of various social and ethnic groupings. Writers and critics have approached the task of theorising Caribbean identity in different ways: some have promoted the concept of unity in diversity, and others have developed more complex models of association across difference.

In a 1997 study of Caribbean poetics, Silvio Torres-Saillant presented the region as ethnically and linguistically fragmented but possessing an 'underlying congruity' which distinguishes it from other places. Caribbean literature, Torres-Saillant argued, is 'one differentiated corpus with an internal logic of its own'.¹¹ In contrast, Antonio Benítez-Rojo and Édouard Glissant have each constructed models of 'Caribbean space' which, rather than adhering to an 'internal logic', are internally unstable (because of ethnic, national and linguistic divisions) and necessarily open-ended.¹² According to each of these theorists, the Caribbean defines itself multiply in relation to a number of external locations including Africa, Asia and Europe, as well as the neighbouring continents of North and South America.

The Caribbean archipelago is 'an island that "repeats" itself, unfolding and bifurcating until it reaches all the seas and lands of the earth', Benítez-Rojo remarked in *The Repeating Island* (1989).¹³ This idea of 'the repeating island' represents the archipelago as a chain, each island a repetition but at the same time different in some way. Benítez-Rojo explored the similarities between communities shaped by the same plantation economy; however, he also emphasised the differences – ethnic, religious, linguistic and political – which not only exist within a regional Caribbean identity but which also constitute it. The concept of the repeating island additionally alludes to the way Caribbean cultures repeat themselves globally, as the Caribbean diaspora spreads across other parts of the world. Benítez-Rojo consequently emphasised the unbounded character of the archipelago, which he saw as both a geographical formation and 'a cultural meta-archipelago without center and without limits'.[14] For Benítez-Rojo, the Caribbean is open to the outside world in a variety of ways – both in terms of its far-reaching influence on other cultures and societies, 'flowing outwards past the limits of its own sea',[15] and also in its ability to incorporate external influences as part of an ongoing process of creolisation.

Benítez-Rojo's notion of the repeating island resonates with Glissant's concept of a Caribbean identity that is as at once 'rooted and open';[16] for both theorists, the region's cultural specificity is negotiated through openness to and dialogue with the outside world. In *Poetics of Relation* (1990), Glissant described the rhizome, a concept appropriated from the work of Gilles Deleuze and Félix Guattari, as 'an enmeshed root system, a network spreading either in the ground or in the air'.[17] The mangrove plant, a species local to the Caribbean region and found in swamps and on shorelines, helps to illustrate Glissant's vision of intertwined peoples and cultures. According to Glissant's 'Poetics of Relation', where 'each and every identity is extended through a relationship with the Other', Caribbean identities are constituted through continually evolving relations with other cultures, both within and beyond the region; they are therefore both fluid and interdependent.[18] Glissant's image of the Caribbean as 'the estuary of the Americas', and Benítez-Rojo's proposal that 'the Antilles are an island bridge connecting, in "another way," North and South America', each conveys a sense of overlapping territories and draws attention to the region's flexible and indistinct boundaries.[19]

In a recent study of postcoloniality and short fiction, Maggie Awadalla and Paul March-Russell have considered some of the ways in which tensions between orality and the literary are played out in different cultural and historical contexts. To illustrate, Awadalla and March-Russell compare short fiction by recent European and American writers (where they suggest 'the form is shadowed by its oral past')[20] with contemporary African short fiction (where writers draw upon living and continually developing modes of a spoken tradition).[21] In the Caribbean, there is a similarly strong connection between contemporary oral and literary cultures, as Olive Senior acknowledges when she refers to the 'continued potency' of the oral as an influence on Caribbean writing.[22] The oral storytelling practices appropriated by the region's writers continue to flourish through many of its popular cultural traditions, including carnival and calypso.

Kenneth Ramchand has read the West Indian short story as 'the most distinctive literary product of the meeting of oral tradition and writing', noting its published precursors ('accidental fictions' to be found in early colonial writings) as well as its oral antecedents of 'song and story', such as anancy stories, stories of obeah and calypsos (all of which have African roots), and 'stories circulating among the descendants of Indians'.[23] Senior similarly observes that '"story" is where the oral and scribal traditions meet',[24] and explores the role of African Caribbean oral culture and 'the Western literary canon' in the shaping of her own style as a short story writer.[25] This is evident in her 1989 story collection *Summer Lightning*, where stories written in standard English alternate with stories written in Jamaican creole, and where modernist devices are used alongside narrative techniques derived from oral storytelling. Ramchand and Senior both suggest that there is something unique about Caribbean short fiction, forged as it is through the merging of various forms of story writing and storytelling, which differentiate it from other uses of the genre. Linking literary influences in Caribbean short fiction to Europe and America, especially, and oral influences to Africa and India, both writers note that the region's history is embedded in the aesthetics of this mode of writing. This in turn highlights the fact that narrative form – like language – is political for Caribbean short story writers.

This chapter analyses four stories out of a much larger body of anglophone Caribbean short fiction. The stories chosen are by writers from different places and backgrounds, each of whom bridges oral and literary cultures in different ways. Jean Rhys, Sam Selvon, Lawrence Scott and Nalo Hopkinson all negotiate multiple cultural traditions in their short story writing. In each case, the Caribbean region's social, cultural and ethnic diversity, generated by its complex history of colonialism, slavery and indenture, is reflected in the form as well as in the content of the stories. The discussion is roughly chronological, beginning with Rhys and concluding with Hopkinson, and the readings locate each story in relation to distinct national storytelling traditions – Dominican legend, Trinidadian calypso, and Jamaican folklore. At the same time, the chapter considers each writer's contribution to a regional aesthetic which, like Glissant's rhizome, is both rooted in the Caribbean and connected to other parts of the world. This aesthetic incorporates what Benítez-Rojo describes as a 'play of differences' of various kinds: national, social, racial, ethnic and gendered.[26]

Jean Rhys's 'Pioneers, Oh, Pioneers' is included in the collection *Sleep it Off Lady* (1976). Published after the period that is usually associated with modernism, the story nonetheless deploys formal and stylistic strategies that are typically associated with modernist literary practice.[27] In 'Pioneers, Oh, Pioneers', some of these strategies – limited perspective, for instance, symbolism, suggestion and narratorial compression – are adapted to fit the setting of late nineteenth-century Dominican society, and are combined with aspects of the island's oral tradition. 'Pioneers, Oh, Pioneers' focuses on the constraints and paranoias of white society in Dominica at the *fin de siècle*. The story's opening scene clearly establishes the split between the white and black communities. Two white girls walking up Market Street observe other women on the road: 'When Rosalie turned her head the few white women she saw carried parasols. The black women were barefooted, wore gaily striped turbans and highwaisted dresses.'[28] Here the seemingly minor detail of dress hints at deeper differences in the women's cultural identity, class background and relationship to the island. The elegance of the white women's parasols, and their function to protect light skin from the sun, is held in direct opposition to the informality of the black women's bare feet, and the close contact between their bodies and the natural world. Additionally, the emphasis on the bright colours of the black women's turbans, set against the unspecified colour of the white women's clothes, suggests a comparable contrast in demeanour between the flamboyance of the black community and the stiff reserve of the white community.

Clothing and colour perform a symbolic function in 'Pioneers, Oh, Pioneers', and provide a subtle reflection on the complex dynamics of Dominican society. Rhys's syntax is allusive and densely packed with meaning, and eschews descriptive commentary or lengthy explanatory passages. The symbolism attached to clothing and colour on the first page extends across the remainder of the story. For example, when the Englishman, Mr Ramage, sings 'baa baa black sheep', his choice of song reinforces the idea – which is already suggested by his clothing – that his unconventional appearance and behaviour marks him out as a black sheep in a white flock. Colour coding also associates Ramage with the black community, prefiguring his later marriage to a 'coloured girl'.[29] This marriage alarms the white community because it threatens to destabilise the strict hierarchies of race and class on the island. Ramage consequently alienates himself from the white – but also the black – community; and his eccentricities lead to isolation, breakdown and, ultimately, death.

Rhys's use of symbolism and suggestion makes 'Pioneers, Oh, Pioneers' a classic example of modernist short fiction; so does her deployment of the experimental technique of 'multiple points of view, all more or less limited and fallible'.[30] Although Rhys's story is narrated in the third person, there are numerous shifts in focalisation and perspective. The narrative voice is unstable, moving between the perspectives of the girl Rosalie, her father Dr Cox, and Mrs Lambton; what is more, towards the end of the story, the narrative voice fragments to include many of the spectators at Ramage's house on the night of his death:

> He went into the house and came out with a shotgun. Then stories differed wildly. He had fired and hit a woman in the front of the crowd ... No, he'd hit a boy at the back ... He hadn't fired at all, but had threatened them.[31]

The lack of consensus displayed in these accounts serves to amplify the tensions between narrative perspectives which have been building since the beginning of the story, tensions which prevent the reader from ever getting to the 'truth' about Ramage and the cause of his death. Significantly, the story does not include Ramage's point of view, and his character remains a construct of other people's comments and perspectives, as well as stories, letters, newspaper articles, gossip and rumour.

The story's inclusion of multiple voices and perspectives can be seen as an illustration of the modernist preoccupation with the process of storytelling, and with the power of stories to shape people's perception of and relations with one another. However, the mode and narrative style of 'Pioneers, Oh, Pioneers' also involves references to the practice of oral storytelling. For Senior, the social activity of gossip is an aspect of the oral tradition which inspires her writing. Senior compares the storytelling conventions of gossip to those of the 'folk song' and claims that '[a]s a short story writer I consider myself a gossip'.[32] As Elaine Savory points out, according to Rhys the 'core of the story' comes from 'Dominican legend',[33] and gossip is a key aspect of the storytelling process with many of the 'facts' that are presented about Ramage established through rumours which circulate within the white and the black communities. Senior explains how 'in traditional cultures, word and stone are symbolically interchangeable'.[34] In 'Pioneers, Oh, Pioneers', Rhys explores the same symbolic connection between words and stones in the scene at Spanish Castle on the night of Ramage's death, when a 'crowd of young men and boys, and a few women, had gone to Ramage's house to throw stones'.[35] The paragraph begins with a description of stone throwing, and ends with an account of the various stories the same crowd casts about Ramage's reaction to events that night. By aligning these two activities, Rhys invites the reader to consider the potentially harmful effects of gossip. 'Pioneers, Oh, Pioneers' portrays gossip negatively, focusing on its capacity to stir up tensions in a polarised society. However, the story also goes some way towards conveying the centrality of gossip – as an aspect of the oral tradition – to Dominican society and culture.

While 'Pioneers, Oh, Pioneers' gestures towards oral storytelling practices in its narrative mode and in its representation of the act of gossip, Sam Selvon's story 'The Cricket Match' is more heavily indebted to the patterns and practices of Caribbean oral culture. 'The Cricket Match' was published in *Ways of Sunlight* (1957). Half of the stories in *Ways of Sunlight* are set in Trinidad; the other half, which include 'The Cricket Match', deal with the experiences of West Indian immigrants in Britain. The influence of Trinidadian storytelling practices can be seen in Selvon's language choice and in his use of narrative strategies. In contrast to the standard English of 'Pioneers, Oh, Pioneers', the characters and the narrator of 'The Cricket Match' speak in a version of Trinidadian creole which is conveyed mainly through syntax and with the aid of idiomatic phrases and words.[36] Selvon's use of Trinidadian English gives the narrative a spoken rather than a written quality. This is enhanced by the story's anecdotal style, announced in the first sentence which begins with the words 'The time when . . .'.[37] This informal construction reinforces the impression of a told tale. Another aspect of the story's anecdotal style is its humour, and at the centre of the story is a joke: feeding off the hype surrounding the success of the West Indies cricket team in the 1950 Test Match at Lord's, a group of immigrants with little skill manage to beat an English team who play regularly and who take the game very seriously.

In an essay on the Indo-Caribbean short story, Frank Birbalsingh identifies humour as the 'most striking feature' of the narrative form, and relates this to Caribbean oral storytelling practices which involve '[l]ighthearted banter, jokes and irreverent wit'.[38] While 'The Cricket Match' is humorous on many levels, much of the story's comic force is derived from the context of the Test Match victory. This event, which marked a 'symbolic victory'[39] of colonised over coloniser as well as the actual victory of the West Indies over England, helped to initiate the flowering of a West Indian 'national consciousness' and is often considered a key moment in Caribbean history. As C. L. R. James points out in *Beyond a Boundary* (1963), cricket originated in Britain and incorporated a nineteenth-century code of conduct which included such qualities as restraint, loyalty, fair play and 'stiff upper lip'.[40] The narrator's suggestion that the West Indies cricket team have 'come to England to show the Englishmen the finer points of the game'[41] is therefore deeply ironic. His playful comment celebrates the triumph of the West Indies team in beating the English at their own game. In developing the comic elements of this story, Selvon draws on the 'tradition of lying, as in the boasting and grandiloquence of the tall tale', a tradition which Ramchand associates with Caribbean oral storytelling practices.[42] The stories Algernon and his friends spin about their knowledge of and proficiency in cricket can be categorised as tall tales, and this is confirmed through the narrator's use of the French creole word 'blague' (which means 'tall story')[43] when he describes how 'the boys' congregate in Algernon's flat to drink tea and engage in 'a lot of blague and argument'.[44] Encouraged by the success of the West Indies team, they invent increasingly implausible anecdotes, 'getting on as if they invent the game'.[45] While their cricketing skills may be questionable, Selvon invites the reader to appreciate their storytelling abilities.

Ramchand presents calypso as another significant component of Caribbean oral storytelling.[46] Calypso first emerged in Trinidad as the music of carnival. It was strongly influenced by African music, as Gordon Rohlehr explains in his study of the history and contexts of calypso in pre-independence Trinidad: '[T]he roots of the political calypso in Trinidad probably lie in the African custom of permitting criticism of one's leaders at specific times, in particular contexts, and through the media of song and story.'[47] Rohlehr alludes to the overlap of song and story in African oral cultures, and considers how this serves as a foundation for the calypsonian's dual role as both a singer and a storyteller. He also draws attention to the satirical function of calypso, where humour is often used as a vehicle for incisive social and political commentary. In 'The Cricket Match', calypso serves as an intertext and as a basis for Selvon's comic style; and Algernon is presented as a calypsonian figure. Referring to the progress of the West Indies cricket team, he asks his colleagues: 'you thought we didn't know how to play the game, eh? That is cricket, lovely cricket.'[48] Algernon then goes on to sing 'a calypso that he make up about the cricket matches they play'.[49] With the words 'cricket, lovely cricket', Selvon includes lyrics from 'Victory Test Match' (1950), a famous calypso by Lord Beginner inspired by the Test Match victory, and signals the place of this calypso as an important reference point for his story.

In 'The Cricket Match', Selvon combines the narrative devices of oral storytelling with the techniques of compression and economy which are particularly associated with the genre of the modern short story. In six pages, Selvon covers the full range of themes which are also explored, albeit in greater detail, in his celebrated novel *The Lonely Londoners* (1956). Despite its brevity, 'The Cricket Match' engages with serious and substantial issues such as geographic and cultural displacement, and the connections and the tensions between national, regional and diasporic identities. This brief sketch about cricket also charts an expansive geography and encompasses significant moments in Caribbean history, dealing as it does with the rise of the British Empire, the export of cricket to the West Indies, and the later association of this sport with a growing West Indian national consciousness within both regionally based and diasporic Caribbean communities. In this respect, 'The Cricket Match' exemplifies Ramchand's argument that Caribbean short stories are a 'product of the meeting of oral tradition and writing'.[50] Moreover, the story's oral qualities – conveyed through language, narrative strategies, comic tone and intertextual references – provide a crucial part of its anti-colonial politics.

Stylistically, Lawrence Scott's 'Ballad for the New World', which also draws on other genres, including memoir and prose poetry, is very different from 'Pioneers, Oh, Pioneers' and 'The Cricket Match'. Scott's story is the title story in *Ballad for the New World and Other Stories* (1994), and opens with the description of a snapshot of 'an all-American-kinda-looking guy'.[51] When this image is repeated later in the story, extra details are added: 'I remember him well', the narrator remarks, 'the all-American-kinda-looking guy on the steps of the sugar-cane estate bungalow with Mutt his dog. Broad-shouldered, his stare holds Baboolal: the white French creole with the Indian boy.'[52] These details convey the picture's, and the story's, rural Trinidadian setting, the young man's cultural background, the influence of American popular culture on his self-styling (his dog Mutt is named after the dog in the *Mutt and Jeff* comic strip), and the object of his 'stare' – an 'Indian boy' who is located outside the frame of the photograph. Each time the narrator describes the picture, he offers further embellishments and deeper insight into its context. Beginning with a focus on the life of his brother (the 'guy' in the snapshot), the narrator's reflections gradually extend outwards to incorporate the wider contexts of the narrator's family, Trinidadian culture and society, the history of the Americas, and world events.

In 'The Philosophy of the Short-story' (1901), Brander Matthews extended Poe's argument on the short story's ideal achievements of 'single effect' and 'unity of effect and impression',[53] arguing that a 'true Short-story' deals with 'a single character, a single event, a single emotion', and is 'complete and self-contained'.[54] 'Ballad for the New World' begins with a 'single character' and a 'single event' encapsulated by the snapshot; however, the narrator goes on to acknowledge the difficulty of keeping his story within these limiting parameters: 'You see, you start telling a story about a guy and then you get to telling a story about a time, a place, a people and a world.'[55] The snapshot provides a starting point for a story about Trinidad, its history, and its relationship to other parts of the world. Rather than capturing a single moment in time, the story presents the reader with a complex temporal framework which incorporates memories from the narrator's past as well as historical events from beyond his life span. It is temporally as well as spatially expansive, ranging from the sixteenth-century conquistadors' 'dream' of Eldorado to the heyday of the plantation, which is remembered with the phrase 'When cocoa was king';[56] it also spans the period from independence in the early 1960s to Trinidad's oil boom a decade later. The story additionally positions Trinidad in relation to a series of global events, including the Second World War and the atomic bombings of Hiroshima and Nagasaki.

In 'The Cricket Match', the influence of calypso is most evident in the story's tone and use of language; in 'Ballad for the New World', by contrast, the conventions of calypso inform the structure of the story. The refrain from Lord Invader's 1943 calypso, 'rum and Coca-Cola . . . working for the Yankee dollar', is quoted at the start of the story, and then again on almost every page; it is also repeated in the story's final line. This gives the narrative an episodic structure similar to that of a calypso, where verses are interspersed with a repeated refrain. 'Ballad for the New World' is also thematically linked to 'Rum and Coca Cola'. Lord Invader's calypso deals with the burgeoning sex trade during the Second World War as a result of the presence of a US naval base in Trinidad. Scott's story similarly refers to the 'Wallerfield American base Camp'[57] and deals with Trinidad-US relations more broadly. Lord Invader's refrain sometimes appears in the story alongside Scott's repeated phrase: 'We were in the shadow of America a long time, a long time.'[58] The story elaborates on this image of Trinidad overshadowed by America in various ways. It explores the considerable influence of American films and music on Trinidadians through references to such figures as Marlon Brando, James Dean, Errol Flynn, John Wayne, Elvis Presley and Frank Sinatra. At the same time, the story examines the unequal power relations between Trinidad and the US with its mention of a US-based oil company's neocolonial hold over Trinidad.[59]

Despite the story's critique of Trinidad-US relations, its alternation between calypso lyrics and allusions to American songs and films leads to a gradual entwining of these intertexts, and in doing so illustrates the extent to which American cinema and music have become part of Trinidadian popular culture. With its emphasis on Trinidad's relations with other parts of the world, as well as its multiple references to American and Trinidadian popular texts, Scott's temporally layered and richly allusive story is anything but complete or self-contained. Instead, like Benítez-Rojo's model of the Caribbean 'flowing outwards past the limits of its own sea',[60] the story strains against its compressed form, and in the process highlights Trinidad's openness to the world. Exploring connections between people, places, times and texts, 'Ballad for the New World' works towards a multiplicity rather than a unity of effect.

In *Skin Folk* (2001), Nalo Hopkinson finds another way of bridging oral and literary cultures through her rewriting of folk tales. Merging the Bluebeard folk tale with Jamaican folklore, Hopkinson's story 'The Glass Bottle Trick' draws on European and African Caribbean oral traditions. The story challenges the patriarchal values underpinning Charles Perrault's original Bluebeard tale, offering a feminist revisioning of the story which builds on other retellings, such as the title story of Angela Carter's *The Bloody Chamber* (1979); Hopkinson extends those retellings, however, by engaging with the power dynamics of race as well as gender within marriage. The setting of 'The Glass Bottle Trick' is geographically and historically non-specific but resembles contemporary Jamaica. It is told from the point of view of a young woman, Beatrice, who has given up her studies and the prospect of a career to marry a wealthy older man, Samuel. Beatrice is pregnant and is uneasy about telling her husband. Alone in their secluded house, which is 'miles away from the closest neighbours',[61] she finds the frozen bodies of his two previous wives, also pregnant, whose spirits Samuel has entrapped in two blue bottles. There are a number of parallels to Perrault's Bluebeard; for example, the setting of an isolated building, the wealth of the Bluebeard figure, his multiple previous wives and his current wife's youthfulness, and the mystery surrounding the locked room containing the murdered wives, the contents of which are revealed at the end of the story. However, there are also crucial differences which distinguish Hopkinson's story from Perrault's tale.

One of these differences is the setting. Hopkinson's story opens with an evocative description which recalls Brathwaite's *History of the Voice*: 'The air was full of storms, but they refused to break ... Another sweltering rainy season afternoon.'[62] The tensions within Samuel's and Beatrice's marriage are conveyed figuratively through this reference to tropical weather. The 'looming rainclouds',[63] which locate the story within the Caribbean, intensify the protagonist's sense of claustrophobia and foreboding as she prepares to inform her husband of her pregnancy. Architectural features of the house, such as its veranda and its 'white gingerbread fretwork',[64] are also characteristic of the region, and the guava tree in the garden further serves to localise the story. Another key difference is Hopkinson's inclusion in the story of mythical figures from Caribbean folklore. In the branches of the guava tree are two blue bottles which contain the spirits of Samuel's dead wives. While the detail of the murdered wives and the impression of 'cobalt light dancing through the leaves'[65] recall the original Bluebeard story, the status of the wives as duppies connects Hopkinson's story to Jamaican oral culture. A duppy is a 'malevolent spirit that may be kept in a bottle, to be released to do harm to somebody'.[66] As Senior explains, the 'concept of duppy is based on an African belief that man has two spirits, or souls', one of which 'lingers on earth' after death.[67] Hopkinson's deployment of Caribbean folklore enables her to retell the Bluebeard story in a way which keeps the murdered wives alive and positions them as potentially triumphant over the Bluebeard figure.

In Perrault's Bluebeard, the living wife is eventually saved by her brothers and subsequently uses Bluebeard's wealth to remarry. In Hopkinson's version, Beatrice accidentally frees the two duppy wives who re-enter the house and begin to resume bodily form by drinking their own blood. The story ends with the suggestion that the duppy wives might save Beatrice from Samuel by killing him; however, this is not certain. Unable to determine at whom their 'fury'[68] is targeted, Beatrice wonders 'would they take revenge on her, their usurper, as well as on Samuel?'[69] By writing these figures from Jamaican folklore into the Bluebeard tale, Hopkinson enacts a shift in the story's gender politics, introducing the prospect of female empowerment. The story's ambiguous ending, in contrast to the closure effected by a marriage in the original Bluebeard story, leaves open the possibility that Beatrice will regain autonomy over her own life.

Hopkinson further alters Perrault's Bluebeard by placing an emphasis on racial as well as on gender identity. Beatrice admires her husband's 'molasses-dark skin' and reflects how 'she had seen the moonlight playing glints of deepest blue in his trim beard'.[70] This reference invites us to compare Samuel with Perrault's Bluebeard. In Perrault's story the name 'Bluebeard' reflects the character's blue blood as a member of the French aristocracy. By contrast, despite his wealth, Samuel is excluded from his country's elite due to the colour of his skin. This leads to an internalisation of racial hatred: Samuel views himself as '[b]lack and ugly',[71] but admires the whiteness of Beatrice, who is of mixed race. In bed with her, he says '"Look how you gleam in the moonlight . . . Beauty. Pale Beauty, to my Beast."'[72] Beatrice responds to being named 'Pale Beauty' by calling Samuel 'Black Beauty'; if he appreciates the ways the moonlight illuminates her pale skin, she 'love[s] the bluish-black cast the moonlight lent him'.[73] Samuel recoils from this partly because he does not like her drawing attention to his skin colour, but possibly also because her observation alters the power relations underpinning their lovemaking, as he is cast as the object of her gaze. The politics of race and gender intersect in this crucial scene.

Hopkinson transforms the Bluebeard tale in 'The Glass Bottle Trick', resituating it within a Caribbean setting, referencing Jamaican folklore, and exploring the overlapping discourses of race and gender. Indeed, Hopkinson's combination of aspects of the European folk tale (Bluebeard, especially, but also Beauty and the Beast, as well as the nineteenth-century children's novel *Black Beauty*) with elements of African Jamaican folklore bears witness to the Caribbean's multiple cultural heritages. Despite the varying styles, backgrounds and settings of Rhys, Selvon, Scott and Hopkinson – Dominica, Trinidad, Jamaica and London – connections can be drawn between each of the stories in terms of themes and narrative strategies. In different ways, each of these stories incorporates elements of the Caribbean's rich practice of oral storytelling – a tradition which is itself influenced by varying strands of African and Indian oral cultures. Rhys's engagement with Caribbean oral storytelling can be identified in her use of gossip, for instance; Selvon's is especially evident in his deployment of language and humour; Scott's is apparent in his use of a Trinidadian calypso as a key intertext and as a structuring device; and Hopkinson's is manifest in her multiple allusions to Jamaican folklore. In addition, each of the stories draws on European and American literary conventions and storytelling practices.

To read these stories within a regional framework is not to homogenise them since, as Benítez-Rojo has remarked, it is the very existence of difference which 'make possible' the idea of a pan-Caribbean regional identity.[74] Nor does it restrict the scope, the reach or the interpretative possibilities of the stories, so long as we think in terms of Glissant's concept of Caribbean identities as at once 'rooted and open',[75] distinct from yet connected with other cultures and societies. Reading short stories in regional terms is not only viable, it is necessary if we are to recognise the different ways that cultural, social and geographic contexts have impacted on the style, the structure and the resonances of this literary form.

Notes

1. Edward Kamau Brathwaite, *History of the Voice* (London: New Beacon, 1984), pp. 9–10.
2. Ibid. p. 10.
3. See, for example: Ian Reid, *The Short Story* (London: Methuen, 1977); and Mary Rohrberger, 'The Short Story: A Proposed Definition', in Charles E. May (ed.), *The New Short Story Theories* (Athens: Ohio University Press, 1994), pp. 80–2.
4. Reid, *The Short Story*, p. 4.
5. See, for example: Clare Hanson, *Short Stories and Short Fictions, 1880–1980* (London: Macmillan, 1995); and Dominic Head, *The Modernist Short Story: A Study in Theory and Practice* (Cambridge: Cambridge University Press, 1992).
6. A 2003 collection of essays on postmodern approaches to the short story opens with the suggestion that 'Poe's chapter remains a critical touchstone for many scholars engaged in short-story theory.' Farhat Iftekharrudin, Joseph Boyden, Joseph Longo and Mary Rohrberger, 'Preface', in Farhat Iftekharrudin et al. (eds), *Postmodern Approaches to the Short Story* (Westport, CT: Praeger, 2003), p. vii.
7. Poe, 'Review of *Twice-Told Tales*', in May (ed.), *New Short Story Theories*, pp. 60–1.
8. W. H. New, *Dreams of Speech and Violence: The Art of the Short Story in Canada and New Zealand* (Toronto: University of Toronto Press, 1987), p. 4.
9. See, for example: F. Odun Balogun, *Tradition and Modernity in the African Short Story: An Introduction to a Literature in Search of Critics* (Westport, CT: Praeger, 1991); Bruce Bennett, *Australian Short Fiction: A History* (Brisbane: University of Queensland Press, 2002); J. H. C. S. Davidson and H. Cordell (eds), *The Short Story in South East Asia: Aspects of a Genre* (London: School of Oriental and African Studies, 1982); Reingard M. Nischik (ed.), *The Canadian Short Story: Interpretations* (Rochester, NY: Camden House, 2007); Lucy Evans, *Communities in Contemporary Anglophone Caribbean Short Stories* (Liverpool: Liverpool University Press, 2014); Lucy Evans, Mark McWatt and Emma Smith (eds), *The Caribbean Short Story: Critical Perspectives* (Leeds: Peepal Tree, 2011).
10. New, *Dreams of Speech and Violence*, p. 12.
11. Silvio Torres-Saillant, *Caribbean Poetics: Toward an Aesthetic of West Indian Literature* (Cambridge: Cambridge University Press, 1997), p. 18, p. 1.
12. Antonio Benítez-Rojo, *The Repeating Island: The Caribbean and the Postmodern Perspective*, trans. James E. Maraniss, 2nd edn (Durham, NC: Duke University Press, [1989] 1996), p. 3.
13. Ibid.
14. Ibid. p. 9.
15. Ibid. p. 4.
16. Édouard Glissant, *Poetics of Relation*, trans. Betsy Wing (Ann Arbor: University of Michigan Press, [1990] 1997), p. 34.
17. Ibid. p. 11.
18. Ibid.
19. Glissant, *Caribbean Discourse, Selected Essays*, trans. J. Michael Dash (Charlottesville: University Press of Virginia, [1981] 1989), p. 139; Benítez-Rojo, *The Repeating Island*, p. 2.

20. Maggie Awadalla and Paul March-Russell, 'Introduction: The Short Story and the Postcolonial', in Maggie Awadalla and Paul March-Russell (eds), *The Postcolonial Short Story* (Basingstoke: Palgrave Macmillan, 2012), p. 2.
21. Ibid. p. 3.
22. Olive Senior, 'The Story as Su-Su, the Writer as Gossip', in *Writers on Writing: The Art of the Short Story* (Westport, CT: Praeger, 2005), p. 50.
23. Kenneth Ramchand, 'The West Indian Short Story', *Journal of Caribbean Literatures*, 1.1 (1997): 23–4.
24. Senior, 'The Story as Su-Su', p. 42.
25. Olive Senior, 'Lessons from the Fruit Stand: Or, Writing for the Listener', *Journal of Modern Literature*, 20.1 (1996): p. 41.
26. Benítez-Rojo, *Repeating Island*, p. 21.
27. Some critics have positioned Rhys's fiction within a Euro-American tradition of literary modernism, while recognising that her work is in some ways at odds with this tradition. See, for example: Sylvie Maurel, *Jean Rhys* (Basingstoke: Macmillan, 1998); Thomas F. Staley, *Jean Rhys: A Critical Study* (London: Macmillan, 1979); Helen Carr, *Jean Rhys* (Plymouth: Northcote House, 1996); Coral Ann Howells, *Jean Rhys* (New York: Harvester Wheatsheaf, 1991).
28. Jean Rhys, 'Pioneers, Oh, Pioneers', in Stewart Brown and John Wickham (eds), *The Oxford Book of Caribbean Short Stories* (Oxford: Oxford University Press, 1999), p. 9.
29. Ibid. p. 12.
30. David Lodge, *The Modes of Modern Fiction* (London: Arnold, 1977), p. 46.
31. Rhys, 'Pioneers, Oh, Pioneers', p. 15.
32. Senior, 'The Writer as Su-Su', p. 50.
33. Elaine Savory, *Jean Rhys* (Cambridge: Cambridge University Press, 1998), p. 165.
34. Senior, 'The Writer as Su-Su', p. 50.
35. Rhys, 'Pioneers, Oh, Pioneers', p. 15.
36. Selvon's narrator and characters speak in a dialect somewhere between standard English and full Trinidadian creole, which is a mixture of English, French and various African languages.
37. Sam Selvon, 'The Cricket Match', in *Ways of Sunlight* (New York: Longman, [1957] 1987), p. 149.
38. Frank Birbalsingh, 'The Indo-Caribbean Short Story', *Journal of West Indian Literature*, 12.1–2 (2004): 123; 126.
39. Stuart Hall, 'Calypso Kings', *The Guardian*, Friday Review, 28 June 2002. Available at <www.theguardian.com/culture/2002/jun/28/nottinghillcarnival2002.nottinghillcarnival> (last accessed 15 April 2018).
40. C. L. R. James, *Beyond a Boundary* (London: Yellow Jersey Press, [1963] 2005), p. 53.
41. Selvon, 'The Cricket Match', p. 149.
42. Ramchand, 'The West Indian Short Story', 24.
43. Richard Alsopp (ed.), *Dictionary of Caribbean English Usage* (Kingston, Jamaica: University of the West Indies Press, 1996), p. 106.
44. Selvon, 'The Cricket Match', pp. 151–2.
45. Ibid. p. 152.
46. Ramchand, 'The West Indian Short Story', p. 24.
47. Gordon Rohlehr, *Calypso and Society in Pre-Independence Trinidad* (Port of Spain, Trinidad: Gordon Rohlehr, 1990), p. 2.
48. Selvon, 'The Cricket Match', p. 149.
49. Ibid.
50. Ramchand, 'The West Indian Short Story', p. 28.

51. Lawrence Scott, 'Ballad for the New World', in *Ballad for the New World and Other Stories* (Oxford: Heinemann, 1994), p. 51.
52. Ibid. p. 58.
53. Poe, 'Review of *Twice-Told Tales*', pp. 60–1.
54. Brander Matthews, 'The Philosophy of the Short-story', in May (ed.), *New Short Story Theories*, p. 73.
55. Scott, 'Ballad for the New World', p. 53.
56. Ibid. p. 54, p. 52.
57. Ibid. p. 55.
58. Ibid. p. 51, p, 53, p. 55.
59. As Jak Peake notes in his analysis of this story, the 'oil company's switch from British to North American, from colonial to neocolonial ownership, appears little more than a shift of hegemonic relations'. Jak Peake, 'Remapping the Trinidadian Short Story: Local, American and Global Relations in the Short Fiction of Earl Lovelace and Lawrence Scott', in Lucy Evans et al. (eds), *The Caribbean Short Story: Critical Perspectives* (Leeds: Peepal Tree, 2011), p. 193.
60. Benítez-Rojo, *The Repeating Island*, p. 4.
61. Nalo Hopkinson, 'The Glass Bottle Trick', in *Skin Folk* (New York: Warner Books, 2001), p. 96.
62. Ibid. p. 83.
63. Ibid.
64. Ibid.
65. Ibid. p. 85.
66. Alsopp, *Dictionary of Caribbean English Usage*, p. 208.
67. Olive Senior, *A-Z of Jamaican Heritage* (Kingston, Jamaica: Heinemann, 1983), p. 52.
68. Hopkinson, 'The Glass Bottle Trick', p. 99.
69. Ibid. p. 101.
70. Ibid. p. 94.
71. Ibid.
72. Ibid.
73. Ibid.
74. Benítez-Rojo, *The Repeating Island*, p. 72.
75. Glissant, *Poetics of Relation*, p. 34.

Bibliography

Alsopp, Richard (ed.), *Dictionary of Caribbean English Usage* (Kingston, Jamaica: University of the West Indies Press, 1996).

Awadalla, Maggie and Paul March-Russell (eds), *The Postcolonial Short Story* (Basingstoke: Palgrave Macmillan, 2012).

Balogun, F. Odun, *Tradition and Modernity in the African Short Story: An Introduction to a Literature in Search of Critics* (Westport, CT: Praeger, 1991).

Bardolph, Jacqueline (ed.), *Telling Stories: Postcolonial Short Fiction in English* (Amsterdam: Rodopi, 2001).

Benítez-Rojo, Antonio, *The Repeating Island: The Caribbean and the Postmodern Perspective*, trans. James E. Maraniss, 2nd edn (Durham, NC: Duke University Press, [1989] 1996).

Bennett, Bruce, *Australian Short Fiction: A History* (Brisbane: University of Queensland Press, 2002).

Birbalsingh, Frank, 'The Indo-Caribbean Short Story', *Journal of West Indian Literature*, 12.1–2 (2004): 118–34.

Brathwaite, Edward Kamau, *History of the Voice* (London: New Beacon, 1984).
Carr, Helen, *Jean Rhys* (Plymouth: Northcote House, 1996).
Davidson, J. H. C. S. and H. Cordell (eds), *The Short Story in South East Asia: Aspects of a Genre* (London: School of Oriental and African Studies, 1982).
Evans, Lucy, *Communities in Contemporary Anglophone Caribbean Short Stories* (Liverpool: Liverpool University Press, 2014).
Evans, Lucy, Mark McWatt and Emma Smith (eds), *The Caribbean Short Story: Critical Perspectives* (Leeds: Peepal Tree, 2011).
Glissant, Édouard, *Caribbean Discourse: Selected Essays*, trans. J. Michael Dash (Charlottesville: University Press of Virginia, [1981] 1989).
— *Poetics of Relation*, trans. Betsy Wing (Ann Arbor: University of Michigan Press, [1990] 1997).
Hall, Stuart, 'Calypso Kings', *The Guardian*, Friday Review, 28 June 2002, <http://www.theguardian.com/culture/2002/jun/28/nottinghillcarnival2002.nottinghillcarnival> (last accessed 15 April 2018).
Hanson, Clare, *Short Stories and Short Fictions, 1880–1980* (London: Macmillan, 1995).
Head, Dominic, *The Modernist Short Story: A Study in Theory and Practice* (Cambridge: Cambridge University Press, 1992).
Hopkinson, Nalo, 'The Glass Bottle Trick', in *Skin Folk* (New York: Warner Books, 2001), pp. 83–101.
Howells, Coral Ann, *Jean Rhys* (New York: Harvester Wheatsheaf, 1991).
Iftekharrudin, Farhat, Joseph Boyden, Joseph Longo and Mary Rohrberger (eds), *Postmodern Approaches to the Short Story* (Westport, CT: Praeger, 2003).
James, C. L. R., *Beyond a Boundary* (London: Yellow Jersey Press, [1963] 2005).
Lodge, David, *The Modes of Modern Fiction* (London: Arnold, 1977).
Lord Beginner, 'Victory Test Match' (1950), <www.espncricinfo.com/westindies/content/story/250996.html> (last accessed 15 April 2018).
Matthews, Brander, 'The Philosophy of the Short-story', in May (ed.), *New Short Story Theories*, pp. 73–80.
Maurel, Sylvie, *Jean Rhys* (Basingstoke: Macmillan, 1998).
May, Charles E. (ed.), *The New Short Story Theories* (Athens: Ohio University Press, 1994).
New, W. H., *Dreams of Speech and Violence: The Art of the Short Story in Canada and New Zealand* (Toronto: University of Toronto Press, 1987).
Nischik, Reingard M. (ed.), *The Canadian Short Story: Interpretations* (Rochester, NY: Camden House, 2007).
Peake, Jak, 'Remapping the Trinidadian Short Story: Local, American and Global Relations in the Short Fiction of Earl Lovelace and Lawrence Scott', in Lucy Evans, Mark McWatt and Emma Smith (eds), *The Caribbean Short Story: Critical Perspectives* (Leeds: Peepal Tree, 2011), pp. 183–98.
Poe, Edgar Allan, 'Review of *Twice-Told Tales*', in May (ed.), *New Short Story Theories*, pp. 59–72.
Ramchand, Kenneth, 'The West Indian Short Story', *Journal of Caribbean Literatures*, 1.1 (1997): 21–30.
Reid, Ian, *The Short Story* (London: Methuen, 1977).
Rohlehr, Gordon, *Calypso and Society in Pre-Independence Trinidad* (Port of Spain, Trinidad: Gordon Rohlehr, 1990).
Rohrberger, Mary, 'The Short Story: A Proposed Definition', in May (ed.), *New Short Story Theories*, pp. 80–2.
Rhys, Jean, 'Pioneers, Oh, Pioneers', in Stewart Brown and John Wickham (eds), *The Oxford Book of Caribbean Short Stories* (Oxford: Oxford University Press, 1999), pp. 9–17.
Savory, Elaine, *Jean Rhys* (Cambridge: Cambridge University Press, 1998).

Scott, Lawrence, 'Ballad for the New World', in *Ballad for the New World and Other Stories* (Oxford: Heinemann, 1994), pp. 51–8.
Selvon, Sam, 'The Cricket Match', in *Ways of Sunlight* (New York: Longman, [1957] 1987), pp. 149–54.
Senior, Olive, *A–Z of Jamaican Heritage* (Kingston, Jamaica: Heinemann, 1983).
— *Summer Lightning and Other Stories* (Harlow: Longman, 1986).
— 'Lessons from the Fruit Stand: Or, Writing for the Listener', *Journal of Modern Literature*, 20.1 (1996): 39–44.
— 'The Story as Su-Su, the Writer as Gossip', in *Writers on Writing: The Art of the Short Story* (Westport, CT: Praeger, 2005), pp. 41–51.
Staley, Thomas F., *Jean Rhys: A Critical Study* (London: Macmillan, 1979).
Torres-Saillant, Silvio, *Caribbean Poetics: Toward an Aesthetic of West Indian Literature* (Cambridge: Cambridge University Press, 1997).

15

THE SHORT STORY AND THE CITY

Philip Coleman

THE TRANSFORMATION OF URBAN space from what Friedrich Engels termed 'the great towns' in the middle decades of the nineteenth century to the 'metropolis' of the twentieth century coincides with an elevation in the short story's status as a literary genre.[1] This is not, perhaps, an obvious connection: why would a writer choose to address the city – evoking as it does ideas of architectural and spatial largeness, sociocultural diversity and openness – in a form that is commonly associated with aesthetic principles of brevity and strict economies of scale? The history of modern literature is full of examples of novels that seek to represent the vastness of cities, from Honoré de Balzac's *Ferragus: Chief of the Devorants* (1833) – which captures what Italo Calvino called 'the monster that is Paris'[2] – to the 'Hibernian Metropolis' of Dublin in James Joyce's *Ulysses* (1922).[3] It is not difficult to appreciate why Balzac, Joyce and others felt that the novel was an appropriate form to contend with the magnitude and multifariousness of the metropolis; as we will see, however, the short story has had its own distinctive relationship to the city, and has made a contribution, quite different from the novel's, to the literature of urban modernity.

In *The Painter of Modern Life* (1863), Charles Baudelaire offered the following analysis of Edgar Allan Poe's 'The Man of the Crowd', a story which for the French author captured the quality of 'life in the capital cities':

> Do you remember a picture (for indeed it is a picture!) written by the most powerful pen of this age and entitled The Man of the Crowd? Sitting in a café, and looking through the shop window, a convalescent is enjoying the sight of the passing crowd, and identifying himself in thought with all the thoughts that are moving around him. He has only recently come back from the shades of death and breathes in with delight all the spores and odours of life; as he has been on the point of forgetting everything, he remembers and passionately wants to remember everything. In the end he rushes out into the crowd in search of a man unknown to him whose face, which he had caught sight of, had in a flash fascinated him. Curiosity had become a compelling, irresistible passion.[4]

In Baudelaire's reading, two key perspectives on the figure of 'The Man of the Crowd' are offered. In the first, he is a man who 'watches the flow of life move by, majestic and dazzling'. He admires 'the eternal beauty and the astonishing harmony of life in the capital cities', and he 'gazes at the landscape of the great city, landscapes of stone, now swathed in the mist, now struck in full face by the sun'.[5] Here, Baudelaire speaks to a sense of urban modernity that recalls an earlier, neoclassical vision of the space of the 'great town' as one of social opportunity and cultural coherence.[6] But elsewhere a different, darker vision of uncertainty and isolation prevails, in which the 'solitary mortal' is left 'roaming the great desert of men' in search of an 'indefinable something we may be allowed to call "modernity"'.[7]

Baudelaire's ambivalence captures the complex of the modern city in Poe's story: a place of rational order and yet impenetrable mystery. In his celebrated interrogation of Poe's story, and of Baudelaire's response to it, Walter Benjamin commented on the way in which Poe's story managed to evoke 'fear, revulsion, and horror . . . something barbaric [that] discipline just barely manages to tame'.[8] Benjamin's point about 'discipline' is interesting if we take it to refer to the precise handling of literary language and form that was central to Poe's aesthetic,[9] for it implies that the short story's ability to 'contain' urban experience is tentative rather than (novelistically) comprehensive – that the form is inherently aware of 'that indefinable something', in Baudelaire's words, that exceeds its own representational limits.

'Containing' the city's multifariousness is a central concern of Poe's urban detective stories, a genre he is widely credited with having invented. 'The Murders in the Rue Morgue', 'The Mystery of Marie Rogêt' and 'The Purloined Letter' – all published in magazines between 1841 and 1844 before they were collected in Poe's *Tales* (1845) – centre on the character of Monsieur C. Auguste Dupin, a shadowy figure who is nonetheless said to possess a 'peculiar analytic ability' that allows him to solve the most puzzling of crimes.[10] The nature of these crimes is often unspeakably gruesome – most notably in 'The Murders in the Rue Morgue' – but they all take place 'amid the wild lights and shadows of the populous city' of Paris.[11] Dupin himself is said to have 'ceased to know or be known' in the city,[12] but the stories depend on their urban setting for a great deal of their atmospheric and thematic resonance.

Like the narrator of 'The Man of the Crowd', Dupin is a remarkable observer of reality and it is this that allows him to develop astonishing powers of deduction in relation to the cases that come before him. However, in 'The Murders in the Rue Morgue' – described by David Van Leer as 'arguably the first detective story'[13] – Dupin knows the difference between mere surveillance and what he terms 'the quality of the observation. The necessary knowledge is that of *what* to observe.'[14] Throughout the stories, the reader follows Dupin as he attempts to solve beguiling mysteries, from the decapitation of a girl in a fireplace to the theft of a love letter from the boudoir of a government minister, but at the same time Poe takes the reader through the streets and districts of Paris, from 'an obscure library in the Rue Montmartre' to a 'secluded' neighbourhood 'opposite the Barrière du Roule'.[15] From his position of withdrawal – living in 'a time-eaten and grotesque mansion [. . .] tottering to its fall in a retired and desolated portion of the Faubourg St Germain'[16] – Dupin seeks to explain and expose the contradictions of the city. Challenging figures of respectable authority (including doctors, policemen and government officials), Poe suggests that the process of urbanisation brings with it a new series of moral, social and political problems. This may have been far from Poe's intention – he was not interested in conveying any kind of didactic or ethical message in his stories – but the specificity of the urban locale in the Dupin tales suggests a degree of strategic contextualisation that cannot be ignored. 'Paris', which Benjamin would later read as the 'capital of the nineteenth century',[17] features in these stories as a puzzle and a problem to be as carefully pondered by Poe's readers as the mysteries dealt with by Dupin.

In 'The Mystery of Marie Rogêt', Poe gives the Parisian setting added significance for his American readers by basing the story on an actual murder that took place in New York, the year before the text was published. In using 'a fictional character to solve a real-life murder',[18] Poe explores the boundaries between fact and fiction, but he also invites readers to compare different kinds of urban experience across the Atlantic. In neither location, the story seems to suggest, is the city a space where any kind of privacy can be obtained:

> Those who know any thing [sic] of the vicinity of Paris, know the extreme difficulty of finding seclusion, unless at a great distance from its suburbs. Such a thing as an unexplored, or even an unfrequently visited recess, amid its woods or groves, is not for a moment to be imagined. Let anyone who, being at heart a lover of nature, is yet chained by duty to the dust and heat of this great metropolis – let any such one attempt, even during the weekdays, to slake his thirst for solitude amid the scenes of natural loveliness which immediately surround us. At every second step, he will find the growing charm dispelled by the voice and personal intrusion of some ruffian or party of carousing blackguards. He will seek privacy amid the densest foliage, all in vain. Here are the very nooks where the unwashed most abound – here are the temples most desecrate. With sickness of the heart the wanderer will flee back to the polluted Paris as to a less odious because less incongruous sink of pollution. But if the vicinity of the city is so best during the working days of the week, how much more so on the Sabbath![19]

This infernal vision of Paris is linked to New York through the character of Marie Rogêt, named for the woman Marie Rogers, a 'shop-girl [. . .] found floating dead in the Hudson'[20] in July 1841, through whose violent death the city is presented by Poe as place of amoral desecration. This is complicated, however, by Poe's recognition of the 'extreme difficulty of finding seclusion, unless at a great distance from its suburbs'. Poe draws attention to the rapid, sprawling growth of cities such as Paris, London and Berlin in the middle of the nineteenth century. At the same time, he suggests that the individual must learn to come to terms with 'the dust and heat of [the] great metropolis' and 'flee back' to it as the only place where his 'sickness of the heart' can be cured. Poe's vision of the city, then, is akin to Baudelaire's conflation of evil and beauty in *Les Fleurs du Mal* (1857). For both artists, the city represents a kind of grotesque spectacle that is a source of intense pleasure and, at the same time, disgust.

Poe's portrait of the city as a 'polluted' space recurs in Herman Melville's series of short prose sketches 'The Encantadas, or Enchanted Isles' (1856), in which an extended urban metaphor is deployed to describe the far-flung Isles. At one point Melville likens the volcanic terrain of one of the Galápagos Islands to an urban scene:

> Take five-and-twenty heaps of cinders dumped here and there in an outside city lot; imagine some of them magnified into mountains, and the vacant lot the sea; and you will have a fit idea of the general aspect of the Encantadas, or Enchanted Isles. A group rather of extinct volcanoes than of isles; looking much as the world at large might, after a penal conflagration.[21]

Based in part on Melville's own experiences as a sailor in the early 1840s, the sketches attempt to provide a kind of history of a lost world, a world that once had at its centre 'a great city', as the narrator puts it in the Fourth Sketch ('A Pisgah View from the Rock'). Signifying, according to the *Oxford English Dictionary*, 'a faint view or glimpse of something unobtainable or distant', the term 'Pisgah' is appropriate not least because of its biblical connotations – in Deuteronomy 3: 27 it is 'the name of the peak on Mount Nebo, from which Moses saw the Promised Land' – but also because it suggests that Melville here foresees the inevitable downfall of all cities and the empires around which they are constructed.

Melville's representations of the city, even in landscapes far removed from the urban centres of Paris, London or New York, are bound up with a wider critique of colonialism and US American expansionism in the nineteenth century. The transposition of an American cityscape onto a Pacific island scene in 'The Encantadas' reflects the sense Melville had of the global reach of the urban imaginary, but it also contributes to his career-long interrogation of what David Kuebrich has called 'the hidden ideology of capitalist production'. According to Kuebrich, Melville had 'an acute personal sense of the discrepancy between the nation's economic practices and its purported democratic and Christian ideals'.[22] Using the city as setting and symbol, Melville translates this 'personal sense' into a political vision of transnational significance in his writing, most notably in stories such as 'Bartleby, the Scrivener' (subtitled 'A Story of Wall-street' on its first publication in 1853) and the diptych 'The Paradise of Bachelors and the Tartarus of Maids' (1855). These stories provide richly detailed descriptions of American and British urban space at mid-century – New York in 'Bartleby, the Scrivener' and London in 'The Paradise of Bachelors' – but an emphasis on the human cost of national economic progress is also registered in a way that gives the stories a strong ethical and political imperative. In 'The Paradise of Bachelors', Melville's account of the city as a space where wealthy men can indulge their fantasies of excess carries with it a moral challenge that has implications for sexual as well as social politics, especially when their privileged urban world is contrasted with the bleak rural New England landscape where women work, as described in 'The Tartarus of Maids'. In 'Bartleby, the Scrivener', the protagonist's withdrawal from urban life is presented as an act of protest against the machinery of modernity that may be contrasted with the solipsism of a character like Poe's Dupin. Like Poe's narrator in 'The Man of the Crowd', however, there is no escape from 'the dust and heat' of the city for Bartleby: when he is asked if he would like 'to travel through the country' or visit Europe he declines both offers, choosing for reasons known only to himself to waste away within the walls of the city that seems to have consumed him.

The stories of Poe and Melville were inextricably bound up with the rapid development in the nineteenth century of magazine publishing on both sides of the Atlantic. The existence of large numbers of periodicals with column inches to fill created an unprecedented market opportunity for story writers; it also, as Andrew Levy has shown, helped establish a sphere of engagement between the short form and urban experience.[23] In Ireland, Sheridan Le Fanu conjured a portrait of Dublin redolent of Poe's Paris or Melville's New York, with his characters experiencing 'strange disturbances' that originated from the city itself.[24] Dublin's streets and suburbs are essential not only to Le Fanu's sense of social space but to the probing of his characters' psychic geographies. The same can be said of London in the work of writers such as George Gissing, Arthur Morrison, Arthur Conan Doyle and Richard Le Gallienne. Poe's influence is particularly evident in the case of Doyle's Sherlock Holmes, of course, the detective-protagonist made famous first in the *Strand* magazine and in subsequent volumes such as *The Sign of Four* (1890) and *The Adventures of Sherlock Holmes* (1892). In his depictions of London, Doyle develops further Poe's conjunction of seaminess and watchfulness. He characterises the city as a space that threatens to devour its inhabitants – 'the monster tentacles which the giant city was throwing out in the country'[25] – while at the same testifying to it as irresistible spectacle, with the detective reflecting a wider *fin-de-siècle* fascination with voyeurism.[26]

Doyle was one among many short story writers who conspired to make urban experience a subject of widespread popular interest at the end of the nineteenth century. Again, the Baudelairean complex is much in evidence. In the work of O. Henry, for example, New York is portrayed as an energetic city teeming with adventure and possibility, the 'melting pot' (a phrase first metaphorised around this time), in which the figure of the 'Cosmopolite in a Café', to use the title of one early story, surveys the lives of the 'four million ... ordinary inhabitants of teeming, turn-of-the-century New York'.[27] Henry's frequently comic presentation of American city life anticipated the work of writers such as Damon Runyon in the 1930s; more common, however, was a darker species of realism, informed by a naturalist world view, as seen in the work of Frank Norris and Stephen Crane. Crane's stories, especially the pieces collected under the title 'New York City, 1892–94', portray the American metropolis as a place of embattlement and hardship whose locus is the slum.[28] Yet as scholars such as Amy Kaplan have shown, Crane's urban writing masks a deep hermeneutic sophistication, with his stories more often tending towards interpretative openness (Baudelaire's 'indefinable' once again) and his realism better regarded as an act of symbolic imagining of the city as a phenomenon of late nineteenth-century capitalism.[29]

Something of the same complexity is evident among other London writers of the period, such as Arthur Morrison, whose *Tales of Mean Streets* (1894), set in the East End slum, echoed Crane's Bowery writing. Morrison's achievement, as Adrian Hunter has argued, was to marry social critique to an understanding of 'the subversive potential of the short story form', capturing the sordidness of slum life in stories that characteristically dealt 'in loose ends, unanswered questions and irresolvable complexes'.[30] In that respect, Morrison's stories look forward to the modernist encounter with the city, as do George Gissing's, many of which were published posthumously. In 'The Light on the Tower', for example, the impressive 'clock tower at Westminster' shines 'steadily a clear, star-like beacon' over 'an expanse of gloom above the city's horizon'.[31] The doubleness of Gissing's image – immense light in a vast gloom – in many ways captures the ambivalence with which late nineteenth-century story writers regarded the city.

In *The Decline of the West* (1918–22), Oswald Spengler prophesied the emergence of what he called 'world-cities', that is, cities 'that have absorbed into themselves the whole content of history'.[32] For Spengler, the 'world-city means cosmopolitanism in place of "home" ... To the world-city belongs not a folk but a mob.'[33] The city is a recurring point of reference for many writers of short stories from the first half of the twentieth century and, indeed, Dominic Head has argued that 'there is a connection between the generic capacities of the short story and the way in which writers have depicted their social world' during this period.[34] For many of these writers, including James Joyce, Virginia Woolf and Katherine Mansfield in the anglophone tradition, the experience of urban modernity in the twentieth century is related to Spengler's presentation of the 'world-city' as a space of homelessness, stalked by a feeling of alienation from both self and world.

Joyce made a major contribution to the shaping of international literary perceptions of the Irish capital in the twentieth century, complicating the Gothic imaginings of Le Fanu before him by dwelling in even more scrupulous detail on the city's social, historical and cultural character. Throughout the stories of *Dubliners*, Joyce provides remarkably detailed portraits of the city and its inhabitants. Indeed, the work is very much about habitation – what it means for people to live in a particular place at a specific moment in history – but the lives of his characters are also often threatened by a pervasive sense of imminent upheaval. This is complicated by the fact that, in story after story, from 'The Sisters' to 'The Dead', Joyce's characters also seem to be locked into certain social situations without any real sense of escape – they are portrayed as victims of a kind of 'paralysis' that Joyce described in a letter in 1904 as afflicting not only the citizens of the Irish capital but the city itself.[35] In doing this, even though his attention often appears to be drawn into the private, emotional lives of his characters, Joyce was critiquing a social and cultural environment that he himself found repressive; but he was also keen to present 'a direct and penetrating view of the city of Dublin in the modernity of the early twentieth century', as Margot Norris has suggested.[36]

In a way, Joyce takes the contradictory impulses of attraction and disgust that one finds in the urban representations of Baudelaire and Poe and translates them into twentieth-century terms. Consider, for example, the way the character of Lenehan observes the city in 'Two Gallants':

> He walked listlessly round Stephen's Green and then down Grafton Street. Though his eyes took note of many elements of the crowd through which he passed they did so morosely. He found trivial all that was meant to charm him and did not answer glances which invited him to be bold. He knew that he would have to speak a great deal, and invent and to amuse, and his brain and throat were too dry for such a task. The problem of how he could pass the hours till he met Corley again troubled him a little. He could think of no way of passing them but to keep on walking.[37]

There are clear echoes of Baudelaire's reading of Poe's 'Man of the Crowd' here – and the fact that Lenehan finds brief solace in a '*Refreshment Bar*' reinforces this intertextual connection – but Joyce's attention to detail in terms of his mapping of the city signals a later, modernist concern with the problem of representation in itself that sets him apart from his Romantic forbears. In Joyce's stories, indeed, narrative momentum and swiftness of observation seem at times to be at odds with the sense of stasis that besets the lives of his characters, further complicating the reader's engagement with stories that are at once obsessively rooted in the Irish capital and, at the same time, expressive of the author's longing to escape from it. In 'Two Gallants', Lenehan seems to know the city intimately and yet, as this passage suggests, he hardly seems to know what to make of it. In this, Joyce identifies an aesthetic problem to do with the representation of the world in art, but he also points to the epistemological question of how the world can be known at all no matter how familiar it may be to those who live in it.

Joyce believed that 'no writer [had] yet presented Dublin to the world', and he claimed that the book 'is not a collection of tourist impressions but an attempt to represent certain aspects of the life of one of the European capitals'.[38] Joyce's insistence that his stories represent 'an attempt' is important here as it emphasises the experimental nature of his work, like much other modernist writing. In this regard, indeed, the stories of *Dubliners* can be read alongside contemporary engagements with London, for example, in the stories of Mansfield and Woolf. In Woolf's story 'The String Quartet', from *Monday or Tuesday* (1921), the narrator begins by observing the networks of transport that convey individuals around the British capital:

> Well, here we are, and if you cast your eye over the room you will see that Tubes and trams and omnibuses, private carriages not a few, even, I venture to believe, landaus with bays in them, have been busy at it, weaving threads from one end of London to the other.[39]

By the end of the story, however, 'London' is replaced by the narrator's envisioning a city that 'has neither stone nor marble; hangs enduring; stands unshakable; nor does a face, nor does a flag greet or welcome'.[40] This moment of urban transcendence is similar to the remarkable movement that occurs in the final paragraph of Joyce's story 'The Dead', in which Gabriel Conroy's observation of snow falling over Dublin leads him to imagine 'snow falling faintly through the universe and faintly falling, like the descent of their last end, upon all the living and the dead'.[41] In both texts, Joyce and Woolf frame moments of intricate realist attention to detail within larger poetic meditations on the ways that urban experience may be conceived in global if not 'universal' terms.

The dialectic between the observation of a public (largely urban) world, on the one hand, and a probing of the inner self, on the other, is also present in many of Katherine Mansfield's short stories, where the conditions of the city create unbearable pressure for individuals in their private lives, no matter how affluent they might be. In 'Bliss', for example, the reader is told of Bertha Young, the protagonist, 'really – she had everything',[42] but her marriage is falling apart and the social group she moves among is held together by delusions of cultural grandeur. 'We are the victims of time and train. We live in Hampstead',[43] says Mrs Norman Knight at the end of the evening. Here, as in other stories, such as 'Pictures' and 'An Indiscreet Journey',[44] Mansfield characterises the city as a centre of precarious late-imperial power, from which even its most comfortable inhabitants are often desperate to escape.

The projection of personal anxieties onto the physical environment of the city by these writers reflects a broader modernist concern with the impact of urban space on human consciousness. But it is important also to recognise how often these existential concerns are paired with a social awareness that the city remains a space rigidly defined and demarcated in terms of social class, despite the opportunities for physical and indeed social mobility it offers. It is a conundrum explored by F. Scott Fitzgerald in many stories that touch on the shifting socio-economic realities in the American city. 'The Rich Boy' is a good example, with its incisive critique of what the narrator calls 'the snobbish and formalized vulgarity of the Gilded Age'.[45] New York provides the setting for many of Fitzgerald's later interrogations of the American Dream. In 'The Lost Decade', published the year before the writer's death, the closing image of the journalist Orrison 'reach[ing] out and press[ing] his thumb against the granite of the building by his side' testifies to the shared reality of the city in a story otherwise concerned with the deep and immersive isolation of one of its inhabitants.[46]

Race relations have, of course, been a major concern of urban writing in twentieth-century America, and the issue has had a significant presence in short fiction. The major demographic and cultural changes triggered by millions of mainly poor black Americans from the South migrating to the urban centres of the North – Chicago, Philadelphia, Washington DC and New York – are reflected in the work of writers such as Jean Toomer and Langston Hughes. In Toomer's case, sections of *Cane* (1923) such as 'Seventh Street' and 'Avey' describe black neighbourhoods in Washington DC during the years after the Great War,[47] while Hughes's depictions of Harlem, especially in his so-called 'Simple' stories (named for their protagonist, Jesse B. Simple), chart the African American urban experience from the Depression through to the Civil Rights era. Toomer's short prose texts are significant in part because of the way that they operate in formal counterpoint to the poems and songs that also comprise *Cane*, but also for the way they expose the violence of racism in the United States. This is something that would be picked up later, though mostly in rural Southern contexts, in the work of Richard Wright, but the stories of Toomer and Hughes describe the experience of African Americans as they attempt to build new lives in the urban centres of the North. Meanwhile Flannery O'Connor, though better known for her stories of the rural South, addresses the urban situation in works such as 'The Geranium', in which an elderly white Southerner is forced to confront his ingrained racial prejudice after he moves to be with his daughter in New York.[48] Here the city becomes the place where white American identity, symbolised in the precarious potted geranium, is confronted with the spectacle of its own demise through the collapsing of racial difference.

If Paris was the capital of the nineteenth century, a claim may be made for New York City as the locus of late twentieth- and early twenty-first-century metropolitan short fiction. From Elizabeth Hardwick's stunningly economical accounts of the city's intellectual milieu during the post-war era – a key example is 'Cross-town', which Darryl Pinckney has described as 'a hymn to the city'[49] – to Donald Barthelme's playful urban fairy tales, to Jay McInerney's exploration of 1980s yuppiedom, New York has in many ways come to stand for the archetypal Spenglerian 'world-city'. In terms of their social concern, many of these stories are not far travelled from the city as it was envisaged by Melville or by Crane. For example, in 'The Queen and I', from his collection *How It Ended* (2000), McInerney has his narrator register the 'suffocating smell of rotting meat [that] hangs over the neighborhood and . . . infiltrates the smug apartments and cafés of Greenwich Village'.[50] The source of the smell is the nearby Meat District, but McInerney's deeper point is the proximity of labour to leisure, which troubles the idea of comfortable urban habitation by making visible the violent source of money that his characters strive to deny. It is a vision of the city remarkably close to that of Melville's Bartleby, in which privacy and commoditisation collide.

This same collision is evident in Don DeLillo's masterly 1994 story 'The Angel Esmeralda', which follows two nuns distributing charity in the South Bronx, amid the 'foragers and gatherers, can-redeemers, the people who yawed through subway cars with paper cups'.[51] Patrolling this 'landscape of vacant lots filled with years of stratified deposits – the age-of-house garbage, the age-of-construction debris and vandalized car bodies. Many years of waste',[52] the nuns come across a homeless young girl, Esmeralda, but she is killed before they can intervene to help her. Soon afterward, the local people are convinced that they can see Esmeralda's face on a billboard advertising orange juice, and a crowd gathers. For one of the nuns, the making of a spectacle of Esmeralda's life is revoltingly exploitative, but for the other nun, the girl's face is a miracle to be witnessed. In these opposing responses, DeLillo returns to the fundamental doubleness of the city first captured by Poe:

> And what do you remember, finally, when everyone has gone home and the streets are empty of devotion and hope, swept by the river wind? Is the memory thin and bitter and does it shame you with its fundamental untruth – all nuance and wishful silhouette? Or does the power of transcendence linger, the sense of an event that violates natural forces, something holy that throbs on the hot horizon, the vision you crave because you need a sign to stand against your doubt?[53]

To an extent, DeLillo's story raises questions about the value of narrative art, and about the 'signs' we produce 'to stand against our doubt'. This self-reflexivity about narrative forms has been more or less visible throughout the history of post-war American short fiction. The questioning was at its most apparent, perhaps, in the 1960s and 1970s, in the work of Donald Barthelme and other so-called experimental postmodernists. In the same way that modernism used the short story to experiment with new possibilities in language and style, these writers and their successors used shorter forms to test the boundaries of genre and narrative representation in the urban setting. Barthelme's famous story 'The Balloon' (1966), for example, can be read as an allegory for the relationship between art and urban experience.[54] In the story, residents of New York City wake up one morning to find a giant balloon floating over the city, covering its streets like an enormous Christo and Jeanne-Claude installation. They set about trying to understand what it is, where it has come from, and what it might be for, but in the end, '[i]t was suggested that what was admired about the balloon was finally this: that it was not limited, or defined'.[55] The balloon promotes an open-ended approach to the interpretation of art that is related to an idea of the city as a zone of heterogeneous possibility and polyphonic discursive practices. No two people need to agree on the meaning of the balloon, not least because of its 'ability [. . .] to shift its shape, to change'.[56] The city also has this ability, even though its inhabitants' lives are often 'rigidly patterned',[57] as Barthelme writes. His stories convey a desire to move beyond the bounds of conventional formal patterns and arrangements, to challenge what urban experience can mean and how it might be written about.

Although later generations of American writers have turned decisively away from Barthelme's particular brand of experimentalism, the heightened self-awareness his work fosters about the expressive power of compressed narrative acts is still in evidence. Indeed, it is difficult not to be reminded of Barthelme when reading, for example, David Foster Wallace's 'The Suffering Channel', a story that explores the transcendent value and meaning of art in the post-9/11 era.[58] Nor would the extreme brevity of the short-short story (addressed in detail in Michael Basseler's chapter) have been likely without the path forged by the 'experimentalists'. In the city stories of Lydia Davis, for instance, the compression of the form itself becomes expressive of the realities of congested living. In 'From Below, as a Neighbor', Davis captures with remarkable formal dexterity, in three tightly woven sentences, the dilemma of self-knowledge that has often been raised as a central preoccupation in artistic engagements with the city in the twentieth century. 'If I were not me and overheard me from below', the piece begins, suggesting a form of radical self-division from the outset ('I' against 'me'), before going on to imagine what it might be like to perceive oneself as one's own neighbour: 'I would say to myself how glad I was not to be her, not to be sounding the way she is sounding, with a voice like her voice and an opinion like her opinion.'[59] Here, the proximity of the other triggers not outwardness but inwardness, and a retreat into agonised forms of self-questioning.

For other contemporary writers, it has been the short story's capacity for rendering historical and ideological richness in a highly circumscribed form that has made it particularly amenable to the city as a subject. One such writer is Mavis Gallant, whose work has lately been the subject of renewed popular and critical interest, and who was a *New Yorker* regular for several decades, beginning in the 1950s.[60] In all, Gallant published more than a hundred stories in the magazine, including many key works reflecting her experiences in post-war Paris. As Michael Ondaatje has put it, '[t]he world Gallant depicts is cosmopolitan'.[61] She is less interested in Parisian local colour than she is in using the French capital to explore her own and other people's experiences of transnational movement and dislocation. In many ways, Gallant's work recasts earlier modernist preoccupations with the 'world-city'; indeed, allusions and references to modernist precursors are frequent in her writing, as in the story 'The Moslem Wife', which is set 'in the business room of a hotel quite near to the house where Katherine Mansfield (whom no one in this hotel had ever heard of) was writing "The Daughters of the Late Colonel"'.[62] For Gallant, however, it is the process of movement *between* cities, as part of an expanded, diasporic experience, that matters. In one of her best-known stories, 'Speck's Idea', a Paris art gallery is blown up by Basque separatists 'who had mistaken it for a travel agency exploiting the beauty of their coast'.[63] Dealing with fascism and the legacies of the Holocaust, the story presents a vision of the modern European city – by implication not just the French capital – in which the racial and ideological struggles of the past cast a long shadow over attempts to accommodate a new multi-ethnic, transnational urban populace.

In Gallant's work, cities are presented as spaces in which identities are multiple and fluid. The same is true of many writers of East Asian ethnicity, such as Vikram Chandra, Bharati Mukherjee and Hanif Kureishi whose explorations of colonial and postcolonial histories, and of migration from east to west, have transformed anglophone short fiction in recent years.[64] In the interlinked stories of *Love and Longing in Bombay* (1997), Vikram Chandra brings the legacy of colonial Bombay into collision with an emerging global Mumbai symbolised by the computer software company for which the narrator works. Many of the stories in Mukherjee's collection *The Middleman* (1988), meanwhile, describe experiences of identity re-formation that are based partly on the ways that characters move between cities, which are often their only points of contact with particular nations. In 'A Wife's Story', in particular, deep personal and cultural rifts are exposed when the character of Panna Bhatt, a married Indian woman living as a student in America, has to manage a visit by her husband, who has been living in India while she has been abroad.[65] Set against the backdrop of New York City which the husband only knows as a tourist but Panna has experienced as an immigrant, Mukherjee's story makes the city the embodiment of a particular kind of conflict and misunderstanding, partly driven by longing for home and the dynamics of diasporic displacement. A version of this theme recurs in Hanif Kureishi's work, much of which explores the personal and intergenerational consequences of migration to post-war England. In 'We're Not Jews', for example, from his collection *Love in a Blue Time* (1997), Kureishi locates a specific episode of abuse within a complex geopolitical web of colonial history, racial violence and postcolonial migration.

As these recent examples suggest, the relationship between the short story and the city is one of continuing expansion and adaptation, and there is every reason to suppose that the form will remain alive to the urban imaginary of the twenty-first-century 'world-city'.

Notes

1. See Friedrich Engels, 'The Great Towns' and Allen J. Scott, 'Metropolis: From the Division of Labor to Urban Form', in Gary Bridge and Sophie Watson (eds), *The Blackwell City Reader*, 2nd edn (Oxford: Wiley-Black, 2010), pp. 11–16, pp. 49–59.
2. Italo Calvino, 'The City as Novel in Balzac', in *Why Read the Classics?*, trans. Martin McLaughlin (London: Vintage, 2010), p. 139.
3. The first section of the 'Aeolus' episode of Joyce's novel has the heading 'In the Heart of the Hibernian Metropolis.' See James Joyce, *Ulysses* (Oxford: Oxford University Press, 1993), p. 112.
4. Charles Baudelaire, *The Painter of Modern Life*, trans. P. E. Charvet (London: Penguin Books, 2010), p. 10.
5. Ibid. p. 14.
6. Giovanni Antonio Canaletto's paintings of cities such as Venice and London in the middle of the eighteenth century are among the best examples of this positive representation of urban modernity. See, for example, his painting *London: Greenwich Hospital from the North Bank of the Thames* (c. 1753). I am grateful to Niamh NicGhabhann for suggesting these examples, and for her editorial assistance in the writing of this essay.
7. Baudelaire, *The Painter of Modern Life*, p. 16.
8. Walter Benjamin, *Illuminations*, trans. Harry Zorn (London: Pimlico, 1999), p. 170.
9. Poe's essay 'The Philosophy of Composition' (1846) contains an elucidation of his aesthetic theory, especially in relation to what he termed 'unity of effect'. See Edgar Allan Poe, *Selected Writings*, ed. G. R. Thompson (London and New York: W. W. Norton, 2004), pp. 675–84.
10. See Edgar Allan Poe, *Selected Tales*, ed. David Van Leer (Oxford: Oxford University Press, 1998), pp. 92–122, pp. 149–92, pp. 249–65.
11. Ibid. p. 95.
12. Ibid.
13. See David Van Leer, note to 'The Murders in the Rue Morgue', in Poe, *Selected Tales*, p. 330.
14. Poe, *Selected Tales*, p. 93.
15. Ibid. p. 95.
16. Ibid.
17. See, for example, Walter Benjamin, 'Paris, the Capital of the Nineteenth Century' (1935), in *The Arcades Project*, trans. Howard Eiland and Kevin McLaughlin (Cambridge and London: The Belknap Press of Harvard University Press, 1999), pp. 3–13.
18. David Van Leer in Poe, *Selected Tales*, p. 332.
19. Poe, *Selected Tales*, pp. 180–1.
20. Van Leer in Poe, *Selected Tales*, p. 332.
21. Herman Melville, *Billy Budd and Other Stories*, ed. A. Robert Lee (London: Everyman, 1993), p. 133.

22. David Kuebrich, 'Melville's Doctrine of Assumptions: The Hidden Ideology of Capitalist Production in "Bartleby"', *The New England Quarterly*, 69.3 (1996): 382.
23. Andrew Levy, *The Culture and Commerce of the American Short Story* (Cambridge: Cambridge University Press, 1993), *passim*.
24. See, for example, the stories 'Strange Disturbances in a House in Aungier Street' and 'Ghost Stories of Chapelizod' in Sheridan Le Fanu, *Irish Ghost Stories of Sheridan Le Fanu*, ed. Patrick F. Byrne (Dublin and Cork: The Mercier Press, 1973), pp. 34–56, pp. 1–33.
25. Arthur Conan Doyle, *The Penguin Complete Sherlock Holmes* (Harmondsworth: Penguin, 2010), p. 99.
26. For a discussion of André Gabriel's Freudian reading of Doyle's stories, where he examines the role of the voyeur, see Christopher Redmond, *In Bed with Sherlock Holmes: Sexual Elements in Arthur Conan Doyle's Stories of the Great Detective* (Toronto: Simon and Pierre, 1984), p. 138.
27. See O. Henry, *100 Selected Stories* (Ware: Wordsworth Editions, 1995), pp. 6–9, p. vii.
28. See Stephen Crane, *Prose and Poetry* (New York: Library of America, 1984), pp. 517–618.
29. See Amy Kaplan's classic study, *The Social Construction of American Realism* (Chicago and London: University of Chicago Press, 1988).
30. Adrian Hunter, *The Cambridge Introduction to the Short Story in English* (Cambridge: Cambridge University Press, 2007), pp. 39–40.
31. George Gissing, *A Victim of Circumstances and Other Stories* (London: Constable, 1927) p. 107.
32. Oswald Spengler, *The Decline of the West*, trans. Charles Francis Atkinson (New York: Oxford University Press, 1991), p. 25.
33. Ibid.
34. Dominic Head, *The Modernist Short Story* (Cambridge: Cambridge University Press, 1992), p. 1.
35. Joyce's letter is quoted by Hans Walter Gabler in his introduction to James Joyce, *Dubliners*, ed. Margot Norris (New York and London: W. W. Norton, 2006), p. xvi.
36. See Norris in her preface to Joyce, *Dubliners*, p. ix.
37. Ibid. p. 45.
38. Ibid p. ix.
39. Virginia Woolf, *Monday or Tuesday* (London: Alma Classics, 2014), p. 49.
40. Ibid. p. 54.
41. Joyce, *Dubliners*, p. 194.
42. Ibid. p. 178.
43. Katherine Mansfield, *Selected Stories*, ed. Angela Smith (Oxford: Oxford University Press, 2002), p. 184.
44. Ibid. pp. 193–200, pp. 60–73.
45. F. Scott Fitzgerald, *The Collected Short Stories* (London: Penguin, 2010), p. 111.
46. Ibid. p. 582.
47. Jean Toomer, *Cane* (New York and London: W. W. Norton, 1988), p. 41, pp. 44–9.
48. Flannery O'Connor, 'The Geranium' in *Collected Works* (New York: Library of America, 1988), pp. 701–13.
49. See Darryl Pinckney, 'Introduction' to Elizabeth Hardwick, *The New York Stories of Elizabeth Hardwick* (New York: New York Review of Books Classics, 2010), p. xxi.
50. Jay McInerney, *How It Ended* (London: Bloomsbury, 2000), p. 166.
51. Don DeLillo, *The Angel Esmerelda* (New York: Scribner, 2011), p. 79.
52. Ibid. p. 75.
53. Ibid. p. 101
54. Donald Barthelme, *60 Stories* (New York: Penguin Books, 1982), pp. 53–8.
55. Ibid. p. 57.

56. Ibid.
57. Ibid.
58. See David Foster Wallace, 'The Suffering Channel' in *Oblivion: Stories* (London: Abacus, 2004), pp. 238–329.
59. Lydia Davis, *The Collected Stories* (London: Penguin Books, 2013), p. 287.
60. On the importance of *The New Yorker*, see Kasia Boddy, *The American Short Story since 1950* (Edinburgh: Edinburgh University Press, 2011), pp. 37–54.
61. See Michael Ondaatje's introduction to Mavis Gallant's *Paris Stories* (New York: New York Review of Books Classics), p. ix.
62. Gallant, *Paris Stories*, p. 79.
63. Ibid. p. 127.
64. See, for example, the stories collected in Bharati Mukherjee's *The Middleman and Other Stories* (New York: Grove Press, 1988) and Hanif Kureishi's *Love in a Blue Time* (New York: Simon & Schuster, 1999).
65. Mukherjee, The Middleman and Other Stories, pp. 23–40.

Bibliography

Barthelme, Donald, *60 Stories* (New York: Penguin Books, 1982).
Baudelaire, Charles, *The Painter of Modern Life*, trans. P. E. Charvet (London: Penguin Books, 2010).
Benjamin, Walter, *The Arcades Project*, trans. Howard Eiland and Kevin McLaughlin (Cambridge and London: The Belknap Press of Harvard University Press, 1999).
— *Illuminations*, trans. Harry Zorn (London: Pimlico, 1999).
Boddy, Kasia, *The American Short Story since 1950* (Edinburgh: Edinburgh University Press, 2011).
Bridge, Gary and Sophie Watson (eds), *The Blackwell City Reader*, 2nd edn (Oxford: Wiley-Blackwell, 2010).
Calvino, Italo, *Why Read the Classics?* trans. Martin McLaughlin (London: Vintage, 2010).
Chandra, Vikram, *Love and Longing in Bombay* (London: Faber and Faber, 1997).
Crane, Stephen, *Prose and Poetry* (New York: Library of America, 1984).
Davis, Lydia, *The Collected Stories* (London: Penguin, 2013).
DeLillo, Don, *The Angel Esmerelda* (New York: Scribner, 2011).
Doyle, Arthur Conan, *The Penguin Complete Sherlock Holmes* (Harmondsworth: Penguin, 2010).
Fitzgerald, F. Scott, *The Collected Short Stories* (London: Penguin, 2010).
Gallant, Mavis, *Paris Stories* (New York: New York Review of Books Classics, 2002).
Gissing, George, *A Victim of Circumstances and Other Stories* (London: Constable, 1927).
Hardwick, Elizabeth, *The New York Stories of Elizabeth Hardwick* (New York: New York Review of Books Classics, 2010).
Head, Dominic, *The Modernist Short Story* (Cambridge: Cambridge University Press, 1992).
Henry, O., *100 Selected Stories* (Ware: Wordsworth Editions, 1995).
Hughes, Langston, *Simple's Uncle Sam* (New York: Hill and Wang, 2000).
Hunter, Adrian, *The Cambridge Introduction to the Short Story in English* (Cambridge: Cambridge University Press, 2007)
Joyce, James, *Ulysses* (Oxford: Oxford University Press, 1993).
— *Dubliners*, ed. Margot Norris (New York and London: W. W. Norton, 2006).
Kaplan, Amy, *The Social Construction of American Realism* (Chicago and London: University of Chicago Press, 1988).
Kuebrich, David, 'Melville's Doctrine of Assumptions: The Hidden Ideology of Capitalist Production in "Bartleby"', *The New England Quarterly* 69.3 (1996): 381–405.

Kureishi, Hanif, *Love in a Blue Time* (New York: Simon and Schuster, 1999).
Le Fanu, Sheridan, *Irish Ghost Stories of Sheridan Le Fanu*, ed. Patrick F. Byrne (Dublin and Cork: The Mercier Press, 1973).
Levy, Andrew, *The Culture and Commerce of the American Short Story* (Cambridge: Cambridge University Press, 1993).
McInerney, Jay, *How It Ended* (London: Bloomsbury, 2000).
Mansfield, Katherine, *Selected Stories*, ed. Angela Smith (Oxford: Oxford University Press, 2002).
Melville, Herman, *Billy Budd and Other Stories*, ed. A. Robert Lee (London: Everyman, 1993).
Morrison, Arthur, *Tales of Mean Streets* (Woodbridge: The Boydell Press, 1983).
Mukherjee, Bharati, *The Middleman and Other Stories* (New York: Grove Press, 1988).
O'Connor, Flannery, *Collected Works* (New York: Library of America, 1988).
Poe, Edgar Allan, *Selected Tales*, ed. David Van Leer (Oxford: Oxford University Press, 1998).
— *Selected Writings*, ed. G. R. Thompson (New York and London: W. W. Norton 2004).
Redmond, Christopher, *In Bed with Sherlock Holmes: Sexual Elements in Arthur Conan Doyle's Stories of the Great Detective* (Toronto: Simon and Pierre, 1984).
Spengler, Oswald, *The Decline of the West*, trans. Charles Francis Atkinson (New York: Oxford University Press, 1991).
Toomer, Jean, *Cane* (New York and London: W. W. Norton, 1988).
Wallace, David Foster, *Oblivion: Stories* (London: Abacus, 2004).
Woolf, Virginia, *Monday or Tuesday* (London: Alma Classics, 2014).

16

The Short Story in Suburbia

Joanna Price

John Cheever, reflecting in 'Why I Write Short Stories', argues that some contemporary art forms have 'lost the language of the landscape', but that the short story is particularly suited to expressing 'the newness in our ways of life' in that landscape. He refers specifically to life in the suburbs and the ephemera that characterise it, which 'confound traditional esthetics'.[1] The 'newness' of the American landscape was, in the post-Second World War period, largely associated with the growth of suburbs. Although suburban landscapes have diversified and proliferated since then, many of the popular images of suburbia derive from the mass-produced housing developments of the post-war period. In the stories of Cheever, John Updike and others associated with *The New Yorker* magazine, an iconography of suburbia was created, and these images become part of a suburban aesthetic and sensibility articulated particularly through the short story form. The concept of the suburbs is essentially spatial and in suburban short stories, this chapter suggests, the spaces of the suburban setting become tied to the spatiality of the short story form.

When he founded *The New Yorker* in 1925, Harold Ross, who remained its editor-in-chief until his death in 1951, intended it to capture the spirit of Manhattan in the 1920s, and to reflect an image of sophistication and urbanity to a largely metropolitan readership.[2] By mid-century, following several decades of growing circulation, that readership had changed dramatically, and was increasingly composed of those whose attachment to the city was tenuous, and often nostalgic. According to Mary F. Corey, the magazine's own market research shows that, by 1959, half of subscribers were recorded as housewives, many of whom lived in the suburbs.[3] To such readers, Corey observes, *The New Yorker* offered either a cherished memory of the urbanity and 'cosmopolitanism' they had left behind, or the image of a sophisticated metropolitan life to which they might aspire.[4] Advertisements for luxury consumer goods spoke to a narrative of prosperous self-improvement and self-reinvention through consumption, while the distinctive *New Yorker* tone – 'knowing, a trifle world-weary, prone to self-consciousness and irony'[5] – performed a commensurate 'commodification of taste and sophistication' which, as Faye Hammill observes, was 'crucial to the sense of verbal privilege' on which *The New Yorker* relied.[6]

The growth years of *The New Yorker* may have coincided with a general increase in the popularity and visibility of the short story across the US,[7] but it was Ross's magazine that became synonymous with a particularly durable and successful version of the form. As Ben Yagoda suggests, *The New Yorker* created its own distinctive brand of short story, one whose hallmarks were 'literary quality', 'brevity' and 'clarity',[8] and which trained 'a specific kind of aesthetic lens on experience'.[9] From the outset,

Ross championed the virtues of 'understatement and subtlety',[10] an ethos perpetuated by William Shawn, who served as editor-in-chief from 1952 until 1987. The stringent word limit on stories enforced brevity,[11] and the insistence on 'pegging', whereby scene-setting material was immediately established, demanded clarity from the outset. This practice contributed to the production of a 'detail-heavy, easily recognisable ... *New Yorker* style'[12] which favoured setting and mood over plot and incident.[13] Formal experimentation along with 'dramatic or surprise endings'[14] were discouraged, and understated emotion strongly preferred.[15]

Recent studies have examined how, through its particular combination of 'entertainment and instruction'[16] in a 'space where art encounters consumerism and pleasure',[17] the magazine was able to cater to the 'middlebrow' tastes of a middle-class readership. The perception of *New Yorker* productions as being middlebrow extends to its short stories. In 1953, Dwight Macdonald observed that 'The "*New Yorker* short story" is a definite genre ... which the editors have established by years of patient, skilful selection' such that they have to 'beg writers not to follow the formula *quite* so closely'.[18] Paul March-Russell describes how the 'story of manners' that *The New Yorker* 'pioneered' in the 1930s, and which 'epitomised' the magazine's short stories of the 1950s and early 1960s, was characteristically 'highly crafted and accessibly told, the attention to living detail ... given shape by the well-made structure, in particular the use of a leitmotif, a recurring image or symbol ... to express the characters' inner feelings'. Cheever's 'The Swimmer' (1964), with its leitmotif of swimming pools, and Updike's 'Flight' (1962), with its leitmotif of escape, exemplify the 'well-made' *New Yorker* short story.[19]

Updike's adeptness in the form reflects his immersion from childhood in the magazine's atmosphere of 'urban romance',[20] as well as his experience of having worked as a Talk of the Town reporter in the 1950s. In all he published 146 short stories in *The New Yorker*, many set in invented places like Olinger, based on the Pennsylvanian small town of Shillington where he grew up, and the suburban Tarbox, based on Ipswich, Massachusetts, where he lived for nearly two decades. His early *New Yorker* stories, such as 'Friends from Philadelphia' and the much-anthologised 'A & P', display his ability to capture nuances of class and character through oblique dialogue, precise attention to detail, and the (then unusual) use of the present tense.[21] But despite the editorial strictures of *The New Yorker*, Updike was able to experiment with a variety of story modes over the decades. One form in which he particularly excelled was the lyric story, several examples of which were re-published in the collection *The Music School* (1966). Updike described such stories as being in the 'abstract-personal' mode,[22] which accurately captures these first-person narratives' qualities of controlled introspection and refracted emotion. In 'Leaves' (1962), for example, a succinct piece of lyrical meditation, the narrator's observations of the sunlight and shadow on the autumnal grape leaves outside his window allow him to reflect on the pain and guilt he feels at the end of his marriage, as well as on the process of writing itself.[23]

Lyric short stories, which focus on 'internal changes, moods and feelings'[24] rather than narrative incident, partake of a long tradition in the short story that runs from Anton Chekhov through European modernists such as James Joyce and Katherine Mansfield, to Updike and Cheever and beyond. Such stories, according to Charles E. May, 'combine the specific details of realism with the poetic lyricism of romanticism'.[25] Lyric stories accentuate the affinity of the short story form with the poem through an emphasis on interiority over plot, the 'pure selection' that produces a 'unified pattern'[26] and 'condensed . . . often figured language'.[27] Such stories illustrate what May has described as the lyric story's 'movement away from the linearity of prose towards the spatiality of poetry',[28] through the use of metaphor and the highly controlled selection of detail as the narrator moves between external objects and his internal landscape. In the work of Updike's fellow *New Yorker* regular, John Cheever, the lyric short story is evolved to accommodate what amounts to an aesthetic of suburbia, in which the spatiality of the short story form becomes embedded in the representation of suburban space and spaces.

Most of the stories in Cheever's so-called 'suburban sequence', gathered together in the 1958 collection *The Housebreaker of Shady Hill and Other Stories*, first appeared in *The New Yorker* between 1953 and 1958. Based in part on the long-established upper-middle-class suburbs of Westchester County, Shady Hill is a bedroom town consisting of different suburban areas, whose demarcation along class lines Cheever indicates in several of his stories. The tensions that arise from the proximity of different types of development are most apparent in 'The Trouble of Marcie Flint'. This story recounts how the local residents are debating whether to allow a public library in Shady Hill. For many of the citizens, who 'have libraries of [their] own', a public repository represents the threat of encroachment by a new, less prosperous housing development nearby. To one upwardly mobile resident of Shady Hill, the prospect of this invasion evokes

> the colorless, hard-pressed people of the Carsen Park project, with their flocks of children, and their monthly interest payments, and their picture windows, and their view of identical houses [which] . . . seemed to threaten her most cherished concepts – her lawns, her pleasures, her property rights, even her self-esteem.[29]

Cheever's Shady Hill performs an intricate double service on the pages of *The New Yorker*. On the one hand, its depiction of wealthy upper-middle-class suburban life was something to which mid-century suburbanites, including *New Yorker* readers, aspired; yet his stories also satirise upper-class stereotyping of the Levittown-type developments – as uniform, vulgar and heavily mortgaged – in which many of those readers themselves lived. In stories such as 'The Swimmer', 'The Housebreaker of Shady Hill', 'O Youth and Beauty' and 'The Country Husband', Cheever reveals the precariousness of the economic position on which suburban class membership rests, and speaks to readers' anxieties about their security as they experienced the re-definition of middle-class status 'around the single-family, privately owned, suburban home'[30] and the ideology of possessive individualism which ownership of that home represented.

Cheever's seminal contribution to the literature of suburbia lies not only in his evocation of the effects of a material reality at a significant moment in the history of the suburbs, but in the aesthetics he forged to explore those effects. By the time he began writing his suburban stories Cheever was already introducing departures from the realism that the *New Yorker* editors preferred, as exemplified by the two critically acclaimed stories 'The Enormous Radio' (1947) and 'Goodbye My Brother' (1951). 'A Vision of the World' (1962) can be read as a further elaboration of his aesthetics and their imbrication with suburbia. The narrator, looking back over the events that have led to his mental disintegration in the suburbs, recounts how he dug up in his garden a can containing a note on which was written: 'I, Nils Jugstrum, promise myself that if I am not a member of the Gory Brook Country Club by the time I am twenty-five years old I will hang myself.'[31] The narrator's interpretation of this note as having been written by 'some farmer's boy' who had worked on the farmland upon which the present suburbs have been built acknowledges the rural and agricultural history that the suburbs have erased, and, later, the aspiration to class mobility held by the writer of the note. The narrator also responds to the emotion expressed by the boy: 'I was moved, as I always am, by these broken lines of communication in which we express our most acute feelings. The note seemed, like some impulse of romantic love, to let me deeper into the afternoon.'[32] His ability to read the emotions expressed in the fragment and to hypothesise their context gives the narrator a sense of 'deep' attunement to the place and moment he occupies. This, as often in Cheever's stories, is suggested by an attentiveness to the nature that the suburbs generally exclude, apart from in localised patches, as here in the case of the narrator's garden, where he notices the smell of the cut grass and the activities of ants, birds and a 'lethal' copperhead nearby.

The narrator's ability to read his landscape and its natural, historical and social striations is immediately interrupted by his arrival at a supermarket: 'I think you may need a camera these days to record a supermarket on a Saturday afternoon. Our language is traditional, the accrual of centuries of intercourse. Except for the shapes of the pastry, there was nothing traditional to be seen at the bakery counter where I waited.'[33] The narrator's bemused enjoyment of the newness and strangeness of the suburban landscape is disturbed, on his return home, by his wife's declaration that, 'I have this terrible feeling that I'm in black-and-white and that I can be turned off by anybody. I just have this terrible feeling that I can be turned *off*.'[34] His wife's expression of feelings of suburban isolation and irrelevance through the metaphor of the television prompts the narrator's recognition of his own suburban captivity: 'I could not bring myself to part with my lawns and gardens . . . while my chains are forged of turf and house paint, they will bind me till I die.'[35] It also provokes a reflection which could be taken as articulating Cheever's suburban aesthetic:

> I was grateful to my wife then for what she had said, for stating that the externals of her life had the quality of a dream. The uninhibited energies of the imagination had created the supermarket, the viper and the note in the shoe-polish can. Compared to these, my wildest reveries had the literalness of double-entry book-keeping.[36]

The 'externals' of the suburban world are dreamlike because of their newness and unfamiliarity and also because of their artificiality. Suburban artefacts, products of 'the uninhibited energies of the imagination' invite, like dreams, decipherment or interpretation. Cheever's stories evoke his characters' attempts to navigate suburban dreamscapes that are at once highly regulated and prescriptive and also, in their newness, uncharted and unread. As Robert Beuka has noted, suburban fiction, including Cheever's, explores the 'struggle to create meaningful attachments to a prefabricated or otherwise artificial place'.[37] In this sense, the suburban landscape comprises dreamlike signs to which Cheever's characters seek to attach emotional and interpretative significance. This landscape both provides the setting for and to some extent produces the often libidinal, nostalgic or fearful desires that Cheever portrays. The stories thus interweave 'literal' or realist descriptions of suburbia with divagations into a phantasmatic or fabular parallel world.

In the suburban aesthetic Cheever creates, the spatiality of the lyric short story form is combined with a thematic and poetic emphasis on space and spaces. Cheever shows how the organisation of everyday life in the post-war suburbs, and the significance attached to different activities, was tied to the arrangement of suburban space. His stories also show how the occupation of these spaces was gendered, with male commuters typically leaving the suburbs by rail or road to work in the city, and his female characters usually inhabiting the spaces around the house. The depiction of domestic spaces often occurs through a male narrator's reflection on how a (house) wife spends her time, and his half-comprehending recognition that her sadness (later to be called 'the problem that has no name' by Betty Friedan[38]) arises at least in part from her confinement and employment within that space. Wives are depicted, for example, navigating 'between the stove and the sink'[39] and adorning a living room which the husband surveys as 'his element, his creation'.[40] These depictions of women's occupation of the suburban home are often rendered in 'a tone of beleaguered ... masculinity' by a narrator who regards himself as trapped by his wife's wish to live there,[41] and to this extent the stories contribute to *The New Yorker*'s 'unremitting subversion of the domestic ideal' which, Mary Corey argues, 'was consistent with its cosmopolitanism'.[42] In Cheever's stories, authorial irony generally accompanies these depictions, although it is the spaces outside the house through which mostly his male characters move that more often offer possibilities of the eventual transformation and transcendence of the norms of suburban life.

Cheever's stories have contributed to the circulation and significance of the most familiar elements of the scenery of suburbia. These are spaces within and outside the house, such as the picture window and the lawn, and spaces associated with the railway (the train car, the platform and the waiting room). Such elements also function as boundaries, both connecting the occupant of the suburban house to the outside world and separating him or her from it. Boundaries are multi-signifying in the ideology and iconography of suburbia. They represent the exclusion of 'others' defined by class and race, thus serving a symbolic function which was particularly potent during the Cold War years. Boundaries also reinforce the suburban subject's identification with the house he owns, consolidating and signifying the possessive individualism that displays his identity as an American. At the same time, they draw attention to his connection with his neighbours, and hence his civic responsibility, and also to his relation to the town or city further afield, where, typically, he works. Many of Cheever's stories explore how suburban social boundaries are created, maintained, transgressed and renewed. Through his characters' negotiation of these boundaries, Cheever reveals not only an ideological (and often topographical) maintenance of social division through class, race, gender and political homogeneity within a development or suburb, but also the pressure to conform exerted by other elements of 1950s American culture. His stories explore his characters' ambivalence towards social boundaries and also the ambiguity of the suburban spaces that demarcate those boundaries.

In 'The Cure', for example, the narrator tries to 'cure' himself of his 'romantic, carnal and disastrous marriage', his wife having left with the children.[43] Alone in the evenings, he positions himself to read in the living room, exposed to view through the picture window. The picture window, the most iconic feature of the suburban house, was designed to enable the occupants of the home to look out at their territory, but it also allows their neighbours to look in at them performing their suburban roles.[44] The window both provides a boundary between inside and outside and private and public and draws attention to the fragility of that boundary.[45] In 'The Cure', the narrator's staging of his reading in an otherwise empty living room presents to view his deviance from the suburban family norm as he realises that he is being observed by someone determined 'to violate my privacy'.[46] The gaze of the voyeur, whose transgression of the boundary represented by the picture window is also enabled by it, dispossesses the narrator not only of the privacy of his home, but also of the boundaries of his identity. Even the lawn, another iconic feature of suburbia, signifying the domestication of wilderness and a 'moat' that separates the suburban subject from his neighbours[47] is defamiliarised by the voyeur's presence. In this particular story, the topographical and subjective boundaries that the voyeur's desires and movements have challenged are reinstated when the narrator's family returns and the voyeur resumes his place 'on the station platform and at the country club'.[48]

Boundaries and their transgression are also vital to the setting, themes and poetics of two of Cheever's best-known suburban stories, 'The Housebreaker of Shady Hill', first published in *The New Yorker* in 1956, and his later, 'generation-defining'[49] story 'The Swimmer', published in *The New Yorker* in 1964. In 'Housebreaker', Johnny Hake's economic dispossession as he loses his job is followed by social displacement in his suburban community. Johnny's 'burglarizing' of his neighbours' houses reveals the flimsiness of the material and moral boundaries that secure the community. However, as Keith Wilhite argues, Johnny's actions show that not only boundaries but also their transgression 'sustain a suburban community', and through such transgressions 'Cheever's suburbanites reaffirm their tenuous positions within the equivocal spaces of suburbia's private geographies'.[50] In 'Housebreaker', Johnny Hake re-embraces his place in the suburban community through a series of ambivalent realisations experienced in ambiguous spaces. Having failed to experience spiritual and moral enlightenment in the church, where he becomes absorbed instead in the sound of a rat 'scraping away at the baseboard',[51] Johnny undergoes a suburban epiphany, a recognition of his place in the suburban landscape, evoked by 'the tie between the wet grass roots and the hair that grew out of my body', and the freedoms that his life and 'possessions' there afford him.[52]

The ambiguity of suburban spaces and boundaries becomes darker in 'The Swimmer'. The story opens with Cheever's depiction of suburbanites' various Sunday rituals at church, on the golf links and tennis courts and at 'the wildlife preserve'. They are connected as an 'imagined community'[53] by the concurrence and weekly repetition of their summer Sunday activities and their common experience of Saturday evening: '"I *drank* too much last night"' is their refrain. Neddy Merrill, the story's protagonist, views with 'a cartographer's eye' the 'string of swimming pools' owned by his neighbours and, optimistically embracing his vision of suburban connectedness, he decides to swim home through them, thereby transforming them into one body, 'the Lucinda River', so-named after his wife.[54] Cheever's depiction of the different swimming pools and the inhabitants on their 'banks' reveals to the reader, however, the social and economic boundaries that serve to isolate rather than include Neddy, an apprehension which belatedly becomes available to him as he arrives at his home to find himself dispossessed, his house locked, dark, empty and neglected.

Cheever's evocation of Neddy Merrill's mythical voyage through suburbia also reveals many of the places through which he travels to be hybrid spaces, as Roger Silverstone has described them. Silverstone argues that suburbia itself is a hybrid: 'Not nature, not culture; not country, not city; suburbia is a physical embodiment of a mythical solution to an essential contradiction.'[55] An in-between space, suburbia both depends upon and denies boundaries between multiple 'dualisms'. Silverstone explains that the 'mythical solution', through which 'essential dualisms, both spatial and temporal, were denied',[56] is created through the 'hybridization' of space and time. The 'hybridization of space' is achieved through the grafting of the countryside or nature onto the urban or artificial. In Cheever's stories the hybridity of such spaces is germane to their significance to the narrator and the reader. In 'The Country Husband', for example, the narrator is required by his wife to participate in her staging of family life on their floodlit stoop for a photograph for their Christmas cards. This spectacle turns night into day, inside into outside and the private into the public as it commodifies 'the family' to passing onlookers.[57] In 'The Swimmer', Neddy Merrill paradoxically draws attention to the artificiality of the swimming pools by trying to turn them into a river. At the same time, some of the pools seem to be more natural than others: the Hallorans' pool, for example, 'was perhaps the oldest in the country, a fieldstone rectangle, fed by a brook. It had no filter or pump and its waters were the opaque gold of the stream.'[58] However, Cheever's evocation of Neddy's journey discloses to the reader the artificiality and hence precariousness not only of the pools but also of the social bonds articulated through their owners, even the naked-swimming and courteous Hallorans.

'The Swimmer', like many of Cheever's stories, also reveals how suburbia embodies 'the hybridization of time', as Silverstone has termed it, where the past is transplanted into the present: for example, family photograph albums evoke a connection to a past that has in fact been severed by the migration to the suburbs.[59] Suburbia erases connections to the past that embed other types of communities in their locale, so the suburban subject is stranded in the present, having only 'ghostly images' to connect him or her to former activities and relationships. In 'The Swimmer', the hybridisation of time is personalised through Neddy Merrill's forgetting and hence denial of a past whose catastrophic consequences gradually become apparent to the reader and finally to Neddy. In other stories, Cheever shows the denial of and severance from the past to be fundamental to the maintenance of suburban community. In 'The Country Husband', for example, Francis Weed's realisation of his family's disinclination to hear about his immediate past – he has just survived the crash landing of an aeroplane – is quickly followed by his recognition of the necessity of oblivion to his social group, which maintains itself through its denial of both troubling recent history and transgressive desires.

Cheever's stories also show how the hybridisation of space and time are interconnected in the suburbs. In 'O Youth and Beauty!' Cash Bentley, haunted by his lost youth, looks out one night through his kitchen window at the 'young people's party' that his neighbours are hosting in their artificially lit garden: 'He feels as if the figures in the next yard are the spectres from some party in that past where all his tastes and desires lie, and from which he has been cruelly removed. He feels like a ghost of the summer evening. He is sick with longing.'[60] Like Silverstone's 'ghostly images', the young people evoke a past that happened elsewhere, his severance from which makes Cash feel dematerialised in his own present. While Cheever does not allow Cash Bentley insight into his own existence, this story, like his other suburban stories, illustrates how the short story favours 'moments of condensed significance, moments in time which allow or enforce a stepping out of routine, out of time', as Kasia Boddy puts it.[61] In Cheever's stories, such moments 'out of time' occur *through* the spaces of suburbia, and the routines whereby his characters inhabit them. In 'O Youth and Beauty!', the epiphany which Cash Bentley does not attain is afforded to the reader. Switching suddenly to the present tense – 'Then it is a summer night, a wonderful summer night' – Cheever transfers his focus from Cash to a community of perspectives that include the reader and culminate in our seeing how a neighbour, through her window:

> glances up at the sky and asks, '*Where* did all the stars come from?' She is old and foolish, and yet she is right: Last night's stars seem to have drawn to themselves a new range of galaxies, and the night sky is not dark at all, except where there is a tear in the membrane of light.[62]

This intimation of wondrous other dimensions of existence opens up through and beyond the suburban spaces and boundaries within which the neighbour is confined. Cheever's description illustrates how, through his poetic images, he gives his stories a dreamlike quality that accompanies and arises out of his evocation of the temporal and spatial co-ordinates of everyday suburban life. It also exemplifies how, for Cheever, 'modern life' was 'rimmed with the marvellous', as Updike has observed.[63] Cheever concludes his visionary description by noting: 'In the unsold house lots near the track a hermit thrush is singing.'[64] Here, as elsewhere in Cheever's stories, the transfiguration of a world experienced through suburban time and space occurs through, or comes to rest in, suburbia's marginal spaces. These are often also neglected man-made or cultivated spaces that nature has reclaimed. In 'The Swimmer', for instance, Neddy Merrill not only swims through his neighbours' pools, but also struggles through thorny hedges, across vacant lots and along the verge and 'grass divider' of a main road. It is in these spaces that Neddy experiences another temporality – in the hours it takes him to swim home, the seasons seem to change as the perhaps 'blighted' leaves change colour and fall and the twilight reflected on a pool late in his journey has 'a wintry gleam'.[65] In his evocation of this alternative temporal dimension, Cheever not only suggests Neddy's psychological disintegration and social fall from grace, but also the possibility of an existence freed from the usual trammels on perception.

After 'The Swimmer', Cheever published only seven more stories with *The New Yorker*. He was increasingly 'mining the element of the fantastic', as Yagoda has observed, while the magazine was for the time being 'still committed to a literary ethos of naturalism, plausibility, and the emotional identification of reader with character'.[66] However, Cheever's poetic evocation of the transformation of his characters' perceptual and emotional relationship to the world through the derealisation of suburban time and spaces, anticipates subsequent suburban fiction published in *The New Yorker* and elsewhere.

Fictional representations of the suburbs in the 1960s continued to explore the effect of social and cultural change as it was registered through the experience of everyday life. In the novel *Revolutionary Road* (1961), Richard Yates portrays the emotional dispossession[67] of his protagonist, Frank Wheeler, and his final repossession of himself as he accepts the consoling familiarity of his work and suburban life. However, the suburban discontent of many of Cheever's housewives takes a darker turn through the narrative of April Wheeler, whose unhappiness with her feminine role eventually leads to her death. Rooted in suburban culture of the 1950s, though poised on a cultural and political threshold, neither the characters nor the novel can foresee the 'revolution' of sexual and cultural values that the new decade will bring.

Suburban short stories of the 1960s likewise evoke this threshold moment as they depict their characters' attempt, in a changing present, to articulate the past with a future they sense but cannot see. From the early 1960s onwards, Updike was a prolific producer of suburban stories, including many of those in a scattered sequence about the couple Richard and Joan Maple which he published, mainly in *The New Yorker*, between 1956 and 1976. Corresponding closely with Updike's own life, the suburban stories chart their characters' initial embrace of the energy and promise of suburban life at a time of changing sexual mores, and the emotions they experience as they undergo infidelity, separation, divorce and re-marriage. In his lyrical evocation of his characters' feelings, Updike often focuses on their reflections on the relationship between the past and the present, as they are expressed through the suburban landscape. In 'Plumbing' (1973), for example, the narrator reflects that in moving to a new house with his new wife and family, 'We think we have bought living space and a view when in truth we have bought a maze, a history, an archaeology of pipes',[68] but that in the house he and his former family have vacated 'the ghosts we have left only we can see'.[69] In 'Separating', Updike evokes Richard Maple's emotions as he spends the spring stalling the moment when he will have to tell his children he is leaving their mother, through the daily repetition of his 'interminable' activities maintaining the tennis court. Characteristically of the lyric short story, Updike fuses Richard's interior and exterior landscape as he contemplates how: 'All spring he had moved through a world of insides and outsides, of barriers and partitions . . . Each moment was a partition, with the past on one side and the future on the other, a future containing this unthinkable *now*.'[70]

The use of the short story form to explore transitional moments,[71] and the connection, in the suburban short story, of such moments to spatial thresholds and boundaries, is also put to dramatic and uncanny effect by Joyce Carol Oates in 'Where Are You Going, Where Have You Been?' (1970). The story of the 'seduction' of Connie, a teenage girl, by a demonic interloper, Arnold Friend, it could be read, as Updike has suggested, as being about 'the call of the counterculture, luring the fifties' restless Connies out from their cramping domestic security and onto the road'.[72] Through Connie's narrative, Oates does indeed suggest the promise of transition to a culture of less restrictive sexual and gender codes, but the uncanny power of the story arises from Connie's ambivalence about crossing a series of thresholds, as well as the ambiguity of Arnold Friend, seducer or potential rapist and murderer. Connie's passage from adolescence into adulthood involves leaving the house and entering various suburban public spaces, by crossing the highway to the shopping plaza and the 'fly-infested' but heady drive-in restaurant. Back at the family home she is tempted to leave, the boundaries of Connie's body and psyche are extended and protected by objects that constitute thresholds in and around the house – the mirror, the telephone, the flyscreen on the kitchen door, the lawn and the driveway. Her family away at a barbecue, Arnold Friend stands outside, cajoling and threatening Connie to leave her now empty home. Oates describes how Connie 'went into the kitchen and approached the door slowly, then hung onto the screen door, her bare toes curling down off the step'[73] and how, with increasing terror, she hesitates at these thresholds. Such thresholds, both inside and outside the house, like Cheever's marginal and boundary spaces, are also liminal spaces, offering the promise – and in Connie's case, possible horror – of revelation and emergence into another place and moment.

Such transitional moments are often preceded by an impasse, whose dramatisation is central to the story, as is illustrated by 'Where Are You Going?' and many of Updike's and Cheever's stories. Lauren Berlant uses the term to designate 'a stretch of time in which one moves around with a sense that the world is intensely present and enigmatic, such that the activity of living demands both absorptive awareness and a hypervigilance that collects material that might clarify things'.[74] The subjects of suburbia are often caught in an impasse, according to Berlant, because they enact the 'cruel optimism' of desiring what is 'actually an obstacle to . . . flourishing',[75] as epitomised by the fantasy of 'the good life' that suburbia enshrines. However, in an impasse, one may be particularly attuned to the present moment which is 'perceived first affectively: the present is what makes itself present to us before it becomes anything else'.[76] For the suburban subject, such attunement to what is unfolding occurs through the ordinary and the everyday, whose affect may be felt as the potential for 'new rhythms of living, rhythms that could, at any time, congeal into norms, forms and institutions'.[77] The transgressions of Cheever's characters, for example, which often express an impasse, offer the reader and sometimes the characters glimpses of new ways of living beyond suburban norms. In 'Where Are You Going?', Connie's response, which Oates evokes as dreaminess, to the affect of various suburban public spaces being transformed by youth and consumer culture, is followed by her vacillation on thresholds within her home until finally Arnold Friend coaxes and intimidates her over the threshold, beyond which stretch ambiguously 'vast sunlit reaches of the land behind him and on all sides of him, so much land that Connie had never seen before and did not recognize except to know that she was going into it'.[78]

An exploration of the relationship between the past and the present, as it is expressed through everyday life, continues to be the subject of suburban short stories in the 1970s and 1980s. Reflection on the past as it affects present-day relationships is a recurrent theme of the short stories of Ann Beattie, a prolific contributor of short stories, many of them suburban, to *The New Yorker* during these decades. It is also the theme of Bobbie Ann Mason's much-anthologised story 'Shiloh', which appeared in *The New Yorker* in 1980. In 'Shiloh', Mason hones the 'minimalist' style which she is regarded as sharing with writers such as Beattie and its perceived originator, Raymond Carver, a style which Mason forges to express her 'democratization' of content as she depicts blue-collar characters and the popular culture which they inhabit. To Leroy Moffitt, Mason's protagonist, the changes that have taken place in his rural home town and his marriage during his years on the road are epitomised by his observation that: 'Subdivisions are spreading across western Kentucky like an oil slick'.[79] The story concludes with Leroy at an impasse as he watches his wife walking along a river: 'Now she turns toward Leroy and waves her arms. Is she beckoning him? She seems to be doing an exercise for her chest muscles. The sky is unusually pale – the color of the dust ruffle Mabel made for their bed.'[80] Hobbled by the injury that has ended his days as a truck-driver, Leroy is unable to move back into the past or forward to catch up with Norma Jean. He notices marital and cultural change affectively, as he tries to reconcile an image of Norma Jean's recent empowerment, (the 'exercise for her chest muscles'), through popular culture's mediation of class mobility and women's liberation, with the domestic and marital continuity his mother-in-law, Mabel, is trying to protect through the dust ruffle she has made for their bed. By ending the story with an impasse, Mason moves away from the epiphany that characterised modernist short stories, but keeps open the possibility of gradual revelation through the understanding which may emerge from affective attention to change. Such endings are characteristic of the suburban short stories of the 'minimalist' writers such as Mason, Beattie and Carver.

In representing Leroy Moffitt's struggle to interpret personal and cultural meaning through the image of the subdivision replacing the readable signs of a more familiar past, Mason articulates a recurring theme of American writing about the suburbs. The difficulty of reading the artefacts which comprise the signifiers of the suburban landscape, which Cheever explored in 'A Vision of the World', has remained insistent as American suburbs have spread and diversified, since the 1950s, to include the 'ruburbs'[81] of Mason's western Kentucky and the de-centralised 'sprawl' typified by Los Angeles. Joan Didion, for example, has described how driving through Los Angeles produces feelings of exhilaration or anxiety because in its apparently homogeneous landscape 'conventional information is missing. Context clues are missing.'[82] The repetition of the same 'laundromats, body shops, strip shopping malls' suggests uniformity as did the iconic houses and spaces of Levittown. For Didion, there is nothing 'to encourage the normal impulse toward "recognition", or narrative connection'.[83]

Suburban fiction has continued to show characters searching for 'narrative connection' in the landscape of suburbia, while responding affectively to microcosmic changes that register in everyday life. In the 'low-rent' suburban landscape of 'motels, back-yard sales, gas stations, night cafés'[84] that recurs in Raymond Carver's short stories, for example, characters frequently respond to the breakdown of familiar narratives with a sense of dissociation from their environment. In 'Why Don't You Dance?' (1981), domestic and suburban space are defamiliarised as a man puts the contents of his house out for a yard sale, reconstructing the interior of his home in his yard. The girl whom he invites to dance there later tries to describe the scene: 'She kept talking. She told everyone. There was more to it, and she was trying to get it talked out. After a time she quit trying.'[85] Just as the girl cannot explain what she has witnessed, so Carver leaves the reader to infer what the man feels about this event and what has caused it from the silences and omissions in the text.[86] The domestic furniture and objects in 'Why Don't You Dance?' become strange and powerful not just because they have been placed in a new and incongruous context, but also because they represent all that Carver does not say about why they are in the yard.

Elsewhere, characters often respond to the artifices and artefacts of the suburban landscape with 'dreaminess', whether this be the narcissistic absorption of Connie in 'Where Are You Going?', the escape into dreams induced by suburban surfaces of Cheever's narrator in 'A Vision of the World', or the 'dreaminess' of Frank Bascombe, the narrator of Richard Ford's novel *The Sportswriter* (1986). Frank pensively embraces the 'mystery' of the everyday and the promise, which he knows to be fictive, offered by the suburban landscape and its consumerist artefacts, as a means of curing himself of the different kind of dreaminess that has afflicted him since the death of his son and the end of his marriage. In post-Second World War short stories, a thematic focus on characters' responses to suburban surfaces that are perceived variously as opaque, rebarbative, enticing or mesmerising, is accompanied by a textual and authorial preoccupation with the suburban world of artifices as one 'of surfaces, textures and signs', as Robert H. Brinkmeyer Jr has put it. Brinkmeyer argues that because 'in their abundance of objects and signs ... suburbs everywhere announce themselves as constructed, as artifacts', they are 'sites of wonder' which invite an imaginative response that will 'transfix and transfigure [and] remake anew'.[87] Such a response to suburbia characterised the mid-century stories of Cheever and Updike, and has continued to shape the poetics of American short stories.

Notes

1. John Cheever, 'Why I Write Short Stories', in *Collected Stories and Other Writings* (New York: The Library of America, 2009), p. 997.
2. Ben Yagoda, *About Town, The New Yorker and the World It Made* (Boston, MA: Da Capo Press, 2000), p. 38.
3. Mary F. Corey, *The World Through a Monocle, The New Yorker at Midcentury* (Cambridge, MA: Harvard University Press, 1999), p. 11.
4. Ibid. p. 9.
5. Yagoda, quoted in Faye Hammill '*The New Yorker*', the Middlebrow, and the Periodical Marketplace in 1925', in Fiona Green (ed.), *Writing for The New Yorker: Critical Essays on An American Periodical* (Edinburgh: Edinburgh University Press, 2015), p. 25.
6. Hammill, '*The New Yorker*', p. 31.
7. Yagoda, *About Town*, p. 152.
8. Ibid. p. 153.
9. Ibid. p. 12.
10. Ibid. p. 162.
11. Ibid. p. 103, p. 162.
12. Sarah Cain, '"We Stand Corrected", *New Yorker* Fact-checking and the Business of American Accuracy', in Green (ed.), *Writing for The New Yorker*, p. 41.
13. Yagoda, *About Town*, p. 152.
14. Kasia Boddy, *The American Short Story Since 1950* (Edinburgh: Edinburgh University Press, 2010), p. 39.
15. Yagoda, *About Town*, p. 238.
16. Hammill, '*The New Yorker*', in Green (ed.), *Writing for the New Yorker*, p. 30.
17. Ibid. p. 18.
18. Dwight MacDonald, quoted in Paul March-Russell, *The Short Story: An Introduction* (Edinburgh: Edinburgh University Press, 2009), p. 84.
19. March-Russell, *The Short Story*, p. 41.
20. Yagoda, *About Town*, p. 302.
21. John Updike, 'Friends from Philadelphia', in *Collected Early Stories*, ed. Christopher Carduff (New York: The Library of America, 2013), pp. 10–17 and Updike, 'A & P', *Collected Early Stories*, pp. 316–22.

22. Robert M. Luscher, 'John Updike', in Alfred Bendixen and James Nagel (eds), *A Companion to the American Short Story* (Malden, MA, Oxford and Chichester: Wiley-Blackwell, 2010), p. 351.
23. Updike, 'Leaves', in *Collected Early Stories*, pp. 422–5.
24. Eileen Baldeshwiler, 'The Lyric Short Story', in Charles E. May (ed.), *The New Short Story Theories* (Athens: Ohio University Press, 1994), p. 231
25. May, *The New Short Story Theories*, p. 199.
26. Ibid. p. 201.
27. Baldeshwiler, 'The Lyric Short Story', p. 231.
28. May, *The New Short Story Theories*, p. 214.
29. John Cheever, 'The Trouble of Marcie Flint', in *The Stories of John Cheever* (Harmondsworth and New York: Penguin, 1982), p. 296.
30. Keith Wilhite, 'John Cheever's Shady Hill, Or: How I Learned to Stop Worrying and Love the Suburbs', *Studies in American Fiction* 34.2 (Autumn 2006): 221.
31. Cheever, 'A Vision of the World', in *The Stories of John Cheever*, p. 512.
32. Ibid. p. 512.
33. Ibid. p. 513
34. Ibid. p. 514.
35. Ibid.
36. Ibid.
37. Robert Beuka, *SuburbiaNation, Reading Suburban Landscape in Twentieth-Century American Fiction and Film* (New York and Basingstoke: Palgrave Macmillan, 2004), p. 17.
38. Betty Friedan, *The Feminine Mystique* (Harmondsworth: Penguin, 1963), p. 13.
39. Cheever, 'The Trouble of Marcie Flint', p. 289.
40. Cheever, 'The Country Husband', in *The Stories of John Cheever*, p. 327.
41. Boddy, *The American Short Story*, p. 41.
42. Corey, *The World Through a Monocle*, p. 152.
43. Cheever, 'The Cure', in *The Stories of John Cheever*, p. 156.
44. See Lynne Spigel, 'From Theatre to Space Ship: Metaphors of suburban domesticity in postwar America', in Roger Silverstone (ed.), *Visions of Suburbia* (London and New York: Routledge, 1997), pp. 217–39.
45. Beuka, *SuburbiaNation*, p. 79.
46. Cheever, 'The Cure', p. 158.
47. Kennth T. Jackson, *Crabgrass Frontier: The Surburbanization of the United States* (New York and Oxford: Oxford University Press, 1985), p. 58.
48. Cheever, 'The Cure', p. 164.
49. Boddy, *The American Short Story*, p. 38.
50. Wilhite, 'John Cheever's Shady Hill', p. 218.
51. Cheever, 'The Housebreaker of Shady Hill', in *The Stories of John Cheever*, p. 263.
52. Ibid. p. 268.
53. See Benedict Anderson's discussion of the modern concept of simultaneity and its relation to the idea of community, specifically the nation, in *Imagined Communities: Reflections on the Origin and Spread of Nationalism* (London and New York: Verso, 1998), p. 24. Beuka also examines Cheever's portrayal of 'imagined community' in 'The Swimmer' through Anderson's related concept of 'horizontal comradeship', in *SuburbiaNation*, pp. 96–7.
54. Cheever, 'The Swimmer', in *The Stories of John Cheever*, p. 603.
55. Silverstone, 'Introduction' to *Visions of Suburbia*, p. 8.
56. Ibid.
57. Cheever, 'The Country Husband', p. 337.
58. Cheever, 'The Swimmer', p. 608.
59. Silverstone, *Visions of Suburbia*, pp. 8–9.
60. Cheever, ''O Youth and Beauty!', in *The Stories of John Cheever*, p. 216.

61. Boddy, *The American Short Story*, p. 101.
62. Cheever, 'O Youth and Beauty!', p. 215.
63. John Updike, *Odd Jobs: Essays and Criticism* (London: Penguin, 1991), p. 112.
64. Cheever, 'O Youth and Beauty!', p. 215.
65. Cheever, 'The Swimmer', p. 610.
66. Yagoda, *About Town*, p. 290.
67. See Catherine Jurca's critique of the white suburban man's sense of dispossession in *White Diaspora: The Suburb and the Twentieth-Century American Novel* (Princeton and Woodstock: Princeton University Press, 2001).
68. Updike, 'Plumbing', in *Collected Early Stories*, p. 693.
69. Ibid. p. 695.
70. John Updike, 'Separating', in *Too Far to Go: The Maples Stories* (New York: Random House-Fawcett, 1979), p. 195.
71. Boddy, *The American Short Story*, p. 100.
72. John Updike, 'Introduction' to *The Best American Short Stories of the Century* (Boston and New York: Houghton Mifflin, 2000), p. xxi.
73. Joyce Carol Oates, 'Where Are You Going, Where Have You Been?' in Tobias Wolff (ed.), *The Vintage Book of Contemporary American Short Stories* (New York: Vintage, Random House, 1994), p. 352.
74. Lauren Berlant, *Cruel Optimism* (Durham, NC and London: Duke University Press, 2011), p. 4.
75. Ibid. p. 1.
76. Ibid. p. 4.
77. Ibid. p. 9.
78. Oates, 'Where Are You Going?', p. 365.
79. Bobbie Ann Mason, 'Shiloh', in *Shiloh and Other Stories* (Lexington: The University of Kentucky Press, 1995), p. 3.
80. Ibid. p. 16.
81. According to R. Z. Sheppard, 'ruburbs' designate places that are 'no longer rural but not yet suburban', quoted by Albert Wilhelm in *Bobbie Ann Mason: A Study of the Short Fiction* (New York: Twayne, 1998), p. 4.
82. Joan Didion, 'Pacific Distances', in *After Henry* (New York: Vintage, Random House, 1993), p. 110.
83. Ibid. p. 111.
84. Robert Macfarlane, 'Back to the Source', *The Guardian*, Saturday, 9 April 2005. Available at <http://www.theguardian.com/books/2005/apr/09/scienceandnature.raymondcarver> (last accessed 15 April 2018), n.p.
85. Raymond Carver, 'Why Don't You Dance?', in *Where I'm Calling From: Selected Stories* (London: The Harvill Press, 1995), p. 130.
86. See Bill Buford's discussion of the effect of 'silences' in the stories of 'dirty realist' writers like Carver, in 'Editorial', in Bill Buford (ed.), *Dirty Realism: New Writing From America* (Cambridge: Granta, 1983), p. 5.
87. Robert H. Brinkmeyer Jr, 'Suburban Culture, Imaginative Wonder, The Fiction of Frederick Barthelme', *Studies in the Literary Imagination* 27.2 (Fall 1994): 113.

Bibliography

Anderson, Benedict, *Imagined Communities: Reflections on the Origin and Spread of Nationalism* (London and New York: Verso, 1998).
Baldeshwiler, Eileen, 'The Lyric Short Story: The Sketch of a History' in Charles E. May, (ed.), *The New Short Story Theories* (Athens: Ohio University Press, 1994).

Berlant, Lauren, *Cruel Optimism* (Durham, NC and London: Duke University Press, 2011).
Beuka, Robert, *SuburbiaNation: Reading Suburban Landscape in Twentieth-Century American Fiction and Film* (New York and Basingstoke, Hampshire: Palgrave Macmillan, 2004).
Boddy, Kasia, *The American Short Story Since 1950* (Edinburgh: Edinburgh University Press, 2010).
Brinkmeyer, Robert H. Jr, 'Suburban Culture, Imaginative Wonder: The Fiction of Frederick Barthelme', *Studies in the Literary Imagination* 27.2 (Fall 1994): 105–14.
Buford, Bill, 'Editorial' in Bill Buford (ed.), *Dirty Realism: New Writing From America* (Cambridge: Granta, 1983), pp. 4–5.
Cain, Sarah, '"We Stand Corrected": *New Yorker* Fact-checking and the Business of American Accuracy', in Fiona Green (ed.), *Writing for The New Yorker: Critical Essays on An American Periodical* (Edinburgh: Edinburgh University Press, 2015), pp. 36–57.
Carver, Raymond. 'Why Don't You Dance?', in *Where I'm Calling From: Selected Stories* (London: The Harvill Press, 1995).
Cheever, John, *The Stories of John Cheever* (Harmondsworth and New York: Penguin, 1982).
— *Collected Stories and Other Writings*. (New York: The Library of America, 2009).
Corey, Mary F., *The World through A Monocle: The New Yorker at Midcentury* (Cambridge, MA and London: Harvard University Press, 1999).
Didion, Joan, 'Pacific Distances' in Joan Didion, *After Henry* (New York: Vintage, Random House, 1993), pp. 110–44.
Friedan, Betty, *The Feminine Mystique* (Harmondsworth: Penguin, 1963).
Green, Fiona (ed.), *Writing for The New Yorker: Critical Essays on An American Periodical* (Edinburgh: Edinburgh University Press, 2015).
Hammill, Faye, '*The New Yorker*, the Middlebrow, and the Periodical Marketplace in 1925', in Fiona Green (ed), *Writing for The New Yorker: Critical Essays on An American Periodical* (Edinburgh: Edinburgh University Press, 2015), pp. 17–35.
Jackson, Kenneth T., *Crabgrass Frontier: The Suburbanization of the United States* (New York and Oxford: Oxford University Press, 1985).
Jurca, Catherine, *White Diaspora: The Suburb and the Twentieth-Century American Novel* (Princeton and Woodstock: Princeton University Press, 2001).
Luscher, Robert M., 'John Updike' in Alfred Bendixen and James Nagel (eds), *A Companion to the American Short Story* (Malden, MA, Oxford and Chichester: Wiley-Blackwell, 2010), pp. 345–65.
Macfarlane, Robert, 'Back to the source', *The Guardian*, Saturday, 9 April 2005, http://www.theguardian.com/books/2005/apr/09/scienceandnature.raymondcarver (last accessed 15 April 2018).
March-Russell, Paul, *The Short Story: An Introduction* (Edinburgh: Edinburgh University Press, 2009).
Mason, Bobbie Ann, 'Shiloh', in *Shiloh and Other Stories* (Lexington: The University Press of Kentucky, 1995).
May, Charles E., 'Chekhov and the Modern Short Story', in Charles E. May (ed.), *The New Short Story Theories* (Athens: Ohio University Press, 1994), pp. 199–217.
— (ed.), *The New Short Story Theories* (Athens: Ohio University Press, 1994).
Oates, Joyce Carol, 'Where Are You Going, Where Have You Been?', in Tobias Wolff (ed.), *The Vintage Book of Contemporary American Short Stories* (New York: Vintage, Random House, 1994), pp. 347–65.
Silverstone, Roger (ed.), *Visions of Suburbia* (London and New York: Routledge, 1997).
Updike, John, *Too Far to Go: The Maples Stories* (New York: Random House-Fawcett, 1979).

— *Odd Jobs: Essays and Criticism* (London: Penguin, 1991).
— 'Introduction' to *The Best American Short Stories of the Century* (Boston, MA and New York: Houghton Mifflin, 2000), pp. xv–xxiv.
— *Collected Early Stories*, ed. Christopher Carduff (New York: The Library of America, 2013).
Wilhelm, Albert, *Bobbie Ann Mason: A Study of the Short Fiction* (New York: Twayne, 1998).
Wilhite, Keith, 'John Cheever's Shady Hill, Or: How I Learned to Stop Worrying and Love the Suburbs', *Studies in American Fiction* 34.2 (Autumn 2006): 215–39.
Yagoda, Ben, *About Town: The New Yorker and the World It Made* (Boston, MA: Da Capo Press, 2000).

17

The Short Story and the Environment

Deborah Lilley and Samuel Solnick

'WHEN WE TRY TO PICK OUT anything by itself, we find it hitched to everything else in the universe.'[1] John Muir's description of the feeling of immanence he experienced in *My First Summer in the Sierra* (1911) also conveys a central issue within ecological thinking: interconnection. Thinking about interconnectivity has provided a challenge to ecocriticism, a critical approach which, to use Timothy Clark's helpful definition, enables 'a study of the relationship between literature and the physical environment, usually considered from out of the global environmental crisis and its revisionist challenge to given modes of thought and practice'.[2] This sense of emerging crisis means that it is no longer enough to posit a vague form of holistic interconnection. It is increasingly important to think about how things are 'hitched' to each other; about which connections – cultural as well as ecological – are most important.

Shifts in environmental awareness mean that traditional ways of describing and understanding the material world, including the places and geographies we find in the short story, need to evolve. The specific locales of Jack London's stories of Yukon mining or Alice Munro's Huron Country, for example, seem less splendidly isolated in the context of the 2015 debates about whether the Yukon or Ontario legislatures should allow fracking. Fracking can release contaminants into the water table that may leach across boundaries and borders, and it leads to the burning of fossil fuels that release greenhouse gases which shift the conditions of the entire biosphere. Ideas of neatly bounded places collapse in the face of such ecological awareness. The distinctions perceived between conceptions of 'the human' and 'the natural', the local and global, become permeable. This chapter focuses on what happens when short stories engage with a changing (sense of) environment. Thinking about the short story and the environment from an ecocritical perspective means working through different conceptions and representations of place (local environments), planet (The Environment writ large), and tradition (a cultural environment). Accordingly, this chapter ranges across spatial and temporal scales, from poetics of place to stories for a degraded world, and from idealised pasts to apocalyptic futures.

Some short stories tackle environmental crisis directly. For example, in the 2011 collection *I'm With the Bears: Stories from a Damaged Planet*, edited by Mark Martin, and including work by T. C. Boyle, Lydia Millet, Kim Stanley Robinson, Nathaniel Rich and Margaret Atwood, the authors rely primarily on a sense of apocalypse to adapt the short story to environmentalist ends. Introduced by the influential environmental critic and activist Bill McKibben, best known for his 1995 polemic *The End of Nature*, the collection begins with the provocative aims of galvanising critical thought and productive action through stories, to provide 'jolts we dearly need'[3] against the political and cultural inertia that has come to characterise the presentation and perception of climate change. In doing so, McKibben states his hope that the collection will win hearts, minds, and – with a portion of the proceeds of the book's sales going to his environmental campaign group www.350.org – funds.

Taking a very different kind of approach to environmental crisis are the 'ecologically conscious' stories identified by Glen A. Love in *The Columbia Companion to the Twentieth Century American Short Story* (2000), which focus on place rather than planet. Pointing to Wendell Berry and Wallace Stegner as examples, Love argues that such writings contrast a sense of alienation between people and place with the value of 'knowing one's geographical place'. Love locates this development within the strand of the short story tradition 'deeply imbued with a distinctive sense of the American land',[4] and traces this back to Washington Irving's Hudson River tales. In doing so, he marks a shift in the tradition towards a more refined awareness of the interrelationships that such places embody.

The multiple ways that short stories have represented and responded to environmental issues resonate with Martin Scofield's suggestion that the short story is particularly amenable to scenarios of crisis, owing to its unity and specificity of theme and focus. Scofield argues that 'the short story frequently – one might almost say typically – takes a moment of crisis as its subject matter: the moment which marks a radical change in the life of an individual, a group or . . . a whole nation'.[5] Given the capacity of environmental crises to register not only upon these categories but between and beyond them, from a cellular to a planetary scale, this chapter explores what a sense of environmental crisis does to the writing and reading of short stories in the Anthropocene: the epoch where humanity operates as a pervasive geophysical force.[6]

The two types of story outlined in the aforementioned collections highlight some of the challenges of representing and interpreting contemporary environmental crises. While the stories described by Love respond on a local and individual level, those collected in *I'm With the Bears* generate a sense of the global and reflect not only upon contemporary environmental maladies but anticipate apocalyptic futures. Yet by relying on the shock tactics of apocalyptic fiction, and seldom interrogating the specific nature of the connections between people, place or planet, Martin's selection of stories betrays certain limitations, too. By contrast, Love's examples illustrate how environmental crises permeate the short story tradition, asking new questions of its representations of and reflections upon place. This approach faces a different sort of limitation. Cataloguing short stories which 'expand our sense of interrelationships to encompass nonhuman as well as human contexts' – such as Eudora Welty's 'A Curtain of Green', Flannery O'Connor's 'A View of the Woods' and Leslie Marmon Silko's 'Lullaby' – Love argues that these stories 'return us to a world that encloses and antedates our culture and social presence' by calling up 'the wisdom of such places and the human need to reconnect with them'.[7] In doing so, he betrays a nostalgia for and an idealisation of the non-human world that is difficult to reconcile with the project of 'expand[ing] our sense of interrelationships' in the light of twenty-first-century ecological crises like climate change, species extinction and pollution.

The scope of these issues exceeds both the shock tactics of *I'm With the Bears* and Love's 'ecologically conscious' reconnections with place. This chapter shows how contemporary short stories grapple with the distortions of space, time and perspective that environmental awareness engenders. It explores not only the ways that environmental crises are represented, but also the ways that the short story's thematic unity and economy of focus can deal with the loosening of the boundaries of place, the blurring of the distinctions between the human and the non-human, and the emerging sense of humans as both changed by and changing their local and global environments.

These interrelated challenges can be seen in the Wyoming stories of Annie Proulx, where environmental issues are woven into the traditions of place writing associated with the 'national art form'[8] of the American short story. Proulx's writing recalls what she has described as the 'golden age of American landscape fiction',[9] fascinated with the local and regional, and epitomised by writers such as Willa Cather, William Faulkner, Flannery O'Connor and John Steinbeck. Proulx's stories locate 'the drive of capitalist democracy on the hunt for resources' associated with the 'pioneer ethos' within the broader legacies of the American place-writing tradition.[10] She brings the wilderness and the frontier – and their related themes of isolation, violence and the struggle for survival – alongside the rural life and 'local colour' of the pastoral homestead. These traditions are supplemented in Proulx's writing by an ecological sensitivity that foregrounds the multifaceted relationships between people and place.

Proulx addressed this complex inheritance in an interview in 2004, explaining that 'I am not people-centric, and I'm appalled at what human beings have done to the planet. I think it would be quite marvelous if human beings disappeared . . . 100 years ago I would have written the great-fight-against-the-elements kind of books, whereas now the landscape has moved from being the great enemy to being the victim.'[11] On the one hand, the sensitivity towards ecology in her stories decentres the human; on the other, it demonstrates the ways that the human and the non-human are deeply enmeshed, problematising the too-easy opposition that Proulx makes above between people and place. The environmental issues that are encountered in her stories, such as pollution and climate change, engage a sense of scale that exceeds the human, while at the same time she is often invested in the minute particularity of the socio-economic issues of specific locales and communities.

As with James Joyce's Dublin and Sherwood Anderson's Winesburg, place plays a central role in Proulx's short fiction. The vast spaces and rural towns of Wyoming depicted in her stories shape the lives of the characters, and the stories themselves. In *Close Range: Wyoming Stories* (1999), the material and cultural hinterlands of the state are imbued with an inescapable sense of the transience and the mutability of physical space and human place. In 'A Lonely Coast', the narrator surveys the landscape and reflects that:

> You think about the sea that covered this place hundreds of millions of years ago, the slow evaporation, mud turned to stone. There's nothing calm in those thoughts. It isn't finished, it can still tear apart. Nothing is finished. You take your chances.[12]

The pace of geologic time evokes an uneasy awareness of the relative impermanence of human life that appears again in 'People in Hell Just Want a Drink of Water'. Against the landscape's 'jags of mountain' and 'tumbled stones like fallen cities', 'the tragedies of people count for nothing'. Although 'the signs of [human] misadventure are everywhere' in the forms of 'fences, cattle, roads, refineries, mines, gravel pits, traffic lights . . . the sun-faded wreathes of plastic flowers marking death on the highway', we are told that 'only earth and sky matter. Only the endlessly repeated flood of morning light.'[13] But while the landscape is shown to exist in a state of flux against which humanity appears inconsequential, the representative sample of human life that Proulx chooses to highlight tells a more complicated story: one of industrial agriculture, oil production and resource extraction. Even the wreath, a reminder of mortality, signals a kind of de-naturalisation: flowers are now made of plastic, an inorganic material that lasts far longer than the people who use it. The story 'Job History' flags up the distortions of scale between human activity and the environmental problems it causes from another angle. Written in a series of short sentences, the story conveys the relentless pace and narrow focus of an individual life, in which an awareness of the global is present but barely registered; 'nobody has time to listen to the news', and when 'a strange hole that has appeared in the ozone layer'[14] is mentioned, ozone is confused with oxygen.

In the collection *Bad Dirt* (2004), ecological concerns are sometimes more direct. In the opening story, 'The Hellhole', a game and fish warden uses a mysterious 'glowing borehole'[15] to dish out rough justice on those he sees as ecologically deviant members of the public. The environmental consciousness that fuels the actions of the warden appears again in the story 'What Kind of Furniture Would Jesus Pick?', albeit in a less crusading fashion. The story explores what Wes Berry calls 'the nexus of economy and ecology'[16] that appears throughout Proulx's writing: in this case, the loss of the 'open country'[17] of ranching thanks to the effects of drought and methane drilling. The environment has changed, the pastoral 'spring wind, fresh and warm and perfumed with pine resin' has become 'erratic, inimical', and 'the country wanted to go to sand dunes and rattlesnakes, wanted to scrape off its human ticks'.[18] The spill of 'poison wastewater'[19] from the methane drilling plant into the dwindling groundwater of the arid landscape results in a 'country of disintegrating communities, endangered species, human and animal misery, toxic wastes, and the wholesale destruction of the sources of life'.[20] Against the backdrop of his degrading environment, the resigned narrator fantasises about the 'simplest round-legged furniture' that Jesus would pick, 'everything pegged, no nails nor screws',[21] envisaging a nostalgic return to a way of life that avoids some of the depredations of modern technology. Berry argues that Proulx's writing conveys optimistic advocacy for 'local economic accountability and community possibility' through the development of 'ecological literacy',[22] and compares this to the fictions of Barbara Kingsolver, Ruth Ozeki and Jane Smiley.

However, such optimism is hard to find in 'Man Crawling Out of Trees', where alienation between people and place is developed through the story of New England emigrants Mitchell and Eugenie. At once entranced and terrified by the environment that they have chosen to live in, Proulx creates an ironic version of the sublime which culminates in Eugenie's failure to help an injured skier stranded in her garden. Her inaction appears representative of a loss of humanity that stems from a fundamental disconnection from her adopted environment on account of a dual sense of wonder and fear. For Mitchell and Eugenie, Wyoming appears 'peripheral to the real world'. Proulx draws upon insect imagery to describe the 'diminution of self' that this perception of place effects, reduced 'to a single gnat isolated from the greater swarm of gnats'.[23] The sense of disconnection between people and place extends to the wider community in the context of the drought and drilling that forms the backdrop to the couple's tale. As Ali Smith comments in a review of *Bad Dirt*, here 'the old rural laws of hospitality before savagery have been broken and there's no going back'.[24]

With their shared sense of alienation from the landscape and the background presence of ecological crisis, Proulx's stories exploit the form of the short story cycle, in which 'stories are both self-sufficient and interrelated'.[25] In *Bad Dirt*, in particular, each story is contained within the narrow scope of the material and personal landscapes of its characters, offering only glimpses of the broader environmental issues with which they are entangled. However, when the stories are read together, their perspectives are extended; these landscapes become visible on a larger scale, new connections emerge, and the signs of pollution and climate change become more visible. By constructing links across the stories, Proulx addresses environmental issues relatively obliquely while consolidating the notion that the fate of people and place are inextricably, inexorably, linked in a world of economic and ecological change. G. K. Chesterton compared the 'fleetingness and fragility'[26] of the short story form to the fragmented experience of modern life. It is significant that the same qualities should be appropriate to depicting environmental crises which, although pervasive and insidious, are often only glimpsed or partially grasped. Environmental issues are seldom addressed comprehensively in their totality; indeed, their diffuse nature makes this difficult to attempt, not least because of the ways that they challenge our sense of causality and confound our sense of scale. The short story offers a means to negotiate the challenges of representing crises such as climate change. In the work of writers such as Proulx, the specificity of the short story's focus allows readers an opportunity to glimpse particular aspects of phenomena like pollution and climate change. In doing so, short stories can replicate the ways that environmental issues are experienced and registered, and the disjointed, fragmented ways that their effects come to be communicated through different media and discourses.

The short story's formal traits offer alternative approaches to ecocritical debates surrounding the representational challenges of landscape and ecology. As Bill McKibben remarks, in the case of climate change, 'the truth is larger than usually makes for good fiction'.[27] For some critics, including Richard Kerridge and Lawrence Buell, the personal focus and timescale of the novel do not easily accommodate the scale or scope of environmental concerns, and crises are often reduced to functions of plot or character development. Accounting for environmental concerns demands narrative strategies that can respond to the particular issues of time and perspective that such concerns precipitate.[28] In contrast to the novel, the flexibility and adaptability of what Adrian Hunter has termed the 'strategic economies'[29] of the short story present opportunities to circumvent some of these problems. The short story is effectively exempted from some of the responsibility to be exhaustive associated with longer prose forms when they try to address the multiple scales of climate change. Instead, the form offers immediacy, flexibility and multiplicity in terms of approach and perspective.

Short story collections in particular provide a suitable form that can avoid the tendency for representations of environmental crises to 'reduce' 'complex long-term issues . . . to monocausal crises'.[30] Though individual stories are themselves only snapshots, collectively they may offer broader and richer reflections of the material and cultural causes and effects of environmental change. Short stories are therefore less likely to 'speak of the environmental crisis – as if "it" were a clear, stable and ahistorical concept'.[31] As Timothy Clark comments, in the case of environmental crisis, 'there is no "it"'.[32]

In a particularly compelling essay, Clark offers a reading of Raymond Carver's story 'Elephant' that explores the way the 'scales' we talk about when we talk about climate change rupture the familiar critical paradigms which are associated with the short story. Clark reads 'Elephant' – in which a man considers his personal and financial obligations before leaving with a friend in 'his big unpaid for car'– on three different 'scales'. The first is a 'critically naïve' personal scale. The second, often evoked in literary criticism, is that of national culture; 'topics prominent in discussions of Carver are broadly located at this scale, such as unemployment and consumer culture as they affect personal relationships, the ideals and realities of American domesticity, that society's materialism, and its concepts of gender, especially masculinity'.[33] Clark then reads the story, particularly the focus on the car, the icon of private fossil fuel transport, on a scale of 600 years (i.e. from 300 years before the 1988 story, to 300 after). On this scale, which stretches from before the Industrial Revolution to a future which will suffer the environmental effects of climate change, characters and settings that 'had seemed harmless on the personal or national scale reappear as destructive doubles of themselves'. Because of what Clark describes as the cumulative 'scale effects' of individual actions (e.g. driving, flying, boiling water), the material infrastructure that dictates people's lives may, in the context of climate change, 'partially displace more familiar issues of identity and cultural representation'. Technology, infrastructure and fossil fuels become politically significant, and ecologically orientated readings have to be more aware of the role of the non-human in the political sphere. This awareness 'decentres human agency, underlining the fragility and contingency of effective boundaries between public and private, objects and persons, the "innocent" and "guilty"'.[34]

Clark admits that his way of reading for 'scale' poses a challenge to critical approaches used to focusing on the plight of the individual: that 'the third scale's tendency to register a person primarily as a physical thing [i.e. as one of millions of comparatively wealthy consumers of energy and resources] is evidently problematic, almost too brutally removed from the daily interpersonal ethics, hopes and struggles that it ironizes'. And yet, Clark's reading does not violate 'Elephant' by reducing the text to the status of ecological example. Rather, Clark zooms between scales, showing how this reading which ruptures individual agency fits with Carver's tone and technique, where the writing's minimalism speaks to 'a late-capitalist society of disjunctive surfaces and personal isolation in which the lack of a completely reliable sense of relation between cause and effect, intention and result, effort and reward, is accompanied by a pervading sense of insecurity'.[35]

Clark's interest in the scale effects of different behaviours, technologies and materials across different registers speaks to one of the most notable aspects of the last decade of ecocriticism – the shift away from a preponderance of phenomenological approaches (particularly those grounded in the late work of Martin Heidegger) towards the increasing prominence of theoretical paradigms which, in some way, address the impact of the non-human on our social and political structures. There is an increasing focus in contemporary ecocriticism on the ways objects, systems and materials confound human attempts to control or even conceptualise them. Without wanting to elide the very real differences between critical approaches, this awareness of the role of the non-human is central to Jane Bennet's 'vibrant materialism', to Timothy Morton and other figures associated with Object Orientated Ontology, to the deconstructive ecocriticism of figures such as Clark and Claire Colebrook, and to those influenced by Bruno Latour's Actor Network Theory.[36]

Perhaps the major contemporary challenge to environmentally aware authors and critics involves finding ways to talk about the macro scales on which climate change operates without neglecting the human scale which is (normally) central to fiction and criticism. One writer who consciously uses the form of the short story to address the tensions that Clark highlights between personal agency and the networks of technologies, lifestyle-choices and everyday behaviours, is Helen Simpson.

Arguably, the most interesting aspect of Simpson's collection *In-Flight Entertainment* (2010) is the way the stories operate collectively as a short story cycle, as this allows the subject of climate change to be addressed from a variety of angles. In the title story, for instance, two men discuss the environmental impact of flying while their plane is rerouted due to a fellow passenger's on-board coronary. The implicit link between the flatlining passenger and the resigned apocalypticism of one of the characters (an environmental campaigner who has given up hope) is one of several recent instances of fiction about climate change that uses a weak heart as a metaphor for a failing or precarious civilisation.[37] The penultimate story in Simpson's collection – which also featured in *I'm With the Bears* – is the epistolary 'Diary of an Interesting Year', set in a global warming-ravaged Britain in 2040. This survivor tale is the sort of apocalyptic narrative still most commonly associated with the term 'cli-fi', the snappy phrase coined by the journalist Dan Bloom to describe climate change fiction.

By including long stories overtly about climate change near the beginning and at the end of the collection, Simpson identifies climate change as a pervasive thematic concern of *In-Flight Entertainment*. The title story throws up several issues which recur through the collection, such as an interest in the environmental cost of particular behaviours and technologies; a figurative relationship between corporeal and planetary health; children as a metonym for the future; and the tension between informed activism and resigned fatalism or denial. Moreover, as Greg Garrard points out, all of the stories 'explore situations of knowing but not acting; hearing truths one had tried to ignore'.[38]

Some of the other stories in the collection address climate change directly. 'Ahead of the Pack' uses the language of personal fitness training to link BMI with carbon emissions, while decrying the hope for easy technological fixes: 'magic solutions like fat-busting drugs and air scrubbers always seem to bring a nasty rash of side effects'. 'Tipping Point', narrated by a frequently flying professor of early modern literature who has recently been dumped by his ecologically concerned girlfriend, shows that despite what some ecocritics would hope, awareness of the arts does not provide a bulwark against environmental exploitation. Rather, literature becomes part of the apparatus of denial: the narrator draws on Milton's *Comus* (1634) and on theories of the Romantic sublime to frame the earth as a 'full and unwithdrawing' resource, against the 'overwhelming natural phenomena' of which humans 'resemble frail figures in a painting by Casper David Friedrich, dwarfed by the immensity of nature'.[39]

As with Clark's reading for scale in Carver, the environmental context that frames Simpson's satirical, acerbic stories means that quotidian behaviours and objects (from aeroplanes to steaks) cast an uncanny shadow, even when they do not seem directly related to climate change. For example, in 'Homework', where the narrator helps her son with an assignment that he should have done earlier, the son's stated admiration for an aunt who 'goes on the best holidays' and owns 'an Audi and a BMW'[40] has, in the context of the collection, a clear environmental barb that heightens our sense of the child's own nascent consumerism with his delight in Nintendo Wii's and Manchester United-branded mugs. But the child also provides us with a junior version of the frequent flier of 'In-Flight Entertainment' and the hypocritical academic of 'Tipping Point' – characters who refuse to act despite what they know, and who cheat in order to allay the consequences. Simpson does not just foreground the environmental impact of her characters' consumption and technologies, she also stresses the ramifications of their pettiness, avarice and selfishness. One can also read the cheating child in 'Homework' as an allegory for society's dithering or greenwashing in the face of environmental necessity. As Garrard explains, 'Simpson's polyvocal treatment of climate change encourages us to see it as an available allegorical meaning even where it seems quite unlikely.'[41]

Speaking of 'In the Driver's Seat', where the narrator is driven too fast by a friend's partner, Garrard asks whether it would 'be too fanciful to interpret this as an oblique commentary on the way that, whatever our personal beliefs or behaviour, we are being dragged along on a "mad, dangerous, out-of-control" climatic journey with little influence over the "driver"?'[42] Given the encouragement to read allegorically that Simpson supplies to her readers, it would seem that such an interpretation is not at all far-fetched. *In-Flight Entertainment* combines humorous tales of everyday life with an allegorical dimension which flattens character and highlights the scale effects of their actions. In doing so, Simpson's stories incorporate the simultaneous considerations of individual and collective, local and global, that typify contemporary environmental consciousness. *In-Flight Entertainment*'s approach is relatively unusual in that, 'Diary of an Interesting Year' aside, Simpson uses the form of domestic realism to explore climate change. This is not the norm. In her useful survey of climate change in literature, Adeline Johns-Putra notes that with the exception of a few novels set in the present,

> overwhelmingly, climate change appears in novels as part of a futuristic dystopian and/or postapocalyptic setting. In such novels, climate change is depicted not just as an internal or psychological problem but for its external effects, often as part of an overall collapse including technological over-reliance, economic instability, and increased social division.[43]

What Johns-Putra says of novels also holds for anthologies of 'cli-fi' short stories such as *I'm With the Bears*, *Loosed upon the World: The Saga Anthology of Climate Fiction* (2015), and *Cli-Fi: Canadian Tales of Climate Change* (2017).

Part of the reason that 'cli-fi' tends toward the apocalyptic and dystopian lies in the fact that the most extreme effects of climate change have yet to occur. However, there is a related question as to how well equipped the realist mode is to cope with climate change or with other environmental issues that operate across space and time. In his study of fiction and climate change, Adam Trexler argues that realist fiction's 'focus on a narrow locale and set of characters compress distributed, global events. It struggles to understand the devastating potential of climate disaster.'[44] In a similar vein, the novelist Amitav Ghosh suggests that, when it comes to climate change, 'the very gestures by which it [the realist novel] conjures up reality are actually concealments of the real'.⁴⁵ In order to generate the texture of everyday life, realist fiction excludes what Ghosh calls the 'improbable'; in this instance, this includes the types of extreme events associated with representations and prognostications of climate change. Realist fiction is generally profoundly anthropocentric, focusing on humans and their interactions, rather than on the non-human world that is central to environmental issues.

Ghosh has been criticised by figures such as Dan Bloom and MacKenzie Wark, who point out that in his discourse on climate writing 'the fiction that takes climate change seriously is not taken seriously as fiction'.⁴⁶ While Ghosh dismisses science fiction as a generic 'outhouse' that exists outside the 'mansions of serious fiction',⁴⁷ the genre has a long-standing tradition of engagement with ecological questions. Science fiction has explored apocalyptic future scenarios, imagined technologies which modify humans' relationships with their environment, and rendered dystopian fears and (eco) utopian possibilities; it also frequently undermines anthropocentric views of existence and time. Indeed, as Urusla K. Le Guin contends, it 'is almost the only kind of story that ever really admits of a world not dominated by human beings (or gods, animals, or aliens who act just like human beings)'.⁴⁸

For Bryan L. Moore, Le Guin's comments exemplify science fiction's capacity to be considered a uniquely 'antianthropocentric' genre.⁴⁹ Moore traces environmental themes back to the earliest science fiction, including the short stories of Jules Verne and H. G. Wells. In Wells's 1897 apocalyptic story 'The Star', for example, the citizens of Earth are too caught up in their everyday lives to realise the danger that they are in from a celestial body moving rapidly towards them. Although there is no collision, the near miss causes catastrophic environmental damage which includes floods from melting ice. The final paragraph sees the narrative zoom away to some observing 'Martian astronomers' who, unable to see the millions of deaths, only note how little the planet appears to have changed. The narrator concludes that this 'only shows how small the vastest of human catastrophes may seem, at a distance of a few million miles'.⁵⁰

The antianthropocentric effect of this shift from a terrestrial to a Martian perspective undermines a belief in the importance of humanity when placed in relation to the vastness of geology and space. In the 1905 story 'The Empire of the Ants', Wells finds another way of challenging humanity's self-importance by suggesting that humans may eventually be usurped by another species: in this case a species of killer Amazonian ants. Both stories suggest a radical antianthropocentric challenge in the face of geophysical and ecological forces. What differentiates these stories from 'cli-fi' and most other more recent environmentally aware science fiction is the fact that humans are not depicted as the authors of their own destruction. Interestingly, when Wells chose to explore the idea of technologically induced destruction in 'A Dream of Armageddon' (1901), the trope he utilised – the flood – is central to biblical and ecological apocalyptic literature. Describing the warplanes that cause Armageddon, the narrator claims that humans 'turn 'em out as beavers build dams, and with no more sense of the rivers they're going to divert and the lands they're going to flood!'.⁵¹ This trope collapses the distinction between humans and other animals to offer a quasi-Darwinian vision of a species which has become maladapted to its surroundings. Crucially, this maladaptation comes through technology.

A comparable sense of humans becoming catastrophically maladapted comes in another early science fiction short story, E. M. Forster's Internet-anticipating 'The Machine Stops' (1909). Forster's tale is an important early example of how science fiction explores environmental questions through images of dystopia and apocalypse. 'The Machine Stops' imagines a society where individuals lead estranged lives, living in solitary cells underground, connected by communication pipes and instant entertainment. People have surrendered any sense of agency to the 'machine' that sustains but also insulates them: 'night and day, wind and storm, tide and earthquake, impeded man no longer. He had harnessed Leviathan. All the old literature, with its praise of Nature, and its fear of Nature, rang false as the prattle of a child.'[52] Inevitably, nature is not so easily divested, and one character, Kuno, leaves the subterranean world for the surface where, before being recaptured by the machine, he catches a glimpse of humans who have escaped this technological nightmare. There is hope, but not for the machine's subjects. The sustaining technology fails, civilisation collapses, and all eventually suffocate. The story is significant not just as an example of technological apocalypse but in the way that Forster presents the gradually deteriorating human environment (at least below ground) as concomitant with an increased alienation from the body. As Kuno remarks, 'we have annihilated not space, but the sense thereof'; according to the narrator, he seeks 'meadows and hills against which he might measure his body'.[53]

Forster's interest in corporeality chimes with an emphasis on embodiment that is a long-held feature of ecocriticism. Aspects of Forster's story can be found in many of the science fiction short stories that Love includes under the heading 'The Blighted Environment' in *The Columbia Companion* – the technological apocalypse of Stephen Vincent Benet's 'By the Waters of Babylon', for example, or the alienation from the body that arises in a dystopia where overpopulation necessitates chemically controlled impotence in Kurt Vonnegut's 'Welcome to the Monkey House'. Another of the tales selected by Love, Rick DeMarinis's 'Weeds', echoes Forster's sense of the organic world's resistance to attempts to coerce or contain it. In 'Weeds' the spraying of herbicides not only sickens humans and animals but leads to uncontrollable, chemical-resistant mutant plants.[54] DeMarinis's story is indebted to Rachel Carson's *Silent Spring* (1962), perhaps the most important foundational text of the modern environmental movement, with its warnings about insect resistance to pesticides and the wider ecological damage that these chemicals cause.[55]

As Joshua David Bellin and others have argued, the power and influence of Carson's text stems from the way she draws on science fiction as well as science fact. Bellin reads *Silent Spring* in the context of popular 'Big Bug' films such as *Them!*, and traces the science fiction sub-genre of marauding insect tales back to Wells's 'The Empire of the Ants'.[56] Moreover, *Silent Spring* actually opens with a science fiction-type story, 'A Fable for Tomorrow', which describes a formerly idyllic town stricken by sickness and animal deaths. 'This town does not actually exist', Carson acknowledges, but a 'grim specter has crept upon us almost unnoticed, and this imagined tragedy may easily become a stark reality we all shall know'.[57] Carson's fable uses a dystopia set in the very near future to explore the negative consequences of behaviour in the present.

This is typical of dystopias which, as Eric C. Otto notes, normally offer an extrapolated version of what already exists in reality by 'following current sociocultural, political, or scientific developments to their potentially devastating conclusions'.[58] In contrast, science fiction utopias function slightly differently and do not tend to have the same predictive or extrapolative dimensions as dystopias. As Fredric Jameson remarks in an analysis of Le Guin, science fiction utopias are 'not a place in which humanity is freed from violence, but rather one in which it is released from the multiple determinisms (economic, political, social) of history itself'.[59] Or to put it another way, science fiction utopias offer a vision of different forms of individual and social being rather than merely dystopic or apocalyptic extensions of the present. Of particular interest to ecocriticism are those ecologically aware utopian visions that have come to be known as 'ecotopias', a term inspired by Ernest Callenbach's 1975 novel *Ecotopia*.

One important science fiction trope related to ecotopia is 'terraforming', the use of technology to make planets habitable or more hospitable. As Chris Pak observes, the term was originally coined by John Williamson, in the short story 'Collision Orbit' (1942), and there are important examples from novelists – such as Frank Herbert's cult novel *Dune* (1965) and Kim Stanley Robinson's *Mars* trilogy (1993–6) – as well as from the short story writers Isaac Asimov, Arthur C. Clarke and Ray Bradbury.[60] Robinson's short story collection *The Martians* (1999) also complements the terraforming narratives of his *Mars* trilogy. While terraforming necessitates some kind of environmental awareness, the manufactured environments that it produces raise political and ethical questions as well as technological and ecological ones: Who will terraform and for whom? Who will benefit? Who will be displaced? Who will bear the economic or ecological cost? Does the attempt to terraform constitute an instance of Promethean overreach that ignores less hi-tech but more politically radical solutions? Such questions have become increasingly pointed in the light of recent speculation into geo-engineering as means of combatting climate change.

Another example of interest in this ecotopian context is Robinson's anthology *Future Primitive: The New Ecotopias*. Published in 1994, this text collects science fiction stories and poetry by a variety of writers including Gary Snyder and Robinson Jeffers. In his introduction, Robinson outlines a shift within science fiction brought about by changing environmental awareness:

> Science fiction responding to the latest advances in contemporary science is beginning to look different, less 'hi tech', more various. All manner of alternative futures are now being imagined . . . they attempt to imagine sophisticated new technologies combined with habits saved or reinvented from our deep past, with the notion that prehistoric cultures were critical in making us what we are, and new things about our relationship to the world that we should not forget.[61]

The anthology is actually more various that Robinson suggests. Some stories, such as Terry Bisson's 'Bears Discover Fire' or Gene Wolfe's '"A Story" By John V. Marsch', explore primitive modes of relation and community. Others have a more dystopian flavour, such as Garry Kilworth's 'Hogfoot Right and Bird-Hands' or Le Guin's 'Newton's Sleep'. Kilworth's story, included under the subsection 'Denial of the Body', describes an old woman who is reliant on an autonomous 'welfare machine'. To alleviate her loneliness, the machine creates pets by removing the woman's body parts and imbuing them with life. One pet kills the woman in its attempts to escape, providing yet another neat image of the biological resisting technological control.

'Newton's Sleep' plays with a dystopic future alongside the possibility, but not the guarantee, of ecotopian transformation. The story depicts a future world suffering the effects of overpopulation and riven with constantly evolving pandemics. In response, a group of individuals try to ensure human survival by forming a colony in a space station, the Special Earth Satellite or 'Spes'. As Tonia L. Payne points out, Spes is the Roman goddess of hope.[62] The title, 'Newton's Sleep', comes from an 1802 letter by William Blake, in which the poet asks to be saved from 'single vision & Newton's sleep'. 'Single vision' stands in contrast to Blake's 'Fourfold Vision' which is 'supreme delight', whereas Newton embodies a blinkered focus on the purely rational as can be seen in Blake's famous 1795 print *Newton*, where the scientist stares at calculations on the floor, blind to the organic world around him.[63] Hearkening back to Blake, Le Guin shows that hope in the face of environmental crisis requires more than rational calculation. Indeed, as in 'The Machine Stops', 'Newton's Sleep' suggests that the organic world and the embodied mind defy attempts at technological control.

The inhabitants of Spes have given up on Earth and the 'stupid, impossible unpredictability'[64] of its weather. They form a closed, heavily vetted space colony of 800 where 'every single person must be fit, not only genetically but intellectually';[65] community members have an average IQ of 165. However, readers are given to understand that the colony's selection process discriminated against black applicants and that, despite the fact that Spes is supposed to be organised on rational principles, racism, gender bias and petty power struggles still exist on the space station. Moreover, the sleep of reason breeds monsters. Although they know that that they have left their home planet behind forever, the inhabitants of Spes increasingly experience a series of psycho-physical hallucinations of the people, animals and landscapes of Earth. The ambiguous end sees the most rational character bloodied by a fall on an imaginary mountain as his daughter tells him 'now we can go down'.[66] It remains unclear if she means back to Earth.

In her much-cited introduction to *The Left Hand of Darkness* (1969), Le Guin argued that 'strictly extrapolative works of science fiction generally arrive about where the Club of Rome arrives: somewhere between the gradual extinction of human liberty and the total extinction of terrestrial life'. Instead, she remarked, what really sets science fiction 'apart from older forms of fiction seems to be its use of new metaphors, drawn from certain great dominants of our contemporary life – science, all the sciences, and technology'.[67] One of her most striking metaphors is included in 'Vaster than Empires and More Slow', a story that borrows both its title and the notion of plant emotions from Andrew Marvell's metaphysical poem 'To His Coy Mistress' (1681).[68] The story sees space travellers encounter a planet which is an interconnected plant super-organism. This wholly alien collective consciousness shifts in response to the emotions of the crew. This is a striking figuration of the mutually affecting relationship between human organisms and their environment on a planetary level. Not only does the super-organism reflect, as Ursula K. Heise argues, 'James Lovelock's well known Gaia hypothesis, according to which Planet Earth constitutes a single overarching feedback system',[69] it also emphasises a kind of second-order systems process where human observers plays a crucial role in shaping the future state of the system they find themselves observing.

The attention towards the non-human world, and the perspectives that it can provide, appears elsewhere in Le Guin's non-science fiction stories. Perhaps the best example is 'Buffalo Gals, Won't You Come Out Tonight' (1987), later collected in *Buffalo Gals and Other Animal Presences* (1990), which incorporates North American trickster mythology in a tale about a girl who, after a plane crash, lives with a society of anthropomorphic animals who refer to themselves as people. In doing so she gains a new perspective on the human world of 'new people' (i.e. human animals), who 'live apart . . . way down our place, they press on it, draw it, suck it, eat it, eat holes in it, crowd it out'.[70] Le Guin deploys an animal narrator in the same way that science fiction sometimes uses alien perspectives, to decentre the human. Other short story writers have used a similar technique. George Saunders's *Fox 8: A Story* (2013), in which an urban fox acquires 'Yuman' language to narrate the collapse of his habitat thanks to the construction of a shopping mall, is a striking instance of such defamiliarisation, as is James Agee's startling 'A Mother's Tale' (first published in *Harper's Bazaar* in 1952), which explores the horrors of meat production from the perspective of cows. Such stories show that the ecological impact of human actions upon the non-human world can be seen in our shopping malls and eateries, as well as in glaciers and rainforests.

One influential author whose short fiction brings together many of the features discussed with a contemporary sense of environmental crisis, particularly in relation to climate change, is Paulo Bacigalupi. Bacigalupi's *Pump Six and Other Stories* (2010) is peppered with the resource shortages, biological modifications, and repressive violence born from changing technologies and environments. The title story shows a future American city losing the capacity to process waste because it no longer understands the technologies that sustain it; the ensuing spread of toxicity means that the populace gradually degenerates into troglodytes. In 'The People of Sand and Slag' set, untypically, in a quite distant future, humans appear to have evolved rather than devolved; these post-humans' bio-technical enhancements allow them to survive on inorganic matter (the titular sand and slag), but leaves them with little sense of compassion or embodied finitude. When they find a dog they cannot look after it; the vulnerable animal initially inspires the sympathy of one of the characters, but the modified humans soon get bored with the dog and kill it.

Two of the stories, 'The Calorie Man' and 'Yellow Card Man', are set in the same fictional universe as Bacigalupi's award-winning 2010 novel *The Windup Girl*, where a collapse in hydrocarbon availability leads to a radically adapted world in which reliance shifts onto low-energy technologies such as foot-powered computers. This situation gives rise to armed and avaricious corporations who seek to perpetuate their monopoly on the high-yield GM crops which provide the calories to motor the kinetic springs that now drive this labour-intensive, wind-up society. As Otto notes, these companies, with their purposefully sterile copyright crops, provide dystopic extrapolations of contemporary agrochemical firms, particularly Monsanto (who, not incidentally, also manufactured the DDT that Carson railed against).[71]

'Pop Squad' brings environmental and bodily change together. Against the backdrop of a warmed world, with a population stabilised by a mandated 'rejoo' serum that effects both immortality and infertility, a detective (and futuristic-noir narrator) has to hunt down and execute the newly born children of those caught neglecting the serum. One mother tells the narrator that she is a 'breeder' because she prefers to see the world through her child's eyes and not the 'dead eyes' of the immortals. Watching the woman breastfeed leaves the narrator unexpectedly aroused and, after a scuffle, he leaves her alone, running out into the night where 'for the first time in a long time, the rain feels new'.[72] This is a different kind of 'rejoo[venation]', as the encounter with birth, desire and death reconnects the human to the embodied finitude of its animal lifeworld – a world from which it has been alienated by biomedical technology.

As in 'The Calorie Man', which ends with the narrator gaining the means to become a 'Johnny Appleseed' who might be able to re-introduce fertile, and therefore uncontrollable, crops back into the corporate ecosystem, there is a certain hopefulness at the climax of 'Pop Squad'. Otto argues that 'Bacigalupi's ecodystopian stories work – that is, instigate ecotopian transformation – by staging a productive tension between what is (im)possible for their protagonists and what is possible for us.'[73] Perhaps it is in this negotiation between the jolting dystopian or apocalyptic and the cautiously hopeful ecotopian that the science fiction short story is most effective in matters of the environment. Not only do the best examples of the genre track alarming possible futures, they also suggest that the technologies, techniques and social formations that might alleviate environmental crisis will have to work with, rather than against, an unpredictable and frequently uncontrollable biological, ecological and cultural inheritance.

In her 2014 article 'Elegy for a Country's Seasons', published around the same time as her environmental short story 'Moonlit Landscape with a Bridge', Zadie Smith describes a 'new normal' where global environmental changes manifesting on a local scale – a superstorm in New York, a washed away train line in Cornwall – no longer seem surprising. She says that despite specific 'local sadness', there is a growing planetary dimension to the various responses and that:

> Sometimes the global, repetitive nature of this elegy is so exhaustively sad – and so divorced from any attempts at meaningful action – that you can't fail to detect in the elegists a fatalist liberal consciousness that has, when you get right down to it, as much of a perverse desire for the apocalypse as the evangelicals we supposedly scorn.[74]

Smith decries biblical self-flagellation and describes herself as 'beginning to turn from the elegiac *what have we done* to the practical *what can we do*'.[75] As the examples discussed in this chapter illustrate, the short story has addressed both what we have done (the ecological results of which are not yet clear) and what we might do in an as-yet undetermined future.

The short story is certainly capable of effecting the 'jolts' that McKibben believes environmental crisis demands. However, rather than relying on shock tactics and stock imagery, the short story generates and accommodates responses to the complex challenges of environmental crises in a variety of ways. In its most interesting examples, the characteristic features of the genre, like its fleeting intensity and its strategic economy, are exploited to address changing circumstances. A genre in which many of the most famous exponents – from Irving to Munro – have had a keen sense of place and setting, has lately been shown to evolve in response to shifts in our cultural and physical environments. These shifts produce new uncertainties in the systems of understanding by which we inhabit and relate to the world, demanding new definitions of the local and the global, the human and the non-human, and the interplay of relations between them.

Many contemporary writers have taken advantage of the short story form to respond to these conditions, offering both direct and oblique approaches to environmental crises. In the process, writers have imagined viewpoints beyond the human and have used the snapshot of the short form, as well as the kaleidoscopic effect of the short story cycle, to realise and reflect scenarios of crisis; they have also moved past apocalyptic paradigms and naïve, nostalgic visions of place to open up both the quotidian nature of environmental crisis and the possibilities of dystopian and ecotopian futures, with new technologies and social formations. In varied and often surprising ways, alternative senses of 'ecological consciousness' have begun to emerge through the fictional environments of the short story.

Notes

1. John Muir, *My First Summer in the Sierra* (Boston, MA: Houghton Mifflin, 1917), p. 158.
2. Timothy Clark, *The Cambridge Introduction to Literature and the Environment* (Cambridge: Cambridge University Press, 2011), p. xiii.
3. Bill McKibben, 'Introduction' in Mark Martin (ed.), *I'm With the Bears: Stories from a Damaged Planet* (London: Verso, 2011), p. 3.
4. Glen A. Love, 'The Ecological Short Story', in Blanche H. Gelfant (ed.), *The Columbia Companion to the Twentieth Century American Short Story* (New York: Columbia University Press, 2000), p. 53.
5. Martin Scofield, *The Cambridge Introduction to the American Short Story* (Cambridge: Cambridge University Press, 2006), p. 10.
6. See Will Steffen et al., 'The Anthropocene: Are Humans Now Overwhelming the Great Forces of Nature?', *Ambio*, 36.8 (December 2007): 614–21.
7. Love, 'The Ecological Short Story', p. 53.
8. Frank O'Connor, *The Lonely Voice: A Study of the Short Story* (London: Macmillan, 1963), p. 13.
9. Annie Proulx, 'Afterword', in Thomas Savage, *The Power of the Dog* (New York: Little, Brown, 2001), p. 285.
10. Ibid.
11. Annie Proulx in Aida Edemariam, 'Home on the Range', *The Guardian*, 10 December 2004. Available at <http://www.theguardian.com/books/2004/dec/11/featuresreviews.guardianreview13> (last accessed 15 April 2018).
12. Annie Proulx, *Close Range: Wyoming Stories* (London: HarperCollins, [1999] 2010), p. 226.
13. Ibid. p. 107, p. 108.
14. Ibid. p. 98, p. 95.
15. Annie Proulx, *Bad Dirt* (London: Fourth Estate, 2004), p. 11.
16. Wes Berry, 'Capitalism vs. Localism: Economies of Scale in Annie Proulx's Postcards and That Old Ace in the Hole', in Alex Hunt (ed.), *The Geographical Imagination of Annie Proulx: Rethinking Regionalism* (Lanham: Lexington, 2009), p. 169.
17. Proulx, *Bad Dirt*, p. 61.
18. Ibid. p. 66, p. 68.
19. Ibid. p. 80.
20. Berry, 'Capitalism vs. Localism', p. 170.
21. Proulx, *Bad Dirt*, p. 86.
22. Berry, 'Capitalism vs. Localism', p. 180.
23. Proulx, *Bad Dirt*, p. 110, p. 125.
24. Ali Smith, 'Earthly Powers: Review of *Bad Dirt* by Annie Proulx' *The Guardian*, 31 December 2004. Available at <http://www.theguardian.com/books/2005/jan/01/fiction.alismith> (last accessed 15 April 2018).
25. Susan Garland Mann, *The Short Story Cycle: A Genre Companion and Reference Guide* (Westport, CT: Greenwood, 1989), p. 15.
26. G. K. Chesterton, *Charles Dickens* (London: Methuen, 1906), p. 85.

27. McKibben, 'Introduction', p. 1.
28. Lawrence Buell, 'Toxic Discourse', *Critical Inquiry*, 24.3 (1998): p. 663; Richard Kerridge, 'Ecothrillers: Environmental Cliffhangers', in Laurence Coupe (ed.), *The Green Studies Reader: From Romanticism to Ecocriticism* (London: Routledge, 2000), p. 243.
29. Adrian Hunter, *The Cambridge Introduction to the Short Story in English* (Cambridge: Cambridge University Press, 2007), p. 2.
30. Greg Garrard, *Ecocriticism*, 2nd edn (London: Routledge, 2012), p. 114.
31. Frederick Buell, *From Apocalypse to Way of Life: Environmental Crisis in the American Century* (London: Routledge, 2003), p. ix.
32. Timothy Clark, 'Some Climate Change Ironies: Deconstruction, Environmental Politics and the Closure of Ecocriticism', *The Oxford Literary Review*, 32.1 (2010): 145.
33. Timothy Clark, 'Scale' in Tom Cohen (ed.), *Telemorphosis: Theory in the Era of Climate Change* (Ann Arbor: Open Humanities Press, 2012), pp. 157–8.
34. Ibid. p. 161, p. 162.
35. Ibid. p. 163.
36. See, for example, Jane Bennett, *Vibrant Matter: A Political Ecology of Things* (Durham, NC: Duke University Press, 2010); Timothy Morton, *Hyperobjects: Philosophy and Ecology After the End of the World* (Minneapolis: University of Minnesota Press, 2013); Claire Colebrook, *The Death of the PostHuman: Essays on Extinction* (Ann Arbor: Open Humanities Press, 2014); and Bruno Latour, *Politics of Nature* (Cambridge, MA: Harvard University Press, 2004).
37. A comparable device can be found in Ian McEwan's *Solar* (2010), Nathaniel Rich's *Odds Against Tomorrow* (2013) and Ben Lerner's *10:10* (2014).
38. Greg Garrard, 'The Unbearable Lightness of Green', *Green Letters: Studies in Ecocriticism*, 17.2 (2013): 182.
39. Helen Simpson, *In-Flight Entertainment* (New York: Knopf, 2010), p. 59, p. 76.
40. Ibid. p. 124.
41. Garrard, 'The Unbearable Lightness of Green', p. 183.
42. Ibid.
43. Adeline Johns-Putra, 'Climate Change in Literature and Literary Studies: From Cli-Fi, Climate Change Theater and Ecopoetry to Ecocriticism and Climate Change Criticism', *Wiley Interdisciplinary Reviews: Climate Change*, 7.2 (2016): 269.
44. Adam Trexler, *Anthropocene Fictions: The Novel in a Time of Climate Change* (Charlottesville, VA: University of Virginia Press, 2015), p. 233.
45. Amitav Ghosh, *The Great Derangement: Climate Change and the Unthinkable* (Chicago: University of Chicago Press, 2016), p. 23.
46. McKenzie Wark, 'On the Obsolescence of the Bourgeois Novel in the Anthropocene', 16 August 2017. Available at <https://www.versobooks.com/blogs/3356-on-the-obsolescence-of-the-bourgeois-novel-in-the-anthropocene> (last accessed 12 September 2017).
47. Ghosh, *The Great Derangement*, p. 66.
48. Ursula K. Le Guin, 'Introduction', in *The Time Machine: An Invention* (New York: Modern Library, 2002), p. xiv.
49. Bryan L. Moore, '"Evidences of Decadent Humanity": Antianthropocentrism in Early Science Fiction', *Nature and Culture*, 12 (2017): 48.
50. H. G. Wells, 'The Star', in *The Complete Short Stories of H. G. Wells* (London: Orion, 2000), pp. 285–9.
51. H. G. Wells, 'A Dream of Armagaddon', *Complete Short Stories of H. G. Wells*, p. 558; see also Moore, '"Evidences of Decadent Humanity"', pp. 50–6.
52. E. M. Forster, 'The Machine Stops' [1909], in *The Machine Stops* (New York: Start, 2012), p. 10.
53. Forster, 'The Machine Stops', p. 17.

54. See Love, 'The Ecological Short Story', pp. 50–5.
55. Rachel Carson, *Silent Spring* (Boston, MA: Houghton Mifflin, [1962] 2002), p. 246.
56. See Joshua David Bellin, 'Us or Them!: Silent Spring and The "Big Bug" Films of the 1950s', *Extrapolation*, 50.1 (January 2009): 147–8.
57. 'The insects are developing strains resistant to chemicals . . . But the broader problem, which we shall look at now, is the fact that our chemical attack is weakening the defenses inherent in the environment itself, defenses designed to keep the various species in check.' Carson, *Silent Spring*, p. 246.
58. Eric C. Otto, '"The Rain Feels New": Ecotopian Strategies in the Short Fiction of Paolo Bacigalupi', in Gerry Canavan and Kim Stanley Robinson (eds), *Green Planets: Ecology and Science Fiction* (Middletown, CT: Wesleyan University Press, 2014), p. 180.
59. Fredric Jameson, 'World-Reduction in Le Guin: The Emergence of Utopian Narrative', *Science Fiction Studies*, 2 (1975): 227.
60. Chris Pak, 'Terraforming 101', *SFRA Review*, 302 (Fall 2012): 6–15.
61. Kim Stanley Robinson (ed.), *Future Primitive: The New Ecotopias* (New York: TOR, 1997), p. 11.
62. Tonia L. Payne, '"We are dirt: we are earth": Ursula Le Guin and the problem of extraterrestrialism', in Catrin Gersdorf and Sylvia Mayer (eds), *Nature in Literary and Cultural Studies: Transatlantic Conversations on Ecocriticism* (Amsterdam: Rodopi, 2006), p. 232.
63. William Blake letter to Thomas Butts, 22 November 1802, in Geoffrey Keynes (ed.), *Blake: Complete Writings* (Oxford: Oxford University Press, 1969), p. 818.
64. Ursula K. Le Guin, 'Newton's Sleep' in Robinson, *Future Primitive*, p. 316.
65. Ibid. p. 322.
66. Ibid. p. 338.
67. Ursula K. Le Guin, *The Left Hand of Darkness* (New York: Ace, 1969), p. xi.
68. Andrew Marvell, 'To His Coy Mistress', in Elizabeth Story Donno (ed.), Andrew Marvell, *The Complete Poems* (Harmondsworth: Penguin, 1972). The poem contains the lines: 'My vegetable love should grow / Vaster than empires and more slow' (p. 50).
69. Ursula K. Heise, *Sense of Place and Sense of Planet: The Environmental Imagination of the Global* (Oxford: Oxford University Press, 2008), p. 19.
70. Ursula K. Le Guin, *Buffalo Gals and Other Animal Presences* (New York: Roc, 1990), p. 43.
71. Otto, '"The Rain Feels New"', p. 183.
72. Paolo Bacigalupi, *Pump Six and Other Stories* (San Francisco: Night Shade Books, 2008), p. 162.
73. Otto, '"The Rain Feels New"', p. 189.
74. Zadie Smith, 'Elegy for a Country's Seasons', *The New York Review of Books*, 61.6 (3 April 2014). Available at <http://www.nybooks.com/articles/archives/2014/apr/03/elegy-countrys-seasons/> (last accessed 15 April 2018).
75. Ibid. (Emphasis in the original.)

Bibliography

Adams, John Joseph (ed.), *Loosed upon the World: The Saga Anthology of Climate Fiction* (New York: Saga Press, 2015).

Agee, James, 'A Mother's Tale', in Robert Fitzgerald (ed.), *The Collected Short Prose of James Agee* (Boston, MA: Houghton Mifflin, 1968), pp. 221–43.

Bacigalupi, Paolo, *Pump Six and Other Stories* (San Francisco: Night Shade Books, 2008).

Bellin, Joshua David, 'Us or Them!: Silent Spring and The "Big Bug" Films of the 1950s', *Extrapolation* 50.1 (January 2009): 145–68.

Bennett, Jane, *Vibrant Matter: A Political Ecology of Things* (Durham, NC: Duke University Press, 2010).

Berry, Wes, 'Capitalism vs. Localism: Economies of Scale in Annie Proulx's *Postcards* and *That Old Ace in the Hole*', in Alex Hunt (ed.), *The Geographical Imagination of Annie Proulx: Rethinking Regionalism* (Lanham, MA: Lexington, 2009), pp. 169–80.

Blake, William, *Blake: Complete Writings*, ed. Geoffrey Keynes (Oxford: Oxford University Press, 1969).

Buell, Frederick, *From Apocalypse to Way of Life: Environmental Crisis in the American Century* (London: Routledge, 2003).

Buell, Lawrence, 'Toxic Discourse', *Critical Inquiry*, 24.3 (1998): 639–65.

Carson, Rachel, *Silent Spring* (Boston, MA: Houghton Mifflin, [1962] 2002).

Chesterton, G. K., *Charles Dickens* (London: Methuen, 1906).

Clark, Timothy, 'Some Climate Change Ironies: Deconstruction, Environmental Politics and the Closure of Ecocriticism', *The Oxford Literary Review*, 32.1 (2010): 131–49.

— *The Cambridge Introduction to Literature and the Environment* (Cambridge: Cambridge University Press, 2011).

— 'Scale' in Tom Cohen (ed.), *Telemorphosis: Theory in the Era of Climate Change* (Ann Arbor, MI: Open Humanities Press, 2012), pp. 148–66.

Colebrook, Claire, *The Death of the PostHuman: Essays on Extinction* (Ann Arbor: Open Humanities Press, 2014).

Edemariam, Aida, 'Home on the Range', *The Guardian*, 10 December 2004, http://www.theguardian.com/books/2004/dec/11/featuresreviews.guardianreview13 (last accessed 15 April 2018).

Forster, E. M., *The Machine Stops* (New York: Start, [1909] 2012).

Garrard, Greg, *Ecocriticism*, 2nd edn (London: Routledge, 2012).

— 'The Unbearable Lightness of Green', *Green Letters: Studies in Ecocriticism* 17.2 (2013): 175–88.

Ghosh, Amitav, *The Great Derangement: Climate Change and the Unthinkable* (Chicago: University of Chicago Press, 2016).

Heise, Ursula K., *Sense of Place and Sense of Planet: The Environmental Imagination of the Global* (Oxford: Oxford University Press, 2008).

Hunt, Alex (ed.), *The Geographical Imagination of Annie Proulx: Rethinking Regionalism* (Lanham: Lexington, 2009).

Hunter, Adrian, *The Cambridge Introduction to the Short Story in English* (Cambridge: Cambridge University Press, 2007).

Jameson, Fredric, 'World-Reduction in Le Guin: The Emergence of Utopian Narrative', *Science Fiction Studies*, 2 (1975): 221–30.

Johns-Putra, Adeline, 'Climate Change in Literature and Literary Studies: From Cli-Fi, Climate Change Theater and Ecopoetry to Ecocriticism and Climate Change Criticism', *Wiley Interdisciplinary Reviews: Climate Change*, 7.2 (2016): 266–82.

Kerridge, Richard, 'Ecothrillers: Environmental Cliffhangers', in Laurence Coupe (ed.), *The Green Studies Reader: From Romanticism to Ecocriticism* (London: Routledge, 2000), pp. 242–52.

Latour, Bruno, *Politics of Nature* (Cambridge, MA: Harvard University Press, 2004).

Le Guin, Ursula K., *The Left Hand of Darkness* (New York: Ace, 1969).

— *Buffalo Gals and Other Animal Presences* (New York: Roc, 1990).

— 'Introduction', in *The Time Machine: An Invention* (New York: Modern Library, 2002), pp. xi–xvi.

Love, Glen. A., 'The Ecological Short Story', in Blanche H. Gelfant (ed.), *The Columbia Companion to the Twentieth Century American Short Story* (New York: Columbia University Press, 2000), pp. 50–5.

McKibben, Bill, 'Introduction' in Mark Martin (ed.), *I'm With the Bears: Stories from a Damaged Planet* (London: Verso, 2011).

Mann, Susan Garland, *The Short Story Cycle: A Genre Companion and Reference Guide* (Westport, CT: Greenwood, 1989).

Martin, Mark (ed.), *I'm With the Bears: Stories from a Damaged Planet* (London: Verso, 2011).
Marvell, Andrew, *The Complete Poems*, ed. Elizabeth Story Donno (Harmondsworth: Penguin, 1972).
Meyer, Bruce (ed.), *CLI-FI: Canadian Tales of Climate Change* (Holstein, ON: Exile Editions, 2017).
Moore, Bryan L., '"Evidences of Decadent Humanity": Antianthropocentrism in Early Science Fiction', *Nature and Culture*, 12 (2017): 45–65.
Morton, Timothy, *Hyperobjects: Philosophy and Ecology After the End of the World* (Minneapolis: University of Minnesota Press, 2013).
Muir, John, *My First Summer in the Sierra* (Boston, MA: Houghton Mifflin, 1917).
O'Connor, Frank, *The Lonely Voice: A Study of the Short Story* (London: Macmillan, 1963).
Otto, Eric C. '"The Rain Feels New": Ecotopian Strategies in the Short Fiction of Paolo Bacigalupi', in Gerry Canavan and Kim Stanley Robinson (eds), *Green Planets: Ecology and Science Fiction* (Middletown, CT: Wesleyan University Press, 2014), pp. 180–91
Pak, Chris, 'Terraforming 101', *SFRA Review*, 302 (Fall 2012): 6–15.
Payne, Tonia L., '"We are dirt: we are earth": Ursula Le Guin and the problem of extraterrestrialism', in Catrin Gersdorf and Sylvia Mayer (eds), *Nature in Literary and Cultural Studies: Transatlantic Conversations on Ecocriticism* (Amsterdam: Rodopi, 2006), pp. 229–48.
Proulx, Annie, 'Afterword', in Thomas Savage, *The Power of the Dog* (New York: Little, Brown, 2001).
— *Bad Dirt* (London: Fourth Estate, 2004).
— *Close Range: Wyoming Stories* (London: HarperCollins, [1999] 2010).
Robinson, Kim Stanley, *The Martians* (London: HarperCollins, 1999).
— (ed.), *Future Primitive: The New Ecotopias* (New York: TOR, 1997).
Saunders, George, *Fox 8: A Story* (London: Bloomsbury, 2013).
Scofield, Martin, *The Cambridge Introduction to the American Short Story* (Cambridge: Cambridge University Press, 2006).
Simpson, Helen, *In-Flight Entertainment* (New York: Knopf, 2010).
Smith, Ali, 'Earthly Powers: Review of *Bad Dirt* by Annie Proulx' *The Guardian*, 31 December 2004, http://www.theguardian.com/books/2005/jan/01/fiction.alismith (last accessed 15 April 2018).
Smith, Zadie, 'Moonlit Landscape with Bridge', *The New Yorker*, 10 February 2014, <http://www.newyorker.com/magazine/2014/02/10/moonlit-landscape-with-bridge/> (last accessed 15 April 2018).
— 'Elegy for a Country's Seasons', *The New York Review of Books*, 61.6 (3 April 2014), <http://www.nybooks.com/articles/archives/2014/apr/03/elegy-countrys-seasons/> (last accessed 15 April 2018).
Steffen, Will, Paul J. Crutzen and John R. McNeill, 'The Anthropocene: Are Humans Now Overwhelming the Great Forces of Nature?', *Ambio*, 36.8 (December 2007): 614–21.
Trexler, Adam, *Anthropocene Fictions: The Novel in a Time of Climate Change* (Charlottesville, VA: University of Virginia Press, 2015).
Wark, McKenzie, 'On the Obsolescence of the Bourgeois Novel in the Anthropocene', 16 August 2017, <https://www.versobooks.com/blogs/3356-on-the-obsolescence-of-the-bourgeois-novel-in-the-anthropocene> (last accessed 15 April 2018).
Wells, H. G., *The Complete Short Stories of H. G. Wells* (London: Orion, 2000).

Part V

Identity and the Short Story

18

Gender and Genre in the Short Story

Ruth Robbins

When you meet a human being, the first distinction you make is 'male or female?' and you are accustomed to make the distinction with unhesitating certainty. (Sigmund Freud)[1]

Genre theory is ... about the ways in which different structures of meaning and truth are produced in and by the various kinds of writing ... by which the universe of discourse is structured. That is why genre matters: it is central to human meaning-making and to the social struggle over meanings. (John Frow)[2]

GENDER AND GENRE ARE related in more ways than one. A glance at the dictionary tells us that the two words were born from the same root word in Latin by way of Old French – *genus*, meaning type or kind. In modern French, *genre* means both gender and genre. That etymological connectedness expands beyond the simple fact of the shared root word: genre is gendered; gender (in literary terms, at least) is also 'genred'. What writers produce and what readers consume is often (but certainly not always) closely aligned to their genders. The 'unhesitating certainty' of gender distinctions in social life of which Freud writes in his 1933 essay on 'Femininity' is also a form of genre reading. His suggestion is that we know a man from a woman by signs that we have learned to read as part of our social training: these signs are biological (facial hair or its lack, deep or high voices, etc.); they are also social – masculinity and femininity are signalled by conventions of clothing and predicted behaviours that attach to the genders in a given society.

John Frow's comments are focused on forms of writing rather than on forms of people, but his comment that genre is 'central to human meaning-making' echoes Freud's focus on the centrality of gender in social interactions beyond the page. This is not accidental. The social learning that goes into telling us both that a given person is male or female and that certain behaviours are expected of us as men or women is part of a continuum in which literary texts also play their part. Texts both reflect in mediated ways an existing social reality, and they are also one means for understanding that reality. And in genre, gender matters from the outset – from the very first 'once-upon-a-time' – of our reading lives. To a very large extent, Freud's comment tells us that we judge people by their covers; this is a judgement that very often also extends to books.

It is important here to make the point that there are least two ways in which the word genre is used in common parlance, because there is a confusion between form (type or kind of writing, for example, prose, poetry, drama) and (sub-)genre (a shared set of generic conventions such as those to be found in the ghost story, the romance, the thriller or the western which provide interpretative clues for the reader, and markets for the writer or publisher or film company). The sense of genre as referring to form is sometimes disallowed by scholars, and is sometimes their central focus. Contemporary criticism of genre tends to focus much more on genre as the sets of subdivisions within the individual form or mode, a tendency which is strongly at play in film studies but which also has its part in literary thought. A play might be a comedy or tragedy or tragicomedy (or many other things). A novel might be a thriller or an 'Aga saga', or a work of science fiction, and so forth. Readers and booksellers really like genre in that sense of subdivision. It tells you what you are buying and what you are selling, provides a safety net against the accidental purchase of an antipathetic kind of story, and helps with the marketing process. As Heta Pyrhönen puts it, rather less cynically and with less attention to the demands of the market:

> Genre theory today signals opportunity and common purpose: genre functions as an enabling device for readers and writers, the vehicle for the acquisition of competence. Familiarity with genre fosters generic competence, that is, an ability (1) to recognize and interpret the codes typical of a given genre; and (2) to perceive departures from it.[3]

The competence that is being described here is both textual and paratextual. It exists both within the individual text, in its plot elements, typologies of character and action, and in its endings, and outside it, in the marginalia of the text, in signs such as the book's cover or the magazine's title, the author's signature, and the associations that the competent reader makes with the publisher's colophon. This competence tells readers what to expect and it alerts us to those moments when our expectations are not met. If Elizabeth Bennet meets a zombie, we know we are outside the generic norms of the ordered social world that Jane Austen's signature is meant to guarantee.

Because of the ways in which short fiction in particular is consumed, the connections between gender and genre are often acutely realised in this form. Publishers are wary of short stories because they sell less reliably than the long-form fiction of the novel. They have habitually been defined as a lesser form on a scale of value which has as much to do with hard cash as it does with aesthetic worth. There are exceptions made for those short fictions which appear on university reading lists: writers such as Henry James, James Joyce, D. H. Lawrence and Katherine Mansfield, whose artful modernist and proto-modernist experiments lend academic respectability to a more usually ephemeral form, have garnered the kind of critical attention that makes them central texts for the university curriculum. Beyond these exceptions, however, short stories often appear as magazine fictions whose reader is typically 'a light, usually female, reader',[4] and in anthologies constructed along lines of national identity (Mary Lord's *The Penguin Best Australian Short Stories*), theme or genre (Michael Newton's *Victorian Fairy Tales*, Michael Cox and R. A. Gilbert's *The Oxford Book of Victorian Ghost Stories*), or gender (Victoria Hislop's *The Story: Love, Loss and the Lives of Women*; Hermione Lee's *The Secret Self: Short Stories by Women*). In the anthology market, there are no collections in the Amazon catalogue entitled *The Masculine Short Story* or *Short Fictions by Men*, which implies both that men have no gendered interests (that they are the norm against which femininity is measured, a judgement that we should all be very wary of accepting); and possibly also particular types of short story are gendered as feminine. There are, by way of contrast, many examples of short fiction collections that bring together women's writing, which suggests that women writers (and readers) are defined by their gender in a way that male readers and writers are not. Even apparently gender-neutral anthologies turn out not to be neutral at all. Statistical analyses of such apparently disinterested titles as V. S. Pritchett's 1981 *The Oxford Book of Short Stories* shows that forty-one stories are collected of which a mere seven are by women writers, a ratio of just under 6:1 male to female (and this is not atypical).[5]

Gender demarcation becomes even clearer when popular genres are in play. Westerns and hard-boiled detective fictions are 'masculine' at least in the sense that they are marketed at men; and romance and cosy detective stories (the ones without too much blood or violence) are feminine in the same way. These demarcations are not quite the concern of this chapter, which focuses rather on the formal qualities of the short story as gendered genre, but they are named here because it is important to understand that the short story itself can be understood as a feminine form, and that its gendered delineation has effects on its production, consumption and reception. Frank O'Connor observed long ago that the short story form was ideal for describing the pains of what he called 'submerged populations' and 'outlaw figures'.[6] His particular concern was with the varieties of spiritual malaise and the discomfort that specifically affect colonised or otherwise impoverished peoples. O'Connor did not mention women at all amongst the examples of 'submerged populations', which, as Mary Eagleton notes in a very important essay, is a highly significant omission.[7] His words, however, also apply to the form as it was adopted by women in the later part of the nineteenth century, and to a range of its subsequent performances in the twentieth century and beyond. O'Connor's comments, Eagleton notes, which image the short story writer as 'non-hegemonic, peripheral, contradictory' is also 'a reflection of the position of women in a patriarchal society'.[8]

Eagleton's essay, 'Gender and Genre' first published in 1989, is a suggestive discussion of how the two terms might be better understood, and a plea for critics to find a mode of feminist criticism in general, and for the short story in particular, which is 'non-essentialist, non-reductive, but [also] subtly alive to the links between gender and genre'.[9] Eagleton points to the fact that value judgements about genre in the past privileged a male canon of good taste and of aesthetic worth, and has made a virtue out of large scale in terms of both word count and subject matter:

> High tragedy, epic poetry, sermons, the philosophical treatise, criticism carry more weight than journals, letters, diaries, even, for the most part, fiction – forms in which women have proliferated. The female forms, we have been told, are less literary, less intellectual, less wide-ranging, less profound.[10]

These judgements, however, are not 'neutral', but are part of a patriarchal narrative that seeks to keep writing and reading women in their place. Eagleton argues that the new fictional form of the novel in the eighteenth century and beyond attracted women writers because it had no tradition of great masters or rigid generic rules to contend with. The education required to emulate the tradition and to abide by the conventions, which were often denied to women in earlier periods, shut them out of the highly valued forms of epic poetry and philosophical debate. But the novel was new and the rules were unformed and women writers and readers leapt into the gap. The short story shares some of these conditions: 'If we are talking about new forms and low status, then the short story is even newer and lower than the novel', Eagleton comments ironically.[11] The woman writer can make her own space in this genre in part because the men weren't bothered.

But in choosing a shorter form, one which was not accorded literary status nor highly regarded by critical opinion, there are dangers for women writers. Eagleton notes a potential analogy between the valuation of the epic (masculine poetic form par excellence, in which the men are all very warlike, and there are hardly any women at all) and the lyric (a form that women were permitted to excel in so long as they did not exceed the boundaries of feminine propriety, for example by discussing their own sexual desires or taking strong political stances). Because the lyric is personal not public, intimate and inward-looking not declamatory and assertive, it is a poetic form that nice girls can write and not sacrifice their niceness. Short fiction often has some of the same attributes as the lyric: as lyric is to epic, so the short story is to the novel. It can be an intimate form, focused on a single incident which values 'the personal, the closely detailed, the miniature' and does not risk a woman writer's status as appropriately feminine. But – and this is the double bind for women writers – if this is what women writers do and the reasons for doing it are focused on maintaining their femininity, 'By implication, the short story becomes both a lesser form and about all women can manage.'[12] This is a double bind that feminist criticism has not always been able to avoid in its own judgements. In the introduction to her 1997 anthology of nineteenth-century women writers of short fiction, *Scribbling Women*, Elaine Showalter undertakes the important work of recovery, anthologising a number of texts that had more or less disappeared from view. (The short story, often having ephemeral publication forms such as magazines, is very prone to disappearance from the record.) But even she almost suggests that the short story was a form that women chose for tactical reasons because the novel 'demanded a commitment of time that many American women could not afford', implying that it was a pragmatic choice, not a deliberate aesthetic one.[13] And for Rebecca Bowler, in a discussion of the woman writer's modernist short stories, writers like May Sinclair, Dorothy Richardson and even Katherine Mansfield, were always ambivalent about the value of the short form's aesthetic claims versus its practical value to them as something to keep an income rolling in: 'short stories were viewed', she writes, 'as a popular and ephemeral product. It was the novels that a writer produced that would create and sustain their reputation and standing in the literary marketplace.'[14]

Because there is so much potentially to say, this chapter is limited to the short story form as it is enacted by women writers who engage with the question of marriage. There are limitations which arise from this choice of writers and theme. For instance, the focus is on heterosexual relationships. It also risks the assumption that the short story is focused on purely domestic issues which somehow attach only to women readers and writers. In 'Gender and Genre', Mary Eagleton, however, points out that romance – of which marriage is generically meant to be the denouement – is a primary case study for a gendered genre because it is 'a form . . . produced almost exclusively by women, for women'.[15] Although there are clearly problems with identifying the romance genre in short fiction (or anywhere else for that matter) as a form with radical potential because of its required ending in monogamous, straight marriages, romance does have some disruptive potential in its expression of the excess of female desire that cannot quite be contained in the usual story. The interest from its audiences is also an expression – perhaps oblique – of that audience's dissatisfaction with an unromantic status quo. She suggests further that women writers are attracted to short fiction not because the form itself is 'known and safe' but because it is 'flexible, open-ended' and may therefore offer 'a transforming potential, an ability to ask the unspoken question, to raise new subject matter'.[16] In similar vein, Sabine Coelsh-Foisner comments that modernist women short story writers 'expressed realms of experience hitherto unnoticed and unexpressed, experimented with modes of perception and style, and opened up disruptive alternative perspectives on life'.[17] More recently Emma Young and James Bailey, who are appropriately careful not to essentialise what women writers can and cannot do, note that some possible characteristics of the woman's short story include an emphasis on 'the politics of time, the significance of the short story's ending, episodic nature and narrative brevity, the open and ambiguous nature of the form ... the relationship between text and reader, and the treatment of character and voice'.[18] They deliberately don't specify further how those emphases might play out or what distinguishes a woman writer or reader's interests in these elements from a man's. There is, though, in these tentative descriptions of what women may write and read about a glimpse of a common understanding of what a gendered version of short fiction might offer: a distinctive point of view which undercuts the old story.

A short story by Lucia Berlin offers a kind of parable both for the writing of a story and for the point of view it might offer – it is called, deliberately signalling its ambivalence, 'Point of View'. A writer considers the value of first-person versus third-person narrative, in a story that she is possibly writing about a doctor's assistant called Henrietta. If Henrietta told her own desperately dull story, which is a recounting of the habits and diurnal activities of her life, she muses, the reader would lose patience and say 'Give me a break.' But if she starts the story in the third person, then the reader will 'read on and see what happens'.[19] In fact, nothing will happen. Henrietta will go to work in her doctor's surgery, a bit in love with him (a classic set up for the doctor and nurse romance), but utterly unappreciated and indeed very badly treated by him. This is the romance plot when it fails to meet its generic goals. It is also the story of the writing of a story in which a woman's experience is placed centre stage – but whether it is the woman *in* the story or the woman who is ostensibly writing the story who is the point of interest is deliberately unresolved. The character, or the narrator, or the writer, goes to bed, watches her neighbours through a steamed-up window. 'In the steam of the glass, I write a word. What? My name? A man's name? Henrietta? Love? Whatever it is, I erase it quickly before anyone can see.'[20] The short form allows the self-assertion and self-expression that come from writing anything at all. It can also be a retreat from the kind of confident statement that prescribes as it inscribes, from the aggressive solidification of ideas and views that amount to a totalising vision. Irresolution gives more freedom than certainty does.

Who the New Woman of the late nineteenth century was very much depended on who was defining her. There were hostile descriptions of her in the contemporary press which emphasised her sexlessness, unattractiveness and stridency. When she was permitted to define herself, however, she was, argues Carol A. Senf, 'a type of well-educated, middle-class woman who was openly critical of the traditional roles established for women, especially marriage and motherhood, and who was influenced by the feminist movement to speak out in favour of equal education for women'.[21] She might also speak of her own desires and needs – though this was rarer, in a context where social and sexual purity for women was a fiercely enforced norm. What is certain, though, is that New Women writers adopted the short story form as a key mode in their struggle for self-expression and social emancipation. The reasons for this choice are not difficult to seek. In part they relate to the material conditions of book publication. Because their focus was on controversial subjects, the New Woman writer was constrained by the aesthetics and market conditions for the production and consumption of long-form fictions. She often turned to more ephemeral markets than those that pertained to the novel, placing her shocking fictions in the smaller circulation specialist magazines. She may well also have been responding to the problem of the novel form itself: as Jane Eldridge Miller has pointed out, for the Victorians, courtship and marriage were the central structural devices of long-form fiction, and marriage was the most usual end point for such fictions, which was constraining for those who wished to explore alternative possibilities for female lives.[22] Because the alternatives were experimental, the experimental short story form was more suitable for exploring them.

Of the New Woman short fictions, probably the most famous is Charlotte Perkins Gilman's 'The Yellow Wall-paper' (1892), which Gilman wrote as a response to her treatment for a uniquely female form of mental distress, post-partum psychosis, following the birth of her son. The story adopts the trappings of the ghost story, one of the most popular genres in nineteenth-century short fiction, in order to chart in fragmented, staccato sentences, the disintegration of its narrator's mind. The story is painful and frightening as a good ghost story should be; but it is also a diagnosis and critique of an unimaginative masculine medical profession which seeks to confine femininity to the domestic sphere, forbidding the narrator to write, and insisting that she ought to be focused on her recovery, not for her own sake but for those of her husband and baby. The story tells how the narrator becomes haunted by the wallpaper in her room, and the story ends with her creeping around the room, trying to free the woman (possibly a reflection of herself) that she imagines has been imprisoned in its monstrous yellow pattern. The story hints that she is driven mad in turn by domesticity, matrimony and maternity.

For Gilman, the choice of short fiction was pragmatic. She wanted to write something that would be read by the doctors who treated her. Writing years later of her intentions, she said that it was written with a purpose and therefore was not literature.[23] The separation that she identifies between politics and aesthetics is not one that many people would now agree with: both the personal and the aesthetic can be highly political. And this story has garnered a great deal of critical attention because it is also very artful, deliberately blurring interpretative certainties so that we cannot be sure whether the narrator is reliable; it thereby unsettles the totalising paradigm of the medical point of view of her case. The narrative is just a few pages; its disorienting effects are produced with a brevity and a misleading simplicity that could not be sustained if it went on much longer. It works in part because it is not couched as a complaint but as a description, apparently without agenda, of what happens. In the end, though, it is like much New Woman fiction, a diagnosis not a prescription for what might be woman's condition in unequal marital relationships and in an unequal social world.

Marriage looms large in New Woman fiction because it is perceived to be an unsatisfactory condition. Despite the many changes to the laws on marriage during the nineteenth century (a series of Married Women's Property Acts, shifts in the balance of power on marriage breakdown to favour the mother over the father in infant custody, and the slow liberalisation of divorce), marriage remained both a staple of romantic fiction and the presumed end of a woman's life-journey. As such it was meant to close down possibilities: 'Readers, she married him, and then she stayed home with the children', so that there is no more story to tell, since narrative apparently demands action, and childcare (mistakenly) is regarded as passive. The assumption that marriage is both a wished-for goal and the end of narrative possibility is often called into question by New Woman writing.

Two stories by George Egerton (pen name of Mary Chavelita Dunne) make this point very effectively. In 'A Cross Line', first published in *Keynotes* (1893), a young married woman who appears to be fond enough of her husband nonetheless toys with the possibilities offered by adultery. In the end she decides against it. In the midst of this story, the unnamed woman also indulges in an astonishing (for the mid-1890s) sexual fantasy, in which she performs, Salome-like, an erotic dance for an audience of thousands of besotted men. The story makes the point that there is a world of possible adventure, including sexual adventure, after the wedding ceremony. In its time, it was regarded as a scandalous. In 'A Cross Line', the reader has to infer the situation that is being described. In 'Wedlock', which appeared in Egerton's second volume, *Discords* (1894) we hear much of the plot from the conversation of two cockney builders working in a working-class London neighbourhood. As they work, they observe the lives around them and comment on the domestic goings-on of a local family, which is heading for disaster because of the mother's habitual drunkenness. The reasons for her alcoholism are not easily explained. They may be the result of poor heredity, one of the builders speculates, drawing on the eugenicist ideas of the times, or they may be the logical outcome of her married life to a brutal man who beats her and who has broken his promises to her. She is his second wife, married by her husband primarily in order to provide a mother to his first wife's children. He promised to let her keep her own child, but had insisted in the end that the child be sent away. In other words, there are biological, social and psychological reasons for her escape into drink. In the midst of the story we meet a second woman, scarcely introduced (unnamed, not socially located), who lodges in the unhappy house. The second woman is a writer who tries – though not very hard – to help the unhappy wife. Because her own life is difficult, however, she has not much sympathy to spare:

> She is writing for money, writing because she must, because it is the tool given to her wherewith to carve her way; she is nervous, overwrought, every one of her fingers seems as if it had a burning nerve knot in its tip . . . she is writing feverishly now, for she has been undergoing the agony of a barren period for some weeks, her brain has seemed arid as a sand plain . . . she has felt in her despair as if she were hollowed out, honeycombed by her emotions, and she has cried over her sterility.[24]

The style here is typical of Egerton. The use of the present tense, which is common in her work, implies that the narrative she is telling is ongoing. There is no distancing of these events into the past. They are happening even now, the tense suggests.

This experimental and elliptical style is more effective in short bursts than in longer fictions; and it has a political force. At the same time, it is also a poetic medium. The story makes use, as in the extract above, of metaphors which direct the reader's mind towards questions of maternity. The blocked writer risks images of herself as 'barren', unable to bring forth her figurative children, which are just as important to her as real children are to biological mothers.

That belief in the importance of her work is partially undermined by the story's shocking conclusion. The wise builder believes that a tragedy is about to happen in the house he has been observing, and he tries to prevent it by keeping a closer watch even when his work is done. However, he is sent on an errand to fetch a doctor for another sick child in the neighbourhood and misses the key moment. The unhappy wife's stepchildren are 'keen-eyed London children' who have 'precocious knowledge of the darker side of life'[25] but they do not see what is coming to them. Child murder is presented metonymically as 'a dark streak' seen dimly in moonlight, which trickles 'slowly from the pool beside the bedside out under the door, making a second ghastly pool on the top of the stairs – a thick, sorghum red, blackening as it thickens'.[26] Where in Thomas Hardy's novel, *Tess of the D'Urbervilles* (1892), published at almost exactly the same time as Egerton's collection, the heroine kills her seducer, Egerton ups the ante: the stepmother kills the children probably in a drunken rage, and we leave the story watching her as she sleeps it off downstairs, dreaming a heavenly but macabre scene where she and her own daughter dance among the open graves of her three stepchildren.

The title of the story tells us that the story is in part about marriage and maternity, but it is also about its alternatives. However, in the current state of play, wedlock is deadlock. The married woman is trapped in a violent situation; the unmarried writer has reached the end of her resources as a writer, and is blocked by her material conditions in a brutal household. Neither alternative is especially attractive, Egerton's story argues. Her concerns with marriage, maternity and the professional woman writer connect her to Gilman's interests, as does the clearly feminist agenda of her fictions. Her choice of the short form, like Gilman's, provides a snapshot diagnosis of social ills, but also like Gilman's tale, Egerton proposes no solution except by implication – something (precisely what is not clear) has to change. And the narrative distortions adopted by both women – the fragmented elliptical telling of the tales, which for Gilman and Egerton is the expression of the discomforts of femininity – points forward to modernist techniques, which resist narrative and closure just at the New Woman short fictions often do.

Katherine Mansfield was exclusively a writer of short stories, and one has to assume that this was a very deliberate choice on her part, not the result of accident, or of it being 'all she could manage'. Where the New Woman writers of short fictions had very definite purposes in their representations of injustices to women, Mansfield's stories are less overt in the message, and more focused on the emotions that circumstances provoke; the politics play more quietly than the feelings. Nonetheless, there is a clear line of inheritance between her works and those of the earlier generation, and the generic choice of the short story is part of that inheritance. Her stories are concerned on the whole with innocent femininity betrayed. Although these betrayals are sometimes apparently purely personal, in most cases the failings of the individual are exacerbated by the social training Mansfield's female protagonists have received; her women or girls are also betrayed by the lessons they have been taught in acceptable codes of femininity, and by the lessons men have learned in masculinity. The short story form enables her to make her point about her characters without stridency or overt preaching.

Mansfield is strongly associated with literary modernism, a mode and period of writing which had many, often contradictory concerns. It is in part a reaction against the conventions of realism which were regarded as unsatisfactory because the clarity of realist motivations and representations were viewed as incongruent with life as it is experienced. It charted a shift from social concerns to more psychological ones, and in Mansfield's case, it saw the expression of fragmented consciousness, in which no single point of view can see the whole picture. Her fiction presents its readers, through inference and implication rather than through direct diegesis, with far more than the characters can ever know about themselves or their own milieu. For Dominic Head, Mansfield's key innovation is in the presentation of characters through a complex mix of direct presentation (what they do and say) and their psychological responses to their world, which often shows them to be mistaken or misled in their views.[27] In a similar vein, Adrian Hunter notes Mansfield's 'omissions' which he identifies as 'characteristic of the modernist short story'.[28] Mansfield uses modernist technique to inscribe a view of life which insists that all interpretation is partial and distorted and all meaning is therefore unsettled. Readers have to fill in the gaps, and the interpretations that they come up with are also partial and distorted, because we can never quite know enough to say definitively what the story has told us. At the end of 'The Garden Party', for example, Laura, who has lived a great deal in the course of a single day, who has understood for the first time that her mother's life is snobbish and narrow, and who has confronted death as well, 'stammers' to her brother: '"Isn't life ... isn't life – " But what life was she couldn't explain.'[29] Laura tries to grasp the significance of her experiences, but has no words to express them because she lacks the vocabulary for describing the emotional impact of the day's events.

Many of Mansfield's stories are about family relationships and romantic attraction (most usually failed in some way) and are characterised by oblique critiques of social norms and conventions. In most cases, though, the critique is less important than the emotions provoked by the social situation. If this technique is derived from New Woman fiction, the emotions conveyed are something new. In one of her most sustained stories, 'Daughters of the Late Colonel' (1922, first published in *The Garden Party and Other Stories*), the question of marriage is approached via that most Victorian of questions: what is a woman to do if she cannot marry? In the immediate aftermath of her father's death, the elder sister, Josephine, experiences an emotion that she cannot name, and which she displaces onto some tiny sparrows on the window ledge:

> Some little sparrows, young sparrows they sounded, chirped on the window-ledge. *Yeep – eyeep – yeep*. But Josephine felt that they were not sparrows, not on the window-ledge. It was inside her, that queer little crying noise ... Ah, what was it crying so weak and forlorn?
>
> If mother had lived, might they have married? But there had been nobody for them to marry. There had been father's Anglo-Indian friends, before he quarrelled with them. But after that she and Constantia never met a single man, except clergymen.[30]

Josephine, in Victorian terms, is a 'relative creature', defined by her relationships with men (her father, her nephew), which is the clear message that the title of the story gives us; and because she is a Victorian, she cannot name the emotion that she feels, the yearning for love and sex, named by her, because of her need to remain respectable, as the desire for matrimony and motherhood. She vaguely knows, but does not articulate, her loss, which is shown to us only by the juxtaposition of new life stirring on the window ledge, while she remains trapped inside tyrannical domesticity, even after her father's death. His petty tyrannies cannot be named by her as tyrannies, for that would render even more starkly the waste of a life under patriarchal rules: her duty to the father has been damaging, but it would be even more destructive to know consciously that he was not worth her sacrifice. All of these messages are implicit in the spaces of the story. The story does not tell us what to think about it all, but simply expresses the stunted lives that the daughters have led, leaving readers to draw their own conclusions about what should be done about situations such as this.

The daughters of the title – like the father by whom they are defined – are Victorian throwbacks, trapped in ideals about duty which belong to another age, leaving them unloved, unlovable and wasted. Theirs is, however, a well-heeled, civilised world. They may be worried about butter being wasted, but they are not actually poor. In a much more stark and violent story, 'The Woman at the Store' (1911), set in the New Zealand wild lands that are a rough equivalent to the American Wild West, three travellers, a woman and two men, meet a woman who runs a general store in the middle of nowhere. They are not sure why, but the atmosphere of this place is strained with barely repressed violence. While one of the trio takes up a most unromantic liaison with the woman at the store, the other two come to realise, via a picture drawn on a scrap of paper by the woman's little daughter, that she has probably murdered her husband and buried him in the field beyond her domain. Her reasons for the killing are clear:

> 'Now you listen to me,' shouted the woman, banging her fist on the table. 'It's six years since I was married, and four miscarriages. I says to 'im, I says, what do you think I'm doin' up 'ere? If you was back on the Coast I'd have you lynched for child murder. Over and over I tells 'im – you've broken my spirit and spoiled my looks, and wot for – that's what I'm driving at. . . . . Oh some days – an' months of them – I 'ear those two words knockin' inside me all the time – "Wot for!"'[31]

This is a very savage kind of existential crisis. A once pretty girl ('Don't forget there's a woman too . . . with blue eyes and yellow hair, who'll promise you something else before she shakes hands with you'[32]), buried by her marriage in the back of beyond, and alternatively pestered and ignored by her husband, has fallen for a romantic lie about marriage, and when she realises what she has lost in the process, she lashes out. Her child is the witness of the crime: 'The kid had drawn the picture of the woman shooting at a man with a rook rifle and then digging a hole to bury him in.'[33] The story does not resolve. One of the men and the woman resume their journey. The other man stays with the woman at the store, who knows – apparently – 125 ways to kiss, which means he is willing to take the risk of a second violent attack. This irresolution, like that of Egerton's story, is an indictment of a world in which such things repeatedly happen, keep happening, always happen.

The further away that the tight bounds of marriage in the nineteenth century are in the twentieth, the more it is possible to treat the theme as matter for satire and even occasionally macabre humour. In Doris Lessing's 'To Room Nineteen' (1963), which narrates the doomed marriage of Matthew and Susan Rawlings, the tone is far less anguished, even though this turns out to be a tragic story. At its outset, Lessing's narrator announces: 'This is a story, I suppose, about a failure in intelligence: the Rawlings' marriage was grounded in intelligence.'[34] The couple have married on rational grounds. They both have lucrative careers, and congratulate themselves for having waited till their late twenties to marry, avoiding the opposing fates of early marriage which leads to regret or later 'desperate or romantic marriages' which are prompted by the fear of being alone. The Rawlings congratulate themselves for being so wise and so modern. They are wrong to be so complacent, and they are not at all modern really, but deeply conventional, with even Matthew's infidelities treading a well-worn path of infatuation followed by trumped-up remorse. Matthew, it would seem, feels reasonably content with his lot, since he has opportunities to seek alternative relationships via his work. But after their children are born, Susan is much less contented, an exemplary victim of the discontent that Betty Friedan defined in *The Feminine Mystique*, as being the condition of large numbers of intelligent middle-class women in the 1950s and 1960s.[35]

Lessing's story typifies a different kind of discontent with marriage. This is not about brutality, waste or lost opportunity, so much as about the possibility that the opportunity taken is the wrong opportunity altogether. Conventional thinking stifles the Rawlings, but its effects on the wife are more extreme than for the husband. While he pursues affairs, she pursues solitude, eventually finding a hotel room in which to sit and be alone, asserting her autonomy through the silence of this slightly sordid space. But if Matthew's (mis)behaviour is conventional, and therefore permitted, Susan's demand for apartness is not. At the story's climax, she is suspected of having an affair by her husband. Because the couple are so 'modern' and so 'intelligent', Matthew suggests that he should meet her lover at a civilised dinner for four with his new mistress. There is no lover and so rather than be found out in the eccentricity of seeking solitude, Susan gases herself in Room Nineteen of the hotel in which she has sought refuge from domesticity.

Lessing's treatment of the Rawlings' marriage is ironic, and her purpose is satirical. Marriage is a convention, not a *grande passion*; a mode of middle-class living, not an individual choice. Her form of address, ostensibly third-person and dispassionate, skewers the people whose lives she narrates by speaking their words and their attitudes for them, as though their attitudes are accepted wisdom so that the irony of the story's denouement is even more pointed. The events of this narrative belie the certitudes and platitudes of the Rawlings' manner of living and thinking, and the story is horrific because they know so little about their own motivations and instincts.

In comparison, another mid-century writer about the mores of marriage, Daphne Du Maurier, focuses on the macabre and the horrific. For her, middle-class marriage is Gothic because it enforces intimacy between often incompatible people. In the apparently safe space of domestic intimacy, horror lurks. In 'The Apple Tree', told – as often the case with Du Maurier, in a pleasing confusing of genders – from the husband's point of view, she narrates the story of a widower who is haunted by his dead wife in the unlikely dryad form of a misshapen apple tree. He sees the shape of her abject body in the boughs and trunk of the tree: 'How often had he seen Midge [his wife] stand like this, dejected.'[36] In one miraculous season, the tree puts forth an astonishing harvest of fruit, which the widower rejects as inedible, but which other people happily eat and enjoy. The remarkable fruiting of the tree seems as if it is a post-mortem offering from a loving but despised wife, but viewed through her husband's jaundiced eyes, it is a repulsive offering: 'The tree was tortured by fruit', we are told; it was 'groaning under the weight of it.'[37] The husband rejects the apples, as a displaced symbol of his wife's fertility; he also rejects the tree which he has cut down, just as he had rejected his wife's life of service to him when she was alive. In revenge, the tree kills him – he catches his foot in its dismembered branches when returning home one evening and dies in his garden of hypothermia in its suffocating embrace, married even beyond the point of death. This is 'a bloody silly way to die' (the quotation is from Du Maurier's masterly weird tale, 'Don't look now!'), but – both Lessing and Du Maurier seem to imply – marriages like these are also a bloody silly way to live.

In the final chapter of their magisterial study of the woman writer's place in the twentieth century, Sandra M. Gilbert and Susan Gubar revisit the fairy story with which, fifteen years earlier, they had begun their first historical consideration of the female tradition, the story of Snow White. In *The Madwoman in the Attic*, they had read this story, retold by the Brothers Grimm, as exemplifying a particular narrative structure in which woman is pitted against woman in the vain attempt to meet lasting male approval.[38] In the story of Snow White, the wicked queen wishes to assert the only power that she has – that of her sexual attractiveness. When that power is threatened by the adolescent sexuality of her stepdaughter, she takes drastic steps to take the girl out of the picture by commissioning her murder. Her punishment for her unnatural step-maternity is to discover that her power will wane anyway because she is ageing (in her culture a woman's value is entirely bound up with her sexual attractiveness), and that her stepdaughter will always survive to usurp her. She finally dances herself to death at Snow White's wedding in red-hot iron shoes. They end this discussion with the question of what the future will hold for Snow White. 'When her Prince becomes a King and she becomes a Queen, what will her life be like?'[39] Is she doomed to relive the story of her mother (dying in childbirth) or her stepmother (ravaged by jealousy and the impotence of middle age)?

When they revisit this story, Gilbert and Gubar imagine a range of possible alternative endings to this traditional story, including a radical lesbian utopia for the Queen and her stepdaughter, a sexless companionate marriage for Snow White to her handsome prince, and a post-structuralist fantasy in which all the characters are happy to admit that they are merely signs and masks, not people at all. In all of this playful recreation of a well-known and well-worn fiction their purpose is to raise an important set of questions about where both feminist criticism and feminist writing might go next: 'how is a woman to achieve personhood in the pleasure palaces of art and the artful palaces of pleasure?'[40] In their choice of a fairy story like 'Snow White' as the pre-text for their discussion – at both the beginning and the end of two very important works of feminist criticism – they signal the persistence of the fairy story's power over women as both readers and writers. They also acknowledge their potential complicity with the narrative it offers of rescue from danger, ending in a marriage that will last happily ever after. The fairy story genre is closely associated with compliant femininity, both in the role models it offers to the girls who read it, and in the maternal situation of its transmission, told as it traditionally is, by *Mother* Goose. For Gilbert and Gubar, this kind of narrative is ripe for retelling in new forms, with new endings and a wider outlook for its heroines. In their critical discussion of Snow White's story, they were already aware that women writers were messing with this narrative form, and borrowing its traditional authority to tell some very different stories.

In the title short story of Margaret Atwood's *Bluebeard's Egg* (1988), a vaguely dissatisfied wife, Sally, married (the irony is very pointed) to a heart specialist, attends evening classes in creative writing. In one class the tutor requires the students to respond to the oral tradition of the folk tale, and narrates a version of the classic tale of male brutality in marriage – 'Bluebeard'. The student assignment for that week is to rewrite the story in a modern setting, with contemporary concerns at its heart. The version of 'Bluebeard' with which they have been presented, however, is a reconstructed version of an oral tale, not the literary fairy-story versions that were remade for eighteenth- and nineteenth-century children. This story is 'much earlier than Perrault's sentimental rewriting of it. In Perrault . . . the girl has to be rescued by her brothers; but in the earlier version, things were quite otherwise.'[41] Following the rule of three, two sisters are taken in turn by Bluebeard, and when they are discovered to have been disobedient by the blood that has appeared on the egg he had required them to guard, they are dismembered and their body parts stored in his secret room. The third sister, using her intelligence, puts the egg away safely before she explores Bluebeard's castle, discovers the secret room, re-members her sisters, and they all escape. This is a tiny part of the story 'Bluebeard's Egg', which, as the narrative unfolds shows us what a modern version of that particular story might consist of. Sally, the wife, is a third wife. Earlier wives have not been murdered but divorced, and Sally, to her intense irritation and self-interested curiosity has no idea about what caused the marital breakdowns, or how she might in turn avoid the same fate. She plays hard at managing domesticity, cooking cordon bleu food and bringing up her husband's children, fearing always that the dissatisfaction she feels with her marriage is her fault, not her husband's. At the story's climax, she realises that it is possible that her husband is a philanderer.

Sally's realisation is reminiscent of a scene in Katherine Mansfield's 'Bliss', where a wife suddenly recognises her husband's infidelity, doubly painful because the object of his new affection is her best friend. All the while this is happening, Sally ponders how she will write her version of 'Bluebeard's Egg', transposed to modern Toronto and narrated from a single point of view: 'They couldn't use the Universal Narrator . . . they had to choose a point of view. It could be the point of view of anyone . . . in the story, but they were limited to one only.'[42] The story in front of us is possibly the story that Sally will eventually write, told from her own point of view, partially aware of both the distortions and the limitations of her standpoint. The universal narrator, often associated with the oral forms of ballad and fairy tale, assumes an omniscience that is the performance of social authority. If you tell the tale from a different, single point of view, and focalise through the eyes of the victim/heroine, the meaning of the story is changed. And if you transpose it to present times, the dubious assumptions of a patriarchal culture are laid bare for diagnosis and possible later reparation. Sally never quite gets to that more emancipatory conclusion. Her endpoint is the terror that her marriage might end, but Atwood has given her readers enough to go on to imagine better endings.

In another example, Jane Gardam's 'The Pangs of Love' (1983), a stroppy teenage mermaid, sick of the story of her older sister whose unrequited passion for a human prince had been immortalised in a story by Hans Christian Andersen, decides to find out for herself, on a purely rational basis, whether romantic love is all it is cracked up to be in the stories and the poems and the models of feminine behaviour that are taught by her mother and sisters. She finds the prince who had deserted her sister for a human bride, and, although he is good looking and 'not at all bad in the bath',[43] she concludes that love, if it means romantic self-sacrifice and feminine passivity in the face of desire, is simply not worth getting into a lather about. She has better things to do with her time: 'I've proved what I suspected. I'm free now – free of the terrible pangs of love which put women in bondage, and I shall dedicate my life to freeing and instructing other women and saving them from humiliation.'[44] Retelling the story with a different end, Gardam's narrative implies, has the potential to change the conditions for women in the real world. Generic conventions can be a trap which alternative narratives can spring.

If marriage is sometimes – or often – the source of women's suffering in short fiction, there is one genre above all for which it is meant to be the desired end point: the fairy tale. This is a genre that is strongly associated with femininity and that is closely aligned to the relationships between mothers and children. In the words of Marina Warner:

> Children . . . who play around the women gossiping are learning the rules of the group; fairy-tales train them in attitudes and aspirations. This can be a conservative influence: the old can oppress the young with their prohibitions and prejudices as well as enlighten them. But the tale-bearing will in either case pass on vital information about the values and beliefs of the community in which they are growing up . . . Stories . . . chart the terrain.[45]

But the form in which we mostly encounter fairy tales is actually a literary rather than an oral tradition, and, although the fashion for writing down oral tales, from the seventeenth century onwards, was begun by women (Madame de Sévigny is the key name), the authors whose stories chart the current terrain were largely men – Perrault and Anderson, name-checked in Atwood and Gardam's stories, and the Brothers Grimm – and were writing in and for very specific contexts. The effect of this on the classic fairy tale is that it fixes a fluid oral tradition to reflect those historical moment's concerns, a fixity that the oral tradition does not share. As Walter J. Ong has pointed out, oral stories are adaptable to new circumstances because they are focused on the present needs of subsistence economies.[46] The stories change as the context does. In subsistence economies, the economic advantages of marriage probably outweighed the potential emotional disadvantages – better to marry than to starve. The ubiquitous perfidy of stepmothers from the tales possibly had its basis in fact – it is a credible outcome of early parental death and the subsequent remarriage of the surviving partner. Those considerations no longer hold quite true in the West, but the persistence of the tropes of fairy-tale fictions in contemporary culture presents readers with conservative versions of femininity (girls need to be rescued by good-looking men, girls are passive in the face of danger, a girl's value is her beauty, a girl's aspiration is for advantageous marriage), that are ripe for rewriting.

There are many examples of feminist rewritings of the fairy tale to better reflect contemporary concerns, the most sustained of which is Angela Carter's collection, *The*

Bloody Chamber (1979). In the narratives that make up this slim volume, Carter toys with generic incongruity, returning to the genre some of the earthy vulgarity that was edited from the record in the tidying up exercises of some of the early written versions. She puts the pussy back into 'Puss-in-Boots' in her version, for instance, in a ribald mixture of Chaucer and Rabelais in which lust rather than romance is the motivating force for couples to come together. She brings to the surface the perversity of Bluebeard ('The Bloody Chamber'), and, as with Atwood's version, the girl is not rescued by a man, but this time by her pistol-packing mama. Carter's concern is with mutually satisfying sexual relations, based on mutual desires and the equality of desiring subjects, including their social equality. Those who seek to dominate are monstrous and sometimes punished, sometimes victorious. There are no lessons about the propriety of female passivity; but nor are virtue and vice necessarily rewarded and punished in the time-honoured fashion. The lessons are more nuanced because they take into account what Merja Makinen describes as 'active, sensual, desiring and unruly' female sexuality,[47] which sometimes means, as in the 'The Bloody Chamber', that the victim of masculine sadism is complicit to some degree in her own victimisation, even almost desires it. In that story, the unnamed protagonist and narrator, for instance, is 'aghast to feel [herself] stirring' with desire when she sees her naked body through the eyes of her monstrous husband:

> And I began to shudder, like a racehorse before a race, yet also with a kind of fear, for I belt both a strange, impersonal arousal at the thought of love and at the same time a repugnance I could not stifle for his white, heavy flesh that had too much in common with the ... arum lilies that filed my bedroom ... those undertakers' lilies, with the heavy pollen that powders your fingers ... The lilies that I always associate with him; that are white. And stain you.[48]

This example shows some of the ways in which this narrative disrupts genre. In the first instance it is written in the first person, where the traditional tale has the authority of impersonal extra-diegetic and omniscient narration. Several other stories share this feature, giving voice to the girl, who tells us how it actually feels to be the heroine of the fairy story – and it's not nearly as comfortable as the tradition would have us believe. The association of monstrous masculinity with the lily, more usually the symbol of pure femininity, is also important. That traditional metaphor is cast adrift from its referential mooring if it is transferred to a man, and if a fuller set of the signifier's meanings are brought to the surface. Rather than pure, this lily is fleshy, it is very highly scented with a sensual, cloying sweet smell, and it stains the unwary who touch it, a comment which is both literal and metaphorical. Its whiteness is not attractive but repellent, leprous even. Alongside the disgust that she expresses, the narrator also expresses curiosity and a compromised desire to experience the sex act. But this is 'impersonal' – it is not about love for a particular man at all but about desire without predetermined object. The story is also concerned with predatory, flesh-consuming masculinity. Finally, because the Duke is a sadist, the connections between sex and death are always writ large in his expressions of desire: lilies are funeral flowers, not bridal ones in this story. The girl-narrator is his prey – a racehorse, even a lamb chop elsewhere in the story, in contrast with his powerful carnivorous desires, which are imaged in recurrent metaphors that associate him with lions or tigers.[49]

The girl's desire takes place in a social context in which the Duke holds all the power. The narrator might have desires, but she is physically, socially and economically in his power unless something happens to disrupt that situation. In the case of 'The Bloody Chamber', that something is the violent incursion of a mother's love. In other stories, the disruption comes from the ingénue's refusal of sexual passivity and dependence in the bedroom or elsewhere, and the realisation of female desire by the male, be he wolf, lion or tiger. Where the traditional literary retellings of folk tales by eighteenth- and nineteenth-century men had disguised some of their sexually violent potential, Carter's stories lay it bare, and sometimes allow the heroine to take a pleasure in it that has usually been denied to her.

In the words of Margaret Atwood, writing about Carter's stories, 'to combat traditional myths about the nature of woman, [Carter] constructs other, more subversive ones'.[50] Part of the force of that subversion is that these new myths are not organised on binary lines of feminine passivity and masculine action. There are, though, quite significant limitations to Carter's vision – no concern with the problems that may attach to different ethnicities, no exploration of sexualities beyond the straight, for instance. Nonetheless, playing with the rules of genre and gender opens up intriguing possibilities for both.

In the introduction to an anthology entitled *Love, Loss and the Lives of Women*, Victoria Hislop makes two important comments, one of which is uncontentious, and the other of which is probably wrong. The first is about the things that a short story can do which a novel cannot. Hislop is very astute about the fact that experiment – with plot, with character, with point of view – is one of the key points of the short story form, and she gives Nicola Barker's 'Inside Information' as an example, a 'shiningly original story' which is told by an unborn child musing about whether or not its mother will be any good at the job. 'Personally', Hislop writes, 'I love the slightly quirky in a short story, but I would probably not be so patient if I had to listen to the voice of a foetus over three hundred pages.'[51] Experiment may well be the defining feature of the short story as genre, at least in its more 'literary' incarnations. Short fiction, by men and women, gives opportunities to try out new points of view. Later in the same introduction, though, Hislop suggests that 'many of the writers in this volume have the ability to leave their gender behind in their writing'. Well, maybe, but probably not. After all, they have been anthologised in this particular publication *because* they are women – there may be no textual marker of their femininity, but the paratextual ones of their names and public personae cannot be ignored. Texts do not just appear without the mediation of a writer, or the contexts of publishers and markets, all of which are gendered. It is also still very hard to imagine an anthology with the title *Love, Loss and the Lives of Men*, which rather implies that gender continues to be genred, since these are 'women's topics', but also that gender continues to be primarily women's work. Genres for people and genders for fiction are still very tangled up as textual formations. Understanding and paying attention to the implications of these knotty problems is one of the key ways in which attention to gender in relation to genre can offer useful insights into both the world and the words that describe it. And there is still much work to do, for men to examine their own genders and their own relationships with other genders more systematically and possibly more sympathetically, and for genders that are not purely binary to make new genres of their own.

Notes

1. Sigmund Freud, 'Femininity', in *The Essentials of Psychoanalysis* (Harmondsworth: Penguin, [1933] 1986), p. 413.
2. John Frow, *Genre* (London: Routledge, 2006), p. 10.
3. Heta Pyrhönen, 'Genre', in David Herman (ed.), *The Cambridge Companion to Narrative* (Cambridge: Cambridge University Press, 2007), p. 112.
4. Paul March-Russell, *The Short Story: An Introduction* (Edinburgh: Edinburgh University Press, 2009), p. 56.
5. To be fair to Oxford University Press, more recent anthologies are a little more even-handedness in their gender representation. For example, A. S. Byatt's collection of *English Short Stories* from 2009 has thirty-eight stories of which a rather more respectable ten are by women. It is still not exactly an even playing field, despite Byatt's own gender. Douglas Dunn's *Scottish Short Stories* from 1996 has thirty-nine stories of which nine are by women. And Philips Hensher's recent anthology, *The Penguin Book of the British Short Story* (2015) contains nineteen female-authored stories out of a total of fifty-four.
6. Frank O'Connor, *The Lonely Voice: A Study of the Short Story*, introduction by Russell Banks (New York: Melville House, [1963] 2004), pp. 18–19.
7. Mary Eagleton, 'Gender and Genre', in Clare Hanson (ed.), *Rereading the Short Story* (Basingstoke: Macmillan, 1989), p. 62.
8. Ibid.
9. Ibid. p. 66.
10. Ibid. p. 57.
11. Ibid. p. 62.
12. Ibid. p. 64.
13. Elaine Showalter (ed.), *Scribbling Women: Short Stories by 19th-Century American Women* (London: J. M. Dent, 1997), p. xxxvi.
14. Rebecca Bowler, 'Potboilers or "Glimpses" of Reality?: The Cultural and the Material in the Modernist Short Story', in Emma Young and James Bailey (eds), *British Women Short Story Writers: The New Woman to Now* (Edinburgh: Edinburgh University Press, 2015), p. 50.
15. Eagleton, 'Gender and Genre', p. 59.
16. Ibid. p. 65.
17. Sabine Coelsh-Foisner, 'Finding a Voice: Women Writing the Short Story (to 1945)', in Cheryl Alexander Malcolm and David Malcolm (eds), *A Companion to the British and Irish Short Story* (Oxford: Wiley Blackwell, 2008), p. 98.
18. Emma Young and James Bailey, 'Introduction' to *British Women Short-Story Writers: The New Woman to Now* (Edinburgh: Edinburgh University Press, 2015), p. 10.
19. Lucia Berlin, 'Point of View', in *A Manual for Cleaning Women* (London: Picador, 2015), p. 50.
20. Ibid. p. 55.
21. Carol A. Senf, 'Introduction' to Sarah Grand, *The Heavenly Twins* (Ann Arbor: University of Michigan Press, 1992), p. viii.
22. Jane Eldridge Miller, *Rebel Women: Feminism, Modernism and the Edwardian Novel* (London: Virago, 1994), pp. 44–5.
23. Charlotte Perkins Gilman, *The Living of Charlotte Perkins Gilman* (Madison: University of Wisconsin Press, [1935] 1990).
24. George Egerton, 'Wedlock', in *Keynotes and Discords*, introduction by Martha Vicinus (London: Virago, 1982), p. 123.
25. Ibid. p. 124.
26. Ibid. p. 144.

27. Dominic Head, *The Modernist Short Story: A Study in Theory and Practice* (Cambridge: Cambridge University Press, 1992), p. 113.
28. Adrian Hunter, *The Cambridge Introduction to the Short Story in English* (Cambridge: Cambridge University Press, 2007), p. 76.
29. Katherine Mansfield, 'The Garden Party', in *The Garden Party and Other Stories* (Harmondsworth: Penguin, 1951), p. 87.
30. Katherine Mansfield, 'Daughters of the Late Colonel', in *The Garden Party and Other Stories*, p. 117.
31. Katherine Mansfield, 'The Woman at the Store', in *The Collected Stories*, introduction by Ali Smith (Harmondsworth: Penguin, 2007), p. 508.
32. Mansfield, 'Woman at the Store', p. 551.
33. Ibid. p. 561.
34. Doris Lessing, 'To Room Nineteen', in Malcolm Bradbury (ed.), *The Penguin Book of Modern British Short Stories* (Harmondsworth: Penguin, 1987), p. 150.
35. Betty Friedan, *The Feminine Mystique* (Harmondsworth: Penguin, [1963] 2010).
36. Daphne du Maurier, 'The Apple Tree', in *The Birds and Other Stories*, ed. and introduction by David Thomson (London: Virago, 2004), p. 144.
37. Ibid.
38. Sandra M. Gilbert and Susan Gubar, *The Madwoman in the Attic: The Woman Writer and the Nineteenth-Century Literary Imagination* (London and New Haven: Yale University Press, 1979), pp. 36–42.
39. Ibid. p. 42.
40. Sandra M. Gilbert and Susan Gubar, *No Man's Land: The Place of the Woman Writer in the Twentieth Century, Volume 3: Letter from the Front* (New Haven and London: Yale University Press, 1994), p. 367.
41. Margaret Atwood, 'Bluebeard's Egg', in *Bluebeard's Egg* (London: Virago, 1988), p. 154.
42. Ibid.
43. Jane Gardam, 'The Pangs of Love', in *The Stories* (London: Abacus, 2014), p. 177.
44. Ibid. p. 183.
45. Marina Warner, *From the Beast to the Blonde* (London: Vintage, Kindle Edition, [1994] 2015), Kindle loc. 1139.
46. Walter J. Ong, *Orality and Literacy: The Technologizing of the Word* (London: Routledge: 1982), pp. 48–9.
47. Merja Makinen, 'Angela Carter's *The Bloody Chamber* and the Decolonisation of Feminine Sexuality', *Feminist Review*, 42 (1992): 9.
48. Angela Carter, *The Bloody Chamber* (London: Vintage, [1979] 2006), p. 11.
49. The Duke has a 'leonine head' (p. 2); 'soles of velvet' and a 'dark mane' (p. 3); he sees his new wife as 'horse flesh' (p. 6); he dresses her as the semblance of a zebra in a black and white striped fur coat (p. 8); and she is 'as bare as a lamb chop' (p. 11) on her wedding night.
50. Margaret Atwood, 'Running with Tigers', in Lorna Sage (ed.), *Flesh and the Mirror: Essays on the Art of Angela Carter* (London: Virago, 1994), p. 122.
51. Victoria Hislop, 'Introduction' to *The Story: Love, Loss and the Lives of Women* (London: Head of Zeus, 2013), n.p.

Bibliography

Atwood, Margaret, *Bluebeard's Egg* (London: Virago, 1988).
— 'Running with the Tigers', in Lorna Sage (ed.), *Flesh and the Mirror: Essays on the Art of Angela Carter* (London: Virago, 1994), pp. 117–35.
Berlin, Lucia, *A Manual for Cleaning Women* (London: Picador, 2015).

Bowler, Rebecca, 'Potboilers or "Glimpses" of Reality?: The Cultural and the Material in the Modernist Short Story', in Emma Young and James Bailey (eds), *British Women Short Story Writers: The New Woman to Now* (Edinburgh: Edinburgh University Press, 2015), pp. 50–65.
Byatt, A. S. (ed.), *The Oxford Book of English Short Stories* (Oxford: Oxford University Press, 2009).
Carter, Angela, *The Bloody Chamber* (London: Vintage, [1979] 2006).
Coelsh-Foisner, Sabine, 'Finding a Voice: Women Writing the Short Story (to 1945)', in Cheryl Alexander Malcolm and David Malcolm (eds), *A Companion to the British and Irish Short Story* (Oxford: Wiley Blackwell, 2008), pp. 96–113.
Cox, Michael and R. A. Gilbert (eds), *The Oxford Book of Victorian Ghost Stories* (Oxford: Oxford University Press, 1991).
Du Maurier, Daphne, *Don't Look Now and Other Stories* (Harmondsworth: Penguin, 1973).
— *The Birds and Other Stories*, ed. and introduction by David Thomson (London: Virago, 2004).
Dunn, Douglas (ed.), *The Oxford Book of Scottish Short Stories* (Oxford: Oxford University Press, 1996).
Eagleton, Mary, 'Gender and Genre', in Clare Hanson (ed.), *Rereading the Short Story* (Basingstoke: Macmillan, 1989), pp. 55–68.
Egerton, George, *Keynotes and Discords*, introduction by Martha Vicinus (London: Virago, [1893; 1894] 1982).
Freud, Sigmund, 'Femininity', in *The Essentials of Psychoanalysis* (Harmondsworth: Penguin, [1933] 1986), pp. 412–32.
Friedan, Betty, *The Feminine Mystique* (Harmondsworth: Penguin, [1963] 2010).
Frow, John, *Genre* (London: Routledge, 2006).
Gardam, Jane, *The Stories* (London: Abacus, 2014).
Gilbert, Sandra M. and Susan Gubar, *The Madwoman in the Attic: The Woman Writer and the Nineteenth-Century Literary Imagination* (London and New Haven: Yale University Press, 1979).
— *No Man's Land: The Place of the Woman Writer in the Twentieth Century, Volume 3: Letter from the Front* (London and New Haven: Yale University Press, 1994).
Gilman, Charlotte Perkins, *The Living of Charlotte Perkins Gilman* (Madison: University of Wisconsin Press, [1935] 1990).
Head, Dominic, *The Modernist Short Story: A Study in Theory and Practice* (Cambridge: Cambridge University Press, 1992).
Hensher, Philip (ed.), *The Penguin Book of the British Short Story* (Harmondsworth: Penguin, 2015).
Hislop, Victoria (ed.), *The Story: Love, Loss and the Lives of Women* (London: Head of Zeus, 2013).
Hunter, Adrian, *The Cambridge Introduction to the Short Story in English* (Cambridge: Cambridge University Press, 2007).
Lee, Hermione (ed.), *The Secret Self: Short Stories by Women* (London: J. M. Dent, 1985).
Lessing, Doris, 'To Room Nineteen', in Malcolm Bradbury (ed.), *The Penguin Book of Modern Short Stories* (Harmondsworth: Penguin, 1987), pp. 150–80.
Lord, Mary (ed.), *The Penguin Best Australian Short Stories* (Harmondsworth: Penguin, 1999).
Makinen, Merja, 'Angela Carter's *The Bloody Chamber* and the Decolonisation of Feminine Sexuality', *Feminist Review*, 42 (1992): 2–15.
Mansfield, Katherine, *The Garden Party and Other Stories* (Harmondsworth: Penguin, [1922] 1951).
— *The Collected Stories*, introduction by Ali Smith (Harmondsworth: Penguin, 2007).

March-Russell, Paul, *The Short Story: An Introduction* (Edinburgh: Edinburgh University Press, 2009).
Miller, Jane Eldridge, *Rebel Women: Feminism, Modernism and the Edwardian Novel* (London: Virago, 1994).
Newton, Michael (ed.), *Victorian Fairy Tales* (Oxford: Oxford University Press, 2015).
O'Connor, Frank, *The Lonely Voice: A Study of the Short Story*, introduction by Russell Banks (New York: Melville House, [1963] 2004).
Ong, Walter J., *Orality and Literacy: The Technologizing of the Word* (London: Routledge, 1982).
Pritchett, V. S. (ed.), *The Oxford Book of Short Stories* (Oxford: Oxford University Press, 1981).
Pyrhönen, Heta, 'Genre', in David Herman (ed.), *The Cambridge Companion to Narrative* (Cambridge: Cambridge University Press, 2007), pp. 109–23.
Senf, Carol A., 'Introduction' to Sarah Grand, *The Heavenly Twins* (Ann Arbor: University of Michigan Press, 1992).
Showalter, Elaine (ed.), *Scribbling Women: Short Stories by 19th-Century American Women* (London: J. M. Dent, 1997).
Warner, Marina, *From the Beast to the Blonde* (London: Vintage, Kindle Edition, [1994] 2015).
Young, Emma and James Bailey (eds), *British Women Short-Story Writers: The New Woman to Now* (Edinburgh: Edinburgh University Press, 2015).

19

Diaspora and the Short Story

Sam Naidu

'Identity is not as transparent or as unproblematic as we think', Stuart Hall remarked some years ago, in an influential intervention on the history of Caribbean migration and the evolution of black British culture. 'Perhaps instead of thinking of identity as an already accomplished fact, we should think, instead, of identity as a "production", which is never complete, always in process, and always constituted within, not outside, representation.'[1] Hall's comments were part of a larger discussion about the need for new concepts or modalities to be formed in order to make sense of the lived realities of identity formation – in particular, expressions of cultural identity – in the latter decades of the twentieth century. The crucial thing, Hall noted, was the need to break from essentialist definitions which are ahistorical, predetermined and the preserve of a select group or community of people. Cultural identity 'is not a once-and-for-all' and 'it is not a fixed origin to which we can make some final and absolute Return'.[2] Rather, Hall stressed the need to move towards more expansive and potentially unsettling ways of thinking about identity as a practice that is always undergoing transformation, that is responsive to an array of influences, and that bears witness to the continuing legacies of colonialism, economic exploitation and slavery in the contemporary world. Cultural identities are constructed in and through history, Hall observed, and are dependent upon the selective use of memory, myth, narrative and other representative strategies for meaning.

A key concept in this discussion was 'diaspora', as a number of commentators on both sides of the Atlantic (including Hall) explored the potential for this term to be revised and extended to speak to the complex and frequently traumatic experiences of different groups of people throughout history. 'If it can be stripped of its authoritarian associations', Paul Gilroy suggested in dialogue with Hall, and shorn of its biblical connotations (the chosen people who are dispersed in the Book of Deuteronomy but who are also promised a future and a divinely sanctioned homecoming, 'the Diaspora'), the term 'may offer a seed capable of bearing fruit in struggles to comprehend the novel sociality of a new millennium'.[3] 'Diaspora' – or rather 'diasporas' – is representative of the lived experiences of peoples who have been variously displaced, transported or forced into exile, Gilroy posited, and of their descendants who carry complex and often conflicting associations with the idea of an ancestral homeland from which they have been sundered. If the idea of return to such a homeland is (or was) an ambition for some, for others it is (or was) undesirable, unrealisable or unimaginable for a host of reasons. 'Like a number of other key concepts that have been deployed to do parallel work', Gilroy counselled,

> hybrid, border, creolization, *mestizaje* and even locality – [diaspora] has a disputed currency in contemporary political life as part of a new vocabulary, a vocabulary that registers the constitutive potency of space, spatiality, distance, travel and itinerancy in human sciences that had been premised upon time, temporality, fixity, rootedness and the sedentary.[4]

Other commentators followed suit, with Steven Vertovec and Robin Cohen, for instance, extending the signifying capacity of the term (tellingly in lower case, 'diaspora', and without the addition of the proper noun) to incorporate 'any population which is considered "deterritorialised" or "transnational"', and which 'originated in a land other than that in which [they] currently reside, and whose social, economic and political networks cross the borders of nation-states, or indeed, span the globe'.[5]

The concept of diaspora has been widely popularised, institutionalised and problematised over the last two decades, and has been variously applied to different types of politics, practices, social groupings and cultural aesthetics. This chapter explores some of the ways a clutch of short story writers from different countries and locations – from India, Nigeria, South Africa and the Caribbean – have grappled with this subject in their work, and have used it to engage with such experiences as isolation, prejudice, migration and hybridity. In many respects, the form of the short story can be considered especially suited to such acts of representation, as it has long been associated with conditions of fragmentation and marginality. Frank O'Connor's discussion of 'submerged population groups'[6] in *The Lonely Voice* is but one of a number of examples where writers and theorists have suggested a particular affinity between the short form and the representation of lives that are marginalised, underrepresented, silenced or rendered subaltern. And the short story might be judged additionally appropriate insofar as it is a form that is intrinsically portable (from periodicals to anthologies, and from little magazines to single-authored collections) and that is often considered an exemplar of the generic principles of cultural fusion (drawing together oral and scribal cultures, and linking traditional folktales with modern literary narratives).

Reflecting on the history of Caribbean writing in English, Louis James has suggested that 'the literature's vitality has drawn deep from the area's flourishing oral culture, from its folktales and performance narratives, its calypsos, and . . . tall stories'.[7] In short stories about Caribbean migration to Britain – particularly stories of the Windrush generation – this energy is typically manifest in the fusion of written traditions with oral rhythms, cadences and creoles. It is fusion which syncretises different cultural practices and which captures the complex and sometimes fraught relationship between the Caribbean and Britain. In 'Let Them Call It Jazz' (1962), Jean Rhys presents a disturbing glimpse of migration from the perspective of a young West Indian woman, Selina Davis. This first-person narrator recounts Selina's experience of poverty and isolation in 1950s London. Selina, who is of mixed race, finds herself destitute and dependent upon the shady Mr Sims, who offers her accommodation in a dilapidated suburban house. As the story progresses, Selina has altercations with racist neighbours, suffers mental breakdown, and ends up incarcerated in Holloway Prison. The story is a bleak indictment of how a migrant character can be subjected to 'misrecognition',[8] in Stuart Hall's telling phrase. 'At least the other tarts that crook installed here were *white* girls',[9] a neighbour is heard to remark, betraying a vulgar racist prejudice which is linked to the unfounded presumption that Selina must be a prostitute.

Rhys makes significant use of Caribbean creole to give voice to Selina and to set her protagonist apart from various English characters who exploit, misunderstand or abuse her. Reflecting on this point (albeit with reference to the concept of 'patois' rather than 'creole'), Kristin Czarnecki explains that 'Selina's patois presents a complex new voice, one that challenges conventional sexual, racial, and class paradigms in its determination not to be silenced.'[10] The story's marked use of creole asserts the validity of Selina's Caribbean identity; it also serves as a distinguishing marker which stresses Selina's cultural 'Otherness' in the diasporic setting – something which refuses to be assimilated by or with the host society. After suffering collapse and then prison, singing becomes a symbol of survival for Selina. While in Holloway, she overhears a fellow inmate sing and this acts as a catalyst for her recovery, as the song Selina hears is believed to have the power to 'jump the gates of the jail easy and travel far, and nobody could stop it'.[11] Selina subsequently begins the process of formulating a diasporic consciousness. Song and patois – along with a love of dancing, a directness of manner, and laughter – are part of her cultural inheritance, and are things she tries to preserve even as she seeks to transform herself into something new. It is striking, therefore, that Selina chooses to whistle rather than to sing at the end of this story, when she discovers that the song that she learned in prison – a song of freedom and resistance – has been commodified into a popular jazz song by a man she taught the melody to. For a moment Selina is unsettled; however, she quickly resigns herself to accept this change. 'So let them call it jazz', she says with a touch of defiance, 'and let them play it wrong. That won't make no difference to the song I heard.'[12] Towards the end of Rhys's story, a stranger asks Selina 'Have you come a long way?' Selina pauses before thinking her response: 'I come so far I lose myself on that journey.'[13] 'Let Them Call It Jazz' dramatises the various processes which collude to erase Selina's cultural identity and to undermine her sense of self-worth. But the story also recounts Selina's fashioning of a new, tougher self which is born out of the recognition that 'I don't belong nowhere really.'[14]

Sam Selvon's *Ways of Sunlight* (1957) also draws on the oral traditions of the Caribbean and interweaves this with the Anglo-American conventions of short fiction. The stories are based on short pieces which Selvon first published in the *Trinidad Guardian*; Selvon subsequently published in *London Magazine* and *New Statesman*, and also converted some of his work into radio scripts which were broadcast by the BBC. As his stories followed this path of publication, Selvon's work demonstrated some of the ways that short fiction can 'surviv[e] within the spaces of elite and popular culture, and [how] this ambiguous existence attests to its political potential'.[15] *Ways of Sunlight* includes nineteen short stories which are divided into two sections. The stories in the first section, 'Trinidad', trace the lives of people of European, African and Indian heritage rubbing shoulders with one another in a complex network of associations in the Caribbean; these associations cause disillusionment and distress for some, but also precipitate positive relationships and new forms of identity to be established. It is the stories in the second section, 'London', however, that fully engage with the subject of migration, as Selvon creates arresting portraits of characters who have travelled from the Caribbean. Referring to Selvon's contemporaneous novel

The Lonely Londoners (1956), Susheila Nasta describes his depiction of London as 'an iconic chronicle of post-war West Indian immigration to Britain', and remarks that this book 'encapsulates the romance and disenchantment of an imagined city that was both magnet and nightmare for its new colonial citizens, a promised land that despite its lure turns out to be an illusion'.[16] Similar comments can be made about *Ways of Sunlight*, where London 'operates paradoxically ... both as a symbol of modernity ... and as a repository of memory that works against that same historical schema'.[17] The city provides a site of convergence for diverse and often opposing pressures in Selvon's fiction, and many of the migrant characters experience discrimination and prejudice while also enjoying formative adventures and fresh possibilities.

In 'Waiting for Aunty to Cough', Selvon's interest in the fate of young Caribbean men is evident, as is his innovative use of language, syntax and humour. Brackley, one of 'the boys'[18] who pepper the stories in *Ways of Sunlight*, is involved in a relationship with a white girl called Beatrice, who lives with her aunt in a London suburb. Brackley escorts Beatrice home every night, and thus begins to 'discover a new world'[19] and to 'extend his geographical knowledge'[20] of the city. The perspective of London that is conveyed through Brackley's creole is male-centred, and offers a strongly gendered experience of migration. Brackley is thrilled to discover new locations, to expand his horizons, and to attempt to fit in with prevailing practices; however, he is also anxious as he travels through London's suburbs with Beatrice. Brackley's adventures in the suburbs are provided with intricate undertones, as he is presented as both an explorer and an interloper by Selvon. In many respects, his experiences are illustrative of the choices available to the young men in *Ways of Sunlight* more generally, as they struggle to make a new life in London. Almost every story in the 'London' section reveals the vulnerability beneath these men's 'adaptive strength',[21] to use Steven Vertovec's and Robin Cohen's useful phrase, and in each story the reader is encouraged to imagine the condition of first-generation migrants – particularly young men – from the Caribbean.

Selvon especially excels in his combination of the oral traditions of the Caribbean with the written conventions of short fiction. Indeed, it is Selvon's creation of a hybrid literary form which has had particular influence on subsequent generations of writers and readers. 'This form is a direct descendant of a Caribbean oral tradition of folk tales', Frank Birbalsingh has observed:

> The discursive, digressive, episodic and anecdotal literary patterns of this tradition, which were originally concerned with the victimization of African slaves and indentured laborers from India, provide a perfect model for Selvon's London stories in which West Indian immigrants are portrayed as marginalized victims or social outcasts.[22]

Selvon's London stories represent Caribbean migrants as marginal and vulnerable. At the same time, though, the stories illustrate some of the ways that members of this community share a camaraderie that is born of the exigencies of displacement and discrimination. As interpretative frames, *Ways of Sunlight* sets the scene of a particular diasporic space – London in the 1950s – and introduces a group of migrant characters whose experiences become the source of their ability to survive and adapt. As a collection, Selvon's stories function 'like a mosaic of portraits or photographs, offering fleeting yet sensitive glimpses into immigrant lives',[23] and provide sustained insights into the perspective of the ubiquitous migrant, poised between vulnerability and fear, nostalgia and promise.

Many of these issues also impinge on the form and the content of short fiction as it has been practised by writers of South Asian origin. Salman Rushdie's *East, West* (1995), recalls the structure of *Ways of Sunlight*, for instance, but is tellingly divided into three sections rather than two ('East', 'West', 'East, West'), with the final section engaging with the processes of hybridisation which are a consequence of migration from one's homeland. 'The Courter', from the third section, 'East, West', is ostensibly about Mary, a 60-year-old ayah or servant from India, and her unlikely romance with Mixed-Up, the porter of the apartment block in which the narrator's family lives. The narrator of the story recalls his migration to London in the early 1960s to attend boarding school; he is subsequently joined by his family and by Mary in England. What prompts the story is a letter the narrator receives many years later from 'an intimate stranger' (Mary's niece in India) which has 'reached out to me in my enforced exile from the beloved country of my birth and moved me, stirring things that had been buried very deep'.[24] Finding himself poised between two worlds, the narrator writes, in effect, an unconventional coming-of-age story about his first 'amorous longings',[25] using the servant's and the porter's burgeoning relationship as a lens through which to view his own experiences of alienation and uncertainty.

This retrospective story allows the narrator to reflect upon his current life and the choices and decisions he has made since he left India as a child. One of the narrator's adolescent objects of desire was his cousin Chandni, who is described as 'a teenage dream, the Moon River come to earth like the Goddess Ganga, dolled up in slinky black'.[26] The description of Chandni is multi-layered, with references included to British and American pop culture, to Hindu mythology, and to an idiomatic form of Indian English; it is also characteristic of Rushdie's approach to the subject of migration, as diasporic identities – and diasporic perspectives and modes of consciousness – are considered both disorienting and richly generative. As Rushdie explained in his much-cited early essay 'Imaginary Homelands' (1981):

> Our identity is at once plural and partial. Sometimes we feel that we straddle two cultures; at other times, that we fall between two stools. But however ambiguous and shifting this ground may be, it is not an infertile territory for a writer to occupy. If literature is in part the business of finding new angles at which to enter reality, then ... our distance, our long geographical perspective, may provide us with such angles. Or it may be that that is simply what we must think in order to do our work.[27]

'The Courter' exemplifies the strength of this thesis, illustrating the complex and often sustaining forms of 'double perspective'[28] that can evolve out of acts of migration. In addition, though, the story shows the tensions that can result from such processes of change – for the narrator and for other, very different migrant characters, like Mary and Mixed-Up.

In 'The Courter', Rushdie – like Selvon – uses demotic speech to connote the complexities of the migrant experience. A ready example is provided when the father

– who is nicknamed the 'Minotaur' – is slapped by a shop assistant for asking for 'nipples'.[29] The proudly anglicised patriarch, who collects copies of *Encyclopaedia Britannica* and *The Reader's Digest*, becomes the butt of a family joke because of his confusion of certain English words. Rushdie uses language – the Indian English spoken by Mary, who cannot pronounce 'p' in English, for instance – to gesture towards the necessity of adaption. Humour is also used to send up other types of Indian migrants (the stereotyped maharajahs who are caricatures of English gentlemen, for example), and even the climactic scene of the story, in which xenophobic thugs accost the narrator's mother and Mary, and then stab Mixed-Up, has an undertone tone of dark comedy.

Reflecting on his first, relatively innocent experience of migration, the adult narrator obliquely comments on his current state of exile, critiquing the relationship that exists between India and England, or East and West. The story portrays the ugly realities of racism and prejudice and includes various emblems of the colonial age, such as Field Marshal Sir Charles Lutwidge-Dodgson – 'an old India hand and a family friend who was supporting my application for British citizenship',[30] and who is appropriately called the Dodo. Colonial patterns of dependency, even sycophancy, are mirrored – but tellingly subverted – in the chess game between the narrator and the Field Marshal. However, just as Selvon sought to refashion London as a diasporic site of possibility, so Rushdie's England is shown to be a place of refuge and hybridisation – it is a cultural melting pot where Mary and Mixed-Up (whose suggestive nickname masks his proper name, Mecir) can meet and court, and where citizenship can be extended to include the Indian-born narrator.

Late in the story, Mary is afflicted with a mysterious heart ailment and it transpires that England 'was breaking her heart, breaking it by not being India'.[31] As a result, she returns to India; this signals the end of an era for the narrator who, like Mary, feels the strain of being away from home. To illustrate his dilemma, the narrator uses the analogy of a tethered horse that is pulled in opposite directions:

> But, I, too, have ropes around my neck, I have them to this day, pulling me this way and that, East and West, the nooses tightening, commanding, *choose, choose*.
>
> I buck, I snort, I whinny, I rear, I kick. Ropes, I do not choose between you . . . I refuse to choose.[32]

With sensitivity, Rushdie captures the determination of the migrant who refuses to choose between birthplace and new home, and who acknowledges that life in and between two locations (the 'East, West' of the third section), while painful and unsettling, can also allow for the fashioning of a new sense of identity. By giving two perspectives and two stories (the narrator's and Mary's), 'The Courter' resists homogenising the experience of migration and rejects any facile attempt at resolution – whether this is conceived through the nostalgia of native return or the uncritical embrace of a vaguely defined multiculturalist aesthetic.

Jhumpa Lahiri's *Interpreter of Maladies* (1999) also exemplifies Avtar Brah's description of diasporas as 'contested cultural and political terrains where individual and collective memories collide, reassemble and reconfigure'.[33] Of the nine stories in Lahiri's debut collection, seven explicitly engage with issues of migration and travel; eight of the stories also deal with relationships and with the theme of marriage. The fragmentary quality of the short story form allows marriage to be viewed from a variety of angles in the collection – from the viewpoint of male and female characters, as well as through the eyes of white American characters (Miranda in 'Sexy', Mrs Croft in 'The Third and Final Continent', Eliot in 'Mrs Sen's') and first- and second-generation Indian characters. The composite result is an image of the migrant as restless and bewildered; at the same time, though, *Interpreter of Maladies* stresses the impact of the migrant on the host society, and the need for a renegotiation of traditional beliefs and practices in such settings. This repeated shifting of focus and location allows for a multi-perspectival approach to the dynamics of migration, and provides a complex engagement with such issues as racism, alterity, the discourse of Orientalism, and the perpetuation of stereotypes.

In 'Mrs Sen's', the central character (a migrant bride from India) experiences multiple forms of displacement, from physical isolation to emotional exile and social ostracisation. Mrs Sen is lonely in America until she meets an 11-year-old boy called Eliot, whom she provides with after-school care. For Mrs Sen 'everything is there',[34] in India; '[h]ere, in this place where Mr Sen has brought me, I cannot sometimes sleep'.[35] Lahiri's story abounds with powerful symbols: a blade brought from India which is used in the preparation of food; blue aerograms which arrive from 'home' with news and local gossip; fish which is reminiscent of Mrs Sen's Bengali heritage; and the act of driving which is associated with mobility and independence, but which also functions as a significant plot device leading to the climax of the story. Mrs Sen, who is learning to drive, is involved in a minor traffic accident; this results in the termination of her job, and the loss of the one relationship she has managed to forge since leaving India.

Mrs Sen represents a type of diasporic consciousness that has not adjusted to or been assimilated with the host culture. Eliot and his mother are representative of the latter social grouping, and a pronounced contrast is established between Eliot's mother and Mrs Sen: Eliot's mother does not understand the codes of hospitality with which Mrs Sen has grown up, and because of her 'Western'[36] palate she rejects Mrs Sen's overtures of friendship. The differences between Eliot, Eliot's mother and Mrs Sen are also emphasised through descriptions of language, food, clothes, furniture, lifestyle and aroma. Although a child, Eliot is sensitive to cultural difference and is sympathetic to Mrs Sen in a way that his mother is not. With time, he comes to understand something of Mrs Sen's predicament; he also learns a little about Indian culture, noting that the vermilion powder Mrs Sen applies to the parting in her hair is a symbol of marriage.[37] The unlikely relationship is mutually comforting: Eliot receives from Mrs Sen the maternal care that he does not get from his mother; and Mrs Sen receives from Eliot the understanding that is lacking in her marriage. Lahiri is careful to signal that this relationship is not sustainable, however, and the bond between Eliot and Mrs Sen is allowed to occupy only a moment in time.

Late in 'Mrs Sens's' the focus of the story shifts from Mrs Sen to Eliot when Eliot's mother decides that the boy is old enough to care for himself. The closing sentence of the story – 'Eliot looked out the kitchen window, at gray waves receding from the shore, and said that he was fine'[38]– encourages the reader to consider loneliness and alienation as a ubiquitous state that is not restricted to migrant or diasporic characters. Just as Rhys's and Selvon's portraits of Caribbean people in England capture a particular form of migrancy as well as a general condition of dislocation and misunderstanding, Lahiri's story comments on a wider sense of what it means to be human and, as Antara Chatterjee contends, 'explores universal complexities of human relationships'.[39] These themes are repeated in other stories in *Interpreter of Maladies* and are also explored in the title story of Lahiri's second collection, *Unaccustomed Earth* (2008). 'Unaccustomed Earth' explores the relationship between two people: Ruma, a 38-year-old Asian American woman who lives in Seattle and who is mother to a young son, Akash; and Ruma's father, who is unnamed, recently widowed, and who left India when he was a young man to study. The story presents two narrative strands, one for each protagonist, and offers insights into how each of the characters negotiates their relationship to India, to America, and to each other; these connections are strained and are described as constituting a 'frail bond'.[40] For Ruma, life in Seattle is lonely, and the death of her mother, who *in absentia* functions as a symbol of the motherland, has left her profoundly bereft. The father's story covers his early experiences of America, and also his memories of his childhood in India. Both father and daughter are shown to struggle with feelings of isolation and dislocation, but for the second-generation Ruma, the 'experience of displacement ... is not associated with immigration'[41] but rather with the legacy of her parents' culture which has diminished in significance over time.

Intergenerational estrangement is the focal point of 'Unaccustomed Earth'. Unexpectedly, the father proves helpful in the domestic sphere, and his presence eases Ruma's anxieties. By teaching his grandson Bengali, and by encouraging the boy to help with him in the garden, the father seeks to bridge the gap with Akash, who is described as an 'American child'.[42] The story ends with a poignant moment of human interconnection, as father and daughter experience revelations about each other which lead to a new-found respect and a shared understanding. For Ruma, in particular, this reconciliation is unexpected and the realisation that her father has adapted to his new home, and to his experience of widowhood, is surprisingly liberating. Most profoundly, the story describes how the children of migrants who grow up in a diasporic setting can become 'foreign'[43] to their parents. Notwithstanding the reconciliations that are achieved, the story concludes with some misgivings about the future as the cultural bonds between parents and children (between the father and Ruma, but also between Ruma and Akash) are set to loosen even further. It is a point that is also voiced in other stories by Lahiri – the final story of *Interpreter of Maladies*, 'The Third and Final Continent', being a case in point, where the unnamed elderly narrator expresses his fears for his American-born son who has begun to lose his Bengali inheritance.

In other settings, the restless fragmentation of the short story form – to paraphrase Nadine Gordimer[44] – has often carried a weighted political significance. The forging of new literary forms and resistance to neocolonial forms of domination have long been the concern of anti-colonial authors in Africa, such as Chinua Achebe and Ngũgĩ wa Thiong'o. However, in his introduction to the recent *Granta Book of the African Short Story* (2011), Helon Habila warns against reductive interpretations of the so-called 'African short story', advising readers to be alert to the multiplicity of styles, techniques and approaches which have been utilised by what he terms 'the post-nationalist generation'[45] of African writers. Habila also encourages readers not to assume that all African short stories are geographically bound, or that they are derived from orature only, but rather to consider the variety of traditions from which stories draw and the increasingly cosmopolitan issues that they reflect. Many of the authors included in his collection, including Chimamanda Ngozi Adichie and Zoë Wicomb, might be considered international in scope and interest, and their stories about migration and diaspora, as Habila suggests, 'capture the range and complexity of African short fiction since independence'.[46]

Adichie's practice of short fiction is overtly political, and engages with some of the challenges faced by young female migrants to Europe and North America; these challenges include objectification, exoticisation and the confluence of racism and sexism. The title story of Adichie's *The Thing Around Your Neck* (2009), for instance, adopts a direct, almost confrontational tone which draws the reader into a poignant exploration of the gendered experience of migration. A sharpness of address is generated through the narrator's decision to speak to the protagonist directly – through use of the second person pronoun, 'you' – and this creates a degree of discomfort in the story, as the narrative observes Akunna (the protagonist) closely and is privy to her every thought and action. The story begins with a description of Akunna's leave-taking in Lagos, and includes reference to the rituals of migration, to a so-called 'visa lottery',[47] and to the poverty of her homeland. Akunna is twenty-two and is dependent upon, and therefore vulnerable to, an 'uncle' in America who has acted as her sponsor. At first, this 'uncle' appears supportive; however, it quickly becomes apparent that he has ulterior motives and when he attempts to exploit Akunna's vulnerability, she is forced to strike out on her own with little more than a green card and her 'uncle's' advice: 'The trick was to understand America, to know that America was give-and-take. You gave up a lot but you gained a lot too.'[48]

Akunna struggles with her experiences in America all the while experiencing intense homesickness for Nigeria. To survive, she effaces her sense of identity and seeks to become 'invisible';[49] however, at night she finds herself figuratively choked by the titular 'thing around her neck' – Akunna's hair, which is exoticised by the white people that she encounters, and which recalls the ropes which bind the narrator of Rushdie's 'The Courter'. The trauma of displacement that is endured by many migrants is captured in this monstrous metaphor, as Akunna's distress is compared to a living creature which physically suffocates her. Akunna finds employment as a waitress and displays filial duty by sending money home to her family; however, her sense of failure prevents her from writing to her parents. Failure is not an uncommon burden for migrants who involuntarily imbibe and consequently contribute to the myth of migration – a myth which relatives and friends in the homeland can also propagate when they fantasise about the migrant's affluence in the new world.

In the course of 'The Thing Around Your Neck', Akunna embarks on a relationship with a privileged white student, and this relationship becomes a medium through which issues of cultural, racial and economic difference are explored. These differences exacerbate Akunna's sense of suffering, but Adichie also suggests the possibility that love might be found – and connection consequently established – between these two young people. However, this is counterbalanced with the experiences of xenophobia and hostility that Akunna and her boyfriend endure, as their relationship elicits responses which are 'a mixture of ignorance and arrogance',[50] as her 'uncle' had previously warned. The story concludes vaguely, and disquietingly, with Akunna's return to Nigeria, when she belatedly learns of her father's death; and it remains unclear whether she will go back to America. In this respect, 'The Thing Around Your Neck' is representative of Adichie's stories more generally which, as Daria Tunca notes, typically make use of 'ambiguous or open endings, perhaps to indicate that the cross-cultural experiences described in her work are complex and on-going processes'.[51]

Zoë Wicomb's *You Can't Get Lost in Cape Town* (1987) also makes innovative use of the short story form. Variously described as a novel, a short story cycle and a story collection, Wicomb's volume invites multiple interpretations, and encourages readers to engage with distinct episodes as well as to appreciate the interrelationship between the stories. Marcia Wright, in her 'Historical Introduction' to the collection, describes the volume as an 'episodic novel' which portrays 'a young coloured woman's coming to age in apartheid-ruled South Africa'.[52] Wicomb's stories can certainly be read as a disjointed, feminist *Bildungsroman*, spanning a thirty-year period, from the 1950s to the 1980s, and focusing upon the character of Frieda Shenton, an aspiring writer. However, the book can equally be interpreted as a series of stand-alone texts, with each element containing an internal coherence and a discrete focus and artistic integrity. The stories can additionally be seen to interconnect and to provide part of a larger cycle. In this respect, it is fitting that Rocío Davis has described the short story cycle as a form that hovers somewhere 'between the novel and the short story';[53] and it is also appropriate that Davis has identified the cycle as 'the perfect medium with which to enact the feeling that one falls "between two stools"':

> Choosing to write a short-story cycle is emblematic of the creative position of post-colonial writers, one that is almost an optical illusion, being two things at the same time and creating total novelty; a metonym for the task of negotiating identity.[54]

From this perspective, Wicomb's deployment of the short story cycle might be considered an articulation of dual inheritance. The choice, as Wicomb stated in an interview in 1990, stems from an attempt to eschew 'the camouflage of coherence that sociopolitical structures are about'.[55]

One of the stories in *You Can't Get Lost in Cape Town*, the autobiographical 'Home Sweet Home', is set in Wicomb's birthplace of Little Namaqualand – 'an impoverished, semiarid area beyond the rich wheat farms and vineyards north of Cape Town'.[56] The story is structured around the gathering of a group of relatives in the Shenton family home, as they prepare to bid farewell to Frieda who is about to emigrate to England. Not only is migration central to the plot, it is also a topic for much of the dialogue of the story. Friends and relatives who previously migrated are discussed, and an uncle's wistful letter from Canada is read aloud. Frieda recalls that uncle's optimistic words which belied his obvious anxiety just before he embarked on his journey: 'Man, there's no problem; we're mos all Juropeens when we get to Canada.'[57] Using the demotic speech of 'coloured' South Africans, Wicomb depicts the myths about migration which abound, showing that migrants frequently hold unrealistic expectations of a better life in their new homes, while those who are left behind cling to fantasies of wealth, opportunity and non-discrimination. At the Shenton gathering, older relatives heap advice on Frieda, who appears as a solitary and introspective young woman, already alienated within her own community. 'Ag, Gerrie, you know this child's always been so', an aunt declares to the assembled crowd.

'Everybody goes to Canada so she wants to go to England where there's nobody, not a soul from South Africa. She's stubborn as a mule; always pulls the other way.'[58] The story ends with Frieda in Cape Town, reading about the 'bright green meadows of Hardy's England',[59] and already thinking herself in England – or rather, already imagining herself in a particular type of England, which is pastoral, anachronistic and fictional. Seeking refuge by the banks of a river, Frieda witnesses the drowning of a mule in quicksand. Given that Frieda was previously compared to a mule, the sense of foreboding that is latent in this incident is not lost on the protagonist, who begins to realise that the journey ahead will be full of peril.

The dangers of migration – and the relationship between migration and writing – is further developed in Wicomb's *The One That Got Away* (2008; revised 2011). Miriam, the young protagonist of 'Raising the Tone', is obsessed with stories and is gripped with a desire to leave home. Through the trope and the practice of storytelling, Wicomb introduces the main action of her narrative, which revolves around the conflict between Miriam and her mother, Cath, who is in exile from apartheid South Africa. The characters are first- and second-generation migrants living in an actual 'liminal zone'[60] in Glasgow, between a development of fancy town houses and an impoverished council estate. 'Everyone should be able to think herself as the subject of a narrative', Miriam remarks early in 'Raising the Tone', 'otherwise people would end up like her mother – stuck in history'.[61] For Miriam, stories have the potential to shape identity and to offer opportunities for invention and independence; however, it slowly becomes clear that Miriam's understanding of the power of stories is poorly informed and politically naïve. Cath's 'old stories of her days as a resistance fighter',[62] and the 'palimpsest of the old story of Africa',[63] are repudiated as 'sentimental nonsense'[64] by her daughter. Cath identifies as African, specifically as South African, and Scotland remains a place of exile not a home. Miriam, on the other hand, is scornful of her mother's past and blithely romanticises about the multicultural values – and the discourse of pluralism, inclusivity and equality – that she believes to exist in her birthplace of Glasgow. These beliefs are tested when immigration officers raid the nearby council estate, and the realities of racial persecution – in Scotland and, by association, in South Africa – dawn on her. 'Raising the Tone', perhaps more than any of the stories examined in this chapter, draws attention to the fraught differences which exist between first- and second-generation migrants. In Wicomb's story, these differences only begin to be reconciled when the younger generation – which is often ignorant about or unsympathetic to the lives of the older generation – comes to appreciate the adaptive strength of its predecessors.

As discussions of diaspora have evolved over the last thirty years, the term has sometimes become shorthand for the 'the world-wide flow of cultural objects, images and meanings'[65] in a contemporary context. If this is akin to more recent conceptualisations of the transnational, diaspora carries additional significance insofar as it is invested with a specific political charge, as it acknowledges the historical conditions of people – of individuals, groups and communities – who have been compelled to migrate at different points in history. The experiences of diasporic peoples have often been pathologised, and have met with ignorance and prejudice; however, they have also allowed for 'variegated processes of creolization'[66] and cultural fusion to be imagined. The stories in this chapter exemplify these difficulties while also exploring the potential for new figurations of identity to be established – and innovative modes of writing to be practised – in diasporic settings. 'The diaspora experience . . . is defined, not by essence or purity', Stuart Hall concluded his seminal discussion of the subject, 'but by the recognition of a necessary heterogeneity and diversity; by a conception of "identity" which lives with and through, not despite, difference; by *hybridity*'.[67] Short fiction, with its own propensity for variety, movement and recombination, provides a crucial vector of this experience.

Notes

1. Stuart Hall, 'Cultural Identity and Diaspora', in Jonathan Rutherford (ed.), *Identity: Community, Culture, Difference* (London: Lawrence & Wishart, 1990), p. 222.
2. Ibid. p. 226.
3. Paul Gilroy, 'Diaspora', *Paragraph*, 17.1 (March 1994): 207.
4. Ibid.
5. Steven Vertovec and Robin Cohen, 'Introduction', in Steven Vertovec and Robin Cohen (eds), *Migration, Diasporas and Transnationalism* (Cheltenham: Elgar, 2001), p. xvi.
6. Frank O'Connor, *The Lonely Voice: A Study of the Short Story* (London: Macmillan, 1963), p. 18.
7. Louis James, 'Writing the Ballad: The Short Stories of Samuel Selvon and Earl Lovelace', in Jacqueline Bardolph (ed.), *Telling Stories: Postcolonial Short Fiction in English* (Amsterdam: Rodopi, 2001), p. 104.
8. Stuart Hall, 'Negotiating Caribbean Identities', *New Left Review*, 1.209 (January–February 1995): 8.
9. Jean Rhys, 'Let Them Call It Jazz', in *The Collected Short Stories* (New York: W. W. Norton, 1987), p. 167.
10. Kristin Czarnecki, 'Jean Rhys's Postmodern Narrative Authority: Selina's Patois in "Let Them Call It Jazz"', *College Literature*, 35 (2008): 20.
11. Rhys, 'Let Them Call It Jazz', p. 173.
12. Ibid. p. 175.
13. Ibid. p. 174.
14. Ibid. p. 175.
15. Maggie Awadalla and Paul March-Russell, 'Introduction: The Short Story and the Postcolonial', in Maggie Awadalla and Paul March-Russell (eds), *The Postcolonial Short Story* (London: Palgrave Macmillan, 2013), p. 8.
16. Susheila Nasta, 'Introduction' to Sam Selvon, *The Lonely Londoners* (London: Penguin, 2006), p. v.
17. Awadalla and March-Russell, 'Introduction', pp. 10–11.
18. Sam Selvon, 'Waiting for Aunty to Cough', in Andrew Salkey (ed.), *West Indian Stories* (London: Faber and Faber, 1968), p. 118.
19. Ibid. p. 119.
20. Ibid. p. 120.
21. Vertovec and Cohen, 'Introduction', p. xviii.
22. Frank Birbalsingh, 'The Indo-Caribbean Short Story', *Journal of West Indian Literature*, 12.1–2 (2004): 125–6.
23. Antara Chatterjee, 'The Short Story in Articulating Diasporic Subjectivities in Jhumpa Lahiri', in Awadalla and March-Russell (eds), *The Postcolonial Short Story*, p. 98.
24. Salman Rushdie, 'The Courter', in *East, West* (London: Vintage, 1995), p. 178.
25. Ibid. p. 187.
26. Ibid. p. 188.

27. Salman Rushdie, 'Imaginary Homelands', in *Imaginary Homelands: Essays and Criticism, 1981–1991* (London: Granta Books, 1991), pp. 15–16.
28. Rushdie, 'Imaginary Homelands', p. 19.
29. Rushdie, 'The Courter', pp. 183–4.
30. Ibid. p. 191.
31. Ibid. p. 209.
32. Ibid. p. 211.
33. Avtar Brah, *Cartographies of Diaspora: Contesting Identities* (London: Routledge, 1996), p. 193.
34. Jhumpa Lahiri, 'Mrs Sen's', in *Interpreter of Maladies* (New York: Houghton Mifflin, 1999), p. 113.
35. Ibid. p. 115.
36. Ibid. p. 118.
37. Ibid. p. 117.
38. Ibid. p. 135.
39. Chatterjee, 'Articulating Diasporic Subjectivities', pp. 97–8.
40. Jhumpa Lahiri, 'Unaccustomed Earth', in *Unaccustomed Earth* (London: Bloomsbury, 2008), p. 37.
41. Chatterjee, 'Articulating Diasporic Subjectivities', p. 105.
42. Lahiri, 'Unaccustomed Earth', p. 23.
43. Ibid. p. 54.
44. Nadine Gordimer, 'The Flash of Fireflies', in Charles E. May (ed.), *The New Short Story Theories* (Athens: Ohio University Press, 1994), p. 265.
45. Helon Habila, 'Introduction' to *The Granta Book of the African Short Story* (London: Granta, 2011), p. viii.
46. Ibid. p. vii.
47. Chimamanda Ngozi Adichie, 'The Thing Around Your Neck', in *The Thing Around Your Neck* (London: Fourth Estate, 2009), p. 115.
48. Ibid. p. 116.
49. Ibid. p. 119.
50. Ibid. p. 116.
51. Daria Tunca, 'Of French Fries and Cookies: Chimamanda Ngozi Adichie's Diasporic Short Fiction', in Kathleen Gyssels and Bénédicte Ledent (eds), *African Presence in Europe and Beyond* (Paris: L'Harmattan, 2010), p. 306.
52. Marcia Wright, 'Historical Introduction' to Zoë Wicomb, *You Can't Get Lost in Cape Town* (New York: The Feminist Press at the City University of New York, 1987), p. vii.
53. Rocío G. Davis, 'Negotiating Place/Re-Creating Home: Short Story Cycles by Naipaul, Mistry, and Vassanji', in Bardolph (ed.), *Telling Stories*, p. 323.
54. Davis, 'Negotiating Place/Re-Creating Home', pp. 323–4.
55. Zoë Wicomb, 'Zoë Wicomb Interviewed by Eva Hunter – Cape Town, 5 June 1990', in Eva Hunter and Craig Mackenzie (eds), *Between the Lines II: Interviews with Nadine Gordimer, Menán du Plessis, Zoë Wicomb, Lauretta Ngcobo* (Grahamstown: National English Literary Museum, 1993), p. 80.
56. Wright, 'Historical Introduction', p. vii.
57. Zoë Wicomb, 'Home Sweet Home', in *You Can't Get Lost in Cape Town* (New York: The Feminist Press at the City University of New York, 1987), p. 84.
58. Ibid. p. 86.
59. Ibid. p. 90.
60. Zoë Wicomb, 'Raising the Tone', in *The One That Got Away* (Nottingham: Five Leaves Publications, [2008] 2011), p. 139.
61. Ibid. p. 135.

62. Ibid. p. 147.
63. Ibid. p. 135.
64. Ibid. p. 138.
65. Vertovec and Cohen, 'Introduction', p. xviii.
66. Ibid.
67. Hall, 'Cultural Identity and Diaspora', p. 235 (emphasis in the original).

Bibliography

Adichie, Chimamanda Ngozi, *The Thing Around Your Neck* (London: Fourth Estate, 2009).
Awadalla, Maggie and Paul March-Russell (eds), *The Postcolonial Short Story* (London: Palgrave Macmillan, 2013).
Birbalsingh, Frank, 'The Indo-Caribbean Short Story', *Journal of West Indian Literature*, 12.1–2 (2004): 118–34.
Brah, Avtar, *Cartographies of Diaspora: Contesting Identities* (London: Routledge, 1996).
Chatterjee, Antara, 'The Short Story in Articulating Diasporic Subjectivities in Jhumpa Lahiri', in Maggie Awadalla and Paul March-Russell (eds), *The Postcolonial Short Story* (London: Palgrave Macmillan, 2013), pp. 96–110.
Czarnecki, Kristin, 'Jean Rhys's Postmodern Narrative Authority: Selina's Patois in "Let Them Call It Jazz"', *College Literature*, 35 (2008): 20–37.
Davis, Rocío G., 'Negotiating Place/Re-Creating Home: Short Story Cycles by Naipaul, Mistry, and Vassanji', in Jacqueline Bardolph (ed.), *Telling Stories: Postcolonial Short Fiction in English* (Amsterdam: Rodopi, 2001), pp. 323–32.
Gilroy, Paul, 'Diaspora', *Paragraph*, 17.1 (March 1994): 207–12.
Gordimer, Nadine, 'The Flash of Fireflies', in Charles E. May (ed.), *The New Short Story Theories* (Athens: Ohio University Press, 1994), pp. 263–7.
Habila, Helon, 'Introduction' to *The Granta Book of the African Short Story* (London: Granta, 2011), pp. vii–xv.
Hall, Stuart, 'Cultural Identity and Diaspora', in Jonathan Rutherford (ed.), *Identity: Community, Culture, Difference* (London: Lawrence & Wishart, 1990), pp. 222–37.
— 'Negotiating Caribbean Identities', *New Left Review*, 1.209 (January–February 1995): 3–14.
James, Louis, 'Writing the Ballad: The Short Stories of Samuel Selvon and Earl Lovelace', in Jacqueline Bardolph (ed.), *Telling Stories: Postcolonial Short Fiction in English* (Amsterdam: Rodopi, 2001), pp. 103–8.
Lahiri, Jhumpa, *Interpreter of Maladies* (New York: Houghton Mifflin, 1999).
— *Unaccustomed Earth* (London: Bloomsbury, 2008).
Nasta, Susheila, *Home Truths: Fictions of the South Asian Diaspora in Britain* (Basingstoke: Palgrave Macmillan, 2002).
— 'Introduction' to Sam Selvon, *The Lonely Londoners* (London: Penguin, 2006), pp. v–xvii.
O'Connor, Frank, *The Lonely Voice: A Study of the Short Story* (London: Macmillan, 1963).
Rhys, Jean, *The Collected Short Stories* (New York: W. W. Norton, 1987).
Rushdie, Salman, *Imaginary Homelands: Essays and Criticism, 1981–1991* (London: Granta Books, 1991).
— *East, West* (London: Vintage, 1995).
Selvon, Sam, 'Waiting for Aunty to Cough', in Andrew Salkey (ed.), *West Indian Stories* (London: Faber and Faber, 1968), pp. 118–24.
Tunca, Daria, 'Of French Fries and Cookies: Chimamanda Ngozi Adichie's Diasporic Short Fiction', in Kathleen Gyssels and Bénédicte Ledent (eds), *African Presence in Europe and Beyond* (Paris: L'Harmattan, 2010), pp. 291–309.

Vertovec, Steven and Robin Cohen (eds), *Migration, Diasporas and Transnationalism* (Cheltenham: Elgar, 2001).

Wicomb, Zoë, *You Can't Get Lost in Cape Town* (New York: The Feminist Press at the City University of New York, 1987).

— 'Zoë Wicomb Interviewed by Eva Hunter – Cape Town, 5 June 1990', in Eva Hunter and Craig Mackenzie (eds), *Between the Lines II: Interviews with Nadine Gordimer, Menán du Plessis, Zoë Wicomb, Lauretta Ngcobo* (Grahamstown: National English Literary Museum, 1993), pp. 79–96.

— *The One That Got Away* (Nottingham: Five Leaves Publications, [2008] 2011).

Wright, Marcia, 'Historical Introduction' to Zoë Wicomb, *You Can't Get Lost in Cape Town* (New York: The Feminist Press at the City University of New York, 1987), pp. vii–xxi.

20

THE QUEER SHORT STORY

Brett Josef Grubisic

I was by myself, and I wanted to meet others like me. I couldn't go down the street saying: 'I'm looking for lesbian friends'. So this was the only way I could think of to do it. That's why I started *Vice Versa*.[1] (Edith Eyde)

IN THE DEBUT ISSUE OF *Sodomite Invasion Review* (1990), founding editor Don Larventz recalled the 'heady days of gay liberation in the 1970s', a decade marked by a 'torrent of poetry, stories, novels, plays, essays and varied mixed forms' that stood in marked contrast to the 'previously silent' eras. While acknowledging a great shift in Western attitudes – 'celebrations where there was hostility and book fairs where there were locked libraries' – Larventz also sensed imminent reversals: 'growing government sentiment in favour of the censorship, remarginalization and exclusion of gay writing and images' and, another 'threat to the liberating effect of gay literature', the corporate capitalist recuperation and assimilation of formerly gay communal imagery.[2] Offering readers 'pleasure and knowledge', the stories, photography, essays and poetry of his 'Magazine of New Writing' – by predominantly Canadian and American male authors such as Alan Alvare, Tony Correia, Dennis Denisoff, Stan Persky, Felice Picano, Scott Watson and Wayne Yung – were positioned as resistance to everyday antagonists. In particular, 'Sodomite Invasion Planned for 1990', a 1988 headline from a Canadian fundamentalist Christian publication alerting British Columbians to an impending international gay and lesbian sporting event, galvanised the editorial board.[3]

Vancouver-based *Invasion* (1990–4) is typical in many respects. Self-consciously political, volunteer-staffed, short-lived, and limited in reach and print run, its ancestors include *Vice Versa* (1947–8), nine issues edited pseudonymously in Los Angeles by 'Lisa Ben' (an anagram of 'lesbian'), and *Arena Three* (1963–72), spearheaded by Londoners Esme Ross-Langley and Diana Chapman. Ordinarily featuring reportage and essays as well as stories and poems, the periodicals take as a given literature's role in liberation activism. There are notable generational differences among the publications, however, reflecting transforming mores. For instance, in 1947 'Lisa Ben', a secretary in Hollywood, necessarily edited in secret; in the 1980s Edith Eyde revealed herself as the magazine's sole producer. Freely distributed in Vancouver, *Invasion* was readily purchased elsewhere in Canada. And while *Vice Versa*, Jan Whitt wrote, 'began primarily to connect isolated, closeted women to one another and provide them with a voice', and Eyde's effort was part of a 'potent social movement',[4] the magazine's legal footing was precarious, unlike *Invasion*'s. Characteristic for the times, in the United States publications addressing homosexuality could be deemed obscene under the Comstock

Act; the change occurred in 1958 with a successful legal challenge to the Post Office's refusal of an edition of ONE Magazine (1953–67) containing 'Sappho Remembered', a 1954 story by 'Jane Dahr' (in fact by 'James Barr', the pseudonym of James Fugaté, the author of 'Death in the Royal Family' (1954), another ONE story) about a lesbian's pursuit of a younger woman with a boyfriend. The Post Office claimed ONE might prove 'lustfully stimulating to the average homosexual reader'; it argued too that the magazine's advertisement for *The Circle*, a Swiss homophile literary magazine, would direct readers to further obscene material.[5]

Collectively, magazines like these are a significant, if now largely unknown and archived, repository of queer short stories. The variety is enormous. Published before the Internet's ubiquity, Alan V. Miller's historical (1890–1990) bibliography of exclusively gay and lesbian periodicals predated online magazines. Nonetheless as of 1990 Miller listed 'over 7200'[6] publications worldwide, including story-publishing magazines like *Tribe, Killer Dyke, Conditions, James White Review, Sinister Wisdom, Moja, Sequel, Azalea, Mighty Real, Ganymede, Maiden Voyage, Flagrant, Sage, Cargo* and *The Furies*. The majority of these publications did not last long enough to celebrate a tenth anniversary. According to Miller's strict methodology of documenting exclusively queer publications, moreover, an updated edition of *Our Own Voices* would disallow the inclusion of theme issues in general interest literary magazines, such as, for example, Edinburgh-based *Gutter Magazine 07* (lesbian and gay short stories (2012)) or London-produced *Litro Magazine*'s '#144: Transgender' (2015).

Surveying the rise of the gay and lesbian press between the 1940s and 1990s, Rodger Streitmatter summarised the role of periodicals: the writers and publications 'served an oppressed minority first by helping gay people identify themselves and then by speaking up and striking back against the powerful forces of prejudice and bigotry'.[7] That process of speaking up continues, whether in defunct queer periodicals with accessible online content like *Lodestar Quarterly* (2002–6), *Polari Journal* (2008–14), and *Mary* (2009–11), or in such newly sprung publications across the globe as *Gertrude* (2009–), *Mused* (2012–), *Plenitude* (2012–), *Glitterwolf* (2012–), *Jonathan* (2012–), *THEM: A Trans Lit Journal* (2013–), *TQ Review* (2015–), and *Chelsea Station* (2015–). Diverse in outlooks and goals, their overall perspectives might be best encapsulated by editor and short story writer Aldo Alvarez (*Interesting Monsters* (2001)), the founder of online literary magazine *Blithe House Quarterly* (1997–2007): 'We have a personal investment in queer culture as we live in it and we want to raise the quality of life for everyone; it's not something we shelve in a small section well-hidden from the rest of the store.'[8]

Larventz's 'previously silent' remark about queer literature implied that the epochs before the success of early 1970s gay liberation activism, and its concomitant 'torrent' of literary endeavour, were defined by the complete absence or invisibility of homosexual discourse in any form.[9] Accepting this, a student of queer literature might assume that only with liberation-era legislative amendments and enhanced social stature could literature representing the wide spectrum of queer subjectivities exist in the public eye. Though pre- and post-liberation serves as a convenient way to demarcate history – with a notable absence on the one side and unencumbered volubility on the other – its accuracy is doubtful. A statement by Mark Mitchell and David Leavitt modifies that neatly bifurcated view. Since the eighteenth century, they claimed, men who were 'sexually attracted to other men – sodomites, pederasts, urnings, Uranians, similsexualists, queers – have constituted a distinct and numerous reading class'.[10] Offering a broad overview of the nineteenth-century West, moreover, Jeffrey Weeks observed that new forms of social regulation and the force of public disapproval that they stimulated instigated resistance in the form of a 'new community of knowledge, if not of life and feeling, amongst many men with homosexual leanings'.[11]

Instead of Larventz's resounding silence, then, literary historians have made the case for queer literature's persistent, if secretive and sporadic, presence. That said, much depends on definitions. As Michael Mason's history of Victorian sexual attitudes observed, sodomy and lesbianism were 'virtually unmentionable topics in any kind of text at this period',[12] while Terry Castle's *The Apparitional Lesbian* noted that 'at least until 1900 lesbianism manifests itself in the Western literary imagination as an absence, as chimera or *amor impossibilia* ... it is reduced to a ghost effect: to ambiguity and taboo'.[13] Accordingly, a lesbian story, as defined by Marilyn R. Farwell – 'the lesbian narrative is not necessarily a story by a lesbian about lesbians but rather a plot that affirms a place for lesbian subjectivity, that narrative space where both lesbian characters and other female characters can be active, desiring agents' – was not, strictly speaking, publishable.[14] Yet, in her pioneering 1956 study Jeannette Foster asserted that the visibility of 'variant women' improved in the nineteenth century, averaging 'better than three per decade',[15] almost all in novels. This minuscule number refers to depictions of female 'variants', women who were 'conscious of passion for their sex, with or without overt expression', and those who were 'merely obsessively attached to other women over a longer period or at a more mature age than is commonly expected'.[16]

Chimeric or 'three per decade', such a status reflects the fact that sexual minority literature developed fitfully over centuries and in cultural contexts that cannot be labelled inclusive, tolerant or indifferent. Alan Bray described common Renaissance attitudes in England as associating homosexuality with the dissolution of godly creation.[17] Surveying British norms in the eighteenth century, Randolph Trumbach observed that the emergent 'sodomitical minority' was linked to despised femininity, and subject to denunciation, arrest, physical violence and blackmail.[18] Discerning 'an entire vocabulary of moral opprobrium' and 'the rise of moral policing and punishment on a new scale' in Victorian England, H. G. Cocks notes as well that homosexual culture remained a 'pervasive feature of urban life'.[19] Likewise, Matt Cook's overview of the era between the First World War and 1967 recognised 'a plurality of queer experiences' in the midst of dominant culture's prosecutions, vilifying public discourses, and collective demonisation of homosexuals as depraved.[20] Addressing Canadian history, moreover, Tom Warner stated that sexual minorities 'managed to exist, largely in secret and always with vulnerability, on the edges of society', and 'Canadian laws, institutions, and social structures, historically, imposed a system of social oppression'[21] well into the early 1970s. Dennis Altman's statement circa 1970 – 'To be a homosexual in our society is to be constantly aware that one bears a stigma'[22] – suggested that the era's coalescing new consciousness was periodic or halting rather than immediate and universal. And inaugurating 'a reclamation of the homosexual past',[23] *Hidden From History* (1989) noted that although repression and marginalisation was often the lot of homosexuals, the popular myth that 'homosexual life in the United States – and elsewhere – before the 1969 Stonewall rebellion consisted of nothing but repression and isolation, opprobrium and closetry'[24] overlooked the richness, resilience and vitality of the suppressed subculture. Speaking in reference to the stories and poetry of Sydney-based *Camp Ink* (1970–7), Jeremy Fisher observed that the Australian state routinely banned gay work until 1969 and that Tasmania did not decriminalise homosexuality until 1997.[25]

Despite the discouraging conditions, scholars such as Lillian Faderman, James Gifford and Axel Nissen discern coded, veiled or discreet literary portrayals of libidinal or romantic same-sex relationships. Surveying 'homoaffectional expression'[26] in magazine fiction, for example, Faderman claimed that previous to the emergence of psychological discourses in the 1920s that largely viewed same-sex affection as a pathology, depictions of chaste female-female love relationships were relatively open. Their number included Margaret Constance Dubois's 'The Lass of the Silver Sword' (1908), Helen Hull's 'The Fire' (1917), Jeanette Lee's 'The Cat and the King' (1919), Os-Anders's 'Karen: A Novel' (1922) and Catherine Wells's 'The Beautiful House' (1912). Faderman categorised Gertrude Stein's 'Miss Furr and Miss Skeene' (1922) as an example of a coded story, and D. H. Lawrence's serialised novel *The Fox* (1922) as exemplifying an ascendant 'medical' view that 'invariably showed lesbian love to be sick'.[27] Mary E. Wilkins Freeman's 'The Long Arm' (1895) illustrated that associating same-sex affection with perversion was not rooted exclusively in discourses of the 1920s, as did another ambiguous but influential depiction of 'lesbian evil',[28] Joseph Sheridan Le Fanu's 'Carmilla' (collected in *In the Glass Darkly* (1872)).

Definitions of homoaffectional expression aside, indirectness and veiling remained key. If the undisguised sensuality of Edith Ellis's 'Dolores' (1909), which fully depicted two sorrowful female characters kissing in silence, draws attention with its rarity, the marked discretion of other stories reflected the norm. From Ivy Compton-Burnett – whose work Jane Rule described as standing 'at the asexual extreme of lesbian sensibility'[29] – to Jane Bowles, masking via 'perfunctorily changing the gender' of characters or 'encoding ... subject matter'[30] offered a means to sidestep censorious social edicts. A heterogeneous assortment of short fiction – including Gertrude Atherton's 'The Striding Place' (1896), Djuna Barnes's 'A Little Girl Tells a Story to a Lady' (1929), H. E. Bates's 'Breeze Anstey' (1937), Elizabeth Bowen's 'The Jungle' (1929), Thomas Burke's 'The Pash' (1926), Josephine Dodge Daskam's 'The Evolution of Evangeline' (1900), Radclyffe Hall's 'Miss Ogilvy Finds Herself' (1934), Sarah Orne Jewett's 'Martha's Lady' (1897), Katherine Mansfield's 'The Jungle' (1929) and Virginia Woolf's 'Moments of Being: Slater's Pins Have No Points' (1928) – serves to indicate the spectrum of portraiture possible within an amorphous term like 'female-female love relationships'.

Discretion was not restricted to lesbian works. In *Dayneford's Library*, for example, James Gifford suggested that while homosexual writing began to cohere during the later nineteenth century, its principal mode was indirectness. He cited Edward Prime-Stevenson's obscure short story 'Out in the Sun' (1913), which describes the library of a turn-of-the-century homosexual that holds a special group of volumes 'crowded into a few lower shelves, as if they sought to avoid other literary society, to keep themselves to themselves, to shun all unsympathetic observation'.[31] Gifford pointed out that homosexual writers seeking to, in effect, write themselves into history nonetheless faced strictures that would never allow sexual otherness 'a platform for open discourse'.[32] Featuring 'suggestive markers'[33] that touched on attraction while simultaneously letting readers 'know the limits of socially acceptable male homosocial desire',[34] the spectral quality recalls Castle's 'apparitional' lesbian subjectivity. Likewise, Chris Packard similarly discerned 'residues' of 'unspoken but known homoerotic desires',[35] an affect 'embedded in gestures, imagery, and figurative codes',[36] from close friendships and nominal male marriage in popular adventure tales like Bret Harte's 'The Luck of Roaring Camp' (1868) and 'Uncle Jim and Uncle Billy' (1898). Nissen utilised the term 'romantic friendship' to describe an assortment of novels and short stories, including Charles Warren Stoddard's 'A South-Sea Idyl' (1869), Thomas Bailey Aldrich's 'Marjorie Daw' (1869) and James Lane Allen's 'Two Gentlemen of Kentucky' (1888).

A multi-genre miscellany of male-centred stories – including Oscar Wilde's 'The Portrait of Mr W. H.' (1889), Ambrose Bierce's 'The Mocking-Bird' (1891), Edwin Emanuel Bradford's 'Boris Orloff' (1893), John Francis Bloxam's 'The Priest and the Acolyte' (1894), Count Stanislaus Eric Stenbock's 'The True Story of a Vampire' (1894), Henry Cuyler Bunner's 'Our Aromatic Uncle' (1895), Frederick Rolfe's 'In Praise of Billy B.' (1897), Jack London's 'In a Far Country' (1899), Henry James's 'The Great Good Place' (1900), Willa Cather's 'The Sculptor's Funeral' (1905) and Charles Kenneth Scott-Moncrieff's 'Evensong and Morwe Song' (1908) – illustrated the modes and strategies of what Gifford named 'resistant discourse'.[37]

An impact of scandalous litigation – from Wilde's conviction for gross indecency to book-related obscenity trials – was a heightened awareness of the material consequences of literary depictions of 'obscene' sexuality and queer identities. As a result of these and other historical prohibitions, writers portraying homosexuality continued to adopt encoding strategies. Robert Phillips, editor of *The Stories of Denton Welch*, described the tactic as a 'Proustian Albertine strategy', changing the 'sex of the protagonist from male to female'[38] in anticipation of censorship concerns. Proustian in style, Welch's *Brave and Cruel* appeared in 1948, the year of his death (at age thirty-three). Mannered but sexually inexplicit short fiction by Ronald Firbank, such as 'A Study in Temperament' (1905) and 'A Study in Opal' (1907), reads as influenced by British Aestheticism generally and Wilde in particular. Reviewers of an implicitly homosexual later work, the 51-page 'Santal' (1921), noted its dandyism, attention to style, and (in a 1955 review) the author's 'discomforting sexual maladjustments'.[39] That aesthetic sensibility (as well as read-between-the-lines quality) is apparent too in the prodigious output of L. P. Hartley, whose 'uses' of homosexuality were studied by Alan Hollinghurst.[40] Hartley's popular collections *The Travelling Grave* (1948) and *The White Wand* (1954) range genre-wise from horror and supernatural to comedy of manners.

Acts of private circulation and writing withheld from publication also remained in practice. Notably, while E. M. Forster published short story collections lacking homosexual characters (like *The Eternal Moment* (1928)), his fiction about sex or romance between men – the novel *Maurice* and such short works as 'Arthur Snatchfold' (written circa 1928) and 'The Obelisk' (written circa 1939) collected in *The Life to Come* (1972) – appeared posthumously. Forster's assessment of these 'indecent writings' varied as well: although he showed them to colleagues, in a diary entry he called them 'positively dangerous to my career as a novelist' and recorded that he burned 'as many as the fire will take'.[41] Glenway Prescott's *Goodbye, Wisconsin* (1928) included 'Adolescence' and 'The Frenchman Six Feet Three' (1942); more sexually explicit, the title piece of *A Visit to Priapus* (2013) appeared after his death in 1987.

Alan Miller's *Our Own Voices* referred to the activism of mid-1950s homophile organisations as the first wave of gay and lesbian liberation; the second began with the broad multinational civil rights movements gaining momentum in the late 1960s. In literary terms, and measuring by short story publication specifically, the mid-century's fitful liberationist accomplishments can be gauged positively in terms of incipient canon formation and relatively increased visibility. A significant impact resulted from flourishing homophile publications – *ONE*'s news-stand and subscriber distribution was 5,000, while *The Ladder* attained 700;[42] mailed internationally, tri-lingual *The Circle* reached 1,900 by 1957;[43] and *Arena Three* peaked near 2,000.[44] With influential Anglo-American social norms predominantly averse to homosexuality, however, mainstream possibilities were largely circumscribed. Craig Loftin described the Cold War era as an 'acutely repressive moment'[45] for sexual minorities characterised by virulent anti-gay sentiments; Weeks noted a marked growth of 'official concern and public anxiety' about 'deviants' over the same period.[46] To illustrate an effect of that virulence, Loftin cited Clarkson Crane's 'Passing Stranger' (1955), a story in *ONE* that was ordinary insofar as it featured loneliness, alienation and 'general gloominess' as well as an indirectness stemming from censorship concerns.[47] Moreover, in the introduction to *The Lesbians Home Journal* (1976), an anthology of twenty stories *The Ladder* published between 1955 and 1972, Coletta Reid summarised that magazine's collective short story output: 'None are lighthearted ... None is happy in that girl-meets-girl-and-lives-happily-ever-after sense. Most are very painful, some despairing, and two raise the possibility of suicide. It is a measure of the oppression under which we live that our stories are dominated by our reactions to society.'[48]

Aside from the cautious public display (and plain paper mail circulation) of homosexual magazines, anthologies from mainstream publishers also appeared. Edited by 'Donald Webster Cory' (the pen name of Edward Sagarin), *21 Variations on a Theme* (1953) reprinted stories by Sherwood Anderson, 'Isabel Bolton' (Mary Britton Miller's pseudonym), Henry James, Wilson Lehr, Naomi Mitchison, Stephen Spender, and Welch, as well as James T. Farrell's light-hearted story of a failed male on male seduction ('A Casual Incident' (1934)), and William Carlos Williams's 'The Knife of the Times' (1932), an account of a married woman's gradual acceptance of her friend Ethel's erotic invitation. Despite the directness of the stories, the book itself – eschewing an introduction and dedicated to 'all those who can identify themselves with ... characters in these stories' – never disclosed the fact that the titular theme is homosexuality. Similarly, nodding to Edward Carpenter's pioneering homophile publications from a half-century earlier (*Ioläus: An Anthology of Friendship* (1902) and *The Intermediate Sex* (1908), which championed 'great writers of the world whose work has been partly inspired by the Uranian love'),[49] *Eros: An Anthology of Friendship* (1961), a volume compiled in the late 1950s, began with an essay by co-editor Patrick Anderson laden with classical references that contextualised the topic – literary depictions of 'any friendship between men strong enough to deserve one of the more serious senses of the word "love"' – within an idealised and decidedly fraternal context; the stories, poems and novel excerpts, representing 'some of the noblest expressions of the greatest minds',[50] celebrated depictions of masculine relationships. Including short pieces from Lawrence, Melville, Proust, Rolfe, Spender, Welch and Wilde as aesthetic exemplars of ostensibly heterosexual male friendship, *Eros* reads as a veiled apologia for male homosexuality that names and champions homosexual authors or themes without incorporating words like 'Uranian' or 'homosexual'.

In contrast, Jeannette Foster's *Sex Variant Women in Literature*, which, Castle pointedly noted, was 'issued privately at her own expense in 1956, at a time when no reputable publisher would touch the subject of female homosexuality',[51] sought to identify modes of female homosocial relations and outline a literary tradition via a history of deviations from the 'heterosexual standard'.[52] Foster, an Institute for Sex Research librarian who worked with Alfred Kinsey, discerned sporadic appearances of 'variant literary expression',[53] and employed the figure of a pendulum to describe dominant culture's fluctuating tolerance of it.[54] Discussing novels and poetry primarily, she listed an assortment of stories by American and English authors, including Harvey O'Higgins's 'Story of Julie Kane' (1924), Naomi Mitchison's 'The Delicate Fire' (1932), Thomas Beer's 'Hallowe'en' (1932), Ethel Richardson's 'The End of Childhood' (1934; writing as Henry Handel Richardson), Isak Dinesen's *Seven Gothic Tales* (1934), Kay Boyle's 'The Bridegroom's Body' (1938), Rhys Davies' 'Orestes' (1946), and John Eichrodt's 'Nadia Devereux' (1951). In *Carol in a Thousand Cities* (1960), a significant mass-market paperback anthology, editor 'Ann Aldrich' (one of Marijane Meaker's pen names) included a story-sized excerpt from *The Price of Salt* (1952), a novel that Patricia Highsmith published under the pseudonym Claire Morgan after her regular publisher rejected it.[55] Released at a time when 'dozens of novels of male and female homosexuality . . . wound matters up with sleeping pills, murder, imprisonment, unbelievable self-reconversion, or the corpse in the swimming pool',[56] the story's hopefulness about lesbian romance stood out as exceptional.

By the mid-1970s Ian Young noted a degree of transforming perspectives in gay male literature; in addition to writers moving beyond the representation of 'little or nothing' related directly to homosexuality in their work, he detected momentum away from the 'semi-obligatory tragedy' to conclude a given work to matter-of-fact, accepting, and occasionally defiant depictions of gay characters.[57] Tennessee Williams's story collections *One Arm* (1948) and *Hard Candy* (1954), which Reed Woodhouse applauds for their refusal of guilt or apology,[58] and Gore Vidal's *A Thirsty Evil* (1956), belong to this category. Even granting that defiant stance, limits existed: queerly modifying a historical anecdote about Tennessee Williams's family, Vidal's story 'Clouds and Eclipses' (written in 1954; published in 2005) was excluded from that mid-century volume. Relatedly, between Gerald Glaskin's bestselling story collections *A Small Selection* (1962) and *The Road to Nowhere* (1967), which featured no overt homosexuality, he published *No End to the Way* (1965) under the alias Neville Jackson. That work, mapping the course of an affair between two men, was banned in his native Australia.

Other significant titles include *Derricks* (1951), the only short story collection by Fugaté (writing as Barr), and James Purdy's *Don't Call Me By the Right Name* (author-published, 1956), *Color of Darkness* (1957) and *Children Is All* (1961). Stories by Graham Greene, Daphne du Maurier, Frank Sargeson and Angus Wilson presented assorted homosexual relationships in direct, if not wholly favourable, light; and Anita Cornwell's 'A Sound of Crying' (1964; her *Black Lesbian in White America* (1983) collected stories, essays and autobiographical sketches) warrants mention as representing a rare instance of a black lesbian writer appearing in print

(*Negro Digest* in this case). Truman Capote's bestselling novella *Breakfast at Tiffany's* (1958) included 'A Diamond Guitar' (1950) and 'A Christmas Memory' (1956). Ranging from homosocial prisoner relationships to the boyhood of a 'sissy', these stories portray homosexuality somewhat obliquely.

The unprecedented popularity of homophobic yet subversive[59] lesbian pulp novels, and the new visibility of legally controversial and sexually explicit novels by Henry Miller, William Burroughs, John Rechy, Hubert Selby Jr and Gordon Merrick, implies an occasional if wide-ranging challenge to conservative sexual mores; so do Alfred Chester's collections *Here Be Dragons* (privately printed in 1955) and *Behold Goliath* (1964). In rejecting one of Chester's stories, 'In Praise of Vespasian' (about a gay man's sexual quests in urban lavatories), however, *Partisan Review* suggested the boundaries of acceptance: 'Our objection is not to the subject or its detail but rather to the rhapsodic treatment.'[60] Other collections offered varied representations. For example, in *A Bachelor's Children* (1962) and *The Cats of Venice* (1965) – and in individual stories such as 'Say to Me Ronald!' (1961), 'The Dream' (1962) and 'My Pal Rembrandt' (1969) – Hal Porter ambivalently explored gay relationships between younger men and their older suitors, whereas in *Tike and Five Stories* (1969), Jonathan Strong presented romantic and fraternal gay relationships without apology. Christopher Bram ('Aphrodisiac' (1979)) praised 'Supperburger', one of *Tike*'s stories, since in it affection between men was 'not treated as sinister, but as tender, sad, with the suggestion that love might work'.[61]

Faderman's claim that '[i]t was not until the early 1970s, with the establishment of lesbian feminist journals and presses, that all the truth could be told without indirection and that love between women could be presented in a positive light'[62] finds supports in Bonnie Zimmerman, who noted that though Cold War-era lesbian fiction was abundant (in the form of pulps with inflammatory titles: *Dyke Farm* and *Lesbian Web of Evil*), the largely conservative and often male-authored genre 'depicted lesbians as tragic, maimed creatures trapped in a world of alcohol, violence, and meaningless sex'.[63] After Stonewall, Zimmerman asserted, lesbian life and literature was never the same, especially because the effective removal of the long silencing of lesbian speech led to a 'flood of intense, immediate, intimate, and sometimes awkward written expression'.[64] She stated that much lesbian fiction – novels and short stories – during this period served a lesbian mythos related to publicly announcing an identity and establishing the fact of a community and history; as such, its genre-like characteristics are evident in an emancipatory literary model that depicts 'good lesbians, bad men, and happy endings'.[65]

Furthermore, literary anthologies from new feminist independent presses (such as Diana, Virago, Naiad and Onlywomen) – *Amazon Expedition* (1973), *The Lesbian Reader* (1975), *The Lesbians Home Journal* (1976), and *True To Life Adventure Stories* (Volume One (1978) and Volume Two (1981)) – underscored the importance of the lesbian periodical network (where many of the pieces first appeared) and the fuller emergence of self-determining lesbian publications. In addition to these multi-genre works, story collections slowly gained in visibility. From Rule's *Theme for Diverse Instruments* (1975) and Ann Allen Shockley's *The Black and White of It* (1980), the first collection of African American lesbian stories, to Red Jordan Arobateau's *Suzie-Q* (1993; the title story was first published in 1978) and Makeda Silvera's *Her Head a Village* (1994), several handfuls of story collections appeared.

The diversity indicates that lesbian stories quickly evolved beyond the 'good lesbians, bad men' phase.

As late as 1984 in *New Lesbian Writing* – a volume of poetry, essays and short stories – editor Margaret Cruikshank remarked on the emergent visibility of lesbian literature, drawing attention to its necessary political and educational purposes in a world of anti-lesbian biases. She also addressed its distinctions from gay male writing, which she typified as emphasising sexual themes and urban settings (in contrast to the liberationist goals, focus on the coming out experience, and non-urban settings of lesbian fiction).[66] Anglo-Canadian writer and editor Ian Young ('A Boy's Book of Wonders' (2004)) evaluated the literary change earlier still. In an introduction signed in 1973, he stated that in planning a volume of contemporary poetry by gay men 'the project seemed impossible to carry out' because 'the aura of taboo was still strong enough to prevent all but a few writers from contributing'; he added that 'quite suddenly, in 1972', the gay liberation gains made in the 1960s began to be felt throughout society, and '"Gay Pride" became not just a slogan but a reality for a significant number of homosexual men and women'.[67] Surveying the background of gay literature, Young observed the familiar bifurcated tradition, with writers addressing gay themes more or less directly and an Anglo-American convention in which authors 'felt obliged to equivocate or conceal',[68] that opened progressively if gradually after the 1930s – with writers such as Spender (*Burning Cactus* (1936)), Isherwood ('An Evening at the Bay' (1933), 'Take It or Leave It' (1942)), and John Lehmann (who as an editor published stories and poems by W. H. Auden, Burroughs and Isherwood) ending what had been 'literally a conspiracy of silence'.[69]

Young's introduction to *On the Line* (1981), the 'first collection of contemporary work, i.e. of gay fiction written since the Stonewall rebellion of 1969',[70] discussed the self-identification of homosexually inclined men and women as emerging in spite of the efforts of the 'spokesmen of convention' to denounce, distort, sneer at and try to dismiss them; 'reflecting both the advances and ambiguities of gay life', the stories, he noted, raised questions relating to the existence and nature of a quantifiable 'gay sensibility' and the value or handicap of identifying as a 'gay writer'.[71] In addition to stories by Americans Purdy, Picano, Edmund White and Whitemore, Young included Canadians and English authors such as Daniel Curzon (*The Revolt of the Perverts* (1978)), Graham Jackson (*Gardens* (1976)), and John Mitzel (*Some Short Stories About People I Don't Like* (1977)). He remarked on the dearth of 'outlets for contemporary short fiction on gay themes' before pointing to the anthology's variety of themes, from generational differences and social oppression to the supernatural and erotic attraction.[72] In a pioneering study of gay male literature, *Playing the Game* (1977), Roger Austen similarly addressed the politics of publication, contending that 'a malicious and inequitable game' had been played in which homophobic critics and publishers either denigrated and ignored novels and short fiction written by or featuring homosexuals, or else created a climate unfavourable to queer writers.[73]

Earlier post-Stonewall anthologies characteristically offered historical surveys and directly served to identify a gay (and to a lesser degree lesbian) cultural tradition and literary canon. For example, like the mid-century anthology *Eros*, editor Stephen Wright's *Different* (1974) gathered stories by 'Phil Andros' (*Below the Belt* (1975); the pen name of Samuel Steward (whose story collection *Pan and the Fire-Bird* appeared in 1930)), Isherwood, James, Lawrence, Vidal and Wilde. Subtitled 'An Anthology of Homosexual Short Stories', it also contained Charles Beaumont's 'The Crooked Man', a science fiction allegory (first published by *Playboy* in 1955) about a world where heterosexuality is an outlawed perversion. In *The Other Persuasion* (1977), which featured stories and excerpts by Paul Bowles, Forster, Hemingway, Lawrence, Proust and Stein, editor Seymour Kleinberg strove to confirm a literary tradition for gays and lesbians while pointing to the difficulty of nomenclature related to both 'gay' and 'gay literature', exploring 'some meanings that [gay] has connoted in the past' and noting 'the changes in meaning, tentative but clear, as we approach the present'.[74] The changes, he observed, related to comforts 'in ghettos' – relative freedom in select metropolitan neighbourhoods but alienation and guilt resulting from exclusion and prejudice most everywhere else.[75] Across three sections of historical punctuation – 'Underground', 'On the Fringe: From Tragedy to Camp', 'Inside: New Directions' – he tracked the trajectory from secretiveness and self-loathing to freedom and acceptance. Beginning with Proust's 'Before Dark' (1893) and concluding with Rule's 'Middle Children' (1975), a story about a contented spectrum of people living in a rooming house owned by a lesbian couple, Kleinberg described a general arc toward a cultural context in which gayness was no longer the central issue. From the stories, he wrote, 'we can learn where we have been, and perhaps that will help us choose where we are going'.[76]

Reed Woodhouse's *Unlimited Embrace* (1998), which charted the modalities of gay fiction between 1945 and 1995, divided fiction into five 'houses': 'ghetto fiction' ('by, for, and about gay men'), proto-ghetto, closet, assimilative and transgressive.[77] Les Brookes's *Gay Male Fiction Since Stonewall* (2009) focused on a political conflict between assimilationism and radicalism – between 'gay life and family life, representing the poles of the homo-heterosexual divide' as being reflected in gay male literature.[78] David Leavitt (*Family Dancing* (1984)), whose characters 'are subsumed within a larger social group and placed within the wider social scene'[79] and Armistead Maupin (whose first novels were serialised as stories beginning in 1974) represent one pole, while Clive Barker (the six-volume Books of Blood story series (1984–5)), Dennis Cooper (*Wrong* (1992)), Andrew Holleran (*In September, The Light Changes* (1999)), and Gary Indiana (*Scar Tissue* (1987)) stood at the other.

Parsing the history of gay fiction anthologies in *Between Men* (2007), Richard Canning noted that from '1978 on, the number of characterizations exploded ad infinitum – if not always for the better, then toward diversity'.[80] In order to chart how much had changed within a few decades he referred to a comment in *The Faber Book of Gay Short Fiction* (1992), where editor Edmund White recalled his teenage experiences reading the limited templates of gay fiction (as either grim psychological case studies or outrageous campy scenes). Canning's 'ad infinitum' is reflected in *Aphrodisiac* (1980), which gathered short fiction from past issues of *Christopher Street* magazine. The *Christopher Street Reader* (1983) and *First Love/Last Love* (1986), reprinting stories by Jane DeLynn, Robert Ferro, Perri Klass, Leavitt, Eleanor Lerman, Purdy and Rule, suggest that Larventz's 'torrent' occurred a full decade after the 1969 watershed. Moreover, Picano's *The New York Years* (2000), which featured stories written in the 1970s and 1980s that initially appeared in *Gay Week*, *Christopher Street*, *Drummer* and *Blue Boy*, highlighted the continuing role of small circulation queer magazines to encourage and publish literary talent. In *The Violet Quill Reader* (1994) – with stories by Americans Christopher Cox, Michael Grumley, Holleran, Picano, White and George Whitmore – editor David Bergman situated the work of the Violet Quill writer's group in late 1970s (and early 1980s New York, just before the emergence of AIDS) between a heterosexual literary mainstream that was uncomfortable with gay themes and a stagnating gay literary tradition whose aesthetic or formal limitations Quill members sought to move beyond; the progression, then, was away from liberatory ideology in a literary package and toward refinement or experimentation.

Though considerably less abundant than novels, the publication of story collections by self-identified gay men increased exponentially. From David Watmough's *Love and the Waiting Game* (1975), Tom Reamy's *San Diego Lightfoot Sue* (1979), Adam Mars-Jones's *Lantern Lecture* (1981) and Richard Walter Hall's *Couplings* (1981) to Ethan Mordden's *I've a Feeling We're Not in Kansas Anymore* (1983) and Tom Wakefield's *Drifters* (1984), collections began to illustrate a remarkable stylistic and thematic diversity. By the mid-1990s, however, Woods noted that if 'the term "gay literature" is to have any practical significance during the present epidemic, it must be defined in such a manner as to include documents relating to the health of gay men'.[81] From anthologies (*Hot Living* (1985), *Brother to Brother* (1991), *Sojourner* (1993)) and numerous stories in annual 'best of' series (*Men on Men* (1986–92)), to short fiction collections – including Mars-Jones and White's *The Darker Proof* (1987), Allan Barnett's *The Body and Its Dangers* (1990), David B. Feinberg's *Spontaneous Combustion* (1991), Richard Hall's *Fidelities* (1992), Peter McGehee's *I.Q. Zoo* (1991), Bernard Cooper's *Guess Again* (2000), and Francisco Ibáñez-Carrasco's *Killing Me Softly* (2005) – the complex, empathetic and painful documentation was, in the matter of a decade, slowed by deaths (authors Barnett, Feinberg, Hall and McGehee; anthology editors Joseph Beam and John Preston) and a lowered mortality rate due to medications.

In 1983, Cruikshank observed a 'marked trend toward specialization'[82] in anthologies. That trend has not abated. Indeed, to date the intrepid collector of sexual minority literary anthologies – volumes that typically mix short stories and novel excerpts with drama, poetry, memoir or essays – could exhibit a library of several hundred titles. Its full inventory would list publications with an international focus (*Boys* (2013) and *The Literature of Lesbianism* (2003)), Anglo-American (*Mae West is Dead* (1984)), North American (*Contra/diction* (1999)), or national and regional ones – the American west coast (*Indivisible* (1991)) and south (*The Queer South* (2014)), among others; Aotearoa/New Zealand in *Subversive Acts* (1991) and *Best Mates* (1997); Australia in *Edge City on Two Different Plans* (1983), *Fruit Salad* (1995), *Penguin Book of Gay Australian Writing* (2002), and *Hold On, I'm Coming* (2012); Canada in *Queeries* (1993) and *No Margins* (2006); Ireland in *Quare Fellas* (1996) and *Coming Out* (2003); and Scotland in *And Thus Will I Freely Sing* (1989), *The Crazy Jig* (1992) and *Out There* (2014). Furthermore, with a notably wide assortment of titles like *Kindred Spirits* (1984), *Finale* (1989), *Flesh and the Word* (1992), *Worlds Apart* (1994), *Queer View Mirror* (1995), *Between Men* (2007), *Unspeakable Horror* (2008) and *Queer Tales* (2012), genre – ranging from literary short stories and flash fiction to erotica, fantasy, horror, suspense and science fiction – would be thoroughly represented. Still others would devote their short fictional examinations to any number of topics, from racial and ethnic categories (*Nice Jewish Girls* (1982), *Compañeras* (1987), *Living the Spirit* (1988), *Shade* (1996), *The Very Inside* (1998), *Q & A* (1998), *Friday the Rabbi Wore Lace* (1998), *Bésame Mucho* (1999), *Take Out* (2000) and *Jewish Gentle* (2011)) to disability (*Eyes of Desire* (1993) and *Staring Back* (1997)) and the queer historical moment itself (*Circa 2000* (2000)).

If the abundance and range of these anthologies signals the appetite of writers, publishers and readers for queer stories, it also speaks to a politicised desire for heightened visibility as well as greater inclusion and representational diversity. There are, in short, further genres to explore and stories to tell. Of the hundreds of queer anthologies, four serve to illustrate these diverse politicised impulses. Joseph Beam's introduction to *In the Life* (1986), a collection of poetry, short stories and essays by writers such as Melvin Dixon ('Boy with Beer' (1978), Craig G. Harris ('Cut Off from Among Their People' (1986)) and Sidney Brinkley ('Passion' (1981)), discussed the need for gay African American male writing in the face of its palpable absence and the preponderance of Caucasian gay authors, whose publications, he wrote, 'cast ominous shadows'[83] over the work of racial minorities. Catherine E. McKinley's introduction to *Afrekete* (1995), featuring short fiction by Jewelle Gomez (*Don't Explain* (1998)) and Carolivia Heron ('The Old Lady' (1994)), positioned her international anthology of prose, essays and poetry as intending to 'recognise and further promote a tradition of Black lesbian writings', and as a corrective, since 'writings by Black lesbians and other lesbians of color have largely been excluded from the collections that have appeared and that have begun to form the "canon" of lesbian and gay writing'.[84] In the prefatory comments of *Black Like Us* (2002), which included stories by Julie Blackwomon (*Voyages Out 2* (1990)) and Randall Kenan (*Let the Dead Bury Their Dead* (1992)), Devon W. Carbado, Dwight A. McBride and Donald Weise described their inclusion strategy and use of the term 'queer' as signifying 'identity and ideological nonconformity – not a particular sexual orientation'. The authors of the volume, then, 'were queer in terms of how they defined and embodied their racial identity, queer in how they articulated and practiced politics, as well as queer in their intimate relationships and sense of sexual identity'.[85] John R. Gordon's foreword in *Black and Gay in the UK* (2014), with stories by Diriye Osman (*Fairytales for Lost Children* (2013)) and Keith Jarrett ('Listening Out for the Sea' (2010)), remarked on the utility of an anthology of literary works representing the 'black British equivalent' to 'very much African-*American* works' ordinarily presented as universal, as well as the value of increasingly diversifying narratives since, along with sexuality, blackness as a 'category and a marker of identity has become less fixed, less monolithic, more interrogated by those it names'.[86]

A detailed selection of contemporary lesbian, gay, bisexual, transgender and queer authors who are also part-time short fiction practitioners effectively illuminates the attractiveness of the elastic form and its capacity to represent diverse points of view. Any alphabetically minded reader could begin with Sandra Alland's *Here's to Wang* (2009) or Donna Allegra's *Witness to the League of Blond Hip Hop Dancers* (2000). After dozens of titles they might conclude with Norman Wong's *Cultural Revolution* (1995) or Marnie Woodrow's *In the Spice House* (1996). Historically unprecedented, this contemporary queer plenitude testifies to the utility of the short story form and the complex of cultural mechanisms that enable their publication.

Notes

1. In Rodger Streitmatter, *Unspeakable: The Rise of the Gay and Lesbian Press in America* (Boston, MA: Faber and Faber, 1995), pp. 2–3.
2. Don Larventz, 'What do men's bodies mean?', *Sodomite Invasion Review* (August 1990), p. 1.
3. In David Morton Rayside, *On the Fringe: Gays and Lesbians in Politics* (Ithaca, NY: Cornell University Press, 1998), p. 185. Rayside described the document as a four-page leaflet distributed by Concerned Citizens for the Family that warned its demographic of 'the new deviant amorality of a highly vocal minority'.
4. Jan Whitt, *Women in American Journalism: A New History* (Chicago: University of Chicago Press, 2008), p. 165.
5. William N. Eskridge, 'Privacy jurisprudence and the apartheid of the closet, 1946–1961', *Florida State University Law Review*, 24.4 (Summer 1997): 760.
6. Alan V. Miller, *Our Own Voices: A Directory of Gay and Lesbian Periodicals, 1890–1990* (Toronto: The Archives, 1991), p. i.
7. Streitmatter, *Unspeakable*, p. xiii.
8. In Kurt Heintz, 'Blithe House Quarterly: publishing queer fiction online', E-Poets Network, 21 May 2004. Available at <www.e-poets.net.> (last accessed 15 April 2018).
9. Larventz, 'What do men's bodies mean?', p. 1.
10. Mark Mitchell and David Leavitt (eds), *Pages Passed From Hand to Hand: The Hidden Tradition of Homosexual Literature in English from 1748 to 1914* (Boston, MA: Houghton Mifflin, 1997), p. xiv.
11. Jeffrey Weeks, *Sex, Politics, and Society: The Regulation of Sexuality Since 1800*, 3rd edn (London: Routledge, 2014), p. 128.
12. Michael Mason, *The Making of Victorian Social Attitudes* (Oxford: Oxford University Press, 1994), pp. 192–3.
13. Marilyn R. Farwell, 'The Lesbian Narrative: "The Pursuit of the Inedible by the Unspeakable"', in George E. Haggerty and Bonnie Zimmerman (eds), *Professions of Desire: Lesbian and Gay Studies in Literature* (New York: MLA, 1995), p. 157.
14. Terry Castle, *The Apparitional Lesbian: Female Homosexuality and Modern Culture* (New York: Columbia University Press), 1993), pp. 30–1.
15. Jeannette Foster, *Sex Variant Women in Literature* (Tallahassee: Naiad Press, 1985), p. 51.
16. Ibid. p. 12.
17. Alan Bray, *Homosexuality in Renaissance England* (London: Gay Men's Press, 1982), p. 30.
18. Randolph Trumbach, 'Modern Sodomy: The Origins of Homosexuality, 1700–1800', in Matt Cook (ed.), *A Gay History of Britain: Love and Sex Between Men Since the Middle Ages* (Oxford: Greenwood, 2007), pp. 77–8.
19. H. G. Cocks, 'Secrets, Crimes and Diseases, 1800–1914', in Cook (ed.), *Gay History of Britain*, p. 107.
20. Matt Cook, 'Queer Conflicts: Love, Sex and War, 1914–1967', in Cook (ed.), *Gay History of Britain*, p. 14.
21. Tom Warner, *Never Going Back: A History of Queer Activism in Canada* (Toronto: University of Toronto Press, 2002), p. 17.
22. Dennis Altman, *Homosexual: Oppression and Liberation* (New York: Outerbridge and Dienstfrey, 1971), p. 1.
23. Martin Duberman et al. (eds), *Hidden from History: Reclaiming the Gay and Lesbian Past* (New York: New American Library, 1989), p. 13
24. Duberman et al., *Hidden from History*, p. 4.

25. Jeremy Fisher, 'Sex, sleaze and righteous anger: the rise and fall of gay magazines and newspapers in Australia', *TEXT*, 25 (April 2014): 3.
26. Lillian Faderman, 'Lesbian magazine fiction in the early twentieth century', *Journal of Popular Culture*, 11.4 (1978), p. 801.
27. Faderman, 'Lesbian magazine fiction', p. 813.
28. Lillian Faderman, *Surpassing the Love of Men: Romantic Friendship and Love Between Women from the Renaissance to the Present* (New York: William Morrow, 1981), p. 288.
29. Jane Rule, *Lesbian Images* (New York: Doubleday, 1975), p. 105.
30. Faderman, *Surpassing the Love*, p. 392.
31. In James Gifford, *Dayneford's Library: Homosexual Writing, 1900–2013* (Amherst: University of Massachusetts Press, 1995), p. 2.
32. Gifford, *Dayneford's Library*, p. 8.
33. Ibid. p. 25.
34. Ibid. p. 27.
35. Chris Packard, *Queer Cowboys: And Other Erotic Male Friendships in Nineteenth-Century American Literature* (New York: Palgrave Macmillan, 2005), p. 9.
36. Ibid. p. 11.
37. Gifford, *Dayneford's Library*, p. 5.
38. Robert Phillips (ed.), *The Stories of Denton Welch* (New York: Dutton, 1985), p. xii.
39. In Steven Moore, *Ronald Firbank: An Annotated Bibliography of Secondary Sources* (Normal, IL: Dalkey Archive, 1996), p. 8.
40. Interviewed by Peter Terzian in *The Paris Review* (214), Hollinghurst refers to his Master's thesis, 'The Creative Uses of Homosexuality in the Novels of E. M. Forster, Ronald Firbank, and L. P. Hartley': 'I think, without wishing to blow my own trumpet, that my thesis was quite an original thing to choose to do. It struck me that here were these gay writers who hadn't been able to publish anything on the subject that was most essential to their lives. And this repression had all sorts of creative implications, as well as limitations – in Forster's case producing a number of original twists on heterosexual comic plots, until in the end, or rather long before the end, he decided he just couldn't carry on writing fiction because he couldn't write about the thing that meant the most to him.'
41. See Oliver Stallybrass, 'Introduction', in E. M. Forster, *The Life to Come and Others Stories* (London: Edward Arnold, 1972), p. xii
42. Streitmatter, *Unspeakable*, p. 28.
43. Maurice Van Lieshout, 'Kries, Der (The Circle)' in George E. Haggerty (ed.), *Gay Histories and Cultures: An Encyclopedia, Volume 2* (London: Routledge, 1999), p. 524.
44. Sebastian Buckle, *The Way Out: A History of Homosexuality in Modern England* (London: I. B. Tauris, 2015), p. 38.
45. Craig M. Loftin, *Masked Voices: Gay Men and Women in Cold War America* (Albany: SUNY Press, 2012), p. 18.
46. Jeffrey Weeks, *Sex, Politics, and Society: The Regulation of Society Since 1800*, 1st edn (London: Longman, 1981), p. 240.
47. Loftin, *Masked Voices*, p. 36.
48. See Coletta Reid, 'Introduction', in Barbara Grier and Coletta Reid (eds), *The Lesbians Home Journal* (Baltimore: Diana Press, 1976), p. 19.
49. Edward Carpenter, *The Intermediate Sex: A Study in Some Transitional Types of Men and Women* [1908] (Project Gutenberg Australia, April 2004), p. 111.
50. Patrick Anderson, 'Introduction' in *Eros: An Anthology of Friendship* (London: Anthony Blond, 1961), p. 8.
51. Terry Castle (ed.), *The Literature of Lesbianism: A Historical Anthology from Ariosto to Stonewall* (New York: Columbia University Press, 2003), p. xix.

52. Foster, *Sex Variant Women*, p. 11.
53. Ibid. p. 354.
54. Ibid. p. 298.
55. Castle, *Literature of Lesbianism*, p. 1025.
56. 'Claire Morgan' [nom de plume of Patricia Highsmith], 'Carol, in a Thousand Cities', in Ann Aldrich (ed.) [nom de plume of Marijane Meaker], *Carol in a Thousand Cities: A Gold Medal Anthology* (Greenwich, CT: Fawcett Publications, 1960), pp. 101–2.
57. Ian Young, *The Male Homosexual in Literature: A Bibliography* (Metuchen, NJ: Scarecrow Press, 1975), pp. 154–5.
58. Reed Woodhouse, *Unlimited Embrace: A Canon of Gay Fiction, 1945–1995* (Amherst: University of Massachusetts Press, 1998), p. 37.
59. Bonnie Zimmerman, *The Safe Sea of Women: Lesbian Fiction 1969–1989* (Boston, MA: Beacon Press, 1990), p. 9.
60. Edward Field, 'The mystery of Alfred Chester' *Boston Review*, March/April 1993. Available at <http://bostonreview.net/archives/BR18.2/field.html> (last accessed 15 April 2018).
61. Christopher Bram, *Mapping the Territory* (New York: Alyson, 2009), p. 30.
62. Faderman, *Surpassing the Love*, p. 405.
63. Zimmerman, *Safe Sea of Women*, p. 9.
64. Ibid. p. 18.
65. Ibid. p. 20.
66. Margaret Cruikshank (ed.), *New Lesbian Writing: An Anthology* (San Francisco: Grey Fox Press, 1984), p. xii.
67. Ian Young (ed.), *The Male Muse: A Gay Anthology* (Trumansburg, NY: Crossing Press, 1973), p. 7.
68. Ibid. p. 8.
69. Ibid. p. 9.
70. Young, *On the Line: New Gay Fiction* (Trumansburg, NY: Crossing Press, 1981), p. 10.
71. Ibid. pp. 5–6.
72. Ibid. p. 9.
73. Roger Austen, *Playing the Game: The Homosexual Novel in America* (Indianapolis: Bobbs-Merrill, 1977), pp. xi–xii.
74. Seymour Kleinberg (ed.), *The Other Persuasion: An Anthology of Short Fiction About Gay Men and Women* (New York: Vintage, 1977), p. x.
75. Ibid. p. xi.
76. Ibid. p. xxi.
77. Woodhouse, *Unlimited Embrace*, pp. 1–2.
78. Les Brookes, *Gay Male Fiction Since Stonewall: Ideology, Conflict, and Aesthetics* (New York: Routledge, 2009), p. 104.
79. Ibid. p. 106.
80. Richard Canning (ed.), *Between Men: Best New Gay Fiction* (Philadelphia: Running Press, 2007), p. xii.
81. Gregory Woods, *A History of Gay Literature: The Male Tradition* (New Haven: Yale University Press, 1998), p. 367.
82. Cruikshank, *New Lesbian Writing*, p. x.
83. Joseph Beam, *In the Life: A Black Gay Anthology* (New York: Alyson, 1986), p. 13.
84. Catherine McKinley, *Afrekete: An Anthology of Black Lesbian Writing* (New York: Anchor, 1995), p. xvi.
85. Devon W. Carbado et al. (eds), *Black Like Us: A Century of Lesbian, Gay, and Bisexual African American Fiction* (San Francisco: Cleis, 2002), p. xiv.
86. John R. Gordon, 'Foreword', in John R. Gordon and Rikki Beadle-Blair (eds), *Black and Gay in the UK* (London: Team Angelica, 2014), p. i.

Bibliography

Altman, Dennis, *Homosexual: Oppression and Liberation* (New York: Outerbridge and Dienstfrey, 1971).
Anderson, Patrick and Alistair Sutherland (eds), *Eros: An Anthology of Friendship* (London: Anthony Blond, 1961).
Austen, Roger, *Playing the Game: The Homosexual Novel in America* (Indianapolis: Bobbs-Merrill, 1977).
Beam, Joseph (ed.), *In the Life: A Black Gay Anthology* (New York: Alyson, 1986).
Bergman, David (ed.), *The Violet Quill Reader: The Emergence of Gay Writing After Stonewall* (New York: St. Martin's Press, 1994).
Bram, Christopher, *Mapping the Territory* (New York: Alyson, 2009).
Bray, Alan, *Homosexuality in Renaissance England* (London: Gay Men's Press, 1982).
Brookes, Les, *Gay Male Fiction Since Stonewall: Ideology, Conflict, and Aesthetics* (New York: Routledge, 2009).
Buckle, Sebastian, *The Way Out: A History of Homosexuality in Modern England* (London: I. B. Tauris, 2015).
Canning, Richard (ed.), *Between Men: Best New Gay Fiction* (Philadelphia: Running Press, 2007).
Carbado, Devon W., Dwight A. McBride and Donald Weise (eds), *Black Like Us: A Century of Lesbian, Gay, and Bisexual African American Fiction* (San Francisco: Cleis, 2002).
Carpenter, Edward, *The Intermediate Sex: A Study of Some Transitional Types of Men and Women* [1908] (Project Gutenberg Australia, April 2004).
Castle, Terry, *The Apparitional Lesbian: Female Homosexuality and Modern Culture* (New York: Columbia University Press, 1993).
— (ed.), *The Literature of Lesbianism: A Historical Anthology from Ariosto to Stonewall* (New York: Columbia University Press, 2003).
Cocks, H. G., 'Secrets, Crimes and Diseases, 1800–1914', in Matt Cook (ed.), *A Gay History of Britain: Love and Sex Between Men Since the Middle Ages* (Oxford: Greenwood, 2007), pp. 107–44.
Cook, Matt, 'Queer Conflicts: Love, Sex and War, 1914–1967', in Matt Cook (ed.), *A Gay History of Britain: Love and Sex Between Men Since the Middle Ages* (Oxford: Greenwood, 2007), pp. 145–78.
Cory, Donald Webster (ed.), *21 Variations on a Theme* (New York: Greenberg, 1953).
Cruikshank, Margaret (ed.), *New Lesbian Writing: An Anthology* (San Francisco: Grey Fox Press, 1984).
Duberman, Martin, Martha Vicinus and George Chauncey (eds), *Hidden from History: Reclaiming the Gay and Lesbian Past* (New York: New American Library, 1989).
Eskridge, William N., 'Privacy jurisprudence and the apartheid of the closet, 1946–1961', *Florida State University Law Review*, 24.4 (Summer 1997): 703–840.
Faderman, Lillian, 'Lesbian magazine fiction in the early twentieth century', *Journal of Popular Culture*, 11.4 (1978): 800–17.
— *Surpassing the Love of Men: Romantic Friendship and Love Between Women from the Renaissance to the Present* (New York: William Morrow, 1981).
Farwell, Marilyn R., 'The Lesbian Narrative: "The Pursuit of the Inedible by the Unspeakable"', in George E. Haggerty and Bonnie Zimmerman (eds), *Professions of Desire: Lesbian and Gay Studies in Literature* (New York: MLA, 1995), pp. 156–68.
Field, Edward, 'The mystery of Alfred Chester', *Boston Review*, March/April 1993, <http://bostonreview.net/archives/BR18.2/field.html> (last accessed 15 April 2018).
Fisher, Jeremy, 'Sex, sleaze and righteous anger: the rise and fall of gay magazines and newspapers in Australia', *TEXT*, 25 (April 2014): 1–12.

Foster, Jeannette, *Sex Variant Women in Literature* (Tallahassee: Naiad Press, [1956] 1985).
Gifford, James (ed.), *Dayneford's Library: Homosexual Writing, 1900–2013* (Amherst: University of Massachusetts Press, 1995).
Gordon, John R. and Rikki Beadle-Blair (eds), *Black and Gay in the UK* (London: Team Angelica, 2014).
Heintz, Kurt, 'Blithe House Quarterly: publishing queer fiction online', E-Poets Network, 21 May 2004, <www.e-poets.net.> (last accessed 15 April 2018).
Kleinberg, Seymour (ed.), *The Other Persuasion: An Anthology of Short Fiction About Gay Men and Women* (New York: Vintage 1977).
Larventz, Don, 'What do men's bodies mean?', *The Sodomite Invasion Review* (August 1990), p. 1.
Lieshout, Maurice van, '*Kreis, Der* (The Circle)', in George E. Haggerty (ed.), *Gay Histories and Cultures: An Encyclopedia, Volume 2* (London: Routledge, 1999), p. 524.
Loftin, Craig M., *Masked Voices: Gay Men and Lesbians in Cold War America* (Albany: SUNY Press, 2012).
McKinley, Catherine E. and L. Joyce DeLaney (eds), *Afrekete: An Anthology of Black Lesbian Writing* (New York: Anchor, 1995).
Mason, Michael, *The Making of Victorian Sexual Attitudes* (Oxford: Oxford University Press, 1994).
Miller, Alan V., *Our Own Voices: A Directory and Lesbian and Gay Periodicals, 1890–1990* (Toronto: The Archives, 1991).
Mitchell, Mark and David Leavitt (eds), *Pages Passed From Hand to Hand: The Hidden Tradition of Homosexual Literature in English from 1748 to 1914* (Boston, MA: Houghton Mifflin, 1997).
Moore, Steven, *Ronald Firbank: An Annotated Bibliography of Secondary Sources* (Normal, IL: Dalkey Archive, 1996).
Morgan, Claire [nom de plume of Patricia Highsmith], 'Carol, in a Thousand Cities', in Ann Aldrich (ed.) [nom de plume of Marijane Meaker], *Carol in a Thousand Cities: A Gold Medal Anthology* (Greenwich, CT: Fawcett Publications, 1960), pp. 101–17.
Nissen, Axel, *Manly Love: Romantic Friendship in American Fiction* (Chicago: University of Chicago Press, 2009).
Packard, Chris, *Queer Cowboys: And Other Erotic Male Friendships in Nineteenth-Century American Literature* (New York: Palgrave Macmillian, 2005).
Phillips, Robert (ed.), *The Stories of Denton Welch* (New York: Dutton, 1985).
Rayside, David, *On the Fringe: Gays and Lesbians in Politics* (Ithaca, NY: Cornell University Press, 1998).
Reid, Coletta, 'Introduction', in Barbara Grier and Coletta Reid (eds), *The Lesbians Home Journal* (Baltimore: Diana Press, 1976), pp. 18–20.
Rule, Jane, *Lesbian Images* (New York: Doubleday, 1975).
Stallybrass, Oliver (ed.), 'Introduction', in E. M. Forster, *The Life to Come and Other Stories* (London: Edward Arnold, 1972), pp. vii–xxi.
Streitmatter, Rodger, *Unspeakable: The Rise of the Gay and Lesbian Press in America* (Boston, MA: Faber and Faber, 1995).
Trumbach, Randolph, 'Modern Sodomy: The Origins of Homosexuality, 1700–1800', in Matt Cook (ed.), *A Gay History of Britain: Love and Sex Between Men Since the Middle Ages* (Oxford: Greenwood, 2007), pp. 77–106.
Warner, Tom, *Never Going Back: A History of Queer Activism in Canada* (Toronto: University of Toronto Press, 2002).
Weeks, Jeffrey, *Coming Out: Homosexual Politics in Britain from the Nineteenth Century to the Present* (London: Quartet Books, 1979).

— *Sex, Politics, and Society: The Regulation of Society Since 1800*, 1st edn (London: Longman, 1981).
— *Sex, Politics, and Society: The Regulation of Society Since 1800*, 3rd edn (London: Routledge, 2014).
Whitt, Jan, *Women in American Journalism: A New History* (Chicago: University of Illinois Press, 2008).
Woodhouse, Reed, *Unlimited Embrace: A Canon of Gay Fiction, 1945–1995* (Amherst: University of Massachusetts Press, 1998).
Woods, Gregory, *A History of Gay Literature: The Male Tradition* (New Haven: Yale University Press, 1998).
Young, Ian, *The Male Homosexual in Literature: A Bibliography* (Metuchen, NJ: Scarecrow Press, 1975).
— (ed.), *The Male Muse: A Gay Anthology* (Trumansburg, NY: Crossing Press, 1973).
— (ed.), *On the Line: New Gay Fiction* (Trumansburg, NY: Crossing Press, 1981).
Zimmerman, Bonnie, *The Safe Sea of Women: Lesbian Fiction 1969–1989* (Boston, MA: Beacon Press, 1990).

21

Disability and the Short Story

Alice Hall

Stephen Kuusisto's *Planet of the Blind* (1998) blurs the boundaries of genre. Marketed as a memoir, the text is divided into fragments of memory that are reminiscent of modernist short fiction; it also includes moments of intense lyricism which stand alone, almost as prose poems. Early in the text, Kuusisto describes his experience of visual impairment as being 'like living inside an immense abstract painting':

> Jackson Pollock's drip canvas *Blue Poles* comes to mind, a tidal wash, an enormous, animate cloud filled with light. This is glacial seeing, like lying on your back in an ice cave and staring up at the cobalt sun.[1]

There is a kaleidoscopic quality to this description which extends throughout *Planet of the Blind*. Kuusisto's writing moves fluidly between different forms of sensory perception and he insists upon the creative potential of a recumbent position. Visual impairment is represented as an intensely physical engagement with the changing quality of light and with one's surroundings. Rather than darkness or lack, it is portrayed as an alternative, potentially transformative way of experiencing the world.

Kuusisto's motif of lying on one's back and staring up at the sky is repeated in many short stories, including D. H. Lawrence's 'The Prussian Officer' (1914) and Virginia Woolf's 'On Being Ill' (1926). For Woolf, the experience of being an 'invalid', on the peripheries of society, leads to an enabling form of sensory acuity. Lying flat allows her to attend to the shifting beauty of the clouds: 'We float with the sticks on the stream . . . irresponsible, disinterested and able, perhaps for the first time in years, to look round, to look up – to look, for example, at the sky.'[2] Her recumbent position reveals 'endless activity . . . [a] gigantic cinema play[ing] perpetually to an empty house'.[3] Woolf's account destabilises the boundary between autobiographical essay and short story but also, like Kuusisto's, challenges the hierarchy of the senses and the boundaries of realism:

> The words give out their scent and distil their flavour, and then, if at last we grasp the meaning, it is all the richer for having come to us sensually first, by way of the palate and the nostrils, like some queer odour.[4]

Lawrence's story also focuses on the relationship between visual perception and the shifting interior consciousness of a single protagonist. Lawrence imagines a scene from the perspective of an orderly who falls from his horse and lies injured and incapacitated in the mountains. The landscape in 'The Prussian Officer' is endowed with a dreamlike beauty in which senses and memories merge to create an overwhelming impression of 'solid unreality' that prefigures Woolf's swirling cinema in the sky: 'There was thick, golden light behind golden-green glitterings, and tall, grey-purple shafts, and darknesses further off, surrounding him, growing deeper.'[5] As in Kuusisto's *Planet of the Blind*, there is an acute awareness of texture, breadth and depth, of 'thick' light and 'deep' darkness.[6]

These brief examples suggest the ways in which a focus on disability can provide new approaches to reading and writing about short stories. Woolf's 'On Being Ill' invites readers to consider the 'undiscovered country' of illness and invalidity in literary writing.[7] 'There is no record', Woolf lamented, of the 'daily drama of the body'.[8] This chapter takes Woolf's challenge seriously, and situates the literary history of the short story in relation to the growing field of disability studies. It suggests that, far from being an 'undiscovered country', representations of disability are central to the work of some of the most celebrated short story writers of the twentieth century, including Raymond Carver, Kenzaburō Ōe, William Faulkner, Flannery O'Connor, D. H. Lawrence and Alice Munro. It argues that short stories are particularly suited to the various experiments with form which recur in cultural representations of disability: the rendering of multisensory forms of perception in literary writing, for example, or the resistance to normative endings.

Short stories invite close attention to the signifying potential of gesture, touch, sound, smell and the surfaces of the body. Today, technological innovations such as voice synthesisers, computer scanners, Braille readers and audiobooks bring with them their own emphases on the physical processes of storytelling while simultaneously making reading and storytelling accessible to a wider audience. They also support the creation of new digital forms, such as Amanda Baggs's 'In my Language', a YouTube video about communication and autism, or Tito Mukhopadhyay's collaboratively produced short stories. New audio-visual and voice-recognition technologies enable the creation of highly experimental texts which borrow from, but also push the boundaries of, more traditional short story forms.

Short stories, alongside other cultural narratives, reflect and actively shape shifting definitions of disability. In the first wave of disability studies in the 1980s, analysing, contesting and debating the 'uses and abuses of language' was understood by scholars and activists not merely as a question of political correctness, but also as a pressing legislative matter which made significant and direct difference to the everyday lives of people with disabilities.[9] More recently, some disability studies theorists have proposed an interactionist model of disability, which seeks to consider the dynamic relationship between medical and social models, and cognitive and physical aspects of disability, and which positions disability studies as intersecting with other theories of race, gender, class, age and sexuality. The model prioritises close reading as a key methodology and as a necessarily politicised process. 'Oppression', Tobin Siebers argues, 'is driven not by individual, unconscious syndromes but by social ideologies that are embodied, and precisely because ideologies are embodied, their effects are readable, and must be read'.[10]

In *Planet of the Blind*, Kuusisto reminds readers that the nature of his visual impairment means that, on a practical level, he necessarily consumes texts in short chunks:

'College is brutally difficult for me. One poem must take the place of the bulky novel I cannot read, or at least not read in a week. I often go home from the library with the few words I've been able to see and absorb still vivid in my imagination.'[11] His descriptions of the reading process are full of pain and lyricism: 'My spastic eye takes in every word like a red star seen on a winter night. Every syllable is acquired with pain.'[12] Reading is not a passive act, it is a multisensory experience in which Kuusisto is active, memorising and imaginatively reconstructing words and stories. This filters through into the form of his writing which is broken down into brief, short story-like fragments, in which every word is significant.

Authors who write about their own experiences of disability, such as Kuusisto, require us to think about reading as an embodied and highly individual process. In the same way, a disability studies perspective confronts us with the ways in which the material and physical conditions of production shape *all* texts:

> Blind hands envision the faces of old acquaintances. Deaf eyes listen to public television. Tongues touch-type letters home to Mum and Dad. Feet wash breakfast dishes. Mouths sign autographs. Different bodies require and create new modes of representation. What would it mean for disability studies to take this insight seriously? Could it change body theory if it did?[13]

However, through representations of cognitive impairment and non-verbal forms of communication, disability studies also invites us to explore difficult questions that go beyond body theory. An example here would be Kenzaburō Ōe's exploration of cognitive impairment and the limits of communication.

This chapter explores short stories that represent physical and cognitive impairments in a range of twentieth-century settings. Like Woolf, who argues that it is 'a new language we need', I suggest that literary disability studies can provide new ways of thinking about even the most widely read short fiction.[14] It also has the potential to energise readers to engage with new authors, fresh theoretical frameworks, and experimental literary forms.

David T. Mitchell and Sharon L. Snyder read disability as a 'crutch upon which literary narratives lean for their representational power, their disruptive potentiality and analytic insight'.[15] Mitchell and Snyder refer to this overarching theory of disability in fiction as a form of 'narrative prosthesis' and suggest that narratives depend on disability as a 'stock feature of characterization' and an 'opportunistic metaphorical device'.[16] Their suspicion of metaphor is a recurring feature of disability studies criticism more generally, with Lennard Davis, for example, highlighting the tendency for disability to be invoked as an easy metaphorical shortcut – a marker of pity, vulnerability or, less frequently, the 'supercrip'.[17]

Michael Bérubé, by contrast, suggests that to strip away disability metaphors seems not only 'queer' and 'counterintuitive' but is in fact 'incompatible with the enterprise of professional literary study'.[18] Etymologically, a metaphor is a carrier of meaning; it is an integral part of the ways in which we think about, understand and communicate human experiences, including disability. Yet, these critical accounts often remain distant from the material realities and difficulties of everyday life with prostheses.

As Siebers suggests, 'frequently, the objects that people with disabilities live with – prostheses, wheelchairs, braces, and other devices – are viewed not as potential sources of pain but as marvelous examples of the plasticity of the human or as devices of empowerment'.[19]

A close reading of literary representations of prosthetics can counter this tendency towards theoretical abstraction or simple idealisation. Short stories such as Flannery O'Connor's 'Good Country People' (1955) and William Faulkner's 'The Leg' (1934) probe the relationship between the material and the metaphorical. Both works invite metaphorical readings of the prosthetic legs that they depict, but both also imagine highly physical, individual experiences of prosthetics, depicting them as sources of pain, shock, sexual pleasure and comic absurdity.

At first, O'Connor appears to use Hulga's prosthesis as a metaphorical shortcut in 'Good Country People': her wooden leg can be read as a straightforward metaphor for the intellectual limitation that she feels, trapped in a claustrophobic domestic setting with her mother, the small-minded Mrs Hopewell. Hulga's physical immobility and her domestic entrapment are aligned with a form of wilful sensory deprivation; her eyes are 'icy blue, with the look of someone who has achieved blindness and means to keep it'.[20] Yet, in a characteristic narrative twist, O'Connor offers readers this reassuring metaphorical crutch, only to pull it away. In the story's climactic scene, Hulga's aloof intellectualism gives way to a combination of morbid curiosity about, and sexual desire for, the Bible salesman, Manley Pointer. The boundary between Hulga's flesh and her wooden leg is a source of fascination for Pointer. At this point in the story, the prosthesis is transformed from an easy metaphor for domestic and social limitation into a highly individual object: an 'artificial limb, in a white sock and brown flat shoe . . . bound in a heavy material-like canvas and ended in an ugly jointure where it attached to the stump'.[21] The boundary between the flesh and prosthesis is the crux of the story: when Hulga allows Pointer to touch and to remove her wooden leg, he steals it and places it out of her reach. At this climactic moment, Pointer's religious rhetoric is replaced by the revelation that he is an atheist; he opens his Bible to reveal that it is hollowed out to allow space for whiskey and pornographic playing cards. Hulga's leg which, until this point, she has taken 'care of . . . as someone else would his soul, in private and almost with her own eyes turned away', is exposed, scrutinised and sexualised.[22] In a story loaded with biblical imagery, the epiphany is not a form of sexual or spiritual transcendence, but rather a return to the body.

Hulga is not represented as a straightforward victim or a stereotypical disabled figure; instead she is rendered as a complex character, stubborn, intelligent and manipulative, yet also vulnerable and highly changeable in just a few pages. O'Connor registers the sensationalist fascination with prosthetics – a fascination that the story itself could be accused of – through Pointer's revelation that he has stolen other personal objects on his travels, including a glass eye. Using the small-scale of the short story, O'Connor draws attention to the detail of everyday material objects, such as wooden legs or glass eyes, as a way of raising fundamental questions about embodiment, faith and disability in a style that is infused with irony and dark comedy.

In 'The Leg', Faulkner also probes the relationship between the material and the metaphorical; like O'Connor, he uses the form of the short story to invite an intense focus on visceral physical details which are also richly symbolic. Faulkner's fragmented narrative describes a body and a mind that have been torn apart by violence in the First World War:

> And my nights were filled too, with nerve- and muscle-ends chafed now by an immediate cause: the wood and leather leg. But the gap was still there, and sometimes at night, isolated by invisibility, it would become filled with the immensity of darkness and silence despite me.[23]

In such passages, Faulkner's narrator conveys a powerful impression of disorientation and physical discomfort, related from a claustrophobic first-person perspective. There is a highly visceral, immediate sense of rawness and pain. Yet, in the course of the story, the narrator also hints at the more abstract, multi-layered metaphorical significance of David's prosthetic leg.

This sense of the symbolic potential of prosthesis connects with Henri-Jacques Stiker's insistence that prosthesis is 'not only the pieces of wood, iron, now plastic that replace the missing hand or foot. It is also the very idea that you can *replace* . . . Replacement, re-establishment of the prior situation, substitution, compensation – all of this now becomes possible language.'[24] Stiker suggests that this 'integrationist ideal' was rooted in the aftermath of the First World War when huge numbers of injured soldiers returned home and tried to re-assimilate into their communities.[25] The expansion of the prosthetics industry was part of a wider shift, from cure towards rehabilitation, in which disability was understood as a deficit, to be covered up in the public sphere, in order to sustain a capitalist fantasy of the physically and economically self-supporting citizen.[26]

In contrast to these wide-ranging historical accounts of prosthesis, William Faulkner's 'The Leg' imagines just a few moments in a soldier's life, as he lies in his hospital bed. The complex form of the story, which moves fluidly between time frames and settings, suggests that these moments are inescapably infused with personal memories and larger historical processes. Faulkner's story explores the difficulty of re-integration and substitution on a social, physical and linguistic level. Just as Faulkner's narrator describes the physical challenges of adapting to his prosthesis, the leg comes to symbolise the difficulties of narrating psychological loss and the impossibility of returning to a prior bodily or mental state. In Faulkner's story, David's prosthesis becomes, paradoxically, a symbol for all that is absent and irreplaceable.

Mitchell and Snyder's account of metaphor suggests that narratives tend to follow an inherently conservative trajectory: 'Our notion of narrative prosthesis evolves out of this specific recognition: a narrative issues to resolve or correct – to "prostheticize" . . . a deviance marked as improper to a social context.'[27] For Mitchell and Snyder, disability not only demands a story, it also requires an explanation which will make the disability disappear or which will cover it up. In this view, disability symbolises a threatening form of bodily and social disorder, which can be temporarily explored through a narrative but which is then removed to ensure a return to the established social norms. Faulkner's 'The Leg' and O'Connor's 'Good Country People' are more radical than this. Both stories represent bodies that are not easily 'prostheticized': they imagine specific examples of the use of prosthetics in everyday life as sometimes painful, embarrassing and difficult to use, and as always supplementary. On a structural level, these stories also refuse to be 'prostheticized'; they resist stereotypical cultural scripts, such as the progress narrative with a hero at its centre. In both stories, open endings are used in particularly powerful ways to render the sense of ongoing emotional and physical rawness. After floundering alone without her wooden leg in the barn, Hulga returns to the oppressive stasis of the kitchen to face yet more of her mother's hollowed out aphorisms and bubbling resentment. Faulkner's wounded soldier remains incapacitated and alone at the end of 'The Leg'. In different ways, O'Connor and Faulkner use the focus of the short story form to draw attention to the details of individual bodies and to depict ongoing situations: lives in flux, unresolved questions, 'incomplete' bodies, and shifting metaphorical meanings. Crucially, both stories resist any urge towards order or closure; at once viscerally material and richly metaphorical, O'Connor and Faulkner depict the everyday lives of people with physical disabilities whose bodies refuse to be easily 'corrected', covered or removed from the narrative frame.

D. H. Lawrence's 'The Blind Man' (1920) and Raymond Carver's rewriting of this story, 'Cathedral' (1981), explore the relationship between blindness and sight, insight and multisensory forms of perception. Like the 'prosthetic' stereotypical metaphors of disability discussed by Mitchell and Snyder, the narrator of Carver's 'Cathedral' initially reads blindness as a form of passive dependency: 'my idea of blindness came from the movies. In the movies, the blind moved slowly and never laughed.'[28] Carver's narrator reminds us that cultural texts, including films, songs, novels and short stories, play an important role in reflecting and also shaping public perceptions of disability. In this context, the process of analysing texts from a literary disability studies perspective becomes, in itself, an act of resistance. Reading from this perspective challenges readers and critics to think beyond the stereotypical cultural scripts or sight-centred epistemologies which can go unquestioned in some prose fiction. The depersonalised title of Lawrence's story invokes the figure of the 'hypothetical blind man' who, Georgina Kleege argues, is a recurring figure in literary theory and philosophy. The 'hypothetical blind man' serves merely as a 'prop for theories of consciousness', and is often used to highlight 'the importance of sight and to elicit a frission of awe and pity which promotes gratitude among sighted theorists for the vision they possess'.[29]

Maurice, the protagonist of Lawrence's story, who is 'totally blind' since arriving back from the war, is initially described in terms that emphasise sensuality and the powerful bond he has with his wife, Isabel: they share 'dark and palpable joy' and an 'unspeakable intimacy'.[30] In the first part of the story, Isabel becomes finely attuned to non-visual forms of knowledge and expression; the narrative encourages readers to attend to 'the noise of her husband's footsteps in the hall', 'the smell of horses', and 'the sound of his voice' which 'seemed to touch her'.[31] Lawrence experiments with a momentary narrative reversal in a scene in which Isabel finds herself plunged into darkness, and into panic, when she goes into an unfamiliar outbuilding of their house; Maurice, meanwhile, works happily and knowledgeably in that environment. Through these opening scenes, Lawrence invites readers to imagine the possibility of deep-rooted affection, communication and empathetic identification between a blind and a sighted character.

The arrival of a visitor, Bertie, disrupts the dominant narrative perspective, complicating Isabel's perception of her husband. Maurice is defamiliarised in the eyes of his wife, and is transformed into a 'hypothetical blindman': 'The blind man was silent . . . Bertie made her conscious of a strangeness.'[32] At this point, the narrative slips into a primarily visual mode, focusing on external appearances and surface details. Maurice's blindness is described as a negation or an absence of visual and imaginative faculties: 'He did not think or trouble much . . . he wanted no intervention of visual consciousness.'[33] In the final scene, Maurice persuades Bertie to trace his eyebrows, to touch his face and to feel his scar. Here, Lawrence explores the significance of touch and the importance of skin as a perceptual surface; he gestures towards a 'new way of consciousness' on Maurice's part, and the possibility of going beyond exclusively visual ways of knowing.[34] For Maurice, this is a transformative moment: he proclaims a newfound friendship with his companion. Bertie, however, feels nothing but 'revulsion'.[35] The image of the smooth, warm, permeable surface of Maurice's skin is replaced by hardened, sharp and fragmented boundaries, as Bertie is described as a 'mollusc whose shell is broken'.[36]

At this point in the text, Lawrence hints at the possibility of going beyond the hardened exterior shell of Bertie, who is depicted as a traditional British gentleman of the period. There are, after all, cracks in that shell. 'The Blind Man', however, is ultimately a story about the breakdown of communication and understanding. In this sense, it chimes with Ato Quayson's wider theory of disability and narrative, which argues that fictional representations of impairment are connected by the ways in which they exhibit a form of 'aesthetic nervousness'. Quayson suggests that these texts share a sense of unease which functions primarily at the level of character, but which also permeates the form of the text and the reader/text relationship. Disability brings about a 'crisis' in representation that 'short-circuits' representation itself.[37] For Quayson, disability presupposes a crisis of language, social marginalisation and an 'interpretive difficulty or impasse'.[38] Like many other modernists, Lawrence pushes at the boundaries of this apparent impasse. He uses blindness as a trope or 'prop' for thinking in abstract ways about the limits of language and the impossibility of empathetic identification with others. However, Lawrence also insists upon the embodied presence of both characters as individuals and explores blindness as an alternative way of being in the world.

In 'Cathedral', Carver rewrites this climactic scene, depicting the triumphant moment of identification which is denied to readers of Lawrence. Carver transposes Lawrence's story into a 1980s American context, and the final scene features Robert, the blind visitor, and the narrator watching a television documentary about architecture. In this unexpected moment of intimacy, the narrator confronts the limits of visual and verbal forms of communication: 'I stared hard at the shot of the cathedral on the TV. How could I even begin to describe it? "I can't tell you what a cathedral looks like. It just isn't in me to do it. I can't do any more than I've done."'[39] In the face of this linguistic crisis of representation, Carver represents a moment of revelation and an alternative form of communication: drawing. The cynicism and prejudices of the narrator are challenged by a unifying moment of shared imagination and creativity: 'his fingers rode my fingers as my hand went over the paper. It was like nothing else in my life up to now.'[40] Closing his eyes, the narrator tries to imagine, for the first time, his companion's perspective. Touch becomes the primary means of communication: 'My eyes were still closed. I knew that. But I didn't feel like I was inside anything . . . "It's really something", I said.'[41] By tracing out the lines of the cathedral together, the two men use the process of representation to form a new level of closeness and understanding.

The process of representation always involves looking away from a subject and then recreating it in the mind's eye, according to Jacques Derrida. In *Memoirs of the Blind* (1993), Derrida analyses portraits of blind people in order to explore the way that memory 'supplements' sight; aesthetic processes of reading, writing and drawing are based on creative moments of not seeing:

> A hand of the blind ventures forth alone or disconnected . . . it feels its way, it gropes, it caresses as much as it inscribes, trusting in the memory of signs and supplementing sight . . . This eye guides the tracing outline; it is a miner's lamp at the point of writing, a curious and vigilant substitute, the prosthesis of a seer who is himself invisible.[42]

Like Carver's narrator, whose perceptions are challenged as he traces the lines of the cathedral on Robert's hand, Derrida focuses on the act of reaching out, touching and re-moulding ideas and images which cannot be seen but which must be imagined. In Lawrence's 'The Blind Man', blindness is connected to a resistance to visual modes of thinking: 'He did not try to remember, to visualise.'[43] Carver's 'Cathedral', by contrast, suggests that an encounter with blindness emphasises the ways in which aesthetic representations require us to remember and to retrace, imagine and fill in the gaps. Kuusisto echoes this sense in which blindness inspires different ways of thinking about processes of representation and multisensory perception: 'as things happen around us we reinvent what we hear like courtroom artists who sketch as fast as they can'.[44] Like Derrida's blind draftsman, Kuusisto insists that 'in reality I cannot see the world by ear, I can only reinvent it for my purposes'.[45] This reconceptualised experience of sound, space and architecture is explored through genre-blurring forms, such as Kuusisto's 'sound postcards' and 'auditory poems'; it is also developed in Carver's short story.

The short story is a particularly pertinent form for exploring such highly significant yet small-scale, everyday epiphanies. The form allows both Lawrence and Carver to engage in thought-experiments, using fictional settings to explore alternative modes of living and consciousness. Like the portraits in Derrida's *Memoirs of the Blind*, the short story allows Lawrence and Carver to capture a particular moment or scene, and to focus on this with a level of intensity which might be lost in a larger-scale painting or novel. Carver's story confronts readers with the limits but also the materiality of writing; words and images are read visually, but they are also understood through touch, traced out on a hand, on a page, or in Braille. 'Cathedral' invites us to reflect upon how, as readers of a short story, we are necessarily implicated in this process of actively reconstructing what remains unwritten, unsaid or unseen.

Kenzaburō Ōe's short fiction takes up the challenge of giving voice to the unspoken. Writing in the context of modern day Japan, Ōe has focused on two key concerns throughout his career, both of which relate to disability. The first is the experiences of victims of the Hiroshima atomic bomb, and the second is his life with his cognitively impaired son, Hikari. In his writing, Ōe frequently returns to the period immediately after Hikari's birth. Born with a brain hernia, Hikari was labelled a 'monster baby'; and Ōe was encouraged by doctors to leave his son to die, without the knowledge of the child's mother. In one sense, Ōe's fiction serves a documentary function: it exposes the deep-rooted prejudices, shocking medical practices, and lack of support for families with disabled children in 1960s Japan, a society in which 'it was considered shameful to even take a handicapped child out in public'.[46] This view of his fiction aligns with the wider disability activism that Ōe has been engaged in since the birth of his son, which includes his participation in World Disabled Person's Day and the interviews that he has done with Hiroshima survivors. *Hiroshima Notes* (1965) is frank about the ongoing effects of impairments caused by the bomb; Ōe describes 'the cataract-clouded eyes of the elderly victims . . . the deformities and handicaps suffered by [the] children . . . the elevated levels of cancer throughout the region, and other lingering effects of radiation'.[47]

On another level, however, Ōe uses fiction, and particularly short stories, to escape from the confines of documentary truth. In 'Aghwee the Sky Monster' (1964), Ōe explores the complexities of his own response to the moral dilemmas that he faced following Hikari's birth. Through the thin veil of fiction, he imagines the consequences for a father who has decided to allow his disabled son to die. 'Aghwee the Sky Monster' tells the story of a young man who is hired to take care of a composer, a 'sentimental madman', who suffers 'delusions about living with a monster'.[48] This 'monster' appears to be the vision of the composer's dead child, visible only to him in a bizarre kangaroo-shaped form that emerges periodically from the sky. This odd image is tinged with intense sadness, as the mother reveals that the name 'Aghwee' was the only sound ever uttered by the child. The father, who has 'fled from reality into a world of phantoms', declines 'to live his own life, just as he declined to let the baby go on living', and ultimately commits suicide.[49] The narrator's description of the father figure as being 'like a traveller who had arrived here in a time machine' provides a fitting metaphor for Ōe's own relationship to his narrative. Through the creative licence of fiction, he imagines himself transported to a different time in his life, living with the consequences of a very different decision about his son's future.[50]

In interviews, Ōe has said that he made his decision to go ahead with the operation to save his son, against the advice of many of the doctors.[51] Yet, the period of indecision and doubt is one that Ōe never allows his readers, or himself, to forget: 'No powerful detergent has allowed me to wash out of my life those disgraceful five weeks, nor do I expect to succeed at this as long as I live.'[52] 'Aghwee the Sky Monster' stands alone in its own right as a short story – or as a 'short novel' in the English translation of the collection's title. But the story also suggests a dialogue with other short stories written by Ōe about the same period in his life in which his son was born and he was asked to determine the child's fate. 'Aghwee the Sky Monster' stands in close relation to *A Personal Matter* (1964) and *Rouse Up O Young Men of the New Age!* (1983). All of these stories depict the same decision-making process but each employs a different timescale and imagines a very different outcome for his son.

The musical metaphor of counterpoint is a particularly fitting way to understand the relationship between these texts, given that it is through music that Hikari, who is largely non-verbal, communicates with his father and the rest of the world. In an interview, Ōe extends this way of thinking about the complex dynamic between his works of fiction, drawing a parallel between the processes of Hikari's musical composition and his own writing: 'I am the kind of writer who writes and rewrites. So one of my main literary methods is "repetition with difference" ... Through elaboration ... composers create new perspectives.'[53] Through this aesthetic of improvisation around a recurring theme, Ōe uses fictional forms to challenge narrative scripts and fixed endings such as the miracle recovery, triumph-over-adversity, or the narrative of overcoming. 'Aghwee the Sky Monster' and *A Personal Matter*, for instance, each represents repetition with difference of his own life story, as Ōe thinks through the consequences of different routes that he could have taken, drafting alternative versions of his own life story, and different versions of himself, in narrative form. As Laura Marcus suggests, fiction here acts as 'a space for more general identification, or the trying out of potentialities and possibilities – what might have been, what could have been, what might yet be'.[54] Reading these stories alongside one another highlights the limits of language and the impossibility of capturing this painful decision-making process within a single narrative frame.

Ōe's fiction draws readers into troubling ethical dilemmas and poses the ongoing question of how he can give voice to his non-verbal son. In this sense, Ōe's writing addresses some of the most pressing and overlooked questions in disability studies today. Mark Osteen suggests that, until recently, the widespread adoption of the social model in disability studies led activists and scholars to focus on sensory and physical rather than cognitive impairments.[55] Focusing on issues of cognitive impairment such as autism or Down syndrome, he argues, challenges understandings of disability as simply a mismatch between the social environment and an individual's physical impairments. Social models of disability borrow heavily from Michel Foucault's understanding of the role of the state in regulating and normalising bodies, through processes of 'subjection' and the techniques of biopower, such as statistics and demographics, sterilisation and eugenics.[56] Yet, this view can also deny people with disabilities a voice; it presents them as 'docile bodies' who have minimal agency in their own self-representation.[57] Ōe's fiction poses these questions in a very practical but also highly creative manner: through his short forms and musical metaphors, he searches for strategies which allow him to go beyond the silenced 'docile bodies' of Foucault, or the 'crisis of representation' described by Quayson, to talk about personal and public experiences of disability in everyday life.[58]

Alice Munro's 'Mrs Cross and Mrs Kidd' also considers this question of self-representation in relation to disability and the loss of voice. As physically disabled inhabitants of a care home, Mrs Cross and Mrs Kidd find themselves marginalised, on the peripheries of their own families and society. The story draws attention to the ways in which dominant Anglo-American models of citizenship regard certain disabled members of society as 'an afterthought', only to be considered 'after the basic institutions of society are designed'.[59] As wives, mothers and inhabitants of a care home, Mrs Kidd and Mrs Cross conceive of themselves, and the community in which they live, merely in terms of waste: 'This is the only place in the county, everything gets dumped here.'[60]

Munro's writing is highly attuned to the irony and absurdity, the tedium, humour and pain of everyday experiences of care. She depicts subtle hierarchies of ability; the two women, for example, look down on the 'Mongoloids' and the 'senile', the 'far gone' and the 'crazies' who are 'locked up in the back wing'.[61] The story focuses on the unspoken nuances that lie just below the surface of the women's conversation: the frictions of class difference, petty jealousies, and small-scale miscommunications. Yet, these seemingly trivial details, Munro suggests, are what make up the fabric of lives and identities. Mrs Kidd and Mrs Cross do not conform to the polarised stereotypes or metaphorical shortcuts of either the hero or the villain; they are rapidly sketched yet carefully crafted characters who, despite the distance between them, come to depend upon each other. This 'dialectic of dependency' between the two women is, however, disrupted by the arrival of a new person into the care home: a man named Jack who, following a stroke, has lost the power of speech.[62] The two women attempt to read Jack's gestures and the surfaces of his body for meaning; 'the whole left side of his body was loose, emptied, powerless', but he has a smile which is 'intelligent, ironic' and 'did not go with his helpless look'.[63] Through the silent figure of Jack, Munro gives a physical, embodied presence to the unspoken words which are central to the plot of the story. Like Ōe, Munro confronts readers with the limits of verbal communication and of writing:

> Mrs Cross brought a pencil and paper, fixed the tray across his chair, tried to see how Jack made out with writing. It was about the same as talking. He would scrawl a bit, push the pencil till he broke it, start to cry. They didn't make progress, either in writing or talking, it was useless. But she was learning to talk to him by the yes-and-no method, and it seemed sometimes she could pick up what was in his mind.[64]

Munro's narrative, which adopts a distinctly depersonalised third-person perspective throughout, suggests the difficulty but also the commitment to try to imagine the interior life of another person. Imagination, reading and interpretation are depicted as key to this ethical imperative. There are moments of non-verbal communication and empathetic identification in the story, such as when Jack uses the picture of the red deer to tell Mrs Cross where he used to live. The story ends, however, with Jack refusing the cosy game that Mrs Cross and Mrs Kidd want him to play; language is reduced to nothing more than a few Scrabble tiles thrown on the floor in silent frustration.

Munro's story, which depicts the tensions between several characters with multiple disabilities, destabilises the notion of any single, unified 'disabled' identity. Her complex characters, and her depiction of the details and tensions of everyday life, call into question universalising narratives of disability as a shared experience or common identity. Identity politics approaches, which seek to celebrate disability as a shared social identity, are put under pressure by intersectional models, in which disability is understood in relation to sexuality, gender, class, race and age. Mrs Cross and Mrs Kidd are mothers, wives, childhood classmates, friends, jealous rivals and reluctant co-habitants, thrown together by chance. Munro's story suggests the ways in which a focus on disability draws attention to some of the most pressing concerns in Western society: the ageing of the baby boomers, longer life expectancies, the privatisation and commodification of care. It also insists on the flexibility of the category of disability, as a fluid identity which most of us are likely to inhabit at some stage in our lives. In an academic context, this revelation also shifts the status of literary disability studies from a marginal, identity-based perspective, to one that is central to fundamental questions about technology, dependency, embodiment and modernity. As Lennard Davis suggests, 'Over time many scholars have come to see [that] the "them" of these identity studies is ultimately the social collectivity of "us" . . . Seeing what appears to be a narrow subject expand to include almost all of literary studies.'[65]

This chapter has explored some of the ways in which disability studies can be understood as a productive perspective for the study of short fiction, particularly for thinking about representations of the body, the ethics of metaphor, non-verbal forms of communication, and multisensory modes of perception. In his classic study of the short story, *The Lonely Voice*, Frank O'Connor suggests that the genre is defined by its representation of 'lonely voices' and 'submerged population groups'.[66] The striking prevalence of characters with disabilities in modern and contemporary short stories certainly increases the cultural visibility of people with impairments, exploring their marginalised positions and challenging their status as a traditionally 'submerged' group in society. Critical metaphors and theories of disability bring to the surface new ways of thinking about short fiction.

However, short fiction can also have a transformative effect on the ways in which the relationship between disability and narrative is understood. To date, literary disability studies has been dominated by analyses of Anglo-American novels. Davis's view of the novel as a normative genre is typical of much scholarship in this area. He suggests that the novel is an inherently conservative form which has the potential to directly inform an individual's world view:

> I am not saying that novels embody the prejudices of society towards people with disabilities. That is clearly a truism. Rather, I am asserting that the very structures on which the novel rests tend to be normative, ideologically emphasising the universal quality of the central character whose normativity encourages us to identify with him or her. Furthermore, the novel's goal is to reproduce, on some level, the semiologically normative signs surrounding the reader, that paradoxically help the reader to read those signs in the world as well as the text. The middleness of life, the middleness of the material world, the middleness of the normal body, the middleness of a sexually gendered, ethnically middle world is created in symbolic form and then reproduced symbolically.[67]

Davis views the novel as one of a number of 'public venues' in which the 'abnormal' is represented and used to bolster hegemonic ideas of the normal in terms of race, class, gender and dis/ability – a theory he refers to as 'enforcing normalcy'.[68] This paradigm has been challenged by some recent scholars through readings of particular novels as sites of resistance to these norms.[69] Short stories, which have received very little critical attention in disability studies to date, offer an additional complication and a different literary lineage to the one that Davis describes. Short fiction is often rooted in physical acts of storytelling, in performance, and face-to-face modes of oral narration. These forms highlight the role of the listener, or the reader, in actively imagining, rewriting or retelling a narrative. For Davis, the novel props up the neoliberal fiction of the definitive white, male, heterosexual, physically and economically self-supporting, autonomous citizen of modernity. Short stories, by contrast, provide the scope for a more expansive model of citizenship through experimentation and innovation. While stories may, of course, reproduce the prejudices and stereotypical shortcuts used in dominant cultural narratives of disability, the fragmented form of the short story means that the idea of a fixed ending, in which order and 'normality' are restored, is always open to question. Often read in a single sitting, short stories invite readers to immerse themselves in the details of everyday life, to attach symbolic and cultural significance to that which has been overlooked, and to play an active part in piecing together narratives and reading unspoken presences.

In 'On Being Ill', Woolf argues that illness and disability inspire new modes of expression: an individual is 'forced to coin words himself, and, taking his pain in one hand, and a lump of pure sound in the other . . . crush them together that a brand new word in the end drops out'.[70] Analysing short fiction from the perspective of disability studies can make us more attuned to the ways in which writers have re-moulded the boundaries of literary form and language. As Woolf suggests, we need new political and critical languages for talking about disability – and not just in English. As the World Health Organisation's 2011 Report on Disability suggested, there is an explosion in the number of people with disabilities; the WHO estimate the number of people with disabilities around the world to be one billion, about 17 per cent of the global population. The majority of these people live in developing countries. Focusing on short fiction from around the world is one way in which cultural disability studies can globalise its perspective and question the hegemony of Western novel forms. Short stories invite us to trace the presence of disability back in time, to think about the very earliest forms of writing, but also to think in creative ways about the practical and aesthetic possibilities of new digital forms such as the YouTube clip, the tweet and the voice synthesiser. As the brief examples from Faulkner, Lawrence, Carver, Ōe and Munro suggest, literary representations of disability open up understandings of identity that are complex and various, embodied and intersectional; each of these short stories invites us to find new vocabularies with which to write, to think and to talk about disability.

Notes

1. Stephen Kuusisto, *Planet of the Blind* (New York: Dial Press, 1998), p. 7.
2. Virginia Woolf, 'On Being Ill', in Hermione Lee (ed.), *On Being Ill* (Ashfield: Consortium, 2002), p. 12.
3. Ibid. p. 14.
4. Ibid. p. 22.
5. D. H. Lawrence, 'The Prussian Officer', in John Worthern (ed.), *The Prussian Officer and Other Stories* (London: Penguin, 1983), p. 19.
6. Ibid.
7. Woolf, 'On Being Ill', p. 3.
8. Ibid. p. 4.
9. Lucy Burke, 'Introduction', *Journal of Literary and Cultural Disability Studies*, 2.1 (2008): i.
10. Tobin Siebers, *Disability Theory* (Ann Arbor: University of Michigan Press, 2008), p. 30.
11. Kuusisto, *Planet of the Blind*, p. 66.
12. Ibid.

13. Siebers, *Disability Theory*, p. 54.
14. Woolf, 'On Being Ill', p. 7.
15. David T. Mitchell and Sharon L. Snyder, *Narrative Prosthesis: Disability and the Dependencies of Discourse* (Ann Arbor: University of Michigan Press, 2001), p. 49.
16. Mitchell and Snyder, *Narrative Prosthesis*, p. 74.
17. Lennard Davis, *Enforcing Normalcy: Disability, Deafness, and the Body* (London: Verso, 1995), p. 106.
18. Michael Bérubé, 'Disability and Narrative', *PMLA*, 120.2 (2005): 570.
19. Siebers, *Disability Theory*, p. 62.
20. Flannery O'Connor, 'Good Country People', in Robert Giroux (ed.), *The Complete Stories* (New York: Farrar, Straus and Giroux, 1971), p. 281.
21. Ibid. p. 297.
22. Ibid.
23. William Faulkner, 'The Leg', in *Dr Martino and Other Stories* (London: Chatto and Windus, 1965), p. 311.
24. Henri-Jacques Stiker, *A History of Disability* (Ann Arbor: University of Michigan Press, 1999), pp. 123–4 (emphasis in the original).
25. Ibid. p. xii.
26. See: Gary L. Albrecht, *The Disability Business: Rehabilitation in America* (Newbury Park: Sage Publications, 1992); David Serlin, *Replaceable You: Engineering the Body in Postwar America* (Chicago: University of Chicago Press, 2004); and Henri-Jacques Stiker, *A History of Disability*.
27. Mitchell and Snyder, *Narrative Prosthesis*, p. 53.
28. Raymond Carver, 'Cathedral', in *Cathedral* (London: Vintage, 2009), p. 196.
29. Georgina Kleege, 'Blindness and Visual Culture: An Eyewitness Account', in Lennard J. Davis (ed.), *The Disability Studies Reader* (New York: Routledge, 2013), pp. 447–8.
30. D. H. Lawrence, 'The Blind Man', in Bruce Steele (ed.), *England, My England and Other Stories* (Cambridge: Cambridge University Press, 1990), p. 46.
31. Ibid. p. 46, p. 5, p. 52.
32. Ibid. p. 57.
33. Ibid. p. 54.
34. Ibid.
35. Ibid. p. 63.
36. Ibid.
37. Ato Quayson, *Aesthetic Nervousness: Disability and the Crisis of Representation* (New York: Columbia University Press, 2007), p. 15.
38. Ibid. p. 14.
39. Carver, 'Cathedral', p. 212.
40. Ibid. p. 214.
41. Ibid.
42. Jacques Derrida and Musée du Louvre, *Memoirs of the Blind: The Self-Portrait and Other Ruins* (Chicago: University of Chicago Press, 1993), p. 3.
43. Lawrence, 'The Blind Man', p. 54.
44. Stephen Kuusisto, *Eavesdropping: A Life by Ear* (New York: W. W. Norton, 2006), p. xi.
45. Ibid.
46. Sarah Fay and Kenzaburō Ōe, 'Kenzaburō Ōe, the Art of Fiction', *The Paris Review*, 183 (Winter 2007). Available at <https://www.theparisreview.org/interviews/5816/kenzaburo-oe-the-art-of-fiction-no-195-kenzaburo-oe> (last accessed 29 June 2018).
47. Kenzaburō Ōe, *Hiroshima Notes,* trans. David L. Swain and Toshi Yonezawa (New York: Grove Press, 1996), p. 22.

48. Kenzaburō Ōe, 'Aghwee the Sky Monster', in *Teach Us to Outgrow Our Madness: Four Short Novels*, trans. John Nathan (New York: Grove Press, 1977), p. 224, p. 245.
49. Ibid. p. 242.
50. Ibid. p. 245.
51. Fay and Ōe, 'Kenzaburō Ōe, the Art of Fiction'.
52. Kenzaburō Ōe, *Rouse up O Young Men of the New Age!*, trans. John Nathan (New York: Grove Press, 2002), pp. 90–1.
53. Fay and Ōe, 'Kenzaburō Ōe, the Art of Fiction'.
54. Laura Marcus, *Auto/Biographical Discourses: Theory, Criticism, Practice* (Manchester: Manchester University Press, 1994), p. 280.
55. Mark Osteen, 'Autism and Representation: A Comprehensive Introduction', in Mark Osteen (ed.), *Autism and Representation* (New York: Routledge, 2008), p. 3.
56. Siebers, *Disability Theory*, p. 55.
57. Michel Foucault, *Abnormal: Lectures at the Collège De France* (New York: Picador, 2003), p. 135.
58. Quayson, *Aesthetic Nervousness*, p. 15.
59. Martha Craven Nussbaum, *Frontiers of Justice: Disability, Nationality, Species Membership* (Cambridge, MA: The Belknap Press and Harvard University Press, 2006), p. 98.
60. Alice Munro, 'Mrs Cross and Mrs Kidd', *The Moons of Jupiter* (London: Vintage, 2007), p. 163.
61. Ibid. pp. 162–3.
62. Michael Davidson, 'Introduction: Dialectics of Dependency', *Journal of Literary and Cultural Disability Studies*, 1.2 (2007): i.
63. Munro, 'Mrs Cross and Mrs Kidd', p. 167.
64. Ibid. p. 171.
65. Lennard Davis, 'Crips Strike Back: The Rise of Disability Studies', *American Literary History*, 11.3 (1999): 500.
66. Frank O'Connor, *The Lonely Voice: A Study of the Short Story* (New York: Melville House, [1963] 2011), p. 17.
67. Lennard J. Davis, 'Constructing Normalcy: The Bell Curve, the Novel, and the Invention of the Disabled Body in the Nineteenth Century', in Lennard Davis (ed.), *The Disability Studies Reader*, 2nd edn (New York: Routledge, 2006), p. 11.
68. Ibid. p. 12.
69. See Alice Hall, *Disability and Modern Fiction: Faulkner, Morrison, Coetzee and the Nobel Prize for Literature* (Basingstoke: Palgrave Macmillan, 2011); and Siobhan Senier, 'Rehabilitation Reservations: Native Narrations of Disability and Community', *Disability Studies Quarterly*, 32.4 (2012).
70. Woolf, 'On Being Ill', p. 7.

Bibliography

Albrecht, Gary L., *The Disability Business: Rehabilitation in America* (Newbury Park: Sage Publications, 1992).

Baggs, Amanda, 'In My Language' (2007), <www.youtube.com/watch?v=JnylM1hI2jc> (last accessed 15 April 2018).

Bérubé, Michael, 'Disability and Narrative', *PMLA*, 120.2 (2005): 568–76.

Burke, Lucy, 'Introduction: Thinking About Cognitive Impairment', *Journal of Literary Disability*, 2.1 (2008): i–iv.

Carver, Raymond, 'Cathedral', in *Cathedral* (London: Vintage, 2009), pp. 196–214.

Davidson, Michael, 'Introduction: Dialectics of Dependency', *Journal of Literary and Cultural Disability Studies*, 1.2 (2007): i–vi.

Davis, Lennard J., *Enforcing Normalcy: Disability, Deafness, and the Body* (London: Verso, 1995).

— 'Crips Strike Back: The Rise of Disability Studies', *American Literary History*, 11.3 (1999), pp. 500–12.

— 'Constructing Normalcy: The Bell Curve, the Novel, and the Invention of the Disabled Body in the Nineteenth Century', in Lennard J. Davis (ed.), *The Disability Studies Reader*, 2nd edn (New York: Routledge, 2006), pp. 3–16.

Derrida, Jacques, and Musée du Louvre, *Memoirs of the Blind: The Self-Portrait and Other Ruins* (Chicago: University of Chicago Press, 1993).

Faulkner, William, *Dr Martino and Other Stories* (London: Chatto & Windus, 1965).

Fay, Sarah and Kenzaburō Ōe, 'Kenzaburō Ōe, the Art of Fiction', *The Paris Review*, 183 (Winter 2007), <https://www.theparisreview.org/interviews/5816/kenzaburo-oe-the-art-of-fiction-no-195-kenzaburo-oe> (last accessed 29 June 2018).

Foucault, Michel, *Abnormal: Lectures at the Collège De France* (New York: Picador, 2003).

Hall, Alice, *Disability and Modern Fiction: Faulkner, Morrison, Coetzee and the Nobel Prize for Literature* (Basingstoke: Palgrave Macmillan, 2011).

Kleege, Georgina, 'Blindness and Visual Culture: An Eyewitness Account', in Lennard J. Davis (ed.), *The Disability Studies Reader*, 4th edn (New York: Routledge, 2013), pp. 447–55.

Kuusisto, Stephen, *Planet of the Blind* (New York: Dial Press, 1998).

— *Eavesdropping: A Life by Ear* (New York: W. W. Norton, 2006).

Lawrence, D. H., 'The Prussian Officer', in John Worthern (ed.), *The Prussian Officer and Other Stories* (London: Penguin, 1983), pp. 1–21.

— 'The Blind Man', in Bruce Steele (ed.), *England, My England and Other Stories* (Cambridge: Cambridge University Press, 1990), pp. 46–63.

Marcus, Laura, *Auto/Biographical Discourses: Theory, Criticism, Practice* (Manchester: Manchester University Press, 1994).

Mitchell, David T. and Sharon L. Snyder, *Narrative Prosthesis: Disability and the Dependencies of Discourse* (Ann Arbor: University of Michigan Press, 2001).

Mukhopadhyay, Tito Rajarshi, *How Can I Talk if My Lips Don't Move?: Inside My Autistic Mind* (New York: Arcade Publishing, 2008).

Munro, Alice, 'Mrs Cross and Mrs Kidd', in *The Moons of Jupiter* (London: Vintage, 2007), pp. 134–59.

Nussbaum, Martha Craven, *Frontiers of Justice: Disability, Nationality, Species Membership* (Cambridge, MA: The Belknap Press and Harvard University Press, 2006).

O'Connor, Flannery, 'Good Country People', in Robert Giroux (ed.), *The Complete Stories* (New York: Farrar, Straus and Giroux, 1971), pp. 280–300.

O'Connor, Frank, *The Lonely Voice: A Study of the Short Story* (New York: Melville House, [1963] 2011).

Ōe, Kenzaburō, 'Aghwee the Sky Monster', in *Teach Us to Outgrow Our Madness: Four Short Novels*, trans. John Nathan (New York: Grove Press, 1977), pp. 223–61.

— *Hiroshima Notes*, trans. David L. Swain and Toshi Yonezawa (New York: Grove Press, 1996).

— *Rouse up O Young Men of the New Age!*, trans. John Nathan (New York: Grove Press, 2002).

Osteen, Mark, 'Autism and Representation: A Comprehensive Introduction', in Mark Osteen (ed.), *Autism and Representation* (New York: Routledge, 2008), pp. 1–47.

Quayson, Ato, *Aesthetic Nervousness: Disability and the Crisis of Representation* (New York: Columbia University Press, 2007).

Senier, Siobhan, 'Rehabilitation Reservations: Native Narrations of Disability and Community', *Disability Studies Quarterly*, 32.4 (2012).
Serlin, David, *Replaceable You: Engineering the Body in Postwar America* (Chicago: University of Chicago Press, 2004).
Siebers, Tobin, *Disability Theory* (Ann Arbor: University of Michigan Press, 2008).
Stiker, Henri-Jacques, *A History of Disability* (Ann Arbor: University of Michigan Press, 1999).
Woolf, Virginia, 'On Being Ill', in Hermione Lee (ed.), *On Being Ill* (Ashfield: Consortium, 2002).

INDEX OF SHORT STORY TITLES

Titles of all other works are included in the main index.

'A & P' (Updike), 257
'Adolescence' (Prescott), 332
'The Adventure of the Speckled Band' (Conan Doyle), 177
'Adventures of a Strolling Player' (Goldsmith), 116
'Afterward' (Wharton), 178
'Again the Antilles' (Rhys), 82
'Aghwee the Sky Monster' (Ōe), 354–5
'Ahead of the Pack' (Simpson), 278
'Alice' (Barthelme), 198
'The Ambitious Guest' (Hawthorne), 30
'The Angel Esmeralda' (DeLillo), 249–50
'The Apple Tree' (du Maurier), 303–4
'Araby' (Joyce), 98
'Art Work' (Byatt), 93, 101–2
'Arthur Snatchfold' (Forster), 332
'At the Bay' (Mansfield), 49, 68
'August Heat' (Harvey), 178

'Ballad for the New World' (Scott), 233–5
'The Balloon' (Bartheleme), 250
'Bartleby, the Scrivener' (Melville), 10, 245, 249

'Bears Discover Fire' (Bisson), 282
'The Beast in the Jungle' (James), 48
'The Beautiful House' (Wells), 331
'Before Dark' (Proust), 337
'The Birth-Mark' (Hawthorne), 181
'The Blind Man' (Lawrence), 351–2
'Bliss' (Mansfield), 50, 248, 305
'The Bloody Chamber' (Carter), 235, 306–8
'The Body Snatcher' (Stevenson), 180
'Boris Orloff' (Bradford), 332
'Branch Line to Benceston' (Caldecott), 179
'The Brazilian Cat' (Conan Doyle), 177
'Breeze Anstey' (Bates), 331
'The Bridegroom's Body' (Boyle), 334
'The Brown Hand' (Conan Doyle), 181
'Buffalo Gals, Won't You Come Out Tonight' (Le Guin), 283–4
'The Buried Alive' (Galt), 180
'By the Waters of Babylon' (Benet), 281

'The Calorie Man' (Bacigalupi), 284–5
'Calypsonian' (Selvon), 83
'Carmilla' (Le Fanu), 331

'The Case of Lady Sannox'
    (Conan Doyle), 181
'A Casual Incident' (Farrell), 333
'The Cat and the King' (Lee), 331
'Cathedral' (Carver), 351–3
'The Chimes' (Dickens), 178
'A Christmas Carol' (Dickens), 178
'A Christmas Memory' (Capote), 335
'A Circle Like Some Circles' (Eggers),
    150–1
'Clouds and Eclipses' (Vidal), 334
'Un Coeur Simple' (Flaubert), 94
'Cold' (Byatt), 204–5
'Collision Orbit' (Williamson), 282
'The Copper Bowl' (Eliot), 183
'The Country Husband' (Cheever),
    258, 262
'The Courter' (Rushdie), 317–18, 321
'The Cricket Match' (Selvon), 232–4
'The Crooked Man' (Beaumont), 337
'A Cross Line' (Egerton), 299
'Cross-town' (Hardwick), 249
'The Crowd' (Bradbury), 166–7, 169
'The Cure' (Cheever), 260–1
'A Curtain of Green' (Welty), 273

'Dante and the Lobster' (Beckett), 98–9
'The Daughter of King Under-Wave'
    (Gregory), 116
'The Daughters of the Late Colonel'
    (Mansfield), 251, 301–2
'Deacon Brodie' (Stevenson), 180
'The Dead' (Joyce), 50, 96–7, 98,
    247–8
'Death in the Royal Family' (Fugaté), 329
'The Delicate Fire' (Mitchison), 334
'The Demon Lover' (Bowen), 219
'A Diamond Guitar' (Capote), 335
'Diary of an Interesting Year' (Simpson),
    278–9
'Doggy Bag' (Sukenick), 194–5
'Dolores' (Ellis), 331
'The Dream' (Porter), 335

'A Dream of Armageddon' (Wells), 280
'The Dreaming Child' (Dinesen),
    168, 170
'The Drover's Wife' (Lawson), 82

'East, West' (Rushdie), 317–18
'The Education of Bunny Smith'
    ('Sapper'), 217–18
'Elephant' (Carver), 277
'The Empire of the Ants' (Wells),
    280–1
'The Encantadas, or Enchanted Isles'
    (Melville), 244–5
'The End of Childhood' (Richardson),
    334
'The Enormous Radio' (Cheever), 258
'An Episode of War' (Crane), 215–16
'Eveline' (Joyce), 98
'An Evening at the Bay' (Isherwood), 336
'Evening Primrose' (Collier), 166–7
'Evensong and Morwe Song'
    (Scott-Moncrieff), 332
'The Evolution of Evangeline'
    (Daskam), 331

'The Facts in the Case of M. Valdemar'
    (Poe), 182
'The Fall of the House of Usher' (Poe),
    161, 180
'The Fire' (Hull), 331
'Fires' (Carver), 60
'The Flash of Fireflies' (Gordimer), 63
'Flight' (Updike), 257
'A Fortnight in France' ('Sapper'), 217
'A Four Hundred-Year-Old Woman'
    (Mukherjee), 64
'The Frenchman Six Feet Three'
    (Prescott), 332
'Friends from Philadelphia'
    (Updike), 257
'From Below, as a Neighbor'
    (Davis), 250–1
'Fugue' (O'Faoláin), 218

'Game' (Barthelme), 198
'The Garden' (Richardson), 49
'The Garden Party' (Mansfield), 50, 301
'The Geranium' (O'Connor), 249
'Girl' (Kincaid), 153–5
'The Glass Bottle Trick' (Hopkinson), 235–6
'The Good Anna' (Stein), 94–6
'Good Country People' (O'Connor), 349–50
'Goodbye My Brother' (Cheever), 258
'The Great Good Place' (James), 332

'Hallowe'en' (Beer), 334
'The Haunted Man' (Dickens), 178
'The Hellhole' (Proulx), 275
'Herbert West – Reanimator' (Lovecraft), 181
'Hogfoot Right and Bird-Hands' (Kilworth), 282
'Home Sweet Home' (Wicomb), 322–3
'Homework' (Simpson), 278–9
'The Hoofed Thing' (Howard), 161
'The Housebreaker of Shady Hill' (Cheever), 258, 261
'How to Write a Blackwood's Article' (Poe), 180

'Il Conde' (Conrad), 48
'I'm the Boy' (Barthelme), 197
'In a Far Country' (London), 332
'In a Station of the Metro' (Pound), 78
'In My Language' (Baggs), 347
'In Praise of Billy B.' (Rolfe), 332
'In Praise of Vespasian' (Chester), 335
'In the Driver's Seat' (Simpson), 279
'An Indiscreet Journey' (Mansfield), 248
'Indissoluble Matrimony' (West), 47
'Inside Information' (Barker), 308
'The Iron Shroud' (Mudford), 180

'Jacqueline Ess: Her Will and Testament' (Barker), 183
'Job History' (Proulx), 275
'The Jungle' (Bowen), 331
'The Jungle' (Mansfield), 331

'Karen: A Novel' (Os-Anders), 331
'Kew Gardens' (Woolf), 49
'The Knife of the Times' (Williams), 333

'The Lass of the Silver Sword' (Dubois), 331
'The Leather Funnel' (Conan Doyle), 182
'Leaves' (Updike), 257
'The Leg' (Faulkner), 349–50
'The Legend of Sleepy Hollow' (Irving), 33
'Lessness' (Beckett), 206
'Let Them Call It Jazz' (Rhys), 214–15
The Light on the Tower' (Gissing), 246
'A Little Girl Tells a Story to a Lady' (Barnes), 331
'A Lonely Coast' (Proulx), 274
'The Long Arm' (Freeman), 331
'The Long Hall on the Top Floor' (Kiernan), 164–5
'The Lost Decade' (Fitzgerald), 248
'The Lottery' (Jackson), 169, 176
'The Lottery in Babylon' (Borges), 167–8
'The Luck of Roaring Camp' (Harte), 331
'Lullaby' (Silko), 273

'The Machine Stops' (Forster), 280–1, 283
'The Magic Poker' (Coover), 206
'The Malice of Inanimate Objects' (James), 179
'Malone Dies' (Beckett), 199–200
'Man Crawling Out of Trees' (Proulx), 275

'The Man in the Bell' (Maginn), 180, 182
'The Man of the Crowd' (Poe), 48, 163–5, 242–3, 245, 247
'Marjorie Daw' (Aldrich), 332
'The Mark of the Beast' (Kipling), 176
'The Mark on the Wall' (Woolf), 48
'Martha's Lady' (Jewett), 331
'Mary Postgate' (Kipling), 217–18
'Me and Miss Mandible' (Barthelme), 198
'A Medical Document' (Conan Doyle), 181–2
'Melanctha' (Stein), 95
'The Midnight Meat Train' (Barker), 165–6, 179
'Miss Brill' (Mansfield), 50
'Miss Furr and Miss Skeene' (Stein), 331
'Miss Ogilvy Finds Herself' (Hall), 331
'The Mocking-Bird' (Bierce), 332
'Moments of Being: Slater's Pins Have No Points' (Woolf), 331
'The Monkey's Paw' (Jacobs), 176–7
'Moonlit Landscape with a Bridge' (Smith), 285
'Morphia' ('Sapper'), 218
'The Moslem Wife' (Gallant), 251
'A Mother's Tale' (Agee), 284
'Mrs Bathurst' (Kipling), 51, 217
'Mrs Cross and Mrs Kidd' (Munro), 355–6
'Mrs Sen's' (Lahiri), 319
'The Murders in the Rue Morgue' (Poe), 243
'My Childhood Friend' (Davis), 152
'My Kinsman, Major Molineux' (Hawthorne), 10
'My Old Man' (Hemingway), 121n
'My Pal Rembrandt' (Porter), 335
'Mysterious Kôr' (Bowen), 51
'A Mystery of Heroism' (Crane), 216
'The Mystery of Marie Rogêt' (Poe), 243–4

'Nadia Devereux' (Eichrodt), 334
'Newton's Sleep' (Le Guin), 282–3
'A Night' (Alcott), 214
'A Night in the Catacombs' (Sandford), 180

'O Youth and Beauty' (Cheever), 258, 262–3
'The Obelisk' (Forster), 332
'An Occurrence at Owl Creek Bridge' (Bierce), 213
'Oh, Whistle, and I'll Come to You, My Lad' (James), 186
'On Being Ill' (Woolf), 346–7, 358
'One of the Missing' (Bierce), 214
'Orestes' (Davies), 334
'Our Aromatic Uncle' (Bunner), 332
'Out in the Sun' (Prime-Stevenson), 331
'The Overcoat' (Gogol), 57–8

'The Painter of Modern Life' (Baudelaire), 48, 242
'The Pangs of Love' (Gardam), 306
'The Paradise of Bachelors and the Tartarus of Maids' (Melville), 245
'The Pash' (Burke), 331
'Passing Stranger' (Crane), 333
'People in Hell Just Want a Drink of Water' (Proulx), 274–5
'The People of Sand and Slag' (Bacigalupi), 284
'The Phantom Coach' (Edwards), 185
'Pictures' (Mansfield), 248
'Pioneers, Oh, Pioneers' (Rhys), 230
'The Pit and the Pendulum' (Poe), 182
'Plumbing' (Updike), 264
'Point of View' (Berlin), 297
'Pop Squad' (Bacigalupi), 284–5
'The Portrait of Mr W. H.' (Wilde), 332
'A Predicament' (Poe), 182
'Prelude' (Mansfield), 49
'The Priest and the Acolyte' (Bloxam), 332

'The Prussian Officer' (Lawrence), 217, 346
'The Purloined Letter' (Poe), 243
'Puss-in-Boots' (Carter), 307

'The Queen and I' (McInerney), 249

'A Radically Condensed History of Postindustrial Life' (Wallace), 151
'Raising the Tone' (Wicomb), 323
'Rappaccini's Daughter' (Hawthorne), 181
'The Reservoir' (Frame), 169
'The Retirement of Signor Lambert' (Conan Doyle), 181
'The Rich Boy' (Fitzgerald), 248
'The Room in the Tower' (Benson), 178

'Santal' (Firbank), 332
'Sappho Remembered' (Dahr/Fugaté), 329
'Say to Me Ronald!' (Porter), 335
'The Sculptor's Funeral' (Cather), 332
'Separating' (Updike), 264
'September Dawn' (O'Connor), 218
'The Sergeant's Private Madhouse' (Crane), 215
'Sexy' (Lahiri), 319
'Shiloh' (Mason), 265–6
'The Signal-Man' (Dickens), 178–9
'The Sisters' (Joyce), 98, 247
'The Smeraldina's Billet Doux' (Beckett), 98
'A Son of the Gods: A Study in the Present Tense' (Bierce), 214
'A Sound of Crying' (Cornwell), 334
'A South-Sea Idyl' (Stoddard), 331
'Speck's Idea' (Gallant), 251
'The Speech of Polly Baker' (Franklin), 15–18
'The Sphinx Without a Secret' (Wilde), 116
'The Squaw' (Stoker), 182–3

'The Star' (Wells), 280
'"A Story" by John V. Marsch' (Wolfe), 282
'Story of Julie Kane' (O'Higgins), 334
'The Story of the Eldest Princess' (Byatt), 204
'Story of Two Highlanders' (Hogg), 15, 18–20
'The Stranger' (Mansfield), 50
'The Striding Place' (Atherton), 331
'The String Quartet' (Woolf), 248
'A Study in Opal' (Firbank), 332
'A Study in Temperament' (Firbank), 332
'The Suffering Channel' (Wallace), 250
'Supperburger' (Strong), 335
'The Surgeon Talks' (Conan Doyle), 181
'The Swimmer' (Cheever), 257–8, 261–3

'Take It or Leave It' (Isherwood), 336
'The Tale' (Conrad), 48
'The Terrible Screaming' (Frame), 168
'The Terror of Blue John Gap' (Conan Doyle), 177
'The Third and Final Continent' (Lahiri), 319, 320
'The Third Generation' (Conan Doyle), 181
'Tipping Point' (Simpson), 278–9
'To Room Nineteen' (Lessing), 303
'The Trains' (Aickman), 179
'The Tree-men of M'Bwa' (Wandrei), 164
'The Trouble of Marcie Flint' (Cheever), 258
'True Short Story' (Smith), 67–8
'The True Story of a Vampire' (Stenbock), 332
'Two Gallants' (Joyce), 247
'Two Gentlemen of Kentucky' (Allen), 332

'Unaccustomed Earth' (Lahiri), 320
'Uncle Jim and Uncle Billy' (Harte), 331
'Usher II' (Bradbury), 161

'Vaster than Empires and More Slow' (Le Guin), 283
'Vienne' (Rhys), 82
'A View of the Woods' (O'Connor), 273
'A Vision of the World' (Cheever), 258–9, 266–7
'A Visit to Priapus' (Prescott), 332

'Waiting for Aunty to Cough' (Selvon), 316
'The Waiting Room' (Aickman), 179
'Wandering Souls' (Ninh), 220
'Wedlock' (Egerton), 299
'Weeds' (DeMarinis), 281
'Welcome to the Monkey House' (Vonnegut), 281

'We're Not Jews' (Kureishi), 251
'What Kind of Furniture Would Jesus Pick?' (Proulx), 275
'Where Are You Going? Where Have You Been?' (Oates), 264–5, 266
'The White Old Maid' (Hawthorne), 33
'Why Don't You Dance?' (Carver), 266
'Why I Write Short Stories' (Cheever), 256
'A Wife's Story' (Mukherjee), 251
'The Wind Blows' (Mansfield), 49
'The Woman at the Store' (Mansfield), 82, 302

'Yellow' (Beckett), 98, 100
'Yellow Card Man' (Bacigalupi), 284
'The Yellow Wallpaper' (Gilman), 298
'Young Goodman Brown' (Hawthorne), 10

General Index

9/11 attacks, 250

Achebe, Chinua, 85, 320
Adams, Henry, 212
Adams, Nick, 80
Adichie, Chimamanda Ngozi, 321–2
The Adventures of Sherlock Holmes (Conan Doyle), 246
Afrekete, 339
Africa, 85, 113, 320–1
Agee, James, 284
Aickman, Robert, 175, 179
Alcott, Louisa May, 214–15
Aldrich, Thomas Bailey, 331
All Hail the New Puritans (Blincoe and Thorne), 117
All the Year Round, 177–8
Allegra, Donna, 339
Allen, James Lane, 332
Altman, Dennis, 330
Alvare, Alan, 328
Amazon, 126, 128, 132–4
The American Short Story (Smith), 27–8
American writing, 10, 57, 61–2, 113, 227
Americentrism, 24, 26–7, 35n
Anand, Mulk Raj, 81
Anderson, Hans Christian, 306
Anderson, Margaret, 79

Anderson, Patrick, 333
Anderson, Sherwood, 80, 100, 274, 333
anthologies, 63–4, 108–19, 294
 and canon formation, 115–17
 cycles and sequences, 93–104
 gay and lesbian, 335–6, 338
 sales and profitability, 108, 111
 thematic, 108, 110
Anthropocene, 273
anthropocentrism, 201, 280
Anticipations (Wells), 179
Antietam, Battle of, 212–13
Anti-Story: An Anthology of Experimental Fiction (Stevick), 61–2, 64, 117
Aphrodisiac (Canning), 337
apocalyptic stories, 272, 279–81
The Apparitional Lesbian (Castle), 330
Apple, 126
architecture, 242
Ardis, Ann, 80
Arena Three, 328, 333
Armstrong, Paul, 44
Arnold, Matthew, 9
Arobateau, Red Jordan, 335
Around the World in Eighty Days (Verne), 136
Artful (Smith), 68

Ashley, Michael, 111
Ashton, Susanna, 29
Asimov, Isaac, 282
The Assassination of Margaret Thatcher (Mantell), 133
Atherton, Gertrude, 331
Atwood, Margaret, 272, 305, 308
audiobooks, 347
Austen, Jane, 294
Austen, Roger, 336
Australian writing, 113
autism, 347, 355
avant-garde, 62, 94, 100
Awadalla, Maggie, 228–9

Bach, J. S., 102
A Bachelor's Children (Porter), 335
Bacigalupi, Paulo, 284–5
Bad Dirt (Proulx), 275–6
Baggs, Amanda, 347
Bahr, Hermann, 45
Bailey, James, 1, 297
Baldeshwiler, Eileen, 43
Baldwin (Lee), 45
Baldwin, Dean, 111, 115
Balfour, A. J., 184
Balzac, Honoré de, 45, 201, 242
Bardolph, Jacqueline, 228
Barker, Clive, 165–7, 175, 179, 183–4, 187, 337
Barker, Nicola, 308
Barnaby Rudge (Dickens), 177
Barnes, Djuna, 331
Barnes, Elizabeth, 16
Barnett, Allan, 338
Baron, Scarlett, 97
Barratt, Nick, 177
Barth, John, 100, 117
Barthelme, Donald, 62, 117, 194, 197, 249
Barthes, Roland, 42, 153
Bates, H. E., 3, 331
Baudelaire, Charles, 48–9, 242–3, 247

Baumbach, Jonathan, 195
Bayou Folk (Chopin), 12
Beattie, Ann, 265–6
Beaumont, Charles, 337
Beckett, Samuel, 98–100, 116, 199–201, 206
Beer, Thomas, 334
'Beginnings: "The Origins and Art of the Short Story"' (Oates), 63–4
Behold Goliath (Chester), 335
Beier, Ulli, 85
Bell, Alice, 135
Bellin, Joshua David, 281
Below the Belt (Andros/Steward), 336
Benet, Stephen Vincent, 281
Benítez-Rojo, Antonio, 228–9, 235–6
Benjamin, Walter, 163, 243
Bennet, Jane, 277
Benson, E. F., 178
Bentley, Nick, 84
Bergman, David, 338
Bergson, Henri, 42, 184
Berlant, Lauren, 265
Berlin, Lucia, 297
Berry, Wendell, 273
Berry, Wes, 275
Bérubé, Michael, 348
Besant, Walter, 46
Between Men (Canning), 337
Beuka, Robert, 259
Beyond a Boundary (James), 232
Bhaskar, Michael, 133
Bierce, Ambrose, 175, 212–16, 332
Binckes, Faith, 81
Birbalsingh, Frank, 232, 316
Bisson, Terry, 282
Black and Gay in the UK, 339
The Black and White of It (Shockley), 335
Black Britishness, 114–15, 213, 339
Black Lesbian in White America (Cornwell), 334
Blackwomon, Julie, 339

Blackwoods Edinburgh Magazine, 110, 177, 180
Blaise, Clark, 67
Blake, William, 203, 283
Blincoe, Nicolas, 117
Bloom, Dan, 278, 280
Bloomsbury Group, 41
Bloxam, John Francis, 332
Bluebeard character, 235–6
Bluebeard's Egg (Atwood), 305
Boddy, Kasia, 110, 127
body/bodies, 40, 180–3, 347, 354–5
bodysnatching, 180–1
Boehmer, Elleke, 81
Bonheim, Helmut, 149
The Books of Blood (Barker), 183
Borges, Jorge Luis, 62, 167–8
boundaries, 260–1, 264–5
Bowen, Elizabeth, 3, 51, 57, 66–7, 75–6, 113, 116, 118, 218–19, 331
Bowler, Rebecca, 296
Bowles, Jane, 331
Bowles, Paul, 337
Boyd, William, 66–7
Boyle, Kay, 334
Boyle, T. C., 272
Bradbury, Ray, 161, 163, 166–7, 169, 282
Bradford, Edwin Emanuel, 332
Brah, Avtar, 318
Bram, Christopher, 335
Brathwaite, Kamau, 68, 236
Brave and Cruel (Welch), 332
Bray, Alan, 330
Breakfast at Tiffany's (Capote), 335
Brettell, Richard, 44
brevity, 147–55
Brief Interviews With Hideous Men (Wallace), 151
Brinkley, Sidney, 339
Brinkmeyer, Robert H., Jr, 267
British Women Short Story Writers: The New Woman to Now, 1, 67

British writing, 65–6, 113, 117–18
Brookes, Les, 337
Brosch, Renate, 150
Broughton, Rhoda, 175, 185
Browning, Robert, 58
Buckley, Chloe, 161
Buell, Lawrence, 276
Buffalo Gals and Other Animal Presences (Le Guin), 283
Bulson, Eric, 85
Bunner, Henry Cuyler, 332
Bunzl, Matti, 10
Burke, Thomas, 331
Burke and Hare, 180–1
The Burned Children of America, 117
Burning Cactus (Spender), 336
Burroughs, William, 335
Butler, Robert Olen, 149
Byatt, A. S., 93–4, 100–2, 204–5

Caillois, Roger, 205
Cain, Tom, 170–1
Caldecott, Andrew, 179
Callenbach, Ernest, 282
Calvino, Italo, 242
calypso, 230, 233–4
Camp Ink, 331
Canby, H. S., 25, 31–2
Cane (Toomer), 249
cannibalism, 165, 167, 177
Canning, Richard, 337
canon formation, 115–17
Can't and Won't (Davis), 149, 152
Canterbury Tales (Chaucer), 193
Capote, Truman, 335
Carbado, Devon W., 339
Caribbean writing, 65, 83–4, 100, 214–15, 227–36
Carleton, William, 116
Caron, James E., 18
Carpenter, Edward, 333
Carson, Rachel, 281
Carter, Angela, 235, 306–7

Carver, Raymond, 50, 60–1, 65, 98, 265–6, 277, 351–3
Castle, Terry, 330, 332, 334
Cather, Willa, 274, 332
The Cats of Venice (Porter), 335
cemeteries, 178
Cézanne, Paul, 44, 95–6
The Challenge of Bewilderment (Armstrong), 44
Chan, Winnie, 77
Chandra, Vikram, 251
Chantler, Ashley, 147
Chapman, Diana, 328
Charters, Ann, 95, 116–17
Chatman, Seymour, 42
Chatterjee, Antara, 320
Chaucer, Geoffrey, 193
Cheap Repository Tracts (More), 12
Cheever, John, 256, 257–8, 260–5, 267
Chekhov, Anton, 41, 60–1, 75, 100, 118, 257
Chester, Alfred, 335
Chesterton, G. K., 45–6, 276
Chickamauga, Battle of, 212–13
Children Is All (Purdy), 334
Childs, Lee, 136
Chopin, Kate, 2, 12, 51
Christianity, 115, 184
Christmas, 178, 186
Chronicles of the Canongate (Scott), 13
Churchill, Suzanne, 77
The Circle, 329, 333
cities, 242–53
Civil Rights era, 249, 333
Civil War (American), 212–15
Clark, Timothy, 2, 24, 51, 272, 276–8
Clarke, Arthur C., 282
class, 114, 184, 258–60, 347
Clifford, James, 12
Cli-Fi: Canadian Tales of Climate Change, 279
climate change, 276–80

Close Range: Wyoming Stories (Proulx), 274
Close Up, 78
closure theories, 76–7
The Club-Book (Picken), 109
Cobbe, Frances Power, 181
Cocks, H. G., 330
Coelsh-Foisner, Sabine, 297
cognitive impairment, 355–6
Cohen, Robin, 214, 316
Cold War, 260, 333, 335
Colebrook, Claire, 278
Collier, John, 166–7
Collins, Michael, 24
Collymore, Frank, 83
colonialism, 82–6, 176–7, 230, 251–2
Color of Darkness (Purdy), 334
The Columbia Companion to the Twentieth Century American Short Story, 273, 281
communication, 148
Compton Burnett, Ivy, 331
Comstock Act, 328–9
Comus (Milton), 278
Conan Doyle, Arthur, 175–7, 181–2, 245
conceptual deviation, 201
Conrad, Joseph, 40, 42, 44, 47, 180
consumerism, 279
Contento, William D., 111
Cook, Matt, 330
Cook, Oscar, 175, 177
Cooper, Bernard, 338
Cooper, Dennis, 337
Coover, Robert, 62, 117, 206
Coppard, A. E., 3, 118
copyright, 13, 132
Corey, Mary F., 256, 260
Cornwell, Anita, 334
Correia, Tony, 328
Cortazar, Julio, 62
Counselman, Mary Elizabeth, 162

counterpoint, 354–5
Couplings (Hall), 338
Cox, Christopher, 338
Crane, Clarkson, 333
Crane, Milton, 112
Crane, Stephen, 40–2, 48, 215–16, 246
CreateSpace, 133, 134
Creative Writing programmes, 59, 62, 64–5, 137
Crews, Frederick, 10
cricket, 232–3
Crowe, Catherine, 184
Cruelty to Animals Act (1876), 180–1
Cruikshank, Margaret, 335, 338
Cuba, 215
Cubism, 40, 96
Cuddy-Keane, Melba, 75
cultural identity, 213–14
Cultural Revolution (Wong), 339
cultural values, 64–5
Cunningham, Alan, 113
Curzon, Daniel, 336
cycles and sequences, 93–104, 322
Czarnecki, Kristin, 214

Dahl, Roald, 163
Danticat, Edwidge, 100
Daskam, Josephine Dodge, 331
Daudet, Alphonse, 45
Davies, Owen, 185
Davies, Rhys, 334
Davis, Lennard, 348, 357
Davis, Lydia, 149, 152–3, 250
Davis, Rocío, 322
Dawson, Frederick T., 33
DDT, 284
death and burial, 178
Debord, Guy, 167, 201
The Decline of the West (Spengler), 246–7
Defoe, Daniel, 113
Degas, Edgar, 44

Deleuze, Gilles, 85, 229
DeLillo, Don, 249–50
DeLynn, Jane, 337
DeMarinis, Rick, 281
Denisoff, Dennis, 328
Depression era, 249
Derricks (Barr/Fugaté), 334
Derrida, Jacques, 353
desire, 307–8
detective fiction, 181, 243, 295
The Development of the American Short Story (Pattee), 31, 33
dialogism, 80–1
diaspora, 313–24
Díaz, Junot, 65, 98, 100
Dickens, Charles, 46, 177–9, 184
Dickerson, Vanessa, 184–5
Didion, Joan, 266
Different (Wright), 336
Digital Fiction Network, 125
digital media, 125–37, 347, 358
Dinesen, Isak, 168–9, 334
disability, 346–58
  as a fluid category, 356–7
  and prosthetics, 349–50
  used as metaphorical shortcut, 348
discrimination, 315–16
Dispatches (Herr), 219
divorce, 264
Dixon, Melvin, 339
The Djinn in the Nightingale's Eye (Byatt), 204
Dombey and Son (Dickens), 179
Dominica, 230
Donoghue, Emma, 114
Don't Call Me By the Right Name (Purdy), 334
The Dover Anthology of Cat Stories, 111
Down syndrome, 355
Dowson, Ernest, 77
Doyle, Laura, 13
Dracula (Stoker), 185

Dream of Fair to Middling Women (Beckett), 98
Drifters (Wakefield), 338
du Maurier, Daphne, 303–4, 334
Dublin, 96–7, 242, 247–8, 274
Dubliners (Joyce), 50, 96–7, 99, 247–8
Dubois, Margaret Constance, 331
Duncan, Ian, 24
Dune (Herbert), 282
Dunn, Maggie, 94
Dunne, Mary Chavelita, 299
The Dunwich Horror (Lovecraft), 161
Dyer, Mary, 17
dystopian stories, 279–81

Eagleton, Mary, 1, 296–7
East End of London, 246
Eco, Umberto, 150
ecocriticism, 278
Ecotopia (Callenbach), 282
Edinburgh University, 181
Education Act (1870), 46
Edwards, Amelia B., 175, 185
Eerie, 164
Egan, Jennifer, 68
Egerton, George, 77, 299
Eggers, Dave, 112, 150–1
Eichrodt, John, 334
Einhaus, Ann-Marie, 3
Einstein, Albert, 42
election, 62–3
Elementals (Byatt), 204
The Elements of the Short Story (Hale and Dawson), 31, 33
Eliot, George, 46, 180
Eliot, George Fielding, 183
Eliot, T. S., 41, 78, 194
Ellis, Edith, 331
The Encyclopedia of Romance, 109
The End of Nature (McKibben), 272–3
Engles, Friedrich, 242
The English Novel 1830–1836 (Garside), 109

Enlightenment, 10, 18
Enon Chapel scandal, 178
Enright, Anne, 65, 116
Ensslin, Astrid, 135
environment, 272–86
e-readers, 125, 127–9, 132
Eros: An Anthology of Friendship, 333–4, 336
erotica, 338
Erskine, Albert, 112
The Eternal Moment (Forster), 332
ethnography, 12
Ette, Ottmar, 155
eugenics, 299
evolutionary development, 30
experimental writing, 61–2, 193–206
Eyde, Edith, 328

Faber and Faber, 75, 85, 118, 218, 337
Facebook, 126
Faderman, Lillian, 331, 335
fairy stories, 109, 304–8
fan fiction, 127, 129
fantasy literature, 129
Farrell, James T., 333
Farwell, Marilyn R., 330
Faulkner, William, 100, 274, 347, 349–50
Federman, Raymond, 195
Feinberg, David B., 338
Felski, Rita, 1, 150
The Feminine Mystique (Friedan), 183, 303
femininity, 293, 296
Ferguson, Suzanne, 42–3
Ferragus: Chief of the Devorants (Balzac), 242
Ferro, Robert, 337
Fiction and the Reading Public (Leavis), 179
Fielding, Henry, 66, 99
film, 211, 234
Firbank, Ronald, 332

First World War, 48, 80, 217, 330
Fisher, Jeremy, 331
Fisher, Mark, 160
Fitzgerald, F. Scott, 248
flash fiction, 111, 120n, 148
Flaubert, Gustave, 42–3, 45, 94, 97, 201
Fludernik, Monika, 102, 152, 200–1
Foley, Martha, 112
folk tales, 109
folklore, 9, 230
Ford, Ford Maddox, 40, 42, 44, 46–7, 78, 82
Ford, Richard, 57, 61–2, 113, 267
Forkel, Johann Nikolaus, 102
Form and Fable in American Fiction (Hoffman), 10
formalism, 10
Forster, E. M., 280–1, 283, 332, 337
Foster, Jeanette, 334
Foucault, Michel, 355
The Fox (Lawrence), 331
Fox, Andrew, 98
Fox 8: A Story (Saunders), 284
fracking, 272
fragmentation, 276
Frame, Janet, 168–9
Frankenstein (Shelley), 181
Franklin, Benjamin, 15–18, 20
Frayling, Christopher, 177
Freeman, Mary E. Wilkins, 185, 331
French literature, 45, 109
Freud, Sigmund, 218, 293
Friedan, Betty, 183, 260, 303
Friedrich, Casper David, 278
Frow, John, 153, 155, 293
Future Primitive: The New Ecotopias (Robinson), 282
Futurism, 40

Gaelic literature, 115–16
Gaia hypothesis, 283
Galápagos Islands, 244
Gallant, Mavis, 251
Galley Beggar Singles, 132
Galt, John, 113, 180
gamification, 135
Ganymede, 329
Garcha, Amanpal, 24
Gardam, Jane, 306
Gardens (Jackson), 336
Gardner, John, 60
Garnett, Edward, 47
Garrard, Greg, 278–9
Garside, Peter, 109
Gasiorek, Andrzej, 41, 46
Gaskell, Elizabeth, 185
Gauguin, Paul, 44
Gautier, Théophile, 46
gay literature, 114, 328, 329–33, 335; *see also* queer short stories
Gay Male Fiction Since Stonewall (Brookes), 337
Gay Pride, 336
gender, 1–2, 59, 114, 236, 259–60, 293–308, 347
'Gender and Genre' (Eagleton), 1, 296–7
genre, 46, 177, 293–308
Gerlach, John, 1, 44, 76–7, 150
German literature, 45, 109
Gertrude, 329
Ghosh, Amitav, 279–80
ghost stories, 178–9, 184–5, 219
Gifford, James, 331–2
gift books, 109–10
Gilbert, Sandra M., 304–5
Gilded Age, 248
Gilman, Charlotte Perkins, 2, 298, 300
Gilroy, Paul, 313–14
Gissing, George, 245–6
Glaskin, Gerald, 334
Gleeson, Sinéad, 111, 116
Glissant, Édouard, 228–30, 237
Glitterwolf, 329
global warming, 278

globalisation, 75–6
GM crops, 284
gods, 176–7
Gods and Fighting Men (Gregory), 116
Gogol, Nikolai, 57–8
Goldberg: Variations (Josipovici), 102–4
Golders Green Crematorium, 178
Goldsmith, Oliver, 116
Gomez, Jewelle, 339
Good, Graham, 149
The Good Soldier (Ford), 47
Goodbye, Wisconsin (Prescott), 332
Gordimer, Nadine, 63, 66, 67, 85, 320
Gordon, David, 129
Gordon, John R., 339
Gothic writing, 163, 177, 179, 182, 187, 212–13, 303
Gourgouris, Stathis, 155
Graff, Gerald, 25, 28, 34
Graves, Robert, 110
Greene, Graham, 334
Gregory, Lady, 116
Greimas, A. J., 42
Grimm Brothers, 9, 12, 304, 306
Grumley, Michael, 338
Guattari, Félix, 85, 229
Gubar, Susan, 304–5
Gutenberg, 127
Gutter Magazine 07, 329

Haas, Robert, 95
Habila, Helon, 320–1
haiku form, 153
Hale, Edward Everett, 25, 31
Hall, Radclyffe, 331
Hall, Richard Walter, 338
Hall, Sarah, 66–7
Hall, Stuart, 313–14, 324
Halpert, Lionel, 82
Hanson, Clare, 3, 43
Hard Candy (Williams), 334
Hardwick, Elizabeth, 249

Hardy, Thomas, 75, 100, 300
Harker, Jonathan, 185
Harland, Henry, 78
Harris, Craig G., 339
Harrison, M. John, 51
Harry Potter books, 148
Harte, Bret, 331
Hartley, L. P., 332
Harvey, W. F., 178
Hawthorne, Nathaniel, 9, 10, 13, 25, 29–31, 33, 40, 76, 227
  as a horror writer, 162, 175, 181
Hawthorne and the Modern Short Story (Rohrherger), 26
Head, Dominic, 2, 43, 76, 246, 301
Heberle, Mark, 219
Hector, 211
Heise, Ursula K., 283
Hejinian, Lyn, 206
Hemingway, Ernest, 67, 79–80, 100, 121n, 337
Henry, O., 246
Hensher, Philip, 57, 65–6, 113, 117
Her Head a Village (Silvera), 335
Herbert, Frank, 282
Herder, Johan Gottfried, 9
Here Be Dragons (Chester), 335
Heron, Carolivia, 339
Herr, Michael, 219
Hidden From History, 330
Highgate Cemetery, 178
Highsmith, Patricia, 334
Hiroshima bombing, 234, 354
Hiroshima Notes (Ōe), 354
Hislop, Victoria, 114, 308
History of New York (Irving), 18
History of the Voice (Brathwaite), 227, 236
Hoffman, Daniel, 10
Hogg, James, 12, 15, 18–20, 113
Holleran, Andrew, 337, 338
Hollinghurst, Alan, 332
Holmes, Sherlock (character), 245–6

Holocaust, 251
Homes, A. M., 117
homosexuality, 331, 336, 340n
Hopkinson, Nalo, 230, 235–6
Hoppenstand, Gary, 212
horror stories, 111, 175–87, 303, 338
The Hound of the Baskervilles (Conan Doyle), 177
Household Words, 112, 177
How It Ended (McInerney), 249
Howard, Robert E., 161
Howe, Irving, 150
Howells, W. D., 108
Hughes, Langston, 114–15, 249
Hull, Helen, 331
Humboldt, Wilhelm von, 9
Hume, David, 40
humour, 66, 318
Hunt, Theodore, 31
Hunter, Adrian, 46, 84, 126, 130, 246, 276, 301
Husserl, Edmund, 42, 44
Hutchinson, Anne, 17
hybridity, 324

iambic pentameter, 227
Ibáñez-Carrasco, Francisco, 338
Ibsen, Henrik, 32
identification, with characters, 58
identity, 213–15, 251
Igbo culture, 85
illustrations, 77, 82
I'm With the Bears: Stories from a Damaged Planet (Martin), 272–3, 278
'Imaginary Homelands' (Rushdie), 317
Imagism, 41, 48
immortality, 284
imperialism, 16, 18–20, 85, 217
Impression: Soleil Levant (Monet), 44
Impressionism, 40–51, 97
In Our Time (Hemingway), 79–80
In the Life (Beam), 339

In the Spice House (Woodrow), 339
Inanimate Alice (Pullinger), 135
incest, 177
India, 317–18
Indiana, Gary, 337
industrialisation, 184, 277
infertility, 284
In-Flight Entertainment (Simpson), 278–9
Ingram, Forrest L., 94
interconnectivity, 272
Internet, 126, 147–8
Interpreter of Maladies (Lahiri), 318–20
Introduction to American Literature (Matthews), 28
Iowa Writers' Workshop, 64
Ipswich (Massachusetts), 257
Irish War of Independence, 218
Irish writing, 9, 65, 111–16, 218
Irving, Washington, 9, 13, 18, 33, 273
ISBNs, 128, 132
Isherwood, Christopher, 336, 337
The Island of Doctor Moreau (Wells), 181
iTunes, 132
I've a Feeling We're Not in Kansas Anymore (Mordden), 338

Jackson, Graham, 336
Jackson, Neville, 334
Jackson, Shirley, 163, 167, 169, 175–6
Jacobs, W. W., 175–6
Jamaica, 230, 236
James, C. L. R., 232
James, Henry, 40–1, 44–6, 75, 77, 113, 184, 294, 332–3, 337
James, Louis, 214
James, M. R., 175, 178–9, 185–6
James, Simon, 78
James, William, 42, 94
Jameson, Fredric, 281
Japan, 353–4

Jarrett, Keith, 339
Jawbreakers, 111–12
Jayanth, Meg, 136
Jeffers, Robinson, 282
Jefferson, Thomas, 18
Jerdan, William, 113
'Jerusalem' (Blake), 203
Jewett, Sarah Orne, 331
Johnson, Charles, 149
Johns-Putra, Adeline, 279
Jolas, Eugene, 85
Joseph, Daniel Samaroo, 84
Joshi, S. T., 161, 163
Josipovici, Gabriel, 102–4, 194, 196–7
Joyce, James, 42, 49–51, 96–100, 218, 242, 246–8, 257, 274, 294
Jump, Harriet Devine, 114

Kaiserling, Count, 102
Kaplan, Amy, 246
Karlin, Wayne, 220
Katz, Steve, 195
Keating, Peter, 77
Kemp, Sandra, 49
Kenan, Randall, 339
Kennedy, A. L., 40, 66–7
Kennedy, Gerald L., 94
Kensal Green Cemetery, 178
Kerridge, Richard, 276
Khue, Le Minh, 220
Kiely, Benedict, 115–16
Kiernan, Caitlín R., 164–5, 170
Kilcup, Karen, 115
Killeen, Jarlath, 184
Killer Dyke, 329
Killick, Tim, 11, 24, 109–10
Kilworth, Garry, 282
Kincaid, Jamaica, 65, 100, 153–5
Kindle, 127, 132–4
King, Stephen, 175, 183
Kingsolver, Barbara, 275
Kinsey, Alfred, 334

Kipling, Rudyard, 51, 176, 217
Klass, Perri, 337
Klee, Paul, 102–3
Kleege, Georgina, 351
Kleinberg, Seymour, 337
Knox, Robert, 181
Koontz, Dean, 134
Kronegger, Elizabeth Maria, 41
Krueger, Kate, 82
Kuebrich, David, 245
Kureishi, Hanif, 251–2
Kuusisto, Stephen, 346–8, 353
Kyk-Over-Al, 83

La Spina, Greye, 162
The Ladder, 333
Ladies' Museum, 110
Lahiri, Jhumpa, 318–19
Lamming, George, 83
landscape fiction, 274–7
Lane, John, 77
language impairment, 356
Lantern Lecture (Mars-Jones), 338
Larsen, Nella, 95–6
Larventz, Don, 328–9
Latham, Sean, 97–8
lawns, 261
Lawrence, D. H., 57, 217, 294, 331, 333, 337, 346–7, 351–2
Lawson, Henry, 82
Le Fanu, Sheridan, 175, 245, 331
Le Gallienne, Richard, 245
Le Guin, Ursula K., 280–4
Leavis, F. R., 40–41
Leavis, Q. D., 179
Leavitt, David, 114, 329, 337
Lee, Hermione, 114, 118
Lee, Jeanette, 331
Lee, Vernon, 45, 77, 185
The Left Hand of Darkness (Le Guin), 283
Lehmann, John, 336
Lehr, Wilson, 333

leitmotifs, 257
Lerman, Eleanor, 337
Leroy, Louis, 44–5
Les Fleurs du Mal (Baudelaire), 244
lesbian literature, 114, 330–1, 334–6, 339
The Lesbians Home Journal, 333, 335
Lessing, Doris, 303
Let's Call the Whole Thing Off (Smith et al.), 110
Levenson, Michael, 46, 78
Levy, Andrew, 3, 25–6, 245
Lewis, Matthew, 182
Lewis, Wyndham, 47, 49, 78
life expectancy, 356
The Life to Come (Forster), 332
light, 275
Lincoln, Abraham, 212
linguistic choice, 41, 61–3
linguistic experimentation, 193–5, 202–4
Lish, Gordon, 60
Litnav, 135
'Little Man' (character type), 58
Loftin, Craig, 333
Lohafer, Susan, 1, 10, 24, 44, 76–7
London, 163, 177, 202, 203, 245–6, 248
London, Jack, 272, 332
London Magazine, 56, 315
The Lonely Londoners (Selvon), 83, 233, 316
The Lonely Voice (O'Connor), 9, 26, 57, 61–2, 65, 68, 214, 357
The Long Gaze Back (Gleeson), 116
Loosed upon the World: The Saga Anthology of Climate Fiction, 279
Lost in the Funhouse (Barth), 100
The Lost World (Conan Doyle), 177
Love, Glen A., 273, 281
Love, Loss and the Lives of Women, 114, 308

Love and Longing in Bombay (Chandra), 251
Love and the Waiting Game (Watmough), 338
Love in a Blue Time (Kureishi), 252
Lovecraft, H. P., 160–5, 170–1, 175, 181, 186
Lovelock, James, 283
Lover, Samuel, 113
Loveswept, 129
Lud Heat (Sinclair), 202
Lulu, 130
Lundén, Rolf, 94
lycanthropy, 176
lyric form, 257–8, 296

McBride, Dwight A., 339
McCracken, Ellen, 125
Macdonald, Dwight, 257
Macfarlane, Robert, 202
McGehee, Peter, 338
McGill, Meredith, 13
MacGuffin, 134, 136
McGurl, Mark, 59, 64, 130
The Machine in the Garden (Marx), 10
McInerney, Jay, 249
MacKay, Claude, 81
McKibben, Bill, 272–3, 276, 285
McKible, Adam, 77
McKinley, Catherine E., 339
McLeod, John, 83
McNamara, Robert, 220
McNeile, H. C., 217–18
Macpherson, Kenneth, 78
McSweeney's Quarterly, 112
The Madwoman in the Attic (Gilbert and Gubar), 304–5
magazines, 46, 56, 66, 83, 85, 298
  digital, 131, 137
  gay and lesbian, 328–9
  'little', 75–86, 126, 130
  in the nineteenth century, 77, 126, 177, 211–12, 245

Maginn, William, 175, 180
Maiden Voyage, 329
'mainstream', 43
Makinen, Merja, 307
Malthusian theory, 178
Mamet, David, 130
mangrove metaphor, 229
Mann, Susan Garland, 80
Mansfield, Katherine, 44, 48, 51, 66–8, 81–2, 113, 246–8, 251, 257, 294, 296, 300–2, 331
Mantel, Hilary, 133
March-Russell, Paul, 56, 77, 100, 108, 110–11, 228–9, 257
Marcus, Ben, 119
Marcus, Laura, 355
Markham, E. A., 65
Marquet, Albert, 82
marriage, 264, 297–300
Mars-Jones, Adam, 338
The Martians (Robinson), 282
Martin, Mark, 272
Martin's Act (1822), 180
Marvell, Andrew, 283
Marx, Leo, 10
Marxism, 75
masculinity, 82, 260
Mason, Bobbie Ann, 61, 265–6
Mason, Michael, 330
Matisse, Henri, 93, 101–2
The Matisse Stories (Byatt), 93
Matthews, Brander, 25–34, 46, 76, 234
Maturin, Charles, 182
Matz, Jesse, 40, 44–5
Maupassant, Guy de, 32, 46, 75, 118
Maupin, Armistead, 337
Maurice (Forster), 332
maximalism, 42
May, Charles E., 1, 10, 11, 24, 26, 150, 257
Meaker, Marijane, 334
meat production, 284
medical ethics, 181

medical fiction, 180–2
Melmoth the Wanderer (Maturin), 182
Melville, Herman, 9, 10, 244–5, 249, 333
memoirs, 346
Memoirs of the Blind (Derrida), 353
memory, 353
Mercier, Vivian, 115–16
Merrick, Gordon, 335
metaphor, 42
metonymy, 42
Mew, Charlotte, 77
microfiction, 148–9
middlebrow, 257
The Middleman (Mukherjee), 251
Miéville, China, 161
Mighty Real, 329
migration, 315–20
Miller, Alan V., 112, 119, 329, 333
Miller, Henry, 335
Miller, Jane Eldridge, 298
Miller, Mary Britton, 333
Millet, Lydia, 272
Milton, John, 278
mimesis, 46
minimalism, 42, 61, 64, 265
Mitchell, David T., 348
Mitchell, Mark, 114, 329
Mitchison, Naomi, 333, 334
Mitford, Mary Russell, 13
Mitzel, John, 336
'mnemonic art', 48
Mobius the Stripper (Josipovici), 196–7
Modern Language Association of America (MLA), 25–7
modernism, 2, 41–4, 50, 57–64, 81, 100, 218, 227, 230–1, 248, 294, 301, 346
'Modernism, Geopolitics, Globalization' (Cuddy-Keane), 75
Molinaro, Ursule, 195
Monet, Claude, 44, 97

money, 56, 66, 109, 128
The Monk (Lewis), 182
Monsanto, 284
montage, 164
Moore, Brian L., 280
Moore, George, 116
Mordden, Ethan, 338
More, Hannah, 12
More Pricks than Kicks (Beckett), 98–9
Moretti, Franco, 14, 85
Morris, Ann, 94
Morrison, Arthur, 245–6
Mortlake Romance, 133
Morton, Timothy, 277
motherhood, 298–300
Mr Penumbra's 24 Hour Bookstore (Sloan), 134
Mudford, William, 180
Mukherjee, Bharati, 64, 251
Mukhopadhyay, Tito, 347
Munro, Alice, 51, 61, 67, 272, 347, 355–6
Murry, John Middleton, 81
music, as metaphor, 354–5
The Music School (Updike), 257
My First Summer in the Sierra (Muir), 268n
'My Last Duchess' (Browning), 58
The Mysteries of London (Reynolds), 180
The Mystery of Dr. Fu-Manchu (Rohmer), 183
mythology, 116

Nagasaki bombing, 234
Nagel, James, 41, 44, 46
Naiad press, 335
Naipaul, V. S., 83, 98, 100
The Narrative Modes (Bonheim), 149
narrative voices, 48, 193–5, 199–205, 231
  anti-narrative, 199
Nasta, Susheila, 316
Nathans, Heather, 14

national literatures, 1, 3, 24
nationalism, 9–12, 14
nativism, 64
naturalism, 184–5
nature, 257, 259
Naylor, Gloria, 114–15
Nelles, William, 149
Neogy, Rajat, 85
neuroscience, 44
New, W. H., 227–8
New Aestheticism, 1
The New Age, 81
New Criticism, 10, 24, 40–1
New Lesbian Writing, 335
The New Short Story Theories (May), 26
New Statesman, 315
New Woman, 297–9, 301
New York, 167, 244–6, 249–51
The New York Years (Picano), 337
The New Yorker, 56–7, 137, 251, 256–8, 263–4
New Zealand, 81–2, 113, 228, 302
New-England Courant, 15
Newton, Isaac, 283
Nigeria, 85
The Nigger of the Narcissus (Conrad), 47
The Night Side of Nature (Crowe), 184
Ninh, Bao, 220–1
Nintendo, 279
Nissen, Axel, 331
Nixon, Mark, 99
No End to the Way (Jackson/Glaskin), 334
Nobel Prize, 75
Norris, Frank, 246
Norris, Margot, 247
North, Michael, 96
Not at Night (Thompson), 186–7
novels, 57, 59, 63, 242, 357
  distinct from short stories, 27, 31, 46, 58, 66, 127
  practical difficulties of writing, 60–1
  three-volume, 46

GENERAL INDEX

Oates, Joyce Carol, 61, 63–4, 118, 264–5, 266
Object Lessons (Stern), 112
Object Oriented Ontology, 277
O'Brien, Edward J., 112
O'Brien, Fitz-James, 175
O'Brien, Tim, 221–2
obscenity trials, 332
occult, 184
O'Connor, Flannery, 65, 249, 273–4, 347, 349–50
O'Connor, Frank, 2–3, 9, 26, 56–62, 66, 115, 118, 214, 218, 295, 357
Ōe, Kenzaburō, 347, 348, 353–5
O'Faoláin, Seán, 3, 118, 218
Ogot, Grace, 85
O'Higgins, Harvey, 334
Öhlschläger, Claudia, 153
The Old Curiosity Shop (Dickens), 177
Olympics, 75
omission, theory of, 79
'On Writing' (Carver), 60
Ondaatje, Michael, 251
One Arm (Williams), 334
ONE Magazine, 329, 333
One Story, 132
The One That Got Away (Wicomb), 323
One Thousand and One Nights, 102
One World: A Global Anthology of Short Stories (Woods), 114
Ong, Walter J., 306
Onlywomen press, 335
Oppenheim, Janet, 184
Orage, A. R., 81
oral storytelling, 57, 65, 214, 231–2, 316
Orientalism, 176–7
Osman, Diriye, 339
Osteen, Mark, 355
O'Sullivan, Michael, 58
The Other Persuasion, 337
The Other Side of Heaven (Karlin), 220
Otto, Eric C., 281, 284–5
Our Own Voices (Miller), 329, 333

Our Village (Mitford), 13
outlaw figures, 295
Owen, Alex, 184
Ozeki, Ruth, 275

Packard, Chris, 331
Pages from the Diary of a Late Physician (Warren), 180
Pak, Chris, 282
Palm-Wine Drinkard (Tutuola), 85
A Pamphlet Against Anthologies, 110
Pan and the Fire-Bird (Steward), 336
pandemics, 282
paper taxes, 211
parenthood, 60–1
Paris, 242–5, 251
The Paris Review, 57
Parisian Sketches (James), 45
Partisan Review, 335
Pascal, Blaise, 58
Pater, Walter, 43, 45, 78
Pattee, Fred Lewis, 25, 31
pay, 56, 66
Payne, Tonia L., 283
The Penguin Book of the British Short Story, 57, 65–6, 117
Perrault, Charles, 235–6, 305–6
Perry, Bliss, 25, 31
Persky, Stan, 328
A Personal Matter (Ōe), 354–5
Pethers, Matthew, 14
phenomenology, 42–4
Phillips, Robert, 332
philology, 9, 28
'The Philosophy of Composition' (Poe), 29
The Philosophy of the Short-story (Matthews), 26–31, 46, 234
Picano, Felice, 328, 336–8
Picken, Andrew, 109, 113
The Pickwick Papers (Dickens), 178
Pilgrimage (Richardson), 49
Pinckney, Darryl, 249

Pissaro, Camille, 44
Planet of the Blind (Kuusisto), 346–8
Playing the Game (Austen), 336
Plomer, William, 81
Ploughshares Solo, 132, 136
Poe, Edgar Allan, 9, 10, 40, 66, 108, 147, 175, 227, 242–5, 247, 250
  on Hawthorne, 76–7
  as a horror writer, 175, 180, 182
  misrepresented by Matthews, 25–8
  poetry, 175, 180
  as a 'weird' writer, 162–3
Poetics of Relation (Glissant), 229
poetry, 31, 58, 60, 66, 175, 180, 211, 227
Polari Journal, 329
political fiction, 321
Pollock, Jackson, 346
pollution, 275–6
population growth, 177–8
Porter, Hal, 335
Portrait of Madame Cézanne (Cézanne), 95
The Postcolonial Short Story (Awadalla and March-Russell), 228
postcolonialism, 2, 10, 58, 64, 83–5, 228–9
post-Impressionism, 49
postmodernism, 20, 60–5, 98, 100, 117, 196, 221, 250
post-nationalism, 320
Pound, Ezra, 34, 41, 47, 78, 97
Pratt, Mary Louise, 2
Prescott, Glenway, 332
Prescott, Linda, 114
Price, Kenneth, 212
The Price of Salt (Highsmith/Morgan), 334
Prime-Stevenson, Edward, 331
Prince, Leah, 108
Pritchett, V. S., 56–7, 60, 62, 112, 118–19, 295

privacy, 261
prizes (literary), 67, 112, 134
The Program Era: Postwar Fiction and the Rise of Creative Writing (McGurl), 59
Propp, Vladimir, 42, 203–5
prostheses, 349–50
Proulx, Annie, 274–6
Proust, Marcel, 333, 337
psychogeography, 201–2
psychology, 42
psychosis, post-partum, 298
publishing industry, 46, 108, 129, 131, 294
  and digital media, 125, 129–30
Pullinger, Kate, 135
Pump Six and Other Stories (Bacigalupi), 284
Purdy, James, 334, 336, 337
Pyrhönen, Heta, 294

Quayson, Ato, 352, 355
queer short stories, 328–39; *see also* gay literature
Quinn, Seabury, 162

race, 64–5, 82–4, 96, 114, 214–15, 217, 230–1, 236, 249–52, 260, 334–9, 347
Radcliffe, Ann, 179–80
radio, 148
railways, 178–9, 188n, 260
Ramchand, Kenneth, 229–30
readers, 14, 28, 127, 295
realism, 49
Reality Hunger (Shields), 147
Reamy, Tom, 338
Rechy, John, 335
regional identity, 227–30
Reid, Coletta, 333
religion, 176–7, 184
Renoir, Jean, 44
The Repeating Island (Benítez-Rojo), 228

The Revolt of the Perverts
    (Curzon), 336
Revolutionary Road (Yates), 264
Reynolds, G. W., 180
rhizome concept, 229–30
Rhys, Jean, 65, 82–3, 113, 214–15,
    230–2
Rhythm, 81–2
Rich, Nathaniel, 272
Richards, Jeffrey H., 14
Richardson, Dorothy, 49, 296
Richardson, Ethel (Henry Handel
    Richardson), 334
Riddell, Charlotte, 185
Riding, Laura, 110
The Road to Nowhere (Glaskin), 334
Robinson, Kim Stanley, 272, 282
Rohlehr, Gordon, 233
Rohmer, Sax, 183
Rohrherger, Mary, 26
The Role of Music in Your Life
    (Five Dials), 135
Rolfe, Frederick, 332
romance genre, 24, 111, 129, 211,
    296–7
Romanticism, 10, 18
Ross, Harold, 256
Ross, Jacob, 114–15
Ross-Langley, Esme, 328
*Rouse Up O Young Men of the New
    Age!* (Ōe), 354
royalties, 133
Rule, Jane, 331, 335, 337
Runyon, Damon, 246
Rushdie, Salman, 317–18, 321
Ruskin, John, 47
Russian Formalists, 194

sacrifice, 177
saga texts, 211
Sagarin, Edward, 333
San Diego Lightfoot Sue (Reamy), 338
Sandford, Daniel Keyte, 180

'Sapper' (H. C. McNeile), 217–18, 221
Sargeson, Frank, 334
Sarraute, Nathalie, 62
Sartre, Jean-Paul, 85
Saunders, George, 117, 284
Saunders, Max, 44
Scheiding, Oliver, 11
Scholes, Robert, 97
Schönbach, Anton E., 27
science fiction, 43, 129, 280–4, 338
Scofield, Martin, 273
Scott, Lawrence, 230, 233
Scott, Walter, 9, 12, 13
Scottish writing, 9, 113
Scott-Moncrieff, Charles Kenneth, 332
Scribbling Women (Showalter), 296
Second World War, 218–19, 234
The Secret Self: Short Stories by Women
    (Lee), 114, 118
Selby, Hubert, Jr., 335
self-publishing, 129–34, 137
Selvon, Sam, 83, 113, 230, 232–3, 236,
    315–18
Senf, Carol A., 297
Senior, Olive, 65, 229–31, 236
Seurat, Georges, 44
Seven Arts, 80
Seven Gothic Tales (Dinesen), 334
Sévigny, Madame de, 306
Sex Variant Women in Literature
    (Foster), 334
sexual mores, 264, 330, 332, 335
sexual oppression, 333
sexual violence, 177, 217
sexuality, 59, 114, 307–8, 347
Shakespeare, William, 162
Shapard, Robert, 111, 148
Sharpey, William, 181
Shaw, Valerie, 43
Shawn, William, 257
Shelley, Mary, 162, 181
The Sheltering Sky (Bowles), 62
Shields, David, 147

Shillington (Pennsylvania), 257
Shockley, Ann Allen, 335
Short Shorts (Howe and Howe), 148
short stories
   advantages over novels, 27, 31–2, 57–8, 60–1
   Americanisation of, 24–7, 35n, 86n, 126, 274
   categorising, 1, 3, 66–7, 76, 227
   definitions, 118–19
   length, 77, 147–55
   as a professional field of study, 26–34
Short Stories and Short Fiction (Hanson), 3
The Short Story (Canby), 31–2
'The Short Story' (Pritchett), 56–7
short-short fiction, 147–55
Showalter, Elaine, 296
Sidgwick, Henry, 184
Siebers, Tobin, 347–8
The Sign of Four (Conan Doyle), 246
The Silent History (app), 136
Silent Spring (Carson), 281
Silko, Leslie Marmon, 273
Silvera, Makeda, 335
Silverstone, Roger, 262–3
Simogo, 135
Simpson, Helen, 278
Simpson, Hyacinth, 83
Simpson, Paul, 193
Sinclair, Ian, 202–3
Sinclair, May, 49, 296
Sinister Wisdom, 329
Sins of the Father (Crews), 10
Situationism, 201
Sitwell, Osbert, 118
Sketchbook of Geoffrey Crayon, Gent (Irving), 13
Sketches by Boz (Dickens), 177, 179
skim reading, 127
slavery, 230
Sleep it Off Lady (Rhys), 230

Sloan, Robin, 134
A Small Selection (Glaskin), 334
Smalley, George, 212–13
Smiley, Jane, 275
Smith, Ali, 67–8, 110, 275
Smith, C. Alphonso, 27–30, 34
Smith, Clark Ashton, 163–4
Smith, Malvern Van Wyk, 217
Smith, Susan Belasco, 212
Smith, Zadie, 285
Snow White, 304
Snyder, Gary, 282
Snyder, Sharon L., 348
Society for Psychical Research (SPR), 184, 186
The Society of the Spectacle (Debord), 167
Sodomite Invasion Review, 328
Some Short Stories About People I Don't Like (Mitzel), 336
The Sound and the Fury (Faulkner), 62
Spanish Inquisition, 182
Spender, Stephen, 118, 333, 336
Spengler, Oswald, 246–7, 249
Spielhagen, Friedrich, 27
spiritualism, 184, 186
The Sportswriter (Ford), 267
Stegner, Wallace, 273
Stein, Gertrude, 80, 82, 94–8, 100, 331, 337
Steinbeck, John, 274
Stephen Hero (Joyce), 50
Stern, Sadie, 112
Sterne, Laurence, 42
Stevenson, Robert Louis, 46, 180–1
Stevick, Philip, 62, 117
Steward, Samuel, 336
Stiker, Henri-Jacques, 350
Stoddard, Charles Warren, 331
Stoker, Bram, 162, 182–3, 185
Stonewall rebellion, 330, 335, 336
Stories of Fatherhood (Tesdell), 111
Stories of Motherhood (Tesdell), 111

The Story and its Writer (Charters), 116–17
Stowell, Peter, 41–2, 44
Strand Magazine, 177, 181, 245
The Strange Case of Dr. Jekyll and Mr Hyde (Stevenson), 180
stream of consciousness, 49
Streitmatter, Rodger, 329
Strong, Jonathan, 335
Studies in Literature and Style (Hunt), 31
A Study in Prose Fiction (Perry), 31
A Study of the Short Story (Canby), 31, 33
submerged populations, 214, 295
suburbs, 177, 256–67
Sudden Fiction (Shapard), 111, 148
Suicide Bridge (Sinclair), 203
Sukenick, Ronald, 194–7, 200
Summer Lightning (Senior), 230
The Supernatural Index (Ashley and Contento), 111
supernatural stories, 178, 219
Surfiction: Fiction Now and Tomorrow (Federman), 195
Suzie-Q (Arobateau), 335
Swift, Jonathan, 66
Symbolism, 41, 49
syphilis, 181

Tate, Trudi, 111
Tales from Blackwood, 110, 112
Tales of Mean Streets (Morrison), 246
Tan, Amy, 64, 66
technology, 75, 277, 284
television, 56–7, 148, 259
Telling Stories: Postcolonial Short Fiction in English (Bardolph), 228
Tender is the Night (Fitzgerald), 62
terraforming, 282
Tesdell, Diana Secker, 111
Tess of the D'Urbervilles (Hardy), 100, 300

Text World Theory, 206
textual cohesion, 195
textual production, 28
textual traffic, 11
Thacker, Andrew, 85
That Glimpse of Truth (Miller), 112–13, 119
Them! (film), 281
Theme for Diverse Instruments (Rule), 335
theosophy, 184
'They All Made Peace – What is Peace?' (Hemingway), 80
The Thing Around Your Neck (Adichie), 321–2
The Things They Carried (O'Brien), 221
Thiong'o, Ngũgĩ wa, 320
A Thirsty Evil (Vidal), 334
Thomas, James, 148
Thompson, Christine Campbell, 186
Thompson, John, 125
Thorne, Matt, 117
Three Lives (Stein), 94–6
Tike and Five Stories (Strong), 335
The Time and Tide Album, 112
Todorov, Tzvetan, 127
Toomer, Jean, 100, 249
'Towards a Philosophy of Transnationalism' (Doyle), 13
TQ Review, 329
the transatlantic review, 78–9, 82
transitional moments, 264–5
translation, 75, 85, 112
transnationalism, 12–14, 75
The Travelling Grave (Hartley), 332
Trevor, William, 50, 115–16
Trexler, Adam, 279
Tribe, 329
Trinidad, 230, 232–5
Tristram Shandy (Sterne), 42
Trois Contes (Flaubert), 94, 97
Trojan War, 211

Trollope, Anthony, 180
True To Life Adventure Stories, 335
Trumbach, Randolph, 330
Tunca, Daria, 322
Tutuola, Amos, 85
Twice-Told Tales (Hawthorne), 13, 29, 40, 76–7, 227
The Twilight Zone, 164
Twitter, 148, 358
Tyler, Anne, 154
Tzara, Tristan, 82

Uganda, 85
Ulysses (Joyce), 42, 57, 242
unity aesthetic, 76
Unlimited Embrace (Woodhouse), 337
Updike, John, 56, 256–7, 264, 267
utilitarianism, 184

Van Dyke, Henry, 25
Van Gunsteren, Julia, 43–5, 49
Van Leer, David, 243
VanderMeer, Ann and Jeff, 161
Verne, Jules, 136, 280
Vertovec, Steven, 214, 316
Vice Versa, 328
Victorian fiction, 177
Victorian Ghosts in the Noontide (Dickerson), 184–5
Victorian Street Society, 181
Vidal, Gore, 334, 337
Vietnam War, 220–1
The Violet Quill Reader, 338
Virago press, 335
visual impairment, 346, 351–3, 354
vivisection, 181
voice synthesisers, 358
Vonnegut, Kurt, 281
Vook, 134
Vorticism, 40
voyeurism, 260
Vu, Truong, 220

W. H. Smith (newsagent), 179, 184
Wakefield, Tom, 338
Walcott, Derek, 83
Walker, Arthur E., 161–2
Wallace, David Foster, 117, 151, 153, 250
Waller, Philip, 177
war stories, 79–80, 111, 211–22
Wark, MacKenzie, 280
Warner, Marina, 306
Warner, Tom, 330
Warren, Robert Penn, 112
Warren, Samuel, 180
Washington DC, 249
The Waste Land (Eliot), 78
Watmough, David, 338
Watson, Scott, 328
Watt, Ian, 41–2, 44
Wattpad, 134
The Waves (Woolf), 49
Ways of Sunlight (Selvon), 232, 315–17
Weeks, Jeffrey, 329
Weiner, Jennifer, 134
weird tales, 160–71
Weird Tales, 160–2, 164, 167, 170
Weise, Donald, 339
Wells, Catherine, 331
Wells, H. G., 179, 181, 280
Welty, Eudora, 273
West, Rebecca, 47
Westchester County, 258
Westerns, 295
Wharton, Edith, 2, 178, 185
Where I'm Calling From (Carver), 60–1
White, Edmund, 336–8
White, Jerry, 177
The White Wand (Hartley), 332
Whitman, Walt, 162
Whitmore, George, 338
Whitt, Jan, 328
Wicomb, Zoë, 321–3

Wide Sargasso Sea (Rhys), 83
Wideman, John Edgar, 130
Wikipedia, 127
Wilde, Oscar, 77, 116, 332–3, 337
wilderness, 274
Wilhite, Keith, 261
Williams, Raymond, 76, 179
Williams, Tennessee, 334
Williams, William Carlos, 34, 333
Williamson, John, 282
Wilson, Angus, 334
The Windup Girl (Bacigalupi), 284
Winesberg, Ohio (Anderson), 80
Winter Evening Tales (Hogg), 13
Witness to the League of Blond Hip Hop Dancers (Allegra), 339
Wolfe, Gene, 282
Wolfreys, Julian, 203
Women, Men and the Great War (Tate), 111
Wong, Norman, 339
Wood, Sarah, 110
Woodhouse, Reed, 334, 337
Woodrow, Marnie, 339
Woods, Molara, 114
Woolf, Virginia, 34, 41, 47–8, 51, 246, 248, 331, 346–8, 358
word choice, 61–3
Wordpress, 131

World Health Organisation, 358
A World of Difference: An Anthology of Stories from Five Continents (Prescott), 114
world systems theory, 14
World War One, 350
Wright, Marcia, 322
Wright, Richard, 95–6, 249
Wright, Stephen, 336
The Writers' and Artists' Yearbook, 130
writing, 34, 299
Wyoming, 274–5

Yagoda, Ben, 256, 263
Yates, Richard, 264
Yeats, W. B., 41, 116, 218
The Yellow Book, 43, 77–8
'Yellow Peril' fiction, 183, 189n
You Can't Get Lost in Cape Town (Wicomb), 322–3
Young, Emma, 1, 297
Young, Ian, 334, 336
Young Adult literature, 129
YouTube, 347, 358
Yung, Wayne, 328

Zimmerman, Bonnie, 335
Zola, Émile, 45, 201

EU representative:
Easy Access System Europe
Mustamäe tee 50, 10621 Tallinn, Estonia
Gpsr.requests@easproject.com

www.ingramcontent.com/pod-product-compliance
Lightning Source LLC
Chambersburg PA
CBHW060334010526
44117CB00017B/2821